Petrarch
& Dante

THE WILLIAM AND KATHERINE DEVERS
SERIES IN DANTE STUDIES

Theodore J. Cachey, Jr., and Christian Moevs, editors
Simone Marchesi, associate editor
Ilaria Marchesi, assistant editor

Petrarch & Dante

Anti-Dantism, Metaphysics, Tradition

Edited by

Zygmunt G. Barański and Theodore J. Cachey, Jr.

with the assistance of Demetrio S. Yocum

University of Notre Dame Press
Notre Dame, Indiana

The poem "Birthday Card," from book four of "The Gardens of Flora Baum,"
is printed with the generous permission of its author, Julia Budenz.
Copyright © 2004 by Julia Budenz.

Library of Congress Cataloging-in-Publication Data

Petrarch and Dante : anti-Dantism, metaphysics, tradition / edited by
Zygmunt Baranski and Theodore Cachey.
    p.   cm. — (The William and Katherine Devers series in Dante studies)
   Includes bibliographical references and index.
   ISBN-13: 978-0-268-02211-2 (pbk. : alk. paper)
   ISBN-10: 0-268-02211-9 (pbk. : alk. paper)
   1. Petrarca, Francesco, 1304–1374—Criticism and interpretation.   2. Petrarca,
Francesco, 1304–1374—Philosophy.   3. Dante Alighieri, 1265–1321—Criticism
and interpretation.   4. Italian literature—To 1400—History and criticism.
5. Ideology and literature—Italy—History—To 1500.   6. Polemics in literature.
I. Baranski, Zygmunt G.   II. Cachey, T. J. (Theodore J.)
  PQ4540.P38   2009
  851'.1—dc22

                                              2009004362

∞ *This book is printed on acid-free paper.*

CONTENTS

The William and Katherine Devers Program in Dante Studies at the University of Notre Dame supports rare book acquisitions in the university's John A. Zahm Dante collections, funds an annual visiting professorship in Dante studies, and supports electronic and print publication of scholarly research in the field. In collaboration with the Medieval Institute at the university, the Devers program has initiated a series dedicated to the publication of the most significant current scholarship in the field of Dante Studies.

In keeping with the spirit that inspired the creation of the Devers program, the series takes Dante as a focal point that draws together the many disciplines and lines of inquiry that constitute a cultural tradition without fixed boundaries. Accordingly, the series hopes to illuminate Dante's position at the center of contemporary critical debates in the humanities by reflecting both the highest quality of scholarly achievement and the greatest diversity of critical perspectives.

The series publishes works on Dante from a wide variety of disciplinary viewpoints and in diverse scholarly genres, including critical studies, commentaries, editions, translations, and conference proceedings of exceptional importance. The series is supervised by an international advisory board composed of distinguished Dante scholars and is published regularly by the University of Notre Dame Press. The Dolphin and Anchor device that appears on publications of the Devers series was used by the great humanist, grammarian, editor, and typographer Aldus Manutius (1449–1515), in whose 1502 edition of Dante (second issue) and all subsequent editions it appeared. The device illustrates the ancient proverb *Festina lente,* "Hurry up slowly."

Theodore J. Cachey, Jr., and Christian Moevs, *editors*
Simone Marchesi, *associate editor*
Ilaria Marchesi, *assistant editor*

Advisory Board

July 20, 2004
Francesco Petrarca
July 20, 1304 – July 18, 1374

————————

Shall I enumerate your lives as three:
That of the mortal flesh, in exile born,
That of the Latin learning not outworn,
That of a sheer immortal poetry?

Is body or is book more real, more key,
more ready after dark for dawning morn?
Latin lasts long beyond its antique bourn.
Art lives in likeness to Romanity.

Your body traveled Alps, took roads to Rome.
The corpus of your work fares farthest ways
Posting to scholars and to sonneteers

Distinctions of the tomb and of the tome:
Those seven decades failed of those two days;
These seven centuries filled all these years.

                    Julia Budenz

ACKNOWLEDGMENTS

This volume is based on a series of seminars given to celebrate the seventh centenary of the birth of Francesco Petrarca (1304–1374), organized by the William and Katherine Devers Program in Dante Studies, and held in the Department of Special Collections of the Hesburgh Library of the University of Notre Dame during the fall of 2004. The series, entitled "Petrarch and Dante," was co-sponsored by the Department of Romance Languages and Literatures and by the Medieval Institute of the University of Notre Dame, and coincided with the distinguished visiting professorship of Zygmunt G. Barański, whose appointment was co-sponsored by the Devers Program in Dante Studies, the Medieval Institute, the Department of Romance Languages and Literatures, and the Ravarino Family Directorship in Italian Studies.

The contributors presented in pairs over several afternoons during the course of the semester. All of the papers stimulated lively debate and discussion among faculty and students. The series was inaugurated in September by Giuseppe Mazzotta of Yale and Justin Steinberg of the University of Chicago. In October, Albert Ascoli of Berkeley and Ronald Martinez of Brown lectured, followed later that month by Zygmunt Barański and Christian Moevs of Notre Dame. Sara Sturm-Maddox of the University of Massachussets, Amherst, and Theodore Cachey of Notre Dame spoke at the last session in November. Teodolinda Barolini of Columbia University was unable to join us in Notre Dame but has generously contributed an essay to the present volume, for which the editors are most grateful. We take this opportunity to thank all the contributors to the volume for their participation and support.

The editors express their warmest gratitude and thanks to the Devers and Ravarino families, whose generosity has made possible the flourishing of Italian Studies at the University of Notre Dame, as well as the "Petrarch and Dante" seminars and the publication of the present volume.

Finally, the editors recognize and thank most warmly and with the greatest admiration Dr. Demetrio S. Yocum, for his expert scholarly, critical, and editorial support in bringing the volume to press.

Zygmunt G. Barański
Theodore J. Cachey, Jr.

PART I

Anti-Dantism

CHAPTER I

Between Petrarch and Dante

Prolegomenon to a Critical Discourse

THEODORE J. CACHEY, JR.

MY CHOICE OF TITLE, MIRRORING THE TITLES OF CANONICAL essays by Natalino Sapegno (1963) and Giuseppe Billanovich (1965), is intended in a heuristic and not a hubristic sense.[1] Rather than reflect an exaggerated self-confidence on my part, it represents in the first place an invitation to anyone interested in what came "between Petrarch and Dante" to turn (or return) to these classic accounts of Italian literary origins. To this essential list I propose to add a more recent essay by Enrico Fenzi, "Tra Dante e Petrarca: Il fantasma di Ulisse" (2004),[2] which takes the Ulysses theme as developed by Petrarch to represent a paradigmatic *trait d'union* "between" Dante and Petrarch, and thus a privileged vantage point from which to compare and contrast the two *auctores*.

The particular tradition of Italian literary history encapsulated by "Tra Dante e Petrarca," which Zygmunt Barański characterizes in this volume as the view that Italian literature is "delicately, though reassuringly, caught between the contrasting possibilities offered by its two great exemplary 'founding fathers,'" will, however, serve here as the basis for observations against the grain of this harmonious critical picture. Informed by the work of the Petrarchan centenary seminars held at the University of Notre Dame in 2004, my essay serves as a prologue-epilogue to our collective reexamination of the question of who and what in fact came between "Petrarch and

Dante," in ideological, historiographical, and rhetorical terms.[3] Indeed, the goal of the seminars was to move beyond the simple juxtaposition of "Dante and Petrarch" or "Petrarch and Dante," as the case may be. As several participants observed, this juxtaposition has sometimes been reduced to more or less neutral (and thus critically inert) descriptions of the pervasive inter-discursive presence of "Dante in Petrarca."[4]

In respectful counterpoint to the perspective provided by an illustrious critical tradition, and bolstered by the contributions of colleagues participating in the Notre Dame seminars (mine was last in the series), I begin by suggesting that Petrarch's deep ideological dissent from Dante can be plausibly linked to the earliest expressions of Trecento anti-*dantismo*[5] discussed by Sapegno, whose critical perspective, however, like most of the Italian critical tradition, elided any connection between these currents and Petrarch. I believe one of the important conclusions to emerge from this volume is that for all Petrarch's claims of respect and admiration for Dante, he ought to be considered within the tradition of Trecento anti-*dantismo*, in particular, for his consistently polemical attitude toward the claims of the *theologus-poeta*, for which there is persuasive evidence throughout his career.

Secondly, I will highlight the way in which the currents of influence that flowed between Petrarch and Boccaccio, which are described by Billanovich primarily in terms of Petrarch's authority vis-à-vis Boccaccio "il più grande discepolo" (the greatest disciple) and the beginnings of Humanism, flowed no less significantly, for the history of vernacular lyric literary history, in the opposite direction from Boccaccio to Petrarch. Boccaccio's provocative championing of Dante represented, in fact, a strong stimulus for Petrarch's renewed engagement with vernacular literature during the Italian phase of his career after 1353. Petrarch's uncompromising, albeit largely dissembled, post-Provence dedication to the vernacular reflects a significant course correction, when considered against the background of his life and works up until and around 1350. The shift becomes especially evident after 1359, the date of the fateful *Familares* 21.15, "To Giovanni Boccaccio, a defense against an accusation by envious people," in which Petrarch famously claimed never to have possessed a *Commedia* before Boccaccio had sent him one copied in his own hand, and to have avoided reading Dante so as not to be unduly influenced by him.[6]

Indeed, once the deep ideological divide that separated Petrarch from Dante is clarified, it becomes apparent that it was none other than Giovanni Boccaccio, the so-called third crown of Florentine eloquence, who came "between" Petrarch and Dante, and who spurred Petrarch to vie ever more strenuously with Dante in the vernacular during the latter part of his career. Petrarch, in fact, almost as a sign of recognition of his debt to Boccaccio on this front, recorded the triumvirate formula for the first time in *Seniles* 5.2, his letter "To the same person [Boccaccio], concerning the obsessive appetite for first place."[7] An appreciation of Boccaccio's influence on Petrarch in the vernacular literary realm is thus enhanced by directly correlating Petrarch's discussions of Dante in these well-known letters from the *Familiares* and the *Seniles* with the history of the making of the *Canzoniere* and the composition of the *Triumphi*. A topographical reconnaissance of occurrences of the Ulysses theme in Petrarch's oeuvre in connection with that history (work pioneered by Fenzi, among others) reveals, for example, that Petrarch's rivalry with Dante in the late 1350s found expression in a famous passage in the first letter on the poet that Petrarch addressed to Boccaccio in 1359, *Familiares* 21.15. As we will see, the subtheme of Ulysses' refusal to return home to Ithaca is evoked both there and in another much less famous, but nonetheless telling, utilization of the same theme in a nearly contemporary passage from the *Itinerarium ad sepulchrum domini Iesu Christi*. The relation between Petrarch and Dante is brought into clearest focus, however, in the most emblematic and moving of Petrarch's rewritings of Dante's figure of Ulysses, in poem number 189, "Passa la nave mia colma d'oblio" (My ship laden with forgetfulness).[8] This originally entered the order of the book as the concluding poem to the first part of the Chigi form of the *Canzoniere* that was undertaken in 1359 under the stimulus of Boccaccio's conversations with Petrarch about Dante.

"Contra Dantem"

In the only explicit mention of Dante *auctor* in all of his works, Petrarch contradicted his predecessor's authority, as if the point of the exercise of reading Pomponius Mela's *Chorografia* were to find an opportunity to challenge his predecessor. Alongside a passage in which the Roman geographer locates Typheus' burial place in Cilicia rather than in Sicily, as Dante was to do in *Paradiso* 8.67–70, Petrarch wrote "Nota contra Dantem."[9] Petrarch's preoccupation with Dante's opinion regarding the point is unusual by any measure, since when it came to locating Typheus, there were numerous and greater authorities than Dante to contend with, including Ovid, who had placed him beneath Aetna. Petrarch, on the other hand, consistent with Horace, Seneca, Lucan, and Claudian, buries Typheus under Ischia in the *Itinerarium,* the *Sine nomine,* and the *Triumphus pudicitie* cited here:[10]

> Non freme così 'l mar, quando s'adira,
> non Inarime, allor che Tipheo piagne,
> né Mongibel, s'Enchelado sospira.
>
> (ll. 112–14)

> Greater his rage than that of the angry sea, / Or that of Ischia [Inarime] when Typhoeus weeps, / Or Aetna's when Enceladus laments.

The geographical dimension of Petrarch's dissent from Dante emerges as an interesting subtheme of this volume. For example, Albert Ascoli shows how Petrarch utilizes in the self-commentary on his eclogue *Parthenias* (*Fam.* 10.4) a modern and more reliable knowledge of biblical geography, based on newly discovered sources such as Pomponius Mela, to indirectly undermine Dante's *auctoritas,* and specifically his predecessor's account of the rivers of the earthly Paradise at the summit of Mt. Purgatory. For our immediate purposes, however, Petrarch's out-of-the-way geographical annotation regarding Typheus' burial site serves simply to illustrate both the "marginality" and the overdetermined character of the emergence of an anti-Dantean attitude in Petrarch's works. The manifestation of this attitude has largely escaped scholarly scrutiny, thanks to a critical tradition concerning the relationship between Dante and Petrarch that, since Boccaccio, has tended to minimize any suggestion of rivalry or incompatibility between the founding fathers of Italian literature. Yet a heightened awareness of the underlying agon that characterized Petrarch's attitude toward Dante can be expected to turn up other intermittent expressions of his indirect ongoing polemic with Dante's authority.

That the equilibrium of Sapegno's title "Tra Dante e il Petrarca," the first in our series of similarly titled essays, is belied by the essay's heavy weighting in favor of Dante is perhaps to be expected, although there is little doubt the imbalance would have irritated Petrarch no end. Indeed, with due respect to father Francesco, father Dante represents the proverbial eight-hundred-pound gorilla in the room of any literary history of Trecento Italy. In this context Sapegno recalled the fact that the domineering presence of Dante in Trecento Italy stimulated strong resistance on ideological grounds, as well as admiration and assent. The two major examples of the anti-Dantean reaction discussed by Sapegno are the allegorical-didactic poem *Acerba,* by the polemically anti-Dantean Cecco d'Ascoli; and what might be considered the culmination of religious suspicion and rejection of Dante during the Trecento, the *De Reprobatione monarchie* of Friar Guido Vernani of Rimini.

Sapegno would never have dreamed of considering Petrarch in relation to either of these two exponents of Trecento anti-*dantismo.* Nevertheless, particularly in the light of evidence presented here by Barański in support of his thesis that Petrarch pursued consistently over many years "the task of dismantling his predecessor's *auctoritas,*" it is perhaps worth considering the question of Petrarch's relation to currents of Trecento anti-*dantismo* during the earliest stage of his literary career. We have already had occasion to mention Albert Ascoli's discussion of Petrarch's first eclogue, *Parthenias.* Ascoli uncovers there an implicit critique of Dante's claims to "the status of *theologus-poeta,* or perhaps better, *scriba Dei*" and a response to the exchange of eclogues that took place between the early humanist Giovanni del Virgilio in Bologna and Dante in Ravenna in the early 1320s, at the same time that Petrarch was studying law in Bologna. Thus one cannot help but wonder whether Petrarch's anti-Dantean attitude went as far back as his days as a law student. Indeed, as Sara Sturm-Maddox recalls in her contribution to this volume, Petrarch, in contrast to Dante, traced his own literary identity as *poeta* and *historicus* back to the early humanists of Padua, especially Albertino Mussato, who had preceded him in obtaining the honor of the laurel crown.[11]

Bologna in the early 1320s was also host to the most prominent and, in the end, tragically vulnerable exponent of early anti-*dantismo,* Cecco d'Ascoli. He was suspended from his professorship of medicine in Bologna by the Inquisitor Lamberto da Cingoli in 1324, and eventually condemned by the Florentine Inquisition and burned at the stake, together with his works, in Florence on September 16, 1327.[12] Cecco's anti-*dantismo* is patent, and several passages from the *Acerba,* in which he expresses skepticism about the poet who "finge, immaginando cose vane" (fakes, imagining vain things), are well known.[13] One in particular deserves further consideration for its generally neglected genealogical relation to what is arguably the most prominent polemical expression of anti-*dantismo* to be found in Petrarch's *Canzoniere.*

While it might seem incongruous on the face of it to associate Petrarch with the Trecento's most rabid exponent of anti-*dantismo,* it is worth recalling, besides the possibility of their biographical intersection at Bologna in the early 1320s, that Cecco d'Ascoli and Petrarch shared a connection to the Colonna family, whose patronage Petrarch first attracted during the early 1320s when both poets were in and out of Bologna. Indeed, in a chapter of *Per moderne carte,* and since then, in his authoritative edition of the *Canzoniere,* Marco Santagata has uncovered extensive traces of Cecco d'Ascoli's poetry in Petrarch's lyric, beginning with the earliest poems dedicated to the Colonna.[14] While Santagata does not make any connection between Petrarch and Cecco's anti-*dantismo,* he highlights Petrarch's utilization of the Dantean turn of phrase "sotto benda" (which derives from Dante's canzone "Doglia mi reca," l. 57) in the envoi of canzone 28 in the *Canzoniere* (l. 113), where it is taken to mean simply "among women." According to Santagata, Petrarch's use of the expression is directly mediated by Cecco d'Ascoli, who had already adopted it in this sense in a misogynistic passage from chapter 9 of book IV of the *Acerba:*[15]

> In donna non fu mai virtù perfetta,
> Salvo in Colei che, innanzi il cominciare,
> Creata fu ed in eterno eletta.
> Rare fiate, come disse Dante,
> S'intende sottil cosa sotto benna:
> Dunque, con lor perché tanto millante?
> Non da virtù viene il parlare inetto.
> Maria si va cercando per Ravenna
> Chi in donna crede sia intelletto.
>
> (ll. 4393–4402)

—————

There was never perfect virtue in a woman, / except in she who before the beginning / was created and chosen in eternity. /

Rarely, as Dante said, / beneath a headband is a subtle thought
understood. / Therefore why do you so exalt them? / Inept
speech does not come from virtue. / He seeks Mary in Ravenna /
He who believes that woman has intellect.

Santagata does not consider the implications of the connection between this
ad personam ("Maria si va cercando per Ravenna") instance of anti-*dantismo*
and one of Petrarch's most directly subversive expressions of skepticism
about Dante's claims for Beatrice, found in the *Canzoniere*'s concluding
canzone 366, "Vergine bella," where Dante's Beatrice is implicitly contrasted
with the Virgin Mary ("vera Beatrice"):

Vergine glorïosa,
donna del Re che nostri lacci à sciolti
et fatto 'l mondo libero et felice,
ne le cui sante piaghe
prego ch'appaghe   il cor, vera beatrice.
(ll. 48–52)

O glorious Virgin, Lady of that King who has loosed our bonds
and made the world free and happy, in whose wounds I pray you
to quiet my heart. O true bringer of happiness.

Nonetheless, the link suggests that the underlying *vis polemica* that informed
the contrast Petrarch drew at the culminating moment of the *Canzoniere*
between the Virgin Mary and any earthly woman traced its genealogical origins directly back to the *Acerba*.[16] This connection between Petrarch's anti-
dantismo and Cecco's might seem tenuous if it were not for the relative
prominence of the passage in question in the collection, and its place within
a broader albeit subtle program pursued throughout Petrarch's lyrics aimed
at subverting Dante's extraordinary and unprecedented claims for Beatrice.
In the context of his examination of the liturgical underpinnings of Petrarch's writings (especially as mediated by Dante) in this volume, Ronald Martinez has further focused for us the anti-Dantean precision of
Petrarch's "vera beatrice." He observes that the expression "is itself a compound of Dante's phrasing, which introduces Beatrice, in Lucia's words,

as 'Beatrice, lode di dio vera' (*Inf.* 2.103) and refers to Christ, in the words of the Croatian pilgrim near the end of the poem, as 'Signor mio Jesu cristo, *Dio verace,* / or fu sì fatta la sembianza vostra' (*Par.* 31.107–8)." But already in canzone 287, Petrarch had reductively relegated Dante and his "love story" to the third heaven, demoting the *"theologus-poeta"* to the same status as Sennuccio, Guittone, Cino, and "Franceschin nostro"; and in the poetic catalogue of the *Triumphus cupidinis* (especially 4.28–38), as Barański observes, "[b]y fixing Beatrice as simply a love poet's lady, the equal of Cino's Selvaggia, Petrarch, as he had done in sonnet 287, denied her role as a heavenly guide and hence once again challenged the *Commedia*'s metaphysical claims."[17] In the light of the skepticism about Beatrice found elsewhere in Petrarch's lyric, there is no reason to doubt that he would have disagreed with Cecco d'Ascoli's attitude toward her as expressed in the *Acerba.* Yet Petrarch's connections to Trecento anti-*dantismo,* beginning with Cecco d'Ascoli, have generally been overlooked, due no doubt to the fact that Petrarch tended to reserve for special occasions the expression of his anti-Dantean animus. In fact, given Dante's status in Trecento culture, Petrarch could only subtly and indirectly take on his predecessor, and seek to undermine him, at the margins, so to speak, of his own works. Moreover, the different bases of Petrarch's own *auctoritas,* rooted as they were in his Latin humanism, led him to express his dissent in an indirect and condescending manner, so as to avoid granting any more credit to Dante than was strictly necessary (even when directly provoked by Boccaccio, he notoriously avoids naming his predecessor in *Familiares* 21.15 and *Seniles* 5.2). This approach is also reflected in Petrarch's idiosyncratic reaction to Dante's *Monarchia,* the second focal point for Trecento anti-*dantismo* recalled by Sapegno in his essay.

In the light of Petrarch's usual strategy of subverting his predecessor without naming him, one should not be surprised if Petrarch never explicitly cited any of his predecessor's Latin works, that is to say, works in the literary realm where Petrarch's preeminence among contemporaries was undisputed.[18] There is ample evidence, on the other hand, of the *Monarchia*'s circulation, and therefore of Petrarch's opportunity to encounter the work, even after the second decade of the Trecento and Guido Vernani's confutation. It is, for example, well known that Petrarch's political idol until around midcentury, Cola di Rienzo, wrote a commentary on the *Monarchia* between 1347 and 1352.[19]

The documentary history of the reception of Dante's political and rhetorical treatises in Latin (including important recent investigations by Corrado Bologna concerning one of the three principal codexes in which the *De vulgari eloquentia* survives, the Berlinese [Berlin, Staatsbibliothek, Lat. fol. 437], containing the *Monarchia,* together with Dionigi da Borgo San Sepolcro's *Commento* on Valerio Massimo)[20] strongly suggests that Petrarch would have known both *De vulgari eloquentia* and *Monarchia.* Indeed, the historian Robert Lerner had already turned up some years ago a passage that is as close to an explicit citation of the *Monarchia* in Petrarch as one can expect to find, at the beginning of the *De sui ipsius et multorum ignorantia,* Petrarch's polemical treatise written in 1367 in response to a group of anonymous contemporary Averroists who had accused him of being an ignorant man.[21]

At the outset of that work the "ignorant man" polemically distinguishes between his own view of human happiness and Aristotle's treatment of the topic, which Dante had strongly endorsed at the beginning of the *Monarchia* when he had opined that it would be superfluous to write about human happiness after Aristotle:

> Nam quem fructum ille qui theorema quoddam Euclidis iterum demonstraret? Qui ab Aristotile felicitatem ostensam reostendere conaretur? Qui senectutem a Cicerone defensam resummeret defensandam? Nullum quippe, sed fastidium potius illa superfluitas tediosa prestaret.

> ---

> For what fruit would a man bear who proved once again a theorem of Euclid's? or who sought to show once again the nature of happiness, which has already been shown by Aristotle? Or who took up the defense of old age, which has already been defended by Cicero? None at all; indeed the tiresome pointlessness of the exercise would arouse distaste.

Thus, Petrarch is offered the opportunity in the *De sui ipsius et multorum ignorantia* to deliver a pointed jab at Dante. He is, in fact, astonished that anyone would think such a thing, much less put it down in writing:

> Et licet multa Ethicorum in principio et in fine de felicitate tractaverit, audebo dicere — clament ut libuerit censores mei — veram illum felicitatem sic penitus ignorasse, ut in eius cognitione, non dico subtilior, sed felicior fuerit vel quelibet anus pia, vel piscator pastorve fidelis, vel agricola. Quo magis miror quosdam nostrorum tractatum illum

aristotelicum sic miratos quasi nefas censuerint, idque scriptis quoque testati sint, de felicitate aliquid post illum loqui, cum michi tamen— audacter forsan hoc dixerim, sed, ni fallor, vere—ut solem noctua, sic ille felicitatem, hoc est lucem eius ac radios, sed non ipsam vidisse videatur. (63–64)

Of happiness he [Aristotle] has indeed said a good deal in the beginning and at the end of his Ethics. However, I will dare to say—and my censors may shout as loud as they please—he knew absolutely nothing of true happiness that any pious old woman, any faithful fisherman, shepherd or peasant is—I will not say more subtle but happier in recognizing it. I am therefore all the more astonished that some of our authors have so much admired that Aristotelian treatise as to consider it almost a crime to speak of happiness after him and that they have borne witness of this even in writing. It may perhaps be daring to say so, but it is true, unless I am mistaken: It seems to me that he saw of happiness as much as the night owl does of the sun, namely its light and rays and not the sun itself.

The indirect allusion to the *Monarchia* has the effect of consigning Dante and his political vision as expressed in that treatise to the same category of scholastic Aristotelianism that Petrarch rejected outright in the *De sui ipsius et multorum ignorantia* and throughout his oeuvre. Nevertheless, even taking this intent into account, the polemical poke at Dante is clearly overdetermined. Singling Dante out in this way reflected Petrarch's private concern with undermining Dante's authority in the literary culture. Although the critique of scholasticism pursued in *De sui ipsius et multorum ignorantia* did not require evoking, even indirectly, the vernacular poet, Petrarch does not miss the opportunity to take a swipe even in the context of a Latin polemic from late in his career, when the controversies surrounding Dante's *Monarchia* were no longer at the forefront of current debate. It is worth recalling in this context that Petrarch wrote *De sui ipsius et multorum ignorantia* at the same time that he was assertively engaged in consolidating his own position as a vernacular poet vis-à-vis Dante. He had been working on the *Triumphi* with renewed conviction and in direct competition with Dante's epic throughout the 1360s; and between the end of 1366 and the beginning of 1367, the year he authored the *De sui ipsius et multorum ignorantia,* he first undertook the organization of the "author's book" of the *Canzoniere,* Vatican Latin manuscript 3195.[22]

The idiosyncratic form that Petrarch's anti-*dantismo* takes vis-à-vis the *Monarchia,* characterized by a kind of surface vulnerability, even peevishness, combined with profound ideological dissent, afforded Lerner in his excellent essay the opportunity to contrast Dante's and Petrarch's divergent brands of humanism. In fact, for Lerner, "Petrarch's attack on Dante's view of Aristotle's *Ethics* and human happiness is at the heart of Petrarch's reaction against Dante."[23] The epistemological optimism of Dante's Aristotelian-Aquinian worldview appeared to Lerner, paradoxically, to be more "humanistic," or modern, at least in the contemporary and colloquial sense of that term, than Petrarch's Augustinian pessimism.[24] This particular point of contact between Dante and Petrarch regarding human happiness is symptomatic of the ideological roots of Petrarch's estrangement from Dante as a poetic authority, a topic variously treated by Giuseppe Mazzotta, Teodolinda Barolini, and Christian Moevs in this volume.

Mazzotta, while recognizing Petrarch's occasional "spasms of crude jealousy," is perhaps the most sanguine of our contributors about the possibility of reconciling Petrarch to Dante. Viewing Petrarch's dialogue with Dante as one between the ancients and the moderns that "is destined never to end," Mazzotta argues that, despite their differences, "Petrarch's modern vision of horizontal self-transcendence flows from a source that is common to both Dante and himself: the Franciscan tradition." Barolini, for her part, provides a meticulous reading of the profound metaphysical valences of Petrarch's poetic vocabulary, especially in relation to the metaphysical theme par excellence of "[s]ingular versus plural, whole versus fragment, the one versus the many." She succeeds in uncovering metaphysical resonances of the *Canzoniere* that inevitably point, however, to the ideological abyss that separated Petrarch from Dante, when one considers the "modern" Petrarch's failure to achieve the kind of metaphysical integration that the *Commedia* described. Moevs contrasts Petrarch's ontologically deracinated subjectivity with Dante's concept of self in terms of an epochal crisis in the metaphysical underpinnings of Christian culture. Thus, for Moevs, Petrarch's culminating vision in the *Triumphus eternitatis,* contrasted with Dante's in *Paradiso* 33, appears a "reduction of the mystical or transcendent or metaphysical to the prosaic [that is] almost Ariostesque in irony."

Moreover, Moevs views Petrarch's rewriting of Dante's Ulysses in *Fam.* 21.15, to which I will return, as Petrarch's way of "stripping Dante of the powerful mythology he created around his own literary project: [Petrarch] is saying that Dante, in reality, did not and could not do more than what Petrarch or any writer can do, which is to establish and stabilize one's presence in the world, the consequence of which is literary glory."

Although the deracinated metaphysical portrait of the Petrarchan self that Moevs provides contributes to our understanding of the desire for literary glory inspiring Petrarch's rivalry with Dante, it perhaps underestimates the extent to which that literary activity represented for him a spiritual practice in its own right. There is little doubt that the vulnerability of the Petrarchan ego, its extreme "suscettibilità," to use an Italian term, made for a life that was full of polemics, all of them at one level or another motivated by Petrarch's need to defend and bolster a precarious sense of identity. In this sense Petrarch's struggles with Dante were central to the construction of a literary sense of self. Nevertheless, it is important to bear in mind that writing for Petrarch itself represented a vehicle for pursuing his own alternative "horizontal" path of spiritual self-transcendence. Thus Petrarch's vernacular lyric poetry articulated, in contrapuntal opposition to the prophetical-poetic claims of Dante's *Commedia*, Petrarch's own experience of transcendent being through the encounter with Laura along a discontinuous and fragmentary itinerary of spiritual development.[25]

Thus, while there is no essential contradiction between the rejection of Laura-Medusa at the end of the *Canzoniere* and the apotheosis of Laura in the final vision of the nearly contemporary *Triumphus eternitatis,* both works, each in its own pointed way, express an unwavering dissent from the claims for Beatrice upon which Dante founded his *Commedia.* Far from an irreconcilable divergence, Petrarch expresses in the *Canzoniere* and the *Trionfi* two perfectly compatible alternative attitudes of the deracinated Petrarchan self vis-à-vis the experience of transcendent being that Laura represented in his life. On the one hand, Laura in the *Canzoniere* is taken to be the Medusa of worldly form to be transcended, while on the other hand, in the *Triumphus eternitatis* she continues to represent the very possibility and promise of that transcendence.[26] In this respect, the culminating vision of the *Triumphus eternitatis,* compared with Dante's in *Paradiso* 33 (with which it shares the identical number of verses), appears to be not so much an expression of Ariostesque irony as a parody in the original sense of that term, that is, a counter-song (the apparent Greek roots of the word are *par-*, which can mean beside, counter, or against, and *-ody,* or song, as in an ode), an imitation that was set in opposition to the original and that expressed Petrarch's own alternative, more humanly vulnerable truth claim.[27]

The specifically ideological basis of Petrarch's rejection of Dante's poetics should not be underestimated. That is to say, the supposed personal issues with Dante, the jealousy of his predecessor that was attributed to him by his contemporaries and against which he archly defended himself in the first of his letters on Dante to Boccaccio, should not obscure for us the fact that his ideological dissent from Dante was substantive. What was at stake was not so much, or in any case not only, poetic glory but rather two divergent views of the relation between the human and the divine, and consequently between literature and divine knowledge. While Petrarch had far less confidence in man's capacity to bridge these gaps in this life than did Dante, his perspective, as is amply demonstrated by Martinez's essay in this volume, was no less profoundly Christian than his predecessor's. Thus it was fundamentally for ideological reasons that Petrarch could never be persuaded by the prophetic truth claims of the *Commedia,* and why he felt authorized, even compelled, to read and rewrite his predecessor against the grain — as we will see, perhaps most emblematically, in the case of Dante's self-authorizing utilization of Ulysses in the *Commedia.*

Given Petrarch's disbelieving attitude toward Dante's poetic claims, it is not surprising that one of his favorite parodic devices in the project of dismantling Dante's authority is reductionism or what Barański terms in his essay "deminutio." The recognition of this kind of pointed "intertextual"[28] intervention through which Petrarch strategically sought to undermine Dante's theological and prophetic claims has been made difficult by the neutral inter-discursiveness that characterizes most of Petrarch's borrowings from Dante, which were due to the rapid and irresistible success of Dante's poetic language as a model for Trecento Italy. Moreover, this rhetorical phenomenon often passes unobserved, due to the anodyne manner in which the relationship between Petrarch and Dante has been received by much of the critical tradition.

To cite one example, when Guglielmo Gorni discovered some years ago that Petrarch had taken the rhyme scheme and even several of the rhyme words of Dante's great canzone of exile, "Tre donne," and used them in his ballad "Di tempo in tempo mi si fa men dura" (*Rerum vulgarium fragmenta* 149),[29] the critic did not consider the possibility that the borrowing could represent anything but an unambiguous homage to the master. For

Gorni, the use of Dante's strophic structure and rhyme words served Petrarch's primary purpose of elevating the status of the ballad and rendering it worthy of entering the austere classicizing precincts of the *Canzoniere*.

Yet this approach ignores the very real possibility that Petrarch sought to undermine Dante's authority by "reducing" to the context of an amorous ballad[30] the structure and rhyme words of the first stanza of "Tre donne," arguably Dante's greatest canzone, the one in which he assumes the self-authorizing status as exile and that led in so many senses directly to the *Commedia*.[31] If one were to accept the notion that Petrarch had knowledge of the *De vulgari eloquentia* (as does Corrado Bologna),[32] the polemical edge of Petrarch's utilization of the scheme from "Tre donne" would emerge even more sharply, for there the *cantio* is defined by Dante as the most privileged and tragic of poetic genres in explicit contrast to the lowly ballad.[33] The subtle nature of Petrarch's reductionism vis-à-vis Dante has conspired with the tendency of Italian literary historiography to mask the underlying *vis polemica* informing Petrarch's attitude toward Dante, and has led scholars as sophisticated as Gorni, Feo,[34] or Fenzi to occasionally overlook its presence. As we will see, the desire to reconcile Petrarch to Dante leads Fenzi to conceive of a Petrarch who is sympathetic to his predecessor, despite persuasive evidence marshaled by Fenzi himself that Petrarch's reuse of Dante's Ulysses reflects a debunking of his predecessor's poetic claims in the *Commedia*. But the evident need of the Italian scholarly tradition to overlook Petrarch's anti-*dantismo* ultimately traces its prestigious origins to the success of Boccaccio's ambitious philological, historiographical, and patriotic program of canonization on behalf of "Florentine" vernacular literature, which required in the first place that Petrarch be reconciled to Dante. The fact that Petrarch's anti-*dantismo* was forced to come to terms with the most enthusiastic of pro-Dantists largely explains its curiously surreptitious and complex character. Petrarch was forced to go underground with his dissent from Dante, and to leave it for posterity to uncover.

BETWEEN PETRARCH AND DANTE: BOCCACCIO

Billanovich's fundamental essay "Tra Dante e Petrarca" describes an *ab origine* opposition between the Tuscan vernacular tradition epitomized by Dante and the earliest phase of Humanism pioneered by Lovato Lovati and Albertino Mussato in Padua, precisely the line that Petrarch was to inherit and carry forward, initially from Provence. (This was the divide that Giovanni del Virgilio had sought to bridge during the 1320s: were Dante to "cease scattering heedlessly his pearls to swine" in the vernacular and instead sing of modern deeds in Latin, not only would del Virgilio personally bestow the laurel crown in Bologna, but Dante would also enjoy the company there of the recently crowned "Phrygian Muso" Albertino Mussato.)[35] Billanovich traces the rapid spread of Petrarch's reputation throughout Italy following the watershed of his coronation as poet laureate in 1341, and the development of Humanism. He describes Boccaccio's contributions to Humanism and to Petrarch's fame in Italy and Florence, beginning with the *De vita et moribus domini Francisci Petracchi de Florentia* (1341). Powerful cultural synergies between Boccaccio and Petrarch were greatly fostered by their personal relationship, which grew more intense after they met for the first time in Florence in 1350. Like that between the later Goethe and Schiller, theirs was to become one of the most significant friendships in literary history.

According to a historiographic commonplace that emerged from this standard account, Boccaccio turned away from the vernacular to embrace Latin Humanism after meeting Petrarch in 1350 in Florence. In fact, most of Boccaccio's works composed after that date were written in Latin, including books that were fundamental for early Humanism, such as the *De casibus virorum illustrium* (1355–63), *De montibus, silvis, fontibus et de nominibus maris liber* (1355–64), *De mulieribus claris* (1361–62), *Genealogia deorum* (1350–74), and the *Buccolicum carmen* (1369–70). According to Dionisotti, the *volgarizzamento* of the second and third decades of Petrarch's Livy that Boccaccio would have completed before their meeting remained without attribution, so as not to offend the fastidious humanistic linguistic sensibilities of Boccaccio's new friend, for whom the very notion of the *volgarizzamento* as a cultural operation was tantamount to casting "heedlessly pearls to swine."[36] Yet, despite his conversion to Petrarch's cultural program and his own impressive contributions to early humanist literature, Petrarch's "first disciple," as Billanovich styled him, never betrayed his faith in Dante, and was not bashful about enthusiastically recommending the father of Tuscan vernacular literature to Petrarch. One can imagine how thrilled Petrarch must have been to encounter Boccaccio's unabated enthusiasm for Dante when they first met in Florence in 1350.

In fact, while joining with Petrarch to promote the cause of Humanism, Boccaccio pursued with no less conviction his own promotion of Dante and his legacy. He wrote in his own hand three extant copies of the *Commedia* between the early 1350s and the early 1370s; and in the last years of his life he undertook a public reading and commentary on Dante's poem in the church of Santo Stefano di Badia. The notes of these lectures have survived as *Le esposizioni sopra la Commedia di Dante* (1373–75), which represent the final testament of a lifelong, unrelenting commitment to Dante and his *Commedia*.

Boccaccio's importance for the tradition of Dante's works is well known. He copied numerous Dantean texts in his manuscript miscellanies or *Zibaldoni,* which preserve three Latin letters (III, X, XII) for which no other copies survive, as well as the most philologically important testimony of the poetic exchange with Giovanni del Virgilio. The *Commedia* that Boccaccio had sent to Petrarch between the summer of 1351 and May 1353, Vatican Latin manuscript 3199, was utilized by Pietro Bembo in his edition of Dante's *Terze rime* published by Aldus Manutius in 1502, and became the vulgata of the poem until the mid-nineteenth century and the edition of Karl Witte (1862). Boccaccio's own "editions" of Dante's poem included other texts and paratexts, among them the *Vita nova,* an anthology of fifteen *canzoni,* brief summaries to accompany the cantos of the *Commedia,* and his own biography of Dante, the *Trattatello in laude di Dante,* which was written to accompany the ensemble. Simon Gilson has recently noted Boccaccio's concern with how Dante and Petrarch might be reconciled and how this aim permeates Boccaccio's *Trattatello*: "[Boccaccio] constantly attempts to juxtapose Dante and Petrarch and to make them complement one another, as he does earlier in the life of Petrarch and later on the pages of his Chigiano manuscript."[37]

Boccaccio's editorial approach to Dante's vernacular writings, meanwhile, reflected a philological attitude toward vernacular literature that was unprecedented and that Petrarch would have recognized and found congenial. It was an approach that applied an incipient humanist textual sensibility to the vernacular sphere, one that represented the beginnings of a response to Petrarch's worries about the uncontrolled nature of the transmission of vernacular texts. These worries emerge as a central preoccupation in both of Petrarch's letters to Boccaccio about Dante. In his contribution to this volume, Justin Steinberg shifts the discussion of *Familiares* 21.15

and *Seniles* 5.2 from a focus on Petrarch's presumed anxieties of influence vis-à-vis Dante to Petrarch's explicitly stated anxieties about textual control over his own vernacular legacy. He shows how Petrarch's preoccupation with the unstable nature of vernacular transmission conditioned the treatment of his own "uncollected" poems, the *disperse,* and influenced not only Petrarch's distinctive development of the theme of "the other woman" that he had inherited from Dante, but also the final ordering of the *Canzoniere* (in particular, the late substitution of *Rvf* 121, the madrigal "Or vedi, Amor, che giovenetta donna," for the ballata "Donna mi vène spesso ne la mente" [E18]).

For our immediate purposes, it is important to recognize that Boccaccio's canonization efforts on behalf of Dante and vernacular literature represented the beginnings of Italian vernacular philology and historiography and, therefore, an institutional response to Petrarch's reservations, anxieties, and fears about the place of vernacular poetry in the culture, including by extension his own "nugellae." It was largely by virtue of his philological and critical efforts that Boccaccio succeeded in reconciling Petrarch to the cause of the vernacular and even to Dante, if only to the extent that Petrarch was thereby stimulated to vie even more strenuously with "ille nostri eloquii dux vulgaris" (the master of our vernacular literature [*Sen.* 5.2.31]).

The most important of Boccaccio's editorial contributions from the perspective of Petrarch and his vernacular legacy was the Chigiano manuscript (Chigi L. VI.176) mentioned by Gilson, which contains the only surviving testimony of the second published form of the *Canzoniere,* also known as the "Chigi" form (1358–63). The fact that Boccaccio brought together in that codex Dante's *Commedia* and Petrarch's *Canzoniere* would have no doubt made a strong impression on Petrarch, as it has on the subsequent tradition and recent criticism. Corrado Bologna, for example, in his history of the classical canon of Italian literature, characterized the Chigi manuscript as "an epoch-defining event, inconceivable to Petrarch's way of looking at things, virtually a necessity in the new horizon opened by Boccaccio, that is, in his integration of Dante and Petrarch." At one level, given his attitude toward Dante, the combination must certainly have been beyond the ken of Petrarch ("impensabile"), as Bologna suggests.[38] Yet at still another level Petrarch must have recognized the implications of Boccaccio's editorial activities for his own vernacular legacy. Together with the conversations with Boccaccio about Dante, they represented a stimulus to continue on his own counter-Dantean vernacular course with renewed determination and conviction. Thus the importance of Boccaccio's Dantean "philology" for subsequent vernacular literary history cannot be underestimated, beginning with its influence on Petrarch. It was no less significant or momentous than Petrarch's on Boccaccio for the history of Humanism. There is, indeed, a kind of balance of reciprocal literary influence to be observed in Boccaccio's turn to Latin, on the one hand, and Petrarch's renewed and intensified engagement with the vernacular in response to Boccaccio's Dante, on the other, as reflected in the compositional histories of the *Canzoniere* and the *Triumphi*.

In fact, the two major letters that Petrarch addressed to Boccaccio concerning Dante coincide with the compositional histories of the *Canzoniere* and the *Triumphi* in such as way as to suggest that their placement in the epistolary collection was meant to underscore for posterity the significance, for Petrarch's vernacular legacy, of the conversation between the two friends about Dante. The first of these, *Familiares* 21.15, was written during the summer of 1359, in the same year in which Petrarch embarked on the Chigi form of the *Canzoniere* (1359–63). He had just published in the previous year the pre-Chigi or Correggio form of the book (1356–58), which is named for its dedicatee Azzo da Correggio, and is generally taken to have been the first published form of the *Canzoniere*. In addition, surviving manuscript annotations point to intensive work on the *Triumphi* toward the end of the 1350s, for which there is also evidence, as we will see, in letters from the *Familiares* written during the same period. Petrarch also composed and published in 1358, among the many projects that engaged him at that time, a pilgrim's guide to the Holy Land, the *Itinerarium ad sepulchrum domini Iesu Christi*, to which I will have occasion to return since, as mentioned earlier, it contains one of the most pointed rewritings of Dante's Ulysses in all of Petrarch's works.

Seniles 5.2, probably written in 1364, was postdated by its ordering in the collection to 1366. This was the very year in which Petrarch started work on the "author's book," Vat. Lat. 3195, that was eventually to contain the definitive form of the *Canzoniere*: the redating of the letter was very likely intended to establish an implicit link to that key moment in the history of the *Canzoniere*.[39] Moreover, it was between 1366 and 1367 that the "forma di Giovanni" of the *Canzoniere* was completed, the next form of the book after Chigi, which is named for the copyist Giovanni Malpaghini, who cop-ied it but abruptly left Petrarch's service in 1367. Petrarch records the episode in nearby letters from book 5 to Donato Albanzani (*Sen.* 5.5 and 5.6), al-most as if he intended to indirectly allude to the completion of the "Gio-vanni form" and his own continuation of the project in these pages of the *Seniles.* That Petrarch was indirectly referencing current developments in his own vernacular project in book 5 of the *Seniles,* especially 5.2 addressed to Boccaccio, is fairly evident. In her contribution to this volume, for ex-ample, Sara Sturm-Maddox takes Petrarch's intriguing reference in *Seniles* 5.2 to an ambitious unfinished work in the vernacular to be an allusion to the project of the *Triumphi,* which continued to be a major focus for Pe-trarch during the 1360s and to the end of his life.[40]

Be that as it may, after Giovanni Malpaghini left Petrarch's service in the spring of 1367, the poet himself continued the work of selecting, revis-ing, ordering, and copying the poems for all the subsequent "forms" of the *Canzoniere,* including the "pre-Malatesta" (1367–72), the "Malatesta" (1371 or 1372 to 4 January 1373), the "Queriniana" (1373), and the final "Vatican redaction" (1373 to 18 July 1374). Far from having given up on the vernacu-lar, as he claims to have done in *Seniles* 5.2, Petrarch was working on both the *Canzoniere* and the *Triumphi* when he wrote that letter, and would continue to do so until his death. During the last year of his life, while still working on the *Triumphus eternitatis,* and perhaps even during his last days, he continued to seek the perfect ordering of the poems, and in the right upper-hand corner of Vat. Lat. 3195 he renumbered the last thirty-one com-positions of the *Canzoniere.*[41] The epistolary exchanges with Boccaccio on Dante thus correspond to the two most important moments in the history of the *Canzoniere,* that is, when Petrarch decided to reopen the project in 1359 following its first publication the year before (which also corresponded to a time of intense dedication to the *Triumphi*), and when he first initiated the assembly of the "author's book" of the *Canzoniere* in 1366. The influ-ence of Boccaccio's promotion of Dante and the nascent vernacular literary tradition on his friend's vernacular development is implicitly commemo-rated by the chronologically congruent placement of these letters in the epistolary.[42]

But to appreciate fully the force of that influence, a brief review of their interactions during the 1350s (discussed more completely by Sturm-Maddox in this volume), is necessary, before examining in somewhat greater detail these two crucial junctures in the progress of Petrarch's vernacular project. Having learned at their first meeting in Florence in 1350 that Petrarch did not possess a copy of the *Commedia*, Boccaccio sent him (between the summer of 1351 and May 1353) what would become know as Vat. Lat. 3199, together with a poem in praise of Dante, "Ytalie iam certus honos," in which Boccaccio heralded Dante as *theologus-poeta*, and worthy of the laurel crown. Boccaccio's provocative promotion of Dante arrived at a time when Petrarch found himself at an important turning point. Their first encounters during the early 1350s (the first meeting in Florence was followed by a visit of Boccaccio's to Petrarch in Padua in the spring of 1352) coincided with preparations and negotiations that would soon lead to Petrarch's definitive move to Italy. The consolidation of the *Canzoniere* into a book, which is conventionally dated from the time of the composition of the proemial poem (1350), also took place at this time. The plan for the *Familiares* dates from the same period, as did the composition of the dedicatory letter of that collection, which is also dated 1350. The first draft of the *Posteritati* is thought to have been written around the same time, probably under the influence of Boccaccio's own precocious biography of Petrarch, the *De vita et moribus domini Francisci Petracchi de Florentia*.[43]

When Boccaccio and Petrarch first met in Florence in 1350, Petrarch was engaged in fashioning for the benefit of contemporaries and posterity an exemplary autobiography figuring his claimed "conversion at forty," somewhat awkward or incongruous remnants of which still survive in his writings. According to these extant traces of the biographical plot that Petrarch was developing around 1350,[44] Petrarch initially planned to present himself to his contemporaries and to posterity as having moved beyond the love story with Laura already in the 1340s, a breakthrough that is foreshadowed in *Familiares* 4.1 (fictionally dated 26 April 1336 but composed between 1350 and 1353) and at the end of book 3 of Franciscus' dialogue with Augustinus in the *Secretum*, which was also fictionally dated (between 1342 and 1343), but actually composed between 1350 and 1353.[45] This same fictional autobiographical scheme informed the penitential structure of the Correggio form of the *Canzoniere*, which took a palinodic rejection of his love for Laura as its point of departure: "et del mio vaneggiar vergogna è 'l frutto / e 'l pentérsi" (and of my raving, shame is the fruit, and repentance [*Rvf* 1, 12−13]).[46]

Indeed, Petrarch reported in the *Posteritati* that he had rejected the fairer sex around his fortieth year (1344): "Mox vero ad quadragesimum etatis annum appropinquans, dum adhuc et caloris satis esset et virium, non solum factum illud obscenum, sed eius memoriam omnem sic abieci, quasi nunquam feminam aspexissem" (As I was approaching my fortieth year, while I still had plenty of ardor and strength, I so completely threw off not only the obscene act, but the very recollection of it, that it seemed I had never looked at a woman [*Sen.* 18.1]). Moreover, in the *Posteritati* he still appeared to stake his literary reputation squarely on the *Africa*. In fact, the coronation, discussed by Sturm-Maddox in this volume, still seemed central to Petrarch's self-portrait in the "Letter to Posterity," at a time when he found himself at a crossroads between Provence and Italy, and on the verge of committing himself to Italy and the second part of his literary career. Yet there is no doubt that Petrarch's renewed encounter with Dante, forced by Boccaccio's enthusiasm, occurred at a propitious moment, and that a change in direction can be traced to the time when Petrarch was first confronted by Boccaccio's Dante. In 1352, the year after his second meeting with Boccaccio in Padua, and the year before his definitive move to Italy, Petrarch probably began in Vaucluse, under the influence of Boccaccio's Dantean *Amorosa visione,* the composition of the *Triumphi.*[47] And as Sturm-Maddox opportunely recalls, it was in the *Amorosa visione* that Boccaccio envisions Dante receiving the laurel crown (*A.V.* 5.70–78), a passage that must have warmed Petrarch's heart.

Petrarch had already claimed by that time, in the "Letter to Posterity," to have abandoned poetry in favor of sacred letters. He did, in effect, abandon the *Africa* and had, for the most part, completed the last of his major poetic works in Latin, the *Bucolicum carmen,* by the end of the 1350s. Nevertheless, in blatant contradiction to the claim that he had abandoned poetry in the *Posteritati,* a renewed commitment to vernacular poetry from the end of the 1350s on clearly emerges, as indicated by even a cursory review of the synthetic chronology of Petrarch's life and works that accompanies Santagata's edition of the *Canzoniere.* It was, in fact, this renewed commitment to vernacular poetry that largely characterized the Italian phase of Petrarch's career and would shape his legacy and reputation for subsequent literary history.

Petrarch must have rapidly come to appreciate during the 1350s the opportunity that the vernacular represented for him in Italy. At the same time, he must also have recognized the formidable opposition that his own anti-*dantismo* would have had to overcome, beginning with his new friend Giovanni Boccaccio, the greatest of Dante's contemporary admirers. In any event, Petrarch appears to have discarded the "conversion at forty" program by the time of their third meeting in Milan in the spring of 1359 and his first letter to Boccaccio on Dante, *Familiares* 21.15, composed the following summer. The first traces of Petrarch's work on the "Chigi" form of the *Canzoniere* date from the fall of that same year. Significantly, this new form of the book abruptly reopened the project of the *Canzoniere* by disrupting the ethical structure that had informed the Correggio redaction, which had been based upon the autobiographical fiction of Petrarch's *mutatio vitae*. The new form, instead, effectively reopened the question of whether the poet's love for Laura was a positive or a negative spiritual force in his life.

The open-ended and ideologically unresolved extension of both parts of the Chigi form left the book, as recorded by Boccaccio in the manuscript he copied in the early 1360s (presumably during his visit with Petrarch in Venice during the spring of 1363), in a precarious state, especially pronounced at the end of the first part, which concluded with the pessimism of Petrarch's most famous shipwreck, "Passa la nave mia colma d'oblio," a composition that would eventually take position 189 in the final order.[48] As noted earlier, this Chigian moment of "horizontal self-transcendence" in the history of the *Canzoniere* corresponds to the same time period in which Petrarch was working on the *Triumphi* with a renewed sense of purpose. The earliest surviving manuscript datings begin in 1356, and Petrarch's enthusiasm in connection with his work on the *Triumphi* is expressed, for example, in *Familiares* 19.16, where Marco Ariani has detected a clear allusion to the project.[49] Both these new beginnings, so to speak, take place in suggestive temporal proximity to the 1359 letter to Boccaccio on Dante, *Familiares* 21.15, when there is plenty of evidence to suggest that Dante was very much on Petrarch's mind. In another famous letter to Boccaccio on imitation, for example, which was written in the same year, namely, *Familiares* 22.2, Ariani has identified a clear allusion to the *Triumphi*, which the critic takes to be among the "inaccessa" of which Petrarch speaks:

> Nolo ducem qui me vinciat sed precedat; sint cum duce oculi, sit iudicium, sit libertas; non prohibear ubi velim pedem ponere et preterire aliqua et inaccessa tentare; et breviorem sive ita fert animus, planiorem callem sequi et properare et subsistere et divertere liceat et reverti.

I do not want a guide who leads me, not one who binds me to him, one who leaves me to use my own sight, judgment and freedom; I do not want him to forbid me to step where I wish to go beyond him in some things, to attempt the inaccessible, to follow a shorter or, if I wish, an easier path, and to hasten or stop or even to part ways and return.

It does not require a great deal of imagination to imagine who the guide is that Petrarch does not need.

An even clearer signal that Petrarch at the end of the 1350s was particularly engaged in taking his own path in counterpoint to Dante's is found in two parallel, nearly contemporary evocations of the Ulysses theme from that period. The most famous of these is in an autobiographical passage from the first letter on Dante to Boccaccio, *Familiares* 21.15, which has quite rightly been interpreted by Gilson, and now in this volume by Moevs and Barański, as containing a veiled critique of Dante:

> Cum avo patreque meo vixit, avo minor, patre autem natu maior, cum quo simul uno die atque uno civili turbine patriis finibus pulsus fuit. Quo tempore inter participes erumnarum magne sepe contrahuntur amicitie, idque vel maxime inter illos accidit, ut quibus esset preter similem fortunam, studiorum et ingenii multa similitudo, nisi quod exilio, cui pater in alias curas versus et familie solicitus cessit, ille obstitit, et tum vehementius cepto incubuit, omnium negligens soliusque fame cupidus. In quo illum satis mirari et laudare vix valeam, quem non civium iniuria, non exilium, non paupertas, non simultatum aculei, non amor coniugis, non natorum pietas ab arrepto semel calle distraheret, cum multi quam magni tam delicati ingenii sint, ut ab intentione animi leve illos murmur avertat.

> He lived with my grandfather and father, being younger than the first, but older than the second with whom on the same day and as a result of the same civil disturbance he was driven from his native land into exile. At such times, fast friendships often develop among victims of similar tribulations, and this was especially true of them since, in addition to a similar fate, they shared common interests and studies. But my father compelled by other matters and by concern for his family,

resigned himself to exile, while his friend resisted and began devoting himself all the more vigorously to his literary pursuits, neglecting all else and desirous only of glory. In this I can scarcely admire and praise him too highly when nothing— not the injustice suffered at the hands of his fellow citizens, not exile, poverty, or the stings of envy, not his wife's love or his devotion to his children— diverted him from his course once he had embarked upon it, when many other great talents, being weak of purpose, would be distracted by the least disturbance.

Petrarch here praises Dante for his single-minded pursuit of glory and implicitly compares him to Ulysses, utilizing terms that echo the very words that Dante had used to condemn Ulysses in the *Inferno*:

> "né dolcezza di figlio, né la pieta
> del vecchio padre, né 'l debito amore
> lo qual dovea Penelopè far lieta,
>   vincer potero dentro a me l'ardore
> ch'i' ebbi a divenir del mondo esperto
> e de li vizi umani e del valore;"
>   (*Inf.* 26.94–99)

> "not tenderness for a son, nor filial duty / toward my aged
> father, nor the love I owed / Penelope that would have made
> her glad, could overcome the fervor that was mine / to gain
> experience of the world / and learn about man's vices, and
> his worth."[50]

Not exile, Petrarch writes, nor stings of envy, nor his wife's love, nor his devotion to his sons could keep Dante from the pursuit of glory. As Gilson has noted, a "pointed differentiation is implied in Petrarch's emphasis upon how Dante pushed aside all matters including family, in the ardent pursuit of fame."[51] The passage evidently traces part of its inspiration to Boccaccio's *Trattatello*, and in particular to a passage in which Boccaccio had emphasized Dante's focus on sacred studies, which Petrarch pointedly alters to a relentless pursuit of fame, while adding the underhanded allusion to Dante's Ulysses.[52] Indeed, as Barański makes clear in his essay in this volume, Petrarch consistently differentiates his own virtue and virtuous motivations from Dante's more questionable poetics fueled by a pursuit of fame. Petrarch even implies in *Familiares* 21.15, according to Barański, that desire for glory motivated Dante to write for a more numerous and less demanding public in the vernacular in the first place: "Dante's pursuit of glory, of wanting to receive the recognition of others (and what others), points to a profound lack of virtue."[53]

The revision of Dante's Ulysses and the sly use of Dante's own invention *contra Dantem* in his letter on Dante addressed to Boccaccio is therefore diametrically opposed to Petrarch's use of the same figure of Ulysses just a year earlier, in a key passage of the *Itinerarium ad sepulchrum domini Iesu Christi* (17.1). There it is the pursuit of virtue, not of glory, fame, or honor, that is described as characteristic of the Ulyssean journey (and by extension, of Petrarch's own journey). The contrast with the motivation that Petrarch will attribute to Dante one year later is evident. When Petrarch addresses to his pilgrim-friend Giovanni Mandelli the exhortation to continue his journey despite nostalgia for home, he may as well have been speaking of his own artistic pilgrimage at the end of the 1350s, urging himself to push beyond his less virtuous predecessor:

Quid vero nunc cogitas? An nondum te desiderium nostri cepit, ut domum, ut patriam, ut amicos invisere animus sit? Credo id quidem, imo ne aliter fieri posse certus sum. Sed nullus est acrior stimulus quam virtutis. Ille nunc per omnes difficultates generosum animum impellit, nec consistere patitur, nec retro respicere cogitque non voluptatum modo, sed honestorum pignorum atque affectuum oblivisci, nichil aliud virtutis spetiem optare, nichil velle, nichil denique cogitare. Hic stimulus qui Ulixem Laertis et Penelopes et Thelemaci fecit immemorem, te nunc nobis vereor abstrahet quam vellemus.

———————

But what are you thinking now? Hasn't the desire to see us again taken you yet; hasn't the desire to return to your home, your fatherland, and friends entered your soul yet? I believe so and am sure it could not be any other way. But there is no greater stimulus than virtue. Virtue inspires the generous soul to overcome every difficulty; it does not suffer one to remain in one place, nor that one should look back; it forces one to forget not only pleasures but also more just duties and affections; it does not allow one to choose anything but the ideal of virtue and it does not allow one to desire or think of anything else. This is the stimulus that made Ulysses forget Laertes, Penelope, and Telemachus, and now keeps you far from us, I am afraid, longer than we should like.

The unambiguous endorsement of the pursuit of virtue as the appropriate and praiseworthy stimulus that made Ulysses stay away from home is in striking contrast with the ambiguity of Petrarch's attributing to Dante one year later the relentless pursuit of glory as the stimulus that made him forget his wife and children. Before turning, however, in the last section of this essay to the wider meta-literary significance of Petrarch's appropriation and rewritings of Dante's Ulysses in his works, we must first consider the state of the *Canzoniere* at the time of the second letter on Dante, *Seniles* 5.2, for the light it can shed on the evolution of Petrarch's attitude toward Dante and toward vernacular literature, and by extension toward his own vernacular poetry.

In the "Giovanni form" of the *Canzoniere*, Petrarch continued to undermine Dante's *auctoritas* by denying him even the title of "poeta," while at the same time clearly signaling his renewed commitment to his own vernacular legacy. Below I provide a map of a segment of Vatican Latin manuscript 3195 showing the complex textual history of reorderings and insertions that Petrarch accomplished in the transition from the Chigi (Ch; 1359–63) to the Giovanni (Gv; 1366–67) to the first phase of the pre-Malatesta (Pmɪ; October 1367–May 1368) forms of the author's book in the first part:

35v	36r	36v	37r	37v	38r	38v	39r	39v
166 (Gv)	170 (Ch)	174 Gv)	178 Ch	182 (Gv)	186 (Gv)	190 (Gv)	*194 (Pmɪ)*	*198 (Pmɪ)*
167 (Gv)	171 (Ch)	175 (Gv)	[ ]* (Gv)	183 (Gv)	187 (Gv)	*191 (Pmɪ)*	*195 (Pmɪ)*	
168 (Gv)	172 (Ch)	176 (Ch)	180 (Gv)	184 (Ch)	188 (Gv)	*192 (Pmɪ)*	*196 (Pmɪ)*	
169 (Ch)	173 (Ch)	177 (Ch)	181 (Gv)	185 (Ch)	189 (Ch)	*193 (Pmɪ)*	*197 (Pmɪ)*	

Completing the Giovanni form required first of all that Petrarch revise the pessimistic ending of the Chigi form, which had concluded with the shipwreck of number 189, "Passa la nave mia," whose original position is indicated in the map by the gap between numbers 178 and 180 that Petrarch had instructed Giovanni Malpaghini to leave blank. It is clear from the map that Petrarch's plan for the Giovanni form was informed, even graphically, by the desire to reestablish equilibrium and achieve balance at the end of the first part of the Giovanni form, values that had been compromised by the ideologically and formally unresolved state of the Chigi *Canzoniere*. The lacuna in the order of the Giovanni form of the book left behind by the shipwreck poem (which had been moved forward to the penultimate position of the Giovanni form) remained unfilled until the first phase of the pre-Malatesta form (Pm1), when Petrarch himself copied number 179, "Geri, quando talor s'adira," into the order of Vat. Lat. 3195.

This particular textual segment of the transition between forms is arguably the most significant in the history of the making of the *Canzoniere*. Petrarch manages in the passage between the Giovanni form and the first phase of the pre-Malatesta form to overcome the shipwreck that had threatened the project at the end of the Chigi form, which had left unresolved the contrast between a positive and negative view of the poet's love for Laura. I have argued elsewhere that Petrarch definitively resolved the unstable ideological structure of the book only during the first phase of the pre-Malatesta form, by inserting number 179, which identified Laura with Medusa: "Andrei non altramente / a veder lei, che 'l volto di Medusa, / che facea marmo diventar la gente" (I would not go to see her otherwise than to see the face of Medusa, which made people become marble [179, 9–11]).[54] Petrarch copied another Medusan poem into the order at the same time, number 197, "L'aura celeste che 'n quell verde lauro": "pò quello in me, che nel gran vecchio mauro / Medusa quando in selce trasformollo" (has the power over me that Medusa had over the old Moorish giant, when she turned him to flint [197, 5–6]). Petrarch thereby established both a structural-ideological link back to an earlier Medusa poem (number 51, "Poco era ad appressarsi agli occhi miei") and, more importantly, a bridge forward to the last poem in the collection, the canzone to the Virgin composed at the same time, in which Laura is explicitly identified with Medusa in opposition to the Mother of God: "Medusa et l'error mio m'àn fatto un sasso / d'umor vano stillante" (Medusa and my error have made me a stone dripping vain moisture [366, 111–12]).

In the context of the present discussion of Petrarch's evolving attitude toward the vernacular, however, I would like to draw attention to the placement of three key metapoetical poems on either side of the blank space left by moving the shipwreck poem in the transition from the Chigi to the Giovanni forms. These metapoetic poems were additions to the Giovanni form that Petrarch precisely positioned in two chiastically structured triptychs, located in the first three positions on pages 35v and 38r, respectively. The triptychs frame, the seam around the shipwreck that Petrarch was concerned with closing between the Chigi and Giovanni forms:

35v	36r	36v	37r	37v	38r	38v
166	170	174	178	182	186	190 (last poem of Giovanni form)
167	171	175	[ ]*	183	187	
168	172	176	180	184	188	
169	173	177	181	185	189	

The triptychs are mirror images of one another. The first metapoetic poem, "S'i' fussi stato fermo a la spelunca" (166), is followed by two love poems, while on the other side of the blank space left by "Passa la nave mia," two metapoetic poems, "Se Virgilio et Homero avessin visto" (186) and "Giunto Alexandro a la famosa tomba" (187), are followed by a love poem:

166	186
167	187
168	188

Besides the graphic and thematic symmetries that are present, Petrarch established by their placement a thematic progression between the poems on either side of the frame that expressed his new attitude toward his vernacular project, consistent with his ongoing work on the *Canzoniere* and the *Triumphi*. In other words, the transition from 166 to 186/187 in the order of the book parallels the unmistakable, albeit dissembled, deeper significance of his contemporary letter addressed to Boccaccio concerning Dante. The first poem, probably a composition from his days in Provence, is recovered by Petrarch and added to the order of the book for the first time here.[55] It combines a dismissal of Dante, to whom Petrarch denies even the title of "poeta" in the first quatrain,[56] with dejection about the prospects of his own Latin poetry, in particular, the *Africa,* while characteristically maintaining the possibility that Jove might yet rain his grace upon him:

> S'i' fussi stato fermo a la spelunca
> là dove Apollo diventò profeta,
> Fiorenza avria forse oggi il suo poeta,
> non pur Verona et Mantoa et Arunca;
>
> ma perché 'l mio terren più non s'ingiunca
> de l'humor di quel sasso, altro pianeta
> conven ch'i' segua, et del mio campo mieta
> lappole et stecchi co la falce adunca.
>
> L'oliva è secca, et è rivolta altrove
> l'acqua che di Parnaso si deriva,
> per cui in alcun tempo ella fioriva.
>
> Così sventura over colpa mi priva
> d'ogni buon fructo, se l'etterno Giove
> de la sua gratia sopra me non piove.

―――――――

If I had stayed in the cave where Apollo became a prophet, Florence would perhaps have her poet today, not only Verona and Mantua and Arunca; but, since my ground produces no more reeds from the water of that rock, I must follow another planet and with my hooked sickle reap thistles and thorns in my field. The olive tree is dry, and the waters have turned elsewhere that flow down from Parnassus and at one time made it flourish. Thus misfortune or my fault deprives me of all good fruit, if eternal Jove does not rain His grace down upon me.

The anti-*dantismo* of this sonnet has been recognized by the commentary tradition since Tassoni ("Mostra di non tener conto alcuno di Dante" [He shows that he has no regard for Dante])[57] and has been reaffirmed by the recent *lectura* of Guglielmo Gorni and Paola Allegretti.[58] What has been overlooked, however, is that the extremely unusual rhyme scheme that departs from "spelunca" is also, ultimately, anti-Dantean in inspiration. The feature completely overlooked, as far as I have been able to determine, is the way in which Petrarch's rare rhymes from "spelunca" ostentatiously echo Dante's hapax use of "spelonca" in rhyme in a passage of the fourth circle of Malebolge (*Inf.* 20.46–51), where the false prophets and soothsayers are punished. Petrarch pointedly recalls in his use of "spelunca" as a rhyme word the infernal example of a Tuscan augur:

> "Aronta è quel ch'al ventre li s'atterga,
> che ne' monti di Luni, dove ronca
> lo Carrarese che di sotto alberga,
>   ebbe tra ' bianchi marmi la spelonca
> per sua dimora; onde a guardar le stelle
> e 'l mar non li era la veduta tronca."
>   (*Inf.* 20.46–51)

> "He who puts his back to that one's belly is Aruns. / In the hills of Luni — where the Carraresi, / who shelter in the valley, work the earth — / he lived inside a cave in that white marble, from which he could observe the sea and stars / in a wide and boundless prospect."

Not only was Dante not a poet in Petrarch's view; he was also a false prophet. Petrarch dismissed Dante not just on stylistic and linguistic grounds and because he wrote in the vernacular rather than Latin, but for ethical and ideological reasons as well.

Poems 186 and 187, on the other hand, rather emphatically express Petrarch's reconciliation with and renewed faith in his own vernacular project:

> Se Virgilio et Homero avessin visto
> quel sole il qual vegg'io con gli occhi miei,

tutte lor forze in dar fama a costei
avrian posto, et l'un stil coll'altro misto:

di che sarebbe Enea turbato et tristo,
Achille, Ulixe et gli altri semidei,
et quel che resse anni cinquantasei
sí bene il mondo, et quel ch'ancise Egisto.

Quel fior anticho di vertuti et d'arme
come sembiante stella ebbe con questo
novo fior d'onestate et di bellezze!

Ennio di quel cantò ruvido carme,
di quest'altro io: et oh pur non molesto
gli sia il mio ingegno, e 'l mio lodar non sprezze!

(186)

———————

If Virgil and Homer had seen that sun which I see with my
eyes, they would have exerted all their powers to give her fame
and would have mixed together the two styles: for which Aeneas
would be angry; and Achilles, Ulysses, and the other demigods,
and he who ruled the world so well for fifty-six years, and he
whom Aegisthus killed, would all be sad. That ancient flower of
virtue and arms, what a similar star he had with his new flower
of chastity and beauty! Ennius sang of him an inelegant song,
I of her; and ah! May my wit not displease her, may she not
despise my praises!

Giunto Alexandro a la famosa tomba
del fero Achille, sospirando disse:
O fortunato, che sí chiara tromba
trovasti, et chi di te sí alto scrisse!

Ma questa pura et candida colomba
a cui non so s'al mondo mai par visse,
nel mio stil frale assai poco rimbomba:
cosí son le sue sorti a ciascun fisse.

Ché d'Omero dignissima et d'Orpheo,
o del pastor ch'anchor Mantova honora,
ch'andassen sempre lei sola cantando,

stella difforme et fato sol qui reo
commise a tal che 'l suo bel nome adora,
ma forse scema sue lode parlando.

(187)

When Alexander came to the famous tomb of fierce Achilles,
he sighing said: "O fortunate one, who found so clear a trumpet,
one who wrote such high things of you!" But this pure and
white dove, whose equal I think never lived in the world, she
resounds very little in my frail style. Thus each one's destiny
is fixed; for she is worthy of Homer and Orpheus and of the
shepherd whom Mantua still honors, worthy to have them
always singing only of her, but a deformed star and her fate,
cruel only in this, have entrusted her to one who adores her
lovely name but perhaps mars her praise when he speaks.

In the transition between the ideologically unresolved and aesthetically still
tentative Chigi form and the resolution and recomposed equilibrium of
the Giovanni form, Petrarch manages to reiterate his disregard for Dante,
suggest that his own ambitions in Latin poetry are a thing of the past, and
reaffirm the validity of his own vernacular poetic enterprise. While rhetorically expressing doubts about his own talent, as was typical for Petrarch,
the worthiness of Laura as an object of poetic celebration is most emphatically asserted in poems 186 and 187; Petrarch justifies his own vernacular
project by an appeal to no less than the authority of Virgil, Homer, and
Orpheus. In an important *lectura* of poems 186 and 187, Vincenzo Fera proposed that their addition to the *Canzoniere* during the Giovanni phase of
elaboration had to do with the fact that Homer, who is mentioned in both
poems for the first and only time in the collection, had entered Petrarch's
library in translation around that time.[59] Yet the architectural precision of
the arrangement of the metapoetic poems in this passage of the book suggests that a deeper, less external intention was at work. Just as Petrarch
strategically ordered the letters in his epistolary to commemorate the his-

tory of his spiritual and intellectual development, so the selection and ordering of the poems in the *Canzoniere* responds to and records the evolution in his thinking about his vernacular legacy as a poet. A moment of reconciliation and recommitment to his vernacular legacy, albeit *contra Dantem*, is expressed and punctually recorded, on the one hand, by the discussion of Dante with Boccaccio in *Seniles* 5.2, and on the other, by the selection and placement of the metapoetic poems that entered the Giovanni form at the end of the first part of the *Canzoniere*.

BETWEEN PETRARCH AND DANTE: ULYSSES

Beyond the richness and precision of its philological reconnaissance of the presence of Ulysses in Petrarch's oeuvre, Enrico Fenzi's 2004 contribution to the "Between Dante and Petrarch" tradition of commentary is fundamental for its discovery that Petrarch's Ulysses ultimately derives his ideological force from Dante's rewriting of the myth. For Fenzi, "Petrarch's Ulysses is essentially Dante's Ulysses, or at least as seen through Dante." He finds that Petrarch, "while basing his evaluation of the figure of Ulysses on classical texts, demonstrates to the end his substantial faithfulness to Dante's vision."[60] In addition, Fenzi's essay provides a vital insight into the motivations that informed Petrarch's appropriation of Dante's Ulysses, and in particular of the Ulyssean journey as a signature theme: Petrarch recognized the sign of his own modernity in Dante's bold rewriting of the myth, which he redirected on an outward-bound trajectory. Petrarch embraces Dante's invention of a Ulysses who never returns home to Laertes, Penelope, and Telemachus: "Ulysses is not that of the tradition, but precisely, that of Dante, he who *does not return*."[61]

But true to the Boccaccian legacy of concern with how to reconcile the two great founders of the traditions of Italian Humanism and vernacular literature, Fenzi, faced with Petrarch's ambiguous praise of a Ulyssean Dante in the first letter to Boccaccio, quite explicitly elides the anti-*dantismo* and resistance that is present in Petrarch's appropriation of Dante's Ulysses: "I don't know how useful it would be, but one might discourse at length on Petrarch's intelligent perfidy in striking his great rival with his own weapons, turning back on its creator the sublime ambiguity of his most controversial creation. Nevertheless, it is best to stick to the serious substance and not the polemics of the discourse. . . ." Rather than explore the nature or the motivation of that perfidious gesture, Fenzi prefers to see Petrarch's attitude as one of admiration for his predecessor as a man. While admitting that Petrarch, in fact, did not endorse the fiction of Dante's own fictional poetic journey, Fenzi concludes that "the operation of Petrarch transforms but essentially remains faithful to the old efficacious topos that states: 'Aristotle was a man and he could err.'"[62]

But such an attempt to reconcile Dante and Petrarch requires that one overlook the way in which Petrarch's ostentatious appropriation of Dante's account of Ulysses's journey (which, one should recall, ends in shipwreck) represented an implicit critique of Dante's utilization of Ulysses in the *Commedia* as a vehicle for authorizing his own poetic journey. As Emilio Pasquini has noted, Petrarch was the first to grasp the manipulative self-authorizing strategy that informed Dante's shipwreck of Ulysses in *Inferno* 26,[63] that is to say, the way in which Dante makes Ulysses and his shipwreck the negative double of himself and his own successful journey. Modern Dante criticism has explored at length this device and found it to be central to the ideological structure of the poem. Yet, while it may be true, as Teodolinda Barolini has argued, that "Ulysses is the lightning rod Dante places in his poem to attract and defuse his own consciousness of the presumption involved in anointing oneself God's scribe,"[64] Petrarch's perfidious praise of Dante for his "non-Ulyssean" pursuit of fame makes clear that for Petrarch, the shipwreck of Ulysses was not sufficient to atone for Dante's presumption. Just as Petrarch implicitly rejected and subverted Dante's self-authorizing vernacular literary history by revising and reordering it in both the *Canzoniere* and the *Triumphi*, so too, he rejected and effectively revised for his own purposes Dante's self-authorization by means of the invention of Ulysses and his shipwreck.

Petrarch's acceptance of the inevitability of shipwreck thus represented, implicitly, a trenchant critique of the elaborate self-authorizing fiction of Dante's *Commedia*, which had based its claim for Dante's successful journey into the afterlife on the shipwreck of Ulysses. In contrast to Dante, Petrarch staked the truth claim for his literature on a stoic acknowledgment of his own human vulnerability and of the inescapability of shipwreck. That Petrarch utilizes every literary means at his disposal to defer inevitable *ruina* thus expresses yet another form of Petrarchan literary resistance to Dante's shipwreck of Ulysses and the literary-ideological system that it supported. For while the wandering journey and shipwreck of Ulysses were for Dante the negative other to the triumph of his own own salvific poetic pilgrimage, Petrarch's stoic deferral of shipwreck allowed him to hold out hope for rescue from his moral abyss. According to an anti-heroic narrative that was implicit and recurring in Petrarch's representations of his moral life, and according to an alternative Christian humanistic poetics conceived in polemical contrast to Dante's, Petrarch repeatedly appeals for deliverance from the depths of his existential predicament, tossed upon the waves, crying out to the Virgin to save him.

Petrarch's appropriation of Dante's Ulysses thus goes to the heart of Petrarch's resistance to Dante and to his theological-poetic system. He rewrites Dante's Ulysses against the grain of Dante's self-authorizing literary construction. It is for this reason that he never uses the figure of the triumphant ocean voyage as a figure for his writing in any of his literary works, as Dante had famously done. Instead, the *Familiares,* for example, begins under the sign of shipwreck, and the burning of Petrarch's letters and poems is likened to the strategy of shipwrecked navigators who lighten their ships in order to survive shipwreck: "mille, vel eo amplius, seu omnis generis sparsa poemata seu familiares epystolas . . . Vulcano corrigendas tradidi. Non sine suspirio quidem—quid enim mollitiem fateri pudeat?—; sed occupato animo quamvis acri remedio succurrendum erat, et tanquam in alto pregravata navis, relevanda preciosarum etiam iactu rerum" (I committed to Vulcan's hands for his correction at least a thousand and more of all kinds and variety of poems and letters . . . I am not ashamed to admit that I did this with a certain tenderness and with many sighs; just as an over-weighted boat in deep waters can be lifted above the billows by discharging overboard even its most precious cargo so it was necessary to render assistance, no matter how drastic, to my preoccupied mind [*Fam.* 1.1.8]).

Petrarch's appropriation of shipwreck as a signature theme is thus "contra Dantem," in the sense that he presents himself in his literature as stoically and serenely contemplating shipwreck, as in the proverbial Lucretian "shipwreck with spectator," even to the point of dispassionately contemplating the inevitability of his own demise. Nothing could be further from Dante's version of Ulysses' shipwreck, hypocritically willed by "altrui" (another), than the ethical authority of Petrarch's Christian stoicism as expressed by Augustinus in the *Secretum.*[65] But no less important, from a literary point of view, to Petrarch's response to Dante's shipwreck of Ulysses is the fact that he rewrites the shipwreck theme in such a way as to avoid as long as possible going under the waves.[66] The focus of the revisions of the Giovanni form cited earlier, for example, can be interpreted in terms of

Petrarch's attempt to contain and overcome the shipwreck threatened by the Chigi form, focused by the shipwreck of poem 189, which found its antidote initially in the Giovanni form in poem 190, and ultimately in the final ordering by the Po river poem 180. Both compositions serve to ward off and defer the shipwreck threatened by "Passa la nave mia."[67] But even in "Passa la nave mia," the most successful and enduring of his treatments of the theme, we find that Petrarch rewrites Ulysses' shipwreck in such a way as to defer ultimate *ruina,* thus holding out hope for ultimate salvation.

> Passa la nave mia colma d'oblio
> per aspro mare, a mezza notte il verno,
> entra Scilla et Caribdi, et al governo
> siede 'l signore, anzi 'l nimico mio;
>
> A ciascun remo un penser pronto et rio
> che la tempesta e 'l fin par ch'abbi a scherno;
> la vela rompe un vento umido eterno
> di sospir', di speranze et di desio.
>
> Pioggia di lagrimar, nebbia di sdegni
> bagna et rallenta le già stanche sarte,
> che son d'error con ignorantia attorto.
>
> Celansi i duo mei dolci usati segni;
> morta fra l'onde è la ragion et l'arte
> tal ch'incomincio a desperar del porto.

———————

My ship laden with forgetfulness passes through a harsh sea, at midnight, in winter, between Scylla and Charybdis, and at the tiller sits my lord, rather my enemy; each oar is manned by a ready, cruel thought that seems to scorn the tempest and the end; a wet changeless wind of sighs, hopes, and desires breaks the sail; a rain of weeping, a mist of disdain wet and loosen the already weary ropes, made of error twisted up with ignorance. My two usual sweet stars are hidden; dead among the waves are reason and skill; so that I begin to despair of the port.

By means of a rhetorical strategy of deferral, which expresses Petrarch's own counter-Dantean conception of the earth-bound place and the humanly delimited function of literature, the presence of the subject called Petrarch endures even to this day, when after seven hundred years he is still "just beginning" to despair of reaching port.

NOTES

1. Natalino Sapegno, "Tra Dante e il Petrarca," in *Storia letteraria del Trecento, La letteratura italiana; Storia e testi* (Milan and Naples: Ricciardi, 1963), 169–96; Giuseppe Billanovich, "Tra Dante e Petrarca," *Italia medioevale e umanistica* 8 (1965): 1–44.

2. Enrico Fenzi, "Tra Dante e Petrarca: Il fantasma di Ulisse," in *Saggi petrarcheschi* (Fiesole: Cadmo, 2003), 492–517.

3. This chapter is based on the last of the lectures in the series, and thus had the benefit of being able to draw on the insights and conclusions of the other contributors. The editors initially thought it would be appropriate to place it last in the order. On reflection, we concluded that it would be more appropriately placed at the beginning, since the essay foreshadows and utilizes different aspects of the other contributions to the seminar while developing its own argument. It should be clear, however, that the chapter is not intended as an introduction to the volume in the conventional sense.

4. For example, Marco Santagata, "Presenze di Dante 'comico' nel *Canzoniere* del Petrarca," *Giornale storico della letteratura italiana* 146 (1969): 163–211, reprinted in Santagata, *Per moderne carte* (Bologna: Il Mulino, 1990), 25–78; Marco Santagata, "Dante in Petrarca," *Giornale storico della letteratura italiana* 157 (1980): 445–52, reprinted in Santagata, *Per moderne carte,* 79–91; Paolo Trovato, *Dante in Petrarca* (Florence: Olschki, 1979); Giorgio Orelli, "Dante in Petrarca," in *Il suono dei sospiri: Sul Petrarca volgare* (Turin: Einaudi, 1990), 124–62; Claudio Giunta, "Memoria di Dante nei *Trionfi,*" *Rivista di letteratura italiana* 11 (1993): 411–52; and Peter Kuon, *L'aura dantesca: Metamorfosi intertestuali nei "Rerum vulgarium fragmenta" di Francesco Petrarca* (Florence: Cesati, 2004). For further bibliography on Petrarch's relationship to Dante, see Barański, "Petrarch, Dante, Cavalcanti" in this volume, n. 1.

5. See Guido di Pino, "L'antidantismo dal Trecento al Quattrocento," *Letture classensi* 5 (1976): 125–48.

6. *Familiares* 21.15, as one might expect, receives focused attention by several contributors to this volume, especially Barański, Mazzotta, Moevs, Steinberg, and Sturm-Maddox. Petrarch's belittling of his vernacular lyrics as "nugae" or "nugellae" (trifles) has become a critical commonplace. See Francesco Petrarca,

Canzoniere, ed. Gianfranco Contini, annotated by Daniele Ponchiroli (Turin: Einaudi, 1968), xv–xvi. Guiseppe Billanovich, *Petrarca letterato. I. Lo scrittoio del Petrarca* (Rome: Edizioni di "Storia e letteratura," 1947), points out that when Petrarch received from Boccaccio the gift of the *Commedia* (Vat. lat. 3199) and Boccaccio's *Amorosa visione,* he uncharacteristically failed to note with an annotation on their cover pages the entry of these texts into his library, nor did he compose letters of thanks that were included in his epistolary, as he did for writings of the Church Fathers and the classics.

7. *Seniles* 5.2 also receives focused attention by several contributors to this volume, especially Barański, Steinberg, and Sturm-Maddox. "Audio senem illum Ravennatem, rerum talium non ineptum iudicem, quotiens de his sermo est semper tibi locum tertium assignare solitum. Si is sordet sique a primo obstare tibi videor, qui non obsto, ecce volens cedo, locus tibi linquitur secundus" (I understand that the old gentleman from Ravenna, a competent judge of such matters, always likes to assign you third place whenever the subject comes up. If this is too lowly, if I appear to block your way to first place, which I do not do, look, I gladly yield and leave second place to you), in Francesco Petrarca, *Senile V 2,* ed. Monica Berté (Florence: Le Lettere, 1998), 32–33.

8. Citations of Francesco Petrarca are from the following texts and translations: *Rerum familiarium libri,* ed. Vittorio Rossi and Umberto Bosco, 4 vols. (Florence: Sansoni, 1933–42); *Letters on Familiar Matters,* trans. Aldo S. Bernardo, 3 vols. (Albany: State University of New York Press, 1975; Baltimore and London: Johns Hopkins University Press, 1982–85); *Petrarch's Guide to the Holy Land: Itinerary to the Sepulcher of Our Lord Jesus Christ,* ed. and trans. Theodore J. Cachey, Jr. (Notre Dame, Ind.: University of Notre Dame Press, 2002); *Canzoniere,* ed. Marco Santagata (Milan: Mondadori, 1996); *Petrarch's Lyric Poems: The "Rime sparse" and Other Lyrics,* trans. and ed. Robert M. Durling (Cambridge, Mass.: Harvard University Press, 1976); *Trionfi, Rime estravaganti, Codice degli abbozzi,* ed. Vinicio Pacca and Laura Paolino (Milan: Mondadori, 1996); *The Triumphs of Petrarch,* trans. Ernest Hatch Wilkins (Chicago: University of Chicago Press, 1962); *De sui ipsius et multorum ignorantia; Della mia ignoranza e di quella di molti altri,* ed. Enrico Fenzi (Milan: Mursia, 1999), translation by Hans Hachod cited from Ernst Cassirer, *The Renaissance Philosophy of Man* (Chicago: University of Chicago Press, 1948), 47–133; Francesco Petrarca, *Secretum,* ed. Enrico Fenzi (Milan: Mursia, 1992); *The Secret by Francesco Petrarch with Related Documents,* ed. Carol E. Quillen (Boston: Bedford St. Martin's, 2003); *Senile V 2,* ed. Berté; *Letters of Old Age,* trans. Aldo S. Bernardo, Saul Levin, and Reta A. Bernardo, 2 vols. (Baltimore: Johns Hopkins University Press, 1992).

9. First noted by Giuseppe Billanovich, "L'altro stil nuovo: Da Dante teologo a Petrarca filologo," *Studi petrarcheschi* n.s. 11 (1994): 1–98 (at 92–93); "Tra Dante e Petrarca," *Italia medioevale e umanistica* 8 (1965): 39–40; Michele Feo, "Petrarca, Francesco," *Enciclopedia Dantesca,* 6 vols., ed. Umberto Bosco, 4:450–58

(at 450). See Ascoli, "Blinding the Cyclops" in this volume, n. 67, for further bibliography and discussion.

10. Petrarch, in placing Typheus beneath Ischia in the *Trionfi* and the *Sine nomine* (consistent with Horace, *Carm.* III 4, 53–58; Seneca, *Herc. Oet.* 1155–59; Lucan V 99–101; Claudian, *De raptu* III 183–87), meant dissenting from the "authority" of Dante (*Par.* 8.67–70; cf. *Inf.* 30.124), who followed Ovid (*Met.* V 346–58) in his placement of Typheus beneath Aetna. While the question of Petrarch's philological-geographical investment as "long-distance specialist" in locating the burial sites of Enceladus and Typheus merits further study, for our immediate purposes, it serves to raise the issue of Petrarch's evolving attitude toward Dante.

11. Ronald Witt has built a case for Petrarch's direct or indirect acquaintance with del Virgilio during his student years in Bologna. See Ronald Witt, *"In the Footsteps of the Ancients": The Origins of Humanism from Lovato to Bruni* (Leiden: Brill, 2000), 236–38: "Petrarch would almost certainly have known of the exchange of bucolic poetry between Dante and Giovanni del Virgilio, which must have been circulating in Bologna in 1320 and 1321"; and see Michele Feo, "Petrarca prima della laurea: Una corrispondenza poetica ritrovata," *Quaderni petrarcheschi* 4 (1987): 50.

12. See Egidio Guidubaldi, "Stabili, Francesco," *Enciclopedia dantesca,* 3:404–5, and, more recently, Justin Steinberg, *Accounting for Dante: Urban Readers and Writers in Late Medieval Italy* (Notre Dame, Ind.: University of Notre Dame Press, 2005), 58–60. Steinberg suggestively discusses intersections between Cecco's condemnation by the Inquisition and the pro-Dante vernacular literary allegiances of the poet-judges involved, including Girardo da Castelfiorentino, a friend and associate of Cino's, Frate Accursio Bonfantini, reported to be the first public lecturer on Dante, and Francesco da Barberino. Steinberg, following Guidubaldi, recalls that several eighteenth-century scholars, including Crescimbeni, Quadrio, and Mazzuchelli, went so far as to attribute Cecco's condemnation and punishment to his anti-*dantismo.*

13. Usually exemplified by the following notorious tercets: "Qui non si canta al modo delle rane, / Qui non si canta al modo del poeta / Che finge, immaginando, cose vane; / Ma qui risplende e luce ogni natura / Che a chi intende fa la mente lieta. / Qui non si gira per la selva oscura. || Qui non veggio né Paolo né Francesca, / Delli Manfredi non veggio Alberico / Che amari frutti colse di dolce esca. / Del Mastin vecchio e nuovo da Verrucchio / Che fece di Montagna, qui non dico, / Né dei Franceschi lo sanguigno mucchio. || Non veggio il Conte che per ira ed asto / Tien forte l'arcivescovo Ruggero / Prendendo del suo ceffo il fiero pasto. Non veggio qui squadrare a Dio le fiche. / Lascio le ciance e torno su nel vero. / Le favole mi fur sempre nemiche" (4669–86). Cited from Cecco d'Ascoli [Francesco Stabili], *L'Acerba [Acerba etas],* ed. Marco Albertazzi (Lavis, Trento: La Finestra Editrice, 2002).

14. The Colonna family is celebrated throughout the *Acerba* as exemplary of true nobility and magnanimity. See Santagata, *Per moderne carte,* 223–45. Traces

of Cecco d'Ascoli turn up in poems of the *Canzoniere* dedicated to the Colonna family (*Rvf* 10, 1–4; 7), which are among the earliest dated poems in the book. A good part of Petrarch's astrological lexicon (although Petrarch was an anti-determinist) derives from Cecco as well. Bestiary and lapidary motifs bearing the signature of Cecco d'Ascoli make their appearance in the *Canzoniere,* including such key elements as the phoenix or the "calamita." Furthermore, Santagata notes that Petrarch shared with Cecco an admiration for Cino's "La dolce vista," at a time before it was canonized by Boccaccio's rewriting of the poem in the *Filostrato* (V 62–65), which is to say, before 1340; for which see also Billanovich, *Petrarca letterato,* 66–67, n. 1.

15. See Santagata, *Per moderne carte,* 242–43.

16. The suggestion was first made by Cecco's early-twentieth-century editor A. Crespi, *L'acerba,* ed. Achille Crespi (Ascoli Piceno: G. Cesari, 1927), as reported by Guidubaldi, "Stabili, Francesco."

17. See Barański, "Petrarch, Dante, Cavalcanti" in this volume, n. 21, for critics who have recently discussed "the ways in which Petrarch used Dante in order to define himself and establish his own cultural superiority."

18. It is reasonable, I think, to suppose that Petrarch knew both the *Monarchia* and the *De vulgari eloquentia,* although he never explicitly cites them, and notwithstanding Barański's caveats about Petrarch's knowledge of Dante's Latin works expressed in these pages. See Barański, "Petrarch, Dante, Cavalcanti," n. 6. See n. 20 below for details of recent research by Corrado Bologna. Earlier, Billanovich expressed the view in *Petrarca letterato* that it was impossible to think that he did not know it (p. 239) and noted, "Argomenti per infirmare la donazione di Costantino molto simili a quelli di *Monarchia* III x e II xii sono esposti nella *Sine nomine* XVII, scritta negli ultimi mesi del 1357" (p. 240).

19. See Pier Giorgio Ricci, "Monarchia," *Enciclopedia dantesca,* 3:993–1004 (at 1002).

20. See Corrado Bologna, "Un'ipotesi sulla ricezione del *De vulgari eloquentia*: Il codice Berlinese," in *La cultura volgare padovana nell'età di Petrarca,* ed. Furio Brugnolo and Zeno Lorenzo Verlato (Padova: Il Poligrafo, 2006), 205–56. For Bologna, "it is not illogical to at least hypothesize that the entire collection was organized by Dionigi himself." He persuasively situates the Berlinese at the court of King Robert of Naples around 1340, within the context of the nascent humanistic cultural milieu that featured prominently not only Petrarch's intimate friend and confessor Dionigi, but also Boccaccio, around the time of Petrarch's coronation. The reception of the *Monarchia* and the *De vulgari eloquentia* expressed a compelling cultural political program linking political power to rhetoric in this environment. In fact, both treatises appear within the codex under the common rubric of a "rectorica Dantis." According to Bologna's reconstruction, Petrarch would have come into contact with the *Monarchia* and the *De vulgari eloquentia* through this joint publication of Dante's political and rhetorical treatises, together with

Dionigi's lengthy commentary on Valerio Massimo's *Dicta e facta* (a commentary whose ideology and inspiration is related to those of Petrarch's own *Rerum memorandarum libri*). See also Corrado Bologna, "Occhi, solo occhi (*Rvf* 70–75)," in *Lectura Petrarca Turicensis. Il Canzoniere. Lettura micro e macrotestuale*, ed. M. Picone (Ravenna: Longo, 2007), 183–205.

21. Robert E. Lerner, "Petrarch's Coolness toward Dante: A Conflict of 'Humanisms,'" in *Intellectuals and Writers in Fourteenth-Century Europe: The J. A.W. Bennett Memorial Lectures, Perugia, 1984,* ed. Piero Boitani and Anna Torti (Cambridge: D. S. Brewer, 1986), 204–25.

22. In fact, he wrote the *De sui ipsius et multorum ignorantia* while sailing on the Po river, and the same theme of writing while traveling by river occurs in *Rvf* 180, which enters the order of the book during this same period, as an antidote to the shipwreck of *Rvf* 189, regarding which see the following discussion in this essay.

23. Lerner, "Petrarch's Coolness," 207.

24. Lerner, "Petrarch's Coolness": "Petrarch's dismissal of Aristotle on happiness was related to his Augustinian view that classical philosophy per se had nothing of independent value to offer the Christian. For Petrarch 'to be a true philosopher is nothing but to be a true Christian' (*Fam.* 17.1). Hence whereas Dante gave Aristotle the last word on happiness, placed Siger of Brabant in Paradise and even quoted Averroës with approval in the *Monarchy* (I,3) Petrarch opposed all the 'crazy and clamorous' scholastics who found intrinsic merits in philosophical works" (222).

25. See Maria Cecilia Bertolani, *Il corpo glorioso: Studi sui Trionfi del Petrarca* (Rome: Carocci, 2001): "il finale dei *Trionfi* va letto alla luce di un intenso clima religioso e filosofico che poi era profondamente mutato nell'arco dei pochi anni tra Dante e Petrarca: gli anni che videro la crisi dell'ottimismo gnoseologico facente capo a san Tommaso. Anche Petrarca condivide la sfiducia nelle possibilità delle facoltà intellettuali di giungere al soprannaturale, e rinnova, contro il tentativo scolastico di conciliare la teologia con la filosofia, le riserve di Agostino, Giovanni di Salisbury, san Bernardo e di tutta la cultura monastica" (137). See also Bertolani's *Petrarca e la visione dell'eterno* (Bologna: Il Mulino, 2005), especially chapter 4, "Nelle profondità della parola: Dal *Canzoniere* al *Trionfo dell'Eternità*," 187–227.

26. Bertolani, *Petrarca e la visione dell'eterno*: "Tuttavia il tema del corpo risorto e quindi della comunità ritrovata occupa in Dante uno spazio secondario rispetto a quello della visione di Dio: il motivo è assente dall'ultimo canto del Paradiso che è invece una celebrazione proprio della *visio Dei intuitive et facialis*. . . . Diversa l'operazione di Petrarca che, attraverso il motivo della resurrezione assunto nel mito laurano, può dunque concertare la sua differenza con il Dante paradisiaco senza per questo doversi confrontare con la potenza visonaria della *Commedia*" (209).

27. Bertolani, *Il corpo glorioso*: "non si deve per questo ritenere, come afferma Ariani seguendo Goffis, Bosco e in ultimo Santagata, che i *Trionfi* si chiudano 'in una dimensione profana': il percorso di Petrarca si ferma ai *visibilia* poiché gli *invisibilia,* giusto il precetto della teologia negativa, non sono conoscibili

direttamente, ma è possible averne una impressione 'vaga' (un aggettivo, questo, costante nei *Trionfi*, riferito in genere a 'mente' e ad 'alma') solo ricorrendo, appunto, ai *visibilia* che, in tal modo, divengono come la scala di Giacobbe che congiunge la terra al cielo" (138).

28. See Cesare Segre, "Intertestuale-Interdiscorsivo: Appunti per una fenomenologia delle fonti," in *La parola ritrovata: Fonti e analisi letteraria,* ed. C. Di Girolamo and I. Paccagnella (Palermo: Sellerio, 1982), 15–28.

29. Guglielmo Gorni, "Le ballate di Dante e di Petrarca," in *Metrica e analisi letteraria* (Bologna: Il Mulino, 1993), 219–42.

30. Other examples of this kind of reductionism are discussed by Michelangelo Picone, "Riscritture dantesche nel *Canzoniere* di Petrarca," *Rivista europea di letteratura italiana* 2 (1993): 115–25.

31. See Ronald L. Martinez, "'Nasce il Nilo': Wisdom, Justice, and Dante's Canzone 'Tre donne intorno al cor mi son,'" in *Dante Now: Current Trends in Dante Studies,* ed. Theodore J. Cachey, Jr. (Notre Dame, Ind.: University of Notre Dame Press, 1995), 115–53.

32. See Bologna, "Occhi, solo occhi (*Rvf* 70–75)," especially 188–91.

33. "Preterea: illa videntur nobiliora esse que conditori suo magis honoris afferunt: sed cantiones magis deferunt suis conditoribus quam ballate; igitur nobiliores sunt, et per consequens modus earum nobilissimus aliorum" (Moreover, those things are seen as more noble that bring greater honour to those who create them; but *canzoni* bring more honour to their creators than *ballate;* therefore they are more noble, and, in consequence, theirs is the noblest form of all) (Dante, *De vulgari eloquentia,* ed. and trans. Steven Botterill [Cambridge: Cambridge University Press, 1996], II.3 [55]).

34. See Barański, "Dante, Petrarch, Cavalcanti," n. 78, which critiques Michele Feo's viewpoint as expressed in "Petrarca, Francesco," *Enciclopedia dantesca,* 4:450–58, that Petrarch's *Sen.* 4.5 addressed to Federico Aretino on how to read the *Aeneid* represents "uno degli sforzi più umanisticamente impegnati a conciliare classico (Virgilio) e moderno (Dante), o meglio a capire, ad assorbire, a sistemare il moderno entro una visione classica" (453).

35. See Dante Alighieri, *Opere minori,* vol. 3, tomo 2, ed. Enzo Cecchini (Milan and Naples: Ricciardi, 1989). English translation by Wilmon Brewer, in Dante Alighieri, *Dante's Eclogues (the Poetical Correspondence between Dante and Giovanni del Virgilio)* (Boston, Cornhill, 1927).

36. Carlo Dionisotti, "Tradizione classica e volgarizzamenti," in *Geografia e storia della letteratura italiana* (Turin: G. Einaudi, 1971), 142–43. The attribution of the *volgarizzamenti* of Livy is, in any event, complex. Billanovich attributed them to Boccaccio and noted their influence on Boccaccio's developing prose style in the vernacular, in *Petrarca letterato,* 86–87 and n. 2. See more recently Maria Teresa Casella, *Tra Boccaccio e Petrarca. I volgarizzamenti di Tito Livio e di Valerio Massimo,* Studi sul Petrarca 14 (Padova: Antenore, 1982), reviewed by Giuseppe Velli, *MLN* 100, no. 1 (1985): 175–77.

37. Simon Gilson, *Dante and Renaissance Florence* (Cambridge: Cambridge University Press, 2005), 25, quotation at 27.

38. ". . . un evento epocale, impensabile nell'ottica di Petrarca, quasi necessario nell'orizzonte nuovo del Boccaccio: in questo cioè proprio nell'integrazione di Dante e Petrarca." Corrado Bologna, *Tradizione e fortuna dei classici italiani* (Turin: G. Einaudi, 1993), 204. See the facsimile edition of the Chigi codex: *Il codice Chigiano L.V. 176 / autografo di Giovanni Boccaccio,* ed. Domenico De Robertis (Rome: Archivi Edizioni; Florence: Fratelli Alinari, 1975).

39. See Vittore Branca, *Studi in onore di Matteo Marengoni* (Florence: Vallecchi, 1957), 30–42, on *Sen.* 5.2, who spoke of "questa lettera scritta, sembra, nell'agosto del '64, ma che il Petrarca, rielaborando il suo epistolario, assegnò all'estate del '66 probabilmente per motivi ideali. Era proprio il periodo in cui pensava più assiduamente ai 'rerum vulgarium fragmenta' e andava maturando in lui il disegno di rivederli e di ordinarli sistematicamente e in maniera in certo senso definitiva, meglio di quanto non avesse fatto sino allora. V'erano stati, sì, già dei tentativi in questo senso e delle divisioni e dei raggruppamenti provvisori; ma è solo nel 1366 che il Petrarca, dopo lunghi dubbi e meditazioni, delinea con risolutezza i criteri e il disegno del suo canzoniere, di cui comincia nel dicembre l'organica sistemazione e trascrizione in quello che oggi è il Codice Vaticano 3195" (38). For the dating of the letter, see most recently Berté, who confirms the 1364 date in "Introduzione," *Senile* V 2, 14 and n. 3.

40. *Sen.* 5.2: "Certe michi interdum, unde coniecturam hanc elicio, de vulgaribus meis, paucis licet, idem agere propositum fuit, fecissemque fortassis, ni vulgata undique iampridem mei ius arbitrii evasissent, cum eidem michi tamen aliquando contraria mens fuisset, totum huic vulgari studio tempus dare, quod uterque stilus altior latinus eo usque priscis ingeniis cultus esset ut pene iam nichil nostra ope vel cuiuslibet addi posset, at hic, modo inventus, adhuc recens, vastatoribus crebris ac raro squalidus colono, magni se vel ornamenti capacem ostenderet vel augmenti. Quid vis? Hac spe tractus simulque stimulis actus adolescentie magnum eo in genere opus inceperam iactisque iam quasi edificii fundamentis calcem ac lapides et ligna congesseram" (Certainly I have sometimes had the idea of doing the same with my vernacular writings, few though they were—that is why I guess this about you; and perhaps I would have done so had they not long ago escaped from my control by being so far-flung, although at times I had also had the self-contradictory idea to devote all my time to vernacular pursuits since the loftier Latin style—both prose and poetry—had been so highly polished by ancient talents that now my resources, or anyone else's, can add very little. On the other hand, this vernacular writing, just invented, still new, showed itself capable of great improvement and development after having been ravaged by many and cultivated by very few husbandmen. Well then, this hope so attracted me and at the time the spur of youth so urged me onward that I undertook a great work in that style; and having laid, as it were, the foundations of that edifice, I gathered the cement and stone and wood [52]). See also, for the interpretation of this passage, Renato Serra, "Dei *Trionfi* di F. Petrarca"

[1904], vol. 2 of *Scritti di Renato Serra,* ed. G. De Robertis and A. Grilli (Florence: Le Monnier, 1938), 43; Umberto Bosco, *Francesco Petrarca,* 3rd ed. rev. (Bari: Laterza, 1973), 216; Carlo Paolazzi, "Petrarca, Boccaccio e il *Trattatello in laude di Dante,*" *Studi danteschi* 55 (1983): 199.

41. Marco Santagata, *I frammenti dell'anima: Storia e racconto nel Canzoniere di Petrarca* (Bologna: Il Mulino, 1992), 341.

42. In fact, many years ago, scholars such as Giuseppe Billanovich, Francesco Mazzoni, and Vittore Branca, each in his own way, noted connections between Petrarch's vernacular literary investments and the correspondence with Boccaccio regarding Dante: Giuseppe Billanovich, *Petrarca letterato,* 167–77; Francesco Mazzoni, "Giovanni Boccaccio fra Dante e Petrarca," *Atti e memorie dell'Accademia Petrarca di Lettere, Arti e Scienze di Arezzo* 42 (1976–78): 15–42; Vittore Branca, *Studi in onore di Matteo Marengoni.* Billanovich's discussion is the classic treatment. Mazzoni's portrays a dynamic of reciprocal influences between the two friends, for example, focused on Boccaccio's sensitivity to Petrarch's concern about the unstable nature of vernacular transmission as made explicit in both his letters to Boccaccio about Dante, and suggesting that this was a principal inspiration for Boccaccio's editorial work on Dante. But Mazzoni viewed the directionality of influence, as has most of the tradition, as primarily from Petrarch to Boccaccio. He did not elaborate on the impact of Boccaccio's editorial activism and promotion of Dante on Petrarch's own vernacular development. Vittore Branca's review of the "nearly forty-year dialogue" between Boccaccio and Petrarch also emphasized the second of Petrarch's two letters to Boccaccio regarding Dante, *Seniles* 5.2, for the light it shed on the making of the *Canzoniere.* He first noted the coincidence of the fictional dating of the letter with the date when Petrarch first undertook, with the assistance of his copyist Giovanni Malpaghini, the organic systemization and transcription of the poet's "author's book," Vat. Lat. 3195.

43. Billanovich, *Petrarca letterato,* 136–41, n. 1.

44. As reconstructed by Santagata in *I frammenti,* "La finzione autobiografica," 76–83.

45. For an introduction to the dating controversy surrounding the *Secretum,* see Francisco Rico, *Vida u obra de Petrarca, I: Lectura del 'Secretum'* (Padova: Antenore, 1974); and Hans Baron, *Petrarch's "Secretum": Its Making and Its Meaning* (Cambridge, Mass.: Medieval Academy of America, 1985).

46. Marco Santagata, *I frammenti,* "Come tanti altri progetti, anche quello di impostare il proprio ritratto ideale sulla conversione a quarant'anni non rimase a lungo sul tavolo di Petrarca. Allo scadere degli anni '50 appare già tramontato. La seconda redazione del *Canzoniere* seguirà un diverso percorso, nel quale i punti di riferimento cronologici legati a quell'evento fittizio perdono ogni rilevanza" (101).

47. Boccaccio had sent Petrarch a copy of his *Caccia di Diana* and of the *Amorosa visione* at the same time that he sent the *Commedia* and "Ytalie iam cer-

tus honus" during that summer of 1351. Based on this fact, Billanovich made the proposal, accepted by Santagata's chronology of Petrarch's life, that the poet first began work on the *Triumphi* at that time. Billanovich, *Petrarca letterato*, 168–72, goes as far as to suggest that Boccaccio is the mysterious unidentified "Tuscan guide." See also Giuseppe Billanovich, "Dalla *Commedia* e dall' *Amorosa Visione* ai *Trionfi*," *Giornale storico della letteratura italiana* 123 (1945–46): 51–52.

48. Santagata, *I frammenti*, "La sua doppia anima [of the Chigi form], il fatto cioè che in esso convivessero a fatica e non senza attriti, due possibili esiti tra loro divergenti, rischiava in effetti di inceppare la crescita ulteriore del libro. E' forse perché quella condizione era oggettivamente paralizzante che la nuova forma evita di scegliere fra l'una o l'altra strada, eludendo il problema di fondo, cioè il dilemma se l'amore per Laura fosse una esperienza moralmente condannabile o un mezzo di perfezionamento spirituale" (259).

49. Francesco Petrarca, *Triumphi*, ed. Marco Ariani (Milan: Mursia, 1988), 6.

50. Dante in the original is cited from the Giorgio Petrocchi edition: Dante Alighieri: *La Commedia secondo l'antica vulgata*, ed. G. Petrocchi (Florence: Le Lettere, 1994 [1966]); the translation is by Robert and Jean Hollander, *Dante Alighieri Inferno* (New York: Doubleday, 2000).

51. Gilson, *Dante and Renaissance Florence*, 33.

52. Enrico Fenzi, "Tra Dante e Petrarca," 510 n. 18: "Petrarca ne abbozza un ritratto [of Dante] che chiaramente deriva da quello del *Trattatello* boccaccesco: 'Non poterono gli amorosi disiri né le dolenti lagrime, né la sollecitudine casalinga, né la lusinghevole gloria dei publici ofici, né il miserabile esilio, né la intollerabile povertà giammai con le lor forze rimuovere il nostro Dante dal principale intento, cioè da' sacri studi'" (first redaction [82]).

53. Barański observes in this volume that "Petrarch expresses a similar opinion, albeit implicitly, regarding Dante's pursuit of literary fame as proof of his lack of virtue both in the *Triumphi* and in *Seniles* 5.2."

54. See Theodore J. Cachey, Jr., "Per una mappa del *Canzoniere: Rvf* 171–179," in *Il Canzoniere. Lettura micro e macrotestuale*, ed. M. Picone (Ravenna: Longo, 2006), 395–414; and "From Shipwreck to Port: *Rvf* 189 and the Making of *Canzoniere*," *MLN* 120, no. 1 (2005): 30–49.

55. Francesco Petrarca, *Canzoniere*, ed. Rosanna Bettarini (Turin: G. Einaudi, 2005), 783.

56. Stefano Asperti notes that Petrarch denies to Dante the title of "poet" (which he reserves for himself and classical poets) twice in the *Canzoniere, Tr. cup.* IV, 25, and *Rvf* 166, 3, in "Dante, i trovatori, la poesia," *Le culture di Dante: Studi in onore di Robert Hollander. Atti del quarto seminario dantesco internazionale, University of Notre Dame (Ind.), USA, 25–27 settembre 2003*, ed. M. Picone, T. Cachey, and M. Mesirca (Florence: Cesati, 2004), 67–68.

57. *Considerazioni sopra le rime del Petrarca*, ed. Alessandro Tassoni (Modena, Cassiani, 1609).

58. Paola Allegretti and Guglielmo Gorni, "Mondo dell'oltretomba e *spelunca* in Petrarca (RVF 161−70)," in *Il Canzoniere. Lettura micro e macrotestuale,* ed. M. Picone (Ravenna: Longo, 2006), 383−93: "è inane il tentativo di attenuare la polemica implicita in questo verso" (390).

59. Vincenzo Fera, "I sonetti CLXXXVI e CLXXXVII," *Lectura Petrarce 7* (1987): 219−43.

60. Enrico Fenzi, "Tra Dante e Petrarca": "l'Ulisse di Petrarca sarebbe essenzialmente l'Ulisse di Dante, o almeno, visto attraverso Dante"; and: "Petrarca invece, sia pur basando la valutazione del personaggio di Ulisse sui testi classici, manifesta sino alla fine la sua sostanziale fedeltà alla visione dantesca"; and "pur avendo tutti i mezzi per correggerla, di fatto accetta la versione di Dante, e a scanso di equivoci ripetutamente la considera come una sorta di archetipo della 'scelta virtuosa' libera da condizionamenti e debolezze" (509).

61. Enrico Fenzi, "Tra Dante e Petrarca": "Ulisse non è quello della tradizione, ma, appunto, quello di Dante. Cioè, essenzialmente, quello che *non ritorna.* Il punto, a mio parere, è decisivo. C'è infatti qualcosa che qui Petrarca riconosce per sempre a Dante (oserei dire, quasi a farne un Omero cristiano): gli riconosce d'aver spezzato la struttura del ritorno che caretterizzava l'esperienza ulissiaca, e dunque di aver spezzato la nozione circolare e pagana del tempo dominata dalla sua sua 'cattiva infinitezza', e di averla raddrizzata e infine ordinata all'unicità e irripetibilità del tempo cristiano" (512).

62. Enrico Fenzi, "Tra Dante e Petrarca": "Non so quanto utilmente, ma certo si potrebbe discorrere a lungo dell'intelligente perfidia petrarchesca che colpisce il grande rivale con le sue stesse armi, ribaltando sul creatore la sublime ambiguità della sua più controversa creatura. Tuttavia, è meglio restare alla sostanza seria, non polemica, del discorso, e osservare che l'operazione di Petrarca trasforma ma però essenzialmente ancora s'affida al vecchio e però efficace topos che recita: 'Aristotele fu un uomo e poté errare'" (515).

63. Emilio Pasquini, "Discussione della relazione di Boitani," in *Dante: Mito e poesia. Atti del secondo Seminario dantesco internazionale,* ed. Michelangelo Picone and Tatiana Crivelli (Florence: Cesati, 1997), 232−33.

64. Teodolina Barolini, *The Undivine Comedy: Detheologizing Dante* (Princeton: Princeton University Press, 1992), 52.

65. "Id autem, ut dixi, facillime consequeris si tue primum mentis compescueris tumultus; pectus enim serenum et tranquillum frustra vel peregrine circumeunt nubes vel circumtonat externus fragor. Itaque velut insistens sicco litori tutus, aliorum naufragium spectabis et miserabiles fluitantium voces tacitus excipies; quantum ve tibi turbidum spectaculum securitas compassionis attulerit, tantum gaudii afferet proprie sortis, alienis periculus collata, securitas" (But, as I said, you would accomplish this most easily if you would first restrain the commotion in your mind. For clouds and clamor surround a serene breast in vain. And so just like one sitting safe and dry on shore, you will watch the shipwrecks of others, and

you will hear in silence the miserable voices of those floundering at sea. And even as you have felt compassion at this chaotic spectacle, so you will feel joy at the security of your fate compared to the dangers of others) (*Secretum* II, 126). For the Lucretian shipwreck with spectator topos, see Hans Blumenberg, *Naufragio con spettatore: Paradigma di una metafora dell'esistenza* (Bologna: Il Mulino, 1985). Lucretius is an indirect source for Petrarch in the *Secretum*: while the text of Lucretius' *De rerum natura* was only discovered by Poggio Bracciolini in 1417, the image circulated widely among religious authors of the Middle Ages.

66. See Theodore J. Cachey, Jr., "'Peregrinus (quasi) ubique': Petrarca e la storia del viaggio," *Intersezioni* 17, no. 3 (December 1997): 369–84: "E' pertanto attraverso l'interiorizzazione della *navigatio vitae* e dei temi del naufragio che Petrarca riesce a sopravvivere al naufragare della storia. La costante rivisitazione del tema crea la distanza necessaria a stabilire una misura di controllo e di restare sulla spiaggia ad osservare a distanza il proprio naufragio. Come nel caso delle metafore del viaggio di terra, potremo dire che Petrarca, attraverso la continua applicazione delle metafore navigative, sia riuscito a svuotare il viaggio di mare della sua mobiltà minacciosa. E questo avviene poiché Petrarca assume tipicamente il ruolo del naufrago e il ruolo dello spettatore. . . . Il brivido, il delirio prodotto da 'Passa la nave mia' è analogo alla gioia della propria incolumità di cui parla Agostino nel *Secretum*, un'estraneità raggiunta attraverso mezzi estetici" (384).

67. See Cachey, "From Shipwreck to Port": "*Rvf* 190 recounts not only a vision of Laura as an emblem of chastity. . . . The poet's fall into the water in the last verse, 'Quand'io caddi ne l'acqua et ella sparve,' whatever one's interpretation of the allegory, represents a recognizably Petrarchan form of shipwreck. It echoes the one recorded in the tercets of *Rvf* 67, and here, as there, appears to signal a moral and spiritual reawakening which in *Rvf* 190 coincides with Laura's 'disappearance,' in marked contrast with the contiguous shipwreck of 189. . . . Sonnet 180 addressed to the Po is no less antidotal with respect to the shipwreck of 189:

> Po, ben puo' tu portartene la scorza
> di me con tue possenti et rapide onde,
> ma lo spirto ch'iv'entro si nasconde
> non cura né di tua né d'altrui forza;

The hemistich 'né di tua né d'altrui forza' at the end of the opening quatrain represents a fairly explicit allusion to the famous 'altrui' responsible for Ulysses' demise in canto 26 of the *Inferno*" (39).

CHAPTER 2

Petrarch, Dante, Cavalcanti

ZYGMUNT G. BARAŃSKI

READING PETRARCH READING DANTE

"Petrarca e Dante"; "Dante in Petrarca"; "Tra Dante e Petrarca": conjunctions and prepositions have played an unexpectedly vital role in determining the critical history of Petrarch's relationship to Dante.[1] The elimination of both grammatical categories in the title of my study marks a deliberate attempt to go beyond the parameters which, to date, have largely defined and, I believe, constrained discussions of Petrarch's attitude toward his great predecessor. The use of the "neutral" comma to link the two poets' names is meant to suggest, first and foremost, a degree of exegetical independence from the scholarly mainstream; indeed, it implies that Petrarch's view of Dante can be assessed outside the interpretive limits imposed by nearly two hundred years of scholarship—a possibility which, as I shall have occasion to explain, the introduction of Guido Cavalcanti's name into the title is also designed to indicate.

As is well known, Petrarch's relationship to Dante was, to say the least, complicated and ambiguous. If, on the one hand, he made few direct references to his father's companion in exile—references whose principal overt aim appears to have been to assert that, in artistic and intellectual terms, little connected him to Dante—on the other, as modern scholarship has so overwhelmingly demonstrated, his writings, beginning with the *Canzoniere,* resound powerfully with Dantean echoes. As a result of such contradictory evidence, critics have been able to put forward radically contrasting explanations of the nature of Petrarch's stance on Dante. Since the fourteenth century, he has been accused of harboring ill-concealed feelings of envy, of disdain, even of hatred toward the author of the *Commedia*. In general, such psychologizing interpretations are based on, and are supposed to account for, the suggestion, first circulated by Petrarch himself, that he had deliberately avoided reading Dante and hence was largely untouched by his influence.[2] In recent years, however, scholars have definitively discredited the notion that Petrarch was somehow immune to Dante by diagnosing the extent to which his predecessor's poetry had infected his artistic system. As a result, scholars have largely left behind the long-held view of a resentful and embittered Petrarch. Instead, those who have continued to judge Petrarch's reaction to the poet of the *Commedia* as problematic have either talked generically of the "distacco che lo separava da Dante" (distance that separated him from Dante)[3] or have explained his recourse to Dante as essentially agonistic in character.[4] Contributions that have stressed Petrarch's dissatisfaction with and "separation" from the "divine poet" can loosely be subsumed under the designation "Petrarch and Dante," where the *and* functions as an adversative preposition: "Petrarch *against* Dante." It was in the decade 1969–79 that perceptions began to change. Thanks to careful intertextual analyses, most notably those of Marco Santagata and of Paolo Trovato,[5] Petrarch's persistent reliance on Dante's poetry and prose — specifically the *rime*, the *Vita nova*, and the *Commedia*[6] — was unveiled for all to see; and, in the ensuing thirty or so years, other critics have added significantly to these pioneering discoveries. In its turn, this fundamental research can be catalogued under the tag "Dante in Petrarch," where the weighty significance of that preposition *in* is more than obvious. This is research of undoubted importance which has irreversibly altered our understanding of Petrarch's dependence on Dante. At the same time, however — and I shall soon return to these matters in greater detail — I find a number of its conclusions somewhat perplexing. In particular, it has encouraged the notion that, since Petrarch, especially in his vernacular writings, borrowed freely from Dante, his standpoint on his illustrious precursor must necessarily have been largely positive, and hence free of ambiguity and criticism. Indeed, it is claimed that Petrarch's relationship to his predecessor was so bereft of tension that the majority of his borrowings from Dante were spontaneously unconscious — marks of an effortless familiarity.[7] As a result, rather than treating Petrarch's rare public statements on Dante as sly declarations of malice—the predominant perspective at least since Foscolo's day[8]—we should read them instead, in harmony with the proof apparently offered by the formal fabric of his poetry, as primarily expressions of appreciation.[9]

The effort to minimize, if not actually to neutralize, the tensions in Petrarch's treatment of Dante conforms well to a deep-seated trend in Italian literary historiography. The idea that Dante and Petrarch represent two distinct yet complementary intellectual and artistic alternatives, which together cover the field of literary endeavor, has its roots once more in the Trecento. It is enough to remember Benvenuto da Imola's lapidary distinction: "Sed certe quanto Petrarcha fuit maior orator Dante, tanto Dantes fuit maior poeta ipso Petrarcha" (But as undoubtedly Petrarch was a greater orator than Dante, so Dante was a greater poet than Petrarch).[10] As a result, it is a critical commonplace to consider Italian literature as delicately, though reassuringly, caught between the contrasting possibilities offered by its two great exemplary "founding fathers"—"Tra Dante e Petrarca"[11]—a condition which not even the third of the *tre corone* could, or wished to, escape. Consequently, Boccaccio too is neatly assigned a representative role. In this grand historiographical narrative, Dante and Petrarch are presented as alternatives, *not* as antagonists. Conversely, however, interpretations that portray Petrarch as motivated by rancor in his judgments of Dante inevitably undermine the cozy picture of a national literary tradition harmoniously guided by its two greatest writers. Such troublesome and disturbing interpretations introduce doubt, strain, and imbalance into the idealized, tidy world of histories of literature, and so, as sources of unease, are prime candidates for elimination. More specifically, as far as the precise argument of this study is concerned, the perception of Dante and Petrarch as colossi bestriding Italian literature tends to isolate both them and their contacts from the cultural environment in which their relationship perforce developed. At most, that other "giant," Boccaccio, is allowed to intrude into their lofty solitude. Thus, the presence of Guido Cavalcanti's name in my title serves as an emblematic reminder of the fundamental importance of that elided context. Indeed, as we shall see, fourteenth-century culture cannot be ignored if we wish to understand Petrarch's reactions not simply to Dante but also to Cavalcanti.

Yet, as a rule, regardless of whether Petrarch's approach to Dante is deemed to have been negative or positive, both critical positions do just that: they tend to discuss the nature of the poet's *dantismo* in a vacuum. In fact, their exegetical rigor and hence their interpretive effectiveness are additionally weakened by other serious shortcomings of method. In general, psychologizing explanations are largely conjectural, unless documentary evidence can be adduced to support their essentially speculative claims. Such proof, in Petrarch's case, is conspicuously lacking. Indeed, the poet vehemently denied being prey to strong adverse sentiments with respect to Dante.[12] To dismiss the significance of his assertions simply by invoking the Freudian unconscious does not seem to me to be the best way of corroborating a problematic, because philologically unsubstantiated, viewpoint. Rather, if we wish to arrive at some idea of Petrarch's attitude toward Dante, we need to start by trying to pick up, however faintly these may reach us, the possible cultural resonances of his comments on his predecessor. To put it a bit differently, before attempting more risky interpretations, we ought first to do our best to consider the possible literal meanings of Petrarch's words, thereby following the sensible example of our medieval forebears who stressed that every reading had to begin from a careful elucidation of the *lictera*.[13] However, a lack of interest in the "letter" of Petrarch's declarations has characterized the debate on his possible ties to Dante. If some scholars have wanted to recognize a profound resentment behind his words, others, behind the very same words, have preferred to hear the strains of admiration—an admiration not necessarily supported by what Petrarch actually says but by the fact that, elsewhere, his writing is rich in borrowings from Dante.

The latter approach seems a strange way to proceed. To equate uncritically the simple fact that an author borrows heavily from a single source with endorsement for that same source does not smack of philological commonsense. Such an approach is especially problematic when used as the basis for establishing what a Trecento writer might have thought about Dante. In the light of the pervasiveness and variety of Dante's impact on fourteenth-century poetry, it is important to move with caution when making claims about the status, and hence possible meaning, of echoes from his writings overheard in the texts of his fellow poets. Thus, some Dantisms are almost certainly indirect, having been mediated, and so largely neutralized, through the verses of others (in Petrarch's case, it is enough to think of the intervening role of Cino).[14] Likewise, Dante's uniquely personal poetic language became closely associated with the general language of Trecento poetry and culture, thereby further loosening its ties to its author. For much of the fourteenth century, Dante's Italian was the literary vernacular of Italy, and as such constituted a common resource. Dante was "everywhere." As Petrarch put it, Dante's *liber* was "sine difficultate parabilis" (easily available) (*Fam.* 21.15.10), and the *Commedia* was appreciated even by *fullones, caupones,* and *lanistae* (fullers, tavern keepers, and woolworkers) (*Fam.* 22).[15] Therefore, if we wish to establish the nature of Trecento reactions to Dante, we ought to try to discriminate, on the basis of their effects and "markedness," between different types of intertextuality. The mere fact of a high incidence of borrowings from Dante, even in a writer as meticulously reflective and as sophisticatedly versed in the ways of *imitatio* as Petrarch, may point to little more than the older Florentine's remarkable contemporary popularity.[16] Moreover, there is no necessary correlation between approval (or, in fact, disapproval) and the degree to which one poet repeats another.[17] Similarly, authors' explicit statements on their peers can be at odds with the recourse they actually make to the works of those same writers. In any case, it is notoriously difficult to be precise about the significance of intertextual evidence. As a norm, therefore, when assessing the relationship between two writers, it would appear prudent to begin by considering any declarations each may have made about the other. Once these have been elucidated, reference points exist against which intertextual practices can be tested and evaluated. This is the approach I intend to pursue in this study by focusing on Petrarch's direct references to Dante in the *Canzoniere,* the *Triumphi,* and the letters.[18] My approach, therefore, is in stark contrast to the tack taken by proponents of "Dante in Petrarch," who, keen to hear everywhere the same tones of admiration, expend little effort in distinguishing between the different ways in which Petrarch had recourse to Dante. In fact, there has been a generalized tendency among scholars of Petrarch, regardless of their take on the specific question of his response to Dante, to "banalize" the poets' relationship either by forcing its multiform aspects—from the intertextual borrowing to the metrical and generic imitation (the *Triumphi*) to the direct comment (*Rer. mem.* 2.83; *Canz.* 287.10; *Tr. Cup.* 4.31;[19] *Fam.* 21.15; *Sen.* 5.2)—into an "unproblematic" totalizing characterization, or by considering individual aspects of his reaction to Dante in isolation. There have thus been limited attempts to explore, first, the possible interrelationships and differences between the different textual forms that record Petrarch's encounter with Dante; second, how in practice Petrarch assembled "his" Dante; third, the implications of this process; fourth, whether Petrarch's construction of Dante is actually as one-dimensional as has been widely assumed; and finally, the extent to which the Petrarchan Dante relates to the different, often conflicting, strands of fourteenth-century reaction to the poet of the *Commedia*. As I hope is becoming evident, by emphasizing matters of context, whether textual, historical, or cultural, the primary aim of this study is to attempt to redress these and related critical shortcomings — shortcomings that have unnecessarily constrained our appreciation of Petrarch's *dantismo*.[20]

Delimiting Dante: "Sennuccio mio, benché doglioso et solo"

Sed esto; non sim dignus cui credatur. Quam tandem veri faciem habet ut invideam illi qui in his [vernacular studies] etatem totam posuit, in quibus ego vix adolescientie florem primitiasque posuerim? ut quod illi artificium nescio an unicum, sed profecto supremum fuit, michi iocus atque solatium fuerit et ingenii rudimentum? Quis hic, precor, invidie locus, que ve suspitio est? Nam quod inter laudes dixisti, potuisse illum si voluisset alio stilo uti, credo edepol — magna enim michi de ingenio eius opinio est — potuisse eum omnia quibus intendisset; nunc quibus intenderit, palam est. (*Fam.* 21.15.21−22)

———————

But let us assume that for some I am deemed unworthy of belief. Yet how true can it be that I am envious of a man who devoted his entire life to those things that were only the flower and first fruits of my youth? How, when what was for him, if not his only occupation, surely his principal one, was for me mere sport, a pastime, a mental exercise? What ground, I ask, could there be for envy or mistrust? In praising him you suggest that he could, if he wished, have used another style; I heartily agree, since I have the highest esteem for his ability, that he could do anything he undertook; but what he did choose to attempt is clear.

What is immediately striking about Petrarch's assessment of Dante's intellectual and literary achievements is that it does not seem appropriate to regard it, in straightforward terms, as either damning or sympathetic. It is even less appropriate to view it as exclusively about Dante. On the one hand, it seems hard to dispute that Petrarch is comfortable recognizing Dante's eminence as a vernacular writer of remarkable *ingenium;* at the same time, however, he is also clearly bent on distinguishing himself from his predecessor. In essence, he, Petrarch, quite early on in life, realized that pursuing a career as a vernacular intellectual was markedly inferior to dedicating himself to Latin studies — a fact that Dante never succeeded in grasping. Thus, as *Familiares* 21.15 demonstrates, it is important to remember, first, that when Petrarch spoke about Dante he was invariably, if not primarily, also speaking about himself;[21] and, second, that he elaborated his two-sided presentation in such a manner that it normally ended up by working to his advantage. To put it a bit differently, Petrarch was not really interested in considering Dante on his merits, though, as we shall see, he was keen to create the impression that this was precisely what he was doing. To attempt to understand Petrarch's attitude to Dante is to be faced with layer upon layer of complication and ambiguity; and, to be sure, there is significantly more that can be said about the passage under discussion — and indeed about the letter as a whole — and I shall return to both in due course. What I should like to stress here, however, is that there is nothing unreflective or emotional, never mind "unconscious," about the way Petrarch carefully evaluated himself and Dante. His rhetorical and discursive structures point to a writer in firm control of his argument — one, in fact, pursuing a deliberate strategy. In the face of Dante's overwhelming contemporary *auctoritas,*[22] Petrarch's intent was not so much to query his "authoritativeness" as to raise questions about its nature and remit. In the fourteenth century, it would have been quite absurd to deny Dante's standing; or, as Petrarch declared, it would have been ridiculous to be envious of him. Petrarch was far too sophisticated a cultural operator and ambitious an intellectual to place himself in direct, and so outlandish, opposition to Dante. Equally, and for the same reasons, he was unwilling to place himself in a condition of passive imitation and doting discipleship in respect of the poet of the *Commedia.* Neither position, it goes without saying, would have done him many favors. He presents himself instead as willing to acknowledge Dante's achievements, though, at the same time, as decidedly unwilling to judge these as absolute, namely, as unreservedly "authoritative." His aim, therefore, appears to have been to redimension and delimit Dante's enormous cultural prestige, thereby opening up a space in which to locate himself and his own work; and much of what follows focuses on just these matters. Contrary, therefore, to what scholars have long and reductively maintained, the issue when examining Petrarch's relationship to Dante is not whether Petrarch was for or against his fellow poet; rather, the vital issue—one much more attune to the cultural circumstances of the Trecento—is what precisely did Petrarch suggest were Dante's achievements and, by extension, what exactly did he think were his failings; and, furthermore, how did he relate his assessment of Dante's strengths and weaknesses, namely, "his" image of Dante, to that other image—of himself—that he was simultaneously and obsessively constructing. I believe that, by offering answers to these questions, we can begin to have a sense of Petrarch's largely self-serving view of his illustrious yet oppressive precursor, as well as an effective yardstick with which to measure his persistent borrowing from Dante.

Given Petrarch's emphasis on Dante's vernacular prowess, it seems reasonable to begin by attempting to establish what kind of vernacular writer he considered the older poet to have been. Only once, and then fleetingly, did Petrarch explicitly name Dante in each of his two major vernacular works, the *Canzoniere* and the *Triumphi*—a reticence which straightway cannot but make one suspicious that, as in *Familiares* 21.15, the Dante presented in their pages will be stripped of a large part of his *auctoritas*. In November 1349, ten years before he penned his famous epistle to Boccaccio refuting accusations that he harbored negative feelings toward Dante, Petrarch commemorated the death of his close friend, Sennuccio del Bene, with the sonnet "Sennuccio mio, benché doglioso et solo" (My Sennuccio, though you have left me alone and sorrowing),[23] number 287 in the *Rerum vulgarium fragmenta*.[24] Remembering one poet, Petrarch alluded to four others, among whom is Dante:

> Ma ben ti prego che 'n la terza spera
> Guitton saluti, et messer Cino, et Dante,
> Franceschin nostro, et tutta quella schiera.
> (ll. 9–11)

But I beg you to salute all in the third sphere: Guittone and messer Cino and Dante, our Franceschino, and all that band.

His strategy is obvious. By locating Dante "in the third sphere," namely the heaven of Venus, and associating him with these particular poets, Petrarch restricted Dante's cultural status to that of a love poet.[25] More specifically, he reduced Dante simply to one such poet among a large "schiera" of erotic versifiers — a radical curtailment of his contemporary image. Nor did Petrarch stop there. He went on to delimit even Dante's standing as a poet of love. Thus, if one compares his treatment of the Florentine with that of the other poets he mentions, Dante emerges yet more dramatically diminished: "Guitton saluti, et messer Cino, et Dante, / Franceschin nostro" (ll. 10–11).[26] It is immediately striking that, unlike his presentation of Cino and Franceschino degli Albizzi, poets of undoubted less exalted luster than the author of the *Commedia,* Dante's name is not qualified by a positive term of appreciation. Furthermore, if, at first sight, the polemical implications of this omission seem to be counterbalanced by the fact that Petrarch placed Dante's name in rhyme position, that is to say in the most privileged part of the line, the polemical intent of his operation returns with all its force when one notes the name, also introduced without an epithet, that is located in the line's other stressed position, namely in its opening. To bracket Dante with Guittone, especially if the aim is to challenge and impose limits on the Florentine's *auctoritas,* is an extremely effective stratagem. It cleverly succeeds in turning Dante against himself: the objections that he had so publicly levied against the Aretine are made to sound hollow and self-serving, given that the two of them are now presented as poetic partners. As a result, and more seriously for Dante's reputation as an "authority," Petrarch raises doubts not just about his critical acumen and self-awareness, but also about his literary prowess. Finally, beyond its direct implications for Dante, Petrarch's approach in sonnet 287 confirms once more his intimate knowledge of his precursor's major vernacular works, the *Vita nova* and the *Commedia* — a knowledge, in fact, without which it would have been impossible for him to carry out his delicately destructive strategy of revision, reduction, and aspersion.[27]

By restricting Dante to love poetry, especially in a poem set in the afterlife, the principal and actual target of Petrarch's attack comes clearly into sight. His intent was to challenge the contemporary obsession with and canonization of the *Commedia* as a text whose "authority" not only matched but also actually outstripped that of the great poets of antiquity. From Petrarch's perspective, he was well within his rights to do this; indeed, as a man whose cultural views had been shaped and refined by his detailed and historically sensitive study of the classics, it was his intellectual duty to un- mask the *Commedia* as a middling vernacular love poet's inevitably flawed attempt at writing an epic; and the *Triumphi* make the same criticism, al- beit in a much more sustained manner.[28] In particular, sonnet 287 calls into question the claims Dante makes throughout the "sacrato poema" (sacred poem)[29] (*Par.* 23.62) as regards the truth and the divinely inspired charac- ter of his account of the other world. When Petrarch described Sennuccio's condition in eternity—"alteramente se' levato al volo. / Or vedi inseme l'un et l'altro polo, / le stelle vaghe et lor viaggio torto" (you have risen high in flight. Now you see both one and the other pole and the wandering stars and their winding journey) (ll. 4–6)—he quite deliberately recalled an em- blematic moment of Dante's celestial journey. After arriving in the heaven of the fixed stars, the pilgrim, like Sennuccio, casts an all-embracing look at the wonder and vastness of creation—a glance which also serves to con- firm the miraculous, and hence true, nature of his experience (*Par.* 22.103–5 for the theme of flight; ll. 118–20 for the divinely sanctioned character of his ascent; and ll. 128–29 and 133–53 for the look at the heavens and down to earth). Yet, it is these fundamental features of the *Commedia* that Petrarch energetically disputes, underlining unambiguously that only Sennuccio, as an inhabitant of Paradise, can actually enjoy such a marvelous vision. This is a privilege that lies beyond the possibilities of the living: "et vedi il veder nostro quanto è corto" (and you see how short our seeing is) (l. 7). This line too is a calque on Dante:

> Or tu chi se', che vuo' sedere a scranna,
> per giudicar di lungi mille miglia
> con la veduta corta d'una spanna?
> (*Par.* 19.79–81)

> Now, who are you that would sit upon the bench and judge
> a thousand miles away with sight short of a span?

Once again the borrowing is highly revelatory. The eagle of justice ac- cuses the *viator* of intellectual presumption; and, by repeating the words of the divine bird, Petrarch accuses Dante of having committed the same error when he composed the *Commedia*—or rather, since the words are Dante's, and as occurs with his association with Guittone, it is the accused who, ironically, charges himself. The subtlety of Petrarch's operation is impressive. Nor does it end here. That Petrarch should have chosen precisely Dante-*personaggio*'s entry into the starry heaven to criticize the *Commedia* has further consequences. The hero who, after rising skywards, looks back was a well-established medieval commonplace—it is enough to think of the *Somnium Scipionis* or even of Petrarch's backward glance on reaching the top of Mount Ventoux (*Fam.* 4.1)—and was closely linked to the idea of the journey of knowledge and enlightenment.[30] By denying the truth of Dante's account, Petrarch concurrently denied both the theological and philosophical claims of the poem; and to undermine the intellectual bases of the *Commedia* was to destroy one of the key elements of Dante's fourteenth-century *auctoritas*. As we have just seen, Petrarch was also intent on contesting the other principal foundation upon which Dante's "authority" was built—his standing, thanks to the *Commedia,* as a poet of exceptional ability. Petrarch's goal is obvious: to dismantle the contemporary image of Dante, divine poet of the afterlife, font of wisdom, and disseminator of truths. As a result, the *Commedia* is no longer a text that readers can trust; and "untrustworthy" authors and texts are most certainly not "authoritative."[31] Specifically, given the immediate context of the *Canzoniere* in which sonnet 287 is located—a context dominated by the death of Laura—Petrarch is most explicitly calling into question Dante's assertions regarding his encounter with the dead Beatrice. By means of sonnet 287's clear-sighted realism, the poet demonstrated, and hence criticized, the inevitably deceptive character of his own visions of and contacts with the deceased Laura—illusory experiences that he had vividly described as real events in the preceding eight sonnets (279–86). In these fantasies, Laura, like Beatrice in the Earthly Paradise, inhabits a *locus amoenus*.[32] Thus, by criticizing himself for having presented illusion as fact, Petrarch extends his criticism to Dante, accusing him of having deceived both himself and his readers when he asserted that he had been reunited with a dead woman.[33]

In sharp contrast, Petrarch portrays himself as a paragon of honesty, as someone with the moral and intellectual strength to acknowledge his mistakes—a clear-sightedness and firmness that are beyond the powers of "his" Dante. By means of sonnet 287, Petrarch not only shattered his and Dante's illusions, but also, and more weightily, endeavored both to expose the "fantasy" of his predecessor's *auctoritas* and to reject the idea, so actively championed by Dante in the *Commedia*, as part of his strategy of "self-authorization," that poetry could go beyond *fictio*—a claim which Dante's own son Pietro also denied.[34] As we shall soon see, the same polemical intent, frequently centered on the same general and specific points as those addressed in "Sennuccio mio, benché doglioso et solo," though naturally with differing emphases, marks Petrarch's approach to Dante elsewhere in his oeuvre. For the moment, however, I should like to stay a bit longer with sonnet 287, and consider further what else it might reveal, especially in broad terms, about Petrarch's relationship to Dante. If Petrarch really was as absorbed in destroying Dante's "authority" as I have maintained, the problem arises as to why he borrowed so heavily, and there is no doubt that he did, from the poet of the *Vita nova* and the *Commedia*. The question is highly pertinent, not least because it is pivotal in any interpretation of Petrarch's attitude to Dante. Having raised it, however, I will desist from dealing with it until I have had the chance to discuss in some depth the *Triumphi* and, probably more importantly, poem 70, "Lasso me, ch'i' non so in qual parte pieghi" (Alas, I do not know where to turn), of the *Canzoniere*—though, as we have just noted, one reason why Petrarch did make such recourse to Dante was to turn Dante's own words against him.

Although this is not the right place to linger on *Rerum vulgarium fragmenta* 70, it does nevertheless have an important bearing on the present discussion of sonnet 287. Canzone 70, the famous canzone *cum auctoritatibus*, in which each of the first four stanzas ends with the opening line of a love poem written by an eminent vernacular poet, constitutes the *Canzoniere*'s major, if not actually sole, explicit statement of poetic genealogy, therefore making it a key point of reference for sonnet 287's metaliterary suggestions. The bonds uniting the two texts are immediately obvious, and not simply because Cino and Dante—naturally, the erotic Dante—are present in both. Canzone 70 defines the *Rerum vulgarium fragmenta* as essentially a Romance amorous poetic collection, if not actually a specifically Italian one, but one with few, albeit culturally noteworthy, models: Arnaut, Cavalcanti, Dante, and Cino. Yet, given the way that their verses easily and "naturally" merge with Petrarch's poetry, functioning essentially as mere adjuncts to his poem, the impression is created, even as regards this quartet, of an influence that is largely fleeting and unproblematic, and therefore of little consequence. Indeed, when Petrarch, in "Sennuccio mio, benché doglioso et solo," introduces, almost *en passant,* another poetic quartet, one which can be seen as a kind of partial complementary addendum to the quartet evoked in the canzone, exactly the same effect is produced. The idea that the poetry of others holds minimal and inconsequential sway over the *Canzoniere* fits neatly with the claim Petrarch made in *Familiares* 21.15 that Dante and other vernacular poets — and it is worth noting how again he fails to discriminate between Dante and the rest — had barely influenced him: "Hoc unum non dissimulo, quoniam siquid in eo sermone a me dictum illius [Dante] aut alterius cuiusquam dicto simile, sive idem forte cum aliquo sit inventum, non id furtim aut imitandi proposito, que duo semper in his maxime vulgaribus ut scopulos declinavi, sed vel casu fortuito factum esse, vel similitudine ingeniorum" (This one thing I do wish to make clear, for if any of my vernacular writings resembles, or is identical to, anything of his or anyone else's, it cannot be attributed to theft or imitation, which I have avoided like reefs, especially in vernacular works, but to pure chance or similarity of mind) (12).

It is vital, I believe, to recognize the consistency — a complex and nuanced rather than one-dimensional consistency, which stretched across many years — of Petrarch's treatment of Dante (and this will become even better apparent once I have examined the letter and the canzone), since it highlights the care with which he undertook the task of dismantling his predecessor's *auctoritas.* And he did this with seemingly logical rigor. Thus, given that, as Petrarch implies in sonnet 287, even the most celebrated of vernacular poets is deeply flawed, it is obvious that, if he had not done his best to avoid the influence of such dubious models, he would have been in breach of his intellectual and artistic duties. The extent to which Dante dominated Petrarch's thinking can be espied not just in the persistence but also in the purposeful precision with which he built himself up while taking his rival apart. Yet, the rigor and logic of Petrarch's operation are ultimately more apparent than real — and I am not just thinking here of the complications introduced into his maneuver by the enormity of his intertextual debt to Dante. Petrarch found himself in the awkward position of attempting simultaneously to conceal his dependence on Dante and to conduct a critique that, as we saw in sonnet 287, was dependent on evoking both the older poet and his poetry, while at the same time suggesting that he was appreciative of his precursor's accomplishments. The tensions inherent in his approach were considerable, since the danger constantly existed that the contradictions in his treatment of Dante would stymie both his revisionary and his self-celebratory goals, thereby seriously damaging his own cultural standing. In such circumstances, the irritation with which Petrarch reacted to those, like Boccaccio, who continued to extol Dante or to accuse him of behaving dishonestly toward his predecessor is understandable. If Dante had not enjoyed the remarkable prestige that he did in the Trecento, it is just about certain that Petrarch would not have been exercised by him, just as he was not especially exercised—as I shall explain in due course—by Cavalcanti. As sonnet 287 adumbrates, it was the weight, absoluteness, and "authority" of the *Commedia* that more than anything troubled Petrarch. In composing the *Canzoniere,* he aimed to create a major vernacular poetic structure that was both independent from and could stand comparison with Dante's "summatic" poem, which, during the fourteenth century, had by and large become normative. Thus Petrarch's hope was to present an alternative mode of writing vernacular poetry. As a result, one way to read the *Rerum vulgarium fragmenta* is as an "anti-*Commedia*."[35] By stressing that Dante's achievement was exclusively as a love poet—a sphere which, at best, had a restricted role in defining his "authority"—and that, in any case, this achievement was fairly limited, Petrarch tried to reduce Dante to such an extent that, as canzone 70 confirms, he could relatively easily subsume him into his "new" lyric model of vernacular literature—the genre where the preeminent voice was of course his own. Paradoxically, in the light of all the energy that Petrarch expended in curtailing Dante's *auctoritas,* it was nevertheless very much to his advantage to be able to suggest that he could absorb and supersede a figure as "authoritative" as the great Florentine. Complexity, self-interest, cultural politics, and contradiction are inescapably intertwined in Petrarch's reaction to Dante; and so it is not at all surprising that scholars should have described his *dantismo* in such sharply contrasting ways.

DELIMITING DANTE: *TRIUMPHUS CUPIDINIS* 4.28–38

There seems little doubt that Petrarch's primary tactic in relation to Dante was to restrict as much as he possibly could the *Commedia*'s cultural power, if not actually to "eliminate" the poem as the defining point of reference in the intellectual and artistic world of Trecento Italy. As long as the *Commedia* was accorded a position of almost absolute dominance, Dante's "authority" was guaranteed and Petrarch could not hope to consolidate his standing as a vernacular poet. Nor was he alone in thinking this. Others in the fourteenth century, including even Boccaccio, felt the oppressive weight of the poem's and its author's *auctoritas*.[36] It was of course in the *Triumphi*, a visionary epic poem written in *terza rima* and chock-full of borrowings from the *Commedia*, that Petrarch most openly grappled with Dante's masterpiece, hoping to bend it to his sway.[37]

The fact that in the *Triumphi*, a work so obviously dependent on the *Commedia*, Petrarch should have referred only once, and then rather curtly, to Dante immediately points to the controversial thrust of his approach:

> Così, or quinci or quindi rimirando,
> vidi gente ir per una verde piaggia
> pur d'amor volgarmente ragionando:
>   ecco Dante e Beatrice, ecco Selvaggia,
> ecco Cin da Pistoia, Guitton d'Arezzo,
> che di non esser primo par ch'ira aggia;
>   ecco i due Guidi che già fur in prezzo,
> Honesto Bolognese, e i Ciciliani,
> che fur già primi, e quivi eran da sezzo;
>   Sennuccio e Franceschin, che fur sì humani,
> come ogni uon vide; e poi v'era un drappello
>   (*Tr. Cup.* 4.28–38)

> And looking then now this way and now that, / I saw people coming along a green field / Speaking of love, but in the common tongue: / Here were Dante and Beatrice, here was Selvaggia, / Here were Cino da Pistoia, Guittone d'Arezzo, / Angry not to be held as first among them all; / Here were both Guidos, once held in high esteem, / Onesto from Bologna, and the Sicilians, / Who, once first, were now no more than last; / Sennuccio and Franceschin, who were so courteous, / As all men saw; and then came a company[38]

The polemical character of his presentation becomes quite explicit when it is noted that, in naming his predecessor, Petrarch made no effort to acknowledge Dante as the author of the *Commedia*, the text that so obviously lies at the basis of his own epic poem. Instead, as in the *Canzoniere*, he portrays Dante as one among a group of Italian love poets—"gente [. . .] d'amor volgarmente ragionando"—a blatant lapse in literary protocol, which would have been flagrant to any medieval reader accustomed to the respectful manner in which epic poets in particular dutifully celebrated their predecessors and admitted the debts they owed them.[39] Petrarch's transgression was glaring since it was committed against an *auctoritas* of such singular standing; nor is there much doubt that the omission was deliberate. It allowed Petrarch to establish effectively and concisely that, however much his poem might resound with echoes of the *Commedia,* the relationship between his and Dante's text was anything but straightforward. As will become apparent, the impression he was keen to foster was that the *Triumphi* stand in clear and direct opposition to the *Commedia,* thereby bringing to the fore those criticisms of Dante's abilities as a writer of epic that remain largely implicit in the *Canzoniere.* Nor does his coupling of Beatrice's name to Dante's—a notable addition with respect to "Sennuccio mio, benché doglioso et solo"—benefit the poet of the *Commedia.* In fact, the opposite is almost certainly true. By fixing Beatrice as simply a love poet's lady, the equal of Cino's Selvaggia, Petrarch, as he had done in sonnet 287, denied her role as heavenly guide and hence once again challenged the *Commedia's* metaphysical claims. Moreover, when made from within an epic poem, such criticism obviously carries that much greater weight than when adumbrated in a lyric collection. Indeed, by presenting his own eschatological experience as a dream-vision—"vinto dal sonno, vidi una gran luce" (Overcome by sleep, I saw a great light) (*Tr. Cup.* 1.11)[40]—Petrarch placed himself in open rivalry to Dante and overtly challenged the idea that his predecessor could have gone bodily on a "viaggio" (voyage) (*Inf.* 1.91) through the afterlife.[41]

In keeping with the precedent set in sonnet 287, the manner in which Petrarch integrated Dante into his brief procession of Italian love poets constitutes a key factor in his programmed *deminutio* of his adversary. A variant of *Triumphus Cupidinis* 3.99—"ché tutti siam macchiati d'una pece" (because we are all stained by a sin)—is extremely revealing in this respect. In the "codice degli abbozzi" (manuscript of drafts), line 99 reads as follows: "ecco qui Dante co la sua Beatrice" (here was Dante with his Beatrice). From once having had a complete line given over to them, in *Triumphus Cupidinis* 4, Dante and his lady are squashed into a hemistich: "ecco Dante e Beatrice." In contrast, Cino and Selvaggia, who immediately follow, comfortably and elegantly spread themselves over a half-line each: "ecco

Selvaggia, / ecco Cin da Pistoia." And I will not even attempt to sound the implications in line 99 of "pece," "sin," replacing "Beatrice." In this instance, I am happy to concede that the problem is best left to the hermeneutic scrutiny of psychoanalytic criticism. It is thus questionable whether the fact that Dante's name appears first in the list is really meant to underline his poetic primacy. On the surface at least, Petrarch seems conventionally to show respect for the foremost poet of the century, as he was to do, with equally studied ambiguity, in *Familiares* 21.15: "Iam qui me aliis iudicandum dabam, nunc de aliis in silentio iudicans, varie quidem in reliquis, in hoc ita, ut facile sibi vulgaris eloquentie palmam dem" (I used to submit my work to the judgment of others, whereas now I judge others in silence, varying in my opinion of them but deeming him the one to whom I would readily grant the palm for vernacular eloquence) (13). It should never be forgotten that Petrarch was keen to present himself as objectively respectful toward, if not entirely persuaded by, Dante's attainments, while concurrently working hard to spread an ever thicker veil of uncertainty around those same attainments and their author. In a context where issues of literary supremacy are to the fore ("che di non esser primo par ch'ira aggia"), Dante's established predominance is undermined not just by the tension that is forged between him and Cino—and, as sonnet 287 confirms, this is not the only time that Petrarch appears to favor Cino over Dante[42]—but also by the fact that, among all the Italian poets mentioned, the two most positively treated are, "shockingly," Sennuccio del Bene and Franceschino degli Albizzi: "Sennuccio e Franceschin, che fur sì humani, / come ogne uon vide." Nor is it likely by chance that Petrarch placed his friends at the end of the sequence. Thus, since the precise logic of the series remains ambiguous— neither strict chronological nor evaluative criteria appear consistently to hold good in it—Sennuccio and Franceschin's strategic placement encourages the thought that, on account of their exclusive "humanity," they can be viewed as moving beyond the poets who precede them. And the pair receives a further boost thanks to their proximity to the "drappello / di portamenti e di volgari strani" (company / foreign in manner and in their vernacular speech) (ll. 38–39), that is to say the Occitan poets, whose broad superiority over their Italian counterparts is made transparent as a result of the sympathetic manner of their treatment and the generosity with which space is allocated to them: nineteen and a half lines (ll. 38–57) as against seven and a half (ll. 31–38). This celebration of Occitan poetic prowess strikes yet another blow against Dante's already shaky vernacular poetic standing and preeminence, as well as the reputation of the Italian lyric in general.[43] Thus, Petrarch's perfunctory nod in his direction is in stark and telling contrast to the powerful, sustained, and unqualified encomium he delivered extolling the lasting legacy of Arnaut's artistic supremacy:

> fra tutti il primo Arnaldo Daniello,
> gran maestro d'amor, ch'a la sua terra
> ancor fa honor col suo dir strano e bello.
> (ll. 40–42)[44]

First of them all was Arnaut Daniel, / Great master in love, who to his land / Still brings honor with the strange beauty of his verse.

However much, in *Triumphus Cupidinis* 4, Petrarch may have been eager to celebrate love poetry in general, there is also no question that he was just as eager to establish that, to-date, Italy had only made a relatively minor contribution to the genre. Thus, he further emphasized the relative insignificance of poetry in Italian by presenting it as dwarfed not only by the Occitans but also, and less problematically, by the poets of antiquity, on whom, conventionally, he lavished the most fulsome praise (ll. 13–27). Consequently, love literature in Italian is reduced to a minor tradition uncomfortably lodged, as Petrarch's actual presentation iconically reveals, between the greats "di chiara fama, / o per antiche, o per moderne carte" (of clear fame, / Either for ancient, or modern pages) (*Tr. Cup.* 4.11–12). It is a tradition, therefore, in urgent need of a major boost if it is ever to stand favorable comparison with the best that the past and the present have produced; and such a boost of course was what Petrarch, who significantly prefaced the pageant by associating himself with its participants (*Tr. Cup.* 4.4–9), planned to provide with the *Canzoniere*. Despite their generic differences, the ideological and metacultural ties and the communality of purpose uniting his two vernacular works are noteworthy. Thus, in direct dialectical tension with *Triumphus Cupidinis* 4, canzone 70 establishes in its very first stanza that Petrarch, unlike other Italian poets, has no difficulty in transcending the Occitan "gran maestro d'amor."[45]

The harmful repercussions for Dante, flawed poet of a flawed tradition, of Petrarch's compressed "history of erotic literature" are more than obvious—and historical systematization and qualitative evaluation were undoubtedly one of the functions that medieval culture assigned to catalogues such as that in *Triumphus Cupidinis* 4.[46] Indeed, when Petrarch put together his poetic procession, I strongly suspect that he was less interested in defining the tradition of erotic literature and even in establishing his own standing than he was in doing as much damage as possible to Dante's reputation. In intertextual terms, the parade is unambiguously constructed with Dante as its primary point of reference.[47] It is Dante, therefore, more than any other poet in *Triumphus Cupidinis* 4, who is being assessed in relation to his peers; and it is his position in the poetic order—and medieval catalogues of authors, I repeat, were invariably hierarchical in character—that is crucially at stake. For instance, just before Dante and Beatrice are introduced, Petrarch writes "vidi gente ir per una verde piaggia" (I saw people coming along a green field) (l. 29), a hendecasyllable which openly recalls the pilgrim's arrival with the "savi" (sages) (*Inf.* 4.110), the five classical poets, inside the "nobile castello" (noble castle) (l. 105): "giugnemmo in prato di fresca verdura" (we came to a meadow of fresh verdure) (l. 111). Petrarch is deliberately evoking the memory of Dante's Limbo, where notoriously the poet had had the temerity to crown himself "sesto tra cotanto senno" (sixth among so much wisdom) (l. 102). Therefore, it is unlikely to be a coincidence that, in the *Triumphus Cupidinis* too, we should discover, a mere few lines earlier, another quintet of poets accompanied by an unexpected sixth:

> Virgilio vidi; e parmi intorno avesse
> compagni d'alto ingegno e da trastullo,
> di quei che volentier già 'l mondo lesse:
>   l'uno era Ovidio, e l'altro era Catullo,
> l'altro Propertio, che d'amor cantaro
> fervidamente, e l'altro era Tibullo.
>   Una giovene greca a paro a paro
> coi nobili poeti iva cantando,
> ed avea un suo stil soave e raro.
>
> (Tr. Cup. 4.19–27)

> I saw Virgil; and it seemed to me that he was surrounded /
> By companions of lofty intelligence and delight, / Whom the
> world once gladly read: / One was Ovid, and the other was
> Catullus, / Another Propertius, who of love sang / Fervidly,
> and another was Tibullus. / A young Greek woman side by
> side / With the noble poets went singing, / And she had her
> own sweet and rare style.

Not only is Dante not a member of this elite of love poets — never mind being the "sixth" member and the symbol of comedy in a pantheon of writers who, by being associated with the major *genera,* embody literature as a whole — but the position he had originally claimed for himself is now reassigned to a woman. The cultural implications of such gender reversal, regardless of Sappho's fame, especially given the ambiguities surrounding women and language in the Middle Ages,[48] do not need further elucidation. Indeed, the deliberately polemical character of Petrarch's operation becomes even more apparent if the links between *suavitas* and comedy are remembered,[49] as well as those between Sappho's "stil soave e raro" and Dante's "dolce stil novo" (sweet new style) (*Purg.* 24.57). The subtle skill and precision with which Petrarch dismantled, even ridiculed, Dante's *auctoritas* are impressive. Without seeming to show overt disrespect for the much admired older poet, Petrarch nevertheless made it more than plain to readers with the right degree of intellectual and cultural preparation — precisely that elite audience whose opinion he wished to influence, and among whom were others who had voiced reservations about the author of the *Commedia* — what he thought both of the contemporary cult of Dante and of the poet's campaign of self-authorization.

Attacking the *Commedia*'s elaborate metaliterary structure, Petrarch had accurately pinpointed the principal means by which Dante had decided to establish and legitimate his *auctoritas.* Thus, by showing up the vanity of Dante's declarations of artistic preeminence and literary "authority," Petrarch compromised the credibility of both the poet and his oeuvre. In addition, and this is important, having unmasked his predecessor's unsustainable pretensions, Petrarch was that much freer to recreate him in terms that could both serve his own purposes of self-authorization and appear to evaluate Dante in a balanced manner. Consequently, if Petrarch emerges as a model of intellectual probity, Dante, on the contrary, appears mired in self-interest. From this perspective, whatever claims Dante had made for himself inevitably sound expedient and exaggerated. Specifically, as Petrarch implies in sonnet 287, Dante's judgments of his fellow writers need to be approached with considerable caution. The poetic pageant in *Triumphus Cupidinis* 4 can therefore be read as a "disinterested" counter to Dante's "selfish" presentation of many of the same poets in the *Commedia*. Indeed, the fact that so much of the procession, as we have begun to see, is openly dependent on some of the poem's most openly metaliterary cantos—*Inferno* 4, *Purgatorio* 11 and 26—underlines its corrective character. Thus, if Dante had referred to Guinizzelli and Cavalcanti in order to promote himself—"cosí ha tolto l'uno a l'altro Guido / la gloria de la lingua; e forse è nato / chi l'uno e l'altro caccerà del nido" (so has the one Guido taken from the other the glory of our tongue; and perhaps he is born who will chase the one and the other from the nest) (*Purg.* 11.97–99)—Petrarch recalls "i due Guidi che già fur in prezzo" for purely literary-historical reasons. Similarly, his definition of Arnaut is more positive and categorical than Dante's ambiguous appreciation filtered through Guinizzelli's inevitably restricted and subjective point of view:

> "O frate," disse, "questi ch'io ti cerno
> col dito," e additò un spirto innanzi,
> "fu miglior fabbro del parlar materno.
>   Versi d'amore e prose di romanzi
> soverchiò tutti; e lascia dir li stolti
> che quel di Lemosí credon ch'avanzi."
>   (*Purg.* 26.115–20)

> "O brother," he said, "the one whom I point out to you with my finger," and he pointed to a spirit ahead, "was a better craftsman of the mother tongue. Verses of love and prose romances, he surpassed them all; and let the fools talk who think that he of Limoges excels."

In any case, unlike Petrarch's sober—I am almost tempted to say "scholarly"[50]—review of Occitan poets, Dante's Arnaut and Giraut de Bornelh are introduced with an acidly polemical intent. Once again, suspicions swarm around Dante's motives for naming other writers; and increasingly the *Commedia* looks like a work written primarily, if not exclusively, so that its author can accumulate literary glory for himself at the expense of his peers. Trapped in its own literary self-absorption, it is a hardnosed exercise in artificially, and therefore improperly, assigning *auctoritas* to the self. It is thus a poem lacking moral purpose—and in the Middle Ages, when literature was regularly defined as a branch of ethics,[51] no more damning a charge could be levied against a text. On the other hand, the *Triumphi* are presented as quintessentially driven by ethical concerns. Petrarch seamlessly passes from the erotic, and hence potentially selfish, poetics of the Occitans—a selfishness of a quite different order, of course, to Dante's egoism—to his own poetics of *charitas:*

> e molti altri ne vidi, a cui la lingua
> lancia e spada fu sempre, e targia ed elmo.
>   E, poi conven che 'l mio dolor distingua,
> volsimi a' nostri, e vidi 'l bon Thomasso,
> [. . .]
> senza 'l qual non sapea movere un passo.
> [. . .]
>   Poco era fuor de la comune strada,
> quando Socrate e Lelio vidi in prima:
> con lor più lunga via conven ch'io vada.
>   O qual coppia d'amici! [. . .]
> [. . .]
>   Con questi duo cercai monti diversi,
> andando tutti tre sempre ad un giogo.
>   (*Tr. Cup.* 4.56–59, 63, 67–70, 73–74)

    And many more I saw, for whom the tongue / Was ever lance and sword, and shield and helmet. / And since I must highlight my pain, / I turned to our people, and saw the good Thomasso, / [. . .] / Without whom I was unable to walk a step. / [. . .] / I had not moved far from the common path, / When I first saw Socrates and Laelius: / With them I must go down a longer road. / Oh what a pair of friends! [. . .] / [. . .] / With these two I sought out different mountains, / all three of us always walking bound to a common yoke.

Friendship, study, ethics: these are the forces that inspire and characterize the *Triumphi*. Petrarch's epic, for all its visionary qualities, is a poem about life rather than literature; and in it literature is never allowed to gain the upper hand on life: "[. . .] che né 'n rima / poria, né 'n prosa ornar assai, né 'n versi, / se, come dee, vertù nuda se stima" (who neither in rhyme / Nor in prose could I celebrate, nor in verse, / If, as it deserves, pure virtue is esteemed) (ll. 70–72). There is nothing calculated and artificial about Petrarch's writing; and it is "living" poetry that brings success and recognition to its author. With a sharp knowing dig at Dante's failure to "prendere 'l cappello" (take the laurel crown) (*Par.* 25.9), Petrarch remembers his own poetic crowning, the reward, once again, for having loved and lived disinterestedly:

> Con costor colsi 'l glorïoso ramo
> onde forse anzi tempo ornai le tempie
> in memoria di quella ch'io tanto amo.
>   Ma pur di lei che 'l cor di pensier m'empie,
> non potei coglier mai ramo né foglia,
> sì fur le sue radici acerbe ed empie
>   (*Tr. Cup.* 4.79–84)[52]

> With them I plucked the glorious branch / With which
> perhaps too soon I decked my brow / In memory of her whom
> I so deeply love. / But yet from her who fills my heart with
> thoughts, / I was never able to pluck branch nor leaf, / So
> bitter and cruel were her roots

Then again, the epic is not poetry of the private sphere; and, if literary decorum is to be maintained, Petrarch must needs leave personal matters, however all-consuming, to one side (or better to his lyrics) and focus, as literary convention required, on matters of universalizing interest—the God of Love and not his love for Laura:

> onde, benché talor doler mi soglia
> come uom ch'è offeso, quel che con questi occhi
> vidi, m'è fren che mai più non mi doglia:

materia di coturni, e non di socchi,
veder preso colui ch'è fatto deo.

(ll. 85–89)

————————

Although I am at times accustomed to complain about
these / Like someone who is offended, what with these eyes /
I saw, is a brake to my ever complaining again: / Matter for
buskin, and not for sock, / To see him captured who is made
a god.

Speaking of *cothurni*, which, in both the ancient and the medieval
worlds, served as a learned metonymy for tragedy, the *stilus* of epic poetry,[53]
Petrarch underscored that he was professionally in control of the *Triumphi*,
and that he knew precisely the correct manner in which to elaborate its epic
subject matter, as well as the appropriate technical vocabulary with which
to discuss his work. Furthermore, to leave no doubt about his competence,
he also deferentially acknowledged Homer and Orpheus as his epic "authorities" (l. 93). Conversely, the poet who had shown little sensitivity and
even less learning when writing epic poetry was, naturally, Dante, who inex-
cusably had committed the bewildering solecism of turning to comedy—
evoked here through the mention of *socci*—when he came to pen his epic,
an elementary lack of judgment which many of his Trecento readers lamented.[54] Far from representing the contemporary vernacular epic at its
best, the *Commedia* was yet another instance of the arrogant presumptu-
ousness of the *moderni*. Thus, rather than being a literary model respectfully to be imitated, the *Commedia* is in fact the embodiment of the *vitia*
that writers need to shun. The *Triumphi*, on the other hand, offer a shining
example of a vernacular text written according to the hallowed conventions
of tradition;[55] and their author stands as an *exemplum* of how the modern
man and the modern writer ought to behave: combining Christian charity
with classical learning.[56]

Petrarch pushed hard to dislodge Dante and the *Commedia* from their
position of "authority"; and it is not hard to imagine the poet, the *Triumphi*
in hand, ready to claim for himself their vacated space. That Petrarch did
not succeed in usurping his rival, or at least not during his lifetime,[57] since
Dante's *auctoritas* was just too powerful, does not in any way invalidate the

allusive subtlety of his corrosive and delimiting revision of the Trecento Dante. Behind a seemingly appreciative veil—the veil of the respectable vernacular love poet—the author of the *Commedia* looms as a monster of incompetence and egoism, ready to trample over the truth and over the reputation of others in order to achieve his ends. Petrarch's Dante is most certainly not an "authority"; if anything, he is that most dangerous of figures, the "false *auctoritas.*"[58] As Petrarch recognized in *Familiares* 21.15, Dante had undeniably managed to dupe the untutored and even many a naively enthusiastic intellectual; however, the truly learned not only were able to see through him, but also had the duty, regardless of the opprobium that their honesty might bring down on their heads, to make their views public.[59] The same pose of scholarly objectivity with respect to Dante thus unites Petrarch's self-presentation in both the epistle and the *Triumphi*. It goes without saying that such a stance was the poet's best bulwark against potential accusations of hypocrisy: namely, that, in denouncing Dante for being selfishly opportunistic, he was just as selfishly looking after his own interests. In any case, further to deflect possible accusations of double standards, Petrarch also underscored that, unlike Dante, he had no need to justify and safeguard his poetic reputation. Others were publicly willing to celebrate his standing, as the brief mention of his crowning in the *Triumphus Cupidinis* confirms.

A common perspective on Dante also unites the *Canzoniere* and the *Triumphi*. Both texts reject as untenable the *Commedia*'s extraordinary metaphysical and literary claims. As a result, they restrict Dante's proficiency to vernacular love poetry,[60] the one area in which Petrarch was prepared to grant his precursor a degree of distinction. What differentiates the *Canzoniere* from the *Triumphi*, however, is the degree of ferocity with which each attacks the *Commedia*. The lyric collection is rather less forceful than the epic. The latter, on account of its generic communality with the "poema sacro" (sacred poem) (*Par.* 25.1), is appropriately more aggressive and open about its polemical intentions. As tradition required, Petrarch critically evaluated Dante's epic from within epic structures. In this respect, rather than being unconscious repetitions or marks of a respectful *aemulatio*, the many borrowings from across the *Commedia* discernible in the *Triumphi* constitute the battleground where Petrarch rescued Dante's "comically" imprisoned epic formulations and restored them to their rightful "tragic" context and register. To have done this in the *Canzoniere* would have been a solecism akin to Dante's disregard for the prescriptions of the *genera di-cendi*. It is thus not surprising that the *Rerum vulgarium fragmenta*'s in-tertextual dependence on the *Commedia* is much more muted and less eye-catching than that of the *Triumphi*.[61] In any case, as I mentioned earlier and will amplify in due course, in the lyric collection Petrarch drew on Dante as a love poet, a decision that inevitably had a fundamental impact on how and what he chose to borrow from the *Commedia*. In addition, in the *Canzoniere*, Petrarch utilized Dante in order to enhance his own work, and there-fore had to be careful not to do excessive damage to his predecessor. He was under no such obligation in the *Triumphi*; indeed, he made it abundantly clear that, regardless of the fact that his poem boomed with echoes of the *Commedia*, Dante's poem, unlike the works of the great classical epic *auctores*, was most definitely not his model. Petrarch was steadfast in main-taining that, however paradoxical, the more he borrowed from Dante, the less he actually owed him: his task was to rewrite the *Commedia* as it ought to have been written if Dante had properly heeded the lessons of the *bella scola*.[62] The care with which the poet approached and finessed his critique of Dante, ensuring that, in each instance, it was appropriate to the text in which he was voicing his disapproval, while at the same time reiterating certain fixed large-scale censures,[63] offers unmistakable evidence of the com-mitment with which he undertook the task of delimiting his burdensome predecessor. If the psychological causes of Petrarch's largely negative reac-tion to Dante remain obscured by conjecture and fancy, the cultural ones, despite the passing of centuries, are somewhat plainer to see, as are the in-tricate and personal means by which the poet transformed these pressures into the stuff of literature.

"Defending" Dante

It is hard to escape the conclusion that, in his vernacular poetry, Pe-trarch, even if obliquely, expressed serious misgivings about Dante and his masterpiece. According to Petrarch, the *Commedia* was a work of lamen-table literary, moral, and intellectual misjudgment, which, rather than es-tablishing and sustaining "authority," was precisely the kind of flawed and deceptive text that someone whose probity was open to question might write. Petrarch went on to reaffirm and further elaborate his doubts, again employing the rhetoric of indirection, in two letters to Boccaccio: *Familiares* 21.15 and *Seniles* 5.2. In terms of my argument, the choice of addressee is highly significant. Boccaccio was an enthusiastic pro-Dante intellectual of the sort that Petrarch was so determined to win over to his camp,[64] since, without the backing of Dante's supporters, whose views represented the majority fourteenth-century position on the poet of the *Commedia,* he could never have hoped to reconfigure the world of Trecento *auctoritas.* It is thus noteworthy, as first Giuseppe Billanovich and then Carlo Paolazzi have gone a long way to demonstrate,[65] that, after having received *Familiares* 21.15, Boccaccio did indeed revise and tone down his celebration of Dante in the *Trattatello.*

Intriguingly, *Familiares* 21.15 was actually born of a failure to persuade. As is well known, Petrarch's letter acts as a reply to a missive, now lost, that he had received from Boccaccio. The *certaldese* had written to his friend soon after their meeting in 1359 in Milan. As is evident from the "Familiar" letter and Boccaccio's *carmen,* "Ytalie iam certus honos" (Already the certain honor of Italy),[66] which had accompanied the missing epistle, its subject matter was almost certainly the thorny one of Dante's greatness — thorny, of course, only as far as Petrarch was concerned. From the surviving texts of the exchange, it is not unreasonable to assume that, as had occurred when the writers had met in 1350 and in 1351,[67] a large part of their Milanese encounter had been spent arguing and disagreeing about Dante's merits. Given the enduring strength of Boccaccio's enthusiasm for Dante, Petrarch must have increasingly realized, and with some discomfort, that something more energetic than his finely allusive poetic criticisms of Dante was required if the Florentine's *auctoritas* was to be significantly disturbed. Instead of embedding his denunciations deep into the ideological nervous system of a universalizing "tragic" *visio* and of a highly personal lyric self-analysis, a more direct approach, one which had Dante at its center, was necessary.

The moment was in fact critical. If, as has been suggestively maintained, a second text had accompanied Boccaccio's letter, namely the first and largely celebratory version of the *Trattatello in laude di Dante,*[68] then the need for a public rebuttal of its encomiastic tones had become pressing. At the same time, Petrarch must have thought that he had a reasonable chance of prevailing over Boccaccio, and so getting him to temper his assessment, since the younger writer himself seemed ready to concede that his enthusiasm was probably excessive: "te michi excusas, idque non otiose, quod in conterranei nostri [. . .] laudibus multus fuisse videare" (you ask pardon, somewhat heatedly, for seeming to praise unduly a fellow country-man of ours) (1). If, on the one hand, Petrarch's treatment of Dante needed to be more vigorous than hitherto, on the other, its polemic — for the reasons I have already discussed — still had to be carefully controlled. *Familiares* 21.15 is thus a model of understated ambiguity.[69] Dante is assessed against the backcloth of contemporary culture, whose sordid state is sharply brought into focus. What initially read like tributes to the poet imperceptibly dissolve into their opposites, especially because they are diluted by being mingled with the corruption of the present. For instance, recognition of Dante's vernacular prowess is undercut by the fact that his use of his mother tongue increasingly appears as a device to gain the support of that uncouth *vulgus* whose shameful antics degrade current intellectual and artistic life, as it is this undiscriminating mass that most loudly celebrates him.[70] Petrarch stresses that, given his *ingenium,* Dante should not have wasted his time on an "ingenii rudimentum" (a mental exercise) (21), which a youthful Petrarch had quickly abandoned as far too trifling. Dante should and could have aimed higher: "Nam quod inter laudes dixisti, potuisse illum si voluisset alio stilo [Latin] uti, credo edepol [. . .] potuisse eum omnia quibus intendisset; nunc quibus intenderit, palam est. [. . .] fuisse illum sibi imparem, quod in vulgari eloquio quam carminibus aut prosa [in Latin] clarior atque altior assurgit" (In praising him you suggest that he could, if he wished, have used another style; I heartily agree [. . .] that he could do anything he undertook; but what he did choose to attempt is clear. [. . .] his style was unequal, for he rises to nobler and loftier heights in the vernacular than in Latin poetry or prose) (22 and 24).[71] In maintaining that Dante so obviously failed to do justice to his talent, Petrarch creates the strong suspicion that his predecessor had chosen to write in the vernacular for less than honorable reasons. Just as seriously, the combination of Dante's choice of language and his apparent wish to reach his untutored audience had led him to make the most basic of writerly errors, and so further debase his *ingenium.* As Giovanni del Virgilio had first lamented several decades earlier,[72] Petrarch too remarks that Dante incongruously clothed "lofty" *materia* in a "low" style: "popularis quidem quod ad stilum attinet, quod ad rem hauddubie nobilis poete" (popular for his poetic style but doubtless noble for his theme) (1). Tellingly, this observation comes at the very beginning of the letter, immediately establishing its basic rhetoric of ambiguity—the *conterraneus* is perplexingly both "popular" and "noble"—and of allusion—the "fellow-citizen" and his work, as happens throughout the epistle, remain unnamed,[73] though it is obvious that, as we have come to expect, Petrarch's barbs, even more than at Dante, are unerringly aimed at the *Commedia*.

Petrarch, who throughout the letter presents himself as a sympathetic, intellectually sophisticated, and disinterested admirer of Dante, is, as such, naturally well within his rights to raise questions regarding his forerunner's recourse to the *vulgaris*. This seems to have been essentially dictated by an all-absorbing Ulyssean desire for glory: "exilio [. . .] ille obstitit, et tum vehementius cepto incubuit, omnium negligens soliusque fame cupidus" (he resisted exile and began devoting himself all the more vigorously to his literary pursuits, neglecting all else and desirous only of glory) (7). Dante, like his Greek anti-hero, was prepared to sacrifice everything and everyone to achieve his aim: "non amor coniugis, non natorum pietas ab arrepto semel calle distraheret" (nothing [. . .] not his wife's love or his devotion to his children—diverted him from his course once he had embarked upon it) (8).[74] Indeed, by appealing so blatantly to the *ineptissimi laudatores*—to the extremely silly admirers—rather than to the intellectual elite, he revealed not just the all-consuming strength of his obsession, but also, more worryingly (and unlike Petrarch), his lack of discrimination and his naked opportunism: "novi enim quanti sit apud doctos indoctorum laus" (for I know how little the praise of the ignorant multitude carries weight with learned men) (22). We are once more in familiar territory. Petrarch is rehearsing again the same accusations as those he had levied against Dante in his poetry. These may very well still be carefully circumscribed; for instance, Petrarch seems to praise his precursor's singlemindedness: "In quo illum satis mirari et laudare vix valeam" (In this I can scarcely admire and praise him too highly) (8); however, his indictments are also less allusive. Thus, Petrarch is almost explicit in charging Dante with immorality, lightly concealing his indictment behind the veil of an optative: "ita dico si quantum delectat ingenio, tantum moribus delectaret" (that is, if his conduct were to please me as much as his genius) (15). Equally, Dante's pursuit of glory, of wanting to receive the recognition of others (and what others), points to a profound lack of virtue: "quod quamvis meritorum gloria ad merendi studium animos excitet, vera tamen virtus, ut philosophis placet, ipsa sibi stimulus, ipsa est premium, ipsa sibi cursus et bravium" (while the glory of deserving men stimulates in the mind an enthusiasm for such glory, true virtue, as philosophers like to say, is its own spur and its own reward, its own way and its own goal) (5).[75]

The letter leaves little doubt that Dante cannot be numbered among the *meriti*. Neither his behavior nor his art is worthy of such an accolade. Indeed, Petrarch is at pains to underscore that Dante is rather less exceptional than is generally believed. Thus, he was not really very different from Petrarch's father ("ut quibus esset preter similem fortunam, studiorum et ingenii multa similitudo" [in addition to a similar fate, they were very similar in studious interests and intellectually] [7]);[76] nor can he serve as a positive role model, as is evident from the fact that, despite being the youthful Boccaccio's "primus studiorum dux et prima fax" (first guide and the light of his youthful studies) (2), he failed to provide his ward with the moral and intellectual wisdom that would have prevented him from committing those many errors which Petrarch feels compelled to list in *Familiares* 21.15; nor, as the young Petrarch had quickly realized, revealing greater acuity than Boccaccio, is he a poet who deserves to be imitated: "sed verebar ne si huius aut alterius dictis imbuerer, ut est etas illa flexibilis et miratrix omnium, vel invitus ac nesciens imitator evaderem" (but I did fear that, were I to immerse myself in his, or any other's, writings, being of an impressionable age so given to indiscriminate admiration, I could scarcely escape becoming an unwilling or unconscious imitator) (11). Petrarch's Dante is a poor teacher, a flawed literary model, a man of dubious ethical standards; he almost stands as an emblem, if not actually a cause, of the corruption of the present. Yet despite all this, there are those who deem him an *auctoritas*. And it is not only the *vulgus* who pays tribute to him in this way. There are intellectuals like Boccaccio who, showing a remarkable lack of discrimination, ally themselves to the mob, thereby besmirching their standing as men of learning: "novi enim quanti sit apud doctos indoctorum laus" (for I know how little the praise of the ignorant multitude carries weight with learned men) (22). Boccaccio—Petrarch is quick to recognize—has an almost sacred duty to recognize his debts to his mentor; however, in acknowledging these, he was not supposed to abandon his critical and ethical faculties. We have at last reached the nub of Petrarch's argument in *Familiares* 21.15. It is less Dante and the *Commedia* that aggravate him than their reception,[77] hence the persistent denigration of the present and the flow of reprimands directed at Boccaccio. Dante was a blatant and unscrupulous seeker after fame;

however, for all his efforts at self-authorization, it is his readers who, nearly half a century after his death, are ultimately responsible for allowing him to continue to exert unjustified sway over the contemporary world.[78] Consequently, they fail to give credit to a more worthy "authority" figure humbly working in their midst; in fact, they attack him without justification and accuse him of harboring feelings of envy and hatred toward their fatally defective idol. Their judgment is, of course, profoundly flawed: "hos ineptissimos laudatores, qui omnino quid laudent quid ve improbent ex equo nesciunt" (these extremely silly admirers who never know why they praise or censure) (16). Among current readers of Dante, only Petrarch is able properly to evaluate him, since, far from blinded by resentment, he neither owes him a debt nor has been taken in by his blandishments: "cum unus ego forte, melius quam multi ex his insulsis et immodicis laudatoribus, sciam quid id est eis ipsis incognitum quod illorum aures mulcet, sed obstructis ingenii tramitibus in animum non descendit" (when perhaps I alone, more than many of these tasteless and immoderate admirers, know the nature of that unknown quality that charms their ears without penetrating their minds since the pathways of intelligence are closed to them) (14). He can estimate both Dante's merits and demerits, praising the former and chastising the latter. Dante's merits, restricted as they are to "immature" and "slight" achievements in the vernacular, cannot but be limited; yet, within this marginal tradition, Dante is the best,[79] and Petrarch is pleased to praise his success and even potentially to defend him: "que ego forsitan, nisi me meorum cura vocaret alio, pro virili parte ab hoc ludibrio vendicarem" (if my many concerns were not so pressing, I might even strive to the best of my powers to rescue him) (16). Petrarch thus comes across as the very ideal of intellectual fair play, approaching others in a spirit of *charitas* but also of moral rectitude. He, not Dante, is the model that the dissolute present ought to be heeding.[80]

Familiares 21.15 is a skillful, tightly constructed piece of writing. It is perfectly pitched to unsettle with its powerful mix of *laus* and *vituperatio*[81] — a mix that is the key to understanding Petrarch's attitude to Dante, and that we as scholars must do our best not to distill, eliminating what we find troubling and unsatisfactory. Yet despite the epistle's impact on Boccaccio — an impact, nevertheless, that should not be exaggerated — its views failed to have a broader effect on Trecento intellectual opinion. *Seniles* 5.2, written between 1365 and 1366 and once more addressed to Boccaccio, offers unambiguous evidence of this state of affairs. It is an even more violent attack on the intellectual, moral, and cultural corruption of the present than the "Familiar" letter[82] — a present in which the triumphs of the ancients are scorned and the foremost intellectual continues to be Dante, "ille nostri eloquii dux vulgaris" (the master of our vernacular literature) (30).[83] This is the only point in the missive where reference is openly, albeit periphrastically, made to Dante, though other elements in it are recognizable as typical of Petrarch's effort to destabilize the poet's contemporary image. Thus, we find mention of the limitations of vernacular culture;[84] of those who "vulgi quoque suffragiis annixi" (rely on the votes of the crowd) (29); and of the fact that "vix quisquam iustus sui operis extimator" (scarcely anyone is a fair judge of his own [creations]) (4), and that "melius tutiusque est operose virtutis auxilio niti quam otiose fame praeconio fidere" (it is better and safer to rely upon the support of active virtue than to count on the praises of idle fame) (39). However, probably the most revealing, one might say, the most emblematic, instance of this subterranean collection of Petrarchan anti-Dante commonplaces is the letter's lapidary title: "de appetitu anxio primi loci atque impatientia secundi deque superbissima modernorum ignorantia" (concerning the obsessive appetite for first place and the dissatisfaction for second place and concerning the arrogant ignorance of the moderns).[85]

The time has come to acknowledge that, for all Petrarch's claims of independence, objectivity, and appreciation, he squarely belonged within the tradition of Trecento anti-*dantismo,* just as, in general, his reaction to the poet of the *Commedia* cannot be detached from Dante's overall fourteenth-century reception. Petrarch most certainly had personal reasons for wanting to redimension his precursor's reputation and *auctoritas*; at the same time, however, he was extremely careful to voice his criticisms in a manner that would find immediate and clear resonance in his world. In this way, not only could he expect his censures to find a receptive audience, but, more astutely, he could also ensure that his opinions, by being grounded in contemporary *dantismo,* would not be dismissed as the jaundiced accusations of an embittered rival, thereby safeguarding that much sought-after pose of "objectivity." That things did not really work out as Petrarch had intended, as evidenced by the ongoing consolidation of Dante's standing in the Tre- and Quattrocento, is, of course, quite another matter, though it does confirm the difficulties that he faced in attempting to challenge Dante's *auctoritas.* Petrarch thus drew on, and to a large extent hid behind, the doubts and criticisms — which, like his, stretched from poetics to ethics and from scholarly competence to behavior — voiced by other contemporary readers.[86] Although the tradition served as the legitimating basis of Petrarch's operation, in practice, he adapted it to his own purposes, amplifying, developing, and, most tellingly, bringing together reservations that, normally, not only were kept apart but also were overshadowed by significantly more generous evaluations of Dante than his. He thus cleverly transformed the communal into the personal. Ultimately, Petrarch's was an extreme form of anti-Dantism, in which idiosyncrasy and tradition merged, and where "defense" was actually attack.

"Disguising" Dante

Having reached this point in my argument, I hope that both the principal lineaments of Petrarch's Dante and the cultural and ideological pressures that helped shape the younger poet's reactions to his illustrious predecessor are becoming apparent. However, given the strength of Petrarch's reservations, what is still far from clear is why, beyond the desire to give a conventional nod in Dante's direction and to exploit his "authority" to his own advantage, the poet granted him so much space in the formal fabric of the *Canzoniere*. The answer, not surprisingly, lies in Petrarch's description of Dante as a certain kind of vernacular love poet. Given the dominant stylistic tenor and the principal thematic and narrative concerns of the *Rerum vulgarium fragmenta,* one instinctively thinks that the Dante who would best fit the demands of the lyric collection is the author of the *Vita nova.* The *libello* and the *Canzoniere* share a preference for formal *dulcedo,* and are lyric love stories centered on a woman who is the source of both crisis and salvation, and whose death has a fundamental impact on her lover, as well as having a profound effect on the narrative and structural organization of each text. Yet, almost certainly because of such similarities, Petrarch, as we shall see, was at pains to conceal and minimize the possible ties between his collection and Dante's "anthology."[87] What Petrarch was never willing to acknowledge was that he owed Dante any kind of significant debt. As a result, there are few easily recognizable echoes in the *Canzoniere* from the stilnovist Dante; in fact, most borrowings from the *Vita nova,* as well as from lyrics belonging to this phase of Dante's poetic career, that scholars have highlighted in the *Rerum vulgarium fragmenta* are either erotic clichés or widely circulating lyric *dantismi.*[88]

To discover the physiognomy of Petrarch's erotic Dante, we need to turn to the evidence offered by the *Canzoniere*'s most open statement of erotic poetics and of literary definition, namely canzone 70, "Lasso me, ch'i' non so in qual parte pieghi," which I have already had occasion briefly to discuss. The poem's importance is immediately obvious both from its strategic position in the Correggio version of the collection[89] and, more significantly, from its being constructed around the opening lines of five canzoni written by five different eminent poets.[90] The *incipit* of each of these canzoni is cited as the *explicit* of one of the five stanzas of "Lasso me." Accordingly, each stanza becomes emblematic of the writer whose line it includes. The poets, in the order in which they are alluded to in the canzone, are Arnaut Daniel, Guido Cavalcanti, Dante, Cino da Pistoia, and Petrarch himself, who closes his poem by citing canzone 23 of the *Canzoniere*, "Nel dolce tempo de la prima etade" (In the sweet time of my first age). Canzone 70, like Petrarch's other Dante-centered texts, is highly complex. As regards its metaliterary connotations, it can be considered from at least three interconnected perspectives: first, it offers an account of the development of Petrarch's attitude to love and poetry about love; second, it reveals the nature of his relationship to the four poets quoted and to that earlier phase of his artistic career symbolized by canzone 23; and third, thanks especially to the stanza in which a particular poet is recalled, it provides a definition of each of his four precursors. As might be expected, this last perspective offers the best insight into the literary erotic identity that Petrarch was keen to allot to Dante.

It is useful to begin by citing the canzone's third, "Dante" stanza in its entirety:

> Vaghi pensier' che così passo passo
> scorto m'avete a ragionar tant'alto,
> vedete che madonna à 'l cor di smalto,
> sì forte, ch'io per me dentro nol passo.
> Ella non degna di mirar sì basso
> che di nostre parole
> curi, ché 'l ciel non vòle
> al qual pur contrastando i' son già lasso:
> onde, come nel cor m'induro e 'naspro,
> *così nel mio parlar voglio esser aspro.*
>
> (ll. 21–30)

Erring thoughts, which thus step by step have led me to such loftily unattainable thoughts, you see that my lady has a heart of such hard stone that I cannot by myself pass into it. She does not deign to look so low as to care about our words, for the heavens do not wish it, and resisting them I am already weary; therefore, as in my heart I become hard and bitter, *so in my speech I wish to be harsh.*[91]

What is immediately striking about this stanza in comparison to the other four is its anomalousness. Dante is being deliberately isolated and tagged as "abnormal." Thus, although in "Lasso me" Petrarch carefully alludes to specific poems, Dante's *petrosa* is the only one of the five canzoni cited whose subject matter and formal qualities find obvious resonance in the stanza that incorporates it. While the other poets' verses seem open to transformation and to being adapted, Dante's poetry, on the other hand, like the "stony lady," seems fixed and unable to change. The inflexibility of the Dantean state is emphasized by a hugely revelatory detail. The fifth line of each stanza, apart of course from the third, opens with a conditional *se* clause, which expresses the wish for a different and improved situation from that sketched in the *fronte,* thereby acknowledging that change is at least a possibility. Indeed, the hope of a better future expressed in the Arnaut and Cavalcanti stanzas[92] — a hope that is absolutely denied in the Dante one — finds reassuring confirmation in the last two stanzas. Here, as the lover begins to take responsibility for his behavior, the aspiration that he might one day be able to exert greater control over his life becomes a very real prospect.[93] For Dante, no such escape from a bleakly depressing condition presents itself. If anything, and again uniquely, his circumstances deteriorate as "his" stanza progresses. The lineaments of Petrarch's erotic Dante are unmistakable. He is represented as the embodiment of a doomed negative sense of love — a sentiment to which he gives expression in a suitably harsh language: "onde, come nel cor m'induro e 'naspro, / così nel mio parlar voglio esser aspro." Dante's complex experience as a love poet, indeed as a vernacular poet, is thus drastically limited to his brief "stony" moment. This is the one point in Dante's career that Petrarch seems willing to acknowledge as being both valid and distinct in terms of the tradition, and as having relevance for his own poetry. Yet, as we have started to see, he ensured that even this, ever so narrow instance of Dante's artistic and intellectual life was heavily circumscribed. Petrarch's Dante is no longer the poet of hope, reform, and salvation, namely the poet of the *Commedia,* but is the damned and eccentric poet of erotic despair, of a lonely hell-like stasis. "Lasciate ogne speranza, voi ch'intrate" (Abandon every hope, you that enter) (*Inf.* 3.9)— the inscription over the gate of Hell seems to have been written exclusively for him. The universalizing *auctoritas* has been transformed into an embittered, self-centered symbol of isolation.

Petrarch was unrelenting in his effort to demolish Dante's Trecento fame. If, on the one hand, fixing his predecessor as *petroso* conformed to his trusted general strategy of *deminutio,* which combined large dollops of *vituperatio* with a sprinkling of *laus,* on the other, such a characterization of his rival also offered specific advantages to the *Canzoniere* and its author. By presenting Dante in this manner, Petrarch was able to distract attention from, if not actually to conceal, the influence that the *Vita nova* had indubitably exercised over his collection. Dante *stilnovista* is overwhelmed by Dante *petroso;* and the *libello*'s formal and ideological features become the exclusive preserve of the *Canzoniere,* thereby allowing Petrarch to enjoy total dominance over the field of vernacular love poetry.[94] In addition, the stress on Dante's "stoniness" further served to sever his ties to the *Commedia;* indeed, given the obvious equation between the *petrose* and the *Inferno,* the "sacrato poema" (*Par.* 23.62) is essentially reduced to its infernal "rime aspre e chiocce" (harsh and grating rhymes) (*Inf.* 32.1). Thus, it is not surprising that the most marked borrowings from Dante in the *Rerum vulgarium fragmenta* are those taken from the canzoni about the *donna petra* and from the first canticle;[95] nor that, as regards the latter, *Inferno* 5, that paradigm of negative love, is the canto most heavily ransacked.[96] Throughout the *Canzoniere,* the same forbidding image of Dante is relentlessly reiterated; and its negativity is further underscored as a result of the infernal and "stony" intertexts being largely used to describe moments of spiritual and psychological crisis.[97] As canzone 70 relates, Dante represents the "other," all that Petrarch has to transcend if he is to reach literary, intellectual, and spiritual maturity. While it is appropriate for him to draw on his own artistic past and on the writings of others in order to continue to develop as a poet and a man, at the same time, if he wants to be artistically and morally successful, he has to shun Dante's Medusan lure.[98] And Petrarch leaves no doubt about this by publicly rejecting Dante's "harshness": "*così nel mio parlar voglio esser aspro. // Che parlo?*" (*so in my speech I wish to be harsh. What* am I saying?) (ll. 30–31). Suggestively, when the poet finally draws explicitly on Dante, it is to highlight the fact that he must cease doing so. Petrarch reduces the great poet of plurilingualism to a flinty, arid, dangerous monotony, while displaying his own skill at controlling the "vario stil" (varied style) (*Rvf* 1.5) necessary to tell his multifaceted story.[99] In this respect, Dante's overwhelming *petrosità* permits the *Canzoniere*, as with its camouflaging of the *Vita nova*, to hide its significant and now well-documented reliance on the *Commedia*'s rich array of "non-harsh" elements, which, as a consequence, rather than recall their original author, appear as a natural part of Petrarch's personal lexicon;[100] and when the origin of such elements in Dante is actually highlighted, this is usually done, as we have seen, to turn them against their creator.[101]

Rather than repression or unconscious repetition, what we are faced with is calculation; and of a very high order at that, as a rapid *explication* of the third stanza of canzone 70 quickly confirms. The stanza, especially if read in Dantean terms, begins ominously and becomes ever more negative. Petrarch's Dante is immediately accused of erroneous thinking ("Vaghi pensier," l. 21), of intellectual presumption and irrationality ("ragionar tant'alto," l. 22). The targets of the attack are familiar: the *Commedia*'s intellectual ambitions and its eschatological claims ("Vaghi pensier' che così passo passo / scorto m'avete a ragionar tant'alto").[102] And Petrarch intensifies his assault: the "Dantean" woman is coldhearted and uncaring, the very antithesis of Beatrice. She refuses to come to her lover's aid, not least because this is forbidden on high: "Ella non degna di mirar sì basso / che di nostre parole / curi, ché 'l ciel non vòle" (ll. 25–27). The precise object of Petrarch's polemic is obvious, and it too is a commonplace of his anti-Dantism: the idea, propagated by both the *Vita nova* and *Inferno* 2, that Beatrice had descended from Heaven to rescue Dante and to confirm him as one of God's chosen. Thus, during the course of the stanza, Petrarch explicitly and repeatedly borrows from the first two cantos of the *Inferno*, beginning with the "passo"-"basso"-"lasso" rhyme (ll. 21, 24, 25, 28).[103] In fact, he only appropriates negative elements, carefully excluding any echo that might recall the cantos' salvific strains.[104] He appears to want to rewrite the opening of the *Commedia* in an exclusively negative key.[105] In canzone 70, therefore, Dante is presented as trapped in a kind of existential hell, alone, and with neither Beatrice nor Virgil, never mind God, ready to come to his rescue. This is a "stony" poet's lonely fate—one which cuts him off from both God and his fellow humans, as well as from the full range of language. Authorization and "authority" cannot but lie far beyond his possibilities. If Petrarch failed to impose his view of Dante in the real world, it was not through want of trying; and, at any rate, within the confines of his own imaginative universe, there is no doubt that the poet of the *Commedia* is unreservedly put in his place. Yet there is also something absurd about Petrarch's effort to bend a whole culture to his will; or perhaps not, given that this is what Dante had so irksomely succeeded in doing.[106]

PETRARCH'S CAVALCANTI (AND DANTE)

It surely cannot have gone unnoticed, not least given the remit of this study, that Petrarch's Dante has all the air of that great, self-acknowledged erotic pessimist, Guido Cavalcanti. The association is suggestive, especially in light of the now widely-held view that, in the *Vita nova* and the *Commedia*, Dante expended much energy to distance himself from his "first friend." Is the confusion between the two, therefore, another instance of Petrarch's deliberate ploy to ruin Dante's reputation, especially given his criticisms of the way in which the older poet had unscrupulously exploited his fellow writers? Was Petrarch, in fact, as a further rebuff to Dante, keen to reexamine Guido's standing after the poet of the *Commedia* had accused him of heresy in *Inferno* 10? The answers to these questions are not as straightforward as they might seem to us today. In the Trecento, Guido's status did not need protecting. Dante's charges had gone almost unnoticed; indeed, not only was Cavalcanti deemed a figure worthy of reverence, if not actually an *auctoritas,* but also he and Dante, on account of their friendship and similarities of temperament, were considered to have been extremely close and to have complemented each other as intellectuals: Guido expert in philosophy, Dante in poetry.[107] In these circumstances, it is obvious that we need to approach Petrarch's treatment of Dante and Cavalcanti in a manner that is sensitive both to the realities of fourteenth-century vernacular culture and to Francesco's idiosyncratic *dantismo.*

Petrarch twice alluded to Cavalcanti in his oeuvre — once by name, the other time metonymically by citing "Donna me prega" (A woman asks me). This is more recognition than he afforded to most *moderni,* and, at first sight, it could be perceived as a mark of respect, an acknowledgment of poetic indebtedness, even an expression of rivalry. However, as so often with hasty impressions, especially as regards Petrarch, things are in fact rather different. Cavalcanti's naming in *Triumphus Cupidinis* 4 — "ecco i due Guidi che già fur in prezzo" (Here were both Guidos, once held in high esteem) (l. 34) — is essentially a device, as we saw, to attack Dante's attitude toward the literary tradition, a state of affairs which thus brings scant personal credit to the two poets being evoked. Furthermore, the use of the past historic — "già fur in prezzo" — underlines the fact that neither Guido is now deemed to be "of value." Equally, Cavalcanti's reappearance in the second stanza of canzone 70 earns him only limited individual advantage. Petrarch certainly does present him as a poet who is part of his vernacular heritage; however, he also portrays him as a "weak" poet, whom he has assimilated, bent to his own needs, and surpassed. More seriously, and as in the *Triumphi*, the main reason why Guido is evoked in the canzone has little to do with his intrinsic merits, but everything with Petrarch's wish to wound Dante. Cavalcanti, in fact, is principally evoked in "Lasso me" as a rhetorical and ideological "strategem" with which Petrarch might delimit the poet of the *Commedia* and constrain him as *petroso*. It is thus striking that in the second stanza we find no trace of the pessimistic Guido. Instead, he is the protagonist of an essentially hopeful mini-narrative. His negative characteristics have all been transferred to Dante. In Petrarch's world, only Dante is the poet of that love from whose "potenza segue spesso morte" (power death often follows);[108] and in his effort to transform the poet of the *Commedia*, he had no misgivings about also misconstruing Cavalcanti's poetic identity. Indeed, he took away from Guido his most distinctive features; and the fact that he cited "Donna me prega," that manifesto of destructive love, in no way undermines his strategy. Quite the contrary: Cavalcanti's great philosophical canzone is actually made to serve as the stanza's optimistic highpoint, thereby putting a seal on the programmed partisanship of Petrarch's approach. There is little here that smacks of disinterested critical appreciation. Everything revolves around polemical and subjective goals. Thus, Guido's loss of his darker qualities is compensated by his eccentrically acquiring Dantean positive traits. Cavalcanti, therefore, is used not only to emphasize Dante's "stony" isolation, but also to confiscate his archetypically "sweet" features, such as the "occhi santi" (holy eyes) (l. 15) and the "dolce mio detto" (my sweet saying) (l. 17),[109] which now become a mark of Guido's erotic and poetic experience.

At Petrarch's hands, Dante is metamorphosed into Cavalcanti; Cavalcanti into Dante. However, the problem remains whether, beyond helping to fix Dante as *petroso,* other polemical intentions lurk behind their rapprochement in canzone 70. Thus, given the customary presentation of Guido and Dante as Florence's "two eyes,"[110] the one complementing the other, Petrarch's treatment of them as antagonists is eccentric, implying at the very least that he had some sense of Dante's animus against his former friend. Interestingly, the first recorded fourteenth-century instance of such an awareness is to be found in the ninth story of the sixth day of the *Decameron,*[111] the famous *novella* of Guido leaping over the *arche,* the "case dei morti" (houses of the dead), in order to flee Betto Brunelleschi and his vacuous companions. Given the impact Boccaccio had on Petrarch's knowledge of and thinking about Dante,[112] it is extremely tempting to hypothesize that it was the *novelliere* who had enlightened Petrarch about the fate that had befallen Guido in the *Commedia.* If this were actually the case, the dialectic that Petrarch had set up between Dante and Cavalcanti would have constituted a subtle and private dig at his friend, reminding him that his beloved Dante was not above acts of selfish calumny, as Boccaccio himself knew better than anyone else. Naturally, as sophisticated a reader as Petrarch did not need Boccaccio to reveal to him Dante's insidious treatment of Guido.[113] If this were a personal discovery, transforming Dante into his reviled "primo amico" (first friend) was a means for Petrarch to confirm, if only to himself, the absolute control that he could exert over his awkward predecessor—a private, sweetly malicious satisfaction.[114] However, the metamorphosis could also serve more public ends. It was a way to ensure that generations of the future would appreciate how insightful he had been, since it was inevitable that other readers would arrive at a recognition of what Dante had done to Cavalcanti. And "posterity," as we know, was always close to Petrarch's heart.

No one is more aware than I am that my arguments have become increasingly hypothetical, and that they have even begun to skirt around that psychologizing type of criticism about which I had something to say earlier. The time is overdue for the philologist to reassert himself. In examining Petrarch's complex interplay between Dante and Guido, one thing is clear: he makes no attempt to deal with Cavalcanti in terms of his typical contemporary standing. As I adumbrated, in the late Middle Ages, Guido's fame resided not in his poetry but in his philosophical abilities. His "authority" was firmly in the field of *scientia;* and Dante's attack, as is obvious from the accusations of heresy, was largely directed at his intellectual reputation and, more specifically, at his identity as a philosophical poet.[115] In fact, Petrarch too seems to have been discomfited by Guido's philosophical prowess. His Guido is a love poet and not a philosopher; and "Donna me prega," the text on which Cavalcanti's *auctoritas* was based, is presented as a celebration of the lover happy at being able to do his lady's bidding. It is hard to imagine a more drastic misrepresentation of Guido's canzone. Unlike Dante, who was convinced that poetry could serve as a vehicle for philosophy, Petrarch was equally adamant that the two must not be confused.[116] His refashioning of Guido, therefore, is not simply a result of his preoccupation with Dante; it is conditioned by other cultural and ideological reasons—the same reasons, in fact, that lie behind one of his principal objections to the *Commedia.*[117] The Cavalcanti that emerges from canzone 70 is the poet of *dulcedo.* This is not an erroneous image of Guido—he undoubtedly did write some poems in the "sweet" register—just a terribly reductive one. As with Petrarch's Dante, so his Cavalcanti too maintains ties with the historical person. Petrarch was too much of a philologist to reshape the tradition more than was absolutely necessary to achieve his personal ends.

At this juncture, it is appropriate to ask how much of Cavalcanti's poetry, whose transmission was erratic and often piecemeal,[118] Petrarch actually knew. Had he only read the "sweet" Guido, thereby nullifying all that I have been saying in this subsection? The idea that he only knew sonnets such as "Biltà di donna" (A woman's beauty) and "Chi è questa che vèn" (Who is she who comes) seems unsustainable, given that he had so publicly quoted "Donna me prega." Nevertheless, I am far from convinced that Petrarch had in fact read the canzone. There is nothing in *Canzoniere* 70 to suggest that he had; while the very few borrowings from "Donna me prega" that commentators have noted in Petrarch's poetry are all lyric clichés.[119] Before it is objected that I have been deliberately and unnecessarily misleading in raising the question of Petrarch's unease at Guido the philosopher, allow me to stress that he did not have to be familiar with "Donna me prega" to be aware of its philosophical prestige. This was a widely established commonplace.[120] Thus, in canzone 70, when Petrarch challenged Cavalcanti's reputation as *saggio,*[121] all he needed to ensure was that no philosophical overtones could be heard in stanza 2. And this is of course what he did. The problem remains, though, whether or not Petrarch knew

Guido's pessimistic verses — and, in the light of what I argued earlier as regards the "petrification" of Dante, this problem is central to the larger question of Petrarch's attitude to his precursor. The simple fact that in canzone 70 he so effectively plays stanzas 2 and 3 off against each other implies that Petrarch had probably read more than just Cavalcanti's "lighter" poetry; and this is confirmed when Guido's intertextual impact on his vernacular poetry is considered.[122] At the same time, I believe that scholars have grossly exaggerated the extent of Petrarch's debts to Cavalcanti, since, as with their claims regarding the influence of "Donna me prega," they have failed to distinguish between erotic *topoi* and precise textual borrowings. This is a question, however, that needs a much fuller treatment than I have the space to dedicate to it here.[123]

"PETRARCH'S DANTE"

Unlike Dante, Guido did not constitute a major cause of concern for Petrarch, though, as he reflected upon the nature of contemporary vernacular culture and his own standing within it, Cavalcanti, or rather Cavalcanti the philosopher, did trouble him enough that he felt obliged to challenge his *auctoritas*. In general, however, Petrarch's public stance toward the *moderni*, beginning with Dante, was one of haughty aloofness. The fact that he referred to his great predecessor so infrequently is a sign of this attitude; and the impression that he was striving to create is obvious. The contemporary world might very well be obsessed with the *Commedia* and its author; he, however, had other, more important matters to address. Furthermore, precisely because he had not permitted Dante to dominate his attention, he had been able to judge him in a balanced and reflective manner. And what he had discovered was troubling. Rather than an *auctoritas*, Dante was of dubious moral standing and limited as a poet and an intellectual. Indeed, his "authority" was a self-fabricated illusion bolstered by a crowd of ignoramuses. At least, this is the myth that Petrarch was keen to propagate. The reality, of course, was very different. The fabric of Petrarch's poetry reveals both the degree to which Dante was continually present in his mind, and the impact that, despite his protestations to the contrary, his predecessor had had on him ever since the 1320s, when, as a student in Bologna, he probably first read the *Commedia*.[124] Given the sophistication with which, in his vernacular poetry, Petrarch manipulated Dantean elements, it is certain that he was acutely aware that his reaction to Dante, based as it was on a mix of limited public interest and substantial covert poetic appropriation, was precariously balanced. Nevertheless, he considered his high-risk strategy a chance worth taking. On the one hand, his approach allowed him to mount a subtle critique of Dante in the present; on the other, it offered him the opportunity to demonstrate to his future readers, as well to the more refined among his contemporaries, that, despite the Trecento's exaggerated canonization especially of the *Commedia,* he had been able to establish intellectual, literary, and moral mastery over his precursor. Ultimately, it was because, in talking about Dante, Petrarch was invariably also talking about himself that his treatment of the older poet was so complex and tense. Petrarch's was, in fact, an extreme reaction to the severe disturbance that hit fourteenth-century Italian culture in the wake of Dante's claims for poetry, for the vernacular, for *scientia,* and most of all for himself. It is thus not at all surprising that Petrarch was extremely sensitive to the multifaceted forms of Trecento *dantismo.* Ironically, he stands as the best confirmation we have of Dante's fourteenth-century *auctoritas,* and of the care with which anyone who wanted to engage with the poet of the *Commedia* had to proceed. Our responsibility as historians of literature is to elucidate the intricacies of Petrarch's response to Dante. In particular, we need to underscore the artificiality and expediency of his response, as well as its calculated subtlety. In speaking of Petrarch and Dante, we are not actually dealing with the relationship between two poets, but rather with one poet's construction of the other: "Petrarch's Dante," to propose a new designation representative of their encounter.[125] Yet, given that it is probably impossible to think about Petrarch's career without also reflecting on the sway that Dante exerted on his development as a writer and as an intellectual, I nearly wrote, and as a Dantist not without a touch of malice, "Dante's Petrarch." To have done so, however, would have been bad philology, or perhaps not.

Notes

I should like to thank Ted Cachey, Simon Gilson, Claire Honess, Daniela La Penna, Giulio Lepschy, Paola Nasti, Michelangelo Picone, and Brian Richardson for their comments on an earlier version of this study, and Anna Barański for her help with some knotty points of Latin.

1. On Petrarch's relationship to Dante, see Claudio G. Antoni, "Esperienze stilistiche petrose da Dante al Petrarca," *Modern Language Studies* 13 (1983): 21–33; Marco Baglio, "Presenze dantesche nel Petrarca latino," *Studi petrarcheschi* n.s. 9 (1992): 77–136; Aldo S. Bernardo, "Petrarch's Attitude toward Dante," *PMLA* 70 (1955): 488–517; Aldo S. Bernardo, "Petrarch, Dante and the Medieval Tradition," in *Renaissance Humanism: Foundations, Forms and Legacy*, vol. 1, *Humanism in Italy*, ed. A. Rabil, Jr. (Philadelphia: University of Pennsylvania Press, 1988), 115–37; Rosanna Bettarini, "Perché 'narrando' il duol si disacerba (Motivi esegetici dagli autografi petrarcheschi)," in *La critica del testo* (Rome: Salerno, 1985), 305–20; Guido Capovilla, "Petrarca e l'ultima canzone di Dante," *Lectura Petrarce* 14 (1994): 289–358; Emilia Chirilli, "Di alcuni dantismi nella poesia volgare di Francesco Petrarca," *L'Alighieri* 16 (1975): 44–74; Annalisa Cipollone, "'Né per nova figura il primo alloro . . .': La chiusa di *Rvf* XXIII, il Canzoniere e Dante," *Rassegna europea di letteratura italiana* 11 (1998): 29–46; Michel David, "Une réminiscence de Dante dans un sonnet de Pétrarque," in *Miscellanea di studi offerta a Armando Balduino e Bianca Bianchi per le loro nozze* (Padua: Seminario di Filologia moderna dell'università, 1962), 15–19; Domenico De Robertis, "Petrarca petroso," *Revue des études italiennes* 29 (1983): 13–37; Domenico De Robertis, "A quale tradizione appartenne il manoscritto delle rime di Dante letto dal Petrarca," *Studi petrarcheschi* n.s. 2 (1985): 131–57; Domenico De Robertis, "Petrarca interprete di Dante (ossia leggere Dante con Petrarca)," *Studi danteschi* 61 (1989): 307–28; Enrico Fenzi, "Tra Dante e Petrarca: Il fantasma di Ulisse," in *Saggi petrarcheschi* (Fiesole: Cadmo, 2003), 492–517; Michele Feo, "Petrarca, Francesco," in *Enciclopedia dantesca* (Rome: Istituto della Enciclopedia Italiana, 1973), 4:450–58; Giulio Ferroni, "Tra Dante e Petrarca," in *Ulisse: Archeologia dell'uomo moderno*, ed. Piero Boitani and Richard Ambrosini (Rome: Bulzoni, 1998), 165–85; Simon Gilson, *Dante and Renaissance Florence* (Cambridge: Cambridge University Press, 2005), 32–40; Claudio Giunta, "Memoria di Dante nei *Trionfi*," *Rivista di letteratura italiana* 11 (1993): 411–52; Bernhard König, "*Dolci rime leggiadre*: Zur Verwendung und Verwandlung stilnovistischer Elemente in Petrarcas *Canzoniere* (Am Beispiel des Sonnetts *In qual parte del ciel*)," in *Petrarca 1304–1374: Beiträge zu Werk und Wirkung*, ed. F. Schalk (Frankfurt am Main: Klostermann, 1975), 113–38; Peter Kuon, *L'aura dantesca: Metamorfosi intertestuali nei "Rerum vulgarium fragmenta" di Francesco Petrarca* (Florence: Cesati, 2004); Robert E. Lerner, "Petrarch's Coolness toward Dante: A Conflict of 'Humanisms,'" in *Intellectuals and Writers in Fourteenth-century Europe*, ed. Piero Boitani and Anna Torti (Tübingen: G. Narr, 1986), 204–25; Bortolo Martinelli, "Dante nei *Rerum vulgarium fragmenta*," *Italianistica* 10 (1981): 122–31; Giorgio Orelli, "Dante in Petrarca," in *Il suono dei sospiri: Sul Petrarca volgare* (Turin: Einaudi, 1990), 124–62; Gioacchino Paparelli, "Due modi opposti di leggere Dante: Petrarca e Boccaccio," in *Giovanni Boccaccio editore e interprete di Dante* (Florence: Olschki, 1979), 73–90; Emilio Pasquini, "Dantismo petrarchesco: Ancora su *Fam.* XXI 15 e dintorni," in *Motivi e forme delle "Familiari" di Francesco Petrarca*,

ed. C. Berra (Milan: Cisalpino, 2003), 21–38; Manlio Pastore Stocchi, "Petrarca e Dante," *Rivista di studi danteschi* 4 (2004): 184–204; Jennifer Petrie, "Dante and Petrarch," in *Dante Comparisons*, ed. E. Haywood and B. Jones (Dublin: Irish Academic Press, 1985), 137–45; Mario Petrini, "Petrarca e Dante," *Critica letteraria* 23 (1995): 365–76; Michelangelo Picone, "Riscritture dantesche nel *Canzoniere* di Petrarca," *Rivista europea di letteratura italiana* 2 (1993): 115–25; Paolo Possiedi, "Petrarca petroso," *Forum italicum* 8 (1974): 523–45; Ezio Raimondi, "Petrarca lettore di Dante," in his *Le metamorfosi della parola: Da Dante a Montale*, ed. J. Sisco (Milan: Bruno Mondadori, 2004), 173–232; Gerhard Regn, "'Allegorice pro laurea corona': Dante, Petrarca und die Konstitution postmittelalterlicher Dichtungsallegorie," *Romanistisches Jahrbuch* 51 (2000): 128–52; Luca Carlo Rossi, "Petrarca dantista involontario," *Studi petrarcheschi* n.s. 5 (1988): 301–16; Luca Carlo Rossi, "Presenze di Petrarca in commenti danteschi fra Tre e Quattrocento," *Aevum* 70 (1996): 441–76; Marco Santagata, *Per moderne carte* (Bologna: Il Mulino, 1990), 25–91; Marco Santagata, *I frammenti dell'anima* (Bologna: Il Mulino, 1992), 199–217; Gennaro Sasso, "A proposito di *Inferno* XXVI 94–98: Variazioni biografiche per l'interpretazione," *La cultura* 40 (2002): 377–96; Sara Sturm-Maddox, "Transformations of Courtly Love Poetry: *Vita Nuova* and *Canzoniere*," in *The Expansion and Transformations of Courtly Literature*, ed. N. B. Smith and J. T. Snow (Athens: University of Georgia Press, 1980), 128–40; Sara Sturm-Maddox, *Petrarch's Metamorphoses: Text and Subtext in the "Rime sparse"* (Columbia: University of Missouri Press, 1985); Giuliano Tanturli, "Il disprezzo per Dante dal Petrarca al Bruno," *Rinascimento* 25 (1985): 199–219; Paolo Trovato, *Dante in Petrarca* (Florence: Olschki, 1979); Aldo Vallone, *Storia della critica dantesca dal XIV al XX secolo,* 2nd ed. (Milan: Vallardi, 1981), 1:133–47; Giuseppe Velli, "Il Dante di Francesco Petrarca," *Studi petrarcheschi* n.s. 2 (1985): 185–99; Giuseppe Velli, "Petrarca, Dante, la poesia classica: *Ne la stagion che 'l ciel rapido inchina* (RVF, L) *Io son venuto al punto de la rota* (Rime, C)," *Studi petrarcheschi* n.s. 15 (2002): 81–98; Nancy J. Vickers, "Re-membering Dante: Petrarch's 'Chiare, fresche et dolci acque,'" *MLN* 96 (1981): 1–11; Nancy J. Vickers, "Widowed Words: Dante, Petrarch, and the Metaphors of Mourning," in *Discourses of Authority in Medieval and Renaissance Literature*, ed. K. Brownlee and W. Stephens (Hanover, N.H.: University Press of New England, 1989), 97–108; Germaine Warkentin, "The Form of Dante's 'libello' and Its Challenge to Petrarch," *Quaderni d'italianistica* 2 (1981): 160–70; Tiziano Zanato, "San Francesco, Pier delle Vigne e Francesca da Rimini," *Filologia e critica* 2 (1977): 177–216.

2. "Odiosum ergo simulque ridiculum intelligis odium meum erga illum nescio quos finxisse [. . .] Ea vero michi obiecte calumnie pars altera fuerat [. . .] nunquam librum illius habuerim [. . .] Factum fateor, sed eo quo isti volunt animo factum nego. Eidem tunc stilo deditus [. . .] verebar ne si huius aut alterius dictis imbuerer [. . .] vel invitus ac nesciens imitator evaderem" (*Fam.* 21.15.9–11). Citations from Petrarch's works are to the following editions: *Canzoniere*, ed. Marco Santagata (Milan: Mondadori, 1996; reference to the commentary is made by

using the editor's surname together with the relevant page numbers); *Rerum familiarium libri,* ed. Vittorio Rossi and Umberto Bosco, 4 vols. (Florence: Sansoni, 1933–42); *Rerum memorandarum libri,* ed. Giuseppe Billanovich (Florence: Sansoni, 1943); *Secretum,* ed. Enrico Fenzi (Milan: Mursia, 1992); *Seniles:* the first four books are quoted from Francesco Petrarca, *Res seniles. Libri I–IV,* ed. Silvia Rizzo with the assistance of Monica Berté (Florence: Le Lettere, 2006), and the remainder from *Seniles,* in *Opera quae extant omnia* (Basle: Henrichus Petri, 1554), 813–1070, with the exception of *Sen.* 5.2, which is cited from Francesco Petrarca, *Senile V 2,* ed. Monica Berté (Florence: Le Lettere, 1998); *Trionfi, Rime estravaganti, Codice degli abbozzi,* ed. Vinicio Pacca and Laura Paolino (Milan: Mondadori, 1996). Citations from Dante's *Commedia* are to the following edition: Dante Alighieri, *La Commedia secondo l'antica vulgata,* ed. Giorgio Petrocchi, 2nd ed., 4 vols. (Florence: Le Lettere, 1994).

3. Giuseppe Billanovich, "L'altro stil nuovo: Da Dante teologo a Petrarca filologo," *Studi petrarcheschi* n.s. 11 (1994): 92.

4. See Lerner, "Petrarch's Coolness toward Dante"; Paparelli, "Due modi opposti"; Sasso, "A proposito di *Inferno* XXVI 94–98"; Tanturli, "Il disprezzo per Dante"; Warkentin, "The Form of Dante's 'libello.'"

5. Marco Santagata, "Presenze di Dante 'comico' nel *Canzoniere* del Petrarca," *Giornale storico della letteratura italiana* 146 (1969): 163–211, reprinted in Santagata, *Per moderne carte,* 25–78; Trovato, *Dante in Petrarca;* Marco Santagata, "Dante in Petrarca," *Giornale storico della letteratura italiana* 157 (1980): 445–52, reprinted in Santagata, *Per moderne carte,* 79–91. See also Chirilli, "Di alcuni dantismi"; Feo, "Petrarca, Francesco"; Kuon, *L'aura dantesca;* Possiedi, "Petrarca petroso"; Zanato, "San Francesco." For important precursors of this type of study, see Lorenzo Mascetta-Caracci, *Dante e il "Dedalo" petrarchesco* (Lanciano: Carabba, 1910), 7–236; David, "Une réminiscence de Dante."

6. There is a lack, in my view, of compelling evidence to support claims that Petrarch had read Dante's remaining Latin and vernacular prose works. Nonetheless, on Petrarch's possible knowledge of Dante's Latin prose writings, see Giuseppe Billanovich, *Petrarca letterato. I. Lo scrittoio del Petrarca* (Rome: Edizioni di "Storia e letteratura," 1947), 16, 239 n. 2; Corrado Bologna, "Occhi, solo occhi (*Rvf* 70–75)," in *Lectura Petrarcae Turicensis. Il Canzoniere. Lettura micro e macrotestuale,* ed. M. Picone (Ravenna: Longo, 2007), 189–91; Lerner "Petrarch's Coolness toward Dante"; Sturm-Maddox in this volume; Velli, "Il Dante di Francesco Petrarca," 187 n. 3, 190–91. At the same time, in this volume, Albert Ascoli makes a sustained and persuasive case as regards Petrarch's likely knowledge of the eclogues. Several other scholars had previously mooted this possibility; for a brief survey of these suggestions, see Baglio, "Presenze dantesche," 94 n. 24. While there is no doubt that Petrarch was intimately familiar with the *Vita nova* and with the *Commedia,* it is harder to establish with the same degree of certainty how many of the *rime* he had actually read (ibid.). The fragmented and mediated nature of the poems' transmission, as

well as the dependence of many of these on erotic and lyric commonplaces, makes such a task difficult, if not actually impossible. At the same time, we can be confident that Petrarch knew a fair number of the *rime*, including distinctive texts such as the *petrose;* see Bologna, "Occhi, solo occhi," 196; De Robertis, "A quale tradizione." As we shall see, what can be asserted rather more confidently is that Petrarch often conflated the "lyric" and the "comic" Dante to construct a reductively generic "vernacular" Dante, whom he then further reduced merely to a love poet. In doing this, he "unphilologically" conflated different moments of his predecessor's poetic career. This operation of *deminutio,* as I shall also attempt to demonstrate, should not be allowed to conceal Petrarch's overwhelming preoccupation with the Dante of the *Commedia.*

7. "L'*imitatio* [di Dante] del P. sarebbe per gli ultimi indagatori un evocare disinteressato della memoria, un riaffiorare naturale, spontaneo, di ritmi e timbri alle zone in cui la liricità si tramuta in onde sonore di parole e sospensioni, di arsi e di tesi. [. . .] La presenza della *Commedia* nel canzoniere sarebbe dunque soprattutto inconsapevole" (Feo, "Petrarca, Francesco," 454–55). This critical tradition has its origins in Hermann Gmelin, "Das Prinzip der *Imitatio* in den Romanischen Literaturen," *Romanische Forschungen* 46 (1932): 83–360, and in Gianfranco Contini's famous 1965 essay "Un'interpretazione di Dante," now in *Varianti e altra linguistica* (Turin: Einaudi, 1970), especially 385–88. Its aim is to confirm Petrarch's claim that any echo from Dante discernible in his poetry was unintended: "Hoc unum non dissimulo, quoniam siquid in eo sermone a me dictum illius aut alterius cuiuscquam dicto simile, sive idem forte cum aliquo sit inventum, non id furtim aut imitandi proposito, que duo semper in his maxime vulgaribus ut scopulos declinavi, sed vel casu fortuito factum esse, vel similitudine ingeniorum, ut Tullio videtur, iisdem vestigiis ab ignorante concursum" (*Fam.* 21.15.12). Several scholars who favor the view that Petrarch's *dantismo* was both largely unconscious and pacific have, surprisingly, made recourse to the Freudian notion of repression, and even to Harold Bloom's influential theory of "anxiety of influence," to support their position. See De Robertis, "Petrarca interprete di Dante," 319; Pasquini, "Dantismo petrarchesco," 34–38; Santagata, *I frammenti dell'anima,* 199; Trovato, *Dante in Petrarca,* 19. What critics who have done this fail to appreciate is that, by introducing concepts such as repression and anxiety into the exegetical mix, they undermine their own case regarding Petrarch's relaxed attitude toward Dante. Intriguingly, though with rather better justification, scholars who consider the poets' relationship to have been largely problematic have also drawn on Bloom's theory; see Roberto Antonelli, "Perché un Libro(-Canzoniere)," *Critica del testo* 6 (2003): 63; Lucia Battaglia Ricci, "Il culto per Dante, l'amicizia con Petrarca," in *Dante e Boccaccio: Lectura Dantis Scaligera 2004–2005 in memoria di Vittore Branca,* ed. E. Sandal (Rome and Padua: Antenore, 2006), 37; Vickers, "Widowed Words," 99.

8. See Ugo Foscolo, "Parallelo fra Dante e Petrarca," in *Saggi e discorsi critici,* ed. C. Foligno (Florence: Le Monnier, 1953), 279–97.

9. See Bettarini, "Perché 'narrando' il duol si disacerba," 316; Capovilla, "Petrarca e l'ultima canzone di Dante," 296; Chirilli, "Di alcuni dantismi," 72–74; De Robertis, "Petrarca interprete di Dante"; Fenzi, "Tra Dante e Petrarca," 515; Feo, "Petrarca, Francesco," 456–57; Giunta, "Memoria di Dante nei *Trionfi*"; Martinelli, "Dante nei *Rerum vulgarium fragmenta*"; Pasquini, "Dantismo petrarchesco"; Santagata, "Presenze di Dante 'comico' nel *Canzoniere*"; Santagata, "Dante in Petrarca"; Velli, "Il Dante di Francesco Petrarca"; Velli, "Petrarca, Dante, la poesia classica." At most, within this critical tradition, some scholars are willing to acknowledge that Petrarch's declarations on Dante were colored by fundamentally respectful "emulative" ambitions (Chirilli, "Di alcuni dantismi," 73) and by his new cultural ideas. I quote one of the most forceful expressions of the latter view: "Le velate allusioni petrarchesche a Dante e lo stesso senso di disagio che pare accompagnarne i pochi frangenti di diretta menzione, vengono cosí oggi ricomposti nella prospettiva di un'innegabile distanza di progetti culturali che porta Petrarca a una sorta di difesa della propria autonomia letteraria di fronte all'imbarazzante poesia dantesca, comunque ampiamente compulsata nonché personalmente filtrata nei propri scritti" (Baglio, "Presenze dantesche," 95 n. 25). Such views have obvious points of contact with the positions of those who, preferring to highlight the problems relating to Petrarch's attitude toward Dante, have talked of his *distacco* from his precursor. In the light of this last observation, this seems the appropriate point to acknowledge that my schematization of the scholarship on Petrarch and Dante—a scheme which adapts suggestions first made by Santagata in his pioneering research (*Per moderne carte*, 79–84)—is precisely that, a schematization, an attempt to offer a broad, though I hope not entirely inaccurate, presentation of the essential features of a long-established and complex critical debate. Especially in recent years, the differences between the two main opposing interpretations have begun to diminish.

10. Benvenuto da Imola, *Comentum super Dantis Aldigherii Comoediam,* ed. James Philip Lacaita, 5 vols. (Florence: Barbera, 1887), 4:309.

11. See in particular Natalino Sapegno, "Tra Dante e il Petrarca," in *Storia letteraria del Trecento* (Milan and Naples: Ricciardi, 1963), 169–96; Giuseppe Billanovich, "Tra Dante e Petrarca," *Italia medioevale e umanistica* 8 (1965): 1–44, a reduced and revised version of which appeared with the title "Il vecchio Dante e il giovane Petrarca," in *Letture classensi* 11 (1982): 99–118. Fenzi's study of the same main title, "Tra Dante e Petrarca: Il fantasma di Ulisse," is not a historical survey, but, as its subtitle suggests, it examines Petrarch's views on Ulysses in the light of Dante's treatment of the classical hero. Equally, Giulio Ferroni's "Tra Dante e Petrarca" explores the treatment of Ulysses in the works of the two writers.

12. "In primis quidem odii causa prorsus nulla est erga hominem nunquam michi nisi semel, idque prima pueritie mee parte, monstratum" (*Fam.* 21.15.7). In fact, as we shall see, the image that Petrarch was keen to project as regards his attitude to Dante was one of respectful yet detached objectivity.

13. On the *lictera* in medieval literary criticism, see Alastair J. Minnis, *Medieval Theory of Authorship,* 2nd ed. (Aldershot: Scolar Press, 1988), 73–159.

14. On Petrarch and Cino, see Armando Balduino, "Cino da Pistoia, Boccaccio e i poeti minori del Trecento," in *Colloquio Cino da Pistoia* (Rome: Accademia Nazionale dei Lincei, 1976), 33–85; Edward L. Boggs, "Cino and Petrarch," *MLN* 94 (1979): 146–52; Santagata, *Per moderne carte*, passim; Franco Suitner, *Petrarca e la tradizione stilnovistica* (Florence: Olschki, 1977), 99–156; Guido Zaccagnini, "Il Petrarca e Cino da Pistoia," in *Convegno petrarchesco* (Arezzo: Accademia Petrarca, 1936), 1:2–21.

15. Translations from the *Familiares* are normally based on Francis Petrarch, *Letters on Familiar Matters,* trans. Aldo S. Bernardo, 3 vols. (Albany: State University of New York Press, 1975; Baltimore and London: Johns Hopkins University Press, 1982–85). At several points, I have modified Bernardo's version to ensure that key Latin (technical) terms are rendered as accurately as possible in English.

16. If Petrarch's borrowings from Dante were mostly of this type, then it would be difficult to challenge the view that his *dantismo* was largely unconscious. It is one of the aims of this study to explore the extent to which Petrarch's recourse to Dante was unreflective.

17. In his excellent article, Manlio Pastore Stocchi notes that "la misura documentabile delle ricorrenze memoriali non è, per sé, correlata a una effettiva disponibilità del Petrarca a riconoscere la grandezza di Dante o a fargli ammettere una reale sintonia d'ingegno e di gusto" ("Petrarca e Dante," 192).

18. I do not intend to examine Petrarch's presentation of Dante in the *Rerum memorandarum libri,* since their "two *novelle* about Dante at the court of Cangrande della Scala, [. . .] though emphasizing his excellence in vernacular poetry, [. . .] essentially modulate some traditional motifs of novelistic literature on the 'proud and disdainful poet'" (Gilson, *Dante and Renaissance Florence,* 37), and hence are somewhat eccentric to his normal treatment of Dante. A few other traces of Petrarch's reaction to Dante have reached us. For his fleeting polemical annotation against Dante in a manuscript of Pomponius Mela, see Billanovich, "Tra Dante e Petrarca," 39–40; on the hitherto undeciphered autograph annotation to *Inf.* 2.24–26 in Vat. lat. 3199, see Armando Petrucci, *La scrittura di Francesco Petrarca* (Vatican City: Biblioteca Apostolica Vaticana, 1967), 48 n. 8, 118. See also note 54 below.

19. Petrarch also refers to Dante in a variant of *Tr. Cup.* 3.99; see the section "Delimiting Dante: *Triumphus Cupidinis* 4.28–38" in this essay.

20. Naturally, there have been some previous attempts, particularly outside Italy, to assess and explain Petrarch's treatment of Dante without downplaying too much the tensions and contradictions that characterize their encounter; see Bernardo, "Petrarch's Attitude toward Dante"; Gilson, *Dante and Renaissance Florence,* 32–40; Kuon, *L'aura dantesca*; Pastore Stocchi, "Petrarca e Dante"; Warkentin, "The Form of Dante's 'libello.'" In particular, Pastore Stocchi declares: "mi avventurerò a suggerire che anche il sofferto rapporto del Petrarca con Dante non possa essere colto nei suoi aspetti più complessi e storicamente significativi attraverso le

mere coincidenze e reminiscenze formali, e vada affrontato invece in una piú integrale visone storico-culturale e persino civile" ("Petrarca e Dante," 192).

21. Kuon, *L'aura dantesca,* is especially good on the ways in which Petrarch used Dante in order to define himself and establish his own cultural superiority: "[i]l concetto di 'riscrittura' implica l'idea di un'imitazione attiva che rovescia la prospettiva dantesca" (52). Other critics too, intent on countering the idea that Petrarch's appropriation of Dante was largely unconscious, have explored the ways in which the poet explicitly used Dantean elements to stress the differences between himself and his predecessor—a strategy that invariably highlights the superiority of his own ideological and artistic solutions; see Gilson, *Dante and Renaissance Florence,* 33–34; Picone, "Riscritture dantesche"; Roberto Mercuri, "Genesi della tradizione letteraria italiana in Dante, Petrarca e Boccaccio," in *Letteratura italiana. Storia e geografia. I. L'età medievale,* ed. A. Asor Rosa (Turin: Einaudi, 1987), 334–44, 360–76; Pastore Stocchi, "Petrarca e Dante," 188; Sturm-Maddox, *Petrarch's Metamorphoses.* See also the section "'Disguising' Dante" in this essay.

22. On Dante's fourteenth-century reception, see at least Gian Carlo Alessio, "La *Comedìa* nel margine dei classici," in *Studi di filologia medievale offerti a D'Arco Silvio Avalle* (Milan and Naples: Ricciardi, 1996), 1–25; Zygmunt G. Barański, *"Chiosar con altro testo": Leggere Dante nel Trecento* (Fiesole: Cadmo, 2001); Saverio Bellomo, "La *Commedia* attraverso gli occhi dei primi lettori," in *Leggere Dante,* ed. L. Battaglia Ricci (Ravenna: Longo, 2002), 73–84; Saverio Bellomo, "Introduzione," in *Dizionario dei commenti danteschi* (Florence: Olschki, 2004), 1–49; Elisabetta Cavallari, *La fortuna di Dante nel Trecento* (Florence: Perrella, 1921; this study needs to be read with a degree of caution); Guido di Pino, "L'antidantismo dal Trecento al Quattrocento," *Letture classensi* 5 (1976): 125–48; Gilson, *Dante and Renaissance Florence,* 21–83; Gioacchino Paparelli, "Dante e il Trecento," in *Dante nel pensiero e nell'esegesi dei secoli XIV e XV. Atti del III Congresso Nazionale di Studi Danteschi* (Florence: Olschki, 1975), 31–70; Marco Petoletti, "La fortuna di Dante fra Trecento e Quattrocento," in *La Divina Commedia di Alfonso d'Aragona re di Napoli. Commentario al codice,* ed. M. Bollati, 2 vols. (Modena: Panini, 2006), 1:159–86; Antonio Enzo Quaglio, Andrea Ciotti, and Bruno Basile, "Commedia," in *Enciclopedia dantesca* (Rome: Istituto della Enciclopedia Italiana, 1971), 2:83–86 and 99–103; Vittorio Rossi, "Dante nel Trecento e nel Quattrocento," in *Scritti di critica letteraria: Saggi e discorsi su Dante* (Florence: Sansoni, 1930), 1:293–332; Bruno Sandkühler, *Die frühen Dantekommentare und ihr Verhältnis zur mittelalterlichen Kommentartradition* (Munich: Max Hueber Verlag, 1967); Aldo Vallone, *Antidantismo politico nel XIV secolo. Primi contributi* (Naples: Liguori, 1974); Vallone, *Storia della critica dantesca,* 1:51–230.

23. Translations of the *Canzoniere* are taken from *Petrarch's Lyric Poems: The "Rime sparse" and Other Lyrics,* trans. and ed. Robert M. Durling (Cambridge, Mass.: Harvard University Press, 1976).

24. Joseph A. Barber, "Il sonetto CXIII e gli altri sonetti a Sennuccio," *Lectura Petrarce* 2 (1982): 21–39; Daniele Piccini, *Un amico del Petrarca: Sennuccio del Bene e le sue rime* (Rome and Padua: Antenore, 2004), xxv–xxxi, xxxiii–xxxix. See also Billanovich, "L'altro stil nuovo," 5–17, 19–22, 24–27, 48–50, 52–67, 74–78, 90.

25. That Petrarch limits Dante to love poetry both in sonnet 287 and in the *Triumphi* (see the following section in this essay) has been previously noted by Gilson, *Dante and Renaissance Florence*, 37–38, and by Trovato, *Dante in Petrarca*, 19. Feo underplays the negative implications of Petrarch's reductive definition: "Omaggio d'occasione che non mira certo a deprimere l'Alighieri confondendolo con altri di minor levatura, ma che è circoscritto senza equivoci al rimatore d'amore" ("Petrarca, Francesco," 450). As regards Petrarch's attempt to "diminish" Dante, Gennaro Sasso writes: "'Letteraria perfidia' sarà espressione troppo cruda; e si dica allora di una tal quale, nei riguardi di Dante, *voluntas minuendi,* quasi che il nascosto proposito fosse di ridurre il grand'uomo nell'ambito di una sua vicenda familiare, in un quadro domestico, dominato bensì dall'esilio, e quindi tragico, ma, appunto, domestico, e richiamato al di qua del suo significato morale e politico" ("A proposito di *Inferno* XXVI 94–98," 391–92).

26. On Petrarch's relationship to the three poets mentioned, see Laura Paolino, "'Ad acerbam rei memoriam': Le carte del lutto nel codice Vaticano Latino 3196 di Francesco Petrarca," *Rivista di letteratura italiana* 11 (1993): 86–92; Daniele Piccini, "Franceschino degli Albizzi, uno e due," *Studi petrarcheschi* n.s. 15 (2002): 129–86; Decio Pierantozzi, "Il Petrarca e Guittone," *Studi petrarcheschi* 1 (1948): 145–65; Suitner, *Petrarca e la tradizione stilnovistica*; Santagata, *Per moderne carte*, 128–37.

27. In sonnet 287, Petrarch is not exclusively curtailing Dante's artistic status. His presentation also diminishes the poetic achievements of Guittone and Cino — an operation which he repeats elsewhere, most notably in the *Triumphi* (see further in this essay). At the same time, it is undoubtedly the case that Petrarch's assault on Dante is of a quite different order from his attack against other poets.

28. See Barański, *"Chiosar con altro testo,"* 153–73. See also Bernardo, "Petrarch's Attitude toward Dante," 506–10, and the following section in this essay.

29. Translations from the *Commedia* are taken, with the occasional slight modification, from Dante, *The Divine Comedy,* trans. John D. Sinclair, 3 vols. (Oxford and New York: Oxford University Press, 1971).

30. For a reading of *Paradiso* 22 from this perspective, see Zygmunt G. Barański, "Canto XXII," in *Lectura Dantis Turicensis. Paradiso,* ed. G. Güntert and M. Picone (Florence: Cesati, 2002), 339–62. On the influence of *Paradiso* 22 in the *Triumphi,* see Giunta, "Memoria di Dante nei *Trionfi*," 416–18, 449.

31. On medieval notions of "authority," see Mary Carruthers, *The Book of Memory* (Cambridge: Cambridge University Press, 1990), 189–220; Marie-Dominique Chenu, "Auctor, actor, autor," *Bulletin du Cange* 3 (1927): 81–86; Minnis, *Medieval Theory of Authorship*; Alastair J. Minnis and Alexander Brian Scott with David Wallace, eds., *Medieval Literary Theory and Criticism, c. 1100–c. 1375*

(Oxford: Clarendon Press, 1988); Alastair J. Minnis, *"Magister Amoris": The "Roman de la Rose" and Vernacular Hermeneutics* (Oxford: Oxford University Press, 2001); Michel Zimmermann, ed., *"Auctor" et "auctoritas": Invention et conformisme dans l'écriture médiévale* (Paris: École des Chartes, 2001); Alastair Minnis and Ian Johnson, eds., *The Cambridge History of Literary Criticism*, vol. 2, *The Middle Ages* (Cambridge: Cambridge University Press, 2005). On Dante and "authority," see Albert Russell Ascoli, "The Vowels of Authority (Dante's *Convivio* IV, vi, 3–4)," in *Discourses of Authority in Medieval and Renaissance Literature*, ed. K. Brownlee and W. Stephens (Hanover, N.H.: University Press of New England, 1989), 23–46; Albert Russell Ascoli, "The Unfinished Author: Dante's Rhetoric of Authority in *Convivio* and *De vulgari eloquentia*," in *The Cambridge Companion to Dante*, ed. R. Jacoff (Cambridge: Cambridge University Press, 1993), 45–66; Zygmunt G. Barański, *"Sole nuovo, luce nuova": Saggi sul rinnovamento culturale in Dante* (Turin: Scriptorium, 1996); Barański, *"Chiosar con altro testo."*

32. On Petrarch's recourse to the episode of Dante's reunion with Beatrice in the Earthly Paradise, see Kuon, *L'aura dantesca*, 85–144.

33. See Zygmunt G. Barański, "'Piangendo e cantando' con Orfeo (e con Dante): Strutture emotive e strutture poetiche in *RFV* 281–90," in *Lectura Petrarcae Turicensis. Il Canzoniere. Lettura micro e macrotestuale*, ed. M. Picone (Ravenna: Longo, 2007), 617–40.

34. See Steven Botterill, "The Trecento Commentaries on Dante's *Commedia*," in *The Cambridge History of Literary Criticism*, vol. 2, *The Middle Ages*, 602–3.

35. See Michelangelo Picone, "Tempo e racconto nel *Canzoniere* di Petrarca," in *Omaggio a Gianfranco Folena*, 3 vols. (Padua: Editoriale Programma, 1993), 1:588–92; Picone, "Riscritture dantesche." See also Kuon, *L'aura dantesca*, 147–48, 213–14; Bortolo Martinelli, "L'ordinamento morale del 'Canzoniere,'" in *Petrarca e il Ventoso* (Bergamo: Minerva Italica, 1977), 217–300.

36. See Zygmunt G. Barański, "'Alquanto tenea della oppinione degli epicuri': The *Auctoritas* of Boccaccio's Cavalcanti (and Dante)," *Zeitschrift für Deutsche Philologie* 13 (2005): 280–325.

37. On the presence of Dante in the *Triumphi*, see Marco Ariani, "Introduzione," in Francesco Petrarca, *Triumphi*, ed. Marco Ariani (Milan: Mursia, 1988), 11–45; Feo, "Petrarca, Francesco," 455–56; Giunta, "Memoria di Dante nei *Trionfi*"; Marco Santagata, "Introduzione," in *Trionfi, Rime estravaganti*, xxv–xxx, xliv–xlviii. See also note 28 above. In the light of the *Triumphi*'s complex and lengthy genesis and composition, it is difficult to date its two references to Dante, and hence to locate these chronologically in relation to Petrarch's other explicit allusions to the poet of the *Commedia*. Scholars now generally agree that Petrarch's main engagement with the *Triumphi* began in the early 1350s.

38. Translations of the *Triumphi* are adapted from *The Triumphs of Petrarch*, trans. Ernest Hatch Wilkins (Chicago and London: University of Chicago Press, 1962).

39. See Kevin Brownlee et al., "Vernacular Literary Consciousness c. 1100–c. 1500: French, German and English Evidence," in *The Cambridge History of Literary Criticism*, vol. 2, *The Middle Ages*, 424–31.

40. Despite their undoubted importance, I do not have the space here to explore further the role played by visionary experiences in Petrarch's response to Dante. It is enough to remember the dramatic appearance of Veritas at the beginning of the *Secretum*—an appearance accompanied by a host of easily recognizable allusions to the *Commedia*, and in particular to its opening canti; see Mercuri, "Genesi," 334–44; Fenzi's notes to his edition of the *Secretum*, 287–90. In this context, it should also not be forgotten that the dream-vision was the tradition to which, in the fourteenth century, many commentators and manuscript illustrators assigned the *Commedia*.

41. On medieval distinctions between otherworldly voyages and visions, see Alison Morgan, *Dante and the Medieval Other World* (Cambridge: Cambridge University Press, 1990); Cesare Segre, *Fuori del mondo* (Turin: Einaudi, 1990), 25–48; Carol Zaleski, *Otherworld Journeys* (New York and Oxford: Oxford University Press, 1987), 26–94. See also Gilson, *Dante and Renaissance Florence*, 39.

42. It is interesting to note that Petrarch was prepared to acknowledge Dante's poetic vernacular primacy in both *Familiares* 21.15 and *Seniles* 5.2 but not in either the *Canzoniere* or the *Triumphi*. When he himself was engaged in writing vernacular poetry, it would seem that Petrarch could not bring himself to declare Dante's primacy, something which he found less difficult to assert when composing Latin prose and addressing cultural and historical issues.

43. On Petrarch and Occitan poetry, see Alessio Fontana, "La filologia romanza e il problema del rapporto Petrarca-trovatori (Premesse per una ripresa del problema secondo nuove prospettive)," in *Petrarca 1304–1374: Beiträge zu Werk und Wirkung*, ed. F. Schalk (Frankfurt am Main: Klostermann, 1975), 51–70; Giuseppe Frasso, "Petrarca, Andrea da Mantova e il canzoniere provenzale N," *Italia medioevale e umanistica* 17 (1974): 185–205; William Paden, "Petrarch as Poet of Provence," *Annali d'Italianistica* 22 (2004): 19–44; Maurizio Perugi, "Petrarca provenzale," *Quaderni petrarcheschi* 7 (1990): 109–92.

44. On Petrarch and Arnaut Daniel, see Maurizio Perugi, *Trovatori a Valchiusa: Un frammento della cultura provenzale del Petrarca* (Padua: Antenore, 1985), 292–314; Maurizio Perugi, "A proposito di alcuni scritti recenti su Petrarca e Arnaut Daniel," *Studi medievali* ser. 3, 32 (1991): 369–84; Santagata, *Per moderne carte*, 157–211.

45. Although modern scholarship has established that the poem cited at the end of the first stanza of "Lasso me" was not actually penned by Arnaut, what is important is that Petrarch considered it to have been composed by the great Occitan poet; see Pietro G. Beltrami, "Appunti su 'Razo e dreyt ay si ·m chant e ·m demori'," *Rivista di letteratura italiana* 5 (1987): 9–39; Carlo Pulsoni, "L'attribuzione della canzone *Drez et rayson es qu'ieu ciant e· m demori*," in his *La tecnica compositiva*

nei "Rerum vulgarium fragmenta": Riuso metrico e lettura autoriale (Rome: Bagatto, 1998), 239–57. See the section "'Disguising' Dante" in this essay for a fuller discussion of "Lasso me."

46. On medieval catalogues of *auctores,* see Birger Munk Olsen, *I classici nel canone scolastico altomedievale* (Spoleto: Centro Italiano di Studi sull'Alto Medioevo Italiano, 1991).

47. See Vinicio Pacca's notes to *Tr. Cup.* 4.13–57 for a general idea of the lines' dependence on Dante.

48. On medieval attitudes to women and language, see Barański, *"Sole nuovo, luce nuova,"* 102–3; Carla Casagrande and Silvana Vecchio, *I peccati della lingua: Disciplina ed etica della parola nella cultura medievale* (Rome: Istituto della Enciclopedia Italiana, 1987); Helena L. Sanson, *"Ornamentum mulieri breviloquentia*: Donne, silenzi, parole nell'Italia del Cinquecento," *The Italianist* 23 (2003): 194–244. See also Eric Jager, *The Tempter's Voice: Language and the Fall in Medieval Literature* (Ithaca and London: Cornell University Press, 1993).

49. See Claudia Villa, *La "Lectura Terentii"* (Padua: Antenore, 1984), 39–42. See also Zygmunt G. Barański, "''nfiata labia' and 'dolce stil novo': A Note on Dante, Ethics, and the Technical Vocabulary of Literature," in *Sotto il segno di Dante: Scritti in onore di Francesco Mazzoni,* ed. L. Coglievina and D. De Robertis (Florence: Le Lettere, 1998), 34.

50. In the context of Petrarch's overall presentation of classical and vernacular poetry, his description of Guittone—"che di non esser primo par ch'ira aggia" (*Tr. Cup.* 4.33)—with its emphasis on the Aretine's frustration at his lowly poetic standing, reads less like a polemical barb than an insightful assessment of the attitude of a poet who, over time, has lost the position of prestige he had once enjoyed.

51. See Judson Boyce Allen, *The Ethical Poetic of the Later Middle Ages* (Toronto: University of Toronto Press, 1982).

52. On poetic crowning, see Michelangelo Picone, "Il tema dell'incoronazione poetica in Dante, Petrarca e Boccaccio," *L'Alighieri* 46 (2005): 5–26. See also the chapters by Ascoli and by Sturm-Maddox in this volume.

53. On tragedy and epic, see Vincent Gillespie, "The Study of Classical Authors from the Twelfth Century to c. 1450," in *The Cambridge History of Literary Criticism,* vol. 2, *The Middle Ages,* 207–23. On tragedy see also Henry Ansgar Kelly, *Ideas and Forms of Tragedy from Aristotle to the Middle Ages* (Cambridge: Cambridge University Press, 1993).

54. On fourteenth-century reactions to Dante's definition of his masterpiece as a comedy, see Barański, *"Chiosar con altro testo,"* 41–97; Henry Ansgar Kelly, *Tragedy and Comedy from Dante to Pseudo-Dante* (Berkeley, Los Angeles, and London: University of California Press, 1989). On medieval ideas of comedy, see also Barański, *"Sole nuovo, luce nuova,"* 129–51; Zygmunt G. Barański, "Dante, the Roman Comedians, and the Medieval Theory of Comedy," in *"Libri poetarum in quattuor species dividuntur": Essays on Dante and 'Genre,'* ed. Z. G. Barański,

Supplement 2, *The Italianist* 15 (1995), 61–99; Karl Heinz Bareiss, *Comoedia: Die Entwicklung der Komödiendiskussion von Aristoteles bis Ben Jonson* (Frankfurt and Berne: Peter Lang, 1982). In his commentary to the *Commedia*, Francesco da Buti, quoting a now lost letter, presents important evidence which confirms Petrarch's dissatisfaction with Dante's choice of *comedía* as his poem's *titulus:* "Messer Francesco Petrarca in una sua epistola che comincia *Ne te laudasse poeniteat* ecc. muove questa questione [as regards the title] e dice: *Nec cur comoediam vocet video*": Francesco da Buti, *Commento di Francesco da Buti sopra la Divina Comedia di Dante Alighieri*, ed. Crescentino Giannini, 3 vols. (Florence: Fratelli Nistri, 1858–62), 1:543.

55. See Barański, *"Chiosar con altro testo,"* 153–73.

56. As is well known, this is the image of himself which Petrarch consistently presented in his oeuvre.

57. Luca Rossi's claim that Petrarch's growing authority in the second half of the fourteenth century "sembra in qualche modo inibire la stesura dei commenti danteschi" (Rossi, "Presenze di Petrarca," 443) is incorrect, as is immediately clear if one consults Bellomo's chronological list of Trecento and Quattrocento commentaries on the *Commedia* (Bellomo, "Introduzione," 17–19).

58. It is noteworthy that, in *Seniles* V.2, Petrarch should have attacked false modern "authorities": "Quanquam quid indoctum vulgus arguo, cum de his quoque qui se doctos vocant tanto et gravior et iustior sit querela, qui, preter multa ridicula, odiosum illud in fine, ignorantie summam superbiam addidere? [. . .] Sed quid, queso, literatos homines excusabit, qui cum veterum non ignari esse debeant, in eadem opinionum cecitate versantur? [. . .] Et hi quoque novis freti ducibus pudendisque" (56, 63, 67).

59. See the following section in this essay.

60. The fact that Petrarch introduced the epic Latin poet *par excellence* into his catalogue of love poets does not mean that, as he did with Dante, he also intended to limit Virgil to the sphere of the erotic. He was simply drawing on an established commonplace, first found in Servius, which interpreted Book 4 of the *Aeneid* as a text concerned with *amor,* thereby associating Virgil with love. In the *Triumphus Fame*, Petrarch ensured that he recognized and celebrated Virgil's status as an epic poet by presenting him as Homer's companion and equal (3.10–17). Servius' definition of Book 4 can be read in *Servii Grammatici qui feruntur in Vergilii carmina commentarii*, ed. Georg Thilo and Hermann Hagen, 3 vols. (Leipzig: Teubner, 1881–87), 1:459.2–5.

61. See the section "'Disguising' Dante" in this essay for a discussion of the *Canzoniere*'s intertextual debts to Dante.

62. It is hard to escape the impression, however, that both the *Triumphi*'s tortuous and precarious composition and its widely recognized weaknesses as an epic poem can ultimately be explained in terms of Petrarch's obsession with Dante. The *Triumphi*'s constant and overt dependence on the *Commedia,* rather than challenge and redimension Dante's poem, is a constant reminder of the lat-

ter's magisterial superiority. To put it somewhat differently, Petrarch failed to find his own epic voice because he was continually drowned out by the more powerful and successful tones of his predecessor. Conversely, in the *Canzoniere*, where he was able effectively to control Dante and to subordinate him to his own needs, Petrarch created a distinctly personal masterpiece.

63. "The other two direct references to Dante in Petrarch's oeuvre, which both occur in his vernacular poetry and date from the late 1340s and early 1350s, reflect more closely the critical stance found later in *Familiares* XXI, 15" (Gilson, *Dante and Renaissance Florence,* 37).

64. On Boccaccio's complex attitude to Dante, which was not unconditionally appreciative, see at least Todd Boli, "Boccaccio's *Trattatello in laude di Dante,* or *Dante Resartus,*" *Renaissance Quarterly* 41 (1988): 389–412; Battaglia Ricci, "Il culto per Dante"; Carlo Delcorno, "Gli scritti danteschi del Boccaccio," in *Dante e Boccaccio: Lectura Dantis Scaligera 2004–2005 in memoria di Vittore Branca,* ed. E. Sandal (Rome and Padua: Antenore, 2006), 109–37; Robert Hollander, *Boccaccio's Dante and the Shaping Force of Satire* (Ann Arbor: University of Michigan Press, 1997); Martin L. McLaughlin, *Literary Imitation in the Italian Renaissance* (Oxford: Clarendon Press, 1995), 50–62; Minnis, Scott, and Wallace, *Medieval Literary Theory,* 453–58. See also n. 112 below.

65. See Billanovich, *Petrarca letterato,* 238, 270; Carlo Paolazzi, *Dante e la "Comedia" nel Trecento* (Milan: Vita e Pensiero, 1989), 167–81. However, see also the reservations expressed in De Robertis, "Petrarca interprete di Dante," 311 n. 7.

66. See *Carmina,* ed. Giuseppe Velli, in Giovanni Boccaccio, *Tutte le opere,* ed. Vittore Branca (Milan: Mondadori, 1992), 5-i (part 1 of vol. 5):386–91, 430–33, 476–80.

67. See Ugo Dotti, *Vita di Petrarca* (Bari: Laterza, 1987), 221–23, 231–36, 330–32; Feo, "Petrarca, Francesco," 451–52.

68. The different versions of the *Trattatello* can be read in *Trattatello in laude di Dante,* ed. Pier Giorgio Ricci, in Giovanni Boccaccio, *Tutte le opere,* ed. Vittore Branca (Milan: Mondadori, 1974), 3:423–538.

69. "Sul fatto che la XXI 15 nasca sotto il segno dell'ambiguità credo non si possa dubitare" (Pasquini, "Dantismo petrarchesco," 27).

70. "[P]opularis quidem quod ad stilum attinet [. . .] ventosisque diu vulgi plausibus agitatam [fax] atque ut sic dixerim fatigatam [. . .] ut vel sic michi odia vulgarium conflent quibus acceptissimus ille est [. . .] et stilus in suo genere optimus" (1, 3, 6, 9).

71. The ambiguity that indelibly marks Petrarch's treatment of Dante is clearly apparent in these interconnected passages. On the one hand, Petrarch appears to acknowledge that Dante could have succeeded as a Latin writer; on the other, he criticizes what his predecessor actually wrote in the classical language. If we can be confident in concluding that *carmina* refers to the eclogues, it is much less clear what Petrarch might have meant by *prosa* (see n. 6 above). If one

were to hazard a guess, among Dante's Latin prose works, the *Monarchia* was the least unlikely text that he might have read. But hard evidence is lacking to bolster such an assumption. It is thus rather more likely that Petrarch's assessment is based not on a direct knowledge of any of Dante's Latin prose works, but simply on an awareness that his predecessor had written such works — a fact that, *inter alia*, he could have learned from the *Trattatello*. In any case, Petrarch's aim is clear: to fix Dante as a vernacular writer whose commitment to composing in Latin was negligible.

72. *Johannes de Virgilio Danti Alagherii [Carmen]*, in Dante Alighieri, *Le Egloghe*, ed. Giorgio Brugnoli and Riccardo Scarcia (Milan and Naples: Ricciardi, 1980), ll. 6–24.

73. Saverio Bellomo has recently suggested that Petrarch's failure to name Dante should not be deemed a "segno di disprezzo" but an instance of that "reticente retorica epistolare, che prevedeva di non nominare le persone ove fosse possibile capire egualmente di chi si parlasse": Saverio Bellomo, "Il sorriso di Ilaro e la prima redazione in latino della *Commedia*," *Studi sul Boccaccio* 32 (2004): 203. I am not persuaded by this suggestion, not only because it goes against the epistle's overall negative treatment of Dante, but also because Petrarch makes it clear that his decision not to name the poet is practical and not rhetorical: "Solent enim plerique michi odium, ut dixi, alii contemptum viri huius obicere, cuius hodie nomine scienter abstinui, ne illud infamari clamitans cunta audiens nichil intelligens vulgus obstreperet" (19). In any case, even this explanation is unpersuasive, since the identity of the *vir* is more than obvious. Petrarch's unwillingness to name Dante is consistent with his customary strategy of granting his precursor as little recognition as possible and of shrouding his achievements in ambiguity. Finally, in Petrarch, anonymity is usually a mark of disdain; it is enough to think of the four false friends condemned in the *De ignorantia* or the nameless "foolish authorities" attacked in *Seniles* 5.2: "Nolo ego nomen facere quibus ipsa res nullum fecit, etsi furor ingens faciat, nolo inter maximos ponere quos inter minimos vidi" (66). As with other aspects of Petrarch's treatment of Dante, *Familiares* 21.15 has elicited contrasting interpretations. Especially by reading the epistle selectively, some scholars have judged it a largely positive assessment of Dante or have attempted to minimize its contradictions; see De Robertis, "Petrarca interprete di Dante," 308–10; Feo, "Petrarca, Francesco," 451–52; Martinelli, "Dante nei *Rerum vulgarium fragmenta*," 122–23; Paolazzi, *Dante e la "Comedia*," 135–46, 154–66; Pasquini, "Dantismo petrarchesco." Others have concentrated primarily on its negative elements; see Paparelli, "Due modi opposti," 77–83; Sasso, "A proposito di *Inferno* XXVI 94–98"; Tanturli, "Il disprezzo per Dante," 200–205. There have been few attempts, in fact, to examine the rhetorical and ideological implications — as I endeavor to do in this section — of the interplay between the letter's positive and negative declarations; notable exceptions to this critical trend are Kuon, *L'aura dantesca*, 16–21; McLaughlin, *Literary Imitation*, 35–37; Pastore Stocchi, "Petrarca e Dante," 184–86; Gilson, *Dante and Renaissance Florence*, 32–37.

74. On the letter's recourse to Dante's Ulysses, see Umberto Bosco, *Dante vicino: Contributi e letture* (Caltanissetta and Rome: Sciascia, 1966), 173–96; Fenzi, "Tra Dante e Petrarca," 509–10; Gilson, *Dante and Renaissance Florence,* 33–34; Pasquini, "Dantismo petrarchesco," 23–27; Sasso, "A proposito di *Inferno XXVI* 94–98," 393–96. See also Michelangelo Picone, "Il sonetto CLXXXIX," *Lectura Petrarce* 9 (1989): 151–77.

75. Petrarch expresses a similar opinion, albeit implicitly, regarding Dante's pursuit of literary fame as proof of his lack of virtue both in the *Triumphi* (see pp. 69–70 of this essay) and in *Seniles* 5.2 (see pp. 80–82). Boccaccio, too, in the *Trattatello*—Petrarch's possible source on this point especially as regards Dante's striving after the "vano favor popolesco"—notes the poet of the *Commedia*'s strong desire for glory. In general, however, Boccaccio is rather more indulgent toward Dante's aspiration than his friend; see first redaction pars. 22, 63 (from where the quotation is taken), and 125.

76. See Gilson, *Dante and Renaissance Florence,* 33–34; Tanturli, "Il disprezzo per Dante," 201.

77. On the "highly partial construction" that is Petrarch's account of the *Commedia*'s reception, see Gilson, *Dante and Renaissance Florence,* 35–37.

78. Petrarch's criticism of Dante's reception cannot but include the commentary tradition on the *Commedia* (although, in the light of our present knowledge, it is impossible to say which, if any, specific commentators the poet might have had in mind when he voiced his censures). Indeed, in *Seniles* 5.2, Petrarch condemns contemporary men of letters who not only do not dedicate themselves to the study of the classics but also undermine these by drawing on modern "authorities": "Sed quid, queso, literatos homines excusabit, qui cum veterum non ignari esse debeant, in eadem opinionum cecitate versantur? Scito me, amice, acri stomaco hec iratum loqui. Surgunt his diebus dyaleticuli non ignari tantum, sed insani et quasi formicarum nigra acies nescio cuius cariose quercus e latebris erumpunt omnia doctrine melioris arva vastantes. Hi Platonem atque Aristotilem damnant, Socratem ac Pythagoram rident. Et, Deus bone, quibus hec ducibus, quam ineptis agunt! Nolo ego nomen facere quibus ipsa res nullum fecit, etsi furor ingens faciat, nolo inter maximos ponere quos inter minimos vidi, horum tamen isti nominibus gloriantur, relictisque fidis ducibus hos sequuntur, qui nescio an post obitum didicerint, certe vivi nec scientiam nec famam ullam scientie habuerunt. Quid de his dicam qui Marcum Tullium Ciceronem, lucidum eloquentie solem, spernunt? Qui Varronem, qui Senecam contemnunt? Qui Titi Livi, qui Salustii stilum horrent, ceu asperum atque incultum? Et hi quoque novis freti ducibus pudendisque" (63–67). It is not difficult to recognize in these words an attack on Dante's literary and cultural canonization. The "esigua tradizione che attribuisce a Petrarca un commento al poema dantesco, collocabile tra la fine del XIV secolo e la prima metà del successivo" (Luca Rossi, "Petrarca dantista involontario," 303) is certainly not based on fact. If its claims were true, this would mean that "Francesco Petrarca, qualificato coi titoli che gli competono [. . .], accetta di farsi servo del poema dantesco e, per

di piú, di soggiacergli nella scelta del volgare; dal momento che il poeta laureato si piega a un compito tanto umile, Dante è degno di tanto omaggio e, dunque, poeta supremo" (ibid., 308). Equally fictitious is Guglielmo Maramauro's claim that "E tanto con l'aiuto de questi expositori, quanto con l'aiuto [. . .] de miser Francesco Petrarca [. . .] io me mossi a volere prendere questa dura impresa [of composing a commentary on Dante]": Guglielmo Maramauro, *Expositione sopra l'"Inferno" di Dante Alligieri*, ed. Pier Giacomo Pisoni and Saverio Bellomo (Padua: Antenore, 1998), Prologo 13. Although Maramauro was certainly in contact with Petrarch, as evidenced by *Seniles* 11.5 and 15.4, the claim that he wrote his commentary with the poet's help represents a typical example of his strategy of exaggerated and fabricated self-aggrandizement; see Barański, *"Chiosar con altro testo,"* 117–52.

As regards Petrarch's attitude to the Dante commentary tradition, *Seniles* 4.5, in which the poet instructs Federigo Aretino on how to read and interpret the *Aeneid,* and which was written in the same years as *Seniles* 5.2, both acts as a reminder of which poets deserve to be celebrated, and serves as a model of how they ought to be studied. It is surprising, therefore, that Michele Feo should have seen in *Seniles* 4.5 "uno degli sforzi più umanisticamente impegnati a conciliare classico (Virgilio) e moderno (Dante), o meglio a capire, ad assorbire, a sistemare il moderno entro una visione classica" ("Petrarca, Francesco," 453). Feo bases his claim on the fact that Petrarch pays considerable attention to the wood of *Aeneid* 1, which in the original is only fleetingly considered (ll. 164–68, 312–14)—a fact which he sees as positively allusive to the "selva oscura" (*Inf.* 1.2). In particular, "[i]l tocco più scopertamente dantesco è l'interpretazione del 'media . . . silva' come *mezzo del cammin di nostra vita* ('circa tempus vitae medium')" (ibid., 453). Petrarch's full description of the wood runs as follows: "Silva vero vita hec, umbris atque erroribus plena perplexisque tramitibus atque incertis et feris habitata, hoc est difficultatibus et periculis multis atque occultis, infructuosa et inhospita et herbarum virore et cantu avium et aquarum murmure, idest brevi et caduca specie et inani ac fallaci dulcedine rerum pretereuntium atque labentium accolarum oculos atque aures interdiu leniens ac demulcens, lucis in finem horribilis ac tremenda adventuque hiemis ceno feda, solo squalida, truncis horrida frondibusque spoliata. Venus obvia silve medio ipsa est voluptas circa tempus vite medium ferventior atque acrior; os habitumque virgineum gerit ut illudat insciis; nam si quis eam qualis est cerneret, haud dubie visu solo tremefactus aufugeret; ut enim nichil blandius, sic nichil est fedius voluptate" (25–26). The weaknesses in Feo's case clearly emerge when Petrarch's complete text is taken into consideration. Thus, the allusion to "vitae medium" refers not so much to the wood as to Venus-*voluptas;* similarly, the differences between Petrarch's rewriting of the Virgilian wood and Dante's "selva selvaggia" (*Inf.* 1.5) are obvious and striking, implying, if anything, a polemical response to the opening of the *Commedia.* Furthermore, the kind of amplification of a relatively minor detail which Feo deems as especially significant is, in fact, typical of medieval exegesis. There is nothing in the epistle to support the idea that it constitutes "uno degli sforzi più umanisticamente impegnati a conciliare classico (Virgilio) e moderno (Dante)." On the other hand, Feo's analysis reveals much about modern scholarship's increasingly frantic efforts to establish that Petrarch had managed to achieve "riconciliazione con Dante" (ibid., 453).

79. It is striking that Petrarch, as is typical of his ambiguous allusiveness in the epistle, fails to be specific as regards Dante's vernacular achievements. The failure explicitly to refer to the *Commedia* is a constant in his writing. It thus does not come as much of a surprise that "quando ottenne quel codice [of the *Commedia*] dal Boccaccio dimenticò le sue abitudini di postillatore zelantissimo e appena depositò su tante e mirabili pagine un unico, microscopico segno di lettura' (Billanovich, "L'altro stil nuovo," 90–91). See also Billanovich, *Petrarca letterato*, 175; Carlo Pulsoni, "Il Dante di Francesco Petrarca: Vaticano latino 3199," *Studi petrarcheschi* n.s. 10 (1992): 155–208.

80. Antonelli is undoubtedly correct to assert that "la sufficienza con cui Petrarca risponde a Boccaccio circa le sue letture dantesche [. . .] rivela [. . .] la coscienza di una consapevole, forte e *autonoma* diversità: quella di un umanista che è poeta volgare ma anche nuovo frequentatore dei classici" (Antonelli, "Perché un Libro(-Canzoniere)," 63).

81. On the centrality of *laus* and *vituperatio* in medieval poetics, see Minnis, Scott, and Wallace, *Medieval Literary Theory*, 282–84. See also the close of Dante's *De vulgari eloquentia* (2.14.2) together with Pier Vincenzo Mengaldo's notes in Dante Alighieri, *De vulgari eloquentia*, ed. Pier Vincenzo Mengaldo, in Dante Alighieri, *Opere minori* (Milan and Naples: Ricciardi, 1979), 2:236–37.

82. For instance, when providing an explanation for Boccaccio's decision to destroy his works, Petrarch writes: "sed indignatione quadam clara, et nobili, aetati inutili ac superbe nihil intelligenti, omnia corrumpenti, quodque est intollerabilis contemnenti, tui iuditium ingenii, surripere voluisset" (50).

83. Translations of the *Seniles* are taken from Francis Petrarch, *Letters of Old Age. "Rerum Senilium Libri" I–XVIII*, trans. Aldo S. Bernardo, Saul Levin, and Reta A. Bernardo, 2 vols. (Baltimore and London: Johns Hopkins University Press, 1992).

84. "[A]t hic, modo [stilus vulgaris] inventus, adhuc recens, vastatoribus crebris ac raro squalidus colono, magni se vel ornamenti capacem ostenderet vel augmenti. Quid vis? Hac spe tractus simulque stimulis actus adolescientie magnum eo in genere opus inceperam iactisque iam quasi edificii fundamentis calcem ac lapides et lignam congesseram, dum ad nostram respiciens etatem, et superbie matrem et ignavie, cepi acriter advertere quanta esset illa iactantium ingenii vis, quanta pronuntiationis amenitas, ut non recitari scripta diceres sed discerpi. Hoc semel, hoc iterum, hoc sepe audiens et magis magisque mecum reputans, intellexi tandem, molli in limo et instabili arena perdi operam meque et laborem meum inter vulgi manus laceratum iri" (52–54).

85. The translation of the title is my own; the original may be found on p. 73 of Berté's edition. On *Seniles* 5.2 see Monica Berté, "Introduzione," in Petrarca,

Senile V 2, 2–31; Feo, "Petrarca, Francesco," 452; McLaughlin, *Literary Imitation,* 37–38; Carla Maria Monti, "Per la *Senile* V 2 di Francesco Petrarca," *Studi petrarcheschi* n.s. 15 (2002): 99–128.

86. See nn. 22 and 54 above.

87. On the structural and ideological similarities and tensions between the *Vita nova* and the *Canzoniere,* see Antonelli, "Perché un Libro(-Canzoniere)," 56–63; Picone, "Tempo e racconto"; Kuon, *L'aura dantesca,* 147–48, 213–14; Martinelli, "L'ordinamento morale"; Regn, "'Allegorice pro laurea corona'"; Sturm-Maddox, "Transformations of Courtly Love Poetry"; Warkentin, "The Form of Dante's 'libello.'" See also De Robertis, "A quale tradizione," 136–37.

88. See, for instance, Capovilla, "Petrarca e l'ultima canzone di Dante," 338.

89. "È dunque ipotizzabile che anche 70, come i principali testi di cornice della redazione Correggio (1, 142, 264), sia stata composta espressamente in funzione della raccolta che P. progetta dopo la morte di Laura e di cui Co sembrerebbe essere la prima organica sistemazione. Dei testi di cornice la canzone ha la rilevanza strutturale: collocata, insieme alle 'cantilene oculorum', a metà delle rime in vita della redazione Co, e subito a ridosso dei testi romani, segna un netto discrimine nella vicenda narrata in quella redazione [. . .]. La svolta consiste in un passaggio da una concezione sensuale e pessimistica dell'amore (che ha nel Dante petroso la sua marca stilistica) a una visone spiritualeggiante che potremmo chiamare stilnovistica, con il conseguente muntamento di segno del personaggio di Laura" (Santagata, 347–48). As I discuss below, "Lasso me" does not simply mark this *svolta* but also explores it through its system of poetic quotations and reminiscences.

90. On canzone 70, see Corrado Bologna, "PetrArca petroso," *Critica del testo* 6 (2003): 367–420; Bologna, "Occhi, solo occhi," 194–97; Rino Caputo, *Cogitans fingo: Petrarca tra "Secretum" e "Canzoniere"* (Rome: Bulzoni, 1987), 119–70; Istvàn Frank, "La chanson 'Lasso me' de Pétrarque et ses prédécesseurs," *Annales du Midi* 66 (1954): 259–68; Santagata, *Per moderne carte,* 327–62.

91. This translation adapts Durling's version.

92. "Ma s'egli aven ch'anchor non mi si nieghi / finir anzi 'l mio fine / queste voci meschine, / non gravi al mio signor perch'io il ripreghi / di dir libero un dì tra l'erba e i fiori: / *Drez et rayson es qu'ieu ciant e· m demori*" (ll. 5–10); "Et s'io potesse far ch'agli occhi santi / porgesse alcun dilecto / qualche dolce mio detto, / o me beato sopra gli altri amanti! / Ma più, quand'io dirò senza mentire: / *Donna mi priegha, per ch'io voglio dire*" (ll. 15–20).

93. "[. . .] e chi m'inganna, / altri ch'io stesso e 'l desir soverchio? / Già s'i' trascorro il ciel di cerchio in cerchio, / nessun pianeta a pianger mi condanna" (ll. 31–34).

94. And it is important to stress that this dominance is presented as total. Although Petrarch closely associated Dante with the "stony" style, this does not mean that he accorded him artistic primacy in this manner. Quite the contrary. By absorbing Dante *petroso* into his own poetry, Petrarch made it clear that, as with other lyric styles, he was the master of the "stony" one too.

95. On Petrarch's debts to the *petrose,* see Antoni, "Esperienze stilistiche petrose"; Bettarini, "Perché 'narrando' il duol si disacerba," 315; Cipollone, "'Né per nova figura il primo alloro . . . ,'" 39–41; De Robertis, "Petrarca petroso"; De Robertis, "A quale tradizione," 139–41; Ferdinando Neri, "Il Petrarca e le rime dantesche della pietra," *La cultura* 8 (1929): 389–404; Possiedi, "Petrarca petroso"; Velli, "Petrarca, Dante, la poesia classica." Petrarch also drew significantly on another of Dante's "negative" *canzoni,* one in fact with considerable ties to the *petrose,* namely the *montanina;* see Capovilla, "Petrarca e l'ultima canzone di Dante"; Trovato, *Dante in Petrarca,* 27.

96. See David, "Une réminiscence de Dante," 16; Kuon, *L'aura dantesca,* 57–83; Pastore Stocchi, "Petrarca e Dante," 188–90; Zanato, "San Francesco," 186–213. On the impact of *Inferno* 5 on the *Triumphi,* see Giunta, "Memoria di Dante nei *Trionfi,*" 434–52; Pastore Stocchi, "Petrarca e Dante," 190–91.

97. See Stefano Benassi, "La vertigine del sublime: Moralità della poesia e razionalità della morale in F. Petrarca," in *Petrarca e la cultura europea,* ed. L. Rotondi Secchi Tarugi (Milan: Editrice Nuovi Orizzonti, 1997), 184; Bettarini, "Perché 'narrando' il duol si disacerba," 319–20; Petrie, "Dante and Petrarch," 138–39.

98. On the importance of the myth of Medusa in Petrarch, see Theodore J. Cachey, Jr., "From Shipwreck to Port: *Rvf* 189 and the Making of the *Canzoniere,*" *MLN* 120 (2005): 44–48; Kenelm Foster, "Beatrice or Medusa," in *Italian Studies Presented to E. R. Vincent,* ed. C. P. Brand, K. Foster, and U. Limentani (Cambidge: W. Heffer & Sons, 1962), 42–56; Sara Sturm-Maddox, *Petrarch's Laurels* (University Park: Pennsylvania State University Press, 1992), 118–19, 164, 220–21. See also Remo Ceserani, "'Petrarca'; Il nome come auto-reinvenzione poetica," *Quaderni petrarcheschi* 4 (1987): 121–37. The possible links in Petrarch between the petrifying Medusa and the "stony" Dante still need to be properly explored.

99. From this perspective, the *Rerum vulgarium fragmenta* can be read both as a classicizing challenge and as an orthodox corrective to the *Commedia*'s transgressive plurilingualism. Considerable research still needs to be undertaken on the *Canzoniere*'s plurilingual character and the relationship of this to Dante.

100. See Capovilla, "Petrarca e l'ultima canzone di Dante," 332–33; Chirilli, "Di alcuni dantismi," 44–48, 54–55; De Robertis, "Petrarca interprete di Dante," 314, 324–28; Feo, "Petrarca, Francesco," 455; Petrini, "Petrarca e Dante," 372; Trovato, *Dante in Petrarca,* 19–20, 31, 157; Zanato, "San Francesco," 177, 183, 196.

101. This strategy is close to Petrarch's programmed use of Dantean elements to underscore the differences between himself and Dante. As I have just mentioned, it is vital to recognize the degree to which Petrarch constructed Dante as the negative antithesis of himself.

102. As characterizes Petrarch's overall approach to Dante, ambiguity stalks the opening of the third stanza. Thus, on first reading, the opening two lines can seem positive, since *vago* in Petrarch can mean "beautiful" and *alto* "sublime." However, the rest of the stanza quickly dismisses this possibility, since its "stony" content requires that the two epithets be assigned negative meanings.

103. The order of the rhyme words in *Inferno* 1 is slightly different: "passo"-"lasso"-"basso" (ll. 26, 28, 30).

104. The following negative elements, which recall *Inferno* 1, are found in stanza three: line 21: "pensier rinova la paura" (l. 6); line 22: the lion's "test' alta" (l. 47) and "perdei la speranza de l'altezza" (l. 54) as a result of the *lupa*'s appearance; line 24: "esta selva selvaggia e aspra e forte" (l. 5); line 25: "rimirar lo passo / che non lascia già mai persona viva" (ll. 26–27) and "basso loco" (l. 61); line 28: "il corpo lasso" (l. 28); line 29: "cosa dura" (l. 4), "esta selva selvaggia e aspra e forte" (l. 5), "di paura il cor compunto" (l. 15), and "la paura [. . .] / che nel lago del cor m'era durata" (ll. 19–20). Santagata's commentary makes no mention of any of the borrowings from *Inferno* 1. He does, however, note two echoes from the *petrose* and one from *Inferno* 11 (351–52).

105. Peter Kuon concludes his analysis of madrigal 54, "Perch'al viso d'Amor portava insegna," by asserting that "[i]l fatto che il ritorno dell'io petrarchesco sia modellato sul 'prologo' della *Commedia* [. . .] sottolinea l'intenzione di portare sulla terra un evento che in Dante si verifica nei regni ultraterreni dell'Inferno e del Purgatorio" (*L'aura dantesca*, 53).

106. My reading of the third stanza of "Lasso me" is diametrically opposed to those interpretations which consider its treatment of Dante as either positive or unproblematic; see, for instance, De Robertis, "Petrarca interprete di Dante," 314.

107. See Zygmunt G. Barański, "Guido Cavalcanti and His First Readers," in *Guido Cavalcanti tra i suoi lettori*, ed. M. L. Ardizzone (Fiesole: Cadmo, 2003), 149–75.

108. Guido Cavalcanti, "Donna me prega,— per ch'eo voglio dire," l. 35, in Guido Cavalcanti, *Rime con le Rime di Iacopo Cavalcanti*, ed. Domenico De Robertis (Turin: Einaudi, 1986).

109. See "Volgi, Beatrice, volgi li occhi santi" (*Purg.* 31.133) and "E io a lui: 'Li dolci detti vostri'" (*Purg.* 26.112).

110. "*son due* [*Inf.* 6. 73] vel jus civile et canonicum quibus justitia ministratur sed falsum est nam intelligit de se et guidone cavalcante qui erant duo oculi florentie": *Commento della Divina Commedia d'anonimo fiorentino del secolo XIV*, ed. Pietro Fanfani, 3 vols. (Bologna: Gaetano Romagnoli, 1866–74), 1:254. See also Barański, "Guido Cavalcanti and His First Readers," 158–61.

111. Barański, "Guido Cavalcanti and His First Readers," 159–60. See also Barański, "'Alquanto tenea della oppinione degli epicuri.'"

112. On the complex ways in which Petrarch and Boccaccio affected each other's thinking about Dante, see Battaglia Ricci, "Il culto per Dante"; Billanovich, *Petrarca letterato*, 57–294; Billanovich, "L'altro stil nuovo," 85–90; Francesco Bruni, *Boccaccio: L'invenzione della letteratura mezzana* (Bologna: Il Mulino, 1990), 405–77; Francesco Mazzoni, "Giovanni Boccaccio fra Dante e Petrarca," *Atti e memorie dell'Accademia Petrarca di Lettere, Arti e Scienze di Arezzo* 42 (1976–78): 15–42; Paolazzi, *Dante e la "Comedia*," 130–221.

113. I am not persuaded, therefore, by Pulsoni's suggestion that, when Petrarch, in "Qui dove mezzo son, Sennuccio mio" (*Rvf* 113), calques Dante's "Guido, i'vorrei," the poet "crea una sorta di parallelismo di 'primi amici' fra il suo Sennuccio e il dantesco Guido" (*La tecnica compositiva*, 138). In keeping with the fact that "Petrarca ricontestualizza alla propria esperienza personale la vicenda di *Guido i' vorrei*" (138), it is rather more likely that he established the equation in order to stress the moral gulf that divided his attitude to friendship from Dante's.

114. This ploy is similar to the way in which, in *Rvf* 287, Petrarch bracketed Dante with Guittone.

115. See Zygmunt G. Barański, "'Per similitudine di abito scientifico': Dante, Cavalcanti, and the Sources of Medieval 'Philosophical' Poetry," in *Science and Literature in Italian Culture: From Dante to Calvino. A Festschrift for Pat Boyde*, ed. P. Antonello and S. Gilson (Oxford: Legenda, 2004), 14–52.

116. See Concetta Carestia Greenfield, "The Poetics of Francis Petrarch," in *Francis Petrarch, Six Centuries Later: A Symposium*, ed. A. Scaglione (Chapel Hill: Department of Romance Languages, University of North Carolina; Chicago: The Newberry Library, 1975), 213–22.

117. Furthermore, as we saw earlier, Petrarch's treatment of Guido conforms to his general intent to reduce all Italian vernacular poetry to love poetry—a strategy that allowed him to present the whole of the preceding poetic tradition as subordinate to his achievements in the *Rerum vulgarium fragmenta*.

118. See Domenico De Robertis, "Nota al testo," in Cavalcanti, *Rime*, 241–50.

119. See Raffaella Pelosini, "Guido Cavalcanti nei *Rerum vulgarium fragmenta*," *Studi petrarcheschi* n.s. 9 (1992): 37; Santagata, 9, 509, 594, 599–600.

120. See Barański, "Guido Cavalcanti and His First Readers," 152, 154, 164–66.

121. On Cavalcanti's philosophical standing in the Trecento, see ibid., 158–60, 164–68.

122. Bettarini, "Perché 'narrando' il duol si disacerba," 308; Pelosini, "Guido Cavalcanti"; Suitner, *Petrarca e la tradizione stilnovistica*, 45–63. See also Santagata's commentary to the *Canzoniere* (references to Cavalcanti are listed in *Indice dei nomi, dei toponimi e dei luoghi letterari*, 1531–32).

123. I examine this question in the book I am completing on Cavalcanti's late-thirteenth- and fourteenth-century reception.

124. Feo, "Petrarca, Francesco," 450. See also Billanovich, "L'altro stil nuovo," 89–90.

125. The designation "Petrarch's Dante" is not completely new. In its Italian form, "Il Dante di Francesco Petrarca," it had been used by Giuseppe Velli in an article of the same name, which appeared in the 1985 issue of *Studi petrarcheschi*. By having recourse to the phrase, Velli did not intend to define Petrarch's reaction to Dante in the tense and complex terms that I have outlined in this study. His aim was to suggest a largely harmonious relationship centered upon the possibility that Petrarch's Dante was (astonishingly) "[u]n Dante classico" (199).

CHAPTER 3

Blinding the Cyclops

Petrarch after Dante

ALBERT RUSSELL ASCOLI

1.

That Petrarch occupies a special place in the history and historiography of the Western tradition is news from nowhere to no one. Still, for all that modern notions of cultural history have frequently located him at a pivotal point between medieval and Renaissance "mentalities" and assigned him a place of privilege in the emergence of a new experience of individual temporality,[1] Petrarch has proved curiously resistant to rigorous historicization in relation to his own immediate context. It has seemed far easier to relate him to authors writing a millennium and more earlier: Virgil, Cicero, Augustine.[2] It is a truism that, notwithstanding the troubadours, the *Scuola Siciliana*, the *Vita nova,* and so on, the modern European lyric "begins" with Petrarch and never strays far from him. Yet it has proven equally difficult to create a plausible set of antecedents for Petrarch's role as the re-founder of a neo-Classical movement, which has come to be known as Humanism.

A specific subset of the historiographical conundrum named "Petrarch" is the problem of his relations to his towering precursor, Dante Alighieri. In a certain sense, recent scholarship has done much to clear up the air of mystery surrounding this genealogy *manqué*. On the one hand, it is now quite clear that Petrarch's Italian oeuvre is shot through with Dantean echoes—of the lyrics, of the *Vita nova,* of the *Commedia*.[3] On the other, the later author's strategy of denying such indebtedness has been laid open for all to see. It goes something like this: "I never read him, and even if I did it was only when I was very young and stupid; his work is OK, but it's written in Italian, which is a vulgar language and hardly worth the trouble he went to—he should only have written brilliant Latin works, like mine" (I paraphrase, very loosely, from *Familiares* 21.15).[4]

Persuasive and exciting as the work on this aspect of the Dante-Petrarch relationship has been, it can hardly be said to have solved the larger problem with which I began, and this for at least two reasons. In the first instance, the relationship has been cast, particularly in North American criticism, as an Oedipal struggle of Petrarch with a titanic literary precursor, one who has been equally difficult, though for quite different reasons, to situate historically.[5] Secondly, and more important for the point of view adopted here, while such scholarship has rejected one of Petrarch's spurious claims—his lack of indebtedness to Dante—it has de facto accepted the other, largely limiting its explorations to the importance of Dante for Petrarch's vernacular lyric oeuvre. At the same time it has remained silent on the possibility that Petrarch was influenced by the Latin Dante, the Dante of *De vulgari eloquentia,* the *Epistole,* the *Monarchia,* the *Quaestio de aqua et terra,* and last, but not for us least, the epistolary *Ecloghae.*

The present essay means to offer the beginnings of a remedy to these latter omissions and thus, at least potentially, to reopen the question of what some of the immediate conditions of possibility for Petrarch's life and works might have been. The foci of my critical attention are two Latin works of Petrarch: the first eclogue, entitled *Parthenias,* of his collection of twelve pastoral eclogues, the *Bucolicum Carmen*; and one of his *Familiar Letters* (*Familiares* 10.4), which accompanies and glosses the eclogue.[6] The reasons for choosing these two texts will become more apparent as we proceed. For the moment it is enough to observe that they are each exemplars of a classical genre—the Virgilian eclogue, which Petrarch is widely credited with refounding, and the Ciceronian-Senecan epistle—and that in the self-reflexive, auto-critical relationship between them (the letter explaining and defending the eclogue) they can be taken—and have been taken—to represent the historical modernity of Petrarchan authorship and selfhood.[7]

What I will suggest, broadly speaking, is that the apparent autochthony of this textual complex conceals deep engagement with and indebtedness to Dante—in the first instance to his vernacular masterpiece, the *Commedia,* but also, perhaps even more surprisingly, to his late and rarely studied Latin epistles written in eclogic form as part of a friendly yet polemical exchange with the Bolognese proto-humanist, Giovanni del Virgilio.[8] I will argue, in fact, that Petrarch's eclogue plus epistle complex is inspired by and attempts to respond to Dante's epistolary eclogues: that the Latin Petrarch is heir not only to a vernacular Dante but to a Latin, humanist one as well. In the process, I will further suggest that it is necessary to see both Petrarch and Dante as indebted to and in dialogue with the Northern Italian humanists of the late Duecento and early Trecento (of whom del Virgilio is a derivative offshoot)—Lovato Lovati and, especially, his great Paduan heir, Dante's contemporary, Albertino Mussato.[9] Among other things, Mussato's coronation with the laurel crown, and Dante's prima facie claims to deserve the same, belie Petrarch's repeated assertions that he was the first poet since Statius to undergo laureation[10]—assertions tantamount to erasing a thousand years of history, which would soon come to be thought of as an age of undifferentiated darkness, a self-canceling historical period, as it were, "that time forgot," and that forgot time in its dreams of eternity.

As we will soon see, there are many ways to relate Petrarch's paired works to Dante's *Ecloghae*: around the questions of Latin versus vernacular literature; of the relation of moderns to ancients; of literary genre and stylistic register; of the practice of self-exegesis; of the relations of these two expatriate Florentine writers to Northern Italian humanism; of specific narrative and figurative patterns and topoi; and so on. The most obvious and important of these is the explicit subject matter of both *Parthenias* and the letter that glosses it: namely, the exploration of possible relationships between poetic writing and sacred, theological writing—identity, complementarity, and/or antagonism. In order to understand what, historically, is at stake for Petrarch in these assorted yet not unrelated topics, and why he finds it necessary both to articulate them in relation to Dante, Mussato, and other immediate precursors and to efface the fact that he does so, we need to begin with a short detour.

2.

In both versions of his *Trattatello in laude di Dante,* Giovanni Boccaccio copies out a Latin epitaph on the poet, which he attributes to Giovanni del Virgilio and says was intended for Dante's tomb in Ravenna. The epitaph was never engraved, and is known to us only through Boccaccio, who is also the only source for the epistolary exchange between del Virgilio and Dante. The exchange first appears in his *Zibaldone laurenziano,* along with a later verse epistle attributed to del Virgilio and directed to Albertino Mussato. It seems fair to say that, for Boccaccio, both the epitaph and the exchange serve as part of a campaign to convince himself and, more importantly, the great friend of his later years, Petrarch, that Dante was not "merely" a vernacular poet but also a key player in the humanist revival of classical Latinity.[11] What Petrarch's response was, we shall see. First, however, let us consider the first eight lines of the epitaph:

> Theologus Dantes, nullius dogmatis expers
> quod foveat claro phylosophya sinu,
> gloria Musarum, vulgo gratissimus auctor,
> hic iacet, et fama pulsat utrumque polum:
> qui loca defunctis gladiis regnumque gemellis
> distribuit, laycis rhetoricisque modis.
> Pascua Pyeriis demum resonabat avenis;
> Amtropos heu! letum livida rupit opus.

––––––––––

> Dante, the theologian, skilled in every branch of knowledge that philosophy may cherish in her illustrious bosom, glory of the Muses, *auctor* most pleasing to the vulgar herd—here lieth and smiteth either pole with his fame; who assigned their places to the dead [in the *Commedia*] and their respective sway to the two swords [Church and Empire, in *Monarchia*] in lay and rhetorical style. At the end he was singing pastoral songs on the Pierian pipes; envious Atropos, alas, broke off the work of joy.[12]

The epitaph is significant for a number of reasons. Del Virgilio's use of the word *auctor* suggests the extraordinary rapidity with which Dante and his works obtained the highest cultural status, a status traditionally reserved for long-dead classical writers and for the human authors of the Bible.[13] Crucially, the verses are composed in Latin and emanate from the stylus of a distinguished professor of classical literature at the oldest and most important academic institution in Italy, the University of Bologna. In other words, Dante's extraordinary, indeed unprecedented, status as modern, vernacular *auctor* is here normalized and institutionalized by a leading representative of the official scholarly culture, who is also closely linked to that early humanist movement which had first emerged in communal Padua, and which would soon find its strongest and most influential voice in the Latin works of Francis Petrarch.

The epitaph is not unequivocally positive, however, and betrays a basic tension within early humanism that would only intensify over the course of the fourteenth century: on the one hand, its commitment to the advancement of modern authors, such as Mussato, to comparability with the classical greats; on the other, its resistance to the new, vernacular literature. In fact, even as the epitaph assimilates Dante to the culture of *auctoritas,* it qualifies his achievement in subtle yet marked ways that would characterize the most prevalent attitude of humanist culture for a century and more to come. Specifically, we should consider the equivocal force of the words "vulgo gratissimus auctor," whose primary meaning must be taken as "the *auctor* most beloved of the vulgar herd," which, yes, posits Dante as *auctor,* but one whose identity as such depends on the ignorant masses who speak only the vernacular, rather than on the approbation of the learned steeped in the Latin classics. Similar is the reference to Dante's "laycis . . . modis" in writing. And it is also significant that, in addition to the *Comedy,* del Virgilio singles out two of Dante's late Latin works, the *Monarchy* and the eclogues, rather than other vernacular achievements.[14] This tension is, we will see, even more explicit in the first of del Virgilio's epistolary poems in the exchange with Dante, which acknowledges his interlocutor's exceptional literary talents but also urges him to turn them to Latin (1.25–34, 41–46).[15] In this connection, it is no accident that del Virgilio in the second of his verse epistles specifically mentions Mussato as an alternative interlocutor (3.80–89) should Dante refuse his invitation of hospitality; or that, at a later date, he would attempt to inaugurate, unsuccessfully, an eclogic exchange with the aging, exiled Mussato, specifically modeled on the earlier one with Dante.[16]

The epitaph, then, serves to suggest an important way in which Petrarch, perhaps spurred on by Boccaccio, could have made an ambiguous connection between his two nearest and most obvious cultural antecedents—Northern proto-humanism and Tuscan lyric poetry—which allowed both for filiation and for opposition. More specifically, del Virgilio in the epitaph as well as in his verse epistles builds a bridge between Dante and Mussato for which the historical and biographical record otherwise offers little support.[17] As regards the textual complex that concerns us here, namely Petrarch's *Parthenias* and *Familiares* 10.4, the critical term in the epitaph is "theologus," applied to Dante by del Virgilio in tandem with *auctor*, and similarly charged. What does del Virgilio mean in using this word? A modern, especially North American, reader is likely to take it as a direct reference to things that Dante says and implies about himself at several points in his oeuvre, allusions which have led Robert Hollander, following in the wake of Charles Singleton, to call Dante a "theologus-poeta." *Theologus* in this sense clearly means "writer or transcriber of the Word of God," that is, a *scriba Dei*, like the human authors of the Bible, rather than an academic theologian, like Aquinas, who writes *about* things divine.[18]

It is far from unreasonable to suggest that del Virgilio could have inferred that Dante thought of himself as a *scriba Dei*. After all, in a passage which Dante echoes in the first of his two eclogues, he refers to his poem as "sacro," a co-production of divine and human hands (*Paradiso* 25.1–12; *Ecloghae* 2.42–44). One is also tempted to adduce the passages, so important for the Hollander-Singleton interpretations, in *Convivio* 2.1 and the *Epistle to Cangrande*, paragraph 7, which notoriously bring biblical and poetic allegory into close proximity and, in the latter case, suggest the applicability of the fourfold model of biblical exegesis to the *Commedia*.[19] Here, however, there is a problem, since the circulation of both was, to judge by the manuscript evidence remaining to us, extremely limited,[20] and they are unlikely to have been known to del Virgilio (or to Petrarch, for that matter, as we will see). Moreover, and this is a point that should be taken seriously, Dante never designates himself as "theologus" or "teologo"—though, as with *auctor*, he would very likely have been pleased by del Virgilio's application of the word to him—nor does he show any signs that he is aware of a contemporary tradition which did claim that poetry was an *alter*-theology.

That tradition, and the one to which del Virgilio is almost certainly referring, derives not from Dante but from Albertino Mussato, whose four verse letters defending poetry (his own and that of the pagan ancients) against its detractors assert that poetry is a kind of theology. In those epistles, Mussato invokes Aristotle to the effect that poets were the first theologians (cf. *Metaphysics* 1.3.983b.28–30), and affirms that true, vatic, poetry is divinely inspired, comparable but decidedly not identical to Scripture.[21] The Aristotelian passage, along with Mussato's poetic gloss on it, became the *loci classici* out of which a flourishing Trecento discourse on poetic theology developed. That discourse was marked by an increasing tendency to specify that poetry (except that of biblical poets, such as David in the Psalms) was not a vehicle for expressing the Word of God, but rather contained allegorical representations of things pertaining to divinity, including God's creatures—the natural world and humanity.[22] It is in this relatively tame sense that del Virgilio apparently intends the word, as suggested by its placement in apposition to the qualifier "ignorant of no doctrine." It is in this sense as well that a number of Dante's most important commentators, including his son Pietro and Giovanni Boccaccio, used the term, presumably in an effort to defuse the more radical claims apparently made by the poet himself.[23] As noted at the outset, Petrarch's pastoral eclogue *Parthenias,* especially as glossed in *Familiares* 10.4, has as its primary topic the relation of poetry and theology as modes of discourse. As we are about to see, both eclogue and letter initially seem to address— transformatively and polemically—the position of Mussato and, perhaps, that of the Dante depicted by del Virgilio's epitaph. We will also see, however, that Petrarch is allusively engaged with Dante's texts: the *Commedia,* as might be expected, and, rather more surprisingly, the two epistolary eclogues.

3.

Whether Petrarch knew del Virgilio's epitaph on Dante, directly or indirectly, is not a matter of concern here, though the probability is that he did.[24] What the previous section established, however, was a cultural context against which to read Petrarch's *Bucolicum Carmen* 1 (*Parthenias*) and *Familiares* 10.4 as successors to the classicism *both* of the northern humanists and of Dante, as well as three key issues raised by these two cultural forces both separately and in the occasional encounters between them:

(1) the problematic "authorization" of modern writers; (2) the ongoing struggle between Latin and vernacular; and (3) the tension between poetry and theology. In what follows I will show how these two works of Petrarch—or rather, this single "hybrid" work, given that, as we shall see, each text is radically dependent upon the other for its significance—engage these issues in a very specific relation to Dante, despite the fact that their overtly designated interlocutors are, on the one hand, Petrarch's brother Gherardo, a Carthusian monk, to whom the letter is addressed, and, on the other, three "ancient" poets—Homer, David the psalmist, and above all Virgil, one of whose names *Parthenias* bears.[25]

Why Dante, however? If Petrarch has a polemical target in the poetry/theology debate, Mussato, as we have seen, seems a much more obvious candidate than Dante. The Latin/Italian question is not broached, at least not overtly, in either *Parthenias* or the commentary on it in the letter. The question of conferring "auctorial" status on the moderns is more promising, especially given that, like the Dante of the *Commedia*, Petrarch assigns Virgil as a guide for his textual alter-ego and, like the Dante of both the *Commedia* and the epistolary *Ecloghae*, he clearly establishes that he is, among other things, imitating Virgil's epic and pastoral works.

We will return to these issues. However, the most obvious grounds for associating *Parthenias* and *Familiares* 10.4 separately, as well as in combination, with Dante are formal. Most notably, the exchange of Latin verse letters initiated by Giovanni del Virgilio, but quickly recast by Dante into the first serious attempt at writing Virgilian bucolic verse in ten centuries,[26] is certainly the proximate model for Boccaccio's[27] and then Petrarch's[28] subsequent, more extensive, and far more influential forays into the pastoral mode. Dante, in other words, has an obvious, if not yet unassailable, claim to at least a mediating role in the genealogy that leads from Virgil's *Eclogues* to the *Bucolicum Carmen.*

Less certain, but still compelling, is the case for Dante as principal model for the pairing of a Latin eclogue with an epistle that glosses it for a third party (Gherardo), who is also included as a character in the autobiographical allegory of the eclogue. Dante's resuscitation of the Virgilian pastoral, in fact, goes one better than his model by fusing it with the epistolary genre, in the double sense that each of his eclogues both dramatizes the receipt of and reaction to a letter from Mopsus, namely del Virgilio, by Tityrus, namely Dante, and also itself constitutes a letter to del Virgilio.[29]

Parthenias is not in itself an epistle, of course, but it is incorporated into one when sent, together with *Familiares* 10.4, to Gherardo—and just as the correspondents Dante and del Virgilio have textual doubles in Tityrus and Mopsus, so Petrarch and Gherardo are doubled by the speakers of *Parthenias*, Silvius and Monicus.

There is another feature of the eclogue and epistle complex that, considered in historical perspective, seems eminently Dantean: namely, its status as a formal self-exegesis. This point, curiously, has not been made previously, perhaps because Petrarch is so consistently self-reflexive in a broad sense that this particular configuration seems just one more example of a uniquely Petrarchan phenomenon, or, perhaps better, a variation on Petrarch's repeated refashioning of St. Augustine's confessional voice. Despite all of the attention that has been drawn to Petrarch's use of Dantean materials, scholars, in fact, have rarely dwelt on the possibility that Petrarch's autobiographical penchant might derive at least in part from Dante's equally pervasive self-staging. Possibly this is because, beyond the use of the first-person singular pronoun, Petrarch's *style* of self-reference seems worlds away from Dante's, for example, in its wholesale rejection of the older poet's penchant for the language and forms of scholastic discourse.

The latter point brings us back to the question of formal self-exegesis, inasmuch as Dante's version of this typically draws upon scholastic models of one sort or another. Throughout his career, in fact, Dante repeatedly assumes the role of privileged interpreter of his own work:[30] in *Vita nova*, in *Convivio*, in the little studied *Epistola* 3 (which accompanies and glosses the sonnet "Io sono stato con amore insieme," addressed to Cino da Pistoia),[31] in *De vulgari eloquentia*, and, most likely, in the so-called *Epistle to Cangrande*.[32] And despite his evident adaptation of the medieval commentary tradition, Dante stands virtually alone among both Latin and vernacular authors in that he writes commentaries on his own works rather than those of others. In the Trecento the practice became more common—Francesco da Barberino, *Documenti d'Amore*, and Boccaccio, *Teseida*, offer notable instances[33]—but it clearly derives from Dante. Petrarch, on the other hand, almost never writes formal glosses on his own work. When he does so in the *Parthenias/Familiares* 10.4 complex, it seems natural that one should look first to Dante as a model, particularly since other key formal features are so plausibly Dantean.

What makes this connection hard to perceive initially is that Petrarch's self-exegesis does not, in its particulars, closely mirror any of the possible

Dantean models—at least not those that Petrarch is likely to have known. In fact, of the five mentioned above, the only one we are sure he had read is the *Vita nova*, while the two that most closely resemble his effort—Dante's *Epistle* 3 plus sonnet and, especially, the *Epistle to Cangrande* plus the initial cantos of *Paradiso*—were most likely unknown to him.[34] However, while the lack of evidence that *Familiares* 10.4 is engaged with the two auto-exegetical texts in which Dante, or at least someone pretending to be Dante, most explicitly addresses the relationship between poetry and theology, namely, *Convivio* 2.1 and the *Epistle to Cangrande*, may be disappointing, it does not affect my argument in substance. The *Vita nova* alone establishes Dante as the progenitor of self-commentary; while the *Commedia* obviously poses the problem of poetry assuming the mantle of theology.

Finally, considering *Familiares* 10.4 apart from *Parthenias* and purely in terms of its place within the macrotext of the epistolary collection as a whole,[35] we can identify at least one more potential connection between Petrarch and Dante. Book 10 is the shortest in the twenty-four-book *Familiares,* consisting of only six epistles. The first of these is also the first and best known of a series of appeals, over the course of the *Familiares,* to Emperor Charles IV to come to Italy and to revive imperial Rome.[36] This letter, evidently, has both ideological and formal ties to the famous letter written by Dante to Emperor Henry VII (Charles' grandfather) at the time of the former's ill-fated foray into the Italian peninsula.[37] Petrarch closes the book with a letter (10.6) directed to Charles' chancellor, John von Neumarkt, whose interest in Petrarch's humanist learning clearly brokered his access to and influence with the emperor.

These two documents, reflecting a basically secular political-cultural mission, surround and bracket four letters of a different kind. *Familiares* 10.2 is a letter to Petrarch's friend "Socrates," expressing concern for the latter's health and welfare and his own sense of the instability of human life, and of the possibility of overcoming its dangers by a retreat into monasticism, like that of Gherardo, who had joined the Carthusian order of Montrieux in 1343.[38] The following three letters are all addressed to Gherardo, and all three meditate anxiously and variously upon the contrast between the experiences of the two brothers and their respective humanist-poetic and monastic-theological vocations. The letters alternate, without definite resolution, between a yearning for the peace and stability of the brother's life and Petrarch's commitment to classical learning and poetic performance.

This formal juxtaposition of "active" and "contemplative" letters is, in fact, a typical ordering principle in the *Familiares*. Book 10 reverses, for example, the structure of *Familiares* book 4, which begins with a great contemplative letter, the so-called "Letter from Mt. Ventoux," and then continues with a series of letters organized primarily around the active life and, in particular, Petrarch's interactions with King Robert the Wise at the time of his coronation as "poet laureate" and his intimate relations with the Colonna family (especially 4.2–8).[39]

Book 4, like book 10, dramatizes the oscillation between worldly, political-cultural concerns and speculative, religiously-oriented interiority. In view of the letters to Robert and to Charles, one is tempted to say that Petrarch had in mind the model of Dante as a poetic titan seemingly able to yoke the political and theological realms together, in implicit comparison to which he both criticizes and values his own hesitant oscillations between worldly and anagogical extremes. As we will see, this oscillation is played out in exquisite detail in the mini-macrotext of *Familiares* 10.4 plus the eclogue it accompanies. Once this is established, we can then turn to the larger intertextual claim that the explicitly loving, and covertly aggressive, relationship to Gherardo expressed in both texts is also, even primarily, a figure for Petrarch's relationship to Dante.

4.

Familiares 10.4 begins by articulating Petrarch's assumption that his brother will be horrified by the accompanying secular poem, which, he imagines, evidently ventriloquizing his own fears, Gherardo will take to be contrary to theology. The first part of the letter (par. 1–9) is thus given over to a defense of the general proposition that "theologie quidem minime adversa poetica est" (poetry is not in the least contrary to theology), with an implied relevance to the specific case of Petrarch's own poem and poetic vocation. The second part of the letter then undertakes an exposition of the poem and is itself divided into three parts: first, a description of the circumstances of its composition (par. 10–12); second, a literal summary of the contents of the poem (par. 13–19); third, an allegorical exegesis of the literal sense (par. 20–34).[40]

At first, the opening defense seems to make the standard use of the claim, attributed by Petrarch, as by Mussato before him, to Aristotle, that

poets were the first theologians.[41] This claim is typically used both to justify the appreciation of non-Christian classical texts as allegorical bearers
of occulted moral and spiritual wisdom (as in the common assertion, which
Petrarch, however, consistently avoided, that Virgil's fourth eclogue prophe-
sies the coming of Christ),[42] and to advance similar claims for moderns
following in their footsteps.[43] Similarly, Petrarch draws upon the defense,
first elaborated by Augustine in the *De Doctrina Christiana* and later developed in rigorous terms by Aquinas, of the figurative and fictive elements,
the "poetic" language, of the Bible.[44] Taken to its extreme, this combination of arguments leads to a convergence, if not coincidence, of poetry and
biblical revelation: on the one hand, the poet striving to approach, or at
least to complement, the discourse of theological truth; on the other, the
Word of God, "Theo-logos," working through the suspect rhetorical devices of poetry.

Nevertheless, while such a convergence may characterize Dante's texts
(e.g., *Convivio* 2.1 and *Purgatorio* 21–22), and perhaps Boccaccio's treatment of Dante as well,[45] Petrarch actively refuses it. He does make explicit
use of both arguments, initially stressing the poetic quality of the Bible:
"theologiam poeticam esse de Deo" (theology [i.e., Scripture] is the poetry
of God [par. 1]) in its use of figure, fiction, and occasionally verse. But he
then immediately and clearly separates poetry from Scripture as to content,
using the Aristotelian *locus classicus* with an emphasis far different from that
of Mussato: "illic de Deo deque divinis, hic de diis hominibusque tracta-
tur, unde et apud Aristotilem primos theologizantes poetas legimus" (that
other discourse deals with God and divine things, this one [poetry] with
gods [i.e., the classical, pagan gods] and men, whence we read in Aristotle
that the first theologizers were the poets [par. 2]). The first theologians,
those who introduced religious worship and ritual, may have been poets
in their use of "exquisite" forms of language (par. 4) to honor the divinity they only dimly perceived, while several of the human authors of
the Bible, above all David, composed their contributions to Scripture in
verse (par. 6). Nonetheless, a clear distinction has now, in the Christian
dispensation, been introduced between poet and theologian. As the allegorical reading of *Parthenias* then makes clear, these two roles are identified, respectively, with the classical poets, above all Homer and Virgil, and
with David as psalmist.[46] The common thread that links the two kinds
of writing and of authorship for Petrarch is the residue of *style* as against
content.[47]

On closer inspection, then, Petrarch's defense of poetry vis-à-vis theology is doubly conservative: in clearly separating the two modes as to content, he refuses and refutes the apparent attempt by some moderns to elevate poetry to a status virtually equivalent to that of theology and even of the Bible itself; and he simultaneously makes classical Latin (and Greek) poetry into the normative model for all verse, thus rejecting any attempt, such as Boccaccio's, to valorize contemporary vernacular poets. In trying to acknowledge the twin normalizing authorities of the Bible and of the classical literary tradition, however, Petrarch ultimately foregrounds significant conceptual problems that he, as an aspiring modern and Latin poet, faces. First of all, he reinstitutes the clear opposition between Scripture and the classics that Dante and Mussato, in their different ways, had tried to efface, and thus must confront the fact that his own desire to write Latin poetry is radically at odds with his insistence on giving the Bible and its interpreters back their specificity and precedence—a struggle which is acted out in his relationship with his beloved brother. Moreover, the very desire to achieve modern poetic greatness by writing a Latin epic, the *Africa*,[48] on a classical subject is inherently anachronistic.

The letter thus constitutes an attack on the *content* that Mussato's theory attributes to poetry and, at least by inference, to the substance of Dante's great poem, even as it appropriates and transforms the poet/theologian dyad that is basic for both of them.[49] The problematization of the relationship between poet and theologian—and the implicit critique of Mussato and Dante—continues in the letter through the use of the most characteristic of Dantean formal devices, auto-commentary and allegoresis, which are deployed to define and defend a modern literary project.

What makes this letter truly stunning in its design and powerfully complex in its mode of signification is how the general defense of poetry, and the allegorical interpretation of *Parthenias* that follows, mirror and mutually interpret one another.[50] The defense sets up a paradigm for the peaceful coexistence of the poet and the theologian, each in his distinct province, which ostensibly will be borne out by the exegesis of the poem. As the exegesis reveals, however, *Parthenias* itself constitutes an unresolved debate *between* theological and poetic perspectives: between the interlocutors Monicus and Silvius; between Gherardo and Petrarch, for whom they are said to stand; and between the classical tradition (embodied by Virgil and Homer) and the biblical poetry of David the psalmist—which Silvius and Monicus, respectively, hold up as paradigms of writing (cf. 10.3, par. 27). In other words, Petrarch entertains the idea of the *poeta-theologus* and/or *theologus-poeta,* only to create a seemingly unbridgeable gap between the theologian and the poet.

Taken on its own terms, *Familiares* 10.4 seems to be the paradigmatic enactment of Petrarch's radical ambivalence, the tension he always feels and never resolves, between secular and religious, active and contemplative, poetic and theological modes of being and expression. In a brilliant piece of close, *intra*-textual reading, which constitutes the point of departure for my own *inter*-textual analysis, Thomas Greene identifies a key motif that distills the agon of Petrarch with his brother as well as within his own thinking.[51] At the beginning of his allegorization, Petrarch explains the appropriateness of the names of the characters in *Parthenias.* Monicus, he says, is suitable to Gherardo because

> quia cum unum ex cyclopibus Monicum dicant quasi monoculum, id quodam respectu proprie tibi convenire visum est, qui e duobus oculis, quibus omnes comuniter utimur mortales, quorum altero scilicet celestia altero terrena respicimus, tu terrena cernentem abiecisti oculo meliore contentus. (par. 20)

> one of the Cyclops is named Monicus, as if he were one-eyed. Such a name seemed [. . .] fitting for you since of two eyes that we mortals usually use, one to gaze upon heavenly things and the other upon earthly ones, you renounced the one that beholds earthly things, being content with the better eye.

In other words, Monicus/Gherardo is identified with the perspective first attributed to theology, which "deals with God and divine things," as against poetry, which deals with "[the pagan] gods and men," and the whole passage thus establishes the specific terms of a doubling between the defense and the allegorization.

Near the end of the allegorization, and herein lies Greene's discovery, the figure of a Cyclops once again becomes crucial. In *Parthenias,* after debating the relative merits of Homer and Virgil, on the one hand, and David, on the other, Silvius shrugs off Monicus' plea for him to listen to the songs of David, who "unum canit . . . Deum, quem turba deorum victa tremit" (sings one God, who makes the vanquished crowd of gods tremble

[100–101]). He will, oxymoronically, experience the will of David's God only "si fata volent" (if the fates allow [100; my translation]), a decidedly non-Christian view of the world. He is drawn away by the love of the Muses, who stimulate him to sing of "sidereum iuvenem genitumque a stirpe deorum" (a youth born of the race of heavenly gods [113]), that is, Scipio Africanus, subject of his still incomplete epic, *Africa*. Silvius, turning the language of pastoral to epic purposes and topics, then asks, "te, Polipheme, tuis iam vi stravisse sub antris" (say, has he not, Polyphemus, by force thrust into your cavern? [115]), a line glossed by the letter as follows:

> Africanus Scipio est, qui in litore afro Poliphemum stravit, hoc est Hanibalem Penorum ducem; sicut enim Poliphemus, sic et Hanibal monoculus fuit post oculum in Italia amissum. (par. 32)

> [It is] Scipio Africanus, who overthrew on the African shore Polyphemus, namely Hannibal, commander of the Carthaginians. Just as Polyphemus had one eye, so did Hannibal after losing an eye in Italy.

Having identified this ironic repetition of the Cyclops imagery, which links the contemplative Monicus to the vicious Hannibal, Greene reveals how Petrarch's overt attitude of respect and devotion to his brother and the theological vocation is subtended by an agonistic hostility.

The significance for the initial defense of poetry of this implied parallelism between Monicus/Gherardo and Polyphemus/Hannibal—within the letter's allegorization, and to an even greater extent within *Parthenias*—is clear.[52] In both texts, Petrarch calls sharp attention to the conflict between the one God, subject of theological poetry, and the pagan gods who tremble in defeat before him, and who are then named as the progenitors of Petrarch's epic protagonist.[53] In other words, the clash of Scipio and Hannibal can be read as a sublimated image of the violent encounter between (classicizing) poetry and (Judeo-Christian) theology, now apparently irreconcilable.

The initial characterization of poetry and theology as using shared stylistic means, especially those of metaphor and "forma . . . exquisita et nova" (exquisite and new forms [par. 4]) to express different but complementary subject matter, dissipates as the potential ideological conflict be-

tween their respective subjects is revealed. That conflict had been anticipated earlier when Silvius tried to deprive David of the defining stylistic
attribute of poetry by deprecating his "vox rauca" (hoarse voice) as against
the stylistic polish of the classical poets (par. 31; cf. *Parthenias* 103). On the
other side, then, would be the stylistic mastery of Virgil in the *Eclogues,*
and of Petrarch's imitation thereof in *Parthenias.* Thus, the intra-textual
conflict is doubled by an inter-textual staging of literary history, or rather
of the history of two kinds of writing, Virgilian and biblical.

The introduction of an intertextual dimension adds further depth to
Greene's seminal reading, but it also creates a perplexity. Polyphemus has
been a traditional figure of the dangerous, uncivilized "other" in the Western epic tradition at least since Homer's *Odyssey,* and, in keeping with his
occupation as shepherd, he also appears in Theocritus' *Idylls,* the founding text of the pastoral tradition. Curiously, however, he and his monstrous brethren make no appearance in Petrarch's supposed model, Virgil's
pastoral *Eclogues.*[54] To the extent that the Polyphemus of Petrarch has classical antecedents, they are the Virgilian and Ovidian rewritings of the
Odyssey in the *Aeneid* (3.588–654) and *Metamorphoses* (14.154–222, see also
13.750–897), respectively. As we will see, however, there is a proximate, pastoral source for the image, which Petrarch both knew and used, while at the
same time taking an imaginative leap even further backward, as he creates
an ideal link between himself and the unknown works of Virgil's great
Greek precursor, Homer.

5.

Prior readings of *Parthenias* and *Familiares* 10.4 have stressed both
their participation in an innovative, humanistic classicism and their representation of an anxious, conflicted, modern self. Without denying the
force of these arguments or the larger discourse of Petrarchan modernity
in which they take part, I would like to stress again the conservative or reactionary tendencies that mingle with and condition the undoubtedly and
distinctively modern features of the text(s). To do this, I believe, it is necessary to probe further the historical genealogy within which the text(s)
are operating and thus to explore to what extent they constitute a reaction
to, even a retreat from, an immediate cultural past (for which Dante and

Mussato stand here), rather than a heroic leap forward from, or dramatic break with, this past. In the balance of this essay, then, I will further explore the narrative of fraternal struggle in *Parthenias* and in *Familiares* 10.4 to suggest, on the one hand, how the generational present (the brothers, Petrarch and Gherardo) tends to be reduced to the subjective struggles of an individual mind, and, on the other, how both of these forms of presentness (familial objective; individual subjective) at once aim to figure and to efface an intergenerational, historical process whereby Petrarch both appropriates and cancels the achievements of his late Duecento–early Trecento precursors.

An important example of this process may be seen at another point in the text where Silvius/Petrarch's hostility toward Monicus/Gherardo appears, in the form of a curious philological quibble. As Monicus attempts to argue the case for David and the Bible as alternatives to the Virgilian and Homeric classics, he is made by Petrarch to display a lack of even a narrowly biblical learning by giving a confused periphrasis for the river Jordan. Monicus first refers to two rivers flowing from a single source, which would, according to a prominent patristic tradition, be appropriate for the Tigris and Euphrates, both real features of Middle Eastern geography, but also, following Genesis 2:10–14, said to be two of the four rivers flowing out of Eden.[55] Monicus then corrects himself to speak of one river flowing from a double source, the Jor and the Dan, combining in the holy river, Jordan. In *Parthenias* the passage is as follows:

> Audisti quo monte duo fons unicus edit
> Flumina? sive ubinam geminis ex fontibus unum
> Flumen aquas, sacrumque caput cum nomine sumit
>   (ll. 62–64)

—————

> Haply you may have heard of the mountain where two
> mighty rivers spring from one source alone, or where there
> pours forth from two fountains one sacred stream which
> from them draws its source and its name and its waters?

In the letter we are presented with the following gloss:

> Fluvii duo uno de fonte, quorum primo quidem Monicus errore decipitur, sunt Tigris et Eufrates, noti amnes Armenie; fluvius autem unus

gemino de fonte, Iordanis et Iudee, quo multi sunt auctores, inter quos Ieronimus, illarum partium sedulus et diuturnus incola. (par. 29)

The two rivers from a single source concerning which Monicus commits his first error are the Tigris and Euphrates, well-known rivers of Armenia; the single river from a double source is the Jordan in Judea about which many authorities, including Jerome, long-time inhabitant of those regions, speak.

The passage has a key thematic role in evoking and defining the problematic relationship of the two brothers, who were earlier said to stem from a single source, their mother's womb (*Parthenias* 4–5: "una fuit genetrix" [one was our progenetrix]), but who risk arriving at two completely different destinations, given the danger in which Silvius is placing his soul (*Parthenias* 5: "at spes non una sepulcri" [but not the same hope for our lives beyond the grave]).[56] Moreover, it also points back to the equivocation in the dialectic of poetry and theology: are they two different modes of serving a single purpose, or do they share a single means, figurative language, but tend to very different ends? Finally, it may be taken as a hint at the obvious: that what the dialogic form of the pastoral presents as two voices is in fact one voice projecting itself as two, disguising and revealing its internal divisions.[57] This point is made clearest in the letter, of course, where Petrarch alone speaks, and Gherardo appears only in the indirect form of what his brother imagines he will think.[58] But it is also particularly apparent if one compares Petrarch's use of the eclogic form with the dialogic model provided by the del Virgilio–Dante exchange.[59]

But why, specifically, focus on this quibble about the two rivers from one source as against one river from two sources? The answer, I believe, is that Petrarch's humanistic learning is being flaunted at the expense of his brother, of medieval Latinity generally, and as we will soon see, of Dante as well. The notion of Tigris and Euphrates stemming from a single source is a medieval topos, with both biblical and classical antecedents, whose foremost *auctoritas* is Boethius' *Consolation of Philosophy*.[60] The topos, however, had it wrong, as a few medieval authors were in fact aware.[61] Petrarch might have come to his own perception of the problem from reading Lucan (*Pharsalia* 3.256–63). More likely, however, he read about the rivers in Pomponius Mela's *Chorographia*, a text he owned and annotated, and which he cites elsewhere in the *Familiares*.[62] When Mela discusses the rivers, he clearly assigns each its own distinct point of origin (3.8.76–77).

This, then, is the scholarly basis of the quibble, but the question remains: why does Petrarch choose to focus on it? The answer, for me, lies in the probable intertextual relationship between Monicus' words and a crucial passage from the end of Dante's *Purgatorio*:

> . . . Ëufratès e Tigri
> veder mi parve uscir d'una fontana,
> e, quasi amici, dipartirsi pigri.[63]
>   "O luce, o gloria de la gente umana,
> che acqua è questa che qui si dispiega
> da un principio e sé da sé lontana?"
>   Per cotal priego detto mi fu: "Priega
> Matelda che 'l ti dica." E qui rispuose,
> come fa chi da colpa si dislega,
>   la bella donna: "Questo e altre cose
> dette li son per me; e son sicura
> che l'acqua di Letè non gliel nascose."
>   E Bëatrice: "Forse maggior cura,
> che spesse volte la memoria priva,
> fatt' ha la mente sua ne li occhi oscura.
>   Ma vedi Eünoè che là diriva:
> menalo ad esso, e come tu se' usa,
> la tramortita sua virtù ravviva."
>   Come anima gentil, che non fa scusa,
> ma fa sua voglia de la voglia altrui
> tosto che è per segno fuor dischiusa;
>   così, poi che da essa preso fui,
> la bella donna mossesi, e a Stazio
> donnescamente disse: "Vien con lui."
>   S'io avessi, lettor, più lungo spazio
> da scrivere, i' pur cantere' in parte
> lo dolce ber che mai non m'avria sazio;
>   ma perché piene son tutte le carte
> ordite a questa cantica seconda,
> non mi lascia più ir lo fren de l'arte.

Io ritornai da la santissima onda
rifatto sì come piante novelle
rinovellate di novella fronda,

puro e disposto a salire a le stelle.

(*Purg.* 33.112–45)

. . . I seemed to see Euphrates and Tigris issuing from
a single fountain and, as if friends, separating slowly.

"O light, o glory of the human race, what water is this,
that spreads forth from one beginning and distances itself
from itself?"

To this request came the answer: "Beg Matelda to tell you."
And here the beautiful lady, like one who frees himself from
blame,

replied: "This and other things I have told him, and I am
sure the waters of Lethe have not hidden them from him."

And Beatrice: "Perhaps a greater care, which often robs
the memory, has darkened the eyes of his mind.

But see Eunoe that pours forth there: lead him to it and,
as is your custom, revive his languishing powers."

As a noble soul makes no excuse but makes another's will
its own as soon any sign discloses it:

So, having taken my hand, the beautiful lady moved, and
to Statius with gracious command she said, "Come with him."

If, reader, I had more space to write, I would continue to
sing in part the sweet drink that could never satiate me,

but because all the pages are filled that have been laid out
for this second canticle, the bridle of art permits me to go no
further.

I returned from the most holy wave refreshed, as new plants
are renewed with new leaves

pure and made ready to rise to the stars.[64]

Dante refers to the Tigris and Euphrates in order to return to the similarly
twinned Lethe and Eunoe, the rivers of forgetfulness and memory, immer-
sions in which frame his experience in Eden.[65] He deftly avoids specifying

whether the former rivers are being compared to the latter, or whether they are just different names for the same ones. In either case, he is playing on the traditional topoi associated with the Tigris and the Euphrates: their shared source and their origin in Eden. The link to Monicus' error comes not only from the fact that they are two rivers from one spring, but also that in both cases they originate on top of a mountain (see again *Parthenias* 62: "Audisti quo monte duo fons unicus edit flumina?" [you may have heard of the mountain where two . . . rivers spring forth from one source alone?]).

In other words, I believe that through Monicus/Gherardo, Petrarch is aiming squarely at Dante's "ignorant," "medieval" adoption of misinformation about which he could have learned the truth not only in classical texts but also from the early Christian Fathers (hence the specific reference to St. Jerome as a source of empirical information about the Jordan).[66] This surmise increases in probability given that Petrarch's annotated text of Mela contains one of his very rare explicit mentions of Dante's name, precisely in the form of a factual correction, a "nota contra Dantem" (note against Dante), on a topic that has interesting affinities with this one.[67] The point that Petrarch insists upon is that the *Chorographia* locates the burial place of the rebellious giant Typheus below the volcanic island of Ischia, rather than beneath Etna, where Dante, following classical authors such as Ovid (*Metamorphoses* 5.346–56), apparently puts it in *Paradiso* 8.67–70.[68]

So much, then, for the specific reference to Tigris and Euphrates. It is not, however, incidental that in quoting the passage in which that reference appears, I included the remainder of canto 33 *Purgatorio* as well. The point is to suggest what Petrarch might have felt were the larger stakes in this error of Monicus/Gherardo/Dante. The vision of the twinned rivers is only a prelude to a culminating experience of cleansing immersion that completes Dante-*personaggio*'s experience of spiritual purification and purgation that began in the very first canto of *Purgatorio* (1.121–36). This profound renewal (the word *novello* and its forms are used three times in two lines in canto 33, namely lines 143–44) then affords Dante unfettered access to the heavens above, that is, to the truest matter of theology.[69] For that matter, this event comes as the immediate sequel to the second of Beatrice's two commissions in as many cantos to return to our world, there to act as a quasi-biblical prophet (indeed, as an Evangelist [bearer of good *news*] in the tradition of John, to judge by the language employed),[70] who will recount the metamorphoses of the allegorical Chariot/Church (*Purgatorio*

32.100–160) and report the imminent advent of a "cinquecento dieci e cinque" (five hundred ten and five; 33.43) along with the vicissitudes of the mystical tree (33.31–78). It remains only to add the obvious: that, both in Petrarch's *Parthenias* and throughout the *Commedia,* the classically-inspired motif of the spring or source points to poetic inspiration, especially in conjunction with a mountaintop that, among other things, figures Parnassus, dwelling place of the Muses.[71] In other words, as much as any other passage in the *Commedia,* this one represents Dante's claim to the status of *theologus-poeta,* or, perhaps better, *scriba Dei*—the very claim that Petrarch is fiercely rejecting in his one-sided polemic with Gherardo.

Through the rivers quibble, then, Petrarch is using Monicus to attack an alternative poetry, like Dante's, that places itself in the tradition of David,[72] the "umile salmista" (humble psalmist) of *Purgatorio* 10.65;[73] a poetry that is avowedly "comic-popular" and thus "rustic,"[74] and that is at the same time patently entering the domain reserved for theology, which "deals with God and divine things"; a poetry, finally, that has extended the domain of pastoral beyond the classical world into sacred history.[75] Finally, it is suggestive that Petrarch should allude to Dante's account of the rivers of memory and forgetfulness while in the process of simultaneously recalling and repressing his illustrious precursor.

Perhaps repression is too strong a word. For if Dante is hidden in the letter and *Parthenias,* he is hidden in plain sight. As I have already suggested, the very combination of poem and authorial gloss is identified more closely with Dante than with any other author known to Petrarch. Moreover, as E. Kegel-Brinkgreve has argued,[76] an allusive contrast between Petrarch's classically-oriented project of neo-Virgilian epic, the *Africa,* and his early flirtation with vernacular poetry is established very early in *Parthenias.* Specifically, Silvius recounts his youthful literary development after a first encounter with Virgil, but before learning of Homer and returning to the path laid down by Virgil:[77]

> . . . Venerat etas
> fortior; audebam, nullo duce, iam per opacum
> ire nemus, nec lustra feris habitata timebam;
> mutatamque novo frangebam carmine vocem,
> emulus, et fama dulcedine tactus.
>
> (15–19)

———

But an age followed after bolder; I dared with no guide to make
my own way into the forest, dense [or "dark, lightless"] as it was,
unafraid of the savage beasts that roamed in it. There, in a voice
now changed, I broke into new song and new measures, lured
by the charm of false glory, driven by keen emulation.

Several elements in this passage connect directly, if in a complex manner,
to what Freccero has called "Dante's prologue scene" and his initial, failed
"journey without a guide."[78] The key of course, is the "opacum / . . . nemus,"
equivalent to Dante's "selva oscura" (*Inferno* 1.1),[79] together with the reference to an encounter with "feris," recalling Dante's three beasts.[80] Petrarch,
in other words, imagines his younger self, even more boldly than Dante,
entering unguided into the uncharted poetic *selva* of vernacular poetry
(hence the "changed voice"). Just like Dante, a guide presents himself—
first Homer, then Virgil—and leads him back onto the right path: in this
case, however, that path is the well-trodden tradition of classical epic.

The ironies here are multiple. Petrarch models himself closely on Dante
in describing his youthful flirtation with vernacular poetry, even as he
shamelessly claims to have had "nullo duce" (no guide) in that enterprise.
Moreover, although he, *just like Dante,* is saved from a perilous wilderness
by the advent of Virgil, for him this salvation entails turning away from a
vernacular *bello stilo* and a grand theological journey in favor of a neo-Latin
epic and, in the specific case at hand, of the Latin eclogic tradition. Given
what we have just seen of Petrarch's allusive manipulations of Dante's claims
to have achieved the perfection of a Christian pastoral, though on an epic
scale, we might conclude that Petrarch is also here polemically reinstituting a distinction between epic and bucolic that Dante seems to have blurred
in his style (by writing a work that ranges from the highest to the lowest
registers), in his choice of subject matter (an epic journey culminating in
the pastoral spaces of Eden and then the eternal Rose), and in the *Commedia*'s double imitation of Virgil as a poet both bucolic and epic (notably in
Purgatorio 22). In *Familiares* 10.4, indeed, Petrarch very specifically states
that the composition of his *Bucolicum Carmen* took the place of work on his
epic *Africa* (par. 10–11). At the same time, however, as will be discussed further below, in *Parthenias* he aligns himself with epic models—with Virgil as epic successor of Homer and with Homer himself—and in conclusion imagines a return to the deferred writing of the *Africa*.[81] It is possible,
furthermore, that the decision to write *twelve* eclogues as against the ten

"aurea mala" (golden apples; *Eclogue* 3.71) of Virgil recalls the twelve books of the *Aeneid*. In other words, while Dante in the *Commedia* undertakes a synthesis of epic and pastoral, Petrarch in *Parthenias* dramatizes an unresolved struggle between the two genres. As we will now see, in fact, even this attitude is in some sense Dantean: the Dante not of the *Commedia*, however, but rather of the Latin epistolary eclogues addressed to Giovanni del Virgilio.

6.

As already mentioned in section 2 of this essay, Giovanni del Virgilio, implicitly in the epitaph and explicitly in his first epistle to Dante, offers a proto-humanist, pre-Petrarchan critique of the use of the vernacular as the principal vehicle for his poetic ambitions. He urges Dante to write instead a long narrative poem in Latin on some contemporary military subject (1.25–34, 41–46), which would apparently lead to his crowning with the poetic laurel (1.35–40), perhaps alluding to Mussato's coronation in Padua four years earlier (1315), and tempts him with the name of "vates," poet-prophet (1.7, 19, 24; cf. 2.31, 36). Dante immediately and firmly rejected del Virgilio's suggestion, but also proved himself capable of following it by couching his reply in the form of a Virgilian eclogue adapted to epistolary form. In this way, as we saw in section 3, Dante Alighieri, and not Giovanni Boccaccio or Francis Petrarch, becomes the first late medieval author to revive the classical mode of pastoral.[82] Moreover, the importance of this achievement in literary historical terms is explicitly emphasized by del Virgilio in his second letter, where he deems Dante worthy of being ranked just behind Virgil: "A, divine senex, a sic eris alter ab illo! / Alter es, aut idem . . ." (Ah, divine old man [Dante], you will be second after him [Virgil]! Rather you are second, or you *are* him [3.33–34])—an assessment that cannot have pleased Petrarch. Nor would he have welcomed del Virgilio's suggestion, in the first letter, that Dante might be worthy of laureation, given Petrarch's reluctance to admit the existence of modern peers deserving of this honor.[83]

The main thrust of this essay is to suggest that Dante's Latin epistolary eclogues, as much as or even more than the Italian *Commedia*, are the object of Petrarchan allusion and imitation in *Parthenias* and *Familiares* 10.4. In section 3, I offered some evidence of formal analogies, including the imitation of the Virgilian pastoral, linking the Petrarchan textual complex to Dante and in particular to the eclogues. Now I would like to suggest that thematic, symbolic, narrative, and even lexical elements confirm that this Latin Dante is not only more of a presence in *Parthenias* than his vernacular avatar, but also more of a presence than Virgil himself, notwithstanding the fact that Petrarch's poem, at least in name, "impersonates" the great Roman *auctor*.[84]

In order to see these links clearly, we should begin by rehearsing the salient details of Dante's part in the exchange with del Virgilio. Dante's reply to del Virgilio's first *epistola metrica* is generally modeled on the first of the Virgilian *Eclogues,* with evident debts to some of the others. Dante speaks in the first person singular under the name of Tityrus, with whom, according to the tradition deriving from Servius' commentary, Virgil himself is identified. Tityrus recounts receiving a letter from Mopsus (del Virgilio) and reveals its contents to his younger companion, Melibeus.[85] For his part, Melibeus figures the sort of unlettered yet intensely curious person of business whom Dante had said in the *Convivio* his vernacular writings are aimed at educating, and whom del Virgilio had ridiculed in his first letter.[86]

Initially telling his protégé that del Virgilio's words are far too lofty for him to understand (echoing, with a certain irony, the humanist's sentiments), Tityrus then gives in to his pleas (2.5–27). Summarizing Mopsus' letter as an invitation to laureation in Bologna (33–35; see also 40–44, 50), he then insists that he fears to go to a place that is "ignara deorum" (ignorant of the Gods [2.41]) and instead, echoing the opening of *Paradiso* 25, imagines a return to Florence, there to be crowned.[87] Furthermore, he points out that Mopsus openly despises his

> comica . . . verba,
> tum quia femineo resonant ut trita labello
> tum quia Castalias pudet acceptare sorores
>
> (2.52–54)

---

lowly comic words, because they sound trite, as if from the lips of lower-class women, and because the Castalian sisters [i.e., the Muses] are ashamed to embrace them [translation mine]

Nonetheless, he says, he will send Mopsus "decem . . . vascula" (ten measures [2.64]) of milk from his "ovis gratissima" (most loved ewe [2.58]).

In section 3, I stressed that the Latin versus vernacular question, which constitutes the central concern of the first half of the del Virgilio–Dante exchange, is not explicitly at issue in the *Parthenias/Familiares* 10.4 duo. In section 4, however, we saw that *Parthenias* is shot through with echoes of the *Commedia* and contains a prominent allusion both to Petrarch's early flirtations with vernacular lyric and to his subsequent reconversion to classical Latin. This, then, is not so far from the balance that Dante strikes in his first eclogue between refusing to renounce the vernacular and his promise of "decem vascula," which del Virgilio, in the epitaph, takes to mean a full-blown *Bucolicum Carmen* modeled on Virgil's.[88] Even more to the point, however, is a tempting structural homology between the narratives of the two works. On the one hand, we find Dante entertaining and rejecting del Virgilio's blandishments to embrace a different and higher form of writing,[89] before reaffirming his commitment to vernacular verse (the "ovis gratissima" that is the *Commedia*). On the other, we find Petrarch/Silvius entertaining and rejecting Monicus/Gherardo's plea to embrace the verse of David, before reaffirming his commitment to the writing of the *Africa*.[90]

The second of Dante's two *Eclogues,* however, clinches the connection. To the first, del Virgilio responded with a letter of his own written in pastoral style, in which he abandoned the critique of vernacular poetry. Now, instead, he urges Dante to visit him in his humble "antrum" (cave) in Bologna (3.47–79), threatening to turn his attentions to "Musone" (i.e., Mussato)[91] if Dante allows his Ravennese patron or unwarranted fears for his safety in Bologna to deter him from the journey (3.80–89). According to the anonymous annotator of the exchange in Boccaccio's *Zibaldone laurenziano,* del Virgilio received a reply a year after his own poem was delivered to Dante, and, in fact, sometime after the latter's death in 1321.[92] Intricately structured, the second Dantean effort contains references to several of Virgil's eclogues,[93] as well as to del Virgilio's second metrical letter, whose ninety-seven verses it pointedly, and perhaps satirically, repeats.[94] After a characteristic *exordium* describing the temporal setting with reference to the golden fleece of Jason (4.1–2),[95] Dante recounts, now in the third person, the story of the same Tityrus in conversation with another shepherd, Alphesibeus.[96] Alphesibeus speaks to Tityrus/Dante of his surprise that Mopsus/del Virgilio is pleased to live among the "arida Ciclopum . . . quod saxa sub Ethna" (parched rocks of the Cyclops under Etna [4.25–27; echoing *Aeneid* 1.201]), a clearly pejorative reference to Bologna and environs, and, in the context of what has been said above, a curious anticipation of Petrarch's critique of Dante's geographical mythography (namely, the question of whether Typheus is buried under Ischia or Etna). Subsequently, the young Melibeus arrives, out of breath, to deliver a musical message from Mopsus — del Virgilio's second verse letter inviting Tityrus to visit him (4.28–43). In response to the pleas of his two companions to remain with them in Pelorus, that is, Ravenna, Tityrus says that while he would rather not abandon them, nonetheless he *would* go for the sake of his love of Mopsus, "ni te, Polipheme, timerem" — were it not that he fears the dangers presented by the Cyclops, Polyphemus (4.43–75, esp. 75).[97] Del Virgilio's second proposal for a visit to Bologna having been elegantly declined, the letter then ends with the curious framing device noted above.

Clearly, del Virgilio's invitation to Dante to join him in his "antrum" parallels Monicus/Gherardo's invitation to Silvius to join him in the "antrum" of Montrieux (del Virgilio 3.3, 48, 53, 65, 78, 82; *Parthenias* 46–49). Similarly, Monicus' assurances about his dwelling place echo del Virgilio's (del Virgilio 3.72–83; *Parthenias* 48–49), while Silvius' refusal is anticipated by that of Tityrus. More obviously still, just like *Parthenias* and *Familiares* 4.10, the Dantean eclogue is positively obsessed with the one-eyed tribe of the Cyclops, especially with Polyphemus — the monstrous opponent of Virgilian Ulysses and Homeric Odysseus, as of Petrarch's Africanus — who dwells in a bloody cave (again, "antrum," Dante 4.47; *Parthenias* 115). In fact, after Tityrus' initial expression of fear, Alphesibeus goes on at some length about the horrors of the savage giant:

> Quis Poliphemon . . . non horreat . . .
> assuetum rictus humano sanguine tingui,
> tempore iam ex illo quando Galathea relicti
> Acidis heu misere discerpere viscera vidit?
> Vix illa evasit: an vis valuisset amoris,
> effera dum rabies tanta perferbuit ira?
> Quid, quod Achemenides, sociorum cede cruentem
> tantum prospiciens, animam vix claudere quivit?
>
> (4.76–83)

Who would not shudder at Polyphemus . . . wont as he is to dye
his jaws in human blood, since that time when Galatea beheld
him tear the flesh of poor deserted Acis—alas miserable one!
[She] scarce herself escaped. Would love's might have kept its
hold when the mad frenzy boiled up in such wrath? And what
of Achmenides [abandoned companion of Ulysses] who only
looking on him [the Cyclops] gory with the slaughter of his
comrades, could scarce keep the breath within his body?

Earlier I mentioned that Petrarch's Polyphemus has no source in Virgil's
Eclogues. Rather, we now see, it was Dante who first plucked this deformed
figure of a shepherd out of the *Metamorphoses* (where the story of Galatea
and Acis is told at 13.750–897),[98] and out of Virgil's retelling of the Homeric Polyphemus episode through the eyes of abandoned Achemenides in
Aeneid 3.588–654 (which Ovid then imitated in *Metamorphoses* 14.154–222). It
was Dante who first placed Polyphemus in the pastoral world. From Dante,
Petrarch almost certainly derived the image;[99] from Dante, he learned to use
the subhuman monstrosity of Polyphemus to represent the otherness of an
alternative way of life, Gherardo's, that he has both loved and rejected.[100]

At the same time, of course, Petrarch turns Dante's monster against its
creator, or rather, turns the creator into his monster, like the Frankenstein
of the movies. Like Gherardo, indeed even more so than Gherardo, Dante
represents for Petrarch alternatives rejected or at least resisted. From Petrarch's point of view, as we have seen, Dante's use of his neo-Virgilian
Eclogues to decline both of Giovanni del Virgilio's invitations was also his
final refusal to accept membership in the new cultural club, neo-Latin humanism, of which he, Petrarch, fully intended to become the *primus inter
pares.* At the same time, Dante, far more than Mussato, whose theories had
relatively little to do with his practice, represents for Petrarch the radical
and menacing fusion of poetry with theology.

In other words, when Petrarch designates Polyphemus as an implicit
substitute and scapegoat for theology and for Gherardo, he is both imitating Dante and adding him to the secret list of those symbolically enfolded in
the Cyclops' all-purpose alterity and monstrosity. In Petrarch's quest to establish his own autonomous identity as poet, which also requires that poetry
be singled out as an autonomous field of activity,[101] Monicus/Gherardo's
theological purity represents a threat, but also a fixed dialectical pole in relation to which Silvius/Francesco can define himself and his vocation.

In many ways, however, Dante represents the proximate historical "condition of possibility" for Petrarch's poetic enterprise. Dante's intense self-reflexivity—as alive in the two autobiographical pastoral epistles as it was in the auto-exegesis of the *Vita nova,* the *Convivio,* and, perhaps, the *Epistle to Cangrande,* and as it was in the *poeta-personaggio* dyad of the *Commedia*—shows the way to Petrarch's different style of self-consciousness, and never more obviously than in the autobiographical poem-gloss pairing of *Parthenias* and *Familiares* 10.4. Dante's resuscitation of Virgil—dramatically in the *Commedia,* "generically" in his eclogic epistles—collapses the difference between classical past and medieval present in ways that Petrarch repeatedly imitates,[102] even as he also appropriates, without acknowledgment, the (proto-)humanism of Lovati, Mussato, and Giovanni del Virgilio. But the lines between past and present are not the only boundaries violated by Dante: he also consistently effaces distinctions, basic for Petrarch, between high and low styles, epic and pastoral, theology and poetry, Latin and Italian. Thus he is not only the single greatest threat to Petrarch's claim to uniqueness, both as reviver of the classical past and as originator of a creative modernity; he also represents a subversion *avant la lettre* of the primary ideological grounds on which Petrarch—at least the Petrarch of *Parthenias* and the letter to Gherardo—stakes such a claim.

7.

Petrarch goes to elaborate lengths in *Familiares* 10.4 to mask the fact that Dante is the source, the *fons,* in a sense both intermediate and primary, of the materials from which *Bucolicum Carmen* 1 and *Familiares* 10.4 are made. Instead, Petrarch clearly means for his readers, contemporary and future, to understand the two works both as expressing his aspiration to join the company of the classical epic poets, Virgil *and* Homer, and as embodying his success in doing so. As he tells the story of how Scipio Africanus defeated Polyphemus/Hannibal—and tells how he has told/will tell that story in the *Africa*—he also fantasizes his own triumph over the immediate cultural past, a triumph seemingly confirmed by the extraordinary prestige he enjoyed during his own lifetime and in the generations that immediately followed it.

The process of masking is at least twofold, and each of the strategies adopted has been converted by scholarship of the last two centuries into a definition of the essence of a period called the "Renaissance." On the one hand, Petrarch turns back to long-dead, far distant, and even, in the case of Homer, literally unreadable (by him) authors,[103] imagining a familial, conversational relationship with them. In this way, following the familiar trope of historical rebirth, the distant past becomes the yesterday of the present, while the empirical "yesterday," the later Middle Ages of Mussato and of Dante, silently falls away into "the dark backward and abysm of time." On the other hand, and at the same time, Petrarch relocates his historical ambivalence and sense of conflict with his immediate precursors into his relationship with his contemporary and "twin," Gherardo, and thence into an interior psychomachia. His obsessive concern with the temporality of an endlessly wavering present moment of indecision between modes of being and of acting paradoxically also releases him from the strict bonds of chronological historicity.

The effacement of Petrarch's contingent, derivative, and uncertain place in recent cultural history—which this essay has represented in the emblematic persons of Mussato, del Virgilio, and Dante—is what is most profoundly at stake in *Parthenias* and *Familiares* 10.4, rather than, as the criticism has more commonly supposed, the emergence of modern subjectivity and/or of secular historical consciousness (though one might argue that the former begets the latter, or *is* in fact this). The Petrarch who emerges from this investigation into the inter- and intra-textual mechanisms of the eclogue-letter pairing is not defined either by his unprecedented recovery of the classical past or by his traumatic discovery of an inner self, but rather by the strategies of avoidance he deploys: strategies which allow him the possibility of "misrecognizing" *who* and even *when* he is by denying his most immediate genealogical filiations.

One final point remains to be made. For the most part, I have treated *Parthenias* and *Familiares* 10.4 as mutually reinforcing elements in an ideologically compact textual complex. I did, however, note one very significant discrepancy between the two—the letter's failure to gloss a key episode in Silvius' account of his poetic apprenticeship, which is also a way of obscuring an important Dantean element of the eclogue. At least one more major shift between the two deserves to be examined. At the end of *Parthenias*, as Giuseppe Mazzotta has observed, Silvius/Petrarch aligns himself with

Orpheus—the arch-poet of antiquity.[104] At the end of *Familiares* 10.4, Orpheus does not appear at all. Why is this?

One might, for example, hypothesize that Orpheus, the poet who descends into the underworld by the power of his song alone, looks too much like the Dante of the *Commedia.* Or one might stress that Orpheus is the poet-theologian *par excellence,* effecting precisely the union that Petrarch seems to be so strenuously resisting in his self-exegesis.[105] In any event, in the letter, as against the eclogue it glosses, Petrarch's ideal predecessor turns out to be Homer, rather than Orpheus, Dante, or Virgil: Homer, whom, he acknowledges, he has only met indirectly, partially, and belatedly (par. 25–26), Homer, whose poetry he will never know *as poetry.* While the Greek poet, whom Dante had named "quel segnor de l'altissimo canto / che sovra li altri com' aquila vola" (that lord of highest song who soars above the others like an eagle [*Inf.* 4.95–96]), represents the heights of poetic fame to which Petrarch yearns to soar, he also constitutes no real threat: no comparison, especially no stylistic comparison, can be made between him and Petrarch, as could be made with either Virgil or Dante.[106]

The latter point is explored more openly by Petrarch in the penultimate letter of the *Familiares,* a letter written *as if in response to* an epistolary complaint originating with "Homer" himself (24.12).[107] The key positioning of that letter as the culmination of the sequence of epistles to the ancients—immediately after the verse epistle (24.11) to Virgil[108]—might even suggest that the twenty-four-book structure of the *Familiares* imitates that of the Homeric epics, and the *Odyssey* in particular,[109] just as we have seen that the twelve-poem sequence of the *Bucolicum Carmen* may allude to the twelve books of the *Aeneid.* At the same time, however, Petrarch specifically stresses that he is unable to imitate Homer's versification as he had done with that of Horace and of Virgil in the immediately preceding letters (par. 4–5).

For this reason as well, it is crucial that Petrarch has chosen to focus on the figure of Polyphemus in *Parthenias* and *Familiares* 10.4, whose defeat, we and he know, came at the hands not of Scipio but of Odysseus/ Ulysses, the trickster and rhetorical genius who saved and established his identity by concealing it behind the name of "Nobody" (a feature of the story on which Petrarch appears to pun in *Parthenias,* when he says: "Nemo antra coactus / nostra petit" [No-one seeks out our caves constrained; 48–49]).[110] Thus, as a number of critics have noted, Petrarch's restless quest for human knowledge and literary fame, his choice of a humanist activism over theological retreat, recalls the itinerary of Dante's most noted infernal humanist, Ulisse,[111] who for Dante was the diabolical yet fascinating other of his own biblical prophetic mission.[112] Petrarch's choice of Homer and Odysseus/Ulysses/Ulisse as his models, which reinforces his cultural and linguistic classicism, again clearly stakes out his opposition to two defining elements of Dante's poetics—its double turn to theology and to the vernacular—even as it reveals yet another hidden debt to his Florentine predecessor. And that double refusal in turn determines the anachronism, and the inevitable failure, of the *Africa,* to which Petrarch had firmly linked his poetic identity, but which even in 1349—the ostensible date of the letter's composition—he had virtually abandoned. In effect, one might say, Petrarch's attempt to reproduce the poetic achievements of Virgil in his own Latin epic based on Roman history gets lost in the space between the unacknowledgeable modernity of Dante (and his Ulisse) and the unreadable, indecipherable pastness of Homer (and his Odysseus).

Paradoxically, of course, despite the fact that Petrarch's modernity in the letter is clearly indebted to Dante's adventures in poetic self-definition, both in Latin (the *Eclogues*) and in Italian (the self-commentaries; the protracted conversation of Dante-*personaggio* with "Virgilio"; the figure of Ulisse), and despite the fact that in fundamental ways his attitudes there are conservative and reactionary, nonetheless, Petrarch still inevitably seems the more modern of the two, precisely in the ambivalence and *réssentiment,* alternately implicit and explicit, conscious or not, that haunt his oeuvre throughout, with *Parthenias* and *Familiares* 10.4 no exceptions to the rule.

NOTES

1. On the paired topoi of Petrarch as "the first modern man" and "the first modern author," see, among others, Arnaud Tripet, *Pétrarque, ou la connaissance de soi* (Genève: Droz, 1967); John Freccero, "The Fig Tree and the Laurel: Petrarch's Poetics," *Diacritics* 5 (1975): 34–40; Ugo Dotti, *Petrarca e la scoperta della coscienza moderna* (Milan: Feltrinelli, 1978); Thomas Greene, *The Light in Troy: Imitation and Discovery in Renaissance Poetry* (New Haven: Yale University Press, 1982); Dolora A. Wojciehowski, *Old Masters, New Subjects: Early Modern and Poststructuralist Theories of Will* (Stanford, Calif.: Stanford University Press, 1995). See also Giuseppe Mazzotta's critique of the critical discourse concerning the Petrarchan

self in "The *Canzoniere* and the Language of the Self," in *The Worlds of Petrarch* (Durham, N.C.: Duke University Press, 1993), 58–79. On the question of Petrarch's verbal invention of the idea of "rinascita" and his embodiment of its various cultural and psychic traits, see Theodor E. Mommsen, "Petrarch's Conception of the Dark Ages," in *Medieval and Renaissance Studies,* ed. Eugene Rice (Ithaca, N.Y.: Cornell University Press, 1959), 106–29; Wallace K. Ferguson, "Humanist Views of the Renaissance," *American Historical Review* 45 (1939): 1–28, and *The Renaissance in Historical Thought* (Cambridge, Mass.: Riverside Press, 1948); Franco Simone, *La coscienza della rinascita negli umanisti francesi* (Rome: Edizioni di Storia e Letteratura, 1949). See also my consideration of this historiographical topos in "Petrarch's Middle Age: Memory, Imagination, History, and the 'Ascent of Mt. Ventoux,'" *Stanford Italian Review* 10 (1991): 5–43.

2. In Dotti's formulation (*Petrarca, 7*), Petrarch is "senza storia." Although Dotti specifically refers to the internal history of Petrarch's *Rvf,* the scholarly tendency, and Petrarch's complicity in it, is more general. To take a recent example of the phenomenon: Carol Quillen's in many ways excellent historicization of Petrarch as reader vis-à-vis Augustine (*Rereading the Renaissance: Petrarch, Augustine, and the Language of Humanism* [Ann Arbor: University of Michigan Press, 1998]) is marred by the absence of any reference to the historical evolution of practices of reading between the fifth and the fourteenth centuries.

3. For Petrarch's specific textual debts to Dante, see Aldo S. Bernardo, "Petrarch's Attitude toward Dante," *PMLA* 70 (1955): 488–517; Giuseppe Billanovich, esp. "L'altro stil nuovo: Da Dante teologo a Petrarca filologo," *Studi petrarcheschi* n.s. 11 (1994): 1–98, and "Tra Dante e Petrarca," *Italia medioevale e umanistica* 8 (1965) 1–44; Marco Santagata, "Presenze di Dante 'comico' nel *Canzoniere* del Petrarca," *Giornale storico della letteratura italiana* 146 (1969): 163–211, and his notes in Francesco Petrarca, *Canzoniere,* ed. Marco Santagata (Milan: Mondadori, 1996) (see esp. the index at 1510–23); Nancy J. Vickers, "Re-membering Dante: Petrarch's 'Chiare, fresche et dolci acque,'" *MLN* 96 (1981): 1–11; Freccero, "The Fig Tree and the Laurel"; Paolo Trovato, *Dante in Petrarca: Per un inventario dei dantismi nei "Rerum vulgarium fragmenta"* (Florence: Olschki, 1979); Franco Suitner, *Petrarca e la tradizione stilnovistica* (Florence: Olschki, 1977); Bortolo Martinelli, "Dante nei *Rerum Vulgarium Fragmenta,*" *Italianistica* 10 (1981): 122–31; G. Paparelli, "Due modi opposti di leggere Dante: Petrarca e Boccaccio," in *Giovanni Boccaccio editore e interprete di Dante,* ed. Società Dantesca Italiana (Florence: Olschki, 1979), 73–90; Margaret Waller, *Petrarch's Poetics and Literary Theory* (Amherst: University of Massachusetts Press, 1980); Giuseppe Velli, "Il Dante di Francesco Petrarca," *Studi petrarcheschi* n.s. 2 (1985): 185–99; Mazzotta, *The Worlds*; Ascoli, "Petrarch's Middle Age," esp. 12–13 and nn.; Marco Baglio, "Presenze dantesche nel Petrarca latino," *Studi petrarcheschi* n.s. 9 (1992): 77–136 (focused on echoes of the *Commedia* in the Latin Petrarch); Enrico Fenzi, "Tra Dante e Petrarca: Il fantasma di Ulisse," in *Saggi petrarcheschi* (Fiesole: Cadmo, 2003), 493–517; Giulio Ferroni, "Tra Dante

e Petrarca," in *Ulisse: Archeologia dell'uomo moderno,* ed. Piero Boitani and Richard Ambrosini (Rome: Bulzoni, 1998), 165–85. See Michele Feo, "Petrarca, Francesco," in *Enciclopedia dantesca,* 6 vols., ed. Umberto Bosco (Rome: Istituto della Enciclopedia Italiana, 1973), 4:450–58, for a judicious review of the relationship, which foregrounds the differences in both style and ideology that separate the two great writers, as well as a rehearsal of the extensive early bibliography on the topic. Additional examples will appear later in this essay.

4. On Petrarch's treatment of Dante in 21.15, see Feo, "Petrarca," in *Enciclopedia dantesca,* 4:451 (and the extensive bibliography on 457–58); Bernardo, "Petrarch's Attitude"; Giuseppe Billanovich, "L'altro stil nuovo," 87–92 passim; Paparelli, "Due modi opposti"; G. Tanturli, "Il disprezzo per Dante del Petrarca," *Rinascimento* 2nd ser. 25 (1985): 199–219; Robert Lerner, "Petrarch's Coolness toward Dante: A Conflict of 'Humanisms,'" in *Intellectuals and Writers in Fourteenth-Century Europe,* ed. Piero Boitani and Anna Torti (Tubingen: G. Narr, 1986), 204–25; Fenzi, "Tra Dante e Petrarca."

5. See Albert Russell Ascoli, *Dante and the Making of a Modern Author* (Cambridge: Cambridge University Press, 2008), chs. 1 and 7.

6. Throughout this essay, references to and quotations from Petrarch's *Bucolicum Carmen* are taken from the Thomas G. Bergin edition (New Haven: Yale University Press, 1974), as are translations of the text. References to the *Familiares* are to the Vittorio Rossi edition (Florence: Sansoni, 1933–42), while translations are adapted from Aldo Bernardo et al. (Baltimore: Johns Hopkins University Press, 1982–85).

7. Although the first poem of the *Bucolicum Carmen* and, to a lesser extent, *Familiares* 10.4 have been the subject of philological discussion (see n. 28 below), as well as of studies dedicated primarily to the history of the eclogic form (see nn. 26–28 below) and to the topos of the "poet-theologian" (see nn. 22, 49 below), neither has received substantial interpretive attention, with the notable exceptions of Bernardo, "Petrarch's Attitude"; Thomas Greene, "Petrarch *Viator*: The Displacements of Heroism," in *The Vulnerable Text: Essays on Renaissance Literature* (New York: Columbia University Press, 1986), 18–45; and Mazzotta, "Humanism and Monastic Spirituality," in *The Worlds of Petrarch,* 147–66. As will appear, I owe a special debt to Greene's reading of 10.4.

8. Citations are to Dante Alighieri, *Le egloghe,* in vol. 2 of *Opere minori,* ed. Enzo Cecchini (Milan and Naples: Ricciardi, 1979). Translations are from Philip H. Wicksteed and Edmund Gardner, *Dante and Giovanni del Virgilio: Including a Critical Edition of Dante's 'Ecloghae Latinae' and of the Poetic Remains of Giovanni del Virgilio* (Westminster: Constable, 1902) with my emendations in brackets. The numeration of the epistles (del Virgilio, 1 and 3; Dante, 2 and 4) follows the traditional usage. On Giovanni del Virgilio in general, see Carlo Battisti, "Le egloghe dantesche," *Studi danteschi* 33 (1955–56): 91–94; Giuseppe Vecchi, "Giovanni del Virgilio e Dante: La polemica tra latino e volgare nella corrispondenza poetica," in

Dante e Bologna nei tempi di Dante, ed. Facoltà di Lettere e Filosofia dell'Università di Bologna (Bologna: Commissione dei Testi in Lingua, 1967), 61–76; Guido Martellotti, "Giovanni del Virgilio," in *Enciclopedia dantesca,* 3:193–94; Giuseppe Billanovich, "Tra Dante e Petrarca," 17–19; Velli, "Sul linguaggio letterario di Giovanni del Virgilio," *Italia medioevale e umanistica* 24 (1981): 137–58; Gary Cestaro, "Giovanni del Virgilio," in *The Dante Encyclopedia,* ed. Richard Lansing (New York: Garland, 2000), 863–64; Ronald Witt, *"In the Footsteps of the Ancients": The Origins of Humanism from Lovato to Bruni* (Leiden: Brill, 2000), 236–38. For some of the small number of works attributed to him independently of the exchange, see his commentary on Ovid's *Metamorphoses* (in Fausto Ghisalberti, ed., "Giovanni del Virgilio espositore delle *Metamorfosi,*" *Giornale dantesco* 34 [1933]: 3–107); the *Diaffonus,* an earlier, non-eclogic verse epistolary exchange with one ser Nuzio marchigiano (in Enrico Carrara, ed., *Atti e memorie della deputazione di storia patria per le provincie di Romagna,* ser. 4, 15 [1925]: 5–54); Paul O. Kristeller, "Un' 'Ars Dictaminis' di Giovanni del Virgilio," *Italia medioevale e umanistica* 4 (1961): 181–200; Gian Carlo Alessio, "I trattati grammaticali di Giovanni del Virgilio," *Italia medioevale e umanistica* 24 (1981): 159–212. The exchange is discussed at length later in this essay. See esp. section 6 as well as nn. 12, 26, 59, 74 below.

9. On the early humanists, see Giuseppe Billanovich, *Petrarca e il primo umanesimo* (Padua: Edizioni Antenore, 1996), and "Tra Dante e Petrarca"; Guido Billanovich, "'Veterum vestigia vatum' nei carmi dei preumanisti padovani," *Italia medioevale e umanistica* 5 (1958): 155–243; Roberto Weiss, *The Renaissance Discovery of Classical Antiquity* (Oxford: Blackwell, 1969); Witt, *"In the Footsteps."* On Mussato specifically, see Alfredo Galletti, "La ragione poetica di Albertino Mussato e i poeti teologi," in *Scritti varii di erudizione e di critica in onore di Rodolfo Renier (con xx tavole fuori testo)* (Turin: Fratelli Bocca, 1912), 331–59; E. R. Curtius, *European Literature and the Latin Middle Ages,* trans. Willard R. Trask (Princeton: Princeton University Press, 1953), 215–21; Gustavo Vinay, "Studi sul Mussato I: Il Mussato e l'estetica medievale," *Giornale storico della letteratura italiana* 126 (1949): 113–59; Manlio Dazzi, *Il Mussato preumanista (1261–1329): L'ambiente e l'opera* (Vicenza: Neri Pozza, 1964); Giuseppe Billanovich, "I primi umanisti e le tradizioni dei classici latini," in *Petrarca e il primo umanesimo,* 124–30; Giorgio Ronconi, *Le origini delle dispute umanistiche sulla poesia (Mussato e Petrarca)* (Rome: Bulzoni, 1976), esp. 20–46; Guido Martellotti, "Mussato," in *Enciclopedia dantesca,* 3:1066–68; Giorgio Padoan, "Tra Dante e Mussato: I. Tonalità dantesche nella *Historia Augusta* di Albertino Mussato, II. A Pisa, la cancelleria imperiale e Dante," *Quaderni veneti* 24 (1996): 27–46; Ronald Witt, "Coluccio Salutati and the Conception of the *Poeta Theologus* in the Fourteenth Century," *Renaissance Quarterly* 30 (1977): 540–42, and *"In the Footsteps,"* 117–73; Jean-Frédéric Chevalier, "Introduction," in Albertino Mussato, *Écérinide, Épitres métriques sur la poésie, Songe,* ed. and trans. Jean-Frédéric Chevalier (Paris: Les Belles Lettres, 2000), esp. xi–xc.

10. For Petrarch's coronation, see *Familiares* 4.2–8 in *Rerum familiarum libri,* vol. 1, trans. and ed. Aldo S. Bernardo (Albany: State University of New York Press,

1975), and the coronation oration (*Collatio laureationis,* in Petrarch, *Scritti inediti di Francesco Petrarca,* ed. Attilio Hortis [Trieste: Tipografia del Lloyd Austro-Ungarico, 1874], 311–28; trans. in Ernest Hatch Wilkins, *Studies in the Life and Works of Petrarch* [Cambridge, Mass.: The Medieval Academy of America, 1955], 300–313). For the claim to uniqueness, see esp. *Familiares* 4.6–7 and the *Collatio* (316–17). One might argue that Petrarch refers specifically to a coronation in Rome—but he also seems to suggest that a Parisian laurel would have been legitimate, if inferior to the Roman one. For Mussato's laureation, see again n. 9 above. We can reasonably infer Petrarch's knowledge of it. His *Epistola Metrica* 2.10.67–74 is suggestive but not conclusive (Giuseppe Billanovich, *Petrarca letterato. I. Lo scrittoio del Petrarca* [Rome: Edizioni di "Storia e letteratura," 1947], 69 and n. 1, 121–22 and n. 1, 148 n. 2, and "L'altro stil nuovo," 86–87). See also Michele Feo, "Petrarca prima prima della laurea: Una corrispondenza poetica ritrovata," *Quaderni petrarcheschi* 4 (1987): 42–46. Petrarch knew some works of Mussato and his teacher Lovato: Giuseppe Billanovich, "I primi umanisti," 124, cites references to Lovato (as poet) and Mussato (as historian) in the *Rerum memorandarum libri,* ed. Giuseppe Billanovich, vol. 14 in *Edizione nazionale delle opere di Francesco Petrarca* (Florence: Sansoni, 1943), 2.61 and 4.118 (cf. 4.39), respectively. See also nn. 22, 49 below, and Witt, "*In the Footsteps,*" 236 and nn. These comments are prior to either of the works discussed here (i.e., 1343–45). The topic of a possible laureation for Dante is raised by del Virgilio in his first epistle to Dante (del Virgilio 1.35–40; Dante 2.33–35 et passim). The *Commedia* also alludes to the possibility of its author undergoing this ceremony or a similar one (*Par.* 1.28–36; *Par.* 25.1–12). See Eduardo Fumagalli, "Canto XXV," in *Lectura Dantis Turicensis. Paradiso,* ed. Georges Güntert and Michelangelo Picone (Florence: Cesati, 2002), nn. 76 and 82.

11. For Boccaccio's key role in promoting and defending Dante, see Giuseppe Billanovich, "La leggenda dantesca del Boccaccio: Dalla lettera di Ilaro al *Trattatello in laude di Dante,*" *Studi danteschi* 28 (1949): 45–144; for his role in mediating Petrarch's attitude toward Dante, see Giuseppe Billanovich, *Petrarca letterato*; Paolazzi, "Petrarca, Boccaccio e il *Trattatello in laude di Dante,*" in *Dante e la "Comedia" nel Trecento* (Milan: Vita e Pensiero, 1989), 131–221 (first published in *Studi danteschi* 55 [1983]: 165–249). See also nn. 12, 23, 24, 28, 43, 59 below; cf. n. 52.

12. Cited from Giovanni Boccaccio, *Trattatello in laude di Dante,* ed. Pier Giorgio Ricci, in *Opera Omnia, Volume III: Amorosa Visione; Ninfale Fiesolano; Vita di Dante,* ed. Vittore Branca (Milan: Mondadori, 1974), 2nd ed., par. 65; 511 (cf. 1st ed., par. 91, 459). The translation is adapted from Wicksteed and Gardner, *Dante and Giovanni del Virgilio,* 174–75. See also Curtius, *European Literature,* 214; Augusto Campani, "Epitafi," in *Enciclopedia dantesca,* 2:710–13. The authenticity of the epitaph, of the exchange between Dante and del Virgilio, and of del Virgilio's later epistolary eclogue to Albertino Mussato have all been disputed. Boccaccio's *Zibaldone laurenziano* is the earliest source for all five epistles, and he is the prime suspect for those who think they are forged. For the relevant portions of the *Zibaldone,* see Giorgio Padoan, "Giovanni Boccaccio e la rinascita dello stile bucolico,"

in idem, *Il Boccaccio: Le muse, il Parnaso, e l'Arno* (Florence: Olschki, 1978), 163–73, building on Enzo Cecchini, "Giovanni del Virgilio, Dante, Boccaccio: Appunti su un'attribuzione controversa," *Italia medioevale e umanistica* 14 (1971): 27–44. Also important are the anonymous annotations to this part of the *Zibaldone,* which are frequently attributed to Boccaccio, though written in a hand other than his (Padoan, "Giovanni Boccaccio," 173–80, 188–91, 197 et passim; and see also nn. 85, 88, 96, 97 below). Boccaccio later compiled an anthology of eclogues that included those of Virgil, Dante, del Virgilio, Petrarch, Checco da Mileto, and himself, as well as the introductory letter to Martin da Signa (Giuseppe Billanovich and F. Cáda, "Testi bucolici nella biblioteca del Boccaccio," *Italia medioevale e umanistica* 4 [1961]: 201–21). The *Epitaph* appears only in the *Trattatello.* However, if the exchange was a Boccaccian forgery, both it and the Mussato eclogue must be so as well, since both refer to Dante's last works as pastorals. The case for forgery was most recently made by Aldo Rossi ("Dante nella prospettiva del Boccaccio," *Studi danteschi* 37 [1960]: 63–139; "Dante, Boccaccio, e la laurea poetica," *Paragone* n.s. 13 [1962]: 3–41; "Il carme di Giovanni del Virgilio a Dante," *Studi danteschi* 40 [1963]: 133–269; "Il Boccaccio autore della corrispondenza Dante-Giovanni del Virgilio," *Miscellanea storica della Valdelsa* 69 [1963]: 130–72; "Dossier di un'attribuzione: Dieci anni dopo," *Paragone* n.s. 36 [1968]: 61–125); Battisti summarizes earlier claims of this kind ("Le egloghe," 64–68), while himself asserting the poems' authenticity. Prominent in the chorus of pro-authenticity scholarship are Giorgio Padoan, reviews of Aldo Rossi essays cited above, in *Studi sul Boccaccio* 1 (1963): 517–40, 2 (1964): 475–507, and 5 (1968): 365–68; Guido Martellotti "Dalla tenzone al carme bucolico: Giovanni del Virgilio, Dante, Boccaccio," in *Dante e Boccaccio e altri scrittori dall'Umanesimo al Romanticismo* (Florence: Olschki, 1983), 82–83 (first published in *Italia medioevale e umanistica* 7 [1964]: 325–36); Martellotti, "La riscoperta dello stile bucolico (da Dante al Boccaccio)," in *Dante e Boccaccio e altri scrittori dall'Umanesimo al Romanticismo,* 91–92 (first published 1966, in *Atti del Convegno di Studi 'Dante e la Cultura Veneta,* 335–46); Martellotti, "Le egloghe," in *Enciclopedia dantesca,* 2:645; Cecchini, "Giovanni del Virgilio"; the "Introduzione" in *Le egloghe,* ed. and trans. Giorgio Brugnoli and Riccardo Scarcia (Milan and Naples: Ricciardi, 1980), xi–xiv, et passim. See also Giuseppe Billanovich, "Giovanni del Virgilio, Pietro da Moglio, Francesco da Fiano," *Italia medioevale e umanistica,* part 1 in 6 (1963): 203–34, part 2 in 7 (1964): 279–324, who explores the complex afterlife of the exchange in the later fourteenth century (pt. 1, 206–10, 221–34, passim); see also Padoan, "Giovanni Boccaccio," 189–91. I will assume the authenticity of both the epitaph and the epistles, although the only requirement for my argument is that Petrarch knew the documents and believed them to be authentic, a claim which much of this essay will substantiate.

   13. On the significance of the appellation *auctor* in the later Middle Ages, see M. D. Chenu, "Auctor, Actor, Autor," *Bulletin du Cange: Archivium Latinitas Medii Aevi* 3 (1927): 81–86, and Alastair J. Minnis, *Medieval Theory of Authorship:*

Scholastic Literary Attitudes in the Later Middle Ages, 2nd ed. (Philadelphia: University of Pennsylvania Press, 1988). For Dante's rehearsal, transformation, and appropriation of the term, see esp. Zygmunt Barański, "Dante Alighieri: Experimentation and (Self-) Exegesis," in *The Cambridge History of Literary Criticism,* vol. 2, *The Middle Ages,* ed. Alastair Minnis and Ian Johnson (Cambridge: Cambridge University Press, 2005), 561–82, and Ascoli, *Dante.*

14. Curtius, *European Literature,* 214–15; Eugenio Chiarini, "I 'decem vascula' della prima ecloga dantesca," in *Dante e Bologna nei tempi di Dante,* ed. Facoltà di Lettere e Filosofia dell'Università di Bologna (Bologna: Commissione dei Testi di Lingua, 1967), 79.

15. See Vecchi, "Giovanni del Virgilio"; also nn. 74, 86, 88, 89 below.

16. The eclogue to Mussato (begun ca. 1325, completed 1327) follows the dialogic model used by Dante but not del Virgilio in their exchange (see also n. 59 below). It opens (8–12) with a tribute to the late "Tityrus" (the name Dante assumes in his eclogues [see nn. 82, 85 below]) as the first pastoral singer since antiquity and seems aimed (as with the earlier exchange too) at gaining recognition from an acknowledged poetic authority, attributing to Alphesibeus/Mussato the desire to see Moeris/del Virgilio receive the same laurel crown as himself (esp. 185–88). Cited from Wicksteed and Gardner, *Dante and Giovanni del Virgilio,* 176–95.

17. For possible connections between the two, see Dazzi, *Mussato,* 68–70; Ezio Raimondi, "Dante e il mondo ezzeliniano," in *Dante e la cultura veneta: Atti del convegno studi organizzato dalla Fondazione Cini,* ed. Vittore Branca and Giorgio Padoan (Florence: L. S. Olschki, 1966), 52–69; Manlio Pastore Stocchi, "Dante, Mussato, e la tragedia," in ibid., 251–62; Martellotti, "Mussato"; Giuseppe Billanovich, "Tra Dante e Petrarca," 8–9 et passim; Fumagalli, "Canto XXV"; Robert Hollander, "Commentary," in Dante Alighieri, *Paradiso,* trans. Robert Hollander and Jean Hollander; introd. and commentary by Robert Hollander (New York: Doubleday, 2007), note to *Paradiso* 9.29–30. Perhaps the most suggestive evidence is Albertino Mussato's *Somnium* (ca. 1319), in *Écérinide, Épitres métriques sur la poésie, Songe,* ed. and trans. Jean-Frédéric Chevalier (Paris: Les Belles Lettres, 2000), a dream-vision of the author's descent into Hell, partly modeled on *Aeneid* 6 and possibly, though not probably, indebted to Dante's *Inferno.* See also n. 9 above and n. 87 below.

18. Both meanings of the word "theologian" were current in Dante's time. One of the many ambiguities of *Convivio* 2.1 concerns which of the two is being used in the key phrase: "[v]eramente li teologi questo senso prendono altrimenti che li poeti; ma . . . mia intenzione è qui lo modo de li poeti seguitare" (2.1.4).

19. Charles Singleton, *Dante Studies 1: Elements of Structure* (Cambridge, Mass.: Harvard University Press, 1954), 62; Robert Hollander, "Dante *Theologus-Poeta,*" *Dante Studies* 94 (1976): 91–136. The authenticity of the *Epistle* (which is in fact not an epistle, but an epistle plus an *accessus* to the *Paradiso* and a commentary on the first lines of the canticle) has been disputed, though recent evidence has

bolstered the case for Dantean authorship (Luca Azzetta, "Le chiose alla *Commedia* di Andrea Lancia, *L'Epistola a Cangrande* e altre questioni dantesche," *L'Alighieri* 44, n.s. 21 [2003]: 5–73). See also Zygmunt Barański, "The *Epistle to Cangrande*," in *The Cambridge History*, 2:583–89, and Albert Russell Ascoli, "Access to Authority: Dante in the *Epistle to Cangrande*," in *Seminario Dantesco Internazionale/International Dante Seminar I*, ed. Zygmunt Barański (Florence: Le Lettere, 1997), 309–52, among many possible. On the one hand, the question of the *Epistle*'s true author is immaterial as regards Petrarch, since all that matters is that he would have believed it to be by Dante. On the other hand, in all likelihood he did not know of its existence (see n. 34 below).

20. See Lino Pertile, "Dante's *Comedy* Beyond the *Stil Nuovo*," *Lectura Dantis* 13 (1993): 47–77, and "Lettera aperta a Robert Hollander sui rapporti tra *Commedia* e *Convivio*," *Electronic Bulletin of the Dante Society of America [EBDSA]* (http://www.princeton.edu/~dante/ebdsa/), October 8, 1996.

21. Mussato's arguments are found in his surviving verse epistles 1, 4, 7, and 18, this last part of an ongoing polemic with Fra Giovannino of Mantua, who helpfully rehearsed his opponent's arguments in a screed edited in Eugenio Garin, ed., *Il pensiero pedagogico dell'umanesimo* (Florence: Giuntine, 1958), 2–19. Until recently, Mussato's *opera omnia* were available in the original and in their entirety only in Johannes G. Graevius, *Thesaurus antiquitatum et historiarum Italiae*, 9 vols. (Leiden: 1704–23), vol. 6, pt. 2, and even the four letters, despite their obvious historical importance, were not easily accessible; now Chevalier has edited them with facing-page French translation (Mussato, *Écérinide*). See Dazzi, *Il Mussato*, 181–95 for Italian translations. For Mussato on poetry, see Galletti, "La ragione poetica"; Vinay, "Studi sul Mussato"; Dazzi, *Il Mussato*, 108–23; Giuseppe Billanovich, "I primi umanisti"; Ronconi, *Le origini*, 20–46; Chevalier, "Introduction," xci–cxvii.

22. On the emergence of the topos of the poet-theologian in the late thirteenth and through the fourteenth century, beginning with Mussato and subsequently rearticulated by Petrarch (*Invectiva Contra Medicum*, ed. and trans. David Marsh, in *Invectives*, I Tatti Renaissance Library Series [Cambridge, Mass.: Harvard University Press, 2003], bk. 3, esp. par. 137–38; *Familiares* 10.4), Giovanni Boccaccio (*Genealogia Deorum Gentilium*, ed. Vittorio Zaccaria, in *Opera Omnia, Volume VII–VIII*, ed. Vittore Branca [Milan: Mondadori, 1998], Preface; 14.8; 15.8; *Trattatello* [1st ed., par. 137–49, esp. 147–48; cf. 2nd ed., par. 90–105]), and then Coluccio Salutati (e.g., *De Laboribus Herculis*), see Curtius, *European Literature*, 214–27; Ronconi, *Le origini*; Charles Trinkaus, *The Poet as Philosopher: Petrarch and the Formation of Renaissance Consciousness* (New Haven: Yale University Press, 1979), esp. 88–105; Witt, "Coluccio Salutati," and *"In the Footsteps"*; Claudio Mésoniat, *Poetica theologica: La 'Lucula Noctis' di Giovanni Dominici e le dispute letterarie tra '300 e '400* (Rome: Edizioni di Storia e Letteratura, 1984); Concetta Carestia Greenfield, *Humanist and Scholastic Poetics, 1250–1500* (Lewisburg, Pa.: Bucknell University Press, 1981), chs. 3–8; Craig Kallendorf, "From Virgil to Vida: The *Poeta*

Theologus in Italian Renaissance Commentary," *Journal of the History of Ideas* 56 (1995): 41–62; Hollander, "Dante *Theologus-Poeta*," makes a useful distinction between the increasingly common "poet-theologian" topos, on the one hand, and, on the other, Dante's claims to be a "Theologian Poet" in a (quasi-)biblical mode.

23. For Boccaccio, see the passages cited in n. 22 above. In both the *Genealogia* (14.22) and the first edition of the *Trattatello* (par. 91, 154–55), he occasionally seems to go beyond his own caveats, identifying Dante's poetry not only as theological in content, but also as virtually identical with Scripture. The second edition of the *Trattatello* is much more cautious on this score (see Ricci, "Introduzione," 433–35), perhaps under the influence of Petrarch. For Pietro see Hollander, "Dante *Theologus-Poeta*," 117 and n.

24. A plausible inference is that he knew it from Boccaccio (see again nn. 11–12 above). See n. 28 below for how and when Petrarch encountered the del Virgilio–Dante exchange. Witt, *"In the Footsteps,"* 236–39, builds a circumstantial case for Petrarch's direct or indirect acquaintance with del Virgilio during his student years in Bologna, and hence for his knowledge of the major figures of early humanism in the north of Italy. See also Padoan, "Giovanni Boccaccio," 162. More generally on Petrarch's time in Bologna, off and on between 1321 and 1326—the years immediately following Dante's death—see Giuseppe Billanovich, "L'altro stil nuovo," 1–5, and "Tra Dante e Petrarca." On Petrarch's early career see also Ernest Hatch Wilkins, *Life of Petrarch* (Chicago: University of Chicago Press, 1961); Feo, "Petrarca prima."

25. Parthenias, "the virginal one," was a nickname assigned to Virgil by his friends, according to both Servius and Donatus (E. Kegel-Brinkgreve, *The Echoing Woods: Bucolic and Pastoral from Theocritus to Wordsworth* [Amsterdam: I. C. Gieben, 1990], 248 n. 32). On Petrarch's relationship to Virgil in general, see Michele Feo, "Petrarca, Francesco," *Enciclopedia virgiliana*, 5 vols. (Rome: Istituto della Enciclopedia Italiana, 1988), 4:53–78; also, Vladimiro Zabughin, *Vergilio nel Rinascimento Italiano: Da Dante a Torquato Tasso*, vol. 1, ed. Stefano Carrai and Alberto Cavarzere, 2 vols., rpt. (Trento: Università degli Studi di Trento, 2000), 21–39; Pierre de Nolhac, *Pétrarque et l'humanisme*, 3 vols. (Paris: Champion, 1907), rpt. 1959, 1:123–62; Giuseppe Billanovich, "Tra Dante a Petrarca." On the structural, narrative, and verbal imitations of Virgil in *Parthenias*, see Kegel-Brinkgreve, *Echoing Woods*, 248; Thomas K. Hubbard, *The Pipes of Pan: Intertextuality and Literary Filiation in the Pastoral Tradition from Theocritus to Milton* (Ann Arbor: University of Michigan Press, 1998), 227–35. See also nn. 42, 46, 56, 72, 82, 84 below.

26. For basic historical-philological information concerning the exchange, see Martellotti, "Le egloghe." Readings of the exchange are in Wicksteed and Gardener, *Dante and Giovanni del Virgilio*; Guido Mazzoni, "Dante e il Polifemo Bolognese," *Archivio storico italiano* 96 (1930): 1–40, rpt. in *Almae luces malae cruces: Studi danteschi* (Bologna: Zanichelli, 1941), 349–72; Battisti, "Le egloghe"; Martellotti, "Dalla tenzone" and "La riscoperta"; Giovanni Reggio, *Le egloghe di Dante*

(Florence: Olschki, 1969); Padoan, "Giovanni Boccaccio"; Cecchini, notes to *Le egloghe*; Brugnoli and Scarcia, notes to *Le egloghe*; Konrad Krautter, *Die Renaissance der Bukolik in der lateinischen Literatur des 14. Jahrhunderts: Von Dante bis Petrarca,* Theorie und Geschichte der Literatur und der Schönen Künste, Texte und Abhandlungen 65 (Munich, 1983); Velli, "Sul linguaggio"; Kegel-Brinkgreve, *Echoing Woods*; Guy Raffa, "Dante's Mocking Pastoral Muse," *Dante Studies* 114 (1996): 271–91; Hubbard, *Pipes of Pan.* See also section 6 of this essay and nn. 8, 12 above and 59, 74 below. On the pastoral genre generally, see Thomas Rosenmeyer, *The Green Cabinet; Theocritus and the European Pastoral Lyric* (Berkeley: University of California Press, 1969); Renato Poggioli, *The Oaten Flute: Essays on Pastoral Poetry and the Pastoral Ideal* (Cambridge, Mass.: Harvard University Press, 1975); Annabel Patterson, *Pastoral and Ideology: Virgil to Valery* (Berkeley: University of California Press, 1987); Paul J. Alpers, *What Is Pastoral?* (Chicago: University of Chicago Press, 1996). For the history of the pastoral eclogue from Virgil to the Renaissance, see Zabughin, *Vergilio nel Rinascimento*; Battisti, "Le egloghe," 72–79 and nn.; Helen Cooper, *Pastoral: Mediaeval into Renaissance* (Totowa, N.J.: Rowman and Littlefield, 1977); Kegel-Brinkgreve, *Echoing Woods*; Hubbard, *Pipes of Pan.* For the ways in which Dante's renewal of the genre, then seconded by del Virgilio, led to imitations by Boccaccio and, most probably, Petrarch, see Giuseppe Billanovich, "Giovanni del Virgilio," 223–24; Martellotti, "Dalla tenzone," "Egloghe," and "La riscoperta"; Padoan, "Giovanni Boccaccio"; Giuseppe Billanovich and Cáda, "Testi bucolici"; Krautter, *Die Renaissance*; Janet Smarr, "Boccaccio pastorale tra Dante e Petrarca," in *Autori e lettori di Boccaccio: Atti del Convegno Internazionale di Certaldo,* ed. Michelangelo Picone (Florence: Cesati Editore, 2002), and "Introduction" and "Notes," in Giovanni Boccaccio, *Eclogues,* ed. and trans. eadem (New York: Garland, 1987).

27. Boccaccio knew of the del Virgilio–Dante exchange at a fairly early date (most likely 1339, according to the detailed case set out by Padoan, "Giovanni Boccaccio," 168 et passim; for his early knowledge of the epitaph, see Carlo Paolazzi, "Dall'epitafio dantesco di Giovanni del Virgilio all'elogio dell' *Amorosa Visione*," in *Dante e la "Comedia" nel Trecento* [Milan: Vita e Pensiero, 1989], 111–30).

28. Giuseppe Billanovich ("Pietro Piccolo da Monteforte tra il Petrarca e il Boccaccio," in *Petrarca e il primo umanesimo,* 473–74) posits that Petrarch learned of the exchange around the time of his first meeting with Boccaccio (ca. 1351), well after the probable date of the first draft of *Parthenias* (1346–47) and the date claimed by Petrarch for the writing of *Familiares* 10.4 (December 2, 1349). Michele Feo, "Di alcuni rusticani cestelli di pomi," *Quaderni petrarcheschi* 1 (1983): 72–73, and "Petrarca prima" (esp. 41–42), however, argues for an earlier knowledge, around 1344, before either had been written. Velli, "Il Dante," 197–98 and nn., points to convincing echoes of the exchange in the *Africa,* thus placing the connection, at latest, in early 1345. Baglio, "Presenze dantesche," 94 n. 24, and Krautter, *Die Renaissance,* 82–85, provide additional evidence for an early dating.

My position too is close to Feo's, and some of the evidence I present tends to reinforce it. In any case, the revisionary process of both *Bucolicum Carmen* and *Familiares* went on well past even Billanovich's proposed date and does not necessarily preclude my claims, since the Dantean components of both might have been introduced at a later stage. On the composition, organization, and dating of the *Bucolicum Carmen,* see Wilkins, *Life,* 57, 61, 158–59; Giuseppe Billanovich, "Giovanni del Virgilio," 209–10; and esp. Nicholas Mann, "The Making of Petrarch's *Bucolicum Carmen,*" *Italia medioevale e umanistica* 20 (1977): 128–35. The manuscript tradition dates from Petrarch's autograph ms. begun in 1357 and only completed in 1366, although a first version of the whole was apparently ready in 1349 (at the time of the epistle to Gherardo). On the dating (often deceptive) of the *Familiares,* see Vittorio Rossi, "Sulla formazione delle raccolte epistolari petrarchesche," *Annali della Cattedra Petrarchesca* 3 (1932): 53–73; as well as my discussion, with bibliography, of the specific dating controversy surrounding 4.1 in "Petrarch's Middle Age," 32 and n. 55 et passim. If Witt is correct (see n. 24 above), it is even possible that Petrarch learned of the exchange directly from del Virgilio as his student in Bologna. In any event, by the time Petrarch wrote *Familiares* 21.15, it seems clear he knew, though he did not openly admire, the only Latin *carmina* written by Dante: "respondi, illum sibi imparem, quod in vulgari eloquio quam *carminibus* [presumably the eclogues] aut prosa [*Monarchia*; *Epistolae*; *Quaestio*; and possibly *De vulgari*] clarior atque altior assurgit" (par. 24). For the interpretation of this passage see, for example, Paolazzi, "Petrarca, Boccaccio," 143, and Krautter, *Die Renaissance,* 82. See n. 84 below for critics who have previously discussed connections between the del Virgilio–Dante exchange and the *Parthenias–Familiares* 10.4 complex.

29. See also n. 59 below.

30. The importance of Dantean "self-exegesis," particularly its formal expression as auto-commentary that mimics patristic and scholastic commentaries on classical authors and the Bible, has been repeatedly stressed in recent Dante criticism. See esp. Gianfranco Contini, "Introduzione alle *Rime* di Dante," in idem, *Un'idea di Dante* (Turin: Einaudi, 1976), 3–20; Luis Jenaro-MacLennan, "Autocomentario en Dante y comentarismo latino," *Vox Romanica* 19 (1960): 82–123; Bruno Sandkühler, *Die frühen Dantekommentare und ihr Verhältnis zur mittelalterlichen Kommentartradition* (Munich: Max Hueber Verlag, 1967); David Wallace, ch. 10, in Alastair J. Minnis and A. B. Scott, with David Wallace, eds., *Medieval Literary Theory and Criticism, c. 1100–c. 1375: The Commentary Tradition* (Oxford: Clarendon Press, 1988); Susan Noakes, *Timely Reading: Between Exegesis and Interpretation* (Ithaca, N.Y.: Cornell University Press, 1988), 68–80 et passim; Thomas Clifford Stillinger, *The Song of Troilus: Lyric Authority in the Medieval Book* (Philadelphia: University of Pennsylvania Press, 1992), chs. 2–3; Ascoli, "Access to Authority" and *Dante,* esp. ch. 4; Deborah Parker, *Commentary and Ideology: Dante in the Renaissance* (Durham, N.C.: Duke University Press, 1993); Barański, "Dante

Alighieri"; Sherry Roush, *Hermes' Lyre: Italian Poetic Self-Commentary from Dante to Tommaso Campanella* (Toronto: University of Toronto Press, 2002).

31. See Ascoli, *Dante*, ch. 2.

32. See n. 19 above.

33. Alastair Minnis, *"Magister Amoris": The "Roman de la Rose" and Vernacular Hermeneutics* (Oxford: Oxford University Press, 2001).

34. Petrarch's knowledge of these works is debatable to varying extents. It is now well-established that he knew from early on both the *Vita nova* and the *Commedia* (see n. 3 above). The *De vulgari eloquentia* was not well nor widely known, though Boccaccio refers to it in both redactions of the *Trattatello in laude di Dante* (1st ed., par. 200; 2nd ed., par. 138), which seems to have been composed between 1351 and 1355, well after the composition dates of both *Parthenias* and *Familiares* 10.4. I have not found a satisfactory answer to the question of a possible knowledge of the *Convivio*, which though limited in circulation, was better known than the *De vulgari* (and, again, it is referred to in both redactions of the *Trattatello*: 1st ed., par. 199; 2nd ed., par. 137). Marco Santagata's notes to his edition of the *Rvf* (Milan: Mondadori, 1996) suggest a number of possible Petrarchan debts to the language of the treatise (see the index, 1517–18). See also n. 40 below. No overt reference to the *Epistle to Cangrande* as such appears before Filippo Villani's commentary on the *Commedia* in the early fourteenth century (see n. 19 above).

35. I adapt the notion of the "macrotext," a larger unitary text containing within itself a number of "microtexts" capable of being read independently, from Maria Corti, *Principi della comunicazione letteraria* (Milan: Bompiani, 1976), 145–47, and *Il viaggio testuale* (Turin: Einaudi, 1978), 185–200; Cesare Segre, *Avviamento all'analisi del testo letterario* (Turin: Einaudi, 1985), esp. 40–42.

36. Other letters addressed to Charles are: 12.1; 18.1; 19.1, 4, 12; 21.7; 23.2, 8, 15, 21. "Petrarch's Private Politics," forthcoming in Albert Russell Ascoli, *"A Local Habitation and a Name": Essays in the Historicity and Historiography of Italian Renaissance Literature* (New York: Fordham University Press), offers a detailed account. I offer a reading of Petrarch's staging of his relationship to Charles.

37. In the complex rhetorical structure of the letter, Petrarch first addresses Charles directly, then imagines him addressed by a female personification of Rome, who in turn imagines him addressed by his grandfather, Dante's ideal emperor, Henry VII (10.1, par. 25–27). This device anticipates the dialogic, ventriloquizing strategies of *Parthenias* and 10.4 (see n. 59 below and the text it accompanies), just as the proffered example of Scipio Africanus' battle against Hannibal (par. 21–23) anticipates the evocation of the hero of Petrarch's *Africa* in both the later letter and the eclogue. It has long been recognized that a shared interest in the revival of Roman political institutions, and a common critique of papal abuses of power, as well as parallels between Dante's appeals to Henry VII and Petrarch's to Charles IV, are among the most prominent intertextual connections between the two authors. Giuseppe Billanovich, *Petrarca letterato*, 165–66 and n. and 239 and n. 2; "Tra Dante e Petrarca," 6 et passim; "L'altro stil nuovo," 87–88, 94–95; Feo, "Petrarca," in *Enci-*

clopedia dantesca, 4:456–57; Velli, "Il Dante di Francesco Petrarca," esp. 187–94; Baglio, "Presenze dantesche," 94 n. 24, 106–9 and nn.; Ronald Martinez, "Petrarch and the Voice of Rome" (unpublished manuscript).

38. On Petrarch's attitude toward Gherardo (and monasticism), see Giles Constable, "Petrarch and Monasticism," in *Francesco Petrarca, Citizen of the World,* ed. Aldo Bernardo (Albany: State University of New York Press, 1980), 53–99; Jean Leclerq, "Temi monastici nell'opera del Petrarca," *Lettere italiane* 43 (1991): 42–54; Mazzotta, "Humanism." In addition to the three letters of book 10, several other *Familiares* are addressed to Gherardo (16.2; 17.1; 18.5) or mention him (4.1; 9.2; 10.2; 13.2; 15.2 and 3; 16.2, 8 and 9). Petrarch's *De otio religioso* is dedicated to Gherardo.

39. Among other links between the two books, in 4.1 Petrarch foregrounds the fact that Gherardo accompanies him on the ascent of Mt. Ventoux and establishes a contrast between his own tormented spirituality and Gherardo's untroubled monastic vocation (see Mazzotta, "Humanism"; Ascoli, "Petrarch's Middle Age").

40. It is possible to find a distant parallel between the organization of 10.4 and the structure of the *Convivio,* which begins with a book that describes the circumstances of composition of the treatise and provides a defense of its language and its content; then, each of the books that follows presents a (vernacular) poem, followed by a literal and, with the interesting exception of bk. 4, an allegorical exegesis thereof (see Ascoli, *Dante,* ch. 2). Needless to say, this structure is available elsewhere in late medieval textuality, though not in the mode of self-exegesis.

41. See nn. 10, 22 above and n. 49 below.

42. For Virgil as prophet, see Domenico Comparetti, *Virgilio nel Medio Evo,* 2 vols., 2nd ed., ed. Giorgio Pasquali (Florence: La Nuova Italia, 1943), and Zabughin, *Vergilio nel Rinascimento,* as well as the vast literature on Dante's adaptation of the motif in *Purgatorio* 22. Witt, "Coluccio Salutati," 543–44 and n. 18, argues, following de Nolhac and Zabughin, that Petrarch consistently avoided the prophetic-theological interpretation of Virgil's fourth *Eclogue,* a position, we will see, in keeping with his attitude toward the theological aspirations of Dante in the *Commedia.* In contrast, Feo, "Petrarca," in *Enciclopedia virgiliana,* 4:72–76, shows a number of points where Petrarch's allegorization of Virgil's poem comes very close to the medieval-prophetic interpretation. On Petrarch's use of allegory more generally in the *Bucolicum Carmen,* see n. 82 below.

43. In this connection, note specifically Boccaccio's repeated assertions that Dante has theological training and that his poetry is theological (*Genealogia,* 14.9 and 22; *Trattatello,* 1st ed., par. 24, 26, 75, 82, 91 [the epitaph], 123, 222 [see also n. 23 above.]). In *Genealogia* 14.9, he also cites both Petrarch's *Bucolicum Carmen* and his own bucolic collection as modern poetic works of real value, but carefully avoids directly linking either of them to theology. On Petrarch, see also *Genealogia* 14.19.

44. See esp. Thomas Aquinas, *Summa Theologiae,* vol. 1, *Christian Theology,* ed. Thomas Gilby (Cambridge: Blackfriars, 1964), Ia, q.1, art. 9, resp. 1. For additional discussion and references, see also Curtius, *European Literature,* 216–17,

223–24, 226; Mesoniat, 15–16 and nn.; Minnis, *Medieval Theory of Authorship*, 230–45 et passim; Minnis et al., eds., *Medieval Literary Theory*, chs. 3 and 6.

45. See n. 23 above.

46. Directly and indirectly, Virgil is referred to at *Parthenias* 13–14, 21–31, 38–39, 60–61, 75–90, and *Familiares* 10.4, par. 24–28, 33; Homer is referred to at *Parthenias* 20–31, 38–39, 60–61, 75–90, and *Familiares* 10.4, par. 25–28; and David is referred to at *Parthenias* 55–60, 70–74, 91–109, and *Familiares* 10.4, par. 6, 28, 31–32. On Petrarch's shifting allegiances within this relatively constant array of the one biblical and the two classical poets, see Feo, "Petrarca," in *Enciclopedia virgiliana*, esp. 4:60, 69–70. See also n. 72 below.

47. See Mazzotta, "Humanism," esp. 152–53, 157–59. See also Bernardo, "Petrarch's Attitude," 501, and Petrarch's extended defense of his style in the *Africa* and the *Bucolicum Carmen* in *Seniles* 2.1 (cf. n. 81 below).

48. Generally on the *Africa*, see Feo, "Petrarca," in *Enciclopedia virgiliana*, 4:67–68; Bernardo, *Petrarch, Scipio, and the "Africa": Humanism's Dream* (Baltimore: Johns Hopkins University Press, 1962).

49. For Petrarch's specific place in the development of the *poeta-theologus* topos, see the studies cited in n. 22 above, as well as Giuseppe Billanovich, *Petrarca letterato*, 121–25 and nn.; Feo, "Petrarca," in *Enciclopedia virgiliana*, 4:72–73; Witt, "Coluccio Salutati," 542–44. Ronconi, *Le origini*, 92, observes that in 10.4 Petrarch derives *poeta* from "exquisite speech" rather than, like Mussato or Boccaccio, linking his art to the divine inspiration of the *vates*. For Petrarch's likely awareness of Mussato's views on poetry, see Giuseppe Billanovich, *Petrarca letterato*, 121–22 n. 1, and "Pietro Piccolo da Monteforte tra il Petrarca e il Boccaccio," in *Petrarca e il primo umanesimo*, 473–74; Feo, "Petrarca," in *Enciclopedia virgiliana*, 4:75–76; Ronconi, *Le origini*, 131–32 n. 39.

50. Both Greene, "Petrarch *Viator*," and Mazzotta, "Humanism," recognize the need to juxtapose the overt defense of poetry at the beginning of the letter with the dramatization of a struggle between poet and theologian in *Parthenias* and in Petrarch's allegorization of that poem.

51. "Petrarch *Viator*," 22–23. Note, in this regard, that the next letter in sequence, *Familiares* 10.5, specifically juxtaposes the external variety of human types with the many internal conflicting tendencies in a single individual (par. 5–7, 16, et passim). See also nn. 57–59 below.

52. Giovanni Cipriani, "Petrarca, Annibale e il simbolismo dell'occhio," *Quaderni petrarcheschi* 4 (1987): 167–84, analyzes Petrarch's recurrent invocation of Hannibal's loss of an eye, in the *Africa*, *Trionfi*, *De viris illustribus*, *Familiares* 10.4, and elsewhere. Rebecca Lenoir's notes to *L'Afrique, 1338–1374* (Grenoble: Éditions Jérôme Millon, 2002), 7.834–38 (pp. 529–30, n. 645), register the textual parallelism between Monicus and Hannibal, arguing, however, that they are opposites (Hannibal's one eye turned not to heaven but to earth). This reading is possible, but, given the dominant opposition of Silvius and Monicus, leads instead to an identification

of the former with the Carthaginian "monster" and leaves intact the subtending notion of violent struggle between the two. The thematic pairing of Monicus-Cyclops in *Parthenias* may be read in conjunction with the titular Argus (again, Robert of Anjou, King of Naples) in the second of the twelve *Bucolicum Carmen* (cf. Cipriani, "Petrarca, Annibale," 180–82). The mythically multi-eyed Argus would seem to represent the "wakefulness" and "multi-tasking" of the representative par excellence of the *vita activa,* who also mediated Petrarch's laureation for the *Africa.* The "Argus"/King Robert who appears in Boccaccio's *Buccolicum Carmen* 3.70–81 and then in opposition to "Polyphemus" in 4.46–60, probably imitates Petrarch (Janet Smarr, "Notes," in Giovanni Boccaccio, *Eclogues* [New York: Garland, 1987], 212, 214; for Boccaccio's Polyphemus, see n. 99 below).

53. In classical myth, the race of the Cyclops is descended from that of the giants, the "sons of the earth," who attempted to storm the Olympian heavens and displace the gods. At the same time, they are also the helpers of Hephaestus/Vulcan as he hammers out the thunderbolts of Jove that the Patriarch of the Gods then uses to quell the rebellion. They thus provide a suitably ambiguous vehicle for Petrarch's purposes in *Familiares* 10.4. On the afterlife of the classical giants in the Middle Ages and Renaissance, see, *inter alii,* John B. Friedman, *The Monstrous Races in Medieval Art and Thought* (Cambridge, Mass.: Harvard University Press, 1981); Walter Stephens, *Giants in Those Days: Folklore, Ancient History, and Nationalism* (Lincoln: University of Nebraska Press, 1989).

54. Polyphemus appears as a comically unsuccessful lover in two of the Theocritan *Idylls,* 6 and 11. Virgil imitates the latter in his second *Eclogue,* from which the Cyclops has, however, disappeared (Hubbard, *Pipes of Pan,* 54, 60, et passim; R. D. Williams' notes to *Eclogue* 2 in *The Eclogues and Georgics* [New York: St. Martin's Press, 1979], 95–99 passim). Servius' commentary on the second *Eclogue* refers to the Theocritan model, but not to the fact that its protagonist is named Polyphemus. His note to line 25, however, does make passing reference to Theocritus' description of a Cyclops. Moreover, as Raffa, "Dante's Mocking," 289 n. 38, observes, Servius glosses a reference to Galatea in the ninth Virgilian *Eclogue* (39; 114 in *Servii Grammatici qui feruntur in Vergilii Carmina Commentarii,* ed. Georg Thilo and Hermann Hagen [Leipzig: B. G. Teubner, 1887]) with a retelling of the Galatea and Acis story borrowed from Ovid, but specifically attributed to Theocritus. It is thus theoretically possible that Petrarch was thinking of Polyphemus as a figure from classical pastoral. As we will see, the case for a Dantean source is stronger.

55. See nn. 60–63, 65–66 below.

56. Compare 10.3, par. 11: "Orabis, frater, ut me quoque iantandem libertati restituat et uno ventre progressos pari fine feliciter"; as well as 10.5, par. 3. Hubbard, *Pipes of Pan,* 228, notes that Petrarch "appropriates the image of Virgilian Meliboeus' twin goats abandoned by their mother [*Eclogue* 1.14–15] and applies it to himself and his brother." Though Gherardo and Francesco were not twins, Petrarch

designates them as such ("quis fata neget diversa gemellis?"; *Parthenias* 4) for evident symbolic purposes. Among the *loci classici* of the literature of rival brothers
are, of course, the biblical tale of Cain and Abel, the Theban struggle of Eteocles
and Polynices, and the Roman rivalry of Romulus and Remus. Probably the most
influential discussion of twinship and fraternal rivalry in the Middle Ages is that
in Augustine's *Civitas Dei*. For recent readings of the significance of the motif,
see René Girard, *Violence and the Sacred*, trans. Patrick Gregory (Baltimore: Johns
Hopkins University Press, 1977); Ricardo J. Quinones, *The Changes of Cain: Violence and the Lost Brother in Cain and Abel Literature* (Princeton: Princeton
University Press, 1991); Regina Schwartz, *The Curse of Cain: The Violent Legacy of
Monotheism* (Chicago: University of Chicago Press, 1997). In telling of the poetic accomplishments of Homer and Virgil in the *Parthenias*, "Silvius" focuses on a
cluster of not two but *three* very different brothers, Jove, Neptune, and Pluto, lords
respectively of the heavens, the oceans, and the underworld (78–90), with a possible further nod to the potentially cosmic differences separating him from Monicus, as well as an ironic preparation for a celebration of the one, though triune, God
of Christianity by Monicus (91–103; on possible del Virgilian and Dantean echoes
in this episode, see n. 84 below). In opposition to these images of contrast within
a natural family lineage is the passage near the beginning of *Parthenias* in which
Petrarch identifies the scene both of Virgil's youthful song and his own early experience of it: "Dulcissimus olim / Parthenias michi, iam puero cantare solebat, / hic
ubi Benacus, vitrea pulcherrimus alvo / persimilem natum fundit sibi" (12–15). Here
the genealogical metaphor with the geographical reference implies that Petrarch is
the "natural" child and heir of Virgil, as against the unnatural contrast between
himself and his sibling. (The doubling of the poet-fathers, "magnus uterque / dignus
uterque coli" [27–28], operates similarly.) Needless to say, the pastoral imagery of
rivers, springs, and even swamps is pervasive in the poem and bears a strong metapoetic burden. In 22.10, as Feo ("Petrarca," in *Enciclopedia virgiliana*, 4:64) notes,
Virgil has become a "brother," at the same time as David has taken his place as *the*
poet in Petrarch's pantheon.

   57. Kegel-Brinkgreve, *Echoing Woods*, 253, makes this point in passing (see
also 271). Mazzotta, *The Worlds*, 9, speaks instead of a general Petrarchan tendency:
"[his] dialogues are metaphorical displacements of monologues, just as monologues are always dialogical," and later observes of the widely various addressees of
book 4 that they "stand for different versions of himself" ("Ethics of Self," in *The
Worlds*, 84). Cf. Hubbard, "Pipes of Pan," 231 n. 39. Compare the well-known passage in *Familiares* 1.1 (also discussed by Mazzotta, "Ethics of Self," 92–93), in which
Petrarch speaks of contradictions in style and content between the various letters
as an effect of the need for the writer to adapt his verbal personality to suit the individual characters and needs of his addressees (par. 27–29). More specifically, in
book 10, letters 3–5, Petrarch oscillates between two related versions of this "multi-
voicing": on the one hand is the appropriation of the voice of the other, his brother

(thus in 10.3, par. 59: "Hec tibi, germane unice, non meo sed peregrino stilo ac prope monastico dictavi, te potius quam me ipsum cogitans"); on the other, the recognition of the otherness within, the fragmentation of the apparently unified self (as in 10.5, par. 5: "Discordant studia tum omnium tum etiam singolorum hominum; fateor et negare non possum, scio alios et me ipsum scio," as well as par. 16–17). Perhaps most telling, in the light of the characterization of Monicus and Gherardo as twins (see previous note), is Monicus' characterization of God's creation of man with body and soul as "geminum munus," which implicitly points to a constituent division within the individual person, further divided by the gift of "artes innumeras" (*Parthenias* 99–100).

58. See esp. 10.4, par. 1: "Si fervorem animi tui novi, iam hinc annexum huic epystole carmen horrueris, quasi professioni tue dissonum adversumque proposito. Noli aliquid temere diffinire; quid enim stultius quam iudicare de incognitis?" Compare *Familiares* 10.3, where Petrarch creates a specific contrast between his own endless "talking," which also figures his writing, and his brother's monastic vow of silence (par. 1–3, 9–11).

59. *Parthenias* follows the Virgilian model, which typically features a dialogue between two or more characters within a single poem, but where relations between the single poems in the collection, as between each poem and its precursor-model (esp. Theocritus), are not made explicit. As Martellotti first emphasized, however, the late medieval revival of the genre has some peculiar features stemming from Dante's radically innovative decision to adapt an existing genre—the Latin verse epistolary exchange previously exemplified, for example, by Lovato Lovati and Mussato, and also by del Virgilio in his earlier "Diaffonus"—to the eclogic model (Martellotti, "Dalla tenzone," 77–78, 82 et passim). Thus, Dante's two eclogues not only contain dramatic dialogues within themselves (along with two different and complex narrational formats), but also engage in dialogue with the del Virgilio poems to which they respond (del Virgilio's one eclogue in the exchange is monologic—i.e., remains within the basic epistolary format—although he would later adopt Dante's strategies when attempting to reproduce the exchange with Mussato). One of Boccaccio's first forays into the genre, an exchange of epistolary eclogues with Checco di Meletto Rossi (two by Boccaccio, one by Checco) seems to be modeled principally on the del Virgilio–Dante exchange, though Boccaccio then would turn to a self-contained collection in the Virgilian manner, almost certainly under the influence of Petrarch, and indeed would convert the second of his eclogic epistles into a free-standing poem, the third, "Faunus," in his sixteen-poem *Buccolicum Carmen* (Martellotti, "Dalla tenzone," 84–89, "La riscoperta," 101–6). See Krautter, *Die Renaissance,* 69–80, and Smarr, "Introduction," esp. xlii, lvii–lviii, for further discussion of the indebtedness of Boccaccio in his eclogic exchange to Dante. By the time of the late letter to Martin of Signa, Boccaccio had excluded Dante and del Virgilio from the eclogic canon altogether (Padoan, "Giovanni Boccaccio," 190). As seen in section 3 in this essay, despite this apparent

contrast between Dante and Petrarch, if one treats *Parthenias* and *Familiares* 4.10 as a unit, the later poet too can be seen to fuse eclogic and epistolary modes.

60. "Tigris et Euphrates uno se fonte resolvunt / et mox abiunctis aquis" (5.1.3−4). This idea is also found earlier in Pliny the Elder, *Historia Naturalis,* 6.9.25, and of course seems to conform to the biblical account of the four rivers of Eden flowing from a single source: "*et fluvius egrediebatur de loco voluptatis ad inrigandum paradisum qui inde dividitur in quattuor capita* / nomen uni Phison ipse est qui circuit omnem terram Evilat ubi nascitur aurum / et aurum terrae illius optimum est ibique invenitur bdellium et lapis onychinus / et nomen fluvio secundo Geon ipse est qui circuit omnem terram Aethiopiae / *nomen vero fluminis tertii Tigris ipse vadit contra Assyrios fluvius autem quartus ipse est Eufrates*" (Genesis 2:10−14; Vulgate edition). See Adolfo Cecilia, "Eufrates," in *Enciclopedia dantesca,* 2:765, and "Tigri," 5:604.

61. Charles Singleton, commentary to *Purgatorio,* in *The Divine Comedy,* 6 vols. (Princeton: Princeton University Press, 1970−75), 822, mentions Roger Bacon's *Opus Maius,* but see n. 66 below.

62. See *Familiares* 1.7, par. 5; 3.1, par. 12−13; 4.1, par. 2; 20.1, par. 22; 20.8, par. 16. I thank Ted Cachey for pointing out the relevance of the *Chorographia* for my argument.

63. Curiously, Dante's word for the movement of the river, "pigro," echoes the word ("pigrus") used by Mela of the Euphrates ("late diffusus in stagna, diu sedentibus aquis *piger* et sine alveo patulus"; par. 77). One might infer the existence of a topos that Dante is activating here to link his mythological Eunoe to the historical-biblical river.

64. Text and translation of the *Commedia* are throughout cited from *The Divine Comedy of Dante Alighieri,* 3 vols., ed. and trans. Robert M. Durling; introd. and notes by Robert M. Durling and Ronald L. Martinez; illus. Robert Turner (Oxford and New York: Oxford University Press, 1996, 2003, forthcoming).

65. The two rivers, their genesis and their function, are described by Matelda in *Purgatorio* 28.121−35. Dante's immersion in Lethe takes place after his "confession" to Beatrice in *Purgatorio* 31 and at the hands of Matelda (91−103). See Charles S. Singleton, *Journey to Beatrice* (Baltimore: Johns Hopkins University Press, 1977), 167−78 and nn., for a moral interpretation of Dante's departure from scriptural authority here. I disagree with Singleton's bald assertion, contrary to the evidence of the text, that Dante does not link Eunoe and Lethe in any way to the traditional rivers of Eden.

66. Petrarch uses Jerome, like Augustine elsewhere, to avoid the recent cultural past. Vittorio Rossi's edition of the *Familiares* gives two very similar references to the topos in Jerome, one of which I quote here: "Iste locus est Caesareae Philippi, ubi Jordanis oritur ad radices Libani, et habet duos fontes, unum nomine *Jor,* et alterum *Dan,* qui simul mixti, Jordanis nomen efficiunt." Cited from St. Jerome's *Commentarium in Evangelium Matthaei,* in Migne, *Patrologia Latina* (Paris:

Vrin, 1844–64) vol. 26, col. 114C–115A. See also *Quaestiones in Genesim,* ibid., vol. 23, col. 960C–961A. In one instance, Jerome asserts, following the biblical tradition, that the Tigris and Euphrates are the third and fourth of the four rivers of the Earthly Paradise mentioned in Genesis 2:10–14 (*Praefatium . . . in Liber Job,* in *Patrologia Latina,* vol. 28, col. 166C). In another, instead, he cites "Sallustius . . . auctor certissimus" to the effect that the sources (plural) of both rivers are found in Armenia, and that thus, he concludes, "animadvertimus aliter de paradiso et fluminibus eius intelligendum." Although the text of 10.4 seems to imply that the reference to Jerome pertains to the Jor-Dan question, it may well be that Petrarch's critique of Monicus' "error" is based not only on his reading of Mela, but also on Jerome's apparent questioning of the belief that the Euphrates originates in Paradise (*Liber de Situ et Nominibus Locorum Hebraicorum,* in *Patrologia Latina,* vol. 23, col. 892B). If this is indeed the case, it would be significant that rather than being a geographical "eye-witness" as the letter suggests, Jerome is in fact dependent for his facts on a classical *auctor,* Sallust. Boccaccio too, in his *De Montibus Silvis, Fontibus, Lacubus, Fluminibus, Stagnis seu Paludibus et de Diversis Nominibus Maris,* ed. Manlio Pastore Stocchi, in *Opera Omnia, Volume VII–VIII,* ed. Vittore Branca (Milan: Mondadori, 1998), 5.397, reviews several accounts of the origins and location of the Euphrates and specifically questions its relationship to Eden; he begs the "one source" question by saying it is "haud longe a fonte Tygris"; his entry on "Tygris," on the other hand, reports the Edenic origin of that river without comment and pairs it conventionally with the Euphrates (5.868).

67. Giuseppe Billanovich, "L'altro stil nuovo," 92–93; "Tra Dante e Petrarca," 39–40. Feo, "Petrarca," in *Enciclopedia dantesca,* 4:450, reviews the limited number of explicit references to Dante, noting further that in none of these does Petrarch treat his illustrious precursor as an *auctor* (on this last point see Giuseppe Velli, *Petrarca e Boccaccio [sic]: Tradizione memoria scrittura,* 2nd ed. [Padua: Antenore, 1995], 3–4; Baglio, "Presenze dantesche," 95 n. 25). See also Luca Carlo Rossi, "Petrarca dantista involontario," *Studi petrarcheschi* n.s. 5 (1988): 302–3 n. 4.

68. See Theodore J. Cachey, "The Place of the *Itinerarium,*" in *Petrarch: A Critical Guide to the Complete Works,* ed. Victoria Kirkham and Armando Maggi (Chicago: University of Chicago Press, 2009). Ironically, in this passage Dante too is correcting the mythological placement of Typheus beneath Etna, by a favorite classical *auctor,* Ovid, not with an alternative myth, as Petrarch does, but rather with a surprisingly modern and "scientific" explanation that the volcano's smoke is caused not by a sleeping giant but by "nascente solfo." Petrarch's correction, in other words, involves a serious misprision of Dante's text.

69. On Dante's staging of his acquisition of poetic-theological authority during the course of the latter cantos of *Purgatorio,* see Ascoli, *Dante,* ch. 7, sects. iii–iv.

70. Hollander, esp. "Dante *Theologus-Poeta,*" 113 and n., and Peter Hawkins, "John is with Me," in idem, *Dante's Testaments: Essays in Scriptural Imagination* (Stanford, Calif.: Stanford University Press, 1999), 54–71, have given particular

attention to the ways in which Dante aligns himself with St. John, to the point of suggesting, in one instance, that the Evangelist agrees with him, Dante, rather than the other way around. See esp. *Purgatorio* 29.92–105, 32.73–82; cf. *Paradiso* 26.

71. On the topos of the source, see David Quint, *Origin and Originality in Renaissance Literature: Versions of the Source* (New Haven: Yale University Press, 1983). *Parthenias* is informed throughout by the imagery of rivers and springs (14–15, 25–26, 34–35, 43, 62–69, 84, 106–7). For fluvial imagery in Dante generally, see Gary Cestaro, *Dante and the Grammar of the Nursing Body* (Notre Dame, Ind.: University of Notre Dame Press, 2003), ch. 2. For Eden as Parnassus, see Ascoli, *Dante*, ch. 7, section iv; also Smarr, "Introduction," xxxviii. Compare also the references in Giovanni del Virgilio (1.22) and Dante's reply (2.54) to the "Castalias . . . sorores," namely, the Muses who haunt the Castalian spring on Mount Parnassus.

72. Bernardo, "Petrarch's Attitude," 503–5, briefly anticipates the idea that in *Familiares* 10.4 David's poetry might recall Dante's. See Feo, "Petrarca," in *Enciclopedia virgiliana*, 4:70, for Petrarch's repeated juxtapositions of David with Virgil, initially in favor of the latter (see again n. 46 above). Famously, in *Familiares* 22.10.7–10, Petrarch claims to have at last turned away from secular *auctores* and toward the sacred, and specifically rejects the earlier comparison of *Parthenias* in favor of Virgil and Homer. Now, he says, "meus poeta David" (par. 7). He would, of course, also eventually compose a series of seven "penitential psalms" in imitation of David.

73. Teodolinda Barolini, *Dante's Poets: Textuality and Truth in the Comedy* (Princeton: Princeton University Press, 1984), 275–78, has succinctly sketched the implied equivalence between Dante and David in *Paradiso*. She observes that in the final cantica David is referred to three times with the periphrastic noun "cantor," which emphasizes that he shares the vocation of song with Dante: *Paradiso* 20.38–39 ("cantor de lo Spirito Santo"; and see the use of "cantor" in a related simile at 20.142); 25.17 ("sommo cantor del sommo duce"); and 32.11–12 ("[i]l cantor che per doglia / del fallo disse *Miserere mei* [*Psalm* 50.3]"). Barolini also points out (277–78) that the last reference contains a direct recall of Dante-*personaggio*'s appeal to Virgil on their first encounter (*Inferno* 1.65), thus linking David and Dante further as sinners redeemed to and by a vocation for singing. I would add that this reference, actually part of a periphrasis for the biblical Ruth, identified as the great-grandmother of the psalmist, reinforces a parallel with Dante as great-great grandson of Cacciaguida. In fact, in this way, it closes an allusive circle that opened with the first use of the key word, "cantor," in *Paradiso*, namely in canto 18.51, where Cacciaguida is called "tra i cantor del cielo artista," preparing the reference to David two cantos later. Finally, to my specific purposes, the first use of the word in the poem as a whole, and the only instance outside the *Paradiso*, is Stazio's reference to Virgilio as "cantor dei bucolici carmi" (*Purgatorio* 22.57; noted by Barolini, 276), forging a proleptic link to David as shepherd-poet and, not incidentally, stressing the

pastoral associations with this highest, yet humblest, type of song. See Stillinger, *Song of Troilus,* on David as poet-figure and model for the *Vita nova* (20, 31–34, 39–41, 67–69). See Minnis, *Medieval Theory,* 43–49 et passim, for David as biblical author and poet in the later Middle Ages.

74. The *Epistle to Cangrande* states that the *Commedia*'s language is stylistically comic, "remissus [est] modus et humilis," because composed in "locutio vulgaris in qua et muliercule comunicant" (par. 10). In Dante's second eclogue, "Tityrus" refers ironically to Mopsus' contempt for his "comica . . . verba" (4.52–54), with a deliberate echo of the del Virgilian adjective "comicomus" (1.13), terms compatible not only with the *Epistle to Cangrande,* but also with *De vulgari eloquentia* 1.1.1 (the vernacular spoken by "mulieres et parvuli"). The "authentic" Dante's principal discussion of "comedy" comes later in *De vulgari eloquentia,* at 2.4.5–6. I will not attempt here to rehearse the vast literature on the "comic" in Dante or its connections to the vernacular. Sufficient to the present purposes are Luis Jenaro-MacLennan, "'Remissus est modus et humilis' (*Epistle to Cangrande,* par.10)," *Lettere italiane* 31 (1979): 406–18; Zygmunt G. Barański, "'Prima tra cotanto senno': Dante and the Latin Comic Tradition," *Italian Studies* 26 (1991): 1–36; Ascoli, "Access"; and the bibliographies included in those essays.

75. For Dante's "return" to Eden as a form of pastoral, see Poggioli, *Oaten Flute,* 135–52. Raffa, "Dante's Mocking," 286 n. 5, offers a review of later critical treatments of the topic, and then asserts that the threat of violence represented by Polyphemus that haunts the pastoral landscape of the Dantean eclogues contrasts with the "true" Christian pastoral of Eden.

76. Kegel-Brinkgreve, *Echoing Woods,* 249, 250–51. See also Krautter, *Die Renaissance,* 116–18.

77. Tellingly, no mention, much less exegesis, of the lines, either literal or allegorical, appears in 10.4. Rather, the initial defense of poetry as "artificiosa . . . et exquisita," and thus radically different from "omni plebeio ac publico loquendi stilo" (10.4, par. 4), implies that poetic language is the antithesis of the "vulgar tongue."

78. John Freccero, "Dante's Prologue Scene," in *Dante: The Poetics of Conversion* (Cambridge, Mass.: Harvard University Press, 1986), 1–28; "Dante's 'Firm Foot and the Journey without a Guide," in ibid., 29–54. For the presence of a Dantean model in the mountain landscape of *Familiares* 4.1 (the "Letter from Mount Ventoux"), see my "Petrarch's Middle Age," esp. 10–12 and nn. Compare the following phrase from Petrarch's letter to Boccaccio on imitation: "Nolo ducem qui me vinciat sed precedat, sint com duce oculi, sit iudicium sit libertas" (*Familiares* 22.2; cited from Cachey, "Place of the *Itinerarium*").

79. Once the Dantean provenance of the imagery has been noted, it is reinforced by additional references, such as the "horrida / silva" and "aerii . . . montes" (31–32). See also Feo, "Petrarca," in *Enciclopedia dantesca,* 4:453–54, for the claim that Petrarch's gloss on the "silvae" of *Aeneid* 1 (164–68, 312–14) is mediated by a recall of the "selva oscura" of *Inferno* 1.

80. I develop a suggestion of Kegel-Brinkgreve, *Echoing Woods* (249, 272−73).

81. Ironically, Petrarch states near the end of *Seniles* 2.1 that he has been criticized for using a higher style than appropriate to pastoral in his *Bucolicum Carmen*. His rebuttal is that he had hoped to have written another work, by implication presumably the *Africa*, in a much higher style (Martellotti, "La riscoperta," 93). Much of the letter is concerned with responding to criticisms relating to the decorum of the *Africa*, and in particular to the inappropriateness of assigning lofty ideas to a youthful speaker, Magone, who functions as an implicit figure for the poetic ambitions, now disappointed, of Petrarch's own early years. Unsurprisingly, in the light of the arguments presented here, *Seniles* 2.1 ends with a typical Petrarchan rant (in the spirit of *Familiares* 21.15) against the truly low style of those (like Dante) who write principally not in Latin but in the vernacular ("tandem vero . . . aliquando, si placet, hos obtrectatores nostros latine loquentes aut scribentes aliquid audiamus, et non semper in angulis inter mulierculas ac fullones vulgaria eructare problemata"). On the tension in *Parthenias* and *Familiares* 10.4, as elsewhere in Petrarch's oeuvre, between epic and pastoral (or lyric more generally), see Greene, "Petrarch *Viator*"; Krautter, *Die Renaissance*, 88−95, esp. 93−94; Smarr, "Introduction," xli−xlii.

82. It is important that Dante also reintroduced and intensified pastoral's characteristic use of topical, and especially political, allegory, which Petrarch would then take to extremes. The association of pastoral and allegory is a critical commonplace (see, for instance, Patterson, *Pastoral and Ideology*). The close connection is usually seen as dating from Servius' pointedly limited recourse to topical allegorical explanations of Virgil's *Eclogues* (see, for example, his note to *Eclogue* 1.1: "et hoc loco Tityri sub persona Vergilium debemus accipere; non tamen ubique, sed tantum ubi exigit ratio" [4]), and as expanding through the medieval Christian allegorizations of the *Eclogues*, especially the fourth. In the use of allegory, Dante's eclogues (not to mention *Purgatorio* 22) go beyond not only Virgil's original texts but also Servius' interpretations of these. Nonetheless, Petrarch is even more clearly committed to pastoral allegory than Dante. In fact, he specifically states that the *Bucolicum Carmen* cannot be understood without an authorial key: "Sed quoniam id genus est quod nisi ex ipso qui condidit auditum, intelligi non possit, ne te inutiliter fatiges, primo quid dicam, deinde quid intendam brevibus explicabo" (*Familiares* 10.4, par. 12); see also *Varia* 42 and the "Preface" to the *Liber sine nomine*. See Martellotti, "La riscoperta," 94−96; Lao Paoletti, *Retorica e politica nel Petrarca bucolico* (Bologna: Libreria Patron, 1974), 60−62 and nn.; Feo, "Petrarca," in *Enciclopedia virgiliana*, 4:67; Cooper, *Pastoral*, 36−37 et passim; Krautter, *Die Renaissance*, 120−27 et passim; Kegel-Brinkgreve, *Echoing Woods*, 243, 252−53, 270; Patterson, *Pastoral and Ideology*, 43−46, cf. 32−35. Boccaccio, in his letter to Fra Martino da Signa (ca. 1374) describing the signifying structure of his own *Buccolicum Carmen*, says that he follows Virgil in the intermittent use of allegory, in contrast with the more thorough-going practice of Petrarch (Martellotti, "La riscoperta," 96). As to the question of a specifically political allegory in pastoral, Patterson, *Pastoral and*

Ideology, 19–59, argues aptly that Petrarch's reading of Virgil is filtered through the politicized lens of Servius' commentary, but omits to note the possible influence of del Virgilio's and Dante's eclogues, which are similarly freighted with political references (see nn. 97, 99 below).

83. See n. 10 above.

84. Without going into detail, Feo, "Petrarca," in *Enciclopedia virgiliana,* 4:67, puts it succinctly: "in principio [per Petrarca] c'è Virgilio, ma tra Virgilio e Petrarca c'è Dante." See n. 28 above on the question of when, in relation to the composition of *Parthenias* and *Familiares* 10.4, Petrarch first encountered Dante's eclogues. A few critics have begun to make the case that *Parthenias* is specifically modeled— verbally, thematically, structurally—on one or more poems in the exchange between Dante and del Virgilio. See notably Krautter, *Die Renaissance,* esp. 86–87; Kegel-Brinkgreve, *Echoing Woods,* 251. Feo, "Petrarca," in *Enciclopedia virgiliana,* 4:70, sees an echo of the *Commedia's* three *cantiche* in the passage describing how both Virgil and Homer "triplicis sortitos numina regni / expingunt . . . fratres" (*Parthenias* 79–80; also cited in n. 56 above). However, rather than making unmediated reference to the "poema sacro," Petrarch's phrase probably conflates Ovid's "triplicis confinia mundi" (*Metamorphoses* 12.40) with del Virgilio's description of the *Commedia* ("evolvens triplicis confinia sortis"; 1.3). Hubbard, *Pipes of Pan,* following a critical proposal rehearsed and dismissed by Thomas G. Bergin, in notes to *Petrarch's "Bucolicum Carmen,"* 224, suggests that *Bucolicum Carmen* 4 also allegorizes Petrarch's relationship to Dante (232–33 and n.).

85. "Melibeus" is identified as one "Ser Dino Perini" by the anonymous annotator of the *Zibaldone* (Wicksteed and Gardner, *Dante and Giovanni del Virgilio,* 222–24). The names of two of the three Dantean protagonists, Tityrus and Melibeus, come from Virgil's first *Eclogue* (Virgil's Meliboeus also appears in the seventh, Tityrus, briefly, in the fifth), while the name Dante applies to del Virgilio, Mopsus, comes from the fifth (on the suitability of the name, see Kegel-Brinkgreve, *Echoing Woods,* 339–40 n. 3). For Servius on Tityrus, see n. 72. In a fine, unpublished seminar paper, Paul Vlajcic has shown that the thematics of exile (Meliboeus) and of city versus country in the Virgilian poem are appropriated and transformed by Dante to suit his own situation (see also Battisti, "Le egloghe," 85). For additional discussion of the relationship of Dante's two *Eclogues* and del Virgilio's one to their Virgilian models, see Wicksteed and Gardner, *Dante and Giovanni del Virgilio,* 207–11; Battisti, "Le egloghe," 81–86; Martellotti, "La riscoperta," 97–98; Cecchini, notes to *Le egloghe,* passim; Brugnoli and Scarcia, notes to *Le egloghe*; Velli, "Sul linguaggio"; Kegel-Brinkgreve, *Echoing Woods,* 244; Raffa, "Dante's Mocking," 274 and nn.; Hubbard, *Pipes of Pan,* 223–27. Hubbard, 227, make the cogent observation that where Dante takes for himself the pastoral name traditionally linked to Virgil, Petrarch, as Silvius, takes on the structural role of Meliboeus, the wandering, dispossessed exile of the first Virgilian eclogue (on this latter point, see also Patterson, *Pastoral and Ideology,* 43). For echoes of other Virgilian works in Dante's eclogues, see Battisti, "Le egloghe," 86–88.

86. This is also the interpretation of Krautter, *Die Renaissance,* 31. *Sed contra,* see Kegel-Brinkgreve, *Echoing Woods,* 242 and n. 10. See *Convivio* 1.1.4 and 13 (cf. 1.9.5) and Richard Lansing, "Dante's Intended Audience in the *Convivio,*" *Dante Studies* 110 (1992): 17–24. For del Virgilio's characterization of the *Commedia*'s audience, see 1.6, 12–19, 21–22, 33–34; for Dante's response, see esp. 2.9–11, 24–26, 52–56, 65–66. See Petrarch, *Familiares* 21.15 and n. 9.

87. "Nonne triumphales melius pexare capillos / et patrio, redeam si quando, abscondere canos / fronde sub inserta solitum flavescere Sarno?" (42–44). Compare *Paradiso* 25.1–9: "Se mai continga che 'l poema sacro / al quale ha posto mano e cielo e terra, / sì che m'ha fatto per molti anni macro, / vinca la crudeltà che fuor mi serra / del bello ovile ov' io dormi' agnello, / nimico ai lupi che li danno guerra; / con altra voce omai, con altro vello / ritornerò poeta, e in sul fonte / del mio battesmo prenderò 'l cappello." Note especially the strong pastoral imagery in the latter passage. On these and other echoes of the *Commedia,* especially in the first Dantean *Eclogue,* see Battisti, "Le egloghe," 68–71, 98–100; Padoan, "Giovanni Boccaccio," 194–95. Cecchini, notes to *Le egloghe,* summarizes what he takes to be a critical consensus that Dante misinterprets del Virgilio's offer (1.35–40), which was not in fact to stage a formal laurel coronation (659). See also n. 10 above and n. 95 below.

88. Dante's promise of "decem . . . vascula" echoes Servius' reference to the interpretation of "aurea mala decem" (Virgil, *Eclogue* 3.71) as the gift of the ten eclogues to Augustus, and has been interpreted to mean either ten Latin eclogues (in imitation of Virgil) or ten cantos (not necessarily the first ten) of the *Paradiso.* Martellotti, "Egloghe," 645, and Cecchini, notes to 2.58 and 64 in *Le egloghe* (668–69), cite some of the partisans on both sides of the question before plumping for the *Paradiso,* along with the scholarly majority. In favor of the *Paradiso* are also Wicksteed and Gardner, *Dante and Giovanni del Virgilio,* 228; Battisti, "Le egloghe," 98–100; Reggio, *Le egloghe,* 21–33; Cooper, *Pastoral,* 34; Kegel-Brinkgreve, *Echoing Woods,* 242 and n.; Hubbard, *Pipes of Pan,* 226–27. For the eclogue option, see Chiarini, "I 'decem vascula' della prima ecloga dantesca," 77–88, and Brugnoli, notes to Dante, *Le egloghe,* 2.58–64, 45–47. I tend to agree with the ten cantos theory, but of more interest here is which option Petrarch would have chosen in reading the exchange—would he have followed the anonymous annotator of the eclogic exchange in Boccaccio's *Zibaldone* in taking the verses as a promise of eclogues? or would he have opted for the "modern" interpretation? The former reading might have been more "threatening," as encroaching on the Latin domain he had defined for himself in opposition to Dante's commitment to the vernacular, and would thus have helped to motivate the repressive textual violence directed against his precursor.

89. For a reading of the two Dantean eclogues "as a defense of his own [vernacular] poetic practice and [an] implicit put-down of del Virgilio" through "a well-developed pattern of classical allusions," see Raffa, "Dante's Mocking" (quotation from 272).

90. Petrarch plays out this same internal/external debate at much great length in his discussions with "Augustinus" in book 3 of the *Secretum*.

91. See Wickstead and Gardner, *Dante and Giovanni del Virgilio*, 234–38.

92. Cited in Cecchini, "Introduzione" to *Le egloghe*, 648.

93. These include, according to Battisti, "Le egloghe," verbal echoes from Virgil's *Eclogues* 1, 2, 3, 5, and 8. See also n. 85 above.

94. On the satirical force of the device, see Raffa, "Dante's Mocking," 275–76. No completely satisfactory interpretive explanation has yet been offered for the curious way in which the poem ends. In 4.95–97, Iollas (Guido da Polenta, Lord of Ravenna, and Dante's host; see del Virgilio, 3.80–83; Virgil, *Eclogue* 2.56–57, and Servius' gloss on the name as "ditior amator, vel eius dominus") is said to have overheard the conversation of Tityrus, Alphesibeus, and Melibeus and to have reported it to an unspecified "us," who then referred it back to Mopsus/del Virgilio (Battisti, "Le egloghe," points out an analogy to the structure of Virgil's *Eclogue* 7). One possible reading is that the final lines were added after Dante's death so that the sequence could be closed and the poem sent on to del Virgilio. But against this hypothesis is the fact that these three lines fill out the number of lines to equal that of del Virgilio's *Eclogue* in a way that the poem earlier makes clear is intentional, by calling attention to the fact that Dante's reference to "centum carminibus" comes in the same line of his poem as del Virgilio's reference to the perfect number "centum" appears in his (respectively, 3.43 and 4.43).

95. As seen in n. 87 above, *Paradiso* 25 also alludes to Jason through the word "vello" (Gian Roberto Sarolli, *Prolegomena alla "Divina Commedia"* [Florence: Olschki, 1971], 401–3; Robert M. Durling and Ronald L. Martinez, *Time and the Crystal: Studies in Dante's "Rime Petrose"* [Berkeley: University of California Press, 1990], 248–49 and nn.), and indeed, Jason as explorer of entirely unknown regions strategically figures Dante's poetic enterprise at the beginning and the end of the *Paradiso* (2.1–18; 33.94–96), with dialectical reference to Ulysses' tragic journey of discovery (*Inferno* 26; and see *Paradiso* 27.82–84). The latter interpretation was first developed by Robert Hollander, *Allegory in Dante's "Commedia"* (Princeton: Princeton University Press, 1969), 220–32; see Ferroni, "Tra Dante e Petrarca," who covers some of the same ground independently. For a less persuasive interpretation of Dante's use of the myth of Jason and the golden fleece in his second eclogue, see Raffa, "Dante's Mocking," 277. Compare Giuseppe Mazzotta, *Dante, Poet of the Desert: History and Allegory in the Divine Comedy* (Princeton: Princeton University Press, 1979), 141–42 and nn.

96. Alphesibeus' name is also glossed by the anonymous annotator of Boccaccio's *Zibaldone*; he is usually identified as "magister Fiducius de Milottis de Certaldo," a physician and philosopher also in exile in Ravenna during this period (Wicksteed and Gardner, *Dante and Giovanni del Virgilio*, 240; Cecchini, notes to *Le egloghe*, 683; Padoan, "Giovanni Boccaccio," 193–94).

97. This figure, about whom the anonymous annotator remains silent, is sometimes identified as King Robert the Wise of Naples, head at this time of the Guelf faction in Italy and de facto overlord of Bologna (Wicksteed and Gardner, *Dante and Giovanni del Virgilio*, 241; Martellotti, "La riscoperta," 95; Cooper, *Pastoral*, 36; Kegel-Brinkgreve, *Echoing Woods*, 245). More often, and more convincingly, it is said to be Fulcieri da Calboli, a fierce persecutor of Ghibellines and Florentine Whites as *podestà* of Florence in 1303, immediately after Dante's exile, who took over the governorship of Bologna in 1321, the period when the *Eclogue* is supposed to have been composed. Dante placed a condemnation of Fulcieri into the mouth of Guido del Duca in *Purgatorio* 14.58–63: "Io veggio tuo nepote [of Guido's fellow penitent, Rinieri da Calboli] che diventa / cacciator di quei lupi in su la riva / del fiero fiume, e tutti li sgomenta. / Vende la carne loro essendo viva; / poscia li ancide come antica belva; / molti di vita e sé di pregio priva." Battisti ("Le egloghe," 104–6), Martellotti ("Le egloghe," 645), and Cecchini (notes to *Le egloghe*, 687–88), all review the question and side cautiously with the majority critical opinion represented, among others, by Guido Mazzoni, "Dante"; Reggio, *Le egloghe*, 35–47; Raffa, "Dante's Mocking," 272–73. On the hostility of Bologna to the White Guelf exiles after 1306, see Wicksteed and Gardner, *Dante and Giovanni del Virgilio*, 226–27.

98. For other Ovidian echoes in Dante's *Eclogues*, see Battisti, "Le egloghe," 88–89; Raffa, "Dante's Mocking," 277–79. Raffa, 281–85, argues that Dante is imitating a connection established by Ovid between Polyphemus and the world of pastoral literature. See again n. 54 above.

99. Boccaccio, *Buccolicum Carmen* 4, "Dorus" (esp. 60–86, 98–108, 135–38) also includes a threatening Polyphemus who stands allegorically for a menacing political figure, in this case Louis of Hungary, persecutor of Queen Joan of Naples (see also n. 52 above). Direct and indirect references to Polyphemus recur in his eclogues 5.57, 126; 6.13–14; 9.101; 15.206–8; 16.22. Boccaccio's poem was probably composed after Petrarch's (1347 or later), and is, I think, equally indebted to Dante for the image (Smarr, "Notes," 216). In any event, the parallels between Petrarch's text and Dante's seem to me more convincing than those between Petrarch's and Boccaccio's.

100. As is well known, Bologna had as much of a special symbolic appeal to Dante for intellectual, poetic, and linguistic reasons as Montrieux did to Petrarch for spiritual ones. For Dante and Bologna, see Ezio Raimondi, "Per una città nell'*Inferno* dantesco," in *Metafora e storia: Studi su Dante e Petrarca* (Turin: Einaudi, 1970), 39–64; Augusto Vasino et al., "Bologna," in *Enciclopedia dantesca*, 1:660–67; Ascoli, *Dante*, ch. 3.

101. See again n. 1 above. While much of Petrarch's work (for example, his discovery and discussion of Cicero's *Pro Archia*) is concerned with establishing the autonomy and privilege of poetry (and of himself as poet-laureate), three of the *Familiares* taken together give a very clear idea of how he goes about systematically

positioning poetry, on the one hand, in opposition to the *vita activa* of kings and emperors (*Familiares* 19.3, describing his visit with the Emperor Charles IV, discussed in my "Petrarch's Private Politics"; see also 4.3 and 7), and, on the other, to the *vita contemplativa* of the religious orders (as in 10.4; but see also 4.1). Perhaps most telling is 13.6, in which he defines at length the uniqueness of the poetic vocation (in the course of denying that Cola di Rienzo, on trial for his life in Avignon, is entitled to a defense, like that of the *Pro Archia*, based on his status as poet).

102. I think particularly of staging dramatic conversations with the ancients as if they were living persons: notably in the *Secretum* and in the letters to ancient authors in *Familiares* 24, which, I believe, are directly modeled on Dante's resuscitation of Virgil in the *Commedia*. See also the discussion of the epistle to Homer in section 7 of this essay.

103. Petrarch's knowledge of Greek, like Boccaccio's, was quite limited, and his knowledge of Homer only indirect (see *Familiares* 10.4, 18.2, 24.12). From at least 1351 on, he possessed a partial manuscript in Greek of Homer, which he could not read. Having come into possession of another and apparently better manuscript in 1353, he and Boccaccio commissioned the Calabrian scholar of Greek, Leontius Pilatus, to undertake a Latin translation of both Homeric epics, which he did between 1359 and 1363. On this topic, see Agostino Pertusi, *Leonzio Pilato fra Petrarca e Boccaccio: Le sue versioni omeriche negli autografi di Venezia e la cultura greca del primo Umanesimo* (Venice: Istituto per la collaborazione culturale, 1964); as well as de Nolhac, *Pétrarque*, vol. 2, 127–88; Giuseppe Billanovich, *Petrarca letterato*, 243–50; Wilkins, *Life*, 101, 136, 162, 164, 190, 197, 200, 207, 215–16. In any event, even assuming an extensive revisionary process, the eclogue-letter pair would have been largely, if not entirely, composed before Petrarch ever saw Pilatus' translation. For the comparisons in Petrarch's work between Homer and Virgil, see Feo, "Petrarca," in *Enciclopedia virgiliana*, 4:70. On the figure of Ulysses in particular, see n. 111 below.

104. Mazzotta, "Humanism," 123.

105. Mazzotta, "Humanism," 154, specifically links Petrarch's Orpheus to the early humanist figure of the "poeta-theologus." See also the preceding chapter in *The Worlds of Petrarch*, "Orpheus, Rhetoric, and Music." On the various interpretations of Orpheus in the Middle Ages and into the early modern period, see August Bück, *Der Orpheus-Mythos in der italienischen Renaissance* (Krefeld: Scherpe, 1961); Friedman, *Orpheus in the Middle Ages* (Cambridge, Mass.: Harvard University Press, 1970); D. P. Walker, *The Ancient Theology* (Ithaca, N.Y.: Cornell University Press, 1972). For Orpheus' relative absence from the *Commedia*, and with him the typical poet-theologian configuration, see Hollander, "Dante *Theologus-Poeta*," 119–20, and Barański, "Notes on Dante and the Myth of Orpheus," in *Dante, mito e poesia: Atti del secondo Seminario dantesco internazionale*, Monte Verità, Ascona, 23–27 giugno 1997, ed. Michelangelo Picone and Tatiana Crivelli (Florence: Cesati, 1999), 133–54. However, as has by now been repeatedly observed, the disappearance

of Virgil in *Purgatorio* 30.49–51 echoes the description of Orpheus' crying out lost Eurydice's name in Virgil's own *Georgics* 4.525–27, just as Dante's "Eurydice" reappears to him, more present in death than she was in life. In addition, Dante specifically aligns himself with Orpheus in *Convivio* 2.1 (par. 3).

106. Of course, in this strategic use of Homer, Petrarch follows a model already brilliantly employed by Dante in *Inferno* 4. See also Velli, "Il Dante," 194–96, for the persuasive argument that the key encounter between Homer and Ennius in book 9 (230–34) of the *Africa*, with its evident goal of placing Petrarch in the epic line they together form, is modeled both on Dante's meeting with Cato (*Purgatorio* 1) and on the encounter between Virgil and Statius (*Purgatorio* 21–22).

107. Wilkins, *Life*, 171–72, briefly describes the episode, attributing the letter from "Homer" to Pietro da Moglio, a literature professor at Bologna. Giuseppe Billanovich, *Petrarca letterato*, 246–48 and nn., and "Giovanni del Virgilio," pt. 1, p. 223 and n., attributes it instead to Boccaccio.

108. It is significant, particularly given his treatment of Dante in 10.4, that Petrarch grudgingly admits Virgil did not do justice to Homer when he failed to name him explicitly as the model for his *Aeneid* (par. 18–25).

109. This point was first made by Giuseppe Billanovich, *Petrarca letterato*, 5, 20, 23.

110. This hypothetical allusion, strongly suggested by Petrarch's language, requires testing, which I have not yet been able to give it, against available medieval retellings of the Ulysses story.

111. I refer to the Dantean character as "Ulisse," to the Latin personage who appears in the classical and medieval Latin tradition as "Ulysses," and to the Homeric hero as Odysseus. Greene, "Petrarch *Viator*," 26, 28, et passim, sees Petrarch comparing himself to both Homer and Ulysses in 10.4 and elsewhere. Cachey ("'Peregrinus (quasi) ubique': Petrarca e la storia del viaggio," *Intersezioni* 17 [1997]: 369–84; "From Shipwreck to Port: *Rvf* 189 and the Making of the *Canzoniere*," *MLN* 120, no. 1 [2005]: 20–39; and "Place of the *Itinerarium*") explores the connection in a broader range of texts, giving special and due emphasis to Petrarch's comparison of himself to the wandering Ulysses in *Familiares* 1.1. See also Feo, "Petrarca," in *Enciclopedia dantesca*, 4:452–53, and "Un Ulisse in Terrasanta," *Rivista di cultura classica e medievale* 19 (1977): 383–88; Fenzi, "Tra Dante e Petrarca"; Ferroni, "Tra Dante e Petrarca"; Waller, *Petrarch's Poetics*, 44–38; Sara Sturm-Maddox, *Petrarch's Laurels* (University Park: Pennsylvania State University Press, 1992), 55–60. Throughout the *Familiares*, Homer is referred to frequently; of particular interest are the references in 1.1; 13.6; 15.4; 21.15; 22.10; 24.4, 11, 12. References to Ulysses are at *Familiares* 1.1; 9.13; 10.3; 13.4; 22.5; 23.2; 24.12 (and to the Cyclops, at 1.7; 9.13; and 12.3). The Petrarch/Silvius/Ulysses comparison is reinforced in other letters of book 10 by a series of direct and indirect references to the Greek hero's marine wanderings (10.2, par. 6; 10.3, par. 2, 4, 5—where Virgil's "ianitor Orci / ossa super recubans antro semesa cruento," *Aeneid* 8.41–42, anticipates Polyphemus, 21, 35, 40–41; 10.5, par. 25). See also n. 106 above.

112. The critical literature on the Dantean Ulysses is vast. Most significant from the perspective adopted here are Freccero, "Dante's Prologue Scene," and "Dante's Ulysses: From Epic to Novel," in *Dante: The Poetics of Conversion* (Cambridge, Mass.: Harvard University Press, 1986), 136–51; Padoan, "Ulisse *fandi fictor* e le vie della sapienza," in idem, *Il pio Enea, l'empio Ulisse* (Ravenna: Longo, 1977), 170–99; Mazzotta, *Dante, Poet of the Desert,* 66–106; Teodolinda Barolini, *The Undivine Comedy: Detheologizing Dante* (Princeton: Princeton University Press, 1992), 48–58, 105–15, et passim; Quint, "Fear of Falling: Icarus, Phaethon, and Lucretius in Paradise Lost," *Renaissance Quarterly* 57 (2004): 847–81.

PART 2

Metaphysics

CHAPTER 4

Petrarch's Dialogue with Dante

GIUSEPPE MAZZOTTA

RELATIONS BETWEEN POETS ARE PROBABLY NEVER UNAMBIGUOUS. In the case of Petrarch, whose voice is marked by contradictions, inconsistencies, and struggles (as a rhetorical form of reinstituting differences between his positions and those of his opponents), ambiguities with respect to Dante can hardly come as a surprise. As scholars have long shown, these ambiguities manifest themselves through the interplay of disclosure and concealment of the influence Dante exercised on Petrarch's poetry, as well as of the prestige of his predecessor. As a matter of fact, Petrarch entered the cultural scene at a time when something like a cult of Dante was in place. Immediately after the latter's death, as we know, Dante was hailed as nothing less than a classic, and his poetry became the object of several distinguished commentaries.

The acknowledgment of Dante in the early fourteenth century was not uniform in nature. His political work, *Monarchia*, inspired "reprobations" from the likes of Guido Vernani and polemics from hierocrats on grounds of its endorsing the Averroistic doctrine of the "double truth" and of dismantling the hierarchical order between Church and Empire. The *Divine Comedy*, on the other hand, gave rise to conflicting interpretations between theologically-minded exegetes and traditional humanists, such as Guido da Pisa and Benvenuto da Imola. The ambiguities Petrarch entertained toward Dante, therefore, cannot be dismissed solely in terms of a modern form of "anxiety of influence," of some private dark resentment toward the fame of the predecessor. Such an interpretive paradigm falsifies the consciously radical, innovative cultural project Petrarch undertakes (a project in which Dante's hierarchical vision plays a limited role), and it conceals what I take to be the essential thrust of Petrarch's thought: to distinguish between two fundamental, complementary ways of viewing poetry as well as the role of the poet/thinker in distinct historical epochs.

The relationship between Petrarch and Dante is destined to keep drawing critical attention exactly because it invests the question of how to understand shifts and ruptures in literary history. Petrarch understood with great clarity the new temper of his times, and he proceeded to articulate the need to reconstruct (and purify) the values of his world. The new times demanded a shift in attitude, an averting the gaze away from and overcoming the forms of Aristotelian and Scholastic logical structure of thought within which Dante developed his thinking. From this standpoint, Petrarch views himself as a modern, one who looks at the world exclusively through the paradigms of modern subjectivity and the will. In his view, character and personalities matter because they shape history. Yet the differences between Dante and Petrarch cannot be explained only through the prism of "romantic" psychology because they are also rooted in the perception of an epochal break in history.

I begin, therefore, by stressing the obvious: that in Petrarch's intellectual and poetic growth, Dante's work remained a steady point of reference, a form of self-orientation, and a stimulus to creative activity. Explicit acknowledgments and echoes of Dante's language and thought can be found everywhere in Petrarch's texts. In the *Canzoniere* (or *Rerum vulgarium fragmenta*), Dante's lexicon is systematically deployed, and Petrarch cites directly one of Dante's songs belonging to the sequence of his *Rime petrose*: "Così nel mio parlar voglio esser aspro."

The citation appears in song 70 of the *Canzoniere,* "Lasso me, ch'i non so in qual parte pieghi," which can be read both as a sketch of Petrarch's construction of the history of the medieval lyric and a reflection on the strategic place Petrarch occupies in that poetic tradition.[1] The overarching argument of the song comes to a head in the motif, which is quite common in Petrarch's poetic corpus, of the poet's doubt about the power of his voice to bend Love to his purposes. Such a voice is referred to as "queste voci meschine" (l. 6), and the plural evokes the wide array of his amorous discourse, the "vario stile" of praise, regret, lament, longing, and so forth, making up the subtle modulations of his poetry. At the same time, the doubt about his powers to persuade the beloved is countered by the poet's authoritative self-insertion in the history of medieval love lyric.

More precisely, the lover's lingering hope that Love may respond to his entreaties leads Petrarch to retrieve what he envisions as the major voices about language and desire in Provençal poetry and in the tradition of the "Sweet New Style." Each stanza of song 70 ends with a quotation of a line from a poem by a poet of the past: Arnaut Daniel's "Drez et rayzon"; Guido Cavalcanti's "Donna mi prega"; Dante's "Così nel mio parlar voglio esser aspro"; and Cino da Pistoia's "La dolce vista e 'l bel guardo soave." The series of poetic echoes ends with Petrarch's self-quotation from his own song 23, "Nel dolce tempo de la prima etade." The geographic (and mythical) space of Provence and Tuscany, which Dante's *De vulgari eloquentia* had cast in terms of their unitary linguistic and poetic history, constitutes the backdrop of Petrarch's self-inscription.

By making himself the endpoint of an ongoing lyric tradition, Petrarch dramatizes the basically innocuous fantasy that he legitimately belongs to and recapitulates the canon of a common mother tongue. The quotations from the voices of the tradition, furthermore, offer a partial solution to the question of solipsism the poem articulates. Petrarch locates himself in an imaginative world inhabited by other poets, and no amount of wishful thinking can force that shared world away. Further, if Dante, with false humility, numbers himself as "sixth" in the line of classical poets stretching from Homer to Virgil, Ovid, Horace, Lucan, and himself (*Inf.* 4.88–102), Petrarch obliquely counts himself as fifth, as it were, among his immediate predecessors or near contemporaries. One need hardly stress that the recognition of the poetic tradition to which he claims to belong does not stifle his voice. As a matter of fact, the romantic fantasies peddled by critics to the effect that Petrarch is overwhelmed and eclipsed by the power of his predecessors have little consistency. If anything, his predecessors' language adds power to his faint speech. Nor can there be any doubt that, of the four poets he mentions in song 70, the shade of Dante looms the largest.

In this song, as a matter of fact, the acknowledgment of Dante goes beyond the overt citation from one of his most peculiar (and not necessarily the most representative) poems, "Così nel mio parlar voglio esser aspro." One rhyme scheme ("alto," "smalto") (ll. 22–23) in Petrarch's song echoes the rhyme scheme in another of Dante's *Rime petrose*, "Io son venuto al punto de la rota," which centers, much like "Così nel mio parlar voglio esser aspro," on a love that shatters the mind and on the harsh, even tragic style of the amorous discourse. By this deliberate strategy of casting Dante as the author of the *petrose*, Petrarch opposes to Dante's harshness his own "sweetness," as if he, not Dante, belonged to the tradition of the "Sweet New Style." It is Dante, not Petrarch, who represents love in the guise of a desperate, imaginative aggression against the unresponsive woman of his desires. But there is no aggression against Dante. If anything, the harshness of Dante's voice turns into a counterpoint to Petrarch's own "Nel dolce tempo de la prima etade." By this move, Petrarch makes Dante the other voice, the voice of the other — a voice that nonetheless he cannot but confront and that at the same time he internalizes.

Song 70 provides a specimen of Petrarch's extensive entanglement with Dante throughout the *Canzoniere*, and this entanglement figures prominently also in the *Trionfi*, which overtly acknowledges Dante's *terza rima* as well as Dante's love for Beatrice. One might recall that the last poem of the *Canzoniere*, which is a prayer to the Virgin (song 366), echoes the final canto of *Paradiso* with its prayer to the "Vergine madre." By giving prominence to this structural feature, Petrarch stages the degree of sameness, punctuated by obvious differences, between their respective experiences: he deliberately brings to a reflective focus the extent of his indebtedness to and deviation from Dante's vision.

So frequent, thus, are the rhetorical modes that Petrarch and Dante share (sonnets, songs, sestinas, *terza rima*, or, as is the case in point, their turning poetry into prayer and vice versa), and so many are the echoes of Dante's poetry in both the *Canzoniere* and the *Trionfi*, that were we to try to limit ourselves to accounting for the debts, conscious or unconscious, that Petrarch incurred, we would risk missing the central point of their relationship: from the very start of his career Petrarch had entered into a dialogue with his predecessor and had kept it going until the very end. Why and what are the modalities of such a dialogue?

Let me say at the outset that the literary manuals of the Italian Trecento do not endorse this line of inquiry. In our time, as much as while he was still alive, Petrarch has been accused of disowning Dante's role in his thinking. The repudiation of his predecessor was raised by Boccaccio himself. As we know, Boccaccio expressed his fear that Petrarch resented his praises of Dante, as if they detracted from Petrarch's own glory. To banish the shadows of slander hanging over him, Petrarch addressed the issue of his problematical relationship with his "fellow countryman" in a letter of the *Familiares* (21.15), which was written in 1359.[2]

The letter makes no mention of Dante's name. Nevertheless, Petrarch protests that he feels no envy either of Dante's achievements or of the popularity he enjoys with the "multitudes" (of which Boccaccio is one). He praises Dante's unwavering pursuit of glory and his commitment to poetry while in exile. He admits keeping his distance from Dante's poetic work out of fear of turning into an "unwilling or unconscious imitator," since he, as much as his predecessor did, writes in the vernacular. He concludes with the statement that, whereas in the past he would submit his work to the judgment of others, now he judges others and "deems him the one to whom I would readily grant the palm for vernacular eloquence" (204).

Were it not for the silencing of the name, Petrarch's letter to Boccaccio would vindicate his claim of recognition of and equanimity toward Dante. But how are we to understand this *reticentia?* That this silence could not be dismissed merely as carelessness is made clear by a letter written to Homer in 1360 (*Fam.* 24.12), a year after writing to Boccaccio about Dante. Petrarch begins by apologizing for his own silence toward the "prince of Greek poetry," but the brunt of the letter consists in the assessment of the relationship between Homer and his epigones or imitators, chief among them Vergil. The reader is irresistibly drawn to the implied homology between the two episodes of literary history. At any rate, Petrarch briefly raises but leaves unsettled the long-standing argument (in which Horace, Propertius, and Macrobius took part) as to which of the two poets, Homer or Vergil, the predecessor and the latecomer, is superior to the other. The burning issue is finally raised: how — Petrarch wonders — is one to understand Vergil's silence about Homer? He ends with the purely arbitrary assertion that Vergil, had he not died prematurely, would have exalted Homer to the "heavens" at "journey's end." If an analogy between Petrarch and Vergil toward their respective "masters" is really implied, it quickly collapses: Petrarch, unlike Vergil, did not die prematurely and yet he kept his silence.

The intricacies of and the ambivalent reasons for this silence force us to ponder the contradictions lodged in Petrarch's posture. Of these reasons, probably the most persuasive is also the most realistic: his all too real desire to dissociate himself from Dante, to replace him, to eclipse and cancel his presence. The phrase "replace Dante" has to be understood as the desire to reconfigure the history of Italian literature, to find a "new place" for one-self even if it were to appear as a displacing of the predecessor. On the other hand, of the several possibilities suggested by this repression of Dante's proper name, two others loom large. It is reasonable to surmise that Dante is not mentioned because of the obviousness of the identity of the person who is being discussed. The silence could also be understood as a strategy to underscore the power of the name (just as Manzoni, say, writes an ode on Bonaparte's death without ever mentioning his name). But there is something far more important revealed by the omission of the name: by his reticence Petrarch avoids saying how much he knows and does not know the true nature of his life-long relationship to Dante. At stake is the truly Socratic question of how much he understood that relationship and how much he knows himself.

The letter to Boccaccio goes a long way in speculating on the complex weave of knowing and not knowing his "countryman." Petrarch informs us that Dante's existence was not unknown to him. It remained enveloped, however, in an aura of mystery, in a contradictory mixture of closeness and distance, knowledge and ignorance. Petrarch recalls seeing Dante only once in his early childhood, yet that memory has not faded. He saw him move within the circle of his family as a friend and an associate. He lived, Petrarch says, with his "grandfather and father, being younger than the first, but older than the second with whom on the same day and as a result of the same civil disturbance he was driven from his native land into exile. At such times, fast friendships often develop among victims of similar tribulations, and this was especially true of them since, in addition to a similar fate, they showed common interests and studies" (203).

The letter opens a new perspective on his relationship to Dante. By installing him within the generational web of his family relations and tying him to shared tragic political memories, Petrarch makes Dante part of his spiritual inheritance, a heritage of family, language, culture, political passions, and grief for a lost common country. In his recollection, Dante stands between his grandfather and his father: he is not an origin, but both a distant source and an immediate resource. As such, he could never be disowned. Were Petrarch to disown him, he would do so at the risk of losing the meaning of his past and the likely or partial knowledge of self the past delivers.

By representing him as a familiar but somewhat old (and thus anti-quated) figure, Petrarch effectively acknowledges that his thinking stems from the knot of language, passions, and historical memories in which Dante's own experiences are rooted. It does not follow that they agree on everything or even on much. That Petrarch disagrees with Dante is made clear by his poem "Vergine bella" (song 366), where, in explicit opposition to Dante's myth of Beatrice as the love messenger leading him to God, he calls Mary "vera beatrice" (1. 52). As I have shown elsewhere, the dis-agreements between them range from questions about the role of the past in history, to the value of medieval encyclopedic organizations of knowl-edge; alternative concepts about philosophy (especially Scholasticism and Averroism, which Petrarch views as neither usable nor instructive); the idea of classical Rome (though they share the particular judgment about the Avignonese papacy); and Petrarch's radical skepticism about the Roman em-pire, which he replaces with the idea of an empire of culture. These differ-ences between them cloak profound similarities. In the pages that follow I will investigate one large area where their respective visions both converge and diverge from each other: the question of subjectivity, around which Pe-trarch erected the great edifice of modernity. As he reconceives the central question of the subject, he is both indebted to and takes his leave of the me-dieval epoch that he identifies with Dante.

To sound the depth of his invention, I look at the *Canzoniere*, which is the language of the self, and I do so in the light of Dante's figurations of the self in the *Vita nova*. Both texts are conceived in the shadow of St. Augus-tine's *Confessions*, as well as in the aftermath of the vast phenomenon of me-dieval autobiographism. They share with Augustine the conviction that the self is constituted by desire, and that the foundation for self-transcendence lies in the endless displacements and shifts of desire. Accordingly, both the *Vita nova* and the *Canzoniere* start with the account of the enigmatic encounter of the poets/lovers with, respectively, Beatrice and Laura. Both of them experience love as an involuntary occurrence, not as a willed one, and as an involuntary occurrence their love carries the mark of necessity. This love mobilizes the faculties of the soul, opens up the domain of the imagi-nation, upsets the assumption of stability of the mind, and forces the lover to think and decipher the signs of love the beloved emits. Above all, this ex-perience allows both Dante and Petrarch to probe the deeper recesses of their selves, provisionally severed from the objective world. As the canon of the "Sweet New Style" has it, this love forms an ascent toward knowledge and God, and yet, at every turn, it threatens to enclose the self further within itself.

The two poets' responses to love and concomitant construction of the self differ widely. Dante's *Vita nova* starts as a book of memory: "In quella parte del libro de la mia memoria dinanzi a la quale poco si potrebbe leggere" (19).[3] Memory presides over the love story, which, at its center, tells of the death of Beatrice. The occurrence triggers Dante's insight into memory's essential limitations. Memory, which for Dante envelops dimensions of space and time, brings about discoveries and revelations. Yet, to yield to its power is tantamount to binding the poet to the inner world of phantasms, to immobilize him within the circle of nostalgia, and to cut him off from the future.[4]

Thus, Dante reverses memory into hope. In the *Vita nova* he employs the future tense only twice. The first time is when he obscurely grasps the premonition of his mortality: "Tu pur morrai" (50). The second time the reference to the future tense is oblique. It occurs in the conclusive chapter (ch. 42) as the poet announces the project of a future work—the *Divine Comedy*—by means of which he will bridge the gulf separating him from the dead Beatrice: "Sì che, se piacere sarà di colui a cui tutte le cose vivono, che la mia vita duri per alquanti anni, io spero di dicer di lei quello che mai non fue detto d'alcuna" (76). Hope, a verb that entails the future, suggests the theological virtue capable of unsettling the direction and the meaning of both past and present. As such, it opens up for the poet/lover possible worlds that are deeper than regions and sediments of memory. It subsumes the empirical dimensions of time into a transcendent order.

In the wake of Augustine's internalization of time, Dante's figuration intimates both that the lover is in time and that time, in the guise of memory, hope, and love, is within the self. No doubt, the *Canzoniere* retrieves the framework of temporality of the self available in both the *Confessions* and the *Vita nova*. Petrarch, however, gives this question a fresh twist. In his lyrical poetry, time does not unfold in a linear direction. It follows the vagaries of memory's association as well as the order of commemorations of past events. At any rate, Petrarch grafts on to these texts the Ovidian myths of Narcissus and Echo as well as the Psalms of David.

A key word in Petrarch's poetry—as it is in the exordium of Dante's *Vita nova*—is "parte." The opening sonnet of the *Canzoniere* describes the poet's mind-change as "quand'era in parte altr'uom da quel ch'i' sono" (l. 4). The sense of the phrase Petrarch envisions places him in a new historical horizon. In the self are parts or regions that the poet seeks to unify into a transcendent whole. The figures in tradition's representations of the self—Augustine, Narcissus, Echo, David—stand for these inner separate regions of the mind, for the many facets of temporal experience that Petrarch tries to bind together. Does he have a perspective enabling him to unify them? If he cannot, by what means can they be unified? Why do they resist any unification?

To answer these questions, let me turn to the two titles for Petrarch's lyrical sequence, *Canzoniere* and *Rerum vulgarium fragmenta*, which, used interchangeably, capture the double impulse of the collection. The term "canzoniere" designates the effort to constitute the "rime sparse" into a definite narrative or book, much as the *Vita nova* does. Petrarch, who was inspired by the *Vita nova*'s coming into being as a book, follows it in another way. Dante's "libello" tells the spiritual itinerary of the protagonist, and it ends with the revelation of the realm where Beatrice dwells in glory. One thread of the *Canzoniere* also tells of the mind's ascent to God. Like the *Vita nova*, the *Canzoniere* focuses on a double apprenticeship. The first is the sentimental education of the lover, who in the *Vita nova* is bent on grasping the elusive essence of the beloved Beatrice. This education mirrors the apprenticeship in the secrets of style by the poet who begins by not knowing much about art (or about love), but who finally announces the project of the book of the future. The *Canzoniere*, by contrast to the *Vita nova*, foregrounds the aesthetic self-creation of the poet for whom Laura is the name of the endless migrations of desire as well as of the pursuit of the poetic laurel: her name, given as an anagram or declined in a number of homophones ("aura," "oro," "laurea") becomes the mask for the shifting objects of desire. The other title, *Rerum vulgarium fragmenta*, recognizes the irreducible, fragmentary structure of the poetic sequence, whereby the parts composing it remain unrelated, broken pieces beginning forever anew.

The decisive event by which Petrarch seeks to unify the poems is the encounter with Laura on Good Friday, April 6, 1327 in the Church of St. Clare in Avignon. Over the course of 366 poems—in imitation of the eternal year—the lover lands on a *terra incognita:* he explores the fluctuations between unsuspected joys and sufferings, movement and stasis, and vanities and contrition of the heart within his own self. The contradictory moods within the self are explored through the myths of Narcissus, Orpheus, Acteon, and Apollo, as well as the voices of the *Confessions,* Dante, and David's Psalms. It may be added that Petrarch read the Psalms with the commentary of Augustine that Boccaccio had sent to him (*Fam.* 18.3).

To be sure, this Davidic dimension of the *Canzoniere* has been almost completely neglected. Nonetheless, it can be shown that it stages the biblical mode of the self (much in the wake of Augustine's self-analysis through the Psalms in the *Confessions*). A confessional sonnet, "Padre del ciel, dopo i perduti giorni" (62), written to commemorate the beginning of Petrarch's passion, juxtaposes it to the passion of the Crucifixion. The line "Miserere del mio non degno affanno" (12), more precisely, echoes David's penitential psalm, *Miserere* (Ps. 50). What is more, Petrarch's rhetorical move follows Dante's own narrative. In *Inferno* 1, the pilgrim, who is lost in a valley, addresses Vergil through the voice of David: "Miserere di me, gridai a lui, / qual che tu sii . . ." (*Inf.* 1.64–65). This penitential dimension, common to their poetry, is not an occasional, inconsequential posture. In fact, both Dante and Petrarch wrote penitential psalms.

One question, however, lingers. From the pilgrim's initial despondency, the *Divine Comedy* shows him rising all the way up to God. Is Dante's vertical transcendence and ordering of experience accessible to Petrarch? Or does Petrarch juxtapose laterally the religious, erotic, and aesthetic fragments of his mind without a hierarchy of values, on the assumption that he lacks a transcendent perspective allowing him to relate the parts to the whole? If so, are the sundry parts equally valuable routes in the journey to God, or is philosophical knowledge valueless to the ends of faith, as Petrarch claims in *De sui ipsius ignorantia*? Does this claim make Petrarch a philosophical skeptic?

It is possible to discern in the *Canzoniere* discreet elements of the desired harmonization of the love for Laura with the poet's desire to behold God's face. Sonnet 362, for instance, climaxes with the line "ch'i' stia a veder et l'uno et l'altro volto" (l. 11): the face of God and the face of Laura do not exclude each other. Yet, Petrarch's complex moral parabola emerges sharply from an analysis of the *Secretum,* which dwells on all these questions haunting the constitution of the self.[5] Written in 1342, the year after Petrarch received the poetic crown in Rome, the *Secretum* breaks a new path in his thinking. At the center of the *Collatio Laureationis,* the speech he deliv-

ered on the steps of the Roman Capitol in 1341, stands the project of founding a new culture that would revive the "discourse of Rome" for the modern age. Now Petrarch pauses and changes direction. He retreats into the
self and makes it the reflective focus of the text. From this standpoint, the
Secretum comes forth as Petrarch's exploratory journey of consciousness
in his interminable quest for self-knowledge. It ends up—one may add
parenthetically—giving legitimacy to the evocation of the historical-Roman
world delineated in the *Collatio*.

   Secretum: De secreto conflicto curarum mearum brings into relief the tortuous path Petrarch follows in this spiritual confession. The title conveys
the inner senses of the text. If "conflict," from *confligo* (to clash), suggests
a disagreement or litigiousness as in a tribunal between two parties, *secretum*, from *secernere* (to divide or separate), implies the solitary practice of
standing apart in an act of self-confrontation, of releasing or secreting what
is yet to be kept hidden from view and is not meant for a wide circulation.
Thus, like voyeurs, the readers are allowed to peek into the world of Petrarch's intimacy and to listen in on his confession, on the contradictory
nature of his consciousness, as it unfolds within an explicitly Augustinian
framework. The *Secretum* starts out, as a matter of fact, as a dialogue between Franciscus, Petrarch's autobiographical self-projection, and a fictional Augustinus, who stands for a highly personal version of the historical St. Augustine.

   What St. Augustine means to Petrarch at this stage can be quickly
sketched. The letter to the Augustinian friar and, until 1338, professor at the
University of Paris, Dionigi di Borgo San Sepolcro (*Fam.* 4.1), signals Petrarch's turn from the experience of curiosity and investigation of the natural world to the Augustinian analysis of the inner self.[6] Through Augustine, Petrarch retrieves the sense of the primacy of the will and of the self,
which is properly a web of discontinuities. By following the teachings of
St. Augustine's *Confessions,* Petrarch explores the domain of the will as the
source of subjectivity and as the gateway to self-knowledge, for it is through
the analysis of the will that any possible intelligibility of the self (and its
projects) can emerge.

   In his mapping the stages of his life's way in the *Secretum,* Petrarch utilizes Augustinus and Franciscus as embodiments of two contrasting perspectives. Accordingly, the dialogue between the two figures casts the text
as an existential quest. As in the love-story with Laura (and more so in the

case of Dante with Beatrice), the gaze of the beloved is the route the lover takes to return to his own self. Augustinus provides the transcendent perspective from which Franciscus descends into the self, judges, and justifies the self. Further, their dialogue, which ranges over a period of three days, takes place in the silent presence of Truth, who first appears as a woman of youthful radiance and beauty.

Truth's appearance to the sleepless Franciscus in the "Proem" is modeled on a variety of sources, such as the figures of *Ratio* in Augustine's two books of *Soliloquia,* the apparition of Venus to Aeneas in the *Aeneid* (I, 327), and, above all, the representation of Lady Philosophy in *De Consolatione Philosophiae.* But there are some differences. Lady Philosophy, for instance, appears to the languishing philosopher to banish the meretricious muses of poetry from his bedside and to instruct him about the order and wisdom of Creation (Fortune, free will, the rationality of the cosmos). In the *Secretum,* by contrast, after an initial self-identification, Truth falls silent and merely witnesses the exchange between her two disciples. We infer, as she stands outside the two interlocutors, that neither can affirm truth's ownership. Thus, a dialogue is needed to bring to light their shared truth. But how are we to understand the enigma of her silence? Is Petrarch implying that language disfigures Truth?

In an early work of Aquinas, *Quaestio disputata de veritate* (written in 1256–57), which can also be read as a bibliographical inventory of different philosophical views about truth (those of Aristotle in the *Metaphysics,* of Boethius, Augustine, Anselm, Avicenna, Isaac Israeli, and Hilary of Poitiers) (Questions 1–10), metaphysical truth is understood in terms of a correspondence between thought and reality. This philosophical background allows us to gauge the singularity and deliberateness of Petrarch's procedure. Truth, far from being understood as *adaequatio,* appears, but reveals itself by cloaking itself in silence. Petrarch tells a fable of Truth (with the double suggestion that we possess fictions of the Truth and that speech reveals and conceals Truth). Thus, silence (even Petrarch's own silence toward Dante) can be understood as the way of resisting the temptations of transforming Truth into a purely rhetorical posture.

As if to dramatize and denounce both the danger in and the human capacity for distorting Truth according to one's own will or whim, Petrarch lies about her. We are told that she lives in a mansion on the peak of Mount Atlas (and Petrarch lies or wrongly boasts that he had described her house in his *Africa*). Conversely, we are also told that she has descended from Heaven. The contradiction about Truth's origin—two views that belong to the claims of poetry and theology—shows that Petrarch is skeptical not about Truth, but about the accounts of the place where she resides. In his view, neither is Truth produced by the poet's own fiction (as if she were an artifact) or one's subjectivity, nor is she explainable, at least a priori, by the transcendent perspective of Augustine.

The claim of a "double truth," advanced by some of Averroes' followers, breaches and falsifies the essential unity of Truth, but there certainly is a double account of her origin. For Petrarch this much is clear: one goes to the Truth (or Truth shows herself forth) when one is engaged in the search of oneself (47), for in the end, Petrarch holds, one converses with one's own soul and experiences only oneself. More importantly, her existence transcends and embraces both the contingent, time-bound perspective of Franciscus and the transcendent vision of Augustinus. Accordingly, the three books of this dialogue investigate the ties binding the two dimensions together: Franciscus and Augustinus, respectively, a modern historical standpoint and a medieval eschatological perspective.

The interplay between these two viewpoints had its first dawning in Dante, and Petrarch alludes to him in a number of significant ways. The tripartite structure of the dialogue; the symbolic value of the number three, which Franciscus discusses in section 2 ("the number three appeals to me enormously, not so much because the three Graces are contained in it, as because it is the number most favored by the divinity") (95–96); the textual echo in the "Proem" to the words with which the pilgrim acknowledges Vergil's guidance in *Inferno* ("tu duca, tu segnore, e tu maestro") (*Inf.* 2.140) to formulate Augustine's submission to the way of Truth ("you are my guide, my counselor, my queen, and my teacher") (38)—these are some elements whereby the shade of Dante hovers over the *Secretum*. Finally, the reference to Boethius' figuration of Philosophy and to Augustine's figure of *Ratio* recalls the point of departure of *Convivio*.[7]

Toward the beginning of the treatise, Dante cites Boethius and Augustine to justify the autobiographical thrust of the philosophical reflection he is undertaking. His speculations are to be conducted as a commentary on his own doctrinal songs. Boethius' and Augustine's examples are mentioned to give dignity to a subjective, seemingly self-referential hermeneutics: "Veramente, al principale intendimento tornando, dico, come è toccato di sopra, per necessarie cagioni lo parlare di sè è conceduto: e questa necessità mosse Boezio di sè medesimo a parlare e questa ragione mosse Augustino ne le sue Confessioni a parlare di sè" (1.2.12–14).

Dante acknowledges and follows the paradigm of his two medieval precursors in the persuasion that their experiences can light his philosophical way and offer a standpoint from which to make intelligible his pursuit of self-knowledge. Petrarch, in turn, offers no facile reversal of Dante. He knows that his compulsion to know himself (which to him is a truly erotic adventure) involves a questioning of the authority of the past in the belief that he may go beyond tradition's ways of thinking. He certainly turns around Philosophy's banishment of poetry in Boethius' text. Thus, in the *Secretum*, he raises a central question, which Dante and the ancients do not: What can antiquity teach the moderns? And how is modernity related to the wisdom of the past? For Franciscus, modernity is crystallized both by the restlessness and digression of the self and by the will of the self to create one's world, to make oneself and so know oneself.

Convivio argues on behalf of the moral virtues on the ground of the purposiveness of actions, and Dante's philosophical hermeneutics follows the path of the Aristotelian-Thomistic *Ethics*. It never probes either the mode of construction of the self (which, in point of fact, the *Vita nova* had uncovered) or the foundation of the intellectual and moral values in life. The *Secretum*'s first question by Augustinus focuses on the dejection and loss of the self: "What are you doing, poor man?" The move doubtless recalls two texts of St. Augustine. In the *Confessions* (4.10), Augustine memorably casts the self as a "quaestio" or a riddle to oneself. In the beginning of his *Soliloquies*, moreover, he writes: "When I had been pondering many different things to myself for a long time, and had for many days been seeking my own self and what my own good was, and what evil was to be avoided, there suddenly spoke to me — what was it? I myself or someone else, inside me or outside me? — at any rate Reason said to me" (23).[8]

In the economy of Augustine's self-analysis, Reason directs the search for God as the proper road to self-knowledge. From this standpoint, the *Soliloquies* rewrites Ovid's myth of Narcissus (88–89). Narcissus lacks self-knowledge, but receives it at the moment of death when he recognizes that he is the very shadow he beholds in the mirror of the water. In the *Canzoniere*, Petrarch is constantly fascinated by the tragic aestheticism of Narcissus and Echo. In the *Secretum*, however, he shifts the ground as he reflects on the strength and weakness of the will. Franciscus' spiritual illness concerns the will. The problems confronting the self are not problems of philosophical self-knowledge or knowledge of the vital human goals. On the contrary, Franciscus has to learn to overcome what St. Paul calls the weakness of the will in order to become his own master: the will is weak to the extent that it cannot regulate itself and submits to the tyranny of the passions.

Consistently, Augustinus, from his metaphysical standpoint, recommends that to overcome oneself, or, as he puts it, to choose the "fig tree" over the "laurel tree" and the myrtle, Franciscus has to make a leap and, in the terms of book 10 of the *Confessions,* surrender the self's claim of power. The leap amounts to the experience of conversion, like that recorded in the *Confessions* and cited in the letter to Dionigi di Borgo San Sepolcro. Franciscus, on his part, hesitates. On the one hand, he rejects the connection between reason and the good; on the other, he acknowledges the sovereignty of the will over the intellect, but he admits that he is powerless to make a choice. If *Convivio's* analysis of moral knowledge strikes Petrarch as inadequate, this is not so for the representation of human activities in the *Divine Comedy*. Book 2 of the *Secretum* reviews the scheme of the seven deadly sins—pride, anger, sloth, lust, gluttony, avarice, and despair—not as psychological, theoretical abstractions available in the traditions of medieval allegory, but as problems of everyday existence. Plainly, Petrarch gives a clear recognition to the moral order of the *Divine Comedy* without, however, mentioning Dante by name. But we cannot be put off the scent. He says he has culled his insights from the theories of classical philosophers (such as Cicero and Seneca) and from "poets."

That the generic "poets" alludes to Dante appears from a number of conceptual elements running through Petrarch's argument. In the *Secretum,* as much as in *Purgatorio,* vices and virtues are tied to the fact of death. This imaginative link between death and ethics works differently in the two texts. *Purgatorio* refuses to view death as a strange event or an otherness coming from the outside. As a matter of fact, Dante internalizes death and makes the soul's moral process occur in its light. In the *Secretum,* by contrast, Petrarch is haunted by the fear of death in the guise of an awareness of the evanescence of beauty and the frailty of the body. He goes so far as to make death the foundation of illusory worldly achievements (as he says by quoting *Purg.* 11.101) (134). But he wills to circumvent death by building monuments to himself.

The second crucial conceptual link between Dante and Petrarch is to be found in the question of freedom as a principle of choice and responsibility for one's actions. In *Purg.* 27, as the pilgrim reaches the Garden of Eden, Dante posits the restoration of free will as the precondition of spiritual conversion. And as the experience of Cato and the pattern of the biblical Exodus underlying the structure of the whole poem show, liberty turns into the end of any significant spiritual quest. In Book 3 of the *Secretum,* Franciscus (whose name bears the resonance of freedom) intuits that Augustinus' request for a spiritual conversion is itself rooted in the depths of liberty. Augustinus makes vertical transcendence the hinge of any possible freedom from the lure of or bondage to earthly goods. Franciscus, on his part, claims the dignity and openness of both the finite world and of human artifacts. He asserts the value of this world. Yet, Petrarch perceives how complex the moral questions he raises can be: he makes the tyranny of the passions the contradictory, paradoxical basis of moral life: "Two unbearable chains," Augustinus tells Franciscus, "hold you in bondage" (101).

Franciscus resists yielding to Augustinus' appeal to free himself from these shackles, and he seems to end in an impasse. His will—so he explains himself—moves in two contrasting directions. By adopting the language of the Stoics (above all, Seneca), he holds that vices and virtues stem from a common seed. It follows that if one extirpates the root of the vices, one also destroys the root of the virtues. Thus, Franciscus resolves that he cannot renounce either the love for Laura or the pursuit of Fame. These two chains turn into wings of the soul. What seemed to be an impasse of the will— such as one finds in the story of Buridan's ass (*Par.* 4.1–9)—comes forth as itself a choice, a way of making finite time part of infinity, and an embracing of liberty as an essential human value. Is this a case of Petrarch's modern sophistry triumphing over the views held by Augustinus and Dante, who hold liberty to be a mode of self-transcendence? How can Petrarch claim to be free while he is in the throes of the passions?

The perception of the kinship between vices and virtues leads Petrarch to argue that his passions actually engender virtuous actions that express themselves through creative works of art. The two loves of Laura and of Fame, the names of self and history, are modes of and ways for self-making, and they describe Petrarch's understanding of freedom as a freedom to make oneself. Such a choice vindicates the Augustinian/Dantesque principle about the power of the will. It acknowledges responsibility for one's actions.

It claims the dignity and openness of the finite world and human artifacts. In effect, in a way that complements the Augustinian emphasis on the value of the beyond, Petrarch adds a modern dimension to the saint's spiritual urgency: the possibility of a horizontal self-transcendence. As Dante himself had shown in *Purgatorio,* the realm of contingency is not separable from the eschatological domain.

In closing, I would like to suggest that Petrarch's modern vision of horizontal self-transcendence flows from a source that is common to both Dante and himself: the Franciscan tradition.[9] It is not as strange as it might seem to think that the figuration of Franciscus preserves something of the original Franciscus, St. Francis. I suggest that in the deeper layers of the *Secretum* an imaginary conversation between the two historical figures, Augustine and Francis, is recorded. Several motifs in the *Secretum* echo the Franciscan legacy: references to various forms of poverty (of language, old age, earthly goods) (67, 74); views of the destitute human condition, whereby man "is born naked and uninformed in need of another's help lacking in wisdom" (77), and always aware of the "unfulfilled need in the heart" (78). From such premises St. Bonaventure articulates the theory of the value of labor, as well as of the lowest artifacts, as steps in the ladder of lights leading to God (see his *De reductione artium ad theologiam*).

From the standpoint of Petrarch as a neo-Augustinian and a Franciscan, an inextricable knot is posited between, on the one hand, history and nature and, on the other, eschatology; between Dante and Petrarch; between ancients and moderns. Their dialogue is rooted in the common, complex soil of the Christian tradition. As this chapter has argued, in this network of echoes and references, Dante, more than anybody else, has become Petrarch's inner voice. He echoes it, and in the process he transforms it. Dante is even a foil against whom Petrarch etches an alternative vision and feels on occasion spasms of crude jealousy—the jealousy of a man who does not get the recognition he craves, and who cannot get any recognition from his predecessor, just as he did not from Laura. And certainly Petrarch yielded to the lure of complacency in casting Dante as an ancient or untimely author, though the fiction allows him to present himself as the modern voice of the self. Clearly, his road to self-knowledge passes through all these stages and shades.

On the face of it, Petrarch has won the day. The modern European lyrical tradition—from Wyatt to Sidney and Shakespeare, from Ronsard to Du Bellay and Louise Labbè, from Garcilaso to Boscan and Sor Juana, from Vittoria Colonna to Bembo, Tasso, and Tansillo, from Leopardi to Nerval — recognizes itself in this self-reflexive poet who is fascinated by his inner shadows and yet, unlike his successors, finds a moral escape route out of his agonizing predicament. But Dante has had his share of followers (Shelley, Pound, Eliot, Mandelstam, Tasso, Ungaretti, Merrill, and, above all, Petrarch). That all his followers tend to view him as "untimely" matters little. From his "untimeliness" — as light emanating from the body of Beatrice — the moderns draw their spiritual energies. In this sense, the dialogue between ancients and moderns is destined never to end.

Notes

1. Quotations from the *Rvf* are taken from Francesco Petrarca, *Canzoniere,* ed. Gianfranco Contini, ann. Daniele Ponchiroli (Turin: Einaudi, 1964).

2. I am quoting from Francesco Petrarca, *Letters on Familiar Matters. Rerum familiarum libri,* trans. Aldo S. Bernardo (Baltimore and London: Johns Hopkins University Press, 1985), vol. 3.

3. I am quoting from Dante Alighieri, *Vita Nuova. Rime,* ed. Fred Chiappelli (Milan: Mursia, 1965).

4. I have discussed these questions in Giuseppe Mazzotta, "The *Vita nuova* and the Language of Poetry," *Rivista di studi italiani* 1 (1983): 1–16.

5. The references to this work are taken from Petrarch's *Secretum,* introd. and ed. Davy A. Carozza and H. James Shey (New York: Peter Lang, 1989).

6. When Petrarch reaches the summit of Mount Ventoux, he reads the following from St. Augustine's *Confessions*: "And they go to admire the summits of mountains and the vast billows of the sea and the broadest rivers and the expanses of the ocean and the revolutions of the stars and they overlook themselves." Bernardo, trans., *Rerum familiarum libri,* 1:178.

7. I quote *Convivio* from Dante Alighieri, *Opere minori,* vol. 1, part 2, ed. Cesare Vasoli and Domenico De Robertis (Milan and Naples: Ricciardi, 1988).

8. St. Augustine, *Soliloquies,* trans. Gerard Watson (Warminster, England: Aris and Phillips, 1990).

9. For a recent argument in favor of Petrarch's Franciscanism, see Marjorie O'Rourke Boyle, *Petrarch's Genius: Pentimento and Prophecy* (Los Angeles: University of California Press, 1991).

CHAPTER 5

Petrarch as the Metaphysical Poet Who Is Not Dante

Metaphysical Markers at the Beginning of *the* Rerum vulgarium fragmenta *(* Rvf *1–21)*

TEODOLINDA BAROLINI

THE FUNDAMENTAL PETRARCHAN PROBLEMATIC, APPARENT IN all his work, is the metaphysical issue of the one and the many. Singular versus plural, whole versus fragment, the one versus the many: this is Petrarch's abiding theme, and it is a metaphysical one. My argument is that Petrarch is a metaphysical poet, and that metaphysical concerns, defined as first principles and ultimate grounds, such as being and time, are Petrarch's abiding concerns. The *Rerum vulgarium fragmenta* is a metaphysical text, in that it engages a metaphysical problematic in both its form and its content. With respect to form, the metaphysical template is built into the shape of the lyric sequence: a form that is based on a dance of part vis-à-vis whole reflects the metaphysician's universal dance of the many vis-à-vis the One.[1] With respect to content, the *Rerum vulgarium fragmenta,* which thematizes fragmentation or multiplicity in its very title (a title that not coincidentally poses the dilemma: do we refer to this text in the plural, as suggested by the plural "fragments," or do we use the singular, as indicated by its being one work, one *canzoniere*?), is a text obsessed with time, the medium that robs us of ontological stillness and wholeness, that subjects us to constant incremental change, and that constitutes the experiential prism through which we humans most emphatically confront multiplicity. I am not suggesting that Petrarch subscribed to a metaphysical system in the sense of a philosophical solution, but I am suggesting that the problems that tugged at him ceaselessly — in particular the nature of time and the existence of the self in time — are metaphysical in nature.[2]

Petrarch's unremitting focus on the one versus the many takes various poetic shapes. Experientially, in terms of lived experience, his one/many focus expresses itself in his intense awareness of how the self gets lost in multiplicity; colloquially, we call this Petrarch's hyper-awareness of the passing of time. Moreover, for Petrarch, steeped in Augustine and having pored over the *Confessions,* it is second nature to link time and language. The self that is lost in the web of time is replicated as the self dispersed through the *rime sparse:* Petrarch self-consciously fashions a spider's web of language — "opra d'aragna" (spider's web [*Rvf* 173.6]) — that mirrors the web of time, of multiplicity. In a text that sets out to harness language's temporal properties, and that carefully deploys narrativity — time in its textual dress — it is not surprising as well to find the poet dramatizing narrative categories. The first of these is the category of beginning.

In this essay I will make the case that the opening poems of the *Rerum vulgarium fragmenta* — by which I mean poems 1–21 — air the major metaphysical concerns of the collection. Poems 1–21 form a unit, together with sestina 22 and canzone 23, that in turn belongs to the larger unit of initiation, poems 1–129; poems 1–23 form a beginning that is itself part of a larger beginning, a micro-*canzoniere* within the larger *canzoniere.*[3] By the time we have reached poem 129, the last canzone of the spectacular sweep of canzoni that begins with 125, we have experienced most of the collection's signature tropes and themes, as well as all of its metrical forms (five of the seven ballate are located between poems 1 and 129, as are all four madrigals). The opening set of 23 poems, which contains at least one subset devoted to beginningness — the introductory sequence 1–5 — is marked off from the larger set of poems 1–129 by its own spectacular culmination: the back-to-back presentation of the collection's first sestina, poem 22, and its first canzone, poem 23 (whose metaphysical depth precludes their treatment here). The conclusion of this set, canzone 23, "Nel dolce tempo de la prima etade," is a micro-text that thematizes firstness — "la prima etade" of the *incipit*—and whose paradoxical theme is that firstness and lastness collapse into the same point, a key theme of a cyclical macro-text that plays the part and the whole against each other in such a way as to problematize the nature of all beginnings and endings.

Many readers have noted that the *Fragmenta* open with a sequence of poems that possesses a narrative thrust, that poems 1–5 provide a prologue to the collection as a whole: poems 2 to 5 provide plot information regarding first the lover's enamorment, the cause and the time of it (2 and 3), and then the beloved, her place of origin and name (4 and 5).[4] Most significantly, this narrative sequence introduces the problematic of time and multiplicity into the text. Poems 1 to 5 are about first things, first times, and first (birth) places: the poet's "**primo** giovenile errore" (first youthful error [1.3]), Love's "**primiero** assalto" (first assault [2.9]), the day when "i miei guai / nel commune dolor s'incominciaro" (my misfortunes began in the midst of the universal woe [3.7–8]), the place where "sì bella donna al mondo nacque" (so beautiful a lady was born to the world [4.14]). Sonnet 2's formulation of Love's "first assault" will recur within the micro-*canzoniere* of poems 1–23: while in sonnet 20 "nel **primier** assalto" (line 14) does not refer to Love, "**primo** assalto" of canzone 23 (line 21) is a precise evocation of the first encounter detailed in sonnet 2. All these "firsts"—including the sound of the first sweet letters of Laura's name ("il suon de' **primi** dolci accenti suoi" [5.4])—find their first epilogue and consummation in canzone 23's "dolce tempo de la **prima** etade."

There are other markers in this prologue sequence of the poet's subjection to multiplicity. The existential significance of "rime **sparse**" in the *incipit* of sonnet 1, "Voi ch'ascoltate in rime sparse il suono," is, as is well known, glossed by the *Secretum*'s "et **sparsa** animae fragmenta recolligam" (I will gather the dispersed fragments of my soul [Book 3, 214]), where we see the metaphor of dispersion used in an explicitly spiritual context, echoing Augustine in the *Confessions*.[5] Moreover, the poet's contrite acknowledgment in the first sonnet of having become a subject of discussion among the populace, in other words of having become famous—"favola fui gran tempo" (10)—is also a way of signifying that he allowed himself to become ever more dispersed, rather than working to stay gathered, to "collect his soul" in the *Secretum*'s language ("Colligere animum" [Book 3, 162]).[6] For fame is nothing but being talked about by the multitude, and as a result the famous person is literally multiplied: "**sparsum** per ora multorum" (dispersed through the mouths of the many [*Secretum*, Book 3, 190]). The word "multorum" in this passage in the *Secretum*, with its suggestion that the self has been utterly consigned to multiplicity, is reinforced by Augustinus in his next remark, in which he defines fame as the breath of the many, "hominum plurimorum" (Book 3, 190). Given this context, the presence of the word "tempo" itself in the phrase "favola fui gran tempo" is only the most explicit of its signifiers of the self's subjection to multiplicity.

Time is the prime agent of our multiplicity. Particularly important for Petrarch — and profoundly metaphysical — is the metaphorical antithesis established in these passages and throughout his writings between whole and gathered versus dispersed and scattered: God is the former, while he is "nusquam integer, nusquam totus" (never whole, never all in one [*Secretum*, Book 1, 68]). In metaphysical terms, *integer* and *totus* versus *sparsus* are metaphorical terms that serve as a description of eternity versus time. We can approach time through the adjective *altro* in verse 4 of sonnet 1, "quand'era in parte **altr'**uom da quel ch'i' sono," frequently read as a trope of conversion (or conversion manqué). We can go further with *altro*, into as it were the metaphysical subsoil of the moral garden of conversion, by remembering that alterity is a key component of time.

Dante cites Aristotle's definition of time from the *Physics* in the *Convivio*: "Lo tempo, secondo che dice Aristotile nel quarto de la Fisica, è 'numero di movimento, secondo prima e poi'" (*Conv.* 4.2.6). "For time is just this," writes Aristotle, "number of motion in respect of 'before' and 'after'" (*Physics* 4.11.219b1): "numerus motus secundum prius et posterius."[7] Time, therefore, comports otherness, difference, nonidentity, nonsimultaneity. To the question, "does [the 'now'] always remain one and the same or is it always other and other?" (*Physics* 4.10.218a9−10), Aristotle replies, "if the 'now' were not different but one and the same, there would not have been time" (4.11.218b27−28): "si non esset **alterum** nunc, sed idem et unum, non esset tempus."[8] For there to be time, there must be the other: the *alterum* as compared to the *unum*, the *prius* and *posterius* as compared to the *nunc*. Time confers motion, change, absence of being, as Aristotle continues to make clear "nel quarto de la Fisica": "For time is by its nature the cause rather of decay, since it is the number of change, and change removes what is" (4.12.221b1−2); "But of time some parts have been while others have to be, and no part of it *is*" (4.10.218a5−6).

Time and multiplicity are causally related to desire, which we experience because of what we lack, as Dante explains in the *Convivio*: "ché nullo desidera quello che ha, ma quello che non ha, che è manifesto difetto" (for no one desires what he has, but what he does not have, which is manifest lack [*Conv.* 3.15.3]). Desire is lack, but also the motion in which we engage in order to fill the lack: "disire, / ch'è moto spiritale" (desire, which is spiritual motion [*Purg.* 18.31–32]). Temporal existence is governed by these laws, by absence of being, by its radical unplenitude, as beautifully expressed in Dante's thirteenth Epistle: "Omne quod movetur, movetur propter aliquid non habet, quod est terminus sui motus [. . .] Omne quod movetur est in aliquo defectu, et non habet totum suum esse simul" (Everything that moves, moves because of what it does not have, which is the end of its motion [. . .] Everything that moves exists in some defect, and does not possess all its being at once [*Ep.* 13.71–72]).

Opposed to the constellation of time/multiplicity/alterity/desire is God, who is precisely not difference but sameness; in the language of the *Confessions,* God is never *aliud* but always *ipsum,* never "other" but "the same and the very same and the very self-same": "qui non es **alias aliud** et **alias aliter,** sed id ipsum et id ipsum et id ipsum" (who art not another in another place, nor otherwise in another place, but the same and the very same and the very self-same).[9] Petrarch's use of the word *altro* throughout the *Frag-menta* bears the consciousness of God as sameness—*id ipsum*—and also of conversion as a process that is profoundly temporal, working through time to go beyond time, marked by a "before" and an "after," a "prius" and "posterius." The archetypal instances of *altro* in this sense are to be found in the *Secretum*'s "Transformatus sum in **alterum** Augustinum" (Book 1, 40), and in the *congedo* of penitential sestina 142, "A la dolce ombra de le belle frondi": "**Altr**'amor, **altre** frondi et **altro** lume, / **altro** salir al ciel per **altri** poggi / cerco, ché n'è ben tempo, et **altri** rami" [Another love, other leaves, and another light, / another climbing to Heaven by other hills / I seek (for it is indeed time), and other branches].[10]

Another word from "Voi ch'ascoltate" with a metaphysical valence is *vario* in the fifth verse, "del **vario** stile in ch'io piango et ragiono" (the varied style in which I weep and speak), an adjective whose *va-* opening reinforces the sonnet's dominant Augustinian message regarding the vanity of all earthly objects of desire, carried by *vano/vaneggiar:* "le **vane** speranze e 'l **van** dolore" (vain hopes and vain sorrow [6]), "et del mio **vaneggiar** vergogna è 'l frutto" (and of my pursuit of the vain, shame is the fruit [12]). Forms of *vario/variare* are a marker of multiplicity in Petrarch's lexicon, as we can see from the *Triumphi,* where they occur almost entirely in the final metaphysically charged *Triumphus Eternitatis* (and, interestingly, in one of the four usages, we find it again closely connected to *vaneggiar:* "la qual va-rietà fa spesso altrui / **vaneggiar**" [*TE* 73–74]).[11] In a passage that reads like a Petrarchan take on Augustine's discussion of time in Book II of the *Confessions,* Petrarch conjures an eternal present in which the inflection of time into past, present, and future will not exist, and there will be none of the temporal markers that "make human life varied and infirm": "né *fia,* né *fu,* né *mai,* né *inanzi,* o *'ndietro,* / ch'umana vita fanno **varia** e 'nferma!" (neither *will be,* nor *was,* nor *never,* nor *before,* nor *after,* which make human life varied and infirm! [*TE* 32–33; italics in original]). Here Petrarch makes explicit the link—a metaphysical link—between time and multiplicity: the inflected forms of the verb "to be" (*fia* and *fu*) represent the inflection of ontology. They signify that being itself is subject to change, while *mai* stands in for the ubiquitous little time-words to which Petrarch, like Augustine, assigns metaphysical importance, and finally, *inanzi* and *'ndietro* are signifiers of time, as we remember from Aristotle's definition of time as "numero di movimento, secondo prima e poi" (*Conv.* 4.2.6).[12]

To say that human life is *varia* is to say that it is subject to multiplicity. Petrarch characterizes multiplicity as that which makes *umana vita* not just *varia* but also *inferma,* for, as the *Secretum* puts it, we are subject to "tanta **varietate** successuum" (such a variety of events [Book 2, 116]). We can appropriately compare Petrarch in this regard to Dante, who has a more robust appreciation for the benefits of multiplicity as an expression of God's sublime act of differentiation, called by theologians *opus distinctionis.* Petrarch, on the other hand, consistently shows that "unease and suspicion in the presence of multiplicity," characteristic of Neoplatonism, which Patrick Boyde claims, mistakenly in my view, for Dante.[13] For Petrarch, as we have seen, a natural linguistic pairing for *vario* is *vaneggiar,* and to be *varia* is also to be *inferma.* Indeed, *inferma,* the adjectival form of the *infermitas* that characterizes human life in its variety and multiplicity, is in rhyme with its antithesis, *ferma,* the epithet for the eternal present in which past, present, and future time are collapsed: "E le tre parti sue vidi ristrette / ad una sola, e quella una esser ferma" (And its three parts I saw compressed to one alone, and that one was still [*TE* 28–29]).

Stability and immobility, the quality of being *ferma,* are key features of the eternal as compared to the temporal: while the temporal is flux and change, that which never stays still ("quel che mai non stette" [*TE* 26]), the eternal is stable ("stabile e ferma" [*TE* 2]), immobile ("in etate immobile et eterna" [*TE* 21]), and—most important for the maker of a collection of lyric poems—it is collected, gathered. Thus, the *Triumphus Eternitatis* defines eternity as "raccolta e 'ntera" (gathered and whole [69]). This characterization of eternity begins by negating the existence of time, which Petrarch does with a spate of the same little time words that litter the *Fragmenta*. Time's cessation is registered linguistically by its hyper-presence, as the poet declares that time and its partitions—"*dianzi, adesso, ier, deman, matino* e *sera*" (*before, right away, yesterday, tomorrow, morning* and *evening* [65; italics in original])—will pass away. There will be no past or future, but only the present. Again, as in the similar passage at *Triumphus Eternitatis* 32–33, Petrarch expresses himself through forms of the verb "to be" and temporal signifiers. He moves from the past and future tenses of "to be" to "only *is*," and from "*before, right away, yesterday, tomorrow, morning* and *evening*" to time words that signify *now,* thus attempting to replace the linearity of time with the simultaneity of the moment: "non avrà loco *fu, sarà,* ned *era,* / ma *è* solo, *in presente,* et *ora,* et *oggi,* / e sola *eternità* raccolta e 'ntera" (there will be no place for *was,* nor *will be,* nor *was being,* but only *is, in the present,* and *now,* and *today,* and only *eternity* gathered and whole [67–69; italics in original]).

The hyper-presence of time in Petrarch's definition of eternity bespeaks anxiety: his language betrays that his focus is on what eternity is not, more than on what it is. The form of this definition of eternity is working against its content. In its substance, however, Petrarch's definition of eternity partakes of the classic theological definition of Boethius, who, in the *Consolation of Philosophy,* notes that God, by definition eternal, is therefore simultaneous. Acknowledging Aristotle's doctrine of infinite time, Boethius yet claims that even if time has no beginning or ending, it cannot be called "eternal"—"aeternum"—because it does not comprehend and embrace all the space of its life at the same time: "simul." Eternity requires simultaneity: "Aeternitas igitur est interminabilis vitae *tota simul* et perfecta possessio" (Eternity therefore is the perfect possession *altogether and at the same time* of an endless life [*Phil. Cons.* 5.6.9–11; italics mine]).[14] Boethius stresses that what is not *simul* is not eternal: endless life is one thing, and God's ability to embrace the whole presence of an endless life together and at the same time is another. Endlessness should be called "perpetual"—"perpetuum"; while only the plenitude of presence in a never fading instant may be called "eternal"—"aeternum." Augustine too had contrasted the still presentness of eternity to the constant movement of time: "But in eternity nothing moves into the past: all is present. Time, on the other hand, is never all present at once" ("non autem praeterire quicquam in aeterno, sed totum esse praesens; nullum vero tempus totum esse praesens" [*Conf.* 11.11]). And for Aquinas, following both Boethius and Aristotle, eternity is a unified and simultaneous whole: "aeternitas est tota simul" (*ST* 1a.10.4).[15]

Philosophically, human life is *varia* for Petrarch not because he is celebrating its infinite variety, but because it is not gathered, simultaneous, and whole. From a philosophical standpoint, in terms of his stated philosophical positions, Petrarch is quite consistent about rejecting the particular for the universal, the creature for the Creator (in the language of the *Secretum*). This is not to say that the particular does not make itself felt—quite the contrary. The *Triumphi* themselves, although describing human life as "varia e 'nferma," end with a vision of Laura: a particular culled from the variety of human life. But, from a philosophical standpoint, *varia e inferma* is a fair representation of Petrarch's consistent stated view (as compared to his practice). In terms of stated positions, in other words, Petrarch does not follow Dante as he walks a tightrope between unity and multiplicity, relishing both the one and the many, keeping always in mind that the one made the many, that "distinctio et multitudo rerum est a Deo" (the difference and multiplicity of things come from God [*ST* 1a.47.1]). As I have tried to show, Dante's is a double allegiance: he works to synthesize Aristotelian sympathy for difference with the Neoplatonic One.[16]

Dante embraces paradox. Both in form and in content he embraces the paradoxes of metaphysics, as dramatized by the vision of *Paradiso* 28, which forces us to conjure the universe as simultaneously "both center and circumference, both the deep (Augustinian) within and the great (Aristotelian) without,"[17] or in modern terms, as both quantum mechanics and general relativity. Petrarch does not embrace paradox, but he does embody it: his form is the vehicle for an anxious celebration of multiplicity that his content attempts to deny. Already we can see the famous Petrarchan *dissidio*, built into the very texture of the web he weaves, in which the warp contradicts the woof and vice versa.

The adjective *vario* appears again in the *Triumphi*, and in a way that reinforces its connection to the many by linkage to another of Petrarch's key metaphysical markers, a usage that is essentially shorthand for evoking the one and the many: constructions based on the contrast of *un* (the one) and *mille* (a thousand). The lovers in *Triumphus Cupidinis* II are "**varii** di lingue, e **varii** di paesi, / tanto che di **mille un** non seppi il nome" (so various in tongue and nation that of a thousand I did not know one name [*TC* II.139–40]). *Mille* is a Petrarchan *senhal* for the many: for the multiplicity of created existence that is contrasted linguistically to the holistic simplicity—the non-variety—of the one. We think, for instance, of the postilla to the draft of *Rvf* 77 and 78, where in order to say that the poems were copied into the *Rerum vulgarium fragmenta* long after their composition, Petrarch writes that they were transcribed "post **mille** annos" (after a thousand years).[18] The repetition of *mille* signifies hyperbolic quantity: in *Triumphus Temporis* the temporal duration of great fame is such that some men are "dopo **mille** anni, / e **mille e mille**, più chiari che 'n vita" (after a thousand years, and a thousand and a thousand, more famous than in life [25–26]). We find a similar usage in the sonnet "Vinse Hanibàl": "che vi può dar, dopo la morte anchora / **mille et mille** anni, al mondo honor et fama" (that can give you, even after death, for a thousand and a thousand years, honor and fame in the world [103.13–14]). Conversely, *mille* can be used to single out the one from the many: Augustinus in the *Secretum* is addressed as "Care michi ex **milibus** Augustine" (Dear to me among thousands, Augustine [*Prohemium*, 24]).[19] Love is frequently connected to the *un/mille* marker, as we saw with the lovers of *Triumphus Cupidinis*. Thus, in *Rvf* 2, in which Petrarch recounts Love's attack on him, Love is said to have punished "in one day a thousand offenses": "Per fare una leggiadra sua vendetta, / et punire in **un dì ben mille** offese" (2.1–2). This association of Love's incursion into his soul with the *un/mille* marker is a primal instance of Laura's metaphysical associations.[20]

The *un/mille* marker is significant because—like Laura herself, as we shall see—it suggests both the one and the many and the dialectic between them. Laura's association with multiplicity—and hence with mortality—is made clear in *Rvf* 5. We noted the series of firsts in the prologue sonnets; we stopped short of noting that with firstness, with beginnings, come also endings and death, implied in the reference to Christ's death in *Rvf* 3 (the cause of the "commune dolor") and fully introduced as early as *Rvf* 5, "Quando io movo i sospiri a chiamar voi." This sonnet, perhaps not coincidentally the first poem to begin with "Quando," is also the first poem to contain the words "il fine": the end. *Rvf* 5 is a famous play on the beloved's name, parsed as LAU-RE-TA, and—far from being a frivolous gesture toward rhetorical virtuosity—it instructs us that narrativity resides in *her*, in her name, represented here as syllabified by time:

> LAUdando s'incomincia udir di fore
> il suon de' primi dolci accenti suoi.
> Vostro stato REal, che 'ncontro poi,
> raddoppia a l'alta impresa il mio valore;
> ma: TAci, grida il fin, ché farle honore
> è d'altri homeri soma che da' tuoi.
>
> (5.3–8)

> When I move my sighs to call you and the name that
> Love wrote on my heart, the sound of its first sweet accents
> is heard without in LAU-ds. Your RE-gal state, which
> I meet next, redoubles my strength for the high enterprise;
> but "TA-lk no more!" cries the ending, "for to do her honor
> is a burden for other shoulders than yours."

In *Confessions* 13.15, angels are able to look upon God's face and read in it "sine syllabis temporum"—"without the syllables of time." The syllabification of Laura's name, by contrast, recalls Augustine's syllabification of the hymn *Deus Creator omnium* as an analogue for time in *Confessions* 11.27. As Augustine sounds out the syllables of the hymn in order to try to grasp the nature of time, so Petrarch's *sospiri* sound out the nature of Laura as a being inexorably temporal. Moreover, Augustine describes his return from ecstatic simultaneity in the vision at Ostia as a falling back into sound, language, and therefore time, in the form of beginnings and endings: "et remeavimus ad strepitum oris nostri, ubi verbum et incipitur et finitur" (we returned to the sound of our own speech, in which each word has a beginning and an ending [*Conf.* 9.10]). Learning from Augustine, who returns from extra-temporal vision at Ostia to the sound of language, and thus to time, in the form of beginnings and endings, Petrarch understands the textual and the temporal to be parallel modalities.

Rvf 5 dramatizes the enmeshedness of time and narrative. Particularly noteworthy are the narrative markers that the poet has linked to the syllables of the beloved's name: LAU with "s'incomincia," RE with "poi," and TA with "il fin." The first syllable corresponds to beginnings, the middle syllable to middles, and the last syllable to endings; thus, to the extent that the text engages a being defined as existing in time, such as Laureta, it engages the temporal/narrative problems of beginnings, middles, and ends. The anomalous spelling of her name as Laureta evokes—in the mature lexicon of the *Fragmenta*—*l'aura* and *rete,* the evanescent caught in the net of time and text, as in *Rvf* 239: "In rete accolgo l'aura" (In a net I catch the air [37]). The ominous "TAci, grida il fin," where *il fin*—the end—shouts "Be silent" to the poet, suggests the ultimate ending and the ultimate silence: the silence of death. The subordination of the poet to the violence of *il fin* also foreshadows the poem's final tercet, where we find that Apollo may disdain the mortal poet's presumptuous attempt to write of the god's evergreen boughs: "se non che forse Apollo si disdegna / ch'a parlar de' suoi sempre verdi rami / lingua mortal presumptüosa vegna" (except that perhaps Apollo is incensed that any mortal tongue should come presumptuous to speak of his eternally green boughs [5.12–14]). The poet's mortality, his non-eternity—his "lingua mortal"—is thus firmly established by *Rvf* 5's conclusion, as well as the link between the last syllable of the beloved's name with finality and with all the many finite things of the world: the opposite of the non-finite plenitude of God.

Laura indeed *is* multiplicity. Her hair (in Italian, we should not forget, *capelli* is plural, like *fragmenta*), scattered to the wind in "**mille** dolci nodi" in *Rvf* 90 (a thousand sweet knots [2]), is the chief of many poetic signifiers of her function as carrier of multiplicity. Unlike Beatrice, who exists in an iconic present tense until she dies, when she is reborn into an even more potent present tense, Laura exists primarily in the past. Her poet does not keep her immune from the passage of time; rather, he uses her to mark the passage of time. Let us consider a paradigmatic sonnet like *Rvf* 90, "Erano i capei d'oro a l'aura sparsi." Here, as frequently throughout his lyric collection, Petrarch uses the traits and motifs of stilnovism—of theologized courtliness—to achieve very different goals from those of Guinizzelli or Dante.

The key to those goals is Petrarch's use of the imperfect tense—a past tense—to capture Laura's traits. Indeed, *Rvf* 90 begins, very subtly but very strongly, with the imperfect of the verb "to be," *Erano:* her hairs of gold *were* scattered by the wind. The imperfect tense, the tense of ongoing incomplete action in the past, is the tense of memory par excellence; it is the tense of narration, in which the "I" captures and caresses the past as he conjures it and holds it in his memory. The "I" and his thought process are the poem's subject (and the only matter to exist in the present); the lady—evanescent, transient, mortal—is the vehicle for catching the "I" in the process, catching him in the web. The imperfect tense that defines Laura in this poem— "Non *era* l'andar suo cosa mortale, / ma d'angelica forma" (Her walk *was* not that of a mortal thing but of some angelic form [9–10; italics mine])— is the marker of her mortality, which functions as a catalyst for the poet to meditate on his own mortality. Her step may not seem mortal, but mortal is precisely what it is, and the "angelic form" she possesses is claimed in a spirit of elegiac hyperbole, not in a spirit of genuine mystical affirmation. She is no longer the Lady as Manifestation of the Transcendent—who exists in a syntactic eternal present, as we can see in Dante's sonnet "Tanto gentile e tanto onesta pare"—but the Lady as Measurer of My Mortality.

For Petrarch, desire is more important as a modality through which to experience the passing of time than it is as an experience in itself. In this respect too he differs from Dante, who is primarily a love poet, in the sense that he is a poet for whom love is a primary experience and for whom understanding the workings of love in human life and in the universe at large is a primary goal. Dante's definition of desire as spiritual motion, "disire, / ch'è moto spiritale" (*Purg.* 18.31–32), is a primary entrance into Dante's thought, glossing the path of life on which we find ourselves in the *Commedia*'s first verse as the path of desire, a path on which we move because propelled by desire, and ultimately showing us that the love and desire that move the individual—"amor mi mosse" (love moved me [*Inf.* 2.72])— move the cosmos as well: "l'amor che move il sole e l'altre stelle" (the love that moves the sun and the other stars [*Par.* 33.145]). Petrarch is a poet for whom understanding the deep springs of desire is secondary to his meditation on what it is to be a self that is caught in the flux of time. Petrarch is in fact always doing what Augustinus in the *Secretum* exhorts him to do: he is always meditating on death, and for him love and desire are merely a means for furthering such a meditation.

Simply stated, my point is that the *Rerum vulgarium fragmenta* are not primarily erotic: erotics are secondary in the *Fragmenta* to multiplicity and time and the subjection of the self to these forces. This is not to say that eros is nonexistent in the *Fragmenta*, but that it is subject to time, which supersedes and vanquishes desire in precisely the way that is dramatized by the *Triumphi*. The *Triumphi* represent existence as a succession of great forces which overcome each other in sequence: love is overcome by chastity, chastity by death, death by fame, fame by time, and finally—in a tellingly flawed bid to step outside of the succession and to trump all successiveness—time is overcome by eternity. In Petrarch's inward-centered lyric sequence, as in the more outward-focused world-historical sequence of triumphs, the object of desire is finally most important as a signifier of the passing of time.

This subordination of eros to a meditation on mortality is already abundantly clear in *Rvf* 12, where Laura's blond hair, which first appears in the preceding poem, the ballata "Lassare il velo," as an erotic fetish, is turned—so early in the *Fragmenta!*—into a marker of mortality.[21] In fact, *Rvf* 12 presages *Rvf* 90, where the captivating tableau of her hair in its sweet knots of multiplicity immediately plunges us into contact with her mortality: "Erano i capei d'oro a l'aura sparsi / che 'n mille dolce nodi gli avolgea, / e 'l vago lume oltra misura ardea / di quei begli occhi ch'or ne son sì scarsi" (Her golden hair was loosed to the breeze, which turned it into a thousand sweet knots, and the lovely light burned without measure in her eyes, which are now so stingy of it [1–4]). The mortality that is explicit in verse 4 of "Erano i capei d'oro," where we confront the dimming of Laura's eyes, and thus the change that has brought about the diminished present tense of "ch'or ne son sì scarsi," is already inscribed into the caressing and elegiac imperfect with which the sonnet begins.

Rvf 12, the sonnet "Se la mia vita da l'aspro tormento," picks up and elaborates on *Rvf* 5's positioning of Laura as a function of time. *Rvf* 12's golden hairs, its "capei' d'oro," are the threads of time, as throughout the *Fragmenta*. Here Petrarch imagines them, in a precise anticipation of "Erano i capei d'oro," where her hair does not change color but the luster of her eyes is dimmed, in the process of changing from gold to silver: "e i cape' d'oro fin farsi d'argento" (and your hair of fine gold made silver [12.5]). This sonnet is threaded with time, and with the language of time, even more densely packed than usual because of the premise: the poet imagines himself and Laura grown old. The result is that we find a language of time that covers the spectrum from the intertextually evocative (the "verdi panni" that the aging Laura puts aside along with her garlands evoke the "green" youth of the lady in Dante's sestina) to the most quintessentially Petrarchan: *Rvf* 12 contains both *oro* (gold) and *ora* (hour), talismanic lexical choices that cluster around the adverb *ora/or* (now), one of the *Fragmenta*'s most frequently used words.[22]

The syllable *or* is ubiquitous, and it functions in the *Rerum vulgarium fragmenta* like the ticking of a clock or the sound of one's breath: it is the very sound of time. (Thus, when in the *Triumphus Eternitatis* Petrarch makes *ora* one of his synonyms for the eternal, he is not only evoking the Boethian *totum simul* but also literally bundling up time into the folds of eternity.)[23] *Or* is also a sound that we encounter immediately, in *Rvf* 1, whose "Ma ben veggio **or** sì come al popol tutto" (9) is reinforced by rhyme words— some of the most common of the *Fragmenta*— that contain the *or* sound: "c**or**e" in verse 2, "err**or**e" in verse 3, "dol**or**e" in verse 6, and "am**or**e" in verse 7.[24]

In *Rvf* 12, the poet imagines a future of at least qualified fulfillment, not of eros in the most obvious sense but of a perhaps even greater longing: the desire to speak of himself to her. He imagines a future when he and Laura will have grown old (a motif that recurs in the *Secretum* as well),[25] in which he will be able to unburden himself of the weight of living in time. This he will do by revealing himself to Laura, recounting to her the story of his sufferings, unraveling for her his existence as a being in time: "ch'i' vi discovrirò de' mei martiri / qua' sono stati gli anni e i giorni et l'ore" (I shall disclose to you what have been the years and the days and the hours of my sufferings [10–11]). In these verses Petrarch conjures a future in which his past— made discrete and quantified through the temporal intervals that mark it, from years, to days, to hours— will be literally "dis-covered" for Laura. And if, concludes the sonnet with a flourish of temporality, age (expressed as "tempo," the passing of time) will no longer permit the satisfaction of eros ("se 'l tempo è contrario ai be' desiri"; if time is hostile to my sweet desires [12]), by communicating with her in this way he will at least receive from Laura some succor of "tardy sighs": "alcun soccorso di tardi sospiri" (some little help of tardy sighs [14]).

We can better gauge the significance of the phrase "alcun **soccorso di tardi** sospiri" when we analyze it as a reconfiguration of Beatrice's fear that she will be too late to help the pilgrim in *Inferno* 2: "e temo che non sia già sì smarrito, / ch'io mi sia **tardi al soccorso** levata" (I am afraid that he may be already so lost that I have risen too late to help him [*Inf.* 2.64–65]).[26] For Dante, lateness is a narrative tool for depicting urgency: he uses lateness— against theological protocol, according to which a blessed soul like Beatrice who sees the future in the mind of God would know full well that she is not too late—to conjure the urgency of Beatrice's willed intervention. Thus, "tardi" is an adverb modifying Beatrice, who fears she is late in offering her "soccorso." For Petrarch, lateness itself has become the topic, as witnessed by the transferral of the epithet, with "tardi" now an adjective modifying "sospiri": "soccorso" will come—if it ever does come—from the "late sighs," the "tardi sospiri." Tardiness takes center stage, while Laura's agency and concern are diminished.

The "tardi sospiri" of *Rvf* 12's conclusion offer our first sighting of the Petrarchan adjective/verb cluster *tardo/tardare*, perhaps the poet's quintessential means for conjuring belatedness: regret for time lost and for a future forever tarnished by what we failed to do in the past. Not for Petrarch the can-do optimism and psychological good health of staying focused on what we can control in the present, of leaving behind what is past and hence irreparable. Deep springs of regret nourish his poetry. They are frequently visible; for me they are most poignantly captured in one of the poet's spare annotations. Above the draft of the sonnet "Mai non vedranno," which became *Rvf* 322, Petrarch wrote: "Responsio mea sera valde"—"My response, late indeed." "Mai non vedranno" was written as a response to Giacomo Colonna's sonnet congratulating Petrarch on receiving the laurel crown in 1341; Giacomo himself died in August 1341, before Petrarch was able to reply to his congratulations. All the regret and belatedness that mark human interactions—all the things we wish we had said before it was forever too late to say them—are contained in the phrase "Responsio mea sera valde."

"Se la mia vita" is an important poem: it inaugurates the lateness that hovers always in the air of the *Fragmenta*, as well as the fusing of future and past, which in the great canzone *Rvf* 126, "Chiare, fresche, et dolci acque," will be compellingly used to create an aura of timeless present. It also works strongly against its predecessor, the ballata *Rvf* 11, "Lassare il velo," to redefine the erotic as the temporal: to temporalize eros. The dynamic between *Rvf* 11 and *Rvf* 12 is worth attending to, for the temporalizing of eros is a signature move of the *Fragmenta*. The care to isolate the metaphysical component of eros, capturing it in his metaphysical net—"In rete accolgo l'aura" (*Rvf* 239.37)—is one that distinguishes Petrarch from other lyric love poets.

One could fairly make the case that Petrarch uses the ballata, as do his predecessors, to import some physicality—in this poem highly deflected by the "veil" whose continual covering presence the lover deplores—into his poetry collection. "Lassare il velo" is the first ballata in the *Fragmenta* (most of the collection's seven ballate are concentrated at the beginning, with five strung between 11 and 63), and it does for erotic physicality what *Rvf* 3, "Era il giorno," does for falling into love: it constructs eros *ab initio* as an exercise in counterproductive behavior and frustration. In "Era il giorno," the poet constructs a literal double bind that trumps the courtly use of *preso* as an expression of being captured by love: he is caught by love on the very day that the sun's rays are discolored out of pity for their Maker ("Era il giorno ch'al sol si scoloraro / per la pietà del suo Factore i rai, / quando i' fui preso"; "It was the day when the sun's rays turned pale with grief for his Maker when I was taken" [3.1–3]), thereby ensuring that he is twice caught—for he is "preso" in a vice of guilt and remorse as well as in a vice of love. Similarly, in "Lassare il velo," the veil is introduced as the agent of frustration. The lover wishes her to reveal herself, but from the moment that she came to know of his great desire, she will not let go the veil with which she keeps herself hidden: "Lassare il velo o per sole o per ombra, / donna, non vi vid'io / poi che in me conosceste il gran desio" (Lady, I have never seen you put aside your veil for sun or for shadow since you knew the great desire in me [11.1–3]).

This theme of desiring to know and withdrawing from being known is Cavalcantian, just as the ballata is Cavalcanti's genre par excellence and *conoscenza* is his word for possession both erotic and meta-erotic: in *Rvf* 11 knowledge is transferred to the lady, so that the Cavalcantian lover's typical failure to achieve *conoscenza* mutates into Laura's punitive self-covering "poi che in me conosceste il gran desio" (3). Petrarch has introduced the veil into the Cavalcantian thematic as the lady's method of wielding control over eros ("sì mi governa il velo"; thus the veil controls me [11.12]), which she does by covering the physical attributes, such as her hair, on which the lover wishes to gaze. And we should remember that the veil motif is closely related to the Diana/Actaeon thematic, made explicit in the extraordinary canzone that culminates the first part of the *Fragmenta*, *Rvf* 23, in which the lover's *conoscenza* is not only denied but also severely punished.

The ballata "Lassare il velo" begins strongly, with the lady's assertion of the control that frustrates the lover: she rejects eros by refusing to let go the veil—"**Lassare** il velo"—either by day or by night ("o per sole o per ombra"). This same infinitive, *lassare*, which in *Rvf* 11 is so forceful a marker of the eros that it rejects, in the sonnet that follows becomes a marker of her mortality, as the aging Laura must "let go" the garlands and green raiment of her youth: "et **lassar** le ghirlande e i verdi panni" (12.6). More striking even is the fading of her hair: the blond hair that in the ballata Laura insists on veiling as soon as Love makes her aware of the poet's feelings— "ma poi ch'Amor di me vi fece accorta, / fuor i **biondi capelli** allor velati" (but since Love has made you aware of me, your blond hair has been veiled [11.8−9])—in *Rvf* 12 has morphed from gold to silver: "e i **cape' d'oro** fin farsi d'argento" (and your hair of fine gold made silver [12.5]). The transition from "biondi capelli" to "cape' d'oro" is telling: *biondo* does not, as *oro* does, evoke *ora,* nor does it belong to a scale of values on which gold degrades to silver.

There is more that one could say about the dynamic between "Lassare il velo" and "Se la mia vita," especially around the theme of self-veiling: the physical self-revelation denied by the beloved in the ballata is achieved in a nonphysical dimension by the lover in the sonnet, whose answer to her covering veil is the process of "dis-covery"—"discovrirò"—whereby he unveils and reveals himself to her. But in our pursuit of *Petrarca metafisico* we shall now go back to *Rvf* 6, "Sì travïato è 'l folle mi' desio," a sonnet about the implacable irresistibility of eros in the spirit of Dante's sonnet "Io sono stato con Amore insieme."[27] Here, as is most often the case with Petrarch, eros is communicated through frustration of desire (as compared, for example, to the aggressive consummation we find in Dante's "Così nel mio parlar"), most emphatically in the identification of the poem's "I" with Apollo as he pursues, gains, and loses Daphne. Thus the perilous analogy between the poet and Apollo, the disdainful god who was introduced by name in *Rvf* 5, is continued beyond the metapoetic into the erotic domain. The lover of *Rvf* 6 is in the grip of a *folle desio* that transports him to his death against his will: "i' mi rimango in signoria di lui, / che mal mio grado a morte mi trasporta" (I remain in his power, as against my will he carries me off to death [6.10−11]). Love's dominance is captured by the pent-up energy of "che mal mio grado a morte mi trasporta," a verse whose furious slowness reflects the self's frustrated resistance and ultimate surrender. But then, in the moment of surrender, the poem turns. The lover rushes headlong to his death—but nothing climactic happens. Or rather, what happens is an anti-climax that only intensifies the previous frustration; he rushes headlong to his death—only to reach the laurel, where one gathers bitter fruit: "che mal mio grado a morte mi trasporta: / sol per venir al lauro onde si coglie / acerbo frutto" (6.11–13).

In its delineation of two bleak alternatives, death or the laurel's bitter fruit, *Rvf* 6 is a precise prolepsis of *Rvf* 22, the sestina that, with the canzone that follows it, serves as the climax or ending of the *Fragmenta's* beginning micro-*canzoniere*. But for the moment I am interested in the use of the word *sol* in "**sol** per venir al lauro" in verse 12 of *Rvf* 6. The *Fragmenta's* first use of *sol* as "sun" belongs to the *incipit* of *Rvf* 3, "Era il giorno ch'al **sol** si scoloraro." Solar imagery begins to be associated with Laura in *Rvf* 4, where her birth is heralded as that of a sun, "ed or di picciol borgo un **sol** n'à dato" (and now from a small village He has given us a sun [4.12]), and is reprised in the elaborate conceit of *Rvf* 9, a sonnet in which the creative effects of a springtime sun on the earth are compared to the effects of Laura's eyes on the lover: "così costei, ch'è tra le donne un **sole**, / in me movendo de' begli occhi i rai / crïa d'amor penseri, atti et parole" (Thus she who among ladies is a sun, moving the rays of her lovely eyes, in me creates thoughts, acts, and words of love [10–12]). Of course her eyes are both solar and not, given that *Rvf* 9 concludes by swerving toward one of the collection's great verses of deprivation: "primavera per me pur non è mai" (spring for me still never comes [9.14]). However she deploys her eyes, for him springtime never comes: the *tronchezza* of the "I" is perfectly reflected in the *verso tronco*, "primavera per me pur non è mai," that seals this poem. And deprivation continues as a theme, for *Rvf* 10 registers the first use of *troncare/tronco*, sutured to the adjective "sol" to signify the deprivation that Giacomo Colonna "alone" can cause, punning on him as an absent sun: "ma tanto ben **sol tronchi** et fai imperfecto / tu che da noi, signor mio, ti scompagne" (But so much good you alone cut short and make imperfect, for you keep yourself, my Lord, far from us [10.13–14]).[28]

The "sol" of *Rvf* 6's "**sol** per venir al lauro" is also connected to loss: it constitutes the text's first instance of the adverb *solo*, "only," and it signifies precisely privation, instead of the plenitude of the sun, which at the same time the homonym evokes. Indeed, we could say that the sun god Apollo of *Rvf* 5 is obliquely present in the *sol* of *Rvf* 6, and that "**sol** per venir al lauro" suggests the moment in which Apollo—*sol*—catches up with Daphne and gets nothing, remaining *sol* (alone). Like the adverb, the adjective *solo/sola*, "alone," can also register privation, although it is an ambivalent signifier: as we shall see, and as already suggested in the *solo* that modifies Giacomo Colonna in *Rvf* 10, it is also capable of denoting the One in its simple fullness. Both erotic privation and erotic fullness are present in *Rvf* 22, the sestina where we find the *Fragmenta*'s most erotically charged uses of the adjective—"'n un **sol** giorno" (in but one day [28]), "**sol** una nocte" (just one night [33])—entwined with the rhyme word *sole*.

This double valence of *sol*—both plenitude and privation—will come to fruition in the sun of the *Triumphus Temporis*, which is not a nourishing presence but a destructive and all-consuming one. Thus, the sun of *Triumphus Temporis* is not the "Almo **Sol**" of *Rvf* 188, not a nurturer. But even the sun of the sonnet "Almo Sol," we remember, belies the descriptor *almo* and is ultimately a grower of shadow, not of life, for it is shadow that grows while the poet speaks: "L'ombra che cade da quel' humil colle [. . .] crescendo mentr'io parlo" (The shadow that falls from that low hill [. . .] growing as I speak [188.9, 12]). The nuance and ambivalence of *Rvf* 188, the conjunction of *almo* with *ombra,* is altogether removed from the sun of the *Triumphi*: the protagonist sun that emerges "sì ratto" from its golden hostel at the outset of *Triumphus Temporis* signals full-blown and uncontrolled temporal anxiety. The transition from verse 1 to verse 2 of *Triumphus Temporis* distills the difference in tone of the *Fragmenta* and the *Triumphi*. From the elegiac *incipit,* "De l'aureo albergo, co l'Aurora inanzi," which is not out of step with many verses of the *Fragmenta,* especially in the later sections of part 1 where Aurora takes the place of Daphne, we move to the uncompromising urgency of "sì ratto usciva il **Sol** cinto di raggi," a verse whose latent anxiety is reinforced and made explicit by the bizarre domesticity of "che detto avresti:—E' si corcò pur dianzi!" (From its golden inn, with the Dawn in front, so fast did the Sun exit banded with rays, that you would have said "He just now went to bed!" [*TT* 1–3]). This third verse, conjuring the whirlwind of adult life in which it seems as though "we just went to bed" as nights bleed into dawn and dawns into nights, gives the full measure of the fearsome yet so familiar *Sol* of the *Triumphus Temporis* (as perhaps the domesticity of the verse gives the measure of the *Triumphi*'s odd modernity).

Petrarch builds much complexity into *sol* as noun, as adverb, and as adjective. This is not surprising given the freighted value of solitude for Petrarch, who penned a treatise entitled *De vita solitaria* on the moral worth of solitude, and yet associates solitude with love and with Laura in the *Fragmenta*. Here too we come back to the core issue of the one/many: solitude is a moral good for Petrarch precisely because it offers the self an opportunity to be collected, rather than to be dispersed in the multiplicity of the crowd. At the same time, Petrarch invests solitude with his typical ambiguity, and so we find that Augustinus in the *Secretum* upbraids Franciscus for seeking solitude: because solitude reinforces his love for Laura (as we see, for example, in *Rvf* 129, the canzone "Di pensier in pensier," where solitude is one element in a recipe for conjuring Laura), Augustinus counsels Franciscus to seek the city crowds as an antidote to love.[29]

Perhaps most significant of the forms from this verbal cluster with respect to the one/many problematic is *solo/sola*, "alone," which as one of Laura's key adjectives carries not the sense of privation but the sense of Neoplatonic plenitude we associate with the end of Plotinus' *Enneads*: "alone unto the Alone I go." We saw precisely this meaning in the *Triumphus Eternitatis*: in eternity "non avrà loco *fu, sarà,* ned *era,* / ma *è* **solo,** *in presente,* et *ora,* et *oggi,* / e **sola** *eternità* raccolta e 'ntera" (67–69; italics in original). For Laura too, the adjective *sola* signals—again with typical Petrarchan ambiguity—that Laura, carrier of multiplicity, is also the opposite of multiplicity: she is alone, she is unique, she is the One. The importance of *sola* can be better gauged if we bear in mind that the final attributes of the Virgin in *Rvf* 366 are "unica et **sola**" (133), and that this designation immediately follows the final definition of the self's condition as time-bound, given that "sì corre il tempo et vola" (time so runs and flies [366.132]). This final rhyme of *sola* with *vola* is a way of indicating the Virgin's ability to redeem our time-boundedness, our multiplicity, through her unicity, her oneness. The Virgin is a beacon of salvation precisely because she is beyond time, beyond multiplicity. Laura is not beyond time and she is not beyond multiplicity; she is indeed, as we have seen, from the beginning of the *Fragmenta* constructed as a being synonymous with multiplicity and also therefore synonymous with mortality, for a being's mortality is precisely that which defines it as one of the many—not *unica e sola*. And yet, through much of the *Fragmenta*, Laura, who denotes time, can also catalyze the lover's ecstatic stepping outside of time.

We encounter *sola* first in *Rvf* 14, modifying death, which "alone can stop the lover's thoughts from pursuing the amorous path that leads to Laura" ("Morte pò chiuder **sola** a' miei penseri / l'amoroso camin che gli conduce" [14.5–6]), and then paradigmatically in *Rvf* 17, which tells us that through Laura "alone the self is divided from the world": "per cui **sola** dal mondo i' son diviso" (4). Here again, as with *Rvf* 5, a sonnet that presents itself as a rhetorical conceit in fact broaches metaphysical issues. The conceit of "Piovonmi amare lagrime dal viso" is meteorological and involves eyes, which have been present—both his and hers—since *Rvf* 3, where her beautiful eyes bind him and Love finds the path open through his eyes to his heart. In "Piovonmi amare lagrime," the tears from his eyes fall like rain from his face when it happens that he turns his eyes toward her— toward the one through whom alone he is divided from the world. At the same time her eyes are also invoked, in an astrological key that recalls her solar eyes in *Rvf* 9; in *Rvf* 17 her eyes are the stars that guide him, "le mie fatali stelle" (my fated stars [17.11]). This is a conceit that anticipates the so-called *canzoni degli occhi* (canzoni of Laura's eyes), *Rvf* 71–73. In *Rvf* 73 Laura's eyes are the beacons and the sole comfort ("conforto **solo**" [73.51]) that guide the self through the sea of love's multiplicity and chaos; her eyes are the two lights that allow the weary helmsman to guide his ship through love's gale of wind:

> Come a forza di vènti
> stanco nocchier di notte alza la testa
> a' duo lumi ch'à sempre il nostro polo,
> così ne la tempesta
> ch'i' sostengo d'Amor, gli occhi lucenti
> sono il mio segno e 'l mio conforto **solo**.
>
> (73.46–51)

As in the force of the winds the tired helmsman at night lifts his head to the two lights that our pole always has, thus in the tempest I endure of love those shining eyes are my constellation and my only comfort.

The question of the lady's role in the *Fragmenta* is a complex one, since she sometimes is presented as the guide she is in *Rvf* 73, and sometimes his love for her is an obstacle on the path to salvation. She is a Beatrice-like figure, for instance, already in *Rvf* 13, the sonnet "Quando fra l'altre donne ad ora ad ora," where we learn that Laura leads to God: from her derives an amorous thought that, as long as one follows it, guides to the highest good

("Da lei ti vèn l'amoroso pensero, / che mentre 'l segui al sommo ben t'invia" [9–10]). However, I say "Beatrice-like" advisedly, since even here what Petrarch is doing is not the same as what Dante does: this strain of Petrarch's love poetry cannot be correctly labeled "stilnovist," as it usually is, since it is not congruent with stilnovism to introduce the concept of physical love as that which all men crave but which Laura's lover is able to devalue.[30] In a true stilnovist sonnet such as Dante's "Tanto gentile e tanto onesta pare," for instance, physical love is a nonissue, a nonpresence in the poem, while in *Rvf* 13 Petrarch conjures "quel ch'ogni huom desia" (11) in order to say that he has been rendered proof against such desire (again, the form working at cross purposes to the content). By the same token, it is instructive to use Dante in evaluating the verse "**per cui sola** dal mondo i' son diviso," which recalls but deviates from Dante's first great tribute to Beatrice in *Inferno* 2: "O donna di virtù, **sola per cui** / l'umana spezie eccede ogni contento / di quel ciel c'ha minor li cerchi sui" (O lady of power, through whom alone the human race rises above all the contents of that heaven whose circles are smallest [*Inf.* 2.76–78]).

Two points need to be made here. The first regards the meaning of Dante's words, around which a dispute has grown as modern commentators have shied away from the traditional—more radical and Dantean—understanding of the verse, whereby "sola per cui" modifies "donna," and therefore have suggested that "sola per cui" modifies "virtù." I heartily endorse Chiavacci Leonardi in her insistence that this interpretation constitutes "a grave critical error."[31] The Dante of the *Vita Nuova*'s canzone "Donne ch'avete intelletto d'amore" was already making theologically hyperbolic claims for his then still-living lady: to resist these claims is to resist the heart of his incarnational poetics. My second point is that Petrarch understands Dante as using the "sola per cui" construction to refer to Beatrice, and reconfigures it to suit his own less incarnational and more Neoplatonic brand of hyperbole. In other words, we can use these two *sola per cui* constructions as indices with respect to the different natures of the transfigured realities to which these ladies give their poets access. Beatrice is an agent for change on earth, the means for humans to surpass morally all other sublunary created beings. Laura operates in a more private dimension: her poet cares less about improving the moral status of other earthlings than he does about separating himself from earth altogether. Laura serves not to transform earth but as the means for separating her poet from it, dividing and removing him from its chaos and multiplicity.

The question of Laura's significance is not one that we can exhaust here. For the time being, it is important to note that *Rvf* 17's "per cui **sola** dal mondo i' son diviso" initiates a meditation on her deep value for the poet. Likewise, the rhyme words *diviso, riso,* and *fiso* in *Rvf* 17 anticipate two important canzoni groups, both of which I view as "metaphysical islands" of particular weight within the *mare magnum* of the *Fragmenta*: the *canzoni degli occhi* and canzoni 125–29. The terms *diviso* and *fiso*, which appear in "Piovonmi amare lagrime dal viso" for the first time, are markers of a meta-erotic and quasi-mystical state. The trigger for this state is frequently Laura's smile, *riso,* which also makes its first appearance here: Laura's "dolce mansueto **riso**" (sweet mild smile [17.5]) quiets the lover's ardent desire. Concentrating on Laura, staring at her intently and fixedly—"mentr'io son a mirarvi intento et **fiso**" (as long as I am intent and fixed on watching you [17.8])—he is released from suffering.

This sequence of events from *Rvf* 17 turns out to be a template for Petrarch's anxious metaphysical quest: in *Rvf* 73 a peace similar to that of heaven moves from the *riso* of her eyes ("Pace tranquilla senza alcuno affanno, / simile a quella ch'è nel ciel eterna, / move da lor inamorato **riso**"; Tranquil peace without any trouble, like that which is eternal in Heaven, moves from their lovely smile [67–69]); to look *fiso* upon her eyes ("Così vedess'io **fiso**"; Might I see thus fixedly [70]) would provide the lover his own brand of Augustinian extra-temporal trance. Like *fiso,* the word *diviso* figures in canzoni with strong metaphysical currents, such as *Rvf* 126, "Chiare, fresche et dolci acque," where the lover achieves an ecstatic state as a result of being cut off—*diviso*—from physical reality through the agency of the lady's attributes, including her *dolce riso:* "Così carco d'oblio / il divin portamento / e 'l volto e le parole e 'l dolce **riso** / m'aveano, et sì **diviso** / da l'imagine vera" (Her divine bearing and her face and her words and her sweet smile had so laden me with forgetfulness and so divided me from the true image [126.56–60]). An early model for the ecstasy-inducing Laura of *Rvf* 73 and *Rvf* 126 is thus provided by *Rvf* 17's "per cui **sola** dal mondo i' son **diviso**" (where too, *diviso* rhymes with *riso*): her plenitude—her oneness—divides him from divisibility, protects him from multiplicity.[32]

The first poems of the *Fragmenta* inaugurate many of the collection's key motifs and concerns. The motif of voyage, for instance, is linked to the metaphysical grounding of this text because it figures forth the linearity—the multiplicity—of the life-experience through time and permits the poet to dramatize the various strategies of the self to defeat time. The *incipit* of *Rvf* 15, the sonnet "Io mi rivolgo indietro a ciascun passo," is emblematic of the self's refusal to move forward that is characteristic of part 1 of the *Fragmenta*, a "non-narrativity" deployed as a means of outsmarting time (according to my formula whereby "in part 1 narrative is avoided because the goal is to stop time, resist death; in part 2 narrative is invoked because in order to preserve her as she was he must preserve her in time").[33] This backward-looking "Orpheus" motif, this stance of *rivolgersi indietro*, moreover, allows the poet to explore the important theme of memory, introducing memory as "part 1's non-forward moving mechanism par excellence": and, indeed, "Io mi rivolgo indietro a ciascun passo" offers the collection's first instances of *ripensare* ("Poi ripensando al dolce ben ch'io lasso"; Then, thinking back on the sweet good I leave behind [15.5]) and *rimembrare* ("Ma rispondemi Amor: Non ti rimembra / che questo è privilegio degli amanti"; But Love replies to me: 'Do you not remember that this is a privilege of lovers' [15.12–13]).

The journey theme of "Io mi rivolgo indietro a ciascun passo," and the journeyer's "corpo stancho ch'a gran pena porto" (weary body which with great effort I carry forward [15.2]), anticipate and contrast with the pilgrimage sonnet that follows, "Movesi il vecchierel canuto et biancho," whose journeyer is also "rotto dagli anni, et dal camino stanco" (broken by the years and tired by the road [16.8]), but where the voyage is uncharacteristically forward rather than backward moving. The strong "Movesi" that launches *Rvf* 16 and the *cammino* that the old man avidly pursues, "seguendo 'l desio" (following his desire [16.9]), tell us that we are in Dantean territory: this is the language of Dante's psychology of desire, according to which life is a pilgrimage on which we are propelled by desire, spiritual motion ("disire, / ch'è moto spiritale" [*Purg.* 18.31–32]). In "Movesi il vecchierel," of course, we are dealing with the exploitation of the old man's belabored pilgrimage toward the Roman icon said to be imprinted with Christ's image (the "Veronica" or "true image"), which in the last tercet is revealed to be an elaborate term of comparison for the lover, who with equal determination pursues his lady's "forma vera": "così, lasso, talor vo cerchand'io, / donna, quanto è possibile, in altrui / la disiata vostra forma vera" (Thus, alas, at times I go searching in others, Lady, as much as is possible, for your longed-for true form [16.12–14]). The profanation of the sacred for which this sonnet is famous does not, however, mean that its metaphysical concerns are not serious; provocatively stripped of a theological context, the self's quest to verify the metaphysical basis of his beloved—her "forma vera"—is all the more exquisitely and urgently etched.

In this essay I have looked at verbal expressions of the *Fragmenta*'s profoundly metaphysical foundation, a foundation that grounds the themes for which the collection is known, such as its psychologizing treatment of love, or its incipient romanticizing of nature. The sonnet "Glorïosa columna in cui s'appoggia," for instance, is cited by Contini for its "così moderna comunicazione con la natura";[34] while I do not disagree, it is important to note that the poet's call to substitute "palazzi [. . .] theatro o loggia" (palaces, theater, or gallery [10.5]) with "un abete, un faggio, un pino" (a fir tree, a beech, a pine [10.6]) engages a dialectic between particulars and universals that is fundamentally metaphysical. The very language "un abete, un faggio, un pino" reveals the underlying query—are we speaking of particular firs, or essence of fir?—a query that radically informs later evocations of Laura, as indeed it informs the issue of her "forma vera" in *Rvf* 16. It is appropriate that this query would be latent in *Rvf* 10, for "Glorïosa columna" is the poem that introduces the marker *columna/colonna* that stands to the Colonna family as *lauro* stands to Laura. These are signs that Petrarch uses to play with the question of particularity versus universality, since "column" and "laurel" can be more readily construed as universals than an individual person or family. These universalizing code-names are treated by Petrarch in ways that continue his program of ambivalence: for on the one hand they work to universalize the particular, but on the other they suggest the fungibility—the non-particularity—of all particulars, which have in common a universal condition of mortality. For instance, the labels are exchanged, with *colonna* in key contexts attached to Laura, as in *Rvf* 126's "gentil ramo ove piacque / (con sospir' mi rimembra) / a lei di fare al bel fiancho **colonna**" (gentle branch where it pleased her [with sighing I remember] to make a column for her lovely side [4–6]). Here the sign that conjures the world of male friendship and patronage crosses over to the female and erotic passion; it is used to elide the world of the column with the world of the laurel.

Nowhere do we see these universals used to achieve a sense of interchangeability and non-particularity more effectively than in the poem of crossing over—of chiasmus—that is *Rvf* 266, the sonnet "Signor mio caro." In *Rvf* 266 Petrarch celebrates both eighteen years of love for Laura and fifteen years of friendship with Cardinal Giovanni Colonna, and chiasmus is the trope that he employs to render Laura and the cardinal fully fungible:

> Carità di signore, amor di donna
> son le catene ove con molti affanni
> legato son, perch'io stesso mi strinsi.
> Un **lauro** verde, una gentil **colonna**,
> quindeci l'una, et l'altro diciotto anni
> portato ò in seno, et già mai non mi scinsi.
>
> (266.9–14)

> Devotion to my lord, love of my lady are the chains where
> with much labor I am bound, and I myself took them on!
> A green Laurel, a noble Column, the latter for fifteen,
> the former for eighteen years, I have carried in my breast
> and have never put from me.

The tercets of this remarkable sonnet feature a double multi-verse chiasmus, in which an ABBA combination is reversed to BAAB through the deployment of three elements referring to the cardinal ("Carità di signore" aligns with "una gentil columna," which aligns with "quindeci l'una") and three elements referring to Laura ("amor di donna" aligns with "Un lauro verde," which aligns with "et l'altro diciotto anni").[35] This protracted double chiasmus is buttressed by two single-verse abba grammatical chiasmi in lines 12 and 13 (the first is a noun/adjective/adjective/noun sequence [*lauro/verde/gentil/columna*], while the second is a number/pronoun/pronoun/number sequence [*quindeci/una/altro/diciotto*]). Moreover, Petrarch reverses grammatical and sexual genders to further suggest interchangeability in this passage: the phrases signifying the male cardinal ("Carità di signore" and "una gentil colomna") are feminine, as underscored by the feminine pronoun that aligns with them in "quindeci l'**una**," while the phrases signifying the female Laura ("amor di donna" and "Un lauro verde") are masculine, as highlighted by "et l'**altro** diciotto anni."

But what is important about this rhetorical play is how it moves us toward thinking of categories, rather than individuals: the categories of noun, adjective, pronoun, and number, the categories of gender, the categories of love and friendship, or—if we switch over from the chains of *Rvf* 266 to the golden chains of the *Secretum*—the categories of love and glory (since both are embedded in the laurel, they can both easily be embedded in the column as well). The distillation of individuals into categories allows Petrarch to manipulate them—like numbers, like figures in a patterned sequence (ABBA, BAAB)—and to consider them in different relationships, in different pairings, in different intellectual contexts: in a word, to consider them abstractly. Indeed, these categories prod us to think abstractly, philosophically, metaphysically. They prod us to think in precisely the way that Alfieri is not thinking when he writes, famously, about the column of *Rvf* 10: "una colonna non cammina" (a column does not walk).[36] Petrarch, held up as a mirror of stylistic perfection, is here taken to task because he got his image wrong—columns don't walk, after all—when what is most interesting about Petrarch is here overlooked: Petrarch is interesting precisely because his cast of mind tends toward the abstract, the universal, the numerical, and the metaphysical, while at the same time his desires remain rooted in the particular, the contingent, the immanent, and the physical.

Petrarch is a metaphysical poet. He does not feign his inclination toward the abstract; it is deeply inscribed into his poetic personality, like the abstract ciphers we are forced to manipulate as we thread our way through the intricate and abstract labyrinth of the *Fragmenta*. He does not feign his inclination toward the abstract any more than he feigns his love for the particular, individual, physical objects that his labyrinth showcases with longing and regret. It is wrong to think that he is in bad faith, as he one moment caresses the *cosa bella mortal* and the next disavows it: the internal Petrarchan fault line of so much critical discourse (the *dissidio* of the *secolare commento*) is essentially his personal metaphysical dance between the one and the many, preserved as poetry, and it is real.

Notes

1. I endeavored to explain the metaphysical properties of the lyric sequence as a form in "The Making of a Lyric Sequence: Time and Narrative in Petrarch's *Rerum vulgarium fragmenta*," *MLN* 104 (1989): 1–38, rpt. in *Dante and the Origins of Italian Literary Culture* (New York: Fordham University Press, 2006), 193–223 (hereafter pages refer to the rpt.). There I discuss metaphysical issues—time, the one and the many—in relation to the construction of a lyric sequence. My goal

now is to unpack the position, expressed in passing in 1989, that "this text is more philosophic than romantic" (205).

2. The common view is that Petrarch rejected metaphysics along with scholasticism and other forms of the medieval mindset: "In place of speculative metaphysical systems, of scientific, especially medical, investigation, of legal codification, he puts grammar, rhetoric, poetry, history, moral philosophy"; see Peter Hainsworth, *Petrarch the Poet: An Introduction to the "Rerum vulgarium fragmenta"* (London: Routledge, 1988), 4. While not without elements of truth, this commonplace requires considerable nuancing.

3. My critical and structural overview of the *Fragmenta* is presented, with a chart, in "The Self in the Labyrinth of Time (*Rerum vulgarium fragmenta*)" in *Petrarch: A Critical Guide to the Complete Works,* ed. Victoria Kirkham and Armando Maggi (Chicago: University of Chicago Press, 2009), 33–62.

4. As Santagata notes in his commentary to sonnet 2: "Se 1 risponde ai canoni dell'*exordium,* la serie 2–5 rispetta quelli dell'*initium narrationis,* con l'utilizzazione di *loci a re* (2 *causa,* 3 *tempus*) e *a persona* (4 *patria,* 5 *nomen*)" (13). See *Canzoniere,* ed. Marco Santagata (Milan: Mondadori, 1996; rev. 2006); all citations are from these editions. Unless I need to render the sense more literally, the excellent translations are those of Robert M. Durling, *Petrarch's Lyric Poems: The "Rime sparse" and Other Lyrics* (Cambridge, Mass., and London: Harvard University Press, 1976). When I use bold rather than italics for emphasis, I am indicating the presence of a "metaphysical marker."

5. The metaphor of the self as dispersed unless gathered in God is fundamental to the *Confessions,* where we find: "et colligens me a dispersione" (recollecting myself from dispersion [*Conf.* 2.1]); "id est velut ex quadam dispersione colligenda" (like being gathered together from dispersion [*Conf.* 10.11]); "in te, quo colligantur **sparsa** mea" (in you, in whom all my scattered parts are gathered [*Conf.* 10.40]); "colligas totum quod sum a dispersione et deformitate hac" (you wholly gather all that I am from this dispersion and deformity [*Conf.* 12.16]). The text of the *Confessions* is from the Loeb edition, 2 vols. (Cambridge, Mass.: Harvard University Press; London: Heinemann, 1976); the translation is R. S. Pine-Coffin's (London: Penguin, 1961).

6. Another example of the use of *recolligere* for the self in the *Secretum* is: "cum diurnis curis relaxatus animus se in se ipsum recolligit" (Book 1, 58). The edition used is that of Enrico Carrara, in *Prose* (Milan and Naples: Ricciardi, 1955).

7. The translation of the *Physics* by R. P. Hardie and R. K. Gaye is from *The Basic Works of Aristotle,* ed. Richard McKeon (New York: Random House, 1941). The Latin for this passage is "hoc enim est tempus, numerus motus secundum prius et posterius." It is cited by Enrico Berti in his article "Fisica," *Enciclopedia dantesca,* 6 vols. (Rome: Istituto dell'Enciclopedia Italiana, 1970–78), 2:933–34, citation 933; for the Latin translation of Aristotle, see *Aristoteles Latinus,* ed. L. Minio-Paluello (Bruges and Paris: Desclée De Brouwer, 1953–78).

8. The Latin text is cited by Cesare Vasoli in his article "Tempo," *Enciclopedia dantesca,* 5:546–51, citation 546.

9. The beautiful translation of the *Confessions* is the 1631 rendition of William Watts in the Loeb edition.

10. See also *Rvf* 62's prayer for conversion to God, "piacciati omai, col Tuo lume, ch'io torni / ad **altra** vita" (let it please you at last that with your light I may return to a different life [5–6]), and sonnet 178's "anti-conversion" to love, rendered as "conven ch'**altra** via segua" (it must follow another path [13]).

11. The other uses in *Triumphus Eternitatis* (*TE*) are *varia* in verse 33, *variar* in verse 41, and *variato* in verse 78, for a total of four. There are also two uses of *vari* in *Triumphus Cupidinis* (*TC*) 2.139. The *Triumphi* are cited in the edition by Marco Ariani (Milan: Mursia, 1988); translations are mine.

12. For Augustine's self-conscious use of "little time words," invoked as a way of delaying conversion, see *Confessions* 8.5: "et undique ostendenti vera te dicere, non erat omnino, quid responderem veritate convictus, nisi tantum verba lenta et somnolenta: 'modo,' 'ecce modo,' 'sine paululum.' sed 'modo et modo' non habebat modum et 'sine paululum' in longum ibat" (You used all means to prove the truth of your words, and now that I was convinced that they were true, the only answers I could give were the drowsy words of an idler—'Soon,' 'Presently,' 'Let me wait a little longer.' But 'soon' was not soon and 'a little longer' grew much longer). This passage from the *Confessions* is imitated by Petrarch in the *Secretum*: "Da michi castitatem, sed noli modo; differ paululum" (Book 2, 80).

13. The citation from Boyde comes from *Dante Philomythes and Philosopher: Man in the Cosmos* (Cambridge: Cambridge University Press, 1981), 219; I cite it in *The Undivine Comedy: Detheologizing Dante* (Princeton: Princeton University Press, 1992), 173.

14. The Latin text of the *Consolation of Philosophy* is cited in the Loeb Classical Library edition, ed. H. F. Stewart and E. K. Rand (Cambridge, Mass.: Harvard University Press; London: Heinemann, 1936). The following discussion is based on Book 5, prose 6.

15. Thomas Aquinas's *Summa Theologiae* is cited in the edition of the Blackfriars, 61 vols. (New York: McGraw-Hill; London: Eyre and Spottiswoode, 1964–81). This citation from *Quaestio* 10, "De aeternitate Dei" (On the eternity of God), is from vol. 2, 1964, ed. and trans. Timothy McDermott, 144. Thomas notes that while eternity is *tota simul,* time contains a before and after: "in tempore autem est prius et posterius" (144). In *Quaestio* 10, article 1, Thomas defends and confirms Boethius' definition of eternity from *Consolation of Philosophy* 5.6. His Aristotelian allegiance, on the other hand, is demonstrated by his discussion of time: in the course of his argument, he notes that we can only come to know eternity by way of time, which "nihil aliud est quam numerus motus secundum prius et posterius" (136).

16. This view is expounded in the *Paradiso* chapters of my *Undivine Comedy.*

17. The citation is from *Undivine Comedy*, 233; the treatment of *Paradiso* 28's paradoxes of form and content extends through 236. An elegant reading of Dante's metaphysics is provided by Christian Moevs, *The Metaphysics of Dante's "Comedy"* (Oxford: Oxford University Press, 2005).

18. The annotation may be found in the famous draft notebook ("codice degli abbozzi") preserved as the codex *Vaticano latino* 3196, which I cite from the useful edition of Laura Paolino: "transcripti isti duo in ordine, post mille annos" (816). See *Trionfi, Rime estravaganti, Codice degli abbozzi*, ed. Vinicio Pacca and Laura Paolino (Milan: Mondadori, 1996).

19. And *mille* as signifier of unending multiplicity is also present in the *Secretum*: for instance, in the description of the pains of Hell as "**mille** suppliciorum, **mille** tortorum genera" (Book 1, 56).

20. Laura is associated with *mille* in the *incipit* of *Rvf* 21, "**Mille** fiate, o dolce mia guerrera." The only other sonnet to start with *mille* is "**Mille** piagge in **un** giorno et **mille** rivi," *Rvf* 177, whose *incipit* uses the *un/mille* marker to define Love as the tour guide that unifies the intricate multiplicity of the Ardenne forest.

21. Hair as a marker of the passing of time is also a motif of the *Secretum*, where Augustinus challenges Franciscus to note the changing ("variari") of his face and the arrival of some white hairs: "nonne vultum tuum variari in dies singulos et intermicantes temporibus canos animadvertisti" (Book 3, 176).

22. *Or* appears 276 times and is the 27th most frequently occurring word in the *Rvf*, while *ora* appears 48 times, for a combined total of 324. See http://www .intratext.com/IXT/ITA1326/. Worth noting as well is that the only nouns with more than 200 occurrences are *amor* (255), *occhi* (251), and *cor* (222), two of which rhyme with *or*.

23. In Boethius' definition of eternity ("Aeternitas igitur est interminabilis vitae *tota simul* et perfecta possessio") the words "tota simul" do not stand alone, since "tota" is an adjective. I have borrowed the handy nominal phrase "totum simul," which so well sums up this definition of eternity as all-at-once-ness, from Benvenuto da Imola, who uses it to gloss Dante's image of the universe bound in one volume in *Paradiso* 33: "*in un volume*, quasi dicat: 'totum simul'" (Guido Biagi, ed., "*La Divina Commedia*" *nella figurazione artistica e nel secolare commento*, 3 vols. [Turin: Unione tipografico-editrice torinese, 1924–29], 3:742).

24. The chains of temporality that bind Franciscus in the *Secretum* are marked by the same **or** sound; they are "Am**or** et gl**or**ia" (Book 3, 132).

25. Augustinus reproves Franciscus for drawing comfort from the idea of his and Laura's mutual old age; see *Secretum*, Book 3, 185.

26. Santagata notes the provenance from *Inferno* 2 but does not analyze it. The text is *La Commedia secondo l'antica vulgata*, ed. Giorgio Petrocchi, 4 vols. (Milan: Mondadori, 1966–67). The translation is Robert M. Durling's, in *Inferno* (New York and Oxford: Oxford University Press, 1996).

27. The lover's mad desire is an uncontrollable steed that cannot be reined in. Sara Sturm-Maddox notes that Dante's sonnet "Io sono stato" is a precedent for

Petrarch's *Rvf* 6, in *Petrarch's Metamorphoses: Text and Subtext in the "Rime Sparse"* (Columbia: University of Missouri Press, 1985), 81–82.

28. I am following Santagata, who opts for Giacomo as the absent Colonna, in place of the traditional choice of Stefano Colonna il Vecchio.

29. Augustinus exhorts Franciscus to avoid solitude, until he feels he has lost all traces of his love sickness: "Tam diu cavendam tibi solitudinem scito, donec sentias morbi tui nullas superesse reliquias" (*Secretum*, Book 3, 172).

30. Referring to this sonnet's "situazione stilnovistica" (59), Santagata shows little appreciation for the ideological divergence from stilnovism captured by a verse like "pocho prezando quel ch'ogni huom desia" (little valuing what other men desire [13.11]). The error of viewing Petrarch as occasionally stilnovist, rather than viewing Petrarch as occasionally echoing and radically transforming stilnovist motifs, occurs throughout his commentary, egregiously in the treatment of the *canzoni degli occhi.*

31. See Anna Maria Chiavacci Leonardi, ed., *Inferno* (Milan: Mondadori, 1991), 61 and 71 for further discussion.

32. The question arises as to whether being *diviso* from everything by Laura is positive or negative for Petrarch. Santagata reads the effect of being *diviso* in *Rvf* 17 as negative ("effetto negativo della passione, denunciato in 360, 46–53 e condannato in *Secr.* III, p. 156 'tristis et amor solitudinis atque hominum fuga'; la stessa connotazione negativa in 292, 3–4 'che m'avean sì da me stesso diviso, / et fatto singular da l'altra gente'"), while also noting that "espressioni analoghe ritornano però anche in accezione del tutto positiva: cf. 323, 30 'che dal mondo m'avean tutto diviso'" (73). While I agree that, like *solo* and *solitario,* to which Santagata is linking *diviso, diviso* can have negative connotations in Petrarch's lexicon, I hold that *diviso* has an ecstatic component not touched on by Santagata's note and that in any case the negative and positive connotations are much more enmeshed than his reading suggests.

33. Barolini, "The Making of a Lyric Sequence," 222; the quote in the next sentence is from 199.

34. Gianfranco Contini, *Letteratura italiana delle origini* (Florence: Sansoni, 1970), 582.

35. ABBA: A = "Carità di signore," referring to Cardinal Colonna; B = "amor di donna," referring to Laura; B = "Un lauro verde," referring to Laura; A = "una gentil colomna," referring to Cardinal Colonna. BAAB: B = "Un lauro verde," referring to Laura; A = "una gentil colomna," referring to Cardinal Colonna; A = "quindeci l'una," referring to Cardinal Colonna; B = "et l'altro diciotto anni," referring to Laura.

36. Cited in the edition of Giosuè Carducci and Severino Ferrari, *Le Rime* (Florence: Sansoni, 1899; rpt. 1957), 12.

CHAPTER 6

Subjectivity and Conversion in Dante and Petrarch

CHRISTIAN MOEVS

CONVERSION, IN THE PARADIGMATIC FORM REALIZED BY SAINT Augustine in both life and literature, is a thematic obsession across much of Petrarch's work, surfacing and resurfacing in works as varied as the *Secretum*, the *Canzoniere*, the *Familiares*, the *De vita solitaria*, the *De otio religioso*, the *Bucolicum Carmen*, the *Itinerarium*, and the *Collatio*, to name but a few. In stark contrast to the Augustinian model, in Petrarch conversion is never done: it remains an unattainable goal, a mirage, a quest only partially fulfilled because never fully willed. While Augustine had given the conversion narrative drawn from his life an unsurpassed literary form, in Petrarch the literary form of the conversion narrative attempts to create a paradigmatic individual life, to construct and stabilize an identity, to generate the voice of a collected soul that says "I." Petarch's exploration of the theme of failed conversion, in relation to the creation and stabilization of a coherent sense of self, is an extraordinarily profound analysis of the nature of the subjective self, when that self experiences itself as radically autonomous, as ontologically deracinated, as not anchored in or continuous with a non-contingent reality or metaphysical ground. The self so pitilessly and acutely anatomized by Petrarch is thus stunningly removed from the self or individual soul as conceived and explored by Dante just a few decades earlier in his works, especially in his own great literary conversion narrative, the *Comedy*. Whether that shift in the understanding of the self between Dante and Petrarch is part of, or representative of, a larger change in Western culture or consciousness as a whole (it has been argued, in various ways, that it is), and if so, what the reasons—historical, philosophical, cultural, social, political, theological, psychological, religious—might be, are beyond the scope of my reflections here.[1] Here I shall briefly set out the problem of failed conversion in a few Petrarchan texts, and then survey the essential features of the Petrarchan self as they emerge in Petrarch's own analysis or literary self-fashioning, against the background of the Dantean understanding of the self. I shall suggest that the key difference between the two, which can account for the characteristic attributes of the literary Petrarchan self, is that while for Dante the self is metaphysically rooted in a non-contingent reality, for Petrarch it is an evanescent locus of thought and desire, irreducibly other than both God and the world. One way of understanding the Petrarchan self is as the dissolution or rejection of the Aristotelian-Neoplatonic understanding of the fundamental metaphysical relations that link the individual to God and to the world. It is perhaps one way of understanding at its birth the whole trajectory of the modern subjective self, through one of its first and greatest analysts, Petrarch.

IN THE FINAL MONTHS OF HIS LIFE, IN 1373–74, PETRARCH renumbers the last poems of the *Canzoniere* to create a new closing sequence. As Marco Santagata has observed,[2] in the new arrangement, the very last poems, from 360 to 366, form a kind of penitential progression, a culminating climax of conversion. As part of that progression, the attention is taken away from Laura and focused explicitly on the poet himself, on the state of his soul and his hope for salvation.

The final sequence is set up by *Rvf* 360, the canzone "Quel antiquo mio dolce empio signore." This canzone replays in an almost humorous vein Petrarch's very serious *Secretum*, which he had written mostly between 1347 and 1353. The *Secretum*, we recall, is a debate between the character Augustinus (modeled on Saint Augustine) and the character Franciscus (modeled on Petrarch himself), in the silent presence of Truth. Among other things, Augustinus accuses Franciscus of loving Laura more than God, with a love that has bound Franciscus to ephemeral mortal earthly pursuits, that has taken his attention away from himself and his salvation, that has led to endless torment, inner conflict, aimless wandering and public infamy, and that has made him squander his gifts and capacity for virtue. Against these accusations, Franciscus insists that Laura is no ordinary mortal, but the image of divine beauty and transcendent virtue; his love for Laura, therefore, is a pure and elevating love; it has fed his love of virtue and made him aspire to the highest things; it is the seed of all he has accomplished and of all his fame; besides, he could not stop loving her if he wanted to. Although Augustinus wears Franciscus down, the *Secretum* ends in a kind of unresolved truce, a sort of stasis or impasse. Franciscus says: "I know . . . that it would be much safer for me to pursue only this one aim now [of attending to myself], and, bypassing the detours, to seize the right path of salvation. But I am not able to restrain my desire." Augustinus answers: "This is our old argument. What you call inability is really a failure of your will."[3] *Rvf* 360, which was probably written around the same time as the *Secretum*, mirrors the *Secretum*: it is a debate between the poet narrator and Lord Love in front of the tribunal of silent Reason. The poet and Lord Love lay out roughly the same arguments that we have mentioned from the *Secretum*, except that the roles are reversed: the same arguments that Augustinus had made against Franciscus, here the poet narrator (Franciscus, so to speak) makes against Lord Love; the same defense that Franciscus had made against Augustinus, here Lord Love makes against the poet narrator, "Franciscus." At the end of the debate, Reason briefly speaks to give her judgment (ll. 156–57): "Piacemi aver vostre questioni udite, / ma più tempo bisogna a tanta lite" (It was a pleasure to have heard your arguments, but more time is needed for such a lawsuit).[4] In other words, again an impasse, a draw, no resolution.

We can make a few observations, then, about *Rvf* 360 in the final ordering of the *Canzoniere*. The first observation is that the closing sequence of poems of the *Canzoniere* is set up by evoking the *Secretum*, the paradigmatic account of Petrarch's *dissidio*, or inner conflict between two great pulls: on the one hand, the aspiration toward conversion and the renunciation of all earthly attachments, desires, ambitions, and memories, in order to love and seek God alone, that is, to seek moral perfection and salvation with a single-minded purpose and focus; on the other hand, the beguiling, bewitching allure of earthly beauty, of mortal love, and the promise of fulfillment in the ephemeral, beautiful, illusory dream of the world of space and time. This split or *dissidio* between these two great pulls is, of course, the great thematic tension of the *Canzoniere* as a whole, and indeed of most of Petrarch's work. Indeed, we can make a second observation about *Rvf* 360: the fact that the roles of the *Secretum* are reversed in the poem, with the result that the poet's voice in effect argues both sides of the issue, makes it clear that the *dissidio* is a split or argument within the poet's own soul, and not between the poet's own earthly inclination and an external religious injunction or obligation, as it could appear from the *Secretum* taken alone. That Augustinus and Franciscus are both Petrarch would of course not escape any careful reader of the *Canzoniere,* given that the *Canzoniere* deploys elaborate strategies to balance and offset the one side or pull against the other, both in the poet's voice. A famous example is the sequence of sonnets 60 through 62: sonnet 61 ("Benedetto sia 'l giorno e 'l mese et l'anno") is perhaps the most ecstatic affirmation of his love that Petrarch ever wrote:

> Benedetto sia 'l giorno, e 'l mese, et l'anno,
> et la stagione, e 'l tempo, et l'ora, e 'l punto,
> e 'l bel paese, e 'l loco ov'io fui giunto
> da' duo begli occhi che legato m'ànno;
>   et benedetto il primo dolce affanno
> ch'i' ebbi ad esser con Amor congiunto,
> et l'arco, et le saette ond'i' fui punto,
> et le piaghe che 'nfin al cor mi vanno.
>   Benedette le voci tante ch'io
> chiamando il nome de mia donna ò sparte,
> e i sospiri, et le lagrime, e 'l desio;
>   et benedette sian tutte le carte
> ov'io fama l'acquisto, e 'l pensier mio,
> ch'è sol di lei, sì ch'altra non v'à parte.

> Blessed be the day and the month and the year and the season and the time and the hour and the instant and the beautiful countryside and the place where I was struck by the two lovely eyes that have bound me;
>   and blessed be the first sweet trouble I felt on being made one with Love, and the bow and arrows that pierced me, and the wounds that reach my heart!

Blessed be the many words I have scattered calling the
name of my lady, and the sighs and the tears and the desire;
    and blessed be all the pages where I gain fame for her,
and my thoughts, which are only of her, so that no other
has part in them!

But that sonnet is sandwiched between *Rvf* 60 ("L'arbor gentil che forte
amai molt'anni"), a sonnet that condemns the Daphnean laurel of love and
poetry and fame, and sonnet 62 ("Padre del ciel, dopo i perduti giorni").
Rvf 62 is one of the most intense of the penitential anniversary poems:

Padre del ciel, dopo i perduti giorni,
dopo le notti vaneggiando spese
con quel fero desio ch'al cor s'accese
mirando gli atti per mio mal sì adorni,
    piacciati omai, col Tuo lume, ch'io torni
ad altra vita et a più belle imprese,
sì ch'avendo le reti indarno tese,
il mio duro adversario se ne scorni.
    Or volge, signor mio, l'undecimo anno
ch'i' fui sommesso al dispietato giogo
che sopra i più soggetti é più feroce:
    miserere del mio non degno affanno;
reduci i pensier' vaghi a miglior luogo;
ramenta lor come oggi fusti in croce.

———————

Father of Heaven, after the lost days, after the nights
spent raving with that fierce desire that was lit in my heart
when I looked on those gestures so lovely to my hurt,
    let it please you at last that with your light I may return
to a different life and to more beautiful undertakings, so that,
having spread his nets in vain, my harsh adversary [the Lord
Love, i.e., the Devil] may be disarmed.
    Now turns, my Lord [this is God, not Lord Love], the
eleventh year that I have been subject to the pitiless yoke
that is always most fierce to the most submissive:

have mercy on my unworthy pain, lead my wandering thoughts back to a better place, remind them that today you were on the Cross.

Thus the third observation we can make about *Rvf* 360 is that it sums up and brings to a climax the great thematic *dissidio* or impasse or tension of the *Canzoniere*, between, on the one hand, wandering in the labyrinth of love, earthly desire, and poetic glory, and on the other, turning resolutely away from the world to focus single-mindedly on salvation and God. In other words, it sets the stage for a resolution of the impasse at the end of the *Canzoniere*, if there is going to be a resolution. A fourth observation we can make about *Rvf* 360 is that it also sets the direction of that resolution, precisely by reversing the roles of Franciscus and Augustinus in the *Secretum*: the poet is now taking the voice of Augustinus and conversion against Franciscus and Love, against his own former self.

Indeed, that is how the end of the *Canzoniere* plays out. As reordered by Petrarch at the end of his life, the final six poems map a progressive conversion *in extremis*.[5] (The number six, given its evocations in the *Canzoniere*, is no accident.) *Rvf* 361 is a meditation on growing old; in *Rvf* 362 Laura (not named) congratulates Petrarch on having changed his habits upon growing old, and she leads him to God, who assures him of salvation; *Rvf* 363 speaks of Laura's death, the end of the poet's love, and his freedom to turn from Lord Love to the Lord God; *Rvf* 364 is a prayer to God, in repentance for the past errors the poet now confesses; *Rvf* 365 intensifies the repentance, for having wasted life loving a mortal thing instead of lifting himself in flight to God, and asks God to bring him from a life in war and storm to an end in peace and port. *Rvf* 366 is of course the great canzone "Vergine bella," in which the glorious attributes that had been Laura's are shifted onto the Virgin, and Laura becomes simply "terra" (earth), "mortal bellezza," and "poca mortal terra caduca" (a bit of passing mortal earth), as well as Medusa. Unlike Laura, the Virgin is "stabile in eterno" (stable in eternity), "unica e sola," "sola al mondo" (one and unique alone), the "vera beatrice" (neither Laura nor Dante's Beatrice), the star above the tempestuous sea of life. She can end the poet's sorrow and finally bring him to peace, as Laura could not.

We seem, then, to have a conversion *in extremis*, put off until the last moment, but better late than never. There are two problems, however.

The first is that the close of the *Canzoniere* is undercut by the opening of the *Canzoniere*, the proemial poem "Voi ch'ascoltate in rime sparse il suono." That proemial poem situates itself as written post-*Canzoniere*: it is a retrospective view of the entire collection, placed at the beginning. As such, it takes a post-conversion perspective: it refers to the poems of the *Canzoniere* as the scattered record of the poet's "primo giovenil errore," his youthful error or wandering, when he was another man from what he is now, and it asks for forgiveness for the *Canzoniere*'s alternation between weeping (for Laura) and reasoning or speaking (his determination to change his life), which were, respectively, a vain sorrow and a vain hope:

> Voi ch'ascoltate in rime sparse il suono
> di quei sospiri ondi'io nudriva 'l core
> in sul mio primo giovenile errore
> quand'era in parte altr'uom da quel ch'i' sono:
> del vario stile in ch'io piango e ragiono,
> fra le vane speranze e 'l van dolore,
> ove sia chi per prova intenda amore,
> spero trovar pietà, nonché perdono.
> Ma ben veggio or sì come al popol tutto
> favola fui gran tempo, onde sovente
> di me medesmo meco mi vergogno;
> et del mio vaneggiar vergogna è 'l frutto,
> e 'l pentérsi, e 'l conoscer chiaramente
> che quanto piace al mondo è breve sogno.

———————

> You who hear in scattered rhymes the sound of those sighs
> with which I nourished my heart during my first youthful error,
> when I was in part another man from what I am now:
> for the varied style in which I weep and speak between vain
> hopes and vain sorrow, where there is anyone who understands
> love through experience, I hope to find pity, not only pardon.
> But now I see well how for a long time I was the talk of
> the crowd, for which often I am ashamed of myself within;
> and of my raving, shame is the fruit, and repentance,
> and the clear knowledge that whatever pleases in the world
> is a brief dream.

I shall not rehearse the critical tradition of this amazingly rich poem here, but note how the wandering anacoluthon of the first eight lines recreates the poet's *errore*, the wandering in the labyrinth of love, and how the "I" gradually emerges as the real subject only in line 8, to then become an almost neurotic self-consciousness in shame, underlined by alliteration, in line 11: "di me medesmo meco mi vergogno," because his vain love has made him the talk of the town, "favola fui gran tempo." Note that the poet *is*, in a sense, sound, rhymes, talk: the scattered rhymes are the sound of sighs (and we hear the sighs onomatopeically in the first lines); the poet asks pardon for the varied style that mirrors his *dissidio*, not for his error itself; he links the words *sono*, *suono*, and *sogno* through rhyme and assonance, as if the "I" itself is but sound, a dream. The poet concludes that the fruit of his amorous ravings is shame and repentance, as well as the clear knowledge that all that the world loves is but a dream, the dream of the *Canzoniere* itself, a dream that poet and reader both are about to caress through hundreds of poems. What then of the poet's conversion? It should be quite clear in line 4: "quand'era in parte altr'uom da quel ch'i' sono." There's a clear "what I was" and "what I am," a past and a present, separated by a metrically isolated principal accent: *altr'uom*, another man. To become another man, to put off the old man and put on the new, is the central topos of conversion; it is explicit in many of the conversion narratives Petrarch relates in the second book of his *De vita solitaria*. When Saint Romuald, for example, turns his vacillating father Sergius back to a religious vocation, Sergius "mira compunctione propositum immutavit; atque ita in virum alterum versus est" (with admirable compunction changed his mind, and became another man), so that he washed his sins with tears, and longed for death to get rid of the weight of the body he had loved and the chains of the earthly life he had desired.[6] Saint Romuald himself in the prime of his life abandoned glory, pleasures, riches, his father, his homeland, the world, and finally himself as he had been, in order to find himself as another person: "et seipsum talem fugiens, ut se alium inveniret."[7] This is apparently what the poet of "Voi ch'ascoltate" presents himself as having done—except for two little words, "in parte," which bring down the whole edifice: "when I was *in part* another man from what I am now." In the Augustinian model, reiterated tirelessly in the *De vita solitaria*, there is no partial conversion: partial conversion is no conversion at all. The first poem of the *Canzoniere* epitomizes with pure Petrarchan ambiguity the impasse of a will to convert that is not entire, not single-minded, not one, that contaminates the new present with the past error. In fact, the poetic voice of the *Canzoniere* will proceed to wander in the labyrinth of vain love and desire for hundreds of poems, seeking an evanescent worldly beauty that will hypnotize centuries of Western poets.

There is also a second problem with the conversion sequence at the end of the *Canzoniere*: as Santagata observes, in the same last months of his life in which Petrarch was rearranging those final poems, he also wrote the *Triumph of Eternity*, the last of the *Triumphi*. The sequence of the *Triumphi* centers on Laura: the poet, through the image of Laura, is conquered by the triumph of the Lord Love; the Lord Love is in turn conquered by the triumph of Chastity in the form of Laura; Laura is overcome by the triumph of Death; Death is overcome by the triumph of worldly Fame (largely through the work of writers, such as Petrarch singing of Laura); Fame in turn is overcome by the triumph of Time, which sweeps away all things, including the writings of poets and historians; but in the end, Time itself is overcome by the triumph of Eternity, which restores what Time and Death had stolen. Thus the first five triumphs take place on earth; the sixth takes place in Heaven, after the Last Judgment.[8] In analogy with the end of the *Canzoniere*, the *Triumph of Eternity* opens with the poet confessing that he should have converted earlier, that he should have opened his eyes sooner, and not waited until the last moment ("più per tempo / deve' aprir gli occhi, e non tardar al fine" [ll. 10–11]). But Petrarch's eternity, as evoked in the *Triumphus Eternitatis*, is a strange affair: it is not a transcendence of time and flux, but rather it is time and flux frozen, fixed, stopped. It is not a beatific vision of the divine light, of pure being or consciousness as the ontological foundation of the world; it is rather a dream that the fleeting world itself could be made a "cosa . . . stabile e ferma" (a stable and steady thing), "un mondo / nuovo, in etate immobile ed eterna . . . più bello e più giocondo" (a new world, in an immoble and eternal state . . . more beautiful and more joyous), an "eternità raccolta e intera" (a collected and integral eternity): in short, a spatiotemporal world that is non-contingent, stable, unchanging, permanently new, whole, dependable, and gathered together (ll. 2, 20–24, 69). It is in a sense the culmination of the *Canzoniere*'s evocations of time suspended and of experience made whole, most famously perhaps in *Rvf* 90 and 126.[9] Past, present, and future collapse in the eternal now of this final vision: "Qual meraviglia ebb'io quando restare / vidi in un punto quel che mai non stette, / ma discorrendo suol tutto cangiare!" (How

I marveled when I saw what never stopped before, but usually changes as it flows, stop in a single instant [*punto*]!) (ll. 25–27).

Petrarch's *punto* in these lines from the *Triumph of Eternity* is almost a send-up of the *punto* that conquers Dante in the closing cantos of the *Paradiso*.[10] Dante's *punto* too is the eternal now, but for Dante that is God himself, the Empyrean that sustains and contains all creation, revealed as a dimensionless point of self-subsistent being and awareness, the ground of all reality. As the ultimate ontological principle, Dante's *punto* is also the self-awareness of the finite intellect turned on itself, through which it comes to know itself as, or as one with, pure consciousness itself, the foundation and being of the world. This idea is part of a long Neoplatonic contemplative tradition that includes, among many others, Pseudo-Dionysius, Richard of St. Victor, St. Bonaventure, and Meister Eckhart.[11] Thus Dante's *punto* is the Christic nexus between time and eternity, between the human and the divine: it is the ultimate point or gateway of revelation, the point through which Saint Bonaventure says, for example, that the mind turned on itself, leaving behind "everything sensible, imaginable, and intelligible," focuses itself on itself, until as pure intelligence and love it passes beyond itself into Truth or pure Being, "totally transferred and transformed into God."[12] As such, Dante symmetrically and ironically contrasts this *punto* of Christic revelation, which conquers him in *Paradiso* 28 ("nel punto che m'avëa vinto" [*Par.* 29.9], "al punto che mi vinse" [*Par.* 30.11]), to the *punto* of text and time that conquered Francesca and Paolo in *Inferno* 5 ("solo un punto fu quel che ci vinse" [l. 132]), ensnaring them in lust and the lure of mortal beauty. The *punto* for Dante thus becomes the moment of conversion, the dimensionless now in which the soul either awakens to its ground or falls under the hypnosis of the senses and mortal desire. Indeed, in his last evocation of the *punto*, the famous Argo simile of *Paradiso* 33, Dante sets up the timeless instant of transcendent understanding, the *lumen gloriae,* against the entire history of human desire and exploration in time ("Un punto solo m'è maggior letargo / che venticinque secoli a la 'mpresa / che fé Nettuno ammirar l'ombra d'Argo" (A single moment brings me more forgetfulness than twenty-five centuries have brought to the enterprise that made Neptune wonder at the *Argo*'s shadow) (*Par.* 33.94–96).[13] It is unlikely that Petrarch did not notice all this when he imported Dante's *punto* into the *Triumph of Eternity* in a constellation of echoes from the last cantos of the *Paradiso.* He chose rather to dismiss it, ignore it, defuse it.

Petrarch's rather off-hand account, in the *Triumph of Eternity*, of how his vision unfolded is almost ironic when compared to the intense, almost agonizing, mystic concentration of intellectual sight in *Paradiso* 33. Petrarch has been thinking, "if these things that heaven turns and governs do not stop, what will come of them after a lot of turning?" ("se non stanno / queste cose che 'l ciel volge e governa, / dopo molto voltar che fine avranno?") (ll. 16–18). He goes on: "Questo pensava, e mentre più *s'interna* / *la mente mia*, veder mi parve un mondo / novo, in etate *immobile ed eterna*..." (This is what I was thinking, and while my mind goes more inward [*s'interna*], I seemed to see a new world, immobile in age and eternal...) (ll. 19–21; italics mine). The word "s'interna" (as well as the phrase "la mente mia" and the stileme "immobile ed eterna") is borrowed from Dante's breathtaking vision, in the last canto of the *Paradiso*, of the intelligible as the foundation of the visible, with its echoes of the Trinity, the book of creation, the Word, the four elements, and the substances and accidents of Aristotelian metaphysics: "Nel suo profondo vidi che *s'interna*, / legato con amore in un volume, / ciò che per l'universo si squaderna: / sustanze e accidenti e lor costume / quasi conflati insieme... / Così *la mente mia*, tutta sospesa, / mirava fissa, *immobile ed attenta*..." (In its depth I saw ingathered, bound by love in one single volume, that which is dispersed in leaves throughout the universe: substances and accidents and their behavior, as though fused together... So my mind, all suspended, gazed fixedly, immobile and alert...") (ll. 85–98; italics mine).[14] Dante is playing on the juncture of the inner and the outer, linked on the one hand (*s'interna*) to the Trinity and its Augustinian interior reflection as will, memory, and intellect, and on the other (*si squaderna*) to the four elements of the exterior world and the senses. This linking of three and four conjures seven, a number that in the medieval tradition evokes the Neoplatonic world soul, which is the nexus between the One and the Many, between the transcendent and the finite, between spirit and matter; in particular, seven is the number of man, as the nexus between the self-subsistent and the contingent, between intellect (a three) and matter (a four). In relation to pure consciousness or being, Dante is saying, everything with finite name and form is ephemeral: substances cannot be distinguished from accidents. Again, Petrarch ignores all this: his reduction of the mystical or transcendent or metaphysical to the prosaic is almost Ariostesque in irony. As another example, consider Dante's penetration into the divine light in *Paradiso* 33, which strains all limits of language and conception (*Par.* 33.52−54, 79−84, 97−105, 109−41), and which has at its center this passage: "E' mi ricorda ch'io fui più ardito / per questo a sostener, tanto ch'i' giunsi / l'aspetto mio col valore infinito. / Oh abbondante grazia ond'io presunsi / ficcar lo viso per la luce etterna, / tanto che la veduta vi consunsi!" (And this, as I recall, gave me more strength / to keep on gazing till I could unite / my vision with the Infinite Worth I saw. / O grace [*grazia*] abounding and allowing me to dare / to fix my gaze on the Eternal Light, / so deep my vision was consumed in It!) (ll. 79−84).[15] Compare Petrarch: "Passa il penser sì come sole in vetro, / anzi più assai, però che nulla il tene; / o qual grazia mi fia, se mai l'impetro, / ch'i' veggia ivi presente il sommo bene . . ." (My thought passes on like sun through glass, indeed quite a bit more, because nothing stops it; O what grace [*grazia*] it would be to me, if I should ever achieve it through prayer, that I might see here present the highest good . . .) (ll. 34−37). Notice Petrarch's echo of the word *grazia;* note that he reduces Dante's contemplative immersion in the *lumen gloriae* to thought, *penser,* which actually precludes beatific vision; note Petrarch's offhand *sommo bene,* which seems almost to refer to his vision or the absence of time (ll. 38−39); Dante uses that phrase six times in the *Commedia* to refer to the transcendent God. In the space of eighteen lines (ll. 19−36) in the *Triumph of Eternity,* Petrarch borrows five key terms or stilemes (*s'interna, la mente mia, immobile ed attenta, un punto, grazia*) from just sixteen lines (ll. 82−97) of Dante's *Paradiso* 33, in order to defuse and set aside the metaphysical and mystical challenge of Dante's text.

Petrarch's eternity is the world scattered in time and space made "raccolta e 'ntera," gathered together and made whole or one; it is the end of hope and memory, the end of the entrapment of the "I" by time, past and future; it is an image of the self made whole. It is above all the home of Laura, redeemed and freed from time; indeed, the *Triumph of Eternity* ends with the beatitude of seeing her: "se fu beato chi la vide in terra, / or che fia dunque a rivederla in cielo!" (if one who saw her on earth was blessed, what will it be like to see her again in Heaven!) (ll. 144−45). In one sense Petrarch has brought us back to the end of Giacomo da Lentini's famous sonnet "Io m'ag[g]io posto in core a Dio servire," in which the poet is torn between his lady and God, and concludes that he would not want to go to Heaven without her ("sanza mia donna non vi voria gire"), but wants salvation just so that he can look at her forever ("ché lo mi teria in gran consolamento, / veg[g]endo la mia donna in ghiora stare").[16] With the last vernacular lines he wrote, Petrarch has wiped out the entire philosophizing and mysticizing history of the Italian lyric that culminates in Dante, everything between the Sicilians and himself; or at least he has wiped out the *Commedia,* and brought us back to the last poem of the *Vita Nova,* "Oltre la spera che più larga gira," in which Dante's sigh ascends to contemplate his lady in heaven. Moreover, in an extraordinary reversal of "Voi ch'ascoltate," the poet's tears for Laura become a mark of honor and rejoicing, not of shame and remorse, and he and Laura become celebrities among the blessed because of those tears, not objects of ridicule and infamy (ll. 85–99). The triumphs of Death and Time are annulled, so that Love, Laura, and Fame are all redeemed and vindicated (ll. 124–45). While the end of the *Commedia* moves from gazing on Beatrice to gazing on the Virgin, and then to seeing God himself, the *Triumph of Eternity* ends with gazing on Laura, undoing even the substitution of the Virgin for Laura at the end of the *Canzoniere.* The *Triumph of Eternity* redeems the earthly mortal dream of space and time, and also of Fame and Love, the two chains that Augustinus had told Franciscus in the *Secretum* precluded his salvation.

We may conclude, then, that the Petrarchan narrator never achieves conversion. He never definitively renounces multiplicity for unity, the world for God. We have also suggested that the self that speaks in Petrarch's works, the narrating voice, is to a peculiar degree a literary construction: indeed, in the proemial sonnet of the *Canzoniere* it seems to have little ontological consistency beyond words, sound, and literature. The self that speaks, fashions and defines itself through the act of writing: as Stephen Greenblatt has observed, "Self-fashioning is always, though not exclusively, in language."[17] In his *I Frammenti dell'anima,* Marco Santagata, drawing on the work of Rico, has traced a compelling history of Petrarch's self-fashioning, which is worth evoking here in a few fundamental elements.[18]

Santagata begins from a remark Franciscus makes at the end of the *Secretum*: after he finishes the great works about other people that Augustinus has just condemned, namely the *De viris illustribus* and the *Africa,* Franciscus will follow Augustinus' advice and turn his attention to himself: "I will attend to myself as far as I am able. I will collect the scattered fragments of my soul [sparsa anime fragmenta recolligam], and I will diligently focus on myself alone."[19] This is the germ of the *Canzoniere,* whose title is of course *Rerum vulgarium fragmenta,* the fragments of vernacular things: it is the effort to make a unity, a coherent self, out of the scattered poems or fragments of his own life, reclaiming them from their haphazard dissemination among the public. The model of this self-construction will be Saint Augustine's life as laid out in the *Confessions*: a conversion narrative, a looking back upon error and wandering, on conflict and dispersive desire, from the new perspective of redemption, penitence, and peace. Hence the division of the *Canzoniere* into two parts, corresponding in its earlier versions to an ideal conversion just before the death of Laura, and even in its later versions to the two poles of error and of repentance; hence also the proemial poem and the final hymn to the Virgin. But the ideology or conception of what conversion is, and the figure of Augustinus himself in the *Secretum*, is more Ciceronian and Senecan and Stoic than Augustinian: it is the ideal of self-control, of collecting oneself through an act of will and reason and of dominating the passions to remain in peace and unperturbed. Following Rico, Santagata argues that Petrarch comes to this decision to refashion himself on the model of Augustine in the early 1350s, after realizing that the *Africa* and *De viris illustribus* are a dead end, and after determining to remake himself as a Christian humanist, a Ciceronian-Augustinian moralist (a project well underway in the *De vita solitaria* and the *De otio religioso*, begun in 1347 and 1346). Thus, he argues, Petrarch would have written the bulk (especially Book 3) of the *Secretum* by 1353, retrodating it internally to 1342, just before an ideal and imaginary conversion in 1344 at age forty. That conversion date is indicated by the famous *Familiares* 4.1, the Ascent of Mount Ventoux, which was probably also written in 1353 but retrodated to Good Friday of 1336. In that letter, Petrarch climbs the mountain when he is about to turn thirty-three, which was Saint Augustine's age when he converted. Petrarch climbs with his brother Gherardo, who goes straight to the top without effort, while Petrarch delays and takes every byway and detour, descending into every valley. When he finally reaches the top of the mountain, Petrarch reads from Augustine's *Confessions* about how people explore the world and neglect themselves, and Petrarch hopes for a changed life by age forty. Petrarch's fortieth year, 1344, is in fact the year after Petrarch's brother Gherardo really does convert (he entered a monastery); it is also the year after the birth of Petrarch's second illegitimate child (it would be hard to feign a conversion before that), and eleven years after 1333, the year Petrarch says he was first given a copy of Augustine's *Confessions*. Similarly, according to Augustine's *Confessions*, Augustine converted eleven years after first reading Cicero's *Hortensius*, the first germ of his own conversion.[20] By the end of the 1350s, Petrarch abandons this fabricated black-and-white conversion narrative for the ever more complex strategies that define the later *Canzoniere*. Yet the basic pattern of that conversion narrative subtends the work to the very end, as we have seen.

I would like to suggest that the two features of the self that we have traced in Petrarch's self-presentation—his failure to achieve conversion and his projection of self as in some sense dependent on words, an elusive and evanescent literary construction—are related to the dissolution of a profound metaphysical understanding that, implicitly or explicitly, had underpinned Christian thought for a millennium. What Petrarch rejects or ignores or finds irrelevant or incomprehensible is the Aristotelian-Neoplatonic metaphysical picture of reality, a picture that sees the individual soul, the world, and God as linked to each other by fundamental ontological relations, so that the soul by its very nature participates directly in the foundational principle of reality: thus in knowing the world, the soul knows it as itself, and by knowing itself, the soul can come to know itself as both the world and God. This understanding of reality reaches perhaps its most perfect and profound expression in Aquinas, Bonaventure, Meister Eckhart, and Dante, just before Petrarch's time. In particular, it is the ground of Dante's cosmological travel narrative.[21]

Two great insights ground Dante's understanding of reality. As metaphysical principles, they both derive from Aristotle, but, absorbed into Neoplatonism, they underlie in various ways most later medieval Christian thought. The first principle is that form gives being to matter: *forma dat esse materiae,* and pure form conceived in itself is pure consciousness or being or actuality. Consciousness (intellect) is thus the ultimate ontological principle, upon which all else depends. Consciousness or pure form is not only transcendent over sensible reality, as Plato would have it, but also immanent in the world: it constitutes the being of the world, which is why the world is intelligible and knowable. A corollary of this principle is that the soul is the form of the body, and gives it being. This corollary dissolves Platonic soul/body dualism, a dualism that identifies the human subject entirely with the soul, and conceives of the soul as trapped in the body, longing to be free of it. The second principle, which is really also a corollary of the first, is the identity of subject and object in the act of intellection, meaning that in knowing or perceiving something, the knower and the thing known are in a deep sense one, because they both share in that form that gives being to the thing.

The heart of these insights is that there is a fundamental connaturality between the human soul and God. Human consciousness is a particular sharing in consciousness itself, in the foundational principle that constitutes the being of the world. Moreover, by knowing things, human consciousness is sharing in the world itself. This means that if the human intelligence or awareness turns away from things and focuses itself on itself, it can come to know itself as one with, as sharing in, the ultimate reality that gives being to the world. It can know itself as in a sense encompassing, immune to and yet one with, the whole changing world of space and time. This is to touch the ground of one's own being, of all being, the utterly one, the utterly simple. Here we have the essence of the entire contemplative tradition up to Dante's time, and the essence of the pilgrim's journey in the *Comedy*. The pilgrim travels from the center of the spatiotemporal world, outwards through all the spheres of creation, ultimately to find himself "outside" the world in the Empyrean, which is the divine conscious reality that encompasses and gives being to the world. To reach the Empyrean is to experience all of space and time within one's own being. In the contemplative tradition, this journey takes the form of entering into oneself, focusing the mind on itself in single-pointed concentration, until ultimately one passes through that point of concentration, so to speak, into the foundational principle of reality, God Himself. The leitmotif of the tradition is the *nosce teipsum,* know yourself; as Saint Augustine says in his *De vera religione,* "noli foras ire, in teipsum redi": do not go outside; return into yourself.[22] As we have seen, this focal point or nexus between the divine and the human, through which the human self is revealed to be in a deep sense one with the foundation of all being, figures large in the last cantos of the *Paradiso.* It is in fact how the divine reality first appears to Dante, as an infinitesimal burning point that conquers Dante and through which he is ushered into the Empyrean.[23]

We have already seen how Petrarch ignores, in his own *Triumph of Eternity,* the metaphysical issues on which Dante builds the last cantos of the *Paradiso.* Petrarch's hostility to metaphysical questions—at least as those questions had been framed and treated in the scholastic tradition—is indeed one of his most sustained polemics; as Charles Trinkaus succinctly puts it, "To Petrarch, the irrelevance of both physics and metaphysics was almost absolute; he couldn't have cared less."[24] Metaphysics, in the non-existential and almost trivialized verbal forms it could take in late scholasticism, seemed to Petrarch, as it would to the humanists after him, the opposite of what was essential or useful to humans living in this world, especially in a time of crisis like the fourteenth century. To irrelevant, marginal, and inconsequential metaphysical and logical disputations, Petrarch opposes an Augustinian-Ciceronian-Senecan moral meditation on oneself, marshaling the resources of history, literature, and a dialogue with elevated minds across the ages to address the real moral problems of human beings in the world and to develop a new vision of Christianity and of humanity in history. For Petrarch and the humanists, this conversation and study would draw on a profound cultivation of eloquence and rhetoric: language, aware of itself, is the medium through which humans express their nature and come to know what they are; known precisely in its details, and deeply in its principles, cultivated language allows minds to converse with each other across the ages; it is also the means of persuasion, through which humans can be moved to develop the potential of their nature, and through which one can become a moral counselor to another. Many of these ideas come into focus in Petrarch's *De sui ipsius et multorum ignorantia,* in which he presents four friends as accusing him of ignorance, which to them largely means ignorance of Aristotle. In one sense, the four friends are perfectly right: Petrarch shows no knowledge or understanding of Aristotle's metaphysics, logic, or physics, either in Aristotle directly or through any scholastic philosopher; he sidesteps in particular the *Metaphysics* and *De anima,* so crucial for Aquinas and Dante in their understanding of the soul's relation to God and to the world. (He does claim and show, on the other hand, knowledge of Aristotle's *Ethics.*)[25] What use, Petrarch asks, is it "to know the nature of beasts and birds and fish and snakes, and to ignore or neglect our human nature, the purpose of our birth, or whence we come and whither we are bound?"[26] Aristotle cannot help us in the pursuit of happiness or understanding, because he "either failed to understand, or understood but ignored, the two things that are absolutely essential to happiness, namely, faith and immortality."[27]

Faith, for Petrarch, is an implicit trust in the Christian promise, a trust in grace and not in one's own merits or power of understanding; it is a refusal to despair (to succumb to *accidia*) despite one's own incapacity to change one's life, to convert as Augustine converted. As Trinkaus observes, for Petrarch "the foundations of religion are psychological, and not epistemological" (or, we might add, metaphysical): faith begins in despair.[28] For Petrarch, Christian faith is not built on the scaffolding of a Neoplatonic metaphysical understanding, as it had been in large measure for Augustine himself: it is rather a trust in the Incarnation and in divine grace as a refuge from *accidia*. Self-knowledge, the meditation on oneself, leads only to the knowledge of one's own inadequacy and misery, to an acute awareness of one's ceaseless, variable, and inconstant thoughts, desires, impulses, and memories; it thus prompts one to throw oneself on God's mercy. Self-knowledge does not itself lead to anything like a contemplative ascent toward the vision of God, as it does in Bonaventure's *Itinerarium mentis in Deum* and in countless texts of the Neoplatonic contemplative tradition, in particular Augustine's *De vera religione*, on which Petrarch's *De otio religioso* is modeled.[29] Thus the *De otio religioso*, entirely structured on the biblical phrase *vacate et videte* (in its original context, "vacate et videte quoniam ego sum Deus," "be still and know that I am God" [Psalm 45.11]), gives virtually every possible meaning to the phrase except what it means in Augustine's *De vera religione*. For Augustine, it means stilling the mind from all thought and imagination, in order to contemplate the One:

> Certainly, we seek the One, and nothing is simpler than that. Let us seek it therefore in simplicity of heart. It is written: *Be still, and know that I am God:* not in the stillness of laziness, but in the stillness of thought, which frees you from space and time. Indeed, the images that come from stimulation and inconstancy do not allow us to see the unchanging unity.[30]

As Augustine explains later, truth dwells inside us; to reach it we must transcend our mutable selves, and even the thinking mind, to strive toward the source where the light of intellect arises.[31] For Richard of St. Victor,

> it is necessary that a person wishing to attain her [Rachel's] embrace [i.e., contemplation] serve seven years, and seven more for her, in order that he may learn to rest not only from evil works but also from useless thoughts. Many, even if they know how to be free of activity in the body, are nevertheless completely unable to be free from preoccupations in the heart. They do not know how to make a Sabbath on the Sabbath and for that reason are not capable of fulfilling what is written in the Psalm: "Be free from preoccupations and see that I am God."[32]

For Petrarch, instead, the phrase sums up a *contemptus mundi* theme, an idealization of the retreat or disengagement from the tempests of the world into the safe port of an ideal monastic solitude, a retreat from which Petrarch presents himself as excluded.[33] To resist degenerate customs is

> laborious and exceedingly difficult for us wretched ones, whose navigation proceeds still uncertain among the stormy billows of the world: indeed, we are swept away by the violence of temporal concerns, and have no other repose except what is granted us by pauses in our sins and preoccupations. For you [the monks to whom he writes], who hold firmly to the port, it is much easier to be prudent and watchful. You have cut the knots of the world, the snares of worldly affairs, the bonds with things; naked and free you have swum out of the many tempests into where you can rest and be free.[34]

Citing the lines quoted above from Augustine on the verse *vacate et videte*, Petrarch interprets them as an exhortation to resist demonic temptations and to contemplate the snares and lures of Satan: "hic nullo strepitu auribus, nullo pulvere rerum transeuntium obstante oculis, omnes hostis dolos tendiculasque prospicite" (here, with no clamour to disturb the ears, no dust of passing things to obstruct your sight, observe attentively all the wiles and snares of the enemy).[35] But Petrarch is also conscious that the tempest of the world is as much inside him as outside: he knows that his incessant efforts to find freedom through flight and travel are hopeless, because he travels with himself; he wishes to put off his cares and his bonds, but that can only be done by putting off himself, an option apparently precluded to him.[36]

For Petrarch, as he presents himself, there can be no escape from the finite self. There is no conversion, and there is no port of peace. The unattainable port he envisions, and of which his brother Gherardo's conversion to monastic life becomes an emblem, is an illusion because he cannot conceive the cessation of thought and desire, or the entering into the ground of the soul's being—pure consciousness or love or being beyond identity—in which alone that port or conversion could consist. Simply put, Petrarch, as he presents himself, cannot stop thinking; because he cannot end the incessant stream of memory, thought, desire, and imagination in his consciousness, he identifies himself with that stream, and not with the consciousness in which it arises. Thus the Petrarchan self as an autonomous and irreducible, albeit unstable, elusive, and evanescent, reality is born. In Petrarch, the thinking subject, the finite ego-center and locus of memory and desire, has become divorced from any deeper reality. No longer ontologically rooted in the foundational principle of the universe, it cannot be surrendered into God. It cannot come to know itself as (one with) God, cannot know the world as itself, and cannot give up itself without ceasing to exist entirely. Hence the ontologically deracinated self, as it emerges in Petrarch's writing, is alienated from both God and the world; it is in existential crisis; it is a fragile and illusory postulate, an evanescent tissue of thought, memory, and desire, in constant danger of dispersion in the flux of space and time.[37] Its very isolation, rootlessness, and instability leads it to an obsessive and anxious preoccupation with itself.

One could argue that Petrarch has discovered and presented the modern subjective self, born fully mature in Petrarch's work and epitomizing the entire history of the self as it will unfold in modernity. Indeed, in Petrarch's pitiless and objective analysis of the subjective self, an analysis as acute and profound as any, one can trace *in nuce* many of the stages and dimensions of subjectivity that will flower in the next six centuries. The standard account of that history of the self (subject, of course, to endless qualifications and reservations and arguments) is elegantly sketched by Roy Porter: the modern "individual" was born in some sense with the Italian Renaissance (as Burckhardt claimed in 1859), became the private space of personal salvation with the Reformation (as Max Weber argued), deepened into a private psychic microcosmos in Montaigne and Shakespeare, and supplied the solipsistic foundation of certainty in Descartes; this autonomous interiority was then explored as a product of education, self-formation, and self-discovery by Locke and Rousseau, spawning the genre of the novel; it became a sacred quest for self-understanding among the Romantics; it exploded into the realm of the unconscious with Freud, to finally "un-do itself" (as Eagleton puts it) as merely a linguistic bewitchment in Wittgenstein, a delusion in Foucault, and a "self-fashioning" (Greenblatt). It is revealed as a cultural, social, literary construction and as the sexist, elitist, and self-indulgent germ of the catastrophes, inhumanities, and slaveries of the twentieth century. The self as an autonomous "thing," as a "private mental theatre" or "inner world" contrasted with an "external world," has come in recent times to seem a source of crisis, a dangerous illusion—which Petrarch's analysis in many ways already suggests it is, and which is what it would have seemed to the Aristotelian-Neoplatonic understanding it replaced.[38]

Let us very briefly set out some of the characteristics of the subjective self as it emerges in Petrarch's work. The first, which I have already treated, is the difficulty or incoherence of conversion, of renouncing the world for God. Conversion in Dante's world, as in Saint Augustine's *Confessions*, is a surrender of the finite self that allows the awakening of the ground of being to itself in us: this is the operation of grace, an awakening that seizes the mind and heart, and takes over our own experience of what we are. Petrarch has an undeniable longing for some such experience, but his idea of conversion, as presented in the *Secretum*, in the *De vita solitaria*, and the *De otio religioso*, becomes almost a parody of Christian conversion.[39] On the one hand (especially in the *Secretum*), it becomes a "macho" act of the will, a trying to force oneself to love God and to despise the world, by constantly meditating on death and mortality; on the other hand (especially in the *De otio religioso*), it becomes a futile waiting or longing for a miracle of grace to rescue one from *accidia*, the despair that arises precisely from the meditation on a subjective self that is rootless, unstable, and incapable of conversion. Either approach only strengthens the self-identification with an autonomous subjective self, the ego, trapping oneself ever more firmly within it. Indeed, for an irreducible subjective self, divorced from both the world and God, there can be no experience of surrender or conversion except by the destruction or abandonment of itself: there is no philosophical or theological framework within which conversion makes sense. The Petrarchan self is caught in a paradoxical circle: despair, *accidia*, throws it toward a longing for conversion; but the *accidia* itself derives from an understanding of self that implicitly precludes conversion. One might say that the *accidia* of the Petrarchan self, which becomes the ground and impulse for his religiosity, is itself a sign of the philosophical incoherence of his religious thought and self-understanding. One might even generalize the picture to argue that Christianity, deprived of its Aristotelian-Neoplatonic philosophical underpinnings and stripped of a picture of reality that breathed life into it for a millennium and that perhaps culminated in Dante, is in danger of becoming philosophically and theologically—indeed, intellectually—incoherent. Hence its growing crisis since the fourteenth century, especially among intellectuals, and its survival largely in forms that deemphasize rigorous philosophy or theology. Hence also the shift whereby the testimony of contemplatives, which had been the experiential core of the Christian tradition, becomes marginalized under the label "mysticism," a term that arises in its modern sense in seventeenth-century France, along with the Enlightenment.[40]

A second characteristic of the Petarchan religious paradox is the separation of intellect, love, and will, with the will becoming almost autonomous from, and primary to, understanding. For Dante and the medieval tradition, whatever the arguments about the relation between will and intellect, moral transformation is always one with growth in both understanding and selfless love. Journeying from the center of the earth through the concentric spheres toward the Empyrean, the pilgrim Dante is encompassing and experiencing more and more of reality as himself. His experience of self is expanding, so to speak, to include more and more of the world: the self grows in understanding, love, and moral perfection together, until, having come to know itself as (one with) pure love-being-awareness, it becomes selfless, merged in love and understanding and will with the divine. For Petrarch, understanding, love, and will are no longer one as integrated faculties (as they were for Augustine). The Petrarchan narrator seeks willpower separately from understanding ("It is better to will what is good than to know what is true," he famously remarks in the *De ignorantia*; "It is more prudent to strive for a good and devout will than a capacious and clear intellect"), and he seeks to will love without understanding: we should love God without trying to know Him.[41] Although God is of course never fully knowable, these maxims would be an impossibility for Dante, for whom love (the experience of the other as oneself) is consequent upon and one with understanding (the recognition of the other as oneself); both depend on sinking oneself into, merging with, the ground of one's being, in which all things are revealed as one. For Dante, understanding ("sight") is logically, although not temporally, prior to love, which subsumes the will:

> tutti hanno diletto
> quanto la sua veduta si profonda
> nel vero in che si queta ogne intelletto.
>   Quinci si può veder come si fonda
> l'esser beato ne l'atto che vede,
> non in quel ch'ama, che poscia seconda . . .

———————

All have delight to the degree that their sight penetrates into the depths of the Truth in which every intellect finds rest. From this you can see how the state of blessedness is founded on the act of vision, not in the act of love, which follows after . . .[42]

A third characteristic of Petrarchan subjectivity is dualism, dualism between the soul and the body, between mind and matter, and between heaven and earth: precisely the polarized existence of the Petrarchan narrative voice. This dualism is what makes Petrarch's religiosity seem retrograde, darker and more fraught than Dante's. In a vivid example from the second book of the *Secretum,* Augustinus likens the body to a dark, humid, and stinking jail, which the soul should hate and try not even to touch, longing only to be free of it.[43] Petrarch's *De otio religioso,* written as counsel to the monks of Gherardo's monastery after Petrarch had visited his brother there, is full of such advice.[44] (Note that Augustinus' view of the body is again a parody of Saint Augustine's view, as developed for example in the *De vera religione,* Petrarch's model for the *De otio.*)[45] This mind/matter dualism, and the understanding of self as a private mental theatre discontinuous with either the world or God, will be enshrined in Cartesianism and its legacy. The paradoxes implicit in this dualism spawn skepticism (the starting point of Descartes' *Meditations*) and the long modern philosophical obsession with epistemology.

A fourth characteristic of the Petrarchan self is *accidia,* so brilliantly dissected by Petrarch in many works, including the *Canzoniere,* but perhaps most stringently in the second book of the *Secretum. Accidia* is fundamentally depression, a loathing of self and of all things, a sense of emptiness, apathy, hopelessness, of nothing to live for, of the vanity of all goals. It includes feelings of anxiety, restlessness, melancholy, and despair; yet it is a depression that has its own kind of voluptuous attraction and morbid pleasure, so that one lacks even the desire to escape from it. This kind of existentialist despair or *ennui* will become a great theme in the history of modernity, from Hamlet and Pascal to Baudelaire and Sartre; in the twentieth century it may be one of the foundations of psychotherapy and psychiatric medicine. One could argue that *accidia* is the intrinsic malady or genetic disease of the modern subjective self: a sign of its instability and paradoxes, of its problematic understanding of itself and its relation to the world.

Accidia is related to neurotic anxiety, a fifth characteristic of the Petrarchan self. As Franciscus tells Augustinus in the *Secretum, accidia* is a feel-

ing of being overwhelmed by the miseries and troubles of the human condition, a sense that everything conspires toward one's destruction: "I am like
someone surrounded by countless enemies who has no way to escape. There
is no hope of mercy or solace. Instead, with weapons aimed at me, with
trenches dug, everything threatens destruction."[46] Unmoored from any ontological foundation and isolated within itself, the ego is acutely aware
of its vulnerability and ephemerality. The subjective self is simply a flow of
thought gathered through memory into a sense of identity: it is a tissue of
memory and desire, of hope and regret, of conflicting impulses dispersed
among all the objects of attention and attraction. The subjective sense of self
is fragile and illusory, as it is in the *Canzoniere.* One can understand much
of Petrarch's writing as an incessant effort to stabilize and define the self, to
rescue it from the flux and multiplicity of space and time. It may be one reason the Petrarchan narrator studies and writes incessantly, by his own testimony sixteen hours a day, every day. If he is not writing, in some sense he
ceases to exist: writing establishes an identity and imposes it in the world
through fame.

The effort to rescue a self from the flux of space and time motivates
some of Petrarch's most obsessive images. Perhaps the most pervasive
image in all of Petrarch's work is that of life as a journey (or rather, an incessant wandering) on a stormy sea or in a flowing river, with the constant
danger of shipwreck and drowning (*naufragio*), along with the constant
search for a port, a point of stability or haven on the shore.[47] The subjective
self is in constant danger of being swept away and dispersed in the sea or
river of change, in the multiplicity and ephemerality of the world and of
thoughts and passions. "What," Petrarch asks in the *De otio religioso,* "is
more like flowing water than the endlessly changing affairs of human beings? . . . They will slip away even more quickly than I write."[48] In this flux
the poet must try to establish a self by an act of will and self-construction
through study and writing. Thus Petrarch often presents himself as writing on the shore of a river (as on the river Sorgue in Valchiusa); in an extraordinary passage in the *De ignorantia,* he presents himself as writing in a
small boat *in* a river, "among the swirling currents of the river Po." "So don't
be surprised," he says, "if my hand or my words falter as I write."[49] It is
through his own effort, and through study and writing, that he overcomes
the current and establishes his identity, namely, his fame: "With oars, sails,
and ropes, I overcome the current of the Po, returning to the Ticino river
and its ancient city of scholars [Pavia]. There . . . I shall resume the mantle

of my former fame. . . ."[50] The sails and oars conjure up Dante's Ulysses of *Inferno* 26, who, instead of lowering his sails in his old age, made wings of his oars, seeking knowledge and virtue, only to end in shipwreck. The Petrarchan narrator *is* Dante's Ulysses, gripped by the idea that if he learns or experiences one more thing, writes one more book, takes one more trip, he will somehow find the stability, understanding, and virtue that he seeks, even in his last days.

Theodore Cachey has traced the strategies through which Petrarch appropriates Dante's Ulysses as a positive image and model, reverses or ignores his tragic end in shipwreck, and suggests that Dante is worthy of praise precisely because he is like Ulysses.[51] If it is through study and writing that the Petrarchan narrator can stand on the dry shore out of the surge, or—if he must be in a boat—conquer the surge to resume his mantle of fame in the city of scholars, then it is also through study and writing that he approaches the goal of life's spiritual pilgrimage. For the Dantean pilgrim that goal is union with God; for the Petrarchan narrator the goal is simply to stave off shipwreck and rescue the subjective self from foundering in the flux of space and time. It is momentarily to placate the tumult within and to assuage one's restlessness and rootlessness. By making Dante the Ulysses whom Dante condemned, Petrarch is in a sense stripping Dante of the powerful mythology he created around his own literary project: he is saying that Dante, in reality, did not and could not do more than what Petrarch or any writer can do, which is to establish and stabilize one's presence in the world, the consequence of which is literary glory.[52] Thus, as Cachey demonstrates, Petrarch's *Itinerarium ad sepulchrum domini nostri Yehsu Christi*, a guide to the Holy Land written for Giovanni Mandelli's pilgrimage to the Holy Sepulcher, in effect also praises Mandelli as a new Ulysses for making the trip. But Petrarch himself, whom Mandelli had asked to accompany him, will not go in person, because he fears shipwreck: instead, he will write a guidebook. He will make the trip, he will be Ulysses, by writing. ("You," he says to Mandelli, "have come this far by oars and by foot on sea and on land: I, plowing this paper with a swift pen.")[53] The tomb of Christ would be the final destination and port of any ideal spiritual journey; betraying its own title, Petrarch's *Itinerarium* never gets there, but ends instead at the tomb of Alexander the Great in Egypt, a monument of fame engendered by restless wandering.[54]

A sixth characteristic of the Petrarchan self is alienation or isolation, from the world, from others, and from God. This alienation gives rise to the unquenchable desire immortalized in the *Canzoniere*— the world, life, love, beauty, God, fulfillment, and peace remain always "other," a shifting mirage always out of reach. But in Petrarch this alienation of the self is also expressed as the obsessive quest for solitude, which absorbs and supplants the futile commitment to conversion. Solitude becomes a fraught and complicated ideal for Petrarch: he layers into it most of his concerns and ambitions and strategies. For Petrarch, solitude is, first of all, the locus of self-fashioning, the locus in which one constructs an ideal unified self: solitude is where one reads and writes. But Petrarch must defuse the challenge of a competing image of solitude: that of anchoritic monasticism, of solitude as the locus of mystical contemplation, of self-knowledge through divine union and rapture.[55] Petrarch needs to present that ideal of mystical solitude and rapture as somehow equivalent to, or subsumed by, a life of classical study and writing and poetry: his own life. In short, he must fuse Mount Sinai into Mount Parnassus, and make them one; the tension between the two mountains represents another version of Petrarch's *dissidio* and his effort to make himself one. In that effort, Petrarch tries to fashion himself as the new Christian humanist and moralist, fusing the classical and the Christian: Petrarch is the Augustinized Cicero, the Senecized Saint Augustine. To effect this is the task of the *De vita solitaria* and the *De otio religioso,* with their carefully balanced classical and religious examples and authorities (although it could be argued that the *De otio* represents the failure of the project). It is also one aim of the *Secretum,* in which Augustinus rarely cites either Saint Augustine or the Bible. Augustinus' authorities are all classical poets and writers: Vergil, Horace, Ovid, Juvenal, Terence, Cicero, Seneca, and of course, Petrarch himself, added to that company of authorities. In fashioning himself as the Augustinized Cicero, Petrarch needs to model Saint Augustine's spiritual conversion from worldly values and pagan error to Christian truth, while at the same time he has to reverse Saint Augustine's cultural conversion away from pagan literature, rhetoric, and Rome to Scripture, preaching, and Jerusalem. In particular, Petrarch must neutralize St. Augustine's *nosce teipsum,* self-knowledge as the contemplative ascent to the divine: by reducing Augustinian self-knowledge to the moral meditation on the subjective self, Petrarch indeed turns St. Augustine into a Seneca or Cicero.

Petrarch also must counter another suspicion. Petrarch seeks solitude not in order to perform austere spiritual practices or rise to the vision of God, or prepare himself through contemplation for redemptive action in the world and service to humanity; rather, he seeks solitude in order to stand on the shore, to read and write and fashion a self that will result in enduring fame.[56] By his own account, Petrarch's solitude requires friends, books, money, virtue, maturity, and health.[57] The suspicion might arise that Petrarch's quest for solitude is self-indulgent. Petrarch is well aware of that suspicion: in answer, he must reclaim the classical ideal of *otium*, again trying to make it equivalent to, or to make it absorb, the religious monastic ideal; he has to assert the need to follow one's own nature and inclination; and he must head off the idea that solitude must result in a spiritual transformation or in action and service in the world. Petrarch brings all three strategies together in discussing Celestine V, the pious hermit who was made pope in 1294, abdicated after five months in order to go back to his cell, and was canonized in 1313. Dante's opinion is clear: Celestine is "colui / che fece per viltade il gran rifiuto" (he who, through cowardice [pusillanimity, contemptible timidity], made the great refusal) (*Inf.* 3.59–60). Dante's Celestine is rejected by both God and the devil, and he lives among the neutrals of *Inferno* 3, with the angels who were for themselves alone ("per sé fuoro"), not even worthy to be properly in Hell. In the *De vita solitaria* Petrarch devotes a disproportionate amount of space to Celestine as an exalted example of the love of solitude. He says that since we all have different inclinations and hence different opinions about the same things, let anyone who wishes attribute the solitary and saintly Celestine's abdication to cowardice or pusillanimity: "Quod factum solitarii sanctique patris . . . vilitati animi quisquis volet attribuat"—a barb obviously aimed at Dante.[58] Celestine's abdication is for Petrarch the gesture of a divine spirit who was fully free, who could despise even the highest office and glory in the world, who turned to heaven and forgot the earth, and who thus returned to himself. The key point is that Petrarch identifies himself and his *otium* with Saint Celestine and his hermitage, although no two souls and lives could be further apart. "Oh," exclaims Petrarch, "If only I could have lived with him! Among so many solitary beings, I would have longed to live only with him in particular. . . . We would have travelled the path of this life with matched steps."[59]

Petrarch as Saint Celestine: it's a stretch, but the equation Petrarch posits between himself and Celestine situates Petrarch's solitude above the papacy, and it makes Petrarch's reading and writing and self-fashioning in Valchiusa equivalent to Saint Celestine's meditation in his hermitage. With

Dante and his world in the background, Petrarch's autonomous subjective self is giving itself authority, sacred dignity, and freedom. It is struggling to emancipate itself, not without crisis, from the obligation to transcend itself through selflessness, an obligation it still feels but cannot understand or fulfill. Above all, that finite self is trying to emancipate itself from any divine or human injunction that contradicts its own natural inclination. In Petrarch, we are watching the painful birth of the modern self and the death of the medieval self: Petrarch is indeed in some sense *altr'uom*, a new man.

Notes

1. One of the best treatments of the question remains Charles Trinkaus, *In Our Image and Likeness: Humanity and Divinity in Italian Humanist Thought*, 2 vols. (Chicago: University of Chicago Press, 1970), 1:3–50, and *The Poet as Philosopher: Petrarch and the Formation of Renaissance Consciousness* (New Haven: Yale University Press, 1979). See also the subtle treatment in Timothy J. Reiss, *The Discourse of Modernism* (Ithaca, N.Y.: Cornell University Press, 1982), esp. 69–107, and *Mirages of the Selfe: Patterns of Personhood in Ancient and Early Modern Europe* (Stanford, Calif.: Stanford University Press, 2003), esp. 269–352; while placing the birth of the "modern self" centuries later (and warning against the anachronistic use of such terms for the medieval period), Reiss sees in Petrarch the tensions that will lead to that birth. Brian Stock, "Reading, Writing, and the Self: Petrarch and His Forerunners," *New Literary History* 26, no. 4 (Fall 1995): 717–30, and Aldo Scaglione, "Classical Heritage and Petrarchan Self-Consciousness in the Literary Emergence of the Interior 'I,'" in *Altro Polo: A Volume of Italian Studies* (Sydney: Fredrick May Foundation for Italian Studies [University of Sydney], 1984), 23–34, trace Petrarch's literary subjectivity to Augustine and Boethius, marked in Petrarch however by a new self-consciousness and conflict. Peter Burke, "Representations of the Self from Petrarch to Descartes," in *Rewriting the Self: Histories from the Renaissance to the Present*, ed. Roy Porter (London: Routledge, 1997), 17–28, Ugo Dotti, "Miti e forme dell' 'io' nella cultura di Francesco Petrarca," *Revue des études italiennes* 29 (1983): 74–85, and Thomas Greene, "The Flexibility of the Self in Renaissance Literature," in *The Disciplines of Criticism: Essays in Literary Theory, Interpretation, and History*, ed. Peter Demetz, Thomas Greene, and Lowry Nelson, Jr. (New Haven: Yale University Press, 1968), 241–64, give historical and literary contextualizations, treating the complex social and cultural factors involved; Pierre Blanc, "Petrarca ou la poétique de l'ego," *Revue des études italiennes* 29 (1983): 122–69, undertakes a psychoanalytic reading of Petrarch.

2. Marco Santagata, *I frammenti dell'anima* (Bologna: Il Mulino, 1992), 333–41.

3. "F: . . . non ignarus, ut paulo ante dicebas, multo michi futurum esse se-
curius studium hoc unum sectari et, deviis pretermissis, rectum callem salutis ap-
prehendere. Sed desiderium frenare non valeo. A: In antiquam litem relabimur,
voluntatem impotentiam vocas." Text cited from Francesco Petrarca, *Secretum: Il
mio segreto,* ed. and trans. E. Fenzi (Milan: Mursia, 1992), 282. Translation based on
Francesco Petrarch, *The Secret,* ed. Carol E. Quillen (Boston: Bedford/St. Martin's,
2003), 148.

4. Text from Francesco Petrarca, *Canzoniere,* ed. Marco Santagata (Milan:
Mondadori, 1996), 1366. Translation based on *Petrarch's Lyric Poems: The "Rime
sparse" and Other Lyrics,* trans. and ed. Robert M. Durling (Cambridge, Mass.:
Harvard University Press, 1976), and Petrarch, *The Canzoniere, or Rerum vulgarium
fragmenta,* trans. Mark Musa (Bloomington: Indiana University Press, 1996); subsequent translations from Durling. For the dating of the poem, see Santagata's survey of the question in his edition, 1366–67.

5. The point is made by Santagata, *I frammenti dell'anima,* 335–40.

6. Petrarch, *De vita solitaria,* in vol. 1 of *Opere latine di Francesco Petrarca,*
ed. and trans. Antonietta Bufano (Turin: Unione tipografico-editrice torinese,
1975), 444. See also Petrarch's account of Augustine's conversion, 414–17.

7. Ibid., 442.

8. "Questi trionfi, i cinque in terra giuso / avem veduto ed alla fine il sesto, /
Dio permettente, vederem lassuso" (Of these triumphs, we have seen five down
on earth, and the sixth, God permitting, we shall see up above): *Triumphus Eternitatis,* ll. 121–23, quoted from Francesco Petrarca, *Rime, Trionfi e poesie latine,* ed.
Ferdinando Neri et al. (Milan and Naples: Ricciardi, 1951), 558.

9. For the time-stopping strategies of the *Canzoniere,* see Teodolinda Barolini, "The Making of a Lyric Sequence: Time and Narrative in Petrarch's *Rerum
vulgarium fragmenta,*" *MLN* 104 (1989): 1–38.

10. See in particular *Paradiso* 28.13–45, 100–114; 29.1–12; 30.10–12, 20–24;
33.94–96.

11. For Dante's treatment of the *punto,* and its relation to the Neoplatonic
contemplative tradition, see my *Metaphysics of Dante's "Comedy"* (New York: Oxford
University Press, 2005), esp. 57–71, 141–46, 152–60, 166–67.

12. " . . . oportet, nos intrare ad mentem nostram, quae est imago Dei ae-
viterna, spiritualis et intra nos, et hoc est ingredi in veritate Dei; oportet, nos transcendere ad aeternum, spiritualissimum, et supra nos aspiciendo ad primum prin-
cipium" (1.2); "ubi in Deum [Franciscus] transiit per contemplationis excessum. . . .
In hoc autem transitu, si sit perfectus, oportet quod relinquantur omnes intellec-
tuales operationes, et apex affectus totus transferatur et transformetur in Deum"
(7.3–4): Saint Bonaventure, *Itinerarium mentis in Deum,* vol. 5 of *Opera omnia* (Ad
Claras Aquas [Quaracchi]: Collegii S. Bonaventure, 1882–1902), quoted in English from *The Soul's Journey into God; The Tree of Life; The Life of St. Francis,* trans.
Ewert Cousins (New York: Paulist Press, 1978), 60, 112–13. ". . . igniculus [sapi-
entiae] est primo congregandus, secundo inflammandus, tertio sublevandus.—

Congregatur autem per reductionem affectionis ab omni amore creaturae . . . Tertio, sublevandus est, et hoc supra omne sensibile, imaginabile, et intelligibile . . . (1.15–17): Saint Bonaventure, *De triplici via,* in vol. 8 of *Opera omnia,* 3–27, quoted in English from *The Triple Way, or Love Enkindled,* in *Mystical opuscula,* trans. José de Vinck (Paterson, N.J.: St. Anthony Guild Press, 1960), 71 [1.15–17].

13. Text cited from Dante Alighieri, *La Commedia secondo l'antica vulgata,* rev. ed., 4 vols., ed. Giorgio Petrocchi (Florence: Le Lettere, 1994). Translations mine.

14. Translation based on *The Divine Comedy,* trans. Charles S. Singleton (Princeton: Princeton University Press, 1973), 3:377.

15. Translation from *The Portable Dante,* trans. and ed. Mark Musa (New York: Penguin Books, 1995).

16. Quoted from Gianfranco Contini, *Poeti del Duecento,* vol. 1, tomo 1 (Milan: Ricciardi-Mondadori, 1995 [Milan and Naples: Ricciardi, 1960]), 80.

17. Stephen Greenblatt, *Renaissance Self-Fashioning from More to Shakespeare* (Chicago: University of Chicago Press, 1980), 9.

18. In particular, Francisco Rico, *Vida u obra de Petrarca, I. Lectura del "Secretum"* (Padova: Antenore, 1974).

19. "Adero michi ipse quantum potero, et sparsa anime fragmenta recolligam, morabor mecum sedulo" (Petrarch, *Secretum,* 282); in English from Quillen's translation, 147.

20. See also Petrarch's conversion narrative, based on Augustine and self-consciously triggered by Augustine's *Confessions,* at the end of the *De otio religioso* (in vol. 1 of *Opere latine,* 802–9).

21. This Aristotelian-Neoplatonic metaphysical understanding and its particular culminating fruition in the work of Dante are the subjects of my *Metaphysics of Dante's "Comedy."*

22. Augustine, *De vera religione,* in *La vera religione, Opere di Sant'Agostino* 6.1 (Rome: Città Nuova, 1995), sect. 39, para. 72 (p. 109).

23. It might be worth observing that Wittgenstein, one of the greatest philosophers of modern times, had a similar insight in the *Tractatus*: the metaphysical subject, the ultimate conscious "I" that grounds the subjective self of attribute, identity, memory, and thought, is not part of the world; it lies outside the world. In the same way the physical eye is not part of its field of vision, but lies outside its field of vision. See Ludwig Wittgenstein, *Tractatus Logico-Philosophicus,* trans. D. F. Pears and B. F. McGuinness (London: Routledge & Kegan Paul, 1961), esp. 5.631–5.641, 6.41–6.54.

24. Trinkaus, *In Our Image,* 1:5.

25. E.g., Francesco Petrarca, *De sui ipsius et multorum ignorantia,* in *Invectives,* ed. and trans. David Marsh, I Tatti Renaissance Library (Cambridge, Mass.: Harvard University Press, 2003), 4.107 (pp. 314–15). Hereafter cited as *De ignorantia.*

26. "Nam quid, oro, naturas beluarum et uolucrum et piscium et serpentum nosse profuerit, et naturam hominum, ad quid nati sumus, unde et quo pergimus, uel nescire uel spernere?" (Petrarch, *De ignorantia* 2.18 [pp. 238–39]).

27. "Illa vero non intellexerit, siue intellecta neglexerit, sine quibus prorsus esse felicitas non potest: fidem scilicet atque immortalitatem" (ibid., 4.50 [pp. 266–67]). Petrarch goes on to say that the former is the case: Aristotle could not have known the Light that entered the world after his time.

28. Trinkaus, *In Our Image,* 1:31. Trinkaus provides a sensitive overview of Petrarchan religiosity in its historical and cultural context, 1:3–50. For Petrarch's *accidia,* see esp. *Secretum,* 40–50, and *De vita solitaria,* 360–65. For a stimulating but problematic account of the relation between Petrarch's religious and poetic vocations, see Marjorie O'Rourke Boyle, *Petrarch's Genius: Pentimento and Prophecy* (Berkeley: University of California Press, 1991).

29. "Et Augustinus in eo libro quem sepe hodie in testimonium arcesso— loquenti enim de otio religioso, quid oportunius quam Vere religionis liber astipuletur—... inquit ..." (And Augustine again in that book that here I often cite as a witness— for one who is speaking of religious repose, what is more opportune than to call in support *The True Religion?*—... says ...) (Petrarch, *De otio religioso,* 610).

30. "Unum certe quaerimus, quo simplicius nihil est. Ergo in simplicitate cordis quaeramus illum. Agite otium, inquit, et agnoscetis quia ego sum Dominus: non otium desidiae, sed otium cogitationis, ut a locis ac temporibus vacetis. Haec enim phantasmata tumoris et volubilitatis, constantem unitatem videre non sinunt" (Augustine, *De vera religione,* 35.65 [p. 100]). My translation.

31. "In interiore homine habitat veritas; et si tuam naturam mutabilem inveneris, transcende et teipsum. Sed memento cum te transcendis, ratiocinantem animam te transcendere. Illuc ergo tende, unde ipsum lumen rationis accenditur" (*De vera religione,* 38 [p. 72]).

32. "Qui enim vult ad ejus [Rachel's] amplexus pertingere, necesse est eum pro ea annis septem, et septem servire, ut discat requiescere, non solum ab operibus malis, sed etiam a cogitationibus supervacuis. Multi siquidem et si sciant vacare corpore, minime tamen praevalent vacare corde, nescientes facere Sabbatum ex Sabbato, et idcirco non valentes implere quod legitur in Psalmo: Vacate et videte, quoniam ego sum Deus (*Psal.* xlv)." Richard of St. Victor, *De gratia contemplationis (Benjamin major),* in *Opera omnia, Patrologiae cursus completus ... series latina,* vol. 196, ed. J. P. Migne (Paris: Migne, 1855), 1.2 (p. 66). Translation from Richard of St. Victor, *The Mystical Ark (Benjamin Major),* in *The Twelve Patriarchs, the Mystical Ark, Book Three of the Trinity,* trans. Grover A. Zinn (New York: Paulist Press, 1979), 1.2 (p. 154).

33. The point is made by Giuseppe Mazzotta in his sensitive treatment of the *De vita solitaria* and *De otio religioso* in *The Worlds of Petrarch* (Durham, N.C.: Duke University Press, 1993), 147–66.

34. "Quod nobis miseris, quibus adhuc inter seculi fluctus anceps navigatio agitur, laboriosum longeque difficile dixerim; nam et estu rapimur rerum temporalium, nec plus otii contingit quam quod nobis peccatorum et occupationum

nostrarum intermissione permittitur. Vobis vero iam portus tuta tenentibus circumspectio provisioque facilior multo est. Abscidistis quidem mundi nodos, negotiorum laqueos, vincula rerum; nudi et liberi multis e tempestatibus enatastis, ubi quiescere liceat et vacare" (Petrarch, *De otio religioso,* 667–68).

35. Petrarch, *De otio religioso,* 670.

36. See esp. *Secretum,* 232–37.

37. Giuseppe Mazzotta has underlined this illusory, elusive, and fragmented nature of the Petrarchan self: "Petrarch seems to call into question in the *Canzoniere* [. . .] precisely the myth of the center and of the centrality of the self" ("The *Canzoniere* and the Language of the Self," in *The Worlds of Petrarch,* 58–79 (quotation, 59).

38. Roy Porter, "Introduction," in *Rewriting the Self,* 1–13; Jacob Burkhardt, *The Civilization of the Renaissance in Italy* (Oxford, Phaidon, 1981 [1859]); Max Weber, *The Protestant Ethic and the "Spirit" of Capitalism and Other Writings,* ed. and trans. Peter Baehr and Gordon C. Wells (New York: Penguin Books, 2002); Terry Eagleton, "Self-Undoing Subjects," in Porter, *Rewriting the Self,* 262–69; Greenblatt, *Renaissance Self-Fashioning.* In *Mirages of the Selfe,* Reiss sees Petrarch as still far from any experience of the "modern self" (see, e.g., 303).

39. In the *De vita solitaria,* Petrarch says of St. Augustine's conversion, "vitam tandem mutare decrevisset" (he decided at last to change his life), "tandem semel de se statuit unde in perpetuum exultaret" (he finally once and for all made a decision about himself that would allow him to rejoice ever after) (*De vita solitaria* 2.4 [pp. 414–17]). This is of course not at all how Augustine's own account of his conversion reads in *Confessions* 8.12–9.4, where Augustine is flooded by an inner light of strength and understanding, and discovers a divine font of joy and peace within himself that makes external goods seem empty shadows. The Petrarchan narrator, on the other hand, keeps wrestling with his passions and his will: "I am unable to lift up the lower parts of my soul, which are still bound to the earth by their passions and fleshly appetites. How often and how mightily I have tried again and again to tear them away!" (*De ignorantia* 5 [p. 331]).

40. See Michel de Certau, "'Mystique' au XVIIe siècle: Le problème du langage 'mystique,'" in *L'homme devant Dieu: Mélanges offerts au Père Henri du Lubac* (Paris: Aubier, 1964), 2:267–91, and Bernard McGinn, *The Foundations of Mysticism* (New York: Crossroad, 1991), 266, 310–13.

41. "Tutius est uoluntati bone ac pie quam capaci et claro intellectui operam dare. . . . Satius est autem bonum velle quam uerum nosse. . . . Multo maxime [errant] qui in cognoscendo, non amando Deo tempus ponunt" (*De ignorantia* 3.111 [pp. 318–19]).

42. *Paradiso* 28.106–11. See also *Paradiso* 14.40–42, 46–51; 10.124–26; 29.139–41. To the degree that souls identify themselves with pure intellect or being, to that extent they can enter into each other, knowing each other as themselves; see, e.g., *Paradiso* 9.73–81.

43. Petrarch, *Secretum,* 113.

44. See, e.g., *De otio religioso,* 717–21.

45. See, e.g., *De vera religione* 23–25 (pp. 44–46), 32–36 (pp. 60–67).

46. "Veluti siquis ab innumeris hostibus circumclusus, cui nullus pateat egressus, nulla sit misericordie spes nullumque solatium, sed infesta omnia, erecte machine, defossi sub terram cuniculi . . ." (*Secretum,* 178); translation from Quillen, 91.

47. For elegant treatments of this theme in Petrarch, see Theodore J. Cachey, Jr., "'Peregrinus (quasi) ubique': Petrarca e la storia del viaggio," *Intersezioni: Rivista di storia delle idee* 17 (December 1997): 369–84, and section 2 of his "From Shipwreck to Port: *Rvf* 189 and the Making of the *Canzoniere,*" in *MLN* 120, no. 1 (January 2005): 30–49. Cachey shows that *Rvf* 189, one of the culminations of the shipwreck theme in all of Petrarch's work, is a nodal point in the evolution and structure of the *Canzoniere.* A related image, also treated by Cachey (see also *Petrarch's Guide to the Holy Land,* ed. and trans. Theodore J. Cachey, Jr. [Notre Dame, Ind.: University of Notre Dame Press, 2002], 29), is that of Italy as the ideal port, the stable center of a life of incessant wandering and travel. Petrarch's return to Italy in 1353 is part of the program of ideal conversion from multiplicity to unity that he is enacting by gathering the scattered rhymes of the *Canzoniere.* But in Petrarch's time "Italy" exists only as a literary construction, an ideal, a postulated unity: the reality of Italy, as Petrarch himself records, is total disunity and incessant war among rival city-states. The tension between the reality of Italy and the ideal of Italy mirrors the tension between Petrarch's dispersed and conflicted self and his will to make it one.

48. "Nam quid, oro, fluenti aque similius quam res hominum sine fine volubiles? . . . sic presentes dicto citius cum suis amatoribus collabentur . . ." (*De otio religioso,* 700); translation from Francesco Petrarch, *On Religious Leisure (De otio religioso),* ed. and trans. S. S. Schearer (New York: Italica Press, 2002), 2.1 (pp. 84–85); see also, e.g., *Secretum,* 196–99, where Augustinus tells Franciscus that if he can placate the tumult within himself, he can stand on the dry shore and listen with compassion to the desperate shouts of the shipwrecked crowd.

49. "Ut noris unde et quo animo tibi hec scribo, inter Padi uertices parua in naui sedeo. Ne mireris si uel manus scribentis uel oratio fluctuat . . ." (*De ignorantia* 6.138 [pp. 340–42]).

50. "Obstantem Padum remis, uelis ac funibus supero, Ticinum repetens, studiosam et antiquam urbem, ubi . . . uestimentum fame uetus inueniam . . ." (*De ignorantia* 6.139 [pp. 342–43]).

51. Cachey, *Petrarch's Guide,* 22–24; see also "From Shipwreck to Port," 37–38.

52. One could argue, as Teodolinda Barolini has, that Dante's Ulysses is Dante's own lightning rod for such a doubt: see Barolini, *The Undivine Comedy: Detheologizing Dante* (Princeton: Princeton University Press, 1992), esp. 48–58, 105–15.

53. "Hactenus tu remis ac pedibus maria et terras, ego hanc papirum calamo properante sulcaverim" (Cachey, *Petrarch's Guide,* 21.0).

54. "Petrarch's conflation of travel and pilgrimage legitimizes his own literary project, which might be described paradoxically as a *Ulyssean pilgrimage* — a pilgrimage to the Center of the World whose final destination is not the fixed Center of the Holy Land but the open-ended Center of the incessantly, heroically wandering Petrarchan self" (Cachey, in *Petrarch's Guide*, 24).

55. On Petrarch and monasticism, see Mazzotta, *The Worlds of Petrarch*, 147–66; Anna Maria Voci, *Petrarca e la vita religiosa: Il mito umanista della vita eremitica* (Rome: Istituto Storico Italiano per l'Età Moderna e Contemporanea, 1983); Giles Constable, "Petrarch and Monasticism," in *Francesco Petrarca, Citizen of the World*, ed. Aldo S. Bernardo (Albany: State University of New York Press, 1980), 53–99.

56. In a summation toward the end of the *De vita solitaria*, Petrarch makes all these goals equivalent, while apparently ranking them: "Sive itaque Deo servire volumus, que una libertas est atque una felicitas; sive artibus bonis ingenium excolere, qui proximus egregius labor est; sive aliquid meditando et scribendo nostri memoriam posteris relinquere, atque ita dierum fugam sistere et hoc brevissimum vite tempus extendere; sive simul hec omnia prestare propositum est nobis, fugiamus, oro, iantandem et id quantulumcunque quod superest in solitudine transigamus, omni studio caventes, ne, dum opem ferre naufragiis videmur, ipsi rerum humanarum fluctibus obruamur, scopulis allidamur." Trans. Bufano: "Therefore, whether we wish to serve God (this is the only free and happy condition); whether we wish to cultivate our genius with noble arts (this is the next-best occupation); whether, by meditating and writing something, we wish to leave our memory to posterity, and thus stop the flight of time and extend the very brief span of our life; whether we propose to do all these things together, let us flee, I beg you, and let us pass in solitude the time that remains to us, however much it is, guarding with all care so that we are not overwhelmed by the billows of human affairs, or cast upon the rocks, while we appear to be bringing help to the shipwrecked" (544–45).

57. See, e.g., *De vita solitaria*, 530–41.

58. *De vita solitaria*, 450–51.

59. "Cum quo utinam vixemus! Quod idcirco precipue de hoc uno inter tot solitarios optaverim . . ."; only a small adjustment in timing was necessary "ut iter hoc vite pariter ageremus" (*De vita solitaria*, 456–57).

PART 3

Tradition

CHAPTER 7

Dante *Estravagante,* Petrarca *Disperso,* and the Spectre of the Other Woman

JUSTIN STEINBERG

IT HAS BEEN MORE THAN TWENTY YEARS SINCE MARCO Santagata, in his article "Dante in Petrarca," lamented that the history of Dante and Petrarch studies can for the most part be summed up as Dante versus Petrarch.[1] Although they were near contemporaries, inhabiting contiguous worlds, as brilliantly illustrated by Giuseppe Billanovich in "Tra Dante e Petrarca," it is difficult today to view both Dante and Petrarch as poets of the Trecento. More often, Dante and Petrarch are removed from history and relocated on a metahistorical plain where, in its crudest version, Dante represents all that was and Petrarch all that would be—medieval versus modern, theological versus humanist, collective versus individual, and so on. In large part, this allegorization of the relationship between Petrarch and Dante is the outgrowth of an already de-historicized treatment of Petrarch's texts. In this treatment, Petrarch is portrayed as a poet "senza storia" (without history)—in Umberto Bosco's famous formulation—whose continuous crises and contradictions make it impossible to trace any development in his work.[2]

Even in his important revision of Bosco's "senza storia" thesis, Santagata limits his analysis to chronicling the influence of Dante on Petrarch during the various phases in the making of the *Canzoniere*. For Santagata, historicizing Dante in Petrarch means above all examining the changing attitudes of the latter toward the former as part of a literary biography and study of influence.[3] What is missing from this account, as well as from the other studies mentioned above (and even from more conceptually-driven studies on the relation between the two poets, such as those by Robert Durling, John Freccero, and Nancy Vickers),[4] is an analysis of how the historical conditions in which Dante's texts circulated might have affected Petrarch's reception of the famous poet. Petrarch would have in fact encountered many different versions of Dante's works: in written form or through oral tradition, in authorized self-collections or as scattered rhymes, in completed texts or as fragments. Given contemporary practices of literary production and dissemination, a proper understanding of the relation of Dante to Petrarch would thus entail first asking the question, "which Dante?" and even, as we shall soon see, "which Petrarch?" In this essay, I argue that in his innovative methods of collecting and preserving his poetry, Petrarch was influenced by the chaotic transmission of Dante's texts and his experience with the various Dantes. As a consequence, the poets differ in how they anthologized their own poetry, and these differences are most evident in their treatment of the "other woman," in how they reframe poetic interludes with ladies other than Beatrice and Laura.

PETRARCH AND THE CIRCULATION OF DANTE'S COLLECTED AND UNCOLLECTED POETRY

Since Santagata and Paolo Trovato first published their groundbreaking findings on Dante *comico* in Petrarch,[5] the importance of Dante's *Commedia* for Petrarch's *rime* has become generally accepted. In spite of this, some aspects of studies on Dante and Petrarch have remained stagnant. Perhaps these studies would be in an altogether different place had scholars looked more closely at Petrarch's *rime disperse*, those poems that, for one reason or another, the poet decided to exclude from his final version of the *Canzoniere*, now Vaticano latino 3195.[6] What is immediately evident even after a cursory reading of the *disperse* is that Dante is ubiquitous in Petrarch's unanthologized poetry. Almost every single poem in the slight corpus cites, tropes, alludes to, or re-invents a situation or passage from Dante's oeuvre. In fact, the question of Petrarch's knowledge of the *Commedia* is easily answered when we glance at the *disperse,* which reveal a Dante-centric Petrarch at every stage of his poetic career.

Petrarch seems, moreover, remarkably unanxious about the influence of Dante in the poems he leaves out of the *Canzoniere,* which complicates the repression thesis for the relationship between the two poets.[7] Scholars often cite artistic rivalry or even Oedipal struggle as the underlying reasons why there are not more explicit references to Dante in the *Canzoniere.* But one critical aspect of Petrarch's uncollected poems casts doubt on these explanations. Many of the *disperse* were exchanged with other poets and form part of poetic exchanges or *tenzoni.* If the critics are right about Petrarch's dark secret, then how does one explain his willingness to expose his debt to Dante to those readers from whom, presumably, he would have especially desired to hide his influences?[8]

Petrarch himself denies that he was jealous of Dante in two important letters to Boccaccio, *Familiares* 21.15 and *Seniles* 5.2. Of course, it would be naive to take Petrarch at his word. No doubt Dante loomed uncomfortably large on the literary scene for the egomaniacal Petrarch. And no doubt the elimination of certain obvious traces of Dante's poetry from the *Canzoniere,* when compared to similar poems among the *disperse,* was the result of careful elaboration and revision, consistent with Petrarch's frequent critiques in his letters of slavish imitation.[9] Still, the current consensus that Petrarch deliberately suppressed his reliance on Dante, both in his poetry and his prose, probably overstates the case. As a result of this critical stance, while scholars have been suspicious (for good reason) of Petrarch's declarations of neutrality toward Dante in his letters to Boccaccio, they have perhaps underestimated the seriousness and significance of what Petrarch does explicitly critique in his great Florentine rival. Judging from these letters, the issue is not so much Dante the individual, or even Dante the poet, but what the overwhelming success of his works had wrought for the contemporary literary field.

In fact, in both of the famous letters, Dante is specifically associated with the problematic circulation of vernacular texts. Speaking, in *Familiares* 21.15, of the contemporary reception of Dante's poetry, Petrarch attacks not the poet, but his readers, whom he observes "illius egregiam stili frontem inertibus horum linguis conspui fedarique" (with their stupid mouths befouling and spitting upon the noble beauty of his lines) (*Fam.* 21.15.17).[10] He is particularly concerned with the increase in textual corruption caused by the widespread popularity and transmission of Dante's work, which has infiltrated even the taverns and public squares. These admirers "et qua nulla poete presertim gravior iniuria, *scripta eius pronuntiando lacerant atque corrumpunt*" (*so mispronounce and lacerate his verses* that they could do no greater injury to a poet) (*Fam.* 21.15.16).[11] Considering the inherent unreliability of this new urban readership, Petrarch worries about the circulation of his own poetry: "Timui enim in meis quod in aliorum scriptis, precipueque huius de quo loquimur" (I feared for my own writing the same fate which I had seen overtake those of others, especially those of the poet of whom we are speaking) (*Fam.* 21.15.17).[12]

In *Seniles* 5.2 the veiled yet unmistakable reference to Dante, "ille nostri eloquii dux vulgaris" (that master of our vernacular literature) (*Sen.* 5.2.30), is similarly framed by discussions of the "market conditions" of vernacular poetry—characterized, on the one hand, by the courtly jongleurs, who traffic in the poetic word, and, on the other, by an increasingly vast and hence untrained general public.[13] Once again, reflection on the mass circulation of Dante's poetry leads Petrarch to a concern for the fate of his own work. In particular, in a passage that echoes the earlier letter to Boccaccio in both content and language, Petrarch explains that—after observing the popular reception of contemporary Italian literature—he has decided to abandon a major project in the vernacular lest he and it suffer the incomprehension of the public:

> Dum ad nostram respiciens etatem, et superbie matrem et ignavie, cepi acriter advertere quanta esset illa iactantium ingenii vis, quanta pronuntiationis amenitas, ut non recitari scripta diceres sed discerpi. Hoc semel, hoc iterum, hoc sepe audiens et magis magisque mecum reputans, intellexi tandem molli in limo et instabili arena perdi operam meque et laborem meum *inter vulgi manus laceratum iri.*

> I then began to observe attentively our age, mother of pride and laziness, and to notice the great talent of the show-offs, the charm of their elocution, so that you would say the words were not being recited but torn to pieces. Hearing this once, twice, many more times, and repeating it to myself more and more, I finally came to realize

that it was a waste of effort to build on soft mud and shifting sand, and that I and my work would be *torn to shreds by the hands of the mob.* (*Sen.* 5.2.53–54)[14]

Finally, even more forcefully than in the letter from the *Familiares*, where Petrarch simply regretted that his vernacular poems had already circulated, the poet here remarks anxiously, several times, that his poems are no longer under his control; they have slipped from his hands and now belong more to the crowd than to him: "non mea amplius sed vulgi potius facta essent" (*Sen.* 5.2.55).

Petrarch's association of the chaotic dissemination of Dante's poetry with his own irretrievable "published" *rime* is highly suggestive for our discussion of the *disperse* and will be examined further below. But first it is worth considering, however briefly, just how Petrarch would have experienced the material circulation of Dante's texts in this period. Simply put, Dante's poetry and especially the *Commedia* revolutionized contemporary reading practices and created a new demand for literature and literary books. Facilitated by a dramatic increase in urban literacy in central and northern Italy, Dante's masterpiece enjoyed a vibrant transmission through a variety of channels—learned and lay, written and oral, public and private.[15]

The demand that drove the production of *Commedia* manuscripts even spawned the creation of a new type of literary book. The elegant "register-book" was written in book-quality cursive handwriting by lay scribes for lay readers. The most famous of these lay scribes was Francesco di ser Nardo da Barberino, whose scriptorium was behind the equally famous series of Dante manuscripts known as the "Danti del Cento."[16] While highly readable and produced in large formats, these Dante manuscripts remained typically unadorned—lacking commentary or glosses—unlike the books created in university and religious environments.[17] In the context of such dramatic changes in contemporary habits of reading and writing, Petrarch must have recognized that Dante's vernacular masterpiece, among many other things, was also a new type of literary commodity. After all, although this fact is easy to overlook among the multiple themes treated in *Familiares* 21.15, the discussion of Dante in the letter originates in the question of why Petrarch, an assiduous collector of rare books, had until then failed to acquire a physical copy of the readily available *Commedia*.

In some sense, the name of Dante functions as an example of synecdoche in the letters for the full range of innovations in the production and consumption of literary texts that Petrarch was forced to negotiate. In a cultural climate where market forces trumped authorial intention and textual integrity (at least according to Petrarch), the artistically possessive poet must have seen the risk for gross misinterpretation of his own work everywhere. Dante of course was already familiar with such risks, and had attempted to mitigate them by collecting his previously disseminated poems into organic narrative accounts. Nevertheless, despite these efforts at self-anthologization, the rapid and doubtless often disorderly reproduction of Dante's texts in the fourteenth century must have made his heterogeneous poetic output seem at odds with a cohesive authorial corpus. According to the initial investigations of Domenico De Robertis, Petrarch likely encountered a manuscript of Dante's *rime* in which the selection and ordering of compositions differed a great deal from the authorial collections of the *Vita Nuova,* the *Convivio,* and the *Commedia.* For example, Petrarch almost certainly encountered the poems from the *Convivio* as *estravaganti,* anthologized alongside Dante's other *canzoni* without narrative context or commentary.[18] Moreover, poems such "Deh, Violetta, che in ombra d'Amore," "I' mi son pargoletta bella e nova," and even the *petrose* to an extent must have always appeared to him as similarly "extravagant," at least in Contini's expanded use of the term to indicate all *rime* excluded from Dante's ideal literary biography.[19]

At several points in his letters, Petrarch similarly discusses the possibility of reframing one's published work in order to regain control over its interpretation. In *Seniles* 5.2, one of the primary reasons Petrarch admonishes Boccaccio for allegedly burning his own Italian poems is that now he will not be able to modify or correct them. That, of course, is exactly what Petrarch does in the *Canzoniere.* He repossesses his published poems (often quite literally requesting their return), reworks them, and reframes them within a penitential narrative that at times dramatically changes their original meanings. In a letter to Pandolfo Malatesta (*Seniles* 13.11) accompanying one of the public redactions of the *Canzoniere,* Petrarch justifies the limited publication of his authorial collection as a response to the appropriation and laceration of his poems by the crowd ("vulgus habet et lacerat").[20] The conspicuous reference to "laceration" recalls the description of Dante's texts being torn to pieces in *Familiares* 21.15 and *Seniles* 5.2. Since this passage was added to the original letter when it was revised for inclusion in the

Seniles collection, the similar language seems intentional. For our purposes, it is crucial that Petrarch's apology for the *Canzoniere* that gradually emerges in *Seniles* 5.2 and 13.11 is based on a dialectic between poems circulated individually in the past and the necessity of collecting and reworking them in the present. I would suggest, moreover, that this apology is articulated in the shadow of Dante because by observing the success and failure of the latter's process of revision, collection, and exclusion, Petrarch learned what to follow and what to avoid in order to preserve his own works for posterity. In the relationship between Dante *estravagante* and Dante *organico* thus lies one of the keys to understanding the relationship of the *disperse* to the *Canzoniere.*

The Other Woman in Dante and the Poetics of Conversion

In many ways, this dialectic between anthologized and unanthologized poems can be observed most clearly in how Dante and Petrarch treat the question of the other woman or women in their poetry. In various poems, Dante and, to a lesser extent, Petrarch were influenced by the troubadour poetic traditions of the *pastorela* and *chanson de change,* in which, in contrast to the poet's lady—lofty and unattainable—the new love interest is often concrete and approachable.[21] Thus in addition to his beloved Beatrice, Dante also addresses poems to "Violetta," an unnamed "pargoletta" (young girl), and "Lisetta," whereas Petrarch falls in love with a woman from Ferrara, just as Guido Cavalcanti had with a lady from Toulouse. Once these poems were published and circulated among contemporaries, they posed an awkward problem for Dante and Petrarch as they constructed their autobiographical personae in the *Commedia* and the *Canzoniere.* Specifically, the high degree of conventionality characteristic of poems about other women, together with the relativism of devotion these poems imply, threatened to undermine the authenticity of their idealized literary autobiographies and the absoluteness of their transcendent love stories.

Dante most directly negotiates the problem of the other woman in his work through the figure of the *donna gentile,* who will serve as an important model for Petrarch as well. As first recounted in the *Vita Nuova,* some time after the first anniversary of Beatrice's death, Dante notices a beautiful young noblewoman watching him from a window, seeming to take pity on him as a result of his downcast condition. Dante's mourning for Beatrice soon comes into conflict with his attraction for this new *donna gentile*, on to whom his subjective desire projects semblances of love, "Color d'amore e di pietà sembianti" (the color of love and semblances of compassion).[22] As with Cavalcanti's "donna di Tolosa," Dante's fascination with the new lady depends on and is justified by her resemblance to Beatrice; she reminds him of Beatrice because both ladies share an amorous pallor (*VN* 36.1). The conflict is decided in favor of Dante's beloved only through the prodding of a visual memorial aid, a waking vision ("una forte imaginazione" [*VN* 39.1]) of Beatrice in her prime.

The *Vita Nuova* is only Dante's first attempt at using narrative to reinterpret lyric poems addressed to other women as a means for integrating them into a coherent literary autobiography. In the *Convivio* we learn that the *donna gentile* was not a lady at all, but an allegorical personification of Lady Philosophy. More important for Petrarch, who most likely was unfamiliar with the prose commentary of the *Convivio*, is the monumental literary self-fashioning Dante accomplishes in the last cantos of the *Purgatorio*. At the end of his "journey to Beatrice," Dante's character is chided by his long departed beloved for having gone astray after her death and interment:

Sì tosto come in su la soglia fui
Di mia seconda etade e mutai vita,
Questi si tolse a me, e diessi altrui.
          (*Purg.* 30, ll. 124–26)[23]

———

As soon as I was on the brink of my second age and
I changed life, this one took himself from me and gave
himself to another/others.

Beatrice specifically accuses him of forsaking the guidance of her visage for false images of the good ("imagini di ben seguendo false" [*Purg.* 30, l. 131]) and of having betrayed her with an unidentified "pargoletta" (young girl) (*Purg.* 31, l. 59).

Scholars have long sought after the identify of this "pargoletta" (suggesting "Violetta," "Lisetta," the *donna pietra*, the *donna gentile*, etc.). However, the dense series of allusions in these cantos to a variety of early poems suggests that Dante intended to leave the identity of the other woman and the exact nature of his betrayal vague. He intended, in other words, to cast a wide net with these allusions, trying to evoke as many poems as possible. In this way, he could incorporate, through a narrative of conversion, the largest number possible of his scattered poetic experiments into a single unifying matrix, a virtual anthology. Paradoxically, these occasional and conventional poems are recovered as the motivation behind a heartfelt confession, thus playing a crucial role in Dante's autobiography and rendering it extraordinarily convincing. Although we need not doubt the sincerity of the existential crisis at the top of Mount Purgatory, it is equally important to recognize that along with saving himself, Dante saves those early poems that might seem to run counter to the salvific narrative of the *Commedia* and the truth claims of his poetic enterprise. The palinode, in essence, allows Dante to suggest that those elements of his work that might seem occasional, conventional, and even inauthentic are in actuality all pieces of an intelligible literary corpus and a cohesive, if fraught, autobiography.[24] (In fact, at least as far back as Boccaccio, who created the first "collected works" of Dante,[25] readers have tried to integrate the unanthologized poems into the moral and artistic framework set out in the autobiographical narratives.)

THE OTHER WOMAN IN PETRARCH'S UNCOLLECTED LYRICS AND THE POETICS OF EXCLUSION

One of the most striking aspects of Petrarch's poetic exchanges with his contemporaries is the frequency with which he refers to the motif of the other woman, at times closely recalling Dante's treatment of the *donna gentile.* In "Se Phebo al primo amor non è bugiardo,"[26] a response to a poem by Pietro Dietisalvi of Siena, Petrarch alludes to a new pleasure, *novo piacer* (l. 2), that resembles his old love. In "Per util, per diletto o per onore," he jokes in a response to Antonio Beccari of Ferrara that, thanks to love's gifts, he has fallen in love not once, but more than twenty-two times.[27] In "Antonio, cosa à fatto la tua terra," written after Laura's death in about 1350, Petrarch marvels to Beccari that a woman from his city, Ferrara, has made him love again, something he never thought possible. Finally, in "Quella che 'l giovenil meo core avinse," a response to a lost poem by Jacopo da Imola, Petrarch comes the closest to reproducing Dante's encounter with the *donna gentile,* in both content and language. In this sonnet, Love once again tempts the poet with a *nova belleza* (new beauty) (l. 5) after the first bond of love has been loosened by Laura's departure from her terrestrial body. Yet he ultimately resists.

Although none of these *disperse* were incorporated into any of the phases of the *Canzoniere,* it would seem clear that outside the confines of his author's book, the autograph manuscript Vaticano latino 3195, Petrarch felt safe to experiment with the destabilizing idea of multiple loves. In his treatment of the other woman, Petrarch specifically focuses on the power of semblances, a key problem already brought out by Cavalcanti's "donna di Tolosa" and Dante's *donna gentile.* In "Quella che 'l giovenil meo core avinse," the memorial image of the first love actually facilitates the new love, instead of coming into conflict with it as in the *Vita Nuova.* Although Petrarch declares in the sonnet that after Laura's death he withstood all temptations, as Ulysses withstood the call of the Sirens, he nonetheless acknowledges that if he did feel any of the old fire, it was because the new objects of his interest recalled the image of a sweetly unyielding Laura:

> Né poi nova belleza l'alma strinse
> né mai luce sentì che fésse ardore,
> se non co la memoria del valore
> che per dolci durezze la sospinse.
> (ll. 5–8)[28]

———

> Since then no new beauty has grasped my soul, nor has it felt
> any light that could make it burn, unless with the recollection
> of that worth which rebuffed it with sweet hardness.

Even more explicitly Dantean (and Cavalcantian) in its evocation of the other woman is "Se Phebo al primo amor non è bugiardo." At the beginning of the sonnet, Petrarch explains that if Apollo is not disloyal to his first love, namely Daphne-Laurel-Laura, then he always has her image in his mind, regardless of any new temptation, *novo piacer* (l. 2), that might come along. Yet the last tercet allows for a potential exception (marked by the adversative "ma" [l. 12]): when this new love object happens to resemble in appearance, "sembianza è forse alcuna de le viste" (l. 13), the first love.

While there are several references to infidelity in Petrarch's poems, they should not be overstated. "Quella che 'l giovenil meo core avinse" only hints at the possibility ("se non co . . .") of other love objects. A negative hypothetical statement similarly introduces the potential of wayward desire in "Se Phebo al primo amor non è bugiardo" (If Phoebus is not a liar toward his first love), distancing the statement from present fact. Still, for readers familiar with Petrarch's monumentalizing of his love for Laura, even the hint that Apollo might be dishonest, "bugiardo," is remarkable, and the term *bugiardo*, of comic origin, is never used in the *Canzoniere*. In the last line of this poem, "so ben che 'l mio dir parrà sospetto" (I know that what I say will seem suspect), Petrarch appears to acknowledge the slippery slope between erotic and literary deceit, how other loves might undermine the authenticity of his love story with Laura, rendering his autobiography "suspect." Indeed, in the *disperse* he seems willing to explore or at least suggest, in a conversation with other poets, the notion that Laura was in fact simply an elaborate myth, a brilliant simulacrum, a "fantasma" as Billanovich put it.[29]

Given the importance of the figure of the other woman in the *disperse*, it is all the more striking that Petrarch excludes references to a similar affair from the *Canzoniere*—an exclusion that is especially conspicuous in the final forms of the collection. Furthermore, he locates his rejection of a potential *donna gentile* at a crucial moment in his autobiographical narrative, shortly after Laura's death, using it to mark his distance from Dante.[30] In the canzone "Amor, se vuo' ch'i' torni al giogo antico" (*Rvf* 270),[31] Petrarch informs Love that the attempts to reclaim him are in vain since Laura is now dead and buried: "Indarno or sovra me tua forza adopre, / mentre 'l mio primo amor terra ricopre" (In vain now you exert your force on me, when the earth covers my first love) (ll. 44–45). The canzone thus firmly contradicts the evidence of a betrayal of Laura recounted in the *dispersa* "Antonio, cosa à fatto la tua terra," where Antonio's *terra*—here used in the sense of "area of provenance"—facilitates the illicit love. Petrarch claims, moreover, that for him to love again, Love would need to disinter and reanimate Laura's dead body—a ghoulish parallel to Dante's reunification with Beatrice in the *Commedia*. The next poem in the *Canzoniere*, the sonnet "L'ardente nodo ov'io fui d'ora in hora" (*Rvf* 271), is even more explicitly in dialogue with Dante and the episode of the *donna gentile*. In this sonnet, Love once again attempts to ensnare Petrarch with the lure of another woman: "un altro lacciuol fra l'erba teso" (another snare set among

the grass) (l. 6). However, the poet's recent exposure to the finality and inevitability of Death—with *Morte* emphasized as the first word of verses 2
and 12—has freed him from this and other future erotic temptations. In
essence, in *Rvf* 270 and 271, Petrarch claims to have learned from Laura's
death what Dante confesses in *Purg.* 30–31 to have failed to grasp from
Beatrice's—namely, that all mortal love objects can offer only false promises of happiness.[32] Even the beautiful members of the beloved end up, as
Beatrice tells Dante, scattered in the ground.

Within the economy of the *Canzoniere*, *Rvf* 270 and *Rvf* 271 directly
follow the laments for Laura's death (*Rvf* 267–69), reproducing the rapidity with which Dante strayed toward the *donna gentile* after Beatrice's
death. Scholars have recently demonstrated the extent to which Petrarch
modeled the opening poems of the second section of the *Canzoniere*—
especially the lament for Laura "Che debb'io far? Che mi consigli, Amore?"
(*Rvf* 268)—on the laments for the departed Beatrice in the *Vita Nuova*.[33]
Yet the obvious similarities between Petrarch and Dante in their respective poetics of mourning only serve to highlight how decisively the poets'
stories diverge in what happens after the death of their beloveds—namely,
Petrarch resists the temptation of a new love while Dante, at least for a
time, yields to it. This ideological and narratological divide reverberates,
in fact, throughout the second half of the *Canzoniere*, where Petrarch insists
on the singularity of his love for Laura in death as in life: "dal mondo a te
sola mi volsi" (from the world to you alone I turned) (*Rvf* 347, l. 13). Instead
of struggling, like Dante, with the false images of good found in other
women ("imagini di ben seguendo false" [*Purg.* 30, l. 131]), he must contend with the non-false images ("imagini non false" [*Rvf* 335, l. 3]) of Laura
herself. And while Dante, at the end of the *Purgatorio*, displaces the darker
aspects of eros onto his other loves, Petrarch, at the end of his own journey,
rejects his own beloved as a petrifying Medusa.

Of course, the differences between how Petrarch and Dante treat the
problem of profane love have long been recognized, most notably Petrarch's
rejection of a stilnovist reconciliation between *eros* and *caritas*.[34] Yet with respect to the question of other women, Petrarch's bypassing of the *donna gentile* episode also has implications for how the two poets differ in their approach to anthologizing their own poetry. In Dante's conversion narrative,
the moral detour toward other women at once helps explain and incorporate into a single authorial corpus numerous poems that might otherwise be
seen as simply occasional, conventional, and unrelated to the autobiographi-

cal narratives found in the *Vita Nuova,* the *Convivio,* and the *Commedia.*
Petrarch was similarly concerned, if not more so, with collecting the fragments of his poetic experience. The penitential narrative constructed by ordering his poems according to biographical criteria — instead of simply according to meter or theme — demonstrates how carefully he studied Dante's
model. At the same time, he likely observed, in the haphazard dissemination of Dante's works, the inherent limitations of a purely narrative reconstruction. The unprecedented popularity of reading and copying Dante in
the Trecento no doubt led at times to a partial disintegration of the author's
carefully constructed anthology of the self.

Petrarch dealt with his anxiety about the uncontrolled circulation of
Dante's (and hence his own) vernacular compositions — an anxiety revealed
repeatedly in his letters — in two primary ways. On the one hand, beyond
the integrating role of narrative, he added the stability of the autograph
manuscript, Vaticano latino 3195, as a means of dictating what can and cannot be considered "Petrarch." At the same time, perhaps due to his greater
control over the material conditions of his literary production, Petrarch
decided to exclude from his official autobiography an entire episode from
his literary life, as if it had never happened. Unlike Dante, he did not seek
to reconcile the poems written about other women, especially when these
compositions, often exchanged with contemporaries, were in conflict with
the reconstructed narrative of the *Canzoniere.*[35] For certain already published poems, he was willing to cede authorial rights to the crowd ("non
mea amplius sed vulgi potius facta essent"), effectively allowing them to
be forgotten with time. Or, to put it another way — borrowing Petrarch's
own terminology from a marginal note in his working papers, the so-called
codice degli abbozzi — in order to "save" many of the poems about Laura
from oblivion, some compositions, such as those about other women, were
"damned."[36]

Although the differences in Petrarch's attitude toward the *donna gentile* in the *disperse* and in the *Canzoniere* are evident, the borders between
his anthologized and unanthologized poems are not entirely seamless. In
particular, the *dispersa* "Quella che 'l giovenil meo core avinse" stands at
a curious midpoint in the development of Petrarch's thinking about the
motif of the other woman. On the one hand, the association of the new
love object with the memorial image of Laura places the sonnet firmly in
the tradition established by Cavalcanti's "donna di Tolosa" and Dante's
donna gentile. In the last tercet, moreover, recalling Beatrice's outburst at

the top of Purgatory, the poet compares the lure of the new women to the call of the Sirens:

Et pur fui in dubbio fra Caribdi et Scilla
et passai le Sirene in sordo legno,
over come huom ch'ascolta et nulla intende.
(ll. 12–14)

———

And yet I wavered between Charybdis and Scylla, and I passed the Sirens in a deaf ship, or like a man who listens without comprehending.

The references to the perils of Ulysses—the sirens and the obstacles of Scylla and Charybdis—also recall the sonnet "Passa la nave mia" (*Rvf* 189), which concluded the first part of the Chigiano redaction of the *Canzoniere*.[37] However, at the end of the penitential narrative of the Chigiano form, the threat of Ulyssean shipwreck represents the dangerous tension between love for Laura and love for God. In the *dispersa* it instead still indicates a potential crisis between the love for Laura and love for other women, more in the spirit of Dante's autobiography.

On the other hand, the primary message of the poem is that Petrarch, unlike Dante, has not succumbed to the lure of the other woman, despite fierce temptation. He has already sailed successfully through the dangerous waters of erotic multiplicity. More specifically, Petrarch claims that, as an old bird, he no longer fears love's net: "nova rete vecchio augel non prende" (a new net does not catch an old bird) (l. 11). This is exactly the lesson from Proverbs 1.17 that Dante failed to learn, according to Beatrice, despite the experience of her death:

Novo augeletto due o tre aspetta
ma dinanzi da li occhi d'i pennuti
rete si spiega indarno o si saetta.
(*Purg.* 31, ll. 61–63)

———

A young bird waits for two or three, but before the eyes of fully-fledged birds, a net is spread or an arrow is shot in vain.

Petrarch's old bird appears to be in direct opposition to Dante's fully-fledged one. In this light, "Quella che 'l giovenil meo core avinse," although perhaps still too ambiguously tied to the figure of the other woman for inclusion in the *Canzoniere*, can nonetheless be seen as an early attempt by Petrarch at distancing his own penitential narrative from Dante's conversion poetics, foreshadowing the narrative turn of *Rvf* 270 and 271.

Further evidence of the transitional nature of "Quella che 'l giovenil meo core avinse" is provided by its redactional history. From a marginal note accompanying the poem in the *codice degli abbozzi,* we learn that, before it was returned to him through a friend, the poet had for a time lost possession of the sonnet and had struggled to recompose it from memory.[38] The attempt to regain control of an already circulated poem, sent out *in mundum* to both Jacopo da Imola (the addressee) and Francesco da Carrara (the friend mentioned in the note) — if not to others — represents part of a larger struggle in Petrarch between the public and private nature of his literary output.[39] In fact, one of the variants of "Quella che 'l giovenil meo core avinse," stemming, most likely, from an earlier version of the poem, gives us a glimpse of the potential significance behind this anxious process of repossession and revision. In the 1544 Aldine *Canzoniere*, the last line of the sonnet reads "com'uom che par ch'ascolti et nulla intende" rather than "over come huom ch'ascolta et nulla intende" as is found in Vaticano 3196.[40] The difference between a man who listens but does not fully comprehend and a man who only appears to be listening is admittedly subtle — yet it is revealing in this context. For, it is the difference between an author glossing his own outward behavior — in this case Petrarch only seemed to be in love with another woman, as Dante claims he only seemed enamored of the screen ladies in the *Vita Nuova* — and an author struggling internally with irrational desire. The contrast in the final version of the sonnet is thus no longer between public perception and individual experience but between a subject and his desires — a psychologizing inward turn that typifies the shift from *rima dispersa* to *rima sparsa*.

The Spectres of the Other Woman and the Literary Marketplace in the *Canzoniere*

If "Quella che 'l giovenil meo core avinse" anticipates the rejection of the figure of the *donna gentile* in *Rvf* 270 and 271, the treatment of the other woman in "Movesi il vecchierel canuto et biancho" (*Rvf* 16) is oddly reminiscent of the *disperse*. Built around an extended simile, the first eleven lines of the sonnet describe an aged pilgrim as he makes his way toward Rome in order to see the holy relic of the Veronica, the cloth that purportedly represents the true image, the *vera icon,* of Christ. Only in the last tercet does Petrarch introduce the second term of comparison, how in the same fashion he seeks in other women, "altrui" (l. 13), the true form, "forma vera" (l. 14), of his lady. As in the *Vita Nuova,* "Movesi il vecchierel" combines the problem of other women with the question of true and false semblances.[41] More specifically, the pilgrim's journey to view the Veronica at the end of his life recalls the pilgrims Dante encounters at the conclusion of his *libello,* recorded in the sonnet "Deh peregrini che pensosi andate" (*VN* 40.9), who are similarly en route to visit the Veronica—that likeness, "exemplo," whose source, "figura," Beatrice now beholds in heaven.[42] "Movesi il vecchierel," however, as one of the earliest poems in the *Canzoniere,* replays the cognitive journey of the *Vita Nuova* in reverse. While Dante organizes the iconic semblances of the *Vita Nuova* into a clear hierarchy of ascent, moving from screen ladies to his lady, from the *donna gentile* to Beatrice in her glory, from the drawing of angels to the Veronica, and from all of these to the beatific vision of Christ, Petrarch spirals downward into multiplicity in "Movesi il vecchierel," descending, in a pattern endemic to the *Canzoniere,* from the face of Christ and his true semblance, to the desired form of Laura, to the memory of her image evoked by other women.

Critics have long recognized the potentially blasphemous nature of Petrarch's simile, of comparing explicitly the images of other women to the Veronica, and implicitly Laura to Christ. Indeed, in a letter to Carlo Gualteruzzi in 1569, Ludovico Beccadelli went so far as to rewrite the last tercet, which he found "troppo ardita e quasi impia" (too bold and almost profane).[43] When read together with *Rvf* 3 and 4—which compare, respectively, Petrarch's first vision of Laura to Christ's passion and her birth to His nativity—"Movesi il vecchierel" can be seen as continuing a dangerous trend of appropriating sacred images and language for profane love.[44] Yet what distinguishes this poem from others that provocatively exploit Christological parallels (and what, I propose, has caused so much anxiety for critics, beginning with Beccadelli) is the suggestion of other illicit loves beyond the narrative of the *Canzoniere.* Various studies of medieval art and literature have demonstrated that, while never officially sanctioned, cross-pollination did occur in this period between religious and secular art, especially between Marian imagery and devotional texts and the courtly love tradition.[45] However, the introduction of plural, indefinite others, "altrui," into the *Canzoniere* threatens the delicate symbiotic relationship between model and antimodel, sacred and profane in the anthology—a system built upon a dialogue, however unorthodox, between two abstract and absolute structures of feeling. Even the suggestion of a plurality of possible loves opens the door to history and relativism, to a Cavalcantian tryst with a woman from Ferrara and to the worldview of "Per util, per diletto o per onore," where "guardando altrui" (looking at others) (l. 14) rhymes comically with "ventidue" (twenty-two) (l. 15). Once the illicit, yet singular love for Laura loses its theological foundation, constructed painstakingly through exclusivity and absoluteness of devotion, it is quickly transformed into just one of many possible human experiences, where the "other" woman becomes simply "another."

As is perceptible—if not conspicuous—in "Movesi il vecchierel," the walls of the *Canzoniere* are surrounded by the ambiguous world of the *disperse*, with their accompanying shadow of erotic and poetic inauthenticity. For our purposes, it is particularly intriguing that in *Rvf* 16 Petrarch situates his problematic relationship to the other woman within the visual discourse of images and likenesses. On the one hand, the veil known as the Veronica represents an authentic portrait, unmitigated by human hands (an *acheiropoieton*), of Christ—nothing less than His true face. Although frequently reproduced as a popular icon, the singularity and sacred presence of the Veronica was guaranteed against any subsequent deflation by its status as a holy touch-relic, a *sudarium*.[46] The semblances of Laura belong to the other end of the iconic scale. Constructed out of subjective human desire and projected onto the form of other women, they are indefinite copies of a distant original.

The rapid pace of image production in this period, combined with the competition among patrons regarding the size, materials, and artistry of commissions, provides an important context for understanding the contrast between the localized, singular, and unreproducible aura of the Veronica and the multiple, scattered copies of Laura. This is not the place to examine how the economic transactions involved in late medieval painting and sculpture breathed new life into the centuries-old debate about the proper role of religious art.[47] However, it is worth noting that Petrarch—as an ardent collector of paintings, rare books, vases, Roman coins, and other aesthetic objects—was at the forefront of changing notions toward the consumption of art in society.[48] The owner of both a portrait of Laura by Simone Martini and a Madonna by Giotto was supremely aware—as evident in numerous passages from the *De remediis utriusque fortunae*—of how easily religious and artistic objects (whether paintings, sculptures, or books) could be translated into market value.[49]

Petrarch must have recognized that his poetry and even his own carefully constructed poetic self risked a similar process of commodification. In his letters to Boccaccio, he bemoans the crowds' appropriation of his poetic property and the base economic uses of his words by the jongleurs. A similar anxiety about how poetry is contaminated by the economic sphere is expressed in "Poco era ad appressarsi agli occhi miei" (*Rvf* 51). Transformed into a statue of jasper by his beloved Medusa, the poet in this sonnet laments that the public will now value him only as an expensive object of exchange: "pregiato poi dal vulgo avaro et scioccho" (prized later by the greedy and ignorant crowd) (l. 11). As critics have rightly noted, the theme of petrification within the *Canzoniere* functions almost as an authorial signature.[50] In this light, Petrarch's attack on the incomprehension of the crowd when faced with an iconic statue (a *petra-arca*) can be read as a critique of the economic debasement of his poetic message. Alongside these more articulated misgivings about the reductive effects of the marketplace on Petrarch's poetic art, the motif of the other woman also hints at the potential arbitrariness of the poet's primary love story—now viewed as a mere simulacrum, reproduced at will for an eager public.

One of Petrarch's responses to the threat of reproduction and commodification of the poetic word is to withdraw to the private sphere, physically repossessing his published work and de-authorizing in his letters those compositions that were no longer under his direct control. In this light, Petrarch's invention (together with his "disciple" Boccaccio) of the autograph, authorial manuscript is even more revolutionary than previously thought,[51] especially when viewed in the context of concurrent phenomena in the visual arts. Just as the proliferation of religious images during the same period was matched by a new role for the irreproducible icon-relic, Petrarch counters the uncontrolled reproduction of his works with the authenticity of his carefully prepared author's book, Vaticano latino 3195. The ultimate, crystallized form of the *Canzoniere,* like a touch-relic emanating from the pen of the author, functions as a sort of profane Veronica, guaranteeing the true face of the artist regardless of the various copies in circulation. The epochal success of Petrarch's strategy is amply demonstrated by the scholarly cult surrounding his autograph papers, dating back at least to Bembo and the sixteenth-century humanists,[52] while the *disperse,* now scattered in libraries throughout the world by the global literary market, lack a proper critical edition.

At the same time, until the very end of his life, Petrarch seems unsure of the best way to deal with those already published poems that engage the theme of the other woman. The traces of the other woman even within the *Canzoniere* show how Petrarch considered incorporating his earlier occasional poems into an all-embracing narrative — as Dante did with his poetics of conversion — instead of solely excluding them from his author's book. In this respect, the excision from the *Canzoniere* of the *ballata* "Donna mi vène spesso ne la mente" marks a final stage in Petrarch's thinking about the motif of the other woman, and is thus a crucial symbolic moment in the making of the *Canzoniere.* Occupying the 121st position in all versions up to the Queriniana, Petrarch decided to remove the *ballata* only in 1373, replacing it with the madrigal "Or vedi, Amor, che giovenetta donna." Although throughout his life he continually added poems to Vaticano latino 3195, this is the only one, as far as we know, that he permanently removed.

"Donna mi vène" recounts a battle in the poet's heart between two ladies, his "donna," presumably Laura, and an "altra donna," whose identity is unknown. Often compared to allegorical poems by Dante such as "Tre donne intorno al cor mi son venute" and "Due donne in cima de la mente mia," it has even more in common with a sonnet from the *Vita Nuova,* "Gentil pensero che parla di vui" (*VN* 38.8), in which Dante's heart wavers between Beatrice and the *donna gentile.* In contrast with *Rvf* 270 or 271, in "Donna mi vène" Petrarch voluntarily consents to the love for another woman just as Dante does in "Gentil pensero"; the verb *consentire* is in fact used in both poems. Nowhere else in his corpus does Petrarch come closer to challenging the exclusivity of his love for Laura.

Though Petrarch was willing to explore the idea of an other woman throughout his career, especially in dialogue with fellow vernacular poets, he decided one year before his death to banish this ambiguous counter-narrative from the final redaction of the *Canzoniere.* Yet having removed "Donna mi vène," the poem he replaces it with, "Or vedi Amor," is no less problematic.[53] Inspired by the first stanza of "Amor, tu vedi ben che questa donna" and the last stanza of "Così nel mio parlar voglio esser aspro," two of Dante's *rime petrose,* it expresses a desire for revenge, "vendetta" (l. 9), against a young disdainful Laura. A similar fantasy of revenge toward an unresponsive beloved, expressed in the language of the *petrose,* can also be found in two *disperse* sent to Giovanni Colonna, especially the violent "Tal cavalier tutta una schiera atterra." The substitution of *Rvf* 121 for "Donna mi vène" evidently represented a choice between two moral low points in Dante's corpus, between the erotic frustration with the *petrosa* and the disloyalty and self-deception involved with the *donna gentile* — two problematic motifs that also characterize the unanthologized Petrarch. The decision to emphasize the pessimism and violence implicit in the *petrose* is consistent with the late inclusions, near the end of the 1360s, of "Geri, quando talor meco s'adira" (*Rvf* 179) and "L'aura celeste che 'n quel verde lauro" (*Rvf* 197), two poems which solidify the idea of Laura as a petrifying Medusa. Both of these poems echo in turn an earlier *dispersa,* "Quando talor, da giusta ira commosso," and Petrarch appears to have long reflected upon their inclusion.[54]

It is not possible, here, to explore all the repercussions of Petrarch's final treatment of these two differing aspects of Dante *estravagante* and Petrarch *disperso.* What seems clear, however, is that at the very least the substitution of *Rvf* 121 for "Donna mi vène" complicates the traditional dichotomy between Laura-Medusa and the Virgin that critics often see as indicative of the end of the *Canzoniere.* Although it now seems evident that Petrarch reinforced the identification of Laura with Medusa in these last stages in the making of the *Canzoniere,* as recently confirmed by Theodore Cachey,[55] that this identification should be read as a conflict between the deadly sensuality of Laura and the divine love for the Virgin is less obvious,[56] especially when we consider not only what Petrarch included in the book, but also what he removed. In fact, a simple contrast between *eros* and *caritas* would have been more effective if Petrarch had left in a *donna gentile* episode, since the worldliness and multiplicity traditionally associated with a figure of the other woman would have stood out against the last prayer to the exalted and singular Virgin.

Petrarch's exact intentions in substituting "Or vedi, Amor" for "Donna mi vène" are, of course, ultimately unknowable. One of its effects, however, can be briefly observed. Unlike the figure of a *donna gentile,* the representation of a Laura *petrosa* need not rely on extratextual references. While allusions to other women send critics searching Petrarch's other works—especially the historically-contingent *disperse*—for context, Laura's stony harshness toward the poet is already one of the primary narrative threads of the *Canzoniere.* In the background of "Or vedi Amor," astute readers may very well be able to detect traces of Dante's *petrose,* or even of the *disperse* exchanged with Giovanni Colonna. More importantly, however, these echoes can be absorbed seamlessly into the macrostructure of Petrarch's conflicted love for Laura. By privileging the intratextual over the intertextual in the last stages of the *Canzoniere,* Petrarch ensures the strikingly modern autonomy of his work, especially when compared to the integrating function of self-citations in Dante's corpus. With an eye, increasingly, on the vast yet unpredictable audience posterity might bring him, Petrarch apparently decided, in the end, to relinquish control over those experimental moments in his poetic career deemed incongruous with the penitential narrative of the *Canzoniere.* He must have assumed that with time they would be forgotten or at least irretrievably dispersed.

Notes

1. In Marco Santagata, *Per moderne carte: La biblioteca volgare di Petrarca* (Bologna: Il Mulino, 1990), 79–91, but originally published in *Giornale storico della letteratura italiana* 157 (1980): 445–52.

2. Umberto Bosco, *Francesco Petrarca,* 3rd ed. (Bari: Laterza, 1965), 7: "Il vero è che noi non possiamo in alcun modo ravvisare una linea di sviluppo, uno svolgimento, non solo nel canzoniere, ma in tutto il Petrarca. Egli è senza storia, se lo si considera, come si deve, nel concreto di tutta l'opera sua." (The truth is that we cannot in any way perceive a line of development or evolution, not only in the *Canzoniere,* but in all of Petrarch. He is without history, if we want to consider him, as we must, in the concrete terms of his entire corpus.) Unless otherwise noted, translations are my own.

3. Santagata, "Presenze di Dante 'comico' nel *Canzoniere* del Petrarca," in *Per moderne carte,* 25–78, but originally published in *Giornale storico della letteratura italiana* 146 (1969): 163–211. In this essay the author traces the frequent borrowing from Dante's texts at the beginning of the *Canzoniere,* to an obscuring of obvious debts in the middle section, to a revival of Dantean poetics in the last section—a trajectory from youthful unselfconsciousness to repression to a return of the repressed.

4. See Robert M. Durling, "Petrarch's 'Giovene donna sotto un verde lauro,'" *MLN* 86 (1971): 1–20; John Freccero, "The Fig Tree and the Laurel: Petrarch's Poetics," *Diacritics* 5 (1975): 34–40; and Nancy J. Vickers, "Re-membering Dante: Petrarch's 'Chiare, fresche et dolci acque,'" *MLN* 96 (1981): 1–11. Also highly suggestive is Durling's introduction to his translation of Petrarch's *rime* in *Petrarch's Lyric Poems: The "Rime sparse" and Other Lyrics* (Cambridge, Mass.: Harvard University Press, 1976).

5. Santagata, "Presenze di Dante 'comico' nel *Canzoniere*," and Paolo Trovato, *Dante in Petrarca: Per un inventario dei dantismi nei "Rerum vulgarium fragmenta"* (Florence: Olschki, 1977).

6. No doubt in part the scholarly neglect of the *disperse* depends on their ambiguous canonical status; they lack an exhaustive critical edition. For this essay I have opted to examine only the poems found in Laura Paolino's highly selective edition of the *disperse* in *Trionfi, Rime estravaganti, Codice degli abbozzi,* ed. Vinicio Pacca and Laura Paolino (Milan: Mondadori, 1996), rather than run the risks of using Angelo Solerti's unreliable, all-encompassing collection of 214 poems in *Rime disperse di Francesco Petrarca o a lui attribuite* (Florence: Sansoni, 1909). For a summary of the textual question of the *disperse,* see the excellent *postfazione* by Paola Vecchi Galli in the reprint of Solerti's edition (Florence: Le Lettere, 1997), 325–401, as well as her entries in *Petrarca nel tempo: Tradizione lettori e immagini delle opere,* ed. Michele Feo (Pontedera [Pisa]: Bandecchi & Vivaldi, 2003), 159–68. See also on the same subject, Santorre Debenedetti, "Per 'le disperse' di Francesco Petrarca," *Giornale storico della letteratura italiana* 56 (1910): 98–106; and Alessandro Pancheri, *"Col suon chioccio": Per una frottola 'dispersa' attribuibile a Francesco Petrarca* (Padua: Antenore, 1993), 3–22.

7. See, for example, the first section of Santagata's *Per moderne carte,* entitled "Dante, il maestro negato," or the section "La rimozione di Dante" in *I frammenti dell'anima: Storia e racconto nel Canzoniere di Petrarca* (Bologna: Il Mulino, 1990), 199–204.

8. In this light, the relatively high number of explicit occurrences of Dante in the early Correggio form of the *Canzoniere* — as underlined by Santagata in "Presenze di Dante 'comico' nel *Canzoniere*" — can in part be explained by the large number of poems this redaction contains (roughly 23 percent) written for and about historical figures. On the "choral" aspect of the Correggio, see Santagata, *I frammenti dell'anima,* especially 158–62.

9. Most famously in *Fam.* 20.2 and 23.19, both to Boccaccio.

10. Latin citations for the *Familiares* from Petrarch, *Le familiari,* ed. Vittorio Rossi, 4 vols. (Rome and Florence: Sansoni, 1933–42). English translation (slightly modified) from Petrarch, *Letters on Familar Matters, Rerum familiarum libri,* trans. Aldo S. Bernardo, 3 vols. (Baltimore and London: Johns Hopkins University Press, 1982–85), 3:205.

11. English translation in Petrarch, *Letters on Familiar Matters,* 3:204. Italics mine.

12. In ibid., 3:205.

13. Latin text of *Seniles* 5.2 from Petrarch, *Senile V 2,* ed. Monica Berté (Florence: Le Lettere, 1998). English translation based on Petrarch, *Letters of Old Age, Rerum senilium libri,* trans. Aldo S. Bernardo, Saul Levin, and Reta A. Bernardo, 2 vols. (Baltimore: Johns Hopkins University Press, 1992), 1:160.

14. English translation from Petrarch, *Letters of Old Age,* 1:162. Italics mine.

15. For a brief discussion, with important bibliography, of the various channels involved in the reception of the *Commedia,* see Corrado Bologna, *Tradizione e fortuna dei classici italiani,* 2 vols. (Turin: Einaudi, 1993), 1:181–99.

16. See Bologna, *Tradizione e fortuna,* 1:194–95, and Armando Petrucci, *Writers and Readers in Medieval Italy: Studies in the History of Written Culture,* ed. and trans. Charles M. Radding (New Haven and London: Yale University Press, 1995), 183–89.

17. For the register-book and other urban vernacular books of the period, see the discussion in Petrucci, *Writers and Readers,* 179–89.

18. See Domenico De Robertis, "A quale tradizione appartenne il manoscritto delle rime di Dante letto dal Petrarca," *Studi petrarcheschi* n.s. 2 (1985): 136–37. This essay is a significant contribution toward better contextualizing Petrarch's reception of Dante.

19. In Dante, *Rime,* liii, ed. Gianfranco Contini (Turin: Einaudi, 1995). All citations of Dante's *rime* from this edition.

20. "Invitus fateor hac etate vulgari iuveniles ineptias cerno; quas omnibus mihi quoque si liceat ignotas velim. Et si enim stilo quolibet ingenium illius etatis emineat: ipsa tamen res senilem dedecet gravitatem. Sed quid possum? Omnia iam in vulgus effusa sunt: legunturque libentius quam que serio postmodum validioribus animis scripsi. Quomodo igitur negarem tibi sic de me merito tali viro: Tamque anxie flagitanti que me invito vulgus habet et lacerat?" (At this age, I confess, I observe with reluctance the youthful trifles that I would like to be unknown to all, including me, if it were possible. For while the talent of that age may emerge in any style whatsoever, still the subject matter does not become the gravity of old age. But what can I do? Now they have all circulated among the multitude, and are being read more willingly than what I later wrote seriously for sounder minds. How then could I deny you, so great a man and so kind to me and pressing for them with such eagerness, what the multitude possesses and mangles against my wishes?) Latin text in Ernest Hatch Wilkins, *The Making of the "Canzoniere" and Other Petrarchan Studies* (Rome: Edizione di storia e letteratura, 1951), 177; translation in Petrarch, *Letters of Old Age,* 2:500.

21. For Dante, see the discussion in Michelangelo Picone, *"Vita Nuova" e tradizione romanza* (Padua: Liviana, 1979), 73–99.

22. *Vita Nuova* 36.4. All citations from Dante, *Vita Nuova,* in *Opere minori* I/1, ed. Domenico De Robertis and Gianfranco Contini (Milan and Naples: Ricciardi, 1984), 27–247.

23. All citations for the *Commedia* from Dante, *La Commedia secondo l'antica vulgata,* ed. Giorgio Petrocchi, 2nd rev. ed., 4 vols. (Florence: Le Lettere, 1994).

24. For a suggestive discussion of the function of the palinode in Dante's work, see Albert Russell Ascoli, "Palinode and History in the Oeuvre of Dante," in *Dante Now: Current Trends in Dante Studies,* ed. Theodore J. Cachey, Jr. (Notre Dame, Ind.: University of Notre Dame Press, 1993), 155–86.

25. See the facsimile edition, Boccaccio, *Il codice Chigiano L.V. 176,* ed. Domenico De Robertis (Rome and Florence: Alinari, 1974), with an important introductory essay by Domenico De Robertis.

26. All citations for the *disperse* from Petrarch, *Trionfi.*

27. The attribution of "Per util, per diletto o per onore" to Petrarch has been recently called into question. See the discussion of the complex question in Gianfranco Contini, "Postilla dantesca," in *Un'idea di Dante: Saggi danteschi* (Turin: Einaudi, 1976), 231–33.

28. Critics are not unanimous in their interpretation of these verses, especially as to whether Petrarch claims to have been moved by other women. See the discussion in Petrarch, *Trionfi,* 651.

29. See also Giuseppe Billanovich's argument that Petrarch invented the character of Laura in a conversation with other poets, in particular with Sennuccio: Billanovich, "Laura fantasma del *Canzoniere,*" *Studi petrarcheschi* n.s. 11 (1994): 149–58.

30. For the importance of the *donna gentile* in the *Canzoniere,* see also Santagata, *I frammenti dell'anima,* 204–7.

31. Citations for the *Canzoniere* from Petrarch, *Canzoniere,* ed. Marco Santagata, 2nd ed. (Milan: Mondadori, 1997). All translations are based on Petrarch, *Petrarch's Lyric Poems.*

32. In particular, it is Beatrice's corrupting body ("carne sepolta" [buried flesh], "le belle membra ... che so' 'n terra sparte" [the lovely members ... that are scattered in the earth] [*Purg.* 31, ll. 48, 50–51]) that Dante fails properly to acknowledge, unlike Petrarch, who underlines, throughout the second part of the *Canzoniere,* that Laura's body is now underground.

33. See, among others, Rosanna Bettarini, "'Che debb'io far? (RVF CCLXVIII),'" *Lectura Petrarce* 7 (1987): 187–99; Ronald J. Martinez, "Mourning Laura in the *Canzoniere*: Lessons from Lamentations," *MLN* 118 (2003): 1–45; and Laura Paolino, "'Ad acerbam rei memoriam': Le carte del lutto nel codice Vaticano Latino 3196 di Francesco Petrarca," *Rivista di letteratura italiana* 11 (1993): 73–102.

34. Petrarch's ultimate rejection of a stilnovist perspective on love and Laura is discussed in Santagata, *I frammenti dell'anima,* 313–16. But these distinctions are by now commonplace. See, for example, Durling's introduction in *Petrarch's Lyric Poems,* 18–26, or Kenelm Foster's influential essay, "Beatrice or Medusa," in *Italian Studies Presented to E. R. Vincent,* ed. C. P. Brand, K. Foster, and U. Limentanti (Cambridge: Heffer, 1962), 41–56.

35. On the fictionalized treatment of time and narrative in the *Canzoniere*, see Teodolinda Barolini, "The Making of a Lyric Sequence: Time and Narrative in Petrarch's *Rerum vulgarium fragmenta*," *MLN* 104 (1989): 1–38.

36. Petrarch appropriates the language of salvation and damnation to talk about his own poetry and his own editorial decisions in a marginal note in the *codice degli abbozzi* next to the sonnet "Voglia mi sprona, Amor mi guida et scorge": "Mirum, hunc cancellatum et damnatum, post multos annos casu relegens absolvi et transcripsi in ordine statim" (Amazing. Rereading by chance this crossed out and condemned poem, after many years, I immediately absolved and transcribed it in order). Transcription from Petrarch, *Trionfi*, 809–10. The poem was in fact "saved," anthologized as *Rvf* 211.

37. For the importance of *Rvf* 189 within the macrostructure of the *Canzoniere*, see Theodore J. Cachey, Jr., "From Shipwreck to Port: *Rvf* 189 and the Making of the Canzoniere," *MLN* 120, no. 1 (2005): 30–49. For the theme of Ulysses, see Picone, "Il sonetto CLXXXIX," *Lectura Petrarce* 9 (1989): 151–77.

38. "ex amici relatu, qui eum abstulerat, et ex memoria primum cui tamen aliquid defuerat." The term "amici" in the note is glossed by Petrarch himself as "d. ca." Critics have tentatively identified Francesco da Carrara as the "domini carrariensis" behind "d. ca." See discussion in Petrarch, *Trionfi*, 649–50.

39. See the chapter "Tra pubblico e privato" in Santagata, *I frammenti dell'-anima*, 253–94.

40. Alternative readings are listed in Petrarch, *Trionfi*, 650.

41. For this section of the essay, I owe a particular debt to Enrico Fenzi's article, "Note petrarchesche: *RVF* 16, *Movesi il vecchierel*," now in Fenzi, *Saggi petrarcheschi* (Fiesole [Florence]: Cadmo, 2003), 17–39.

42. For a discussion of the visual semiotics at the end of *Vita Nuova*, see the chapter "Peregrinus amoris: La metafora finale" in Picone, *Vita Nuova*, 129–92.

43. Cited in Petrarch, *Canzoniere*, 71.

44. See Fenzi, *Saggi petrarcheschi*, 24–26, and Santagata, *I frammenti dell'-anima*, 226.

45. See, for example, Michael Camille, *The Gothic Idol: Ideology and Image-Making in Medieval Art* (Cambridge: Cambridge University Press, 1989), 311–16.

46. See Hans Belting, *Likeness and Presence: A History of the Image before the Era of Art*, trans. Edmund Jephcott (Chicago: University of Chicago Press, 1994), 208–24.

47. See at least the fundamental discussions in the chapters "The Image in Urban Life" and "The End of the Private Image at the End of the Middle Ages" in Belting, *Likeness and Presence*, 377–457.

48. Gianfranco Contini underlines Petrarch's aesthetic consumerism in "Petrarca e le arti figurative," in *Francesco Petrarca, Citizen of the World*, Proceedings of the World Petrarch Congress, Washington, D.C., April 6–13, 1974, ed. Aldo S. Bernardo (Padua: Antenore; Albany: State University of New York Press, 1980), 126–27. For additional discussions of Petrarch and the visual arts, see

Michael Baxandall, *Giotto and the Orators: Humanist Observers of Painting in Italy and the Discovery of Pictorial Composition, 1350–1450* (Oxford: Clarendon Press, 1971), 51–66; and Bettini, "Tra Plinio e sant'Agostino: Francesco Petrarca sulle arti figurative," in *Memoria dell'antico nell'arte italiana,* ed. Salvatore Settis (Turin: Einaudi, 1984), 1:221–67.

49. The recent commodification of books, which is related to similar phenomena in the visual arts, is expressed most succinctly by a personified Reason in the *De remediis utriusque fortunae* (1.43): "Nam ut quidam disciplinae, sic alii voluptati et iactantiae libros querunt. Sunt qui hac parte suppellectilis exornent thalamos, quae animos exornandis inuenta est, neque aliter his utantur, quam Corinthiis vasis aut tabulis pictis ac statuis, caeterisque de quibus proxime disputatum est. Sunt qui obtentu librorum avaritiae inserviant, pessimi omnium non librorum vera pretia, sed quasi mercium aestimantes. Pestis mala sed recens, et quae nuper divitum studiis obrepsisse videatur, quae unum concupiscientiae, instrumentum atque una ars accesserit" (Some seek books for study, others seek them for pleasure and for ostentation. There are those who decorate their rooms with furniture devised to decorate their minds, and they use books as they use Corinthian vessels or paintings or statues and the like, which we discussed before. There are those who by obtaining books satisfy their greed. They are the worst of the lot who do not appreciate the true value of books but regard them as merchandise—a foul and recent pest which now seems to have infected the desires of the rich, providing avarice with yet another tool and another trick). Latin text from *Francisci Petrarchae operum: Tomus I–VI* (Ridgewood, N.J.: Gregg Press, 1965). The English translation is from Petrarch, *Petrarch's Remedies for Fortune Fair and Foul,* trans. Conrad H. Rawski, 5 vols. (Bloomington and Indianapolis: Indiana University Press, 1991), 1:138.

50. See Remo Ceserani, "'Petrarca': Il nome come auto-reinvenzione poetica," *Quaderni petrarcheschi* 4 (1987): 121–37.

51. See the highly suggestive discussion on the relationship between Petrarch and the autograph manuscript in Petrucci, *Writers and Readers,* 145–68 and 189–94, where the author suggests that the private "author's book" was in part a reaction to the uncontrolled and amateurish quality of manuscript production at this time.

52. Beccadelli succinctly characterizes this sacral approach to Petrarch's autograph papers: "sono come reliquie sante conservati" (they are preserved like sacred relics). Text cited in Pancheri, *"Col suon chioccio,"* 12.

53. By relocating "Or vedi, Amor, che giovenetta donna" from its original position between sonnets 243 and 244, Petrarch further ensures that the "giovenetta donna" named in the madrigal is identified with Laura and not some new *pargoletta* (since in canzone 127 Laura *giovenetta* has already become a "donna"). See Laura Paolino, "Sui madrigali di Petrarca (RVF 52, 54, 106, 121)," *Italianistica: Rivista di letteratura italiana* 30 (2001): 318–19. Paolino's discussion of how Pe-

trarch transforms the meaning of his occasional madrigals when they are included in the *Canzoniere* has several parallels with the process discussed in this essay.

54. See Rosanna Bettarini, "Perché 'narrando' il duol si disacerba. (Motivi esegetici dagli autografi petrarcheschi)," in *La critica del testo: Problemi di metodo ed esperienze di lavoro* (Rome: Salerno, 1985), 317–18; Cachey, "From Shipwreck to Port," 44–48; and Petrarch, *Trionfi,* 665.

55. Cachey, "From Shipwreck to Port," 44–48.

56. As in Foster, "Beatrice or Medusa."

CHAPTER 8

Dante, Petrarch, and the Laurel Crown

SARA STURM-MADDOX

WITH REGARD TO POETIC CORONATION, ITALIAN POETS OF THE fourteenth century received from antiquity a double legacy: one part an individual, literary sanction, the other a collective, historical one. Ovid's tale in the *Metamorphoses* of Apollo's pursuit of a nymph who was transformed into a laurel tree culminates in the god claiming the tree as his own, initiating its significance in the recognition of inspired achievement. Then there is the ritual with which Ovid's Apollo also associates the laurel: the jubilant popular acclaim of triumphant heroes in ancient Rome. In fourteenth-century Italy, a series of events—both textual and historical—brought the theme to the fore in the aspirations of some of the most fervent practitioners of the poetic art. While the two strands, poetic and historical, are frequently intertwined, both in the works of the poets and in critical assessments of their attitudes, attention to the distinction between them sheds light on the issues of preeminence and public recognition that concerned the three greatest poets of the Trecento: Dante Alighieri, Francesco Petrarca, and the self-proclaimed disciple of them both, Giovanni Boccaccio.

MUSSATO AND DANTE: VARIATIONS ON A THEME OF CORONATION

In 1315, in Padua, Albertino Mussato was awarded a triple crown of laurel, ivy, and myrtle for his achievement as historian and poet. His *De gestis*

Henrici VII Caesaris was an ambitious endeavor treating very recent history: the life of the emperor Henry VII from his arrival in Italy in late 1310 until his death at Buonconvento three years later.[1] The Paduans were also eager to reward Mussato for his tragedy *Ecerinis,* which evoked the tyrannization of their city under Ezzelino da Romano in the preceding century. Following Mussato's coronation in the Palazzo Comunale, on Christmas Day the Paduans were summoned to a patriotic festival, a public reading of the *Ecerinis.* Denouncing the crimes of a former Ghibelline tyrant, the play served as political propaganda to fuel the city's resistance to assaults led by another powerful Ghibelline lord, Can Grande della Scala of Verona. Thus did Mussato become the hero as well as the poet laureate of Padua.[2]

The *Inferno* of the Florentine exile Dante Alighieri was circulated a year before Mussato's *Ecerinis,* his *Purgatorio* in the year of the Paduan's coronation. In 1319, while living in Ravenna and at work on the *Paradiso,* Dante received a poetic epistle in Latin from Giovanni del Virgilio, a poet and respected professor at the University of Bologna, praising his poem "triplicis confinia sortis / indita pro meritis animarum, sontibus Orcum, / astripetis Lethen, epiphoebia regna beatis" (unfolding the regions of three-fold fate assigned according to deserts of souls, Orcus to the Guilty, Lethe to them that seek the stars, the realms above the sun to the blest) (*Carm.* 1.5).[3] But del Virgilio also asserted that despite its extraordinary merits, Dante's great poem written in the "language of the market-place" could be expected to garner no fame higher than the clamor of the crowd. "Cast not in prodigality thy pearls before the swine," del Virgilio urges. Rather, why not undertake a great poem in Latin on the tumultous events of contemporary Italy, the "mighty toils of men," which Dante alone was able to extol?[4] Thus might Dante truly set himself apart, and Giovanni promised to present him proudly in Bologna, crowned with laurel, to receive the ovations of a learned and discerning public.

The proposal could hardly have been more timely for Dante, who in the opening canto of the *Paradiso* invokes Apollo to help him merit at last the coveted accolade:

> O buono Appollo, a l'ultimo lavoro
> fammi del tuo valor sì fatto vaso,
> come dimandi a dar l'amato alloro.
>
> (*Par.* 1.13–15)

O good Apollo, for this last labor make me such a vessel of
your worth as you require for granting your beloved laurel.[5]

If he succeeds in depicting "l'ombra del beato regno / segnata nel mio capo"
(the image of the blessed realm which is imprinted in my mind) (*Par.*
1.23–24), he tells Apollo,

> vedra'mi al piè del tuo diletto legno
> venire, e coronarmi de le foglie
> che la materia e tu mi farai degno.
>> (*Par.* 1.25–27)

---

you shall see me come to your beloved tree and crown me with
those leaves of which the matter and you shall make me worthy.

Michelangelo Picone suggests that this scene, in which the author receives
the laurel crown upon completion of his work, assumes the value of an ar-
chetype and marks the beginning of an Italian literary tradition.[6] The verses
themselves echo a similar invocation of Apollo in the *Achilleid* by Statius,
who hopes for a second crown, of laurel, to follow that of myrtle he had already received for the *Thebaid*—a reward that his shade evokes in an encounter with Dante and Virgil in the *Purgatorio.*[7]

Dante's reply to Giovanni was a pastoral eclogue in Latin, deemed
by its editors to be "surely one of the most precious and revealing documents which ever threw light on the character of a great man."[8] In the
poem, Dante in the persona of a shepherd recalls having reported Giovanni's invitation to an unlearned companion. "Quid facies?" (What wilt
thou do?) the companion demands; "tu tempora lauro / semper inornata
per pascua pastor habebis?" (wilt thou forever wear thy temples unadorned
with laurel, a shepherd on the pasture lands?) (*Carm.* 2.34–35, 154). Ah
no, says Dante-shepherd, who avers that it would be much better to receive the crown of laurel and ivy when he has completed his threefold
poem and, as he hopes, returned to his ancestral home on the Arno.
In the meantime, he hopes to convince Giovanni of the worthiness of
the vernacular *Commedia* by sending him ten completed cantos of the
Paradiso.[9]

While Giovanni does not mention Mussato's recent coronation, his poetic epistle presupposes it as the model for the revival of the classical tradition of the laurel crown. Dante does not acquiesce. He does not acknowledge Giovanni's disparaging comment on the unlearned audience unfit to be offered a great poem, nor indeed does he respond directly to the implication that only a great work in Latin could merit the crown. As Cecil Grayson argues, the poet who had penned the *De vulgari eloquentia* during the early years of his exile apparently did not find the vernacular and Latin to be "mutually exclusive or incompatible."[10] Furthermore, having depicted himself early in the *Inferno* as one welcomed into a group of great poets, including four Latins and the Greek Homer, Dante is now confident that the *Paradiso* in progress will fully justify his linguistic choice.[11] With regard to the circumstances appropriate for the bestowal of the honors, Giovanni's implicit invitation to follow in the footsteps of Mussato must have caused Dante to reflect, despite differing political affinities, on the similarities between his experience of public life and that of the Paduan laureate.[12] Like Dante in Florence, Mussato had held public office in Padua and repeatedly served his city as ambassador, and in Padua he had been honored and acclaimed. While political circumstances may well have contributed to Dante's stated reluctance to abandon his secure haven in Ravenna in order to receive the crown in Bologna as Giovanni proposed, the Florentine exile makes his acceptance of a formal coronation contingent upon his reconciliation with his own city, a polity that had wrongfully and cruelly excluded him.

Dante seems much more confident of the merits of his great poem than of achieving a coronation in Florence "prima che morte tempo li prescriba" (before death appoint his time to him) (*Par.* 24.6), for in the same canto he imagines an alternative, celestial version enacted by Saint Peter, following his fervent profession of faith: "così, benedicendomi cantando, / tre volte cinse me, sì com' io tacqui, / l'appostolico lume al cui comandò / io avea detto: sì nel dire li piacqui!" (so, singing benedictions on me, the apostolic light at whose bidding I had spoken encircled me three times when I was silent, I so pleased him by my speech) (*Par.* 24.151–54). Nonetheless, at the opening of *Paradiso* 25—the canto in which he will be examined on the theological virtue of Hope—he discloses that he has not renounced his hope for an earthly coronation in his native city, although he did not envision this honor as being like that of Mussato:

Se mai continga che 'l poema sacro
　　al quale ha posto mano e cielo e terra,
　　sì che m'ha fatto per molti anni macro,
vinca la crudeltà che fuor mi serra
　　del bello ovile ov'io dormi' agnello,
　　nimico ai lupi che li danno guerra;
con altra voce omai, con altro vello
　　ritornerò poeta, e in sul fonte
　　del mio battesmo prenderò il cappello.
　　　　　　　　　　　　　　(*Par.* 25.1–9)

If ever it comes to pass that the sacred poem to which heaven
and earth have so set hand that it has made me lean for many
years should overcome the cruelty from the fair sheepfold where
I slept as a lamb, an enemy to the wolves which war on it, with
changed voice now and with changed fleece a poet will I return,
and at the font of my baptism will I take the crown.

When in 1321 Dante was splendidly adorned to receive the accolades
due a great poet, these cantos of the *Paradiso* had not been made public, and
the setting was not Florence but Ravenna. The occasion was his funeral.
Ravenna's ruler Guido Novello, who had befriended him, pronounced the
funeral oration, proposing to honor him with an "egregia sepultura [. . .]
che, se mai alcuno altro suo merito non l'avesse memorevole renduto a' fu-
turi, quella l'avrebbe fatto" (so magnificent a sepulcher that if no merit of
his own should render himself memorable to posterity, this of itself would
do so). According to the account in Boccaccio's *Life of Dante*, many illustrious poets sent verses to adorn the monument, but due to reversals of
fortune, it was never finished.[13]

PETRARCH THE POET LAUREATE: VARIATIONS ON THE LAUREL CROWN

Petrarch, the son of another Florentine exile, wrote that he had conceived the desire for the laurel crown at an early age.[14] That desire no doubt

increased, if it did not originate, during the period of his legal studies in Bologna, which, while renowned for its law faculty, appears also, as John Ahern writes, to have been at that time "the principal center of diffusion of the *Commedia*," such that if he "did not already know of the great work in progress, notaries, students, and professors in Bologna would soon have mentioned the still-incomplete poem, whose author lived in nearby Ravenna."[15] Among his fellow students was Dante's son Pietro Alighieri, later author of a commentary on the *Commedia*;[16] among the professors was Giovanni del Virgilio.

In Avignon, to which he returned after his father's death, Petrarch undertook a major philological endeavor, the restoration of the Decades of Livy's *Ab Urbe condita libri*. The Paduan philologist and pre-humanist Lovato Lovati had brought together the Decades, and the poet laureate Mussato had imitated the work. Through close contact with intellectual circles in Padua, Petrarch added to his rapidly expanding library a collection of Lovato's poems and all the major works of Mussato: the *Historia Augusta*, another historical work on Italy after the death of Henry VII, and the *Ecerinis*.[17] Following a sojourn in Rome in 1337, during which he sought out further classical texts, Petrarch's focus on historical works intensified. A sonnet later included in the *Rerum vulgarium fragmenta*, probably written in 1338, requests aid in obtaining material necessary for the completion of a new work, "la tela novella ch'ora ordisco" (the new cloth that now I prepare to weave). With this aid, he tells his unnamed correspondent,

> i' farò forse un mio lavor sì doppio
> tra lo stil de' moderni e 'l sermon prisco
> che (paventosamente a dirlo ardisco)
> in fin a Roma n'udirai lo scoppio.
>
> (*Rvf* 40.5–8)

> I shall perhaps make a work so double between the style of
> the moderns and ancient speech that (fearfully I dare to say it)
> you will hear the noise of it even as far as Rome.[18]

The work to which Petrarch alludes is most likely the *Africa*, begun, like the *De viris illustribus*, in 1338–39.[19] In both the *Africa* and the *Secretum*, as E. H. Wilkins notes, there is mention of a "liber historiarum" from the time of Romulus, referred to in the *Secretum* as an "opus immensum" set aside when the *Africa* was begun.[20] That immense work, not further identified, is very probably the *De viris,* whose preface sheds much light on Petrarch's "sustained reflection on himself in the role of historian of Roman antiquity."[21] In the *Secretum,* written in the years immediately following his coronation, he refuses to set aside an urgent work-in-progress, "Preclarum nempe rarumque opus et egregium" (illustrious, rare and outstanding *opus*) (*Secretum* 3.15.2), even though his interlocutor Augustinus warns him of his inordinate love of earthly glory.[22]

His desire for a poetic coronation was soon fulfilled. In 1340 one invitation arrived from the chancellor of the University of Paris, Roberto de' Bardi, a Florentine later described by the laureate as a friend and "illustri viro . . . rebus meis amicissimo" (an illustrious man . . . well acquainted with my activities) (*Fam.* 4.4.1), and another from Rome, following Petrarch's avowal to distinguished and influential individuals of his interest in achieving the award.[23] At that time, his works that had circulated were almost entirely in Latin, and few in number, including, notably, material later included in the *De viris illustribus* and bits of the *Africa.* Petrarch reports in his late *Epistola Posteritati* ("Letter to Posterity") (*Sen.* 18.1) that he had read passages from the latter to King Robert of Anjou in Naples during the "examination" staged at his own request to establish his worthiness to receive the laurel crown, adding that with regard to a larger public the work was eagerly anticipated but not already known.[24]

Petrarch's choice of Rome as the venue for the ceremony partook of a cultural strategy combining the achievement of literary glory with the civic mission of the poet.[25] His procession, following his coronation on the Capitoline, to place his laurel crown on the altar of St. Peter's is evocative of Dante's pious veneration of the ancient city, reflected in Beatrice's identification of Paradise as "quella Roma onde Cristo è Romano" (that Rome whereof Christ is Roman) (*Purg.* 32.102). The nature of Petrarch's association of his own myth-in-the-making with the established one of the Eternal City, however, is apparent in an extraordinary (but not atypical) declaration to Giacomo Colonna concerning the two invitations he had received: "cum me tantillum certatim due maxime urbes exposcerent, Roma atque Parisius, altera mundi caput et urbium regina, nutrix altera nostri temporis studiorum" (I in my insignificance was eagerly implored by two of the greatest cities, Rome and Paris, one the capital of the world and queen of cities, the other the mother of the studies of our time) (*Fam.* 4.6.5). That "insignificance" is somewhat qualified in a tribute, written shortly after the coronation, to King Robert: "Novo nuper beneficio desertas Pyerides obligasti, quibus hoc meum quantulumcunque est ingenium solemniter consecrasti; ad hec et urbem Romam et obsoletum Capitolii palatium insperato gaudio et insuetis frondibus decorasti" (Recently you obliged the abandoned Muses with new kindness by solemnly consecrating to them this talent of mine, however small. To this end you decorated the city of Rome and the decaying palace of the Capitoline with unexpected joy and unusual foliage) (*Fam.* 4.7.1).

In the *Africa,* the poet Ennius is honored along with the conquering hero:

> Ipse coronatus lauro frondente per urbem
> Letus iit totam Tarpeia rupe reversus.
> Ennius ad dextram victoris, tempora fronde
> Substringens parili, studiorum almeque Poesis
> Egit honoratum sub tanto auctore triumphum.

> ─────────

> Wearing his crown of laurel, Scipio
> comes down again from the Tarpeian rock
> and traverses once more the joyous town.
> Upon the right hand of so great a guide
> Stands Ennius, his temples also girt
> with like triumphal crown, to celebrate
> great learning and sustaining poesy.
> (*Afr.* 9.398–402)[26]

Thus the new poet Petrarch represents himself many centuries later striving to follow the "precious traces" of Scipio and Ennius, "to imitate / with similar crown, like site, and glorious name, / the ancient heroes and their dignities / sublime" (*Afr.* 9.567–70). His choice of venue in which to receive the crown would thus be unlike either that of Mussato or that of Dante, but similar to that of Scipio and Ennius—and that of Statius, who had received his coronation for the *Thebaid* in Rome, as he explains in the *Commedia*:

"Tanto fu dolce mio vocale spirto, / che, tolosano, a sé mi trasse Roma, / dove mertai le tempie ornar di mirto" (So sweet was my vocal spirit that me, a Toulousan, Rome drew to itself, where I was deemed worthy to have my brows adorned with myrtle) (*Purg.* 21.88–90). Like Statius, Petrarch would come to the ancient capital from afar, his poetic supremacy confirmed by the "call to Rome."

It was very probably in imitation of Mussato's coronation that Petrarch imagined—or, as Giuseppe Billanovich puts it, "si costruì"—his own formal ceremony that took place on the Capitoline in April 1341.[27] With his *De gestis Henrici VII Caesaris,* Mussato had set the example for the kind of Latin composition that Giovanni del Virgilio unsuccessfully urged on Dante: a work celebrating the tumultuous events of contemporary Italy; Henry VII, whose deeds Mussato recorded, had had enormous significance for his generation, in particular for the Florentine exiles, including Dante and Petrarch's father.[28] The diploma, or *Privilegium laureae,* that was ceremonially read and awarded to Petrarch at his coronation, to which he himself contributed substantially,[29] acclaims him, like Mussato before him, as both *poeta* and *historicus.* The most ambitious and significant work he had undertaken prior to his coronation, the epic *Africa,* celebrates one of the greatest heroes of imperial Rome, Scipio Africanus, whose deeds he declared insufficiently rewarded by public memory. The *Privilegium* ratifies the poet's honors awarded to him by both the sponsorship of King Robert and the acclaim of the Roman people, and his *Epistolae metricae* written in 1342–44 repeatedly associate King Robert with his desire to complete the *Africa.*[30] Even if we take into account the strong current of mythmaking in Petrarch's *Posteritati,* the extent to which he there associates the epic poem with the coronation suggests that, as Stephen Murphy comments, "in his own mind, Petrarca *laureatus* was the poet of the *Africa.*"[31]

The *Collatio laureationis,*[32] the oration that Petrarch pronounced when accepting the honor, also suggests the connection between the crowning and the *Africa.* Thus, the probable source of the *Collatio*'s brief listing of the awards conferred on poets is Virgil's seventh eclogue, where it is epic poetry that gains Apollo's laurels.[33] Petrarch uses a Virgilian text to portray himself as striving to scale the heights of Parnassus in pursuit of the laurel,[34] and refers his audience to the first book of Ovid's *Metamorphoses,* where Apollo decrees that the laurel "ducibus Latiis aderis, cum laeta Triumphum / vox canet et visent longas Capitolia pompas" (will accompany

the generals of Rome, when the Capitol beholds their long triumphal processions, when joyful voices raise the song of victory) (560).[35] Thereafter
the *Collatio* insistently associates great poets with great military leaders as
protagonists in the pursuit of glory, referring repeatedly to the laurel crown
as bestowed upon "cesaribus et poetis," before citing directly, near the end of
the oration, Statius' phrase in the *Achilleid* from which Petrarch's formula
derives.[36] The association is featured also in the *Africa*, where the military
leader Scipio and the poet Ennius are both crowned with laurels in Rome.[37]
Petrarch was no doubt aware that Dante had preceded him in making
the link when, invoking Apollo's aid in the *Paradiso*, he effected the slight
transformation of Statius' "vatumque ducumque" into caesars and poets:
"Sì rade volte, padre, se ne coglie / per trïunfare o cesare o poeta, / colpa e
vergogna de l'umane voglie" (So rarely, father, are they gathered, for triumph of caesar or of poet—fault and shame of human wills) (*Par.* 1.28–30).
Petrarch's own emphasis, however, is unmistakably different, as when he
writes to Giacomo Colonna from Rome where he is about to receive the
crown that he had long been "scito me lauree delphice cupidine—que olim
clarorum Cesarum et sacrorum vatum singulare et precipuum votum fuit"
(driven by the desire for the Delphic laurel!—which once was the unique
and special object of desire of outstanding rulers and of sacred seers)
(*Fam.* 4.6.5).

   Nowhere in these documents is there mention of Petrarch's own vernacular rhymes. A number of them were already well known, however, notably by some of the distinguished patrons who knew of his desire for the
laurel crown.[38] His readers would have been well aware of the association
of that desire with the Ovidian story of Apollo's pursuit of an inaccessible
beloved and her metamorphosis into the laurel that he then claimed as his
own, which was the central element in the lyrics that formed the earliest
nucleus of the *Rerum vulgarium fragmenta*.[39] That Petrarch was far more
ambivalent about the association of the laurel and Laura than about his
proud claim to the laurels awarded by ancient Rome is evident in a number
of the poems themselves, and in particular in the dialogue he writes in the
Secretum between the Petrarchan persona Franciscus and his interlocutor
Augustinus. The saint attributes the poet's cultivation of the symbolic laurel to an infatuation with the beauty both of Laura and of her name: "Quam
ob causam tanto opere sive caesaream sive poeticam lauream" (Had you
any liking for the laurel of empire or of poetry), he declares, it was "quod illa

hoc nomine vocaretur, adamasti" (because the name they bore was hers) so that "ex eoque tempore sine lauri mentione vix ullum tibi carmen effluxit" (there is hardly a verse from your pen but in it you have made mention of the laurel) (*Secretum* 3.7.5). Augustinus, not without protest from Franciscus, condemns this fixation as "alienate mentis insaniam" (the sign of a distempered mind).[40]

Boccaccio: Disciple of Two Poets

Interest in the new vernacular poetry was particularly intense in Naples when Giovanni Boccaccio initiated his own poetic career there in the 1330s. One of his mentors was the stilnovist poet Cino da Pistoia, friend of both Dante and Petrarch. Boccaccio's early sonnets demonstrate his familiarity with the *Vita Nuova* and the first cantos of the *Inferno,* and his early admiration for Petrarch is featured in an epistle transcribed in his manuscript known as the *Zibaldone laurenziano*;[41] his first acquaintance with Petrarch's lyrics, he reports in a late letter, had caused him to burn his own youthful vernacular poems.[42] After his return to his native Florence in the winter of 1340–41, his interest in both poets intensified, and Petrarch's coronation in Rome in 1341, closely following upon the examination by King Robert in Naples, attracted his immediate and sustained attention. He pored over the *Privilegium* and the *Collatio laureationis,* and in the months following he began what became his biography of Petrarch, the *De vita et moribus Domini Francisci Petracchi de Florentia.*[43] Presenting him only as poet, "in facultate poetica approbatu," Boccaccio may not have understood the implications of the *Privilegium*'s qualification of the honoree as "poeta e historicus."[44] On the other hand, although the coronation documents make no mention of Petrarch's vernacular lyrics, Boccaccio reads his ardent expressions of love for a lady named Laura (Lauretta) allegorically as his love for the laurel crown.[45] Petrarch might have contested the allegorical reading, as he emphatically denied a similar allegation by his patron and friend Giacomo Colonna,[46] but Boccaccio's supplement would hardly have surprised him.

In any case, Boccaccio did not make Latin composition an essential criterion for the award of the laurel crown. Very soon after his biographical tribute to the newly-crowned Petrarch, Boccaccio staged a ceremonial coronation for Dante in the *Amorosa Visione,* a work written, like his earlier *Comedia delle Ninfe,* in Dantean *terza rima.*[47] The Boccaccio-narrator is witnessing a series of allegorical triumphs when his attention is captured by a wonderful celebration ("così mirabile festa"):

> Dentro del coro delle donne adorno,
> in mezzo di quel loco ove facieno
> li savii antichi felice soggiorno,
>   rimirando, vid'io di gioia pieno
> onorar festeggiando un gran poeta,
> tanto che 'l dire alla vista vien meno.
>   Aveali la gran donna mansueta
> posta d'alloro una corona in testa,
> e di ciò ciascun' altra parea lieta.
>
> <div align="right">(<i>A.V.</i> 5.70–78)</div>

Within the graceful group of ladies, in the midst of that place where the ancient wise men were happily dwelling, as I gazed again, in full gladness, I saw such joyous honors bestowed upon a great poet that telling must fall short of sight. That great, serene lady had placed on his head a crown of laurel, for which all the other ladies seemed to rejoice.

Boccaccio's celestial guide, presiding at this ceremony, identifies the honored figure for him as "Dante Alighier fiorentin," who was "the glory of the Muses while he lived." In the following canto, which is filled with echoes of encounters in the *Commedia,* Boccaccio offers Dante this tribute:

> Vivrà la fama tua, e ben saputa,
> gloria de' Fiorentin, da' quali ingrati
> fu la tua vita assai mal conosciuta!
>
> <div align="right">(<i>A.V.</i> 6.13–18)</div>

Your fame shall endure, well recognized, glory of the Florentines; to those ingrates your life had little enough repute!

While a very personal tribute follows, to "il maestro dal qual io / tengo ogni ben, se nullo in me sen posa" (the master from whom I take every good thing, even if it does not perdure in me), it is here, Vittore Branca observes, that Dante for the first time is "consecrated as a 'classic.'"[48]

During his residence in Romagna in the 1340s, Boccaccio acquired not only other texts by and concerning Dante but also the works of Giovanni del Virgilio, including the latter's poetic correspondence with Dante.[49] He transcribed into the *Zibaldone laurenziano* not only that correspondence, but also Giovanni's eclogue to Albertino Mussato, which he annotated with observations on poetic coronation.[50] He understood the cultural significance of Petrarch's emphasis in his coronation speech on the rebirth of classical poetry, and composed an eclogue in imitation of Petrarch's "Argus," a lament for the death of King Robert who had restored the glory of the laurel crown—to which Boccaccio too, albeit tentatively, aspired.[51] But he also pondered the fundamental question raised by Giovanni del Virgilio in his poetic epistle to Dante, namely that of the status of the *volgare* in relation to the laurel crown, and he knew of Dante's defense of the vernacular in the *De vulgari eloquentia* and his defense of his own use of the mother tongue in the *Convivio*. Boccaccio's interest in the question is confirmed by another work copied into the same *Zibaldone*, the so-called Letter of Frate Ilaro.[52] The letter purports to be a monk's account of a brief visit by Dante to his monastery during which the poet, responding to Ilaro's surprise that the great work in progress was cast in the vernacular, disclosed the reason. He had indeed begun to compose the *Commedia* in Latin—he cited its opening verses, duly included by Ilaro in his letter—but had then abandoned that option because the public, and even those nobles who might sustain him in his work, would have found it inaccessible. Many questions have been raised about the authenticity of the letter; Billanovich argues that it may have been composed by Boccaccio himself.[53]

LATIN OR VERNACULAR LAURELS?

Petrarch first met Boccaccio several years later in Florence, in 1350, when he passed through the city on his way to Rome to observe the Jubilee year. In the following year Boccaccio visited Petrarch in Padua. We do not know to what extent they discussed Dante, but it was probably following this encounter that Boccaccio sent his new friend a copy of the *Commedia*, accompanied by a metrical Latin epistle, "Ytalie iam certus honos," urging Petrarch to praise and honor their Florentine precursor.[54] That he may have anticipated a particular objection from Petrarch is suggested by his affirmation—in keeping with the letter of "Frate Ilaro"—that contrary to what some envious critics might argue, Dante could well have written the *Commedia* in Latin, but had chosen instead to demonstrate the potential of the vernacular. There is no record of Petrarch's response, either to the gift or to the epistle.[55]

In 1359 Boccaccio paid another, extended visit to Petrarch, this time in Milan. That Dante was a major topic of their discussions may be deduced from Petrarch's *Fam.* 21.15 that he addressed to Boccaccio some months later, in which he responds to his friend's praises of Dante and explicitly denies any ill will or envy on his own part toward their great precursor. In this famous letter, Petrarch broke a prolonged silence concerning Dante, a silence that may well have prompted speculation about his attitude toward the exiled poet. Changed circumstances may have played a part; by 1359, Marco Santagata points out, he was no longer closely tied to the papal curia and to other prominent ecclesiastical figures for whom Dante was a highly controversial individual, and his new protectors, the Visconti of Milan, were Ghibellines who did not hesitate to turn the developing political myth of Dante to their own advantage.[56]

It has also long been assumed, as is suggested by the opening sentences of *Fam.* 21.15, that the letter was written in response to a now-lost letter from Boccaccio, who feared he had offended his host in Milan by his enthusiastic admiration for Dante. Giuseppe Billanovich has proposed a different scenario, that the much-discussed epistle responds just as well to the *De origine, vita, studiis et moribus viri clarissimi Dantis Aligerii florentini poete illustris et de operibus compositis ab eodem,* often referred to as the *Trattatello in laude di Dante.*[57] One of the most interesting features of this "little treatise," probably begun sometime in the early 1350s,[58] is its illustration of the convergence between Boccaccio's continuing veneration for Dante and his new enthusiasm for Petrarch. On the one hand, as Victoria Kirkham shows, he honors Dante by constructing a subtle parallelism between the Florentine poet's life and that of Virgil.[59] Some sections of the work's first redaction, on the other hand, appear to be patterned on Boccaccio's own recent life of Petrarch; the comment on Dante's lack of loquaciousness, for example, uses

almost the same words, though in the vernacular, that he had used to describe Petrarch.[60] Todd Boli adduces considerable evidence that the work
deliberately implies or exaggerates similarities between Petrarch and Dante,
using as sources either Petrarch's works or discussions of these with their
author.[61]

Among the most remarkable of these implied similarities is the ambi-
tion to achieve earthly glory, and with it the honor—and the ceremony—
of the laurel crown. It is to that desire that Boccaccio attributes Dante's
fervent devotion to poetry: "E perciò, sperando per la poesì allo inusitato
e pomposo onore della coronazione dell'alloro poter pervenire, tutto a lei
si diede e istudiando e componendo" (As a result, hoping to attain the unusual and glorious honor of being crowned with laurel, he devoted himself
wholeheartedly to the study and composition of poetry) (*Trat.* 125–26).[62]
This striving is underlined in the account of a dream attributed to Dante's
pregnant mother, that an infant born in a green meadow, nourished by
the berries falling from a laurel tree, would become a shepherd who desired
nothing but the laurel's leaves (*Trat.* 16–18).[63] The bucolic image resonates
curiously with Petrarch's own early self-representations, with which Boccaccio was familiar: the solemn *Collatio* he presented on the occasion of his
coronation depicts him as a poet beneath his laurel, "sub lauro mea." And
in the *Africa,* as the Greek poet Homer foretells the greatness of a Petrarch
yet to be born to the Latin poet Ennius, they glimpse the object of their
prospective admiration writing beneath the boughs of a laurel, with whose
leaves "he seems about to bind his locks."[64]

That these foreshadowings of future poetic triumph suggest no distinction between composition in Latin or in the vernacular supports the
hypothesis that the *Trattatello* was written in an attempt to convince readers, Petrarch perhaps foremost among them, that Dante's composition of
the *Commedia* in the vernacular in no way diminished his greatness. Again
Boccaccio affirms, excerpting from the letter of "Frate Ilaro," that while
Dante had begun the *Commedia* in Latin, he had had excellent reasons
for turning to the vernacular. In addition to making his poem accessible to
a larger public, he had chosen to demonstrate the potential of the *volgare*
with such success that poetry, long dead, had been brought back to life.
Repeatedly affirming Dante's desire for the laurels and his worthiness of
the award, Boccaccio is confident that had fortune favored the poet's return to Florence, he would have realized his hope to receive the laurel crown
in his native city.[65]

In *Fam.* 21.15, "purgatio ab invidis obiecte calumnie" (a defense against an accusation by envious people), Petrarch addresses the issue of vernacular composition and the question of his own regard for Dante in a curiously circuitous way. The epistle opens with the protestation that he could not have been offended by Boccaccio's praise of "conterranei nostri — popularis quidem quod ad stilum attinet, quod ad rem hauddubbie nobilis poete" (a fellow countryman of ours who is popular for his poetic style but doubtless noble for his theme) — a countryman who remains nameless throughout. On the contrary, he writes: "Age ergo, non patiente sed favente me, illam ingenii tui facem, que tibi in hoc calle, quo magnis passibus ad clarissimum finem pergis, ardorem prebuit ac lucem, celebra et cole, ventosisque diu vulgi plausibus agitatam atque ut sic dixerim fatigatam" (Continue, not with my sufferance alone but with my approval to honor and cherish that beacon of your intellect who has afforded you ardor and light for this pathway that you have been treading with giant steps toward a glorious goal; raise high with sincere praise worthy alike of you and of him that torch long buffeted and, I would say, wearied by the windy applause of the multitude) (*Fam.* 21.15.3). Only then does he address an opinion "ut non tantum falso, sicut de se ipso et Seneca Quintilianus ait, sed insidiose etiam penitusque malivole apud multos" (that has been not only falsely, as Quintilian remarks of himself and of Seneca, but insidiously and maliciously circulating) (*Fam.* 21.15.6).

As in so much of the correspondence that he carefully collected into volumes, Petrarch is writing here not only to his addressee, but to posterity. With the pretext of approving Boccaccio's initiatives in praise of Dante, he moves to the larger context of a public assessment of his own attitude toward their great precursor. After noting the reasons that would incline him to love and not hate his father's fellow exile, he evokes the particular "accusation" that he, an avid book-collector, had not acquired a copy of the *Commedia* in his youth: "ardentissimus semper in reliquis, quorum pene nulla spes supererat" (while always hunting passionately for other books with little hope of finding them), he writes, "in hoc uno sine difficultate parabili, novo quodam nec meo more tepuerim" (I was strangely indifferent to this one which was new and easily available) (*Fam.* 21.15.10). These two characterizations of Dante's "book" are not as neutral as they might appear: both draw attention away from Dante to Petrarch, as reminders that the latter had distinguished himself from an early age by his often-successful search for codices of venerated ancient texts. During his years in Avignon, as John Ahern observes, Petrarch had become "a precocious, exigent biblio-phile, familiar with a variety of elegant formats, for whom the undoubtedly unprepossessing copies of individual canticles [of Dante's poem], probably in notarile script, then circulating in Bologna could only provoke scorn."[66] Both the "newness" and the "easy availability" of the *Commedia* have a dis-paraging ring that could hardly have been missed by Boccaccio, an ardent admirer of Petrarch's library as well as of his scholarship.

Petrarch then provides another explanation which, while he claims it to be different, in fact is closely related to the first. "Eidem tunc" (At that time), he writes, "stilo deditus, vulgari eloquio ingenium exercebam; nichil rebar elegantius necdum altius aspirare didiceram, sed verebar ne si huius aut alterius dictis imbuerer, ut est etas illa flexibilis et miratrix omnium, vel invitus ac nesciens imitator evaderem" (I too was devoted to the same kind of writing in the vernacular; I considered nothing more elegant and had yet to learn to look higher, but I did fear that, were I to immerse my-self in his, or any other's, writings, being of an impressionable age so given to indiscriminate admiration, I could scarcely escape becoming an unwill-ing or unconscious imitator) (*Fam.* 21.15.11).[67] The claim that he had for that reason avoided reading Dante, while generally accepted for centuries, is belied by the profound and now well-documented impact of the *Commedia*, not only on his *Rerum vulgarium fragmenta*, the work for which he is now best remembered,[68] but also on his Latin works from his earliest composi-tions to his last.[69]

Yet another reason is forthcoming, however, one that refocuses the question from the merits of vernacular composition, whether Petrarch's own or Dante's, to that of its reception. "[U]bi unum, quod locus exigit, non silebo" (Here may be the proper place to mention), Petrarch writes, "fuisse michi non ultimam causam hanc stili eius deserendi, cui adolescens incubueram; timui enim in meis quod in aliorum scriptis, precipueque huius de quo loquimur" (that this was not the least of my reasons for abandon-ing his style of composition to which I devoted myself as a young man, for I feared for my writings what I saw happening to the writings of others, and especially of this poet about whom we speak) (*Fam.* 21.15.17); that fear has since proven well-founded, he adds, since "in his ipsis paucis que michi iuveniliter per id tempus elapsa sunt, vulgi linguis assidue laceror, indig-nans quodque olim amaveram perosus" (a few pieces that slipped from my youthful pen are constantly being mangled by the multitude's recitation, something that is so vexing as to make me hate what I once loved) (*Fam.* 21.15.18). However heartfelt this protestation, it is, like his further affirmation that composition in the vernacular had been for him "iocus atque solatium . . . ingenii rudimentum" (a mere sport, a pastime, a mental exercise) (*Fam.* 21.15. 21), subject to the overwhelming evidence, in both the *Rerum vulgarium fragmenta* and the *Trionfi,* that any such aversion was of very short duration.[70]

In *Fam.* 21.15, Petrarch may have been breaking his relative "public" silence about Dante, but not about his own vernacular rhymes; the attitude emphatically affirmed here was not unknown to Boccaccio. Probably in 1350, late in the year in which he and Boccaccio first met in person, Petrarch addressed to his new friend an *epistola metrica* in which he declared his intent that his works be "paucisque placere contenti" (content to please a few friends) (*Ep. met.* 3.17), avoiding the vain applause of a larger public.[71] He sent the poem to Boccaccio in early 1351 along with *Fam.* 11.2, which explains that it had been composed "festinante quidem calamo" (with a truly hasty hand) (*Fam.* 11.2.2), then lost and rediscovered, in response to a poem from Boccaccio lamenting that some of Petrarch's poems had fallen "inter vulgares etiam profanosque" (into the hands of the general public and evil men) (*Fam.* 11.2.1), while Boccaccio himself had difficulty in acquiring them. In another *epistola metrica* of 1350, the poem addressed to Barbato da Sulmona that he designated as the *proemio* to his collected *metriche,* he protested that he would like to hide his youthful rhymes, since he was so much changed that they seemed to him like those of another, but could not do so because Fate had intervened and his poems were on everyone's lips; even as he complained of the ensuing clamor and praise, he yielded to his friend's repeated request for copies of some of the poems.[72]

The declarations in *Fam.* 21.15, then, are among many signs that Petrarch's vernacular *rime* were essentially a private undertaking, their circulation protected from what he termed the mangling of the mob and restricted to a few well-chosen friends. In the context of this letter, apparently written to deny allegations of his envy of Dante, his avowal of having long ago abandoned vernacular poetry serves to erase the suggestion of competition in the comparison with Dante that would inevitably be part of present and future assessments of his work. Just as Petrarch makes no mention of his *rime sparse,* or scattered rhymes, in his unfinished autobiographical *Posteritati,* which foregrounds the relation between the *Africa* and his coronation

in Rome,[73] he writes in *Fam.* 21.15 "for the record"—a record whose terms
and content he is intent to establish. Even Boccaccio will admit, he writes,
that Dante "in vulgari eloquio quam carminibus aut prosa clarior atque
altior assurgit . . . nec rite censentibus aliud quam laudem et gloriam viri
sonat" (rose to greater heights in the vernacular than in Latin poetry or
prose . . . nor does it redound to anything but his praise or glory in the
minds of sensible judges) (*Fam.* 21.15.24).[74] As Boccaccio had indeed already
argued this in a variety of ways in the *Trattatello,* Petrarch returns to the initial topic of his letter by enjoining his friend to pursue his informed praise
of Dante, in part to put an end to the distortions to which the favor of the
"vulgo" had subjected the latter's work.[75] His "explanation" of his own attitude, on the other hand, opens the way for the attribution of two poetic
crowns: one the "palm for vernacular eloquence" earned by a great endeavor
addressed to a popular audience, and the other a tribute for preeminence
in Latin composition on an exalted theme worthy of a coronation like that
of the ancients. The latter, Boccaccio and through him others were to understand, was the tribute Petrarch had received in Rome, the tribute upon
whose uniqueness he insisted. Shortly after his coronation, he had written to King Robert in *Fam.* 4.7.2 that "lauree morem non intermissum
modo tot seculis, sed ibi iamprorsus oblivioni traditum, aliis multum diversis curis ac studiis in republica vigentibus, nostra etate renovatum te duce,
me milite" (the custom of the laurel crown, which has not only been inter-
rupted for so many centuries, but here actually condemned to oblivion as
the variety of cares and problems grew in the republic, has been renewed in
our own age through your leadership and my involvement).

PETRARCH'S VERNACULAR TRIUMPHS: THE *TRIONFI*

The themes that most concern us in *Fam.* 21.15 are taken up again years
later in Petrarch's *Sen.* 5.2, also addressed to Boccaccio.[76] Its pretext is the
author's indignation at a report that Boccaccio had long ago burned his
vernacular rhymes upon becoming acquainted with Petrarch's. After a series of reprimands to his friend, he imagines another motive as justification for Boccaccio's reported deed: an "indignatione quadam clara et nobili,
etati inutili ac superbe, nichil intelligenti, omnia corrumpenti, quodque
est intolerabilius contemnenti" (noble, glorious indignation that made you

wish to snatch any judgment of your talent from a worthless and arrogant age that understands nothing, corrupts everything, and—what is even more intolerable—scorns everything) (*Sen.* 5.2.22).[77] Here he displays the fear of violation by the public, already alleged in *Fam.* 21.15 as his reason for abandoning his own youthful vernacular rhymes, in yet more graphic terms: "meque et laborem meum inter vulgi manus laceratum iri" (I and my work would be torn to shreds by the hands of the mob) (*Sen.* 5.2.25)—an audience then likened to the snake lying in the runner's path which obliges him to change his course. Now the culpable parties include not only the "indoctum vulgus" (unlearned multitude) (*Sen.* 5.2.26), whose response to works in the vernacular he had feared, but also "reges qui . . . ut in his sic in virtute et gloria se superioribus pares putant" (the rulers who view themselves equal to their betters in valor and glory) (*Sen.* 5.2.28). The most egregious offenders, however, are men of letters and men of the cloth "qui se doctos vocant" (who call themselves learned) (*Sen.* 5.2.26)—"iudicibus seu tyrannis" (judges and tyrants) (*Sen.* 5.2.37) for whom Petrarch's scathing indictment has an apocalyptic ring: "iam non scolas sed latissimas urbes replent et vicos impediunt ac plateas, ut ipse michi sepe irascar, qui sic modo his proximis annis ultoribus irascebar exhaustumque flebam orbem. Viris enim forsan, fatear" (Not only do they fill the schools, but even the largest cities; they so crowd the streets and squares that I often reproach myself for my anger against these last years of retribution [the plagues] and for my lament over a world that has been emptied, I would perhaps admit, of its real men) (*Sen.* 5.2.37). Already in his *Epistolae metricae* 2.8, probably written in 1344,[78] he had lamented that with the death of King Robert of Naples, to whom he had intended to dedicate the *Africa,* he had become deprived of his proper audience and had considered throwing the work into the fire—as Boccaccio is reported in *Sen.* 5.2 to have done with his vernacular poems. There is no mention of coronation in the epistle, and no trace of the world in which Petrarch had earned the sponsorship of the learned King Robert, the unanimous acclamation of the Roman people, and, of course, the laurel crown.

This darkening picture of the writer's world is the backdrop for the topic to which *Sen.* 5.2 is presumably devoted, "de appetitu anxio primi loci" (the obsessive appetite for first place), and in particular the question of rivalry between men of letters. The issue of Petrarch's alleged envy of Dante is transposed here into an examination of Boccaccio's attitude toward Petrarch. The parallel with the earlier letter continues with the attribution to Boccaccio of an early interest in the vernacular like that which Petrarch had reported about himself in *Fam.* 21.15. He has learned, Petrarch tells his friend, that "prima etate hoc vulgari stilo unice delectatum, plurimum in eo cure ac temporis posuisse" (in your early youth, fascinated solely by the vernacular style, you devoted the most time and care to it) (*Sen.* 5.2.8); however, the urge to continue writing in this style had been cooled, not by fear of the unworthy public, but by reading Petrarch's vernacular rhymes. Was it "an sui ipsius contemptrix humilitas, an supra alios sese efferens superbia" (self-deprecating humility or a pride that feels superior to others) (*Sen.* 5.2.9) that had prompted Boccaccio's destruction of his own poems? The discussion rapidly expands to encompass Dante, as Petrarch admonishes Boccaccio not to allow pride to make him unable to accept second or third place, "Ut ego etenim te antistem (cui utinam par essem!), ut te precedat ille nostri eloquii dux vulgaris" (or that I should surpass you when I wish to be your equal, or that the master of our vernacular literature should be preferred to you) (*Sen.* 5.2.15).[79]

Petrarch of course knew very well that Boccaccio had not abandoned vernacular composition, just as Boccaccio knew that Petrarch had not abandoned it as he had reported in *Fam.* 21.15.[80] The point of his introducing his and Boccaccio's youthful vernacular poetry here is to return to the topic of his own early aspirations. The allusion is tantalizing. "[A]liquando" (At times), he confides,

> contraria mens fuisset totum huic vulgari studio tempus dare, quod uterque stilus altior latinus eousque priscis ingeniis cultus esset ut pene iam nichil nostra ope vel cuiuslibet addi posset, at hic, modo inventus, adhuc recens, vastatoribus crebris ac raro squalidus colono, magni se vel ornamenti capacem ostenderet vel augmenti. Quid vis? Hac spe tractus simulque stimulis actus adolescentie, magnum eo in genere opus inceperam, iactisque iam quasi edificii fundamentis, calcem ac lapides et ligna congesseram.

> I had also the self-contradictory idea to devote all my time to vernacular pursuits since the loftier Latin style — both prose and poetry — had been so highly polished by ancient talents that now my resources, or

anyone else's, can add very little. On the other hand, this vernacular writing, just invented, still new, showed itself capable of great improvement and development after having been ravaged by many and cultivated by few husbandmen. Well then, this hope so attracted me and at the same time the spur of youth so urged me onward that I undertook a great work in that style; and having laid, as it were, the foundations of that edifice, I gathered the cement and stone and wood. (*Sen.* 5.2.23–24)

The "great work" to which Petrarch refers is very probably the unfinished *Trionfi*, begun early in his poetic career.[81] To evoke the *Trionfi* in *Sen.* 5.2 is particularly apt because it is a work that links the vernacular Petrarch to both Dante and Boccaccio. Like Boccaccio's *Amorosa Visione* (to which it is also much indebted), it is composed in the *terza rima* of the *Commedia* and adopts myriad thematic, stylistic, and linguistic elements from Dante's poem. While Boccaccio envisions a coronation for Dante in the *Amorosa Visione*, in the *Trionfi* Dante is glimpsed in Cupid's retinue together with Beatrice, among other couples "volgarmente ragionando" (speaking of love, but in the common tongue). While participating as a captive in that same procession, the poet-narrator affirms having acquired the laurel crown: "colsi 'l glorioso ramo / onde forse anzi tempo ornai le tempie / in memoria di quella ch'io tanto amo" (I plucked the glorious laurel branch wherewith — perhaps too soon — I decked my brow, remembering her whom I so deeply love).[82]

With the *Trionfi*, as Zygmunt Barański concludes, Petrarch was in essence attempting a vernacular epic "which could match the refinement of his classical forebears by following their example in a rhetorically appropriate manner," and his choice to compose a poem of such ideological and formal ambitions in the vernacular suggests that "his seeming 'contempt' for the *volgare* has all the air of a well-rehearsed pose."[83] Petrarch's commitment to the project of the *Trionfi*, whose last two "triumphs" were written in the last two years of his life, belies the implied exclusivity of his choice of Latin proclaimed in *Fam.* 21.15 and reiterated in *Sen.* 5.2; the *Triumphus eternitatis* (Triumph of Eternity) in particular draws abundantly on the *Paradiso* and does nothing to conceal Petrarch's immense debt to Dante. The *Trionfi* also attests to the close connection between Petrarch's Latin and his vernacular works.[84] The opening apostrophe in *Rvf* 263 to the "arbor vittoriosa triunfale, onor d'imperadori et di poeti" (Victorious triumphal tree, the honor of emperors and of poets) is only the most obvious of the intertextual elements deliberately connecting the *Trionfi*, his works in praise of the great heroes of antiquity, and the lyric collection.[85]

THREE CROWNS OF FLORENCE

Boccaccio did indeed continue his praise of Dante, as Petrarch encouraged him to do in *Fam.* 21.15. During his late years in Certaldo, he produced two new redactions of the *Trattatello*, the so-called shorter and longer *Compendio*, in which he focuses his praise almost exclusively on Dante's worthiness of the "vernacular palm."[86] His final work was also devoted to Dante: the *Esposizioni sopra la Comedia di Dante* was published from his notes for the lectures he was commissioned to present in Florence beginning in late 1373. On the whole, the *Esposizioni* sound a note more optimistic than that of Petrarch's *Sen.* 5.2 concerning the future of illustrious works, whether in Latin or in the vernacular.[87] Remaining faithful to his aim of affirming the preeminence of both his two "masters," Boccaccio now relies on the praise of poetry itself, which "solamente a' nobili ingegni se stessa concede" (concedes itself only to the noblest minds), to exalt Dante along with Petrarch as modern poets worthy to share the exalted title of *poeta* with the great poets of antiquity. He declares that Petrarch, choosing the path of Latin composition, has filled every land where Latin is known with his "maravigliosa e splendida fama" (marvelous and splendid fame), while Dante, "la luce del cui valore è per alquanto tempo stata nascosa sotto la caligine del volgar materno" (the light of whose merit has for a while been hidden beneath the mist of the maternal vernacular), "è cominciato da grandissimi litterati ad essere disiderato e ad aver caro" (has begun to be sought out and held in high esteem by the greatest of men of letters).[88]

Time, Boccaccio suggests hopefully in the *Esposizioni*, was proving Giovanni del Virgilio mistaken in his claim that only by composing a great poem in Latin could Dante win the acclaim of a deserving audience. Two postscripts to his exchanges with Petrarch on composition in Latin or in the vernacular are particularly suggestive. Very late in life, Petrarch translated Boccaccio's tale of the faithful and devoted Griselda (*Decameron* 10.10) into Latin, so that it could be circulated to what he considered to be its appropriate audience of learned readers, and his enthusiastic praise contributed to heightened interest in the *Decameron* as a whole.[89] And Boccaccio anticipated the judgment of posterity in associating his friend, in a final tribute following his death, with the vernacular poets of love: "Or con Sennuccio e con Cino e con Dante / vivi, securo d'etterno riposo" (Now you live with Sennuccio and Cino and Dante, sure of eternal rest).[90] Over time, the issues of ceremonial poetic coronation and of preeminence so earnestly engaged, each in his own way, by Dante, Petrarch, and Boccaccio gave way to the now-customary designation of the "three crowns of Florence": the image of the city itself crowned with their enduring fame.

NOTES

1. The work, otherwise known as the *Historia Augusta,* covers the period from 1311 until the emperor's death.

2. See Jean Frédéric Chevalier, ed. and trans., in Albertino Mussato, *Ecérinide, Epîtres métriques sur la poésie, Songe* (Paris: Les Belles Lettres, 2000), xii–xiii. On Mussato's spirited epistles defending the exalted status of poetry, see Giorgio Ronconi, *Le origini delle dispute umanistiche sulla poesia (Mussato e Petrarca)* (Rome: Bulzoni, 1976), 17–59.

3. The Latin citation is from Giovanni del Virgilio, Carmen 1 to Dante Alighieri, in Philip H. Wicksteed and Edmund G. Gardner, *Dante and Giovanni del Virgilio* (Westminster: Archibald Constable & Co., 1902), 146. The English translation is from the reprint (New York: Haskell House, 1970), 146–47. Hereafter citations are to the 1970 reprint.

4. Ibid., 149. For the recent struggles that Del Virgilio identifies in mythological guise, see 215–20.

5. Citations and translations of the *Commedia* are from *The Divine Comedy,* trans. Charles S. Singleton (Princeton: Princeton University Press, 1970–75), 3 vols.

6. Michelangelo Picone, "Il tema dell'incoronazione poetica in Dante, Petrarca e Boccaccio," *L'Alighieri* n.s. 25 (2005): 11.

7. *Achilleid* I.8–10; *Purg.* 21.88–90. Picone emphasizes the importance of this evocation of Statius' honors for the theme of poetic coronation that is subsequently sounded throughout the *Paradiso* and inspires both Petrarch and Boccaccio ("Il tema dell'incoronazione poetica," 8).

8. Wicksteed and Gardner, *Dante and Giovanni del Virgilio,* 123–24.

9. Ibid., Carmen 2, 152–57; citation, 155.

10. Cecil Grayson, "*Nobilior est vulgaris*: Latin and Vernacular in Dante's Thought," in *Centenary Essays on Dante, by Members of the Oxford Dante Society* (Oxford: Clarendon, 1965), 73–74.

11. For the episode in Limbo, see *Inf.* 4.73–102.

12. On their "striking analogies and differences," see Wicksteed and Gardner, *Dante and Giovanni del Virgilio,* 123–24.

13. Giovanni Boccaccio, *Trattatello in laude di Dante,* first redaction, in Boccaccio, *Vita di Dante,* ed. Pier Giorgio Ricci (Milan: Mondadori, 2002), paragraphs 87–89. Ricci notes that the "ornamenti poetici" are mentioned in other sources; for instance, the *Ottimo Commento* records that at his funeral Dante was "a guisa di poeta onorato" (*Trattatello* 134 n. 382).

14. "Visum est michi tandem lauream poeticam, quam a teneris annis optaveram, sibi potissimum debere" (*Rerum memorandum libri,* ed. Giuseppe Billanovich, vol. 14 of *Edizione nazionale delle opere di Francesco Petrarca* [Florence: Sansoni, 1943], 1.37.14–16). For other affirmations of Petrarch's early pursuit of the laurel crown, see Ernest H. Wilkins, *The Making of the "Canzoniere" and Other Petrarchan Studies* (Rome: Edizioni di Storia e Letteratura, 1951), 25–27.

15. John Ahern, "What Did the First Copies of the *Comedy* Look Like?" in *Dante for the New Millenium,* ed. Teodolinda Barolini and H. Wayne Storey (New York: Fordham University Press, 2003), 4–5. For evidence of the circulation of the poem in Bologna, see 6–7.

16. See Michele Feo, "Petrarca, Francesco," in *Enciclopedia dantesca,* 6 vols., ed. Umberto Bosco (Rome: Istituto dell'Enciclopedia Italiana, 1973), 4:450–51.

17. See Giuseppe Billanovich in Billanovich and Claudio Scarpati, "Da Dante al Petrarca e dal Petrarca al Boccaccio," in *Il Boccaccio nelle culture e letterature nazionali,* ed. Francesco Mazzoni (Florence: Olschki, 1978), 589–92.

18. The *Rvf* are cited from Robert L. Durling, trans. and ed., *Petrarch's Lyric Poems: The "Rime sparse" and Other Lyrics* (Cambridge, Mass.: Harvard University Press, 1976).

19. Both the addressee of the sonnet and the "new" work to which it refers are disputed. For a review of both questions, see Santagata's notes to the poem in Francesco Petrarca, *Canzoniere,* ed. Marco Santagata (Milan: Mondadori, 1996), 219–23.

20. Wilkins, *The Making of the "Canzoniere,"* 32–33.

21. Giuseppe Mazzotta, *The Worlds of Petrarch* (Durham and London: Duke University Press, 1993), 123.

22. See Aldo Bernardo, *Petrarch, Scipio and the "Africa": The Birth of Humanism's Dream* (Baltimore: Johns Hopkins University Press, 1962), 2–3, 163.

23. On his communications with Bishop Giacomo Colonna, his great patron, and Dionigi da Borgo San Sepolcro, see E. H. Wilkins, *Life of Petrarch* (Chicago: University of Chicago Press, 1961), 25–26. Latin citations are from *Le familiari,* ed. Vittorio Rossi and Umberto Bosco, 4 vols. (Florence: Sansoni, 1933–42); English citations are from *Letters on Familiar Matters,* trans. Aldo S. Bernardo, 3 vols. (Albany: State University of New York Press, 1975; Baltimore and London: Johns Hopkins University Press, 1982–85).

24. *Letters of Old Age. Rerum senilium libri I–XVIII*, 2 vols., trans. Aldo S. Bernardo, Saul Levin, and Reta A. Bernardo (Baltimore: Johns Hopkins University Press, 1992), 2:677.

25. Its aim is to "far coincidere la gloria letteraria con la missione civile del letterato": Marco Ariani, *Petrarca* (Rome: Salerno editrice, 1999), 39.

26. The Latin citation is from Nicola Festa, ed., Francesco Petrarca, *L'Africa* (Florence: Sansoni, 1926), 276. The English translation is from *Petrarch's "Africa"*, trans. Thomas G. Bergin and Alice S. Wilson (New Haven: Yale University Press, 1977), 237. See Stephen Murphy, "Petrarch's *Africa* and the Poets' Dream of Glory," *Italian Quarterly* 9 (1991): 79.

27. Billanovich, "Da Dante al Petrarca e dal Petrarca al Boccaccio," 592.

28. The exiles had hoped that the arrival in Italy of Henry VII, the count of Luxembourg, to be crowned emperor and to assert imperial control over the region against the Guelph League led by Florence, would make possible their return to the city.

29. See E. H. Wilkins, "The Coronation of Petrarch," in *Studies in the Life and Works of Petrarch* (Cambridge, Mass.: Medieval Academy of America, 1955), 300–313.

30. *Epistolae metricae* 2.1, 9, 10, 12 and 16; in 2.9 he writes that the *Africa* was to be dedicated to the king. See Bernardo, *Petrarch, Scipio and the "Africa"*, 88–90.

31. Stephen Murphy, *The Gift of Immortality: Myths of Power and Humanist Poetics* (Madison, Wisc.: Farleigh Dickinson University Press, 1997), 90–91; Murphy notes that Petrarch's contemporaries, including Boccaccio and Coluccio Salutati, affirmed the connection between the *Africa* and the coronation in urging the publication of the poem (91–93).

32. See Carlo Godi, "La 'Collatio Laureationis' del Petrarca nelle due redazioni," *Studi petrarcheschi* n.s. 5 (1988): 1–58.

33. See Jonathan Usher, "Boccaccio ghirlandaio: L'incoronazione universale del *Decameron*," in *Studi sul canone letterario del Trecento: Per Michelangelo Picone*, ed. J. Bartuschat and L. Rossi (Ravenna: Longo, 2003), 148.

34. "Sed me Parnasi deserta per ardua dulcis / raptat amor" (*Georgics* 3.291). In the explication of his first eclogue, addressed to his brother Gherardo, Petrarch represents himself as ardently struggling to scale the hill of Glory in the footsteps of Virgil and Homer (*Fam.* 10.4).

35. *Le metamorfosi/Publio Ovidio Nasone*, Libro I, introd. Gianpiero Rosati, trans. Giovanna Faranda Villa (Milan: Biblioteca Universale Rizzoli, 2001). The English translation is from *The Metamorphoses of Ovid*, Book I, trans. Mary M. Innes (London: Penguin, 1955), 44.

36. See Murphy, *The Gift of Immortality*, 79–82.

37. In a vernacular lyric Petrarch invokes the leaves of the laurel, "sola insegna al gemino valore" (sole ensign of the twin deservings), to witness his suffering occasioned by love (*Rvf* 161, 5–6). It is also repeated in *Ep. met.* 2:10: "Sunt

laurea certa Poëtis / Caesaribusque simul parque est ea gloria utrisque" (Murphy, *The Gift of Immortality,* 81 and n. 42).

38. See Carlo Calcaterra, *Nella selva del Petrarca* (Bologna: Cappelli, 1942), 94–99.

39. On the Ovidian subtext of the earliest "version" of the *Rvf,* see Sara Sturm-Maddox, *Petrarch's Metamorphoses: Text and Subtext in the "Rime sparse"* (Columbia: University of Missouri Press, 1985), 9–38.

40. Both Latin citations are from the following edition: *Secretum,* introd., trans., and notes by Ugo Dotti (Rome: Archivio Guido Izzi, 1993), 144–45; the English translation is from *Petrarch's Secretum,* trans. William H. Draper (London, 1911), 134.

41. Florence, Biblioteca Medicea Laurenziana 29.8. The letter, "Mavortis miles extrenue," is termed by E. H. Wilkins a "pseudo-letter," an "embellished version" of what Boccaccio had heard from Dionigi da Borgo San Sepolcro, who had known Petrarch in Avignon; see Ernest Hatch Wilkins, "Boccaccio's Early Tributes to Petrarch," *Speculum* 38 (1963): 80.

42. *Ep.* XIX, to Pietro Piccolo, in Giovanni Boccaccio, *Opere latine minori,* ed. A. F. Massèra (Bari: Laterza, 1928).

43. Giovanni Boccaccio, *De vita et moribus Domini Francisci Petracchi de Florentia,* ed. Renata Fabbri, in Giovanni Boccaccio, *Tutte le opere,* ed. Vittore Branca (Milan: Mondadori, 2002), 1.897–911. For 1341–42 as the probable date of composition, see Giuseppe Billanovich, *Petrarca letterato. I. Lo scrittoio del Petrarca* (Rome: Edizioni di "Storia e letteratura," 1947), 74–79; Giuseppe Velli, "Il *De vita et moribus domini Francisci Petracchi de Florentia* del Boccaccio e la biografia del Petrarca," *MLN* 102 (1987): 32–38.

44. Billanovich suggests that he may at the time have been unfamiliar with the ambitious project of the *De viris illustribus.* See *Petrarca letterato,* 79.

45. "Laurettam illam allegorice pro laurea corona quam postmodum est adeptus, accipiendam existimo." Boccaccio, *De vita,* in *Opere latine minori,* ed. Massèra, 243.

46. "What in the world do you say?" he demands. "That I invented the splendid name of Laura so that it might be not only something for me to speak about but occasion to have others speak of me; that indeed there was no Laura on my mind except perhaps the poetic one for which I have aspired as is attested by my long and untiring studies?" (*Fam.* 2.9).

47. Cited from Giovanni Boccaccio, *Amorosa Visione,* bilingual edition, trans. Robert Hollander, Timothy Hampton, and Margherita Frankel (Hanover and London: University Press of New England, 1986).

48. Vittore Branca, "Introduction," in *Amorosa Visione,* xiii.

49. See Vittore Branca, *Boccaccio: The Man and His Works,* trans. Richard Monges (New York: New York University Press, 1976), 72–73.

50. For these texts in relation to Boccaccio's "passion for coronations," see Usher, "Boccaccio ghirlandaio," 148–49.

51. Boccaccio, *Opere latine minori,* ed. Massèra, 12–15; see Guido Martellotti, "Dalla tenzone al carme bucolico," *Italia medioevale e umanistica* 7 (1964): 335.

52. The letter is addressed to Uguccione della Faggiuola. For a recent edition see Saverio Bellomo, "Il sorriso di Ilaro e la prima redazione in latino della *Commedia,*" *Studi sul Boccaccio* 32 (2004): 206–9.

53. Giuseppe Billanovich, "La leggenda dantesca del Boccaccio," *Studi danteschi* 27 (1948): 59–75. Bellomo, after a detailed review of the question, associates it with the school of Giovanni del Virgilio, perhaps even with Giovanni himself; see "Il sorriso di Ilaro," 209–35.

54. Massèra, *Opere latine minori,* 96–97. On the dating of the *metrica* see A. F. Massèra, "Di tre epistole metriche boccaccesche," *Giornale dantesco* 30 (1927): 31–36.

55. See Feo, "Petrarca, Francesco," 451.

56. Marco Santagata, *I frammenti dell'anima* (Bologna: Il Mulino, 1993), 201–2; for Petrarch's relations with the Colonna, see 162–65.

57. See Billanovich, *Petrarca letterato,* 238–39; text in Boccaccio, *Vita di Dante.* Carlo Paolazzi assembles the evidence that *Fam.* 21.15 responds, at least in part, to the first version of Boccaccio's life of Dante; see his "Petrarca, Boccaccio, e il *Trattatello in laude di Dante,*" *Studi danteschi* 55 (1983): 165–249.

58. Todd Boli argues instead for a date following Boccaccio's later visit to Petrarch in 1359; see "Boccaccio's *Trattatello in laude di Dante,* or *Dante Resartus,*" *Renaissance Quarterly* 41 (1988): 399 n. 28. For a summary of studies of the complex textual history of the work, see Giovanni Boccaccio, *The Life of Dante (Trattatello in laude di Dante),* trans. Vincenzo Zin Bollettino (New York and London: Garland, 1990), xxi–xxvii.

59. See Victoria Kirkham, "The Parallel Lives of Dante and Virgil," *Dante Studies* 110 (1992): 233–53.

60. Velli, "Il *De vita et moribus domini Francisci Petracchi,*" 35.

61. Boli, "Boccaccio's *Trattatello,*" 389–412.

62. Ibid., 404–7; translations from Bollettino, *The Life of Dante.* Boli demonstrates that Boccaccio's discussion of poetry at this point derives from the "Petrarchan conception of the literary vocation" in Petrarch's letter to his brother Gherardo, *Fam.* 10.4.

63. For this dream in both Boccaccio and Benvenuto da Imola, see Zygmunt G. Barański, "A Note on the Trecento: Boccaccio, Benvenuto, and the Dream of Dante's Pregnant Mother," in *Miscellanea di Studi Danteschi in memoria di Silvio Pasquazi,* 2 vols., ed. Alfonso Paoletta et al. (Naples: Federico & Ardia, 1993), 1:69–82.

64. *Africa,* 9.295–300; trans., 230. See the chapter "Sub lauro mea" in Calcaterra, *Nella selva del Petrarca,* 89–107.

65. "[S]e tanto gli fosse stata la Fortuna graziosa, che egli fosse giammai potuto tornare in Firenze, nella quale sopra le fonti di San Giovanni s'era disposto di coronare" (par. 126).

66. Ahern, "What Did the First Copies . . . Look Like?" 5.

67. Another very interesting letter to Boccaccio in that same year raises again the question of unconscious imitation, suggesting that a degree of discomfort or anxiety may underlie Petrarch's protestation, although the letter directly engages Petrarch's reading of Virgil and Ovid rather than of a vernacular author; see *Fam.* 22.2, "De imitandi lege."

68. Among many recent studies, see Marco Santagata, "Presenze di Dante 'comico' nel *Canzoniere* del Petrarca," now in *Per moderne carte: La biblioteca volgare di Petrarca* (Bologna: Il Mulino, 1990), 25–78; Sturm-Maddox, *Petrarch's Metamorphoses*, 39–94.

69. A particularly salient example is a critical passage in the *Africa*, already noted, concerning poetic ancestors: the scene in which the poet Ennius recounts to the hero Scipio his dream of an encounter with ancient Homer effectively recalls the encounter in *Purgatorio* 21–22 of Statius and Virgil with Dante as their intermediary and interpreter. See Velli, "Il Dante di Francesco Petrarca," in *Petrarca e Boccacccio* [sic]: *Tradizione memoria scrittura*, 2nd ed. (Padua: Antenore, 1995), 68–71, and Marco Baglio, "Presenze dantesche nel Petrarca latino," *Studi petrarcheschi* n.s. 9 (1992): 91–92.

70. On expressions of Petrarch's "aristocratic scorn," see Giuliano Tanturli, "Il disprezzo per Dante dal Petrarca al Bruni," *Rinascimento* 25 (1985): 199, 203–4.

71. In Francesco Petrarca, *Rime, Trionfi e poesie latine*, ed. Ferdinando Neri et al. (Milan and Naples: Ricciardi, 1951), 794.

72. *Ep. met.* 1.1, "ad Barbatum Sulmonensem"; in ibid., 706–11.

73. "Ma nelle *Posteritati* per le rime non c'è posto. Chi potrebbe pensare a queste nugae dinanzi al filosofo morale e allo storico delle antiche gesta?" (Enrico Carrara, "L'Epistola 'Posteritati' e la leggenda petrarchesca," in *Studi Petrarcheschi e altri scritti* [Turin: Bottega d'Erasmo, 1959], 62).

74. This confident judgment is, of course, a tacit admission that he is sufficiently familiar with Dante's works to make such an assessment.

75. Paolazzi, "Petrarca, Boccaccio, e il *Trattatello*," 183.

76. Bernardo, *Letters of Old Age*, 1:157–66.

77. Latin citations from this letter are from the following edition: *Francesco Petrarca Le senili*, ed. and trans. Ugo Dotti (Turin: Aragno, 2004), 582.

78. See E. H. Wilkins, *The "Epistolae metricae" of Petrarch* (Rome: Edizioni di Storia e Letteratura, 1956), 29. The *metrica* was sent with Petrarch's epitaph for King Robert.

79. Bernardo, *Letters of Old Age*, 1:160. This and other references suggest, although the evidence is not conclusive, that Petrarch knew Dante's Latin treatise on vernacular eloquence, the *De vulgari eloquentia*. For the known dissemination of the work in the fourteenth century, see Pier Vincenzo Mengaldo, *Linguistica e retorica di Dante* (Pisa: Nistri-Lischi, 1978), 23–25. See also Zygmunt G. Barański, "The Constraints of Form: Towards a Provisional Definition of Petrarch's *Triumphi*," in *Petrarch's Triumphs: Allegory and Spectacle*, ed. Konrad Eisenbichler and Amilcare A. Iannucci (Ottawa: Dovehouse Editions, 1990), 70–71.

80. In 1360, the year following his first exchange of letters with Boccaccio about Dante, Petrarch had released for circulation a new, reordered and expanded form of his lyric "fragments" (Vaticano Chigiano L. V. 176); in 1373, the year before his death, another expanded form was sent to Pandolfo Malatesta, and yet other additions followed.

81. For this identification see, among others, Umberto Bosco, *Francesco Petrarca* (Bari: Laterza, 1971), 216.

82. The *Triumph of Love*, in *The Triumphs of Petrarch*, trans. Ernest Hatch Wilkins (Chicago: University of Chicago Press, 1962), 28, 30.

83. Barański, "The Constraints of Form," 72–73.

84. See Amilcare A. Iannucci, "Petrarch's Intertextual Strategies in the *Triumphs*," in *Petrarch's Triumphs: Allegory and Spectacle*, ed. Konrad Eisenbichler and Amilcare A. Iannucci (Ottawa: Dovehouse Editions, 1990), 3–10.

85. Sara Sturm-Maddox, "*Arbor vittoriosa triunfale*: Allegory and Spectacle in the *Rime* and the *Trionfi*," in *Petrarch's Triumphs: Allegory and Spectacle*, ed. Konrad Eisenbichler and Amilcare A. Iannucci (Ottawa: Dovehouse Editions, 1990), 113–34. For the association of the laurel with the triumphal motif, see 128–29.

86. Ibid., 214–28. Ricci comments on the attenuation of the identification of poetry and theology in the later versions (*Vita di Dante*, xiii–xv).

87. Giorgio Padoan, *L'ultima opera di Giovanni Boccaccio: Le "Esposizioni sopra il Dante,"* Pubblicazione della Facoltà di lettere e filosofia, Università di Padova, 34 (Padua: Cedam, 1959), 36–40; translations mine.

88. Giovanni Boccaccio, *Esposizioni sopra la Comedìa di Dante*, ed. Giorgio Padoan (Milan: Mondadori, 1965); translations mine. The scorn in Giovanni del Virgilio's warning to Dante not to "cast his pearls before swine" nonetheless reasserted itself in the accusation to Boccaccio that he had wronged the Muses by undertaking to make high poetry more accessible to the "volgo"; Boccaccio devoted four sonnets (*Rime* 122–25) to his response. See Giorgio Padoan, "Il Boccaccio 'fedele' di Dante," in *Il Boccaccio le Muse il Parnaso e l'Arno* (Florence: Olschki, 1978), 239; Luigi Surdich, *Boccaccio* (Bari: Laterza, 2001), 288.

89. *De Obedientia ac Fide Uxoria, Sen.* 17.3. See Branca, *Boccaccio: The Man and His Works*, 172–73.

90. *Rime* CXXVI, 9–10; translation mine. On this and other responses by Boccaccio to Petrarch's death, see Branca, *Boccaccio: The Man and His Works*, 188–90.

CHAPTER 9

Places and Times of the Liturgy from Dante to Petrarch

RONALD L. MARTINEZ

IN A CELEBRATED LETTER, *FAMILIARES* 6.2, PETRARCH RECOUNTS perambulations with the Dominican Giovanni Colonna through Rome, possibly shortly after the poet's coronation on 8 April 1341.[1] In the letter, which has long been taken as in some sense marking the "beginning of the Renaissance," a review of locations marking the history of ancient Rome is followed by a run of places known for miracles and martyrdom; the effect is to register the transformation of the pagan city into the capital of Christendom.[2] The reported walks, surveying monuments both within and without the Aurelian walls (Sta. Agnese, for example), are implausible, and scholars rightly insist that they reflect Petrarch's reading as much as his walking. Yet, although Petrarch rehearses Aeneas' visit to the site of Rome in the *Aeneid* and evokes the ancient Roman *via Triumphalis* leading to the Capitol,[3] it is likely that the more immediate models for his progresses were Christian. The oldest Roman public progress, the papal *possessio*, part of the papal coronation ceremony since the ninth century, had been suspended after Pope Clement V in 1305 snubbed Rome as the papal seat.[4] More recent, and still vivid in memory, were the routes followed by the Jubilee pilgrims of 1300 in obtaining plenary indulgences.[5] But most familiar would have been the stational liturgies of Advent and Easter, when the pope offered Mass on specified days and in specified churches in the city.

Already centuries old in Petrarch's day, stational liturgies had grown and persisted because of a need, resembling that of the *possessio* itself, to extend the presence and authority of the bishop of Rome into the *disabitato,* the sparsely inhabited parts of the city where a number of ancient titular churches were located, as well as to the great basilicas without the walls.[6] Through such a processional liturgy, the consecration and shaping of mere durative time effected by the liturgy with the reenactment of the life of Christ *in illo tempore* could be extended to the city's geography: stational processions disseminated to the entire city a consistent liturgical order anchored in St. Peter's and in the Lateran. In the case of Petrarch's letter, too, what begins as an excursion through an imagined ancient Rome winds up as a pilgrimage to martyrs' tombs.[7]

Not that Petrarch's routes duplicate or even substantially overlap known processional itineraries — although some six of the dozen Christian sites Petrarch mentions do figure on published stational lists, while others, it has been noted, are found in the *Mirabilia urbis Romae,* a text designed for pilgrims.[8] Petrarch's letter rather establishes his and Colonna's personal memories of Roman and Christian monuments as the basis for reimagining Rome as a Christian city resting on pagan foundations.[9] And as Rome has become Christian, as Augustus has foreseen the birth of Christ and the foundation of Sta. Maria in Aracoeli, so Petrarch himself, though saturated with classical learning, claims he is nevertheless fully a disciple of Christ. The beginning of the letter, in which Petrarch maintains that his Christian faith transcends three classical philosophical sects, prepares the final section, in which Petrarch wrestles evasively with Colonna's request that the poet's magisterial lectures on the liberal and mechanical arts, delivered while contemplating the city from the roof of the Basilica of Maxentius, might be set down in writing. That Petrarch should put off his friend's request by protesting his need for the leisure in Vaucluse if he is to embark on such a formidable task hints at the demanding labor of synthesizing the history of Rome and the *summa* of learning; however, it does not call into question the implication that this is Petrarch's job, for which the letter serves as a kind of propaedeutic.[10]

Thus, in a Rome desolate due to the Avignon papacy and the economic decline of the fourteenth century, and in lieu of the abrogated *possessio* (or, we could add, in lieu of an imperial coronation, which would not occur until that of Charles IV in 1355), Petrarch and Colonna fashion, first in their conversations, and then in Petrarch's text, a memory-theater of pagan and Christian *loca sancta*. The poet appropriates rituals of the medieval Church for a private processional liturgy on behalf of a greater, imaginary Rome whose refounders are Colonna and Petrarch himself, with Petrarch assigning to himself principal responsibility for antiquity, and to Colonna, a Dominican, responsibility for the Christian centuries.[11] The first line of the letter ("Deambulabamus Rome soli") inaugurates a series of three imperfects that articulate the letter,[12] marking it as both a spatial excursion and an iteration of rhetorical places. Writing of the stational liturgy as a memorial system, Mary Carruthers observes that "the journey thus provided a walk-through, in processional order, of the city as memorized network, for clergy, laity, and neophytes alike. Each basilica was a node of this network, a site for memory-making: and at other seasons other churches were incorporated into the stational schemata."[13] Carruthers also calls attention to the traditional homology between rhetorical *ductus*, the way a written passage "marches on" through figure and trope, and the conduct of processions and liturgies: that is, she writes, "the concept of *ductus* nourished not only meditation but also the public rhetoric of the liturgy 'mapped' within the architectural complexes of the monastic church and cloister."[14]

Petrarch's letter accordingly begins with his self-comparison to the Peripatetics whose "wanderings" were also philosophical discussions (*Fam.* 6.2.1: "meum quidem obambulandi perypateticum morem nosti" [you are indeed acquainted with my peripatetic habit]), and indeed his text realizes the homology of rhetorical and ambulatory *ductus* in an exemplary way: not only the imperfects noted above, but terms such as *procedo* (6.2.4) and *quo pergo* (6.2.14), refer to both discursive and physical mobility, as do the reiterated demonstratives *hic, hoc* (e.g., 6.2.5: "hic Evandri regia" [here was the palace of Evander]) for the various *loca sancta* of Roman and Christian antiquity, simultaneously the *loci citati* of Petrarch's reading and scholarship.[15] The "place" itself evokes Petrarch's eloquence (6.2.17, "ipse locus hortabatur" [the very place encouraged me]); and only the place itself can recall it (6.2.18, "redde mihi locum, illud otium, illam diem" [Give me back that place, that idle mood, that day]). Memory, place, and discourse are indivisible, and they entail, in the great summary that Colonna desires of Petrarch, an entire curriculum, an entire history. The appropriation of a stational liturgical procession to Petrarch's discursive reconstruction of Rome sacralizes both the spatial and temporal dimensions of the city; yet, as the last part of the letter makes plain, recovery of the memorial "places" of Rome—*de locis insignibus urbis Rome,* reads the rubric of Petrarch's letter—ultimately depends solely on the knowledge, will, and industry of Petrarch the author.

Yet in dividing the proposed scholarly labor of recovering Rome with Giovanni Colonna di Gallicano, a Dominican, Petrarch adumbrates a distinction between his own brand of philological humanism, focused on the classics, and the religiously oriented culture of Colonna. In a sense that will occupy us considerably in this chapter, the division of labor marks Petrarch's need to distinguish himself from the religious vocation and perspective even as he was drawn to it and to those who practiced it.[16]

From any perspective, Petrarch's *reductio ad seipsum* of both the survival of ancient Rome and its secular traditions of public ritual is a bold stroke. It is one for which the only possible precedent in the fourteenth century is the case of Dante, where, in works both in Latin and the vernacular, a systematic appropriation of poetic, philosophical, and theological authority is achieved.[17] Indeed, returning to the beginning of the letter, Petrarch's positioning of himself between ancient philosophy and the truth of the Resurrection that the pagan philosophers unhappily never knew, is a gesture reminiscent of *Convivio* 3.22.14−18. In that passage, Dante compares philosophical sects to the three Marys of Mark 16.1−7 who approach the sepulchre early on Easter Sunday,[18] only to be informed that Christ has preceded them into Galilee—by which Dante establishes that the Stoics, Epicureans, and Academic philosophies, signifying the virtues of the active life, fell short of reaching the goal of beatitude, attainable only through the exercise of the intellectual virtues.[19] Dante's text is itself in part dependent on liturgical sources, for his account features the two texts, Mark 16.1−7 and Matthew 28.1−7, that furnish the gospel readings and Antiphons for Matins and Lauds and the Vigil Mass on Easter eve and Mass on Easter Sunday. But Dante's choice of biblical episodes for his parable of philosophers on the hunt for truth is also the scene familiar to Christians since at least the tenth century as the *Quem quaeritis* dialogue dramatized during the nocturnal Office of Easter Sunday, a text often claimed as the prototype of medieval drama.[20] Dante's philosophical allegory might be thought of as a trope on the liturgical trope: in the *Convivio* scriptural characters are played not by deacons and canons, as in *Quem quaeritis* performances, but by representatives of the pagan philosophical sects; but it is important to note that Dante's freedom in adapting the scriptural text derives in part from the license implied by the tropes themselves.[21] Petrarch's discriminations resemble Dante's distantiation of the philosophical sects from beatitude ("lo salvatore"),[22] and the later poet focuses not on the scriptural scene at the tomb but on the larger transformation of Rome's fabric from pagan to Christian.[23] Although Petrarch's direct knowledge of Dante's *Convivio* is unlikely, for my purposes here the letter to Colonna exemplifies how Petrarch assimilates the collective practices of the liturgy to his self-construction (and self-promotion) as a man of letters, and how this assimilation is, somewhat paradoxically, filtered through what will prove to be predominantly Dantean precedents in adapting liturgy to literary compositions.[24]

Of course, Petrarch did not need Dante to teach him how to assimilate and adapt liturgical and paraliturgical texts, practices, and gestures to a literary project: this makes his adherence to Dante's example the more striking, as I hope my argument will show. Despite Petrarch's sporadic fulfillment of the duties of the clerical benefices (canonries, an archdeaconate) from which he obtained his living, he knew intimately the liturgy of the Mass and Office as well as more specialized rituals.[25] Moreover, we know that his acquaintances and places of residence put him in frequent contact with the religious life and its liturgy. During his residences in Milan Petrarch resided next to Sant'Ambrogio and San Simplicio, whose services he could overhear, and twice visited a Carthusian establishment nearby in Garegnano, where he attended devotions with the brothers; in Padua his residence was in the Cathedral close.[26] Indeed, Petrarch's spatial and experiential proximity, but stubborn moral marginality, to the professed religious life is a persistent theme in his life and work, even a constitutive aspect of his peculiar subjectivity, and has been well described,[27] although the role of liturgy has in this respect been touched upon only briefly.[28]

Although Petrarch counted among his friends and correspondents members of nearly all the religious orders in existence at the time,[29] the role of liturgy in shaping the schism of Petrarch's inner life is most dramatically manifest in the course of his relations with his brother Gherardo.[30] Because Gherardo had once been a sighing lover like Petrarch himself,[31] Gherardo's vocation as a Carthusian *renditus* in 1343 defined the path of renunciation that Petrarch might have, but did not, take. In letters to Gherardo (*Fam.* 10.3–5), in the first eclogue of the *Bucolicum carmen,* and allegorically in the letter on the ascent of Mount Ventoux (*Fam.* 4.1.9–13), Petrarch represents Gherardo's cenobitic life as the virtuous leg of the Pythagorean *bivium* or crossroads of moral choice.[32] Yet Petrarch kept the strict religious life within striking distance. In his treatise *De vita solitaria,* he juxtaposes the anxious cares of a man of the world with the tranquillity of the solitary who is punctual in singing the daily Office.[33] When a canon living within the cathedral in Padua, Petrarch was technically required to repeat the daily Office in choir; with respect to other benefices, he had, as a *litteratus,* the option of reciting the Office privately or merely repeating the Psalms.[34]

Material evidence of Petrarch's devotions has survived in the form of the large breviary, bought in Milan, which he bequeathed in his testament to the priest Giovanni da Bocheta and ultimately to the cathedral of Padua.[35] Petrarch's volume, in its present state,[36] includes the Temporal or Office Breviary, Kalendar, choir or ferial Psalter, Sanctoral, Common of Saints, and the Office of the Virgin (incomplete), along with other insertions.[37] Petrarch unquestionably used his breviary, or similar liturgical book, as his correspondence attests. He claims that he kept his psalter under his pillow,[38] and that his settled habit in mature life was to rise at midnight, recite Matins and probably Lauds, and write, often until dawn.[39] Boasting of his moral amendment, he writes to his brother: "I have become so assidous in reciting, thanks to God, the daily and nocturnal praises of Christ, that even during these very short nights dawn has not found me asleep or silent, however exhausted I might be by my long vigils." In the same passage, the poet recalls being singularly pleased by verses from Psalm 118: "I rise at midnight to confess to you" and "Seven times in the day I have said your praises."[40] Indeed, reciting the Office linked him with his brother Gherardo's monastic habits, especially when doing so at the hour when, as Petrarch says, we are most in solidarity with Christ because he endured his scourging at that hour.[41] Such penitential moments represented Petrarch's daily confrontation with the divergent loves for which Augustine chastises Franciscus in the *Secretum,* the "two adamantine chains" of his cultivation of letters in pursuit of fame and the obsession with Laura.[42]

Both in his letters to Gherardo and allegorically in the first Eclogue, Petrarch juxtaposed his errant erotic pursuit to the living example set by his brother and, at the level of literature, by the rougher and ruder but ultimately nobler and more beautiful text of the Psalms, that is, of the liturgy.[43]

Indeed, so focused was Petrarch on the Office as a fulcrum of his relation-ship to his brother that he represents his divergence from Gherardo's com-mitment as their dissonant singing of a psalm verse (commonly used both as an Antiphon at Tuesday Vespers and as a Versicle preceding Confession). It is as if their diverging destinies were incompatible uses in performing the Office. Wondering how their paths diverged, Petrarch writes: "what other reason can it be if not that, our bonds having been equally broken, what fol-lowed was unequal: 'our help in the name of the Lord'? Why have we con-cluded in such discord this Davidic Psalm begun in such harmony?"[44] That the psalm verse in question plays a part in the ordination ceremonies of clerics may explain Petrarch's use of it to mark the differences of his life as a mere tonsured cleric from Gherardo's severe discipline.[45] In defining his relationship to Gherardo and to regular clergy in general, Petrarch con-structed a chiasmus, persistently characterizing the religious, who are in fact bound by a rule, as free of bondage, but thinking of himself as bound.[46] There are several such instances in Petrarch's long letter recalling his life to-gether with his brother before Gherardo's turn to the contemplative life.[47]

We will see later how this dissonance drives Petrarch to frame his wish to escape his attachment to Laura in the terms of the desire of the ancient just to be freed from their confinement in Limbo. For the present, if it is true, as Albert Ascoli argues in this volume, that Monicus—that is, Gherardo—is in Petrarch's first Eclogue a stand-in for "moral Dante," Petrarch's juxta-position of his own errancy to the firmness of Gherardo would suggest a complex relationship to Dante's focused moral engagement as a writer.[48] And since Gherardo advocates that Silvius, that is, Petrarch, read the Psalms of David rather than Virgil or Homer, the Eclogue might be interpreted as Petrarch's disguised wrestling with Dante's exemplary status as author of the *poema sacro,* a poem in which David appears as "cantor dello spirito santo" (*Par.* 20.38) and thus as a model for Dante's poem insofar as it, too, is a kind of *teodia* (*Par.* 25.73), which, like the Psalms, transcends comedy and tragedy.[49] The fact that David is a *cantor* and that the suffix of *teodia* speci-fies song, *cantus,* reminds us that David's psalmody is sung, is liturgical. In-deed, in the *Commedia,* David's appearance as "umile salmista" as he dances before the Ark alludes to his role in establishing liturgical music and song,[50] and Petrarch's first Eclogue specifies that David's psalmody is liturgical be-cause it is nocturnal (the reference is to Matins, the most elaborate noctur-nal Office).[51]

Despite Silvius-Petrarch's stated deferral of attention to psalmody in the first Eclogue, Petrarch the author probably took up the Davidic option before completing the *Bucolicum carmen* in 1347,[52] given that his sample of Davidic poetry in *Ecl.* 1.91–109 is textually close to the fourth of the seven penitential psalms that he composed before 1350. Thought by some scholars to have been stimulated by Gherardo's vocation in 1343, the *Salmi* were ultimately sent to Sagremor de Pommiers upon his entrance into the Cistercian order, along with a copy of the *De otio religioso* that had been composed for and dedicated to Gherardo and the Carthusians.[53] Petrarch's psalms were, readers agree, inspired by the seven penitential psalms of the liturgy (Pss. 6, 31, 37, 50, 101, 129) typically recited during Lent, during rituals of penance, and in connection with the Offices for the sick, the dying, and the dead. Centered on the *Miserere* (Ps. 50) and drawn from the whole span of psalms, the traditional seven penitentials are a microcosm of the Psalter itself, though slanted toward penitence rather than praise. Indeed, the idea of a sevenfold recitation of psalms was thought to be at the origin of the Hours of the Office itself, as Petrarch well knew; along with the reference to nocturnal rising to praise God mentioned above, Petrarch cites in writing to Gherardo the passage from Ps. 118.164 that suggests seven occasions of praise during the day: "So much was I pleased by the words of the Psalmist: 'Seven times I have praised you during the day' that since I took up this habit no activity has distracted me from it, not even once." The two passages were traditionally taken to refer to the totality of the noctural and diurnal Office.[54] That Petrarch's seven psalms preserve their relationship to the liturgical singing of the psaltery is confirmed by Petrarch's use, as if in a Choir Psalter used in the liturgy, of the new doxology to end his versions ("Gloria patri . . . sicut in principio," etc.), whereas the scriptural book of Psalms is traditionally articulated by the Old Testament doxology.[55]

The internal ordering of the material in Petrarch's versions echoes, with creative variation, some of the emphases that conventionally organize the seven penitentials.[56] In the traditional seven, the fourth and central one, Psalm 50, the *Miserere*, is preceded by three psalms pleading for divine leniency (the first and third begin with "ne in furore tuo arguas me" [punish me no more in your anger]) and is followed by three that beg God to hearken to his petitioner (each begins, or nearly, "Exaudi orationem meam" [Lord, hear my prayer]). In Petrarch's series the fourth and central psalm offers a hymn of praise for the creation and the Creator's provision for his creatures—much like the material attributed to David by Monicus in Petrarch's first Eclogue—surrounded by two groups of three psalms. This does not, however, diminish the import of the penitential cry *Miserere*, given that the first Petrarchan psalm begins and ends with a similar expression ("Heu michi misero"), and this sentiment is echoed throughout the series, such that the *Miserere*, the central of the seven penitential psalms, marks the incipit and defines the recurring theme of Petrarch's suite.[57] The other recurring emphasis in the series is Petrarch's plea to be rescued from his moral abyss in terms that suggest the Office for the Dead and Christ's rescue of the just from Hell; this implicit narrative in Petrarch's representation of his moral life will concern me in detail below.[58]

Petrarch's was not the first adaptation of penitential psalmody by an individual author, though it did begin the fashion of such personalized versions.[59] A likely precedent is found in the distribution through Dante's penitential *Purgatorio* of phrases from seven different psalms.[60] Dante's system is organized around three appearances of verses from the *Miserere*, the "central" penitential psalm, such that there are seven psalms employed, but nine instances of psalm use overall (a detail doubtless pleasing to the author). The symmetrical arrangement of the seven penitentials is suggested for Dante's grouping in *Purgatorio* by having the psalm verses fall into two groups divided by a central instance consisting of a single word, *Delectasti*, drawn from Psalm 91, in praise of the Creator and His creation. This use of Psalm 91 may have inspired Petrarch's choice of his fourth and central psalm, which treats, we saw, a similar theme. Moreover, if the first and last of Dante's psalm fragments are excluded (that is, those from Psalms 113 and 78, with "historical" references to the Exodus and the Babylonian captivity), the central seven psalm citations, beginning with the *Miserere* sung in *Purg.* 5.24, form a system dominated by the three verses drawn from Psalm 50, and which, in conjunction with the incipit of Psalm 31 ("beati quorum tecta sunt peccata" [Happy the sinner whose fault is removed]), includes a verse from a traditional penitential psalm in the first, third, fifth, and final positions.[61] In this way, both Dante and Petrarch reflect the mixture of penitence and praise that characterizes the book of Psalms as a whole.

Much more work is needed on Petrarch's expressive and parodic uses of liturgical allusion, but a number of passages in Petrarch's letters have been identified where liturgical allusion is clearly material to the meaning expressed in the letter. Writing in the *Familiares* (13.6) to Francesco Nelli, Petrarch sarcastically refers to the pact by which Emperor Charles IV handed Cola di Rienzo over to Pope Innocent IV for prosecution as "mirum commercium" (astonishing exchange), thereby altering the words beginning the Antiphon for the feasts of the Circumcision and the Purification, "O admirabile commercium," referring to the Incarnation, by which divine and human came to be one in Christ.[62] Petrarch's explicit parody of the liturgy—he refers in the passage to the balance of the Antiphon, which he neither dares nor wishes to repeat—mocks how the two chief authorities in Europe, so often rivals, are for once unanimous in denying Cola his freedom.[63] This vein of Petrarchan satire is most abundantly represented in the *Liber Sine nomine,* the invectives against the contemporary Babel of Avignon that Petrarch left unsigned and without identified addressees. The seventh letter, in which Petrarch expresses his enthusiasm for the possible rescue of Italy, is entirely constructed around scriptural allusions, including Psalm 43.23, "Exurge domine, quare obdormis" (Arise, why sleepest thou, O Lord), which furnishes the Mass introit for Sexagesima Sunday, where, appropriately enough for Petrarch's *Sine nomine,* it alludes, along with that liturgy as a whole, to the widowhood of the Church.[64] Petrarch concludes the letter with what is perhaps the most familiar liturgical phrase of all, the plea to God to help his devotee—"Domine in adiutorium meum intende" (God, come to my assistance)—from the dialogue between priest and chorus that begins Matins and possibly every hour of the Office: again, Petrarch calls attention to the liturgical formula: "Adesto, spes nostra, et, quod quotidie iteramus, in adiutorium nostrum intende ac festina!" (Be with us, our hope, and as we say every day, hasten to our aid!).[65] As in the curious collection of the *Sine nomine* generally, Petrarch here grafts onto the communal discourse of the liturgy an explicitly personal communication and petition, which nevertheless circulates without his signature, a gesture that at once protected Petrarch and his correspondents from reprisal and aggrandized the authorial voice as an impersonal witness, an everyman who spoke as the conscience of Italy. The Dantean model that Petrarch emulates is unmistakable: the extraordinary authorial digression in *Purg.* 6.70–139, where the contiguous verse from Psalm 43.25 ("quare faciem tuam avertis" [Why do you hide your face]) is applied to Italy's political sorrows: "son li occhi tuoi rivolti altrove?" (6.120) and indeed to the widowed state of Rome (6.112–13, "Roma che piange / vedova e sola").[66]

Such a rhetorical use of the liturgical text to at once depersonalize and authorize Petrarch's voice also informs his shrewd use of the Sanctoral in the massive letter of 1366, constituting an entire book of the *Seniles* (bk. 7), urging Urban V to return to Rome. The letter is an archive of devices that might persuade a recalcitrant Avignon pope to come home, but the final, exquisite touch is Petrarch's dating of the letter on the 29th of June, the feast of Saints Peter and Paul, to which Petrarch had already called attention in the body of the letter by vividly imagining the pope's delight in celebrating the liturgy in the city of the apostles on a day peculiarly flattering to the papacy.[67] But it is not merely flattering. Petrarch is also calling Urban's attention to the sacrifices made by the patron saints and protectors of the city, who had both, according to tradition, laid down their lives for the Church, for the *sponsa Christi*, on that same day. Their sacrifices are recalled in the liturgical texts, as is Peter's liberation from the Mamertine prison by the angel of the Lord—circumstances that Petrarch wanted Urban to keep firmly in mind as the pontiff considered freeing himself from the toils of Avignon.[68]

On a larger scale, affecting important works such as the *Triumphi* and the *Canzoniere*, is Petrarch's adaptation of aspects of the liturgy of Advent and of the Harrowing of Hell. Like his contemporaries, Petrarch knew well the text of Isaiah 9.2, "populus qui ambulabat in tenebras, vidit lucem magnam; habitantibus in regione umbrae mortis, Lux orta est eis" (the people who walked in darkness have seen a great light; a light has dawned for those dwelling in the land of the shadow of the dead). This text is recited in modified form to herald the approach of the Redeemer in the liturgy of Advent, both in the antiphon "O oriens" to the Magnificat at Vespers on 21 December, and as a reading at Christmas Matins.[69] As liturgical commentary made clear, included among those who "walked in darkness" were the just souls awaiting their redeemer in the darkness of Limbo.[70] Petrarch adopts the earlier part of the same verse—"for those who inhabit the region of the shadow of death, a light has dawned"—to begin the last chapter of the *De otio religioso*, the book he dedicated to Gherardo, in order to mark that goal of human desire to which the Carthusian monks of Montrieux are clearly devoted, but which was denied to the philosophers of antiquity,[71] as it was to Dante's *spiriti magni* in Limbo. Petrarch uses the text from Isaiah again for the first few verses of the first *Triumphus*, when the triumphal car of Amor first strikes the speaker's eyes:

Ivi fra l'erbe, già del pianger fioco,
vinto dal sonno, *vidi una gran luce,*
e dentro assai dolor con breve gioco.
    Vidi un vittorioso e sommo duce,
pur com'un di color che 'n Campidoglio
triumfal carro a gran gloria conduce.
            (*Triumphus cupidinis* 1.10–15;
            emphases mine)

The irony of Petrarch's use is obvious: the light breaking is not that of Christ's Advent to souls imprisoned in Limbo, but the light of Amor's triumph, arriving like a victorious general who will subject the speaker to the love of Laura. The passage as Petrarch has it contrasts not only with Advent liturgy but with passages in Dante that rely on that liturgy. Petrarch's "di pianger fioco" echoes the pilgrim's first sight of Virgil, "chi per lungo silenzio parea fioco" (*Inf.* 1.63),[72] and the subsequent sight of Limbo, where only a small light shines (*Inf.* 4.68–69: "foco / ch'emisperio di tenebre vincia"), but where the victorious Christ had once come, as Virgil reports, to harrow souls from Hell: "vidi un possente, di segno di vittoria coronato" (*Inf.* 4.53–54).[73]

Although the most recent commentary on the *Triumphi* dismisses as "merely verbal" a liturgical or scriptural influence on Petrarch's "una gran luce," Marco Ariani justifiably annotates the words as a translation of Isaiah's verse.[74] Given that the very first lines of the *Triumphi* evoke the Good Friday inception of Petrarch's love ("quel giorno / che fu principio a sí lunghi martiri," *TC* 1.2–3), the presence of other liturgical allusion seems anything but farfetched. And as later discussion will show, the narrative of Christ descending to Hell to liberate the souls in Limbo was a significant constant in Petrarch's construction of his own persistent need for liberation from the "adamantine chains" that bound him to Laura and to the pursuit of fame. There is thus good reason to think that the text of Isaiah 9.2, and the narrative of Christ liberating the just from Hell, were much on Petrarch's mind as he began the *Triumphi.*

Like the other works studied thus far, the *Triumphi* adapt liturgical loci already filtered through precedents established by Dante. For example, Dante's account of the *Paternoster* in *Purgatorio* 11.1 ("Padre nostro *che nei cieli stai*") is minimally modified by Petrarch for the second hemistich of *Triumphus mortis* 1.70 ("Come piace al Signor *che'n cielo stassi*"), and the account at *Triumphus cupidinis* 4.49–51 of the poet Folco di Marsiglia, also a character in Dante's *Paradiso,* as one who changed for the better at the end of life ("ed a l'estremo / cangiò per miglior patria abito e stato") echoes the tardy conversions of characters in the *Purgatorio,* including a poet like Guinizelli (*Purg.* 26.93: "per ben dolermi prima ch'a lo stremo").[75] The protagonist's vision of Beatrice's death in the *Vita nuova,* which commentators have identified as informing the account of Laura's passing in *Triumphus mortis* 1.141–56, is more extensively overhauled.[76] Dante's account is informed by the liturgy for the dying, and the same prayers commending the soul (*commendatio animae*), which call for the dying to be spared affliction by Satan, determine Petrarch's reference to the absence of demons at Laura's deathbed (*TM* 1.154–55: "Nesun de gli adversarii fu sí ardito / ch'apparisse già mai con vista oscura").[77] The implicit narrative of Petrachan bondage to Laura that winds its way through the first three of the *Triumphi* will return to concern us further below.

With its structure of superseding pageants culminating in the triumphs of Time and Eternity, the *Triumphi* point to the consciousness of labile temporal existence as the absolutely dominant theme of Petrarch's work, including of course the collection of vernacular lyrics conventionally referred to as the *Canzoniere.* The articulation of the collection in terms of anniversary poems that mark the thirty-one years of the poet's bondage (of which twenty-one years are during Laura's lifetime, beginning on Good Friday 1327); the spacing throughout the collection of the nine sestine, whose form evokes traditional numerological understanding of the number six as symbolizing human embeddedness in time; and recurring references to years, days and nights, hours, and moments (*Rvf* 211, 12–13: "Mille trecento ventisette, a punto / su l'ora prima, il dì sesto d'aprile") are familiar to readers. If Petrarch could conceive the space and time of both ancient and Christian Rome mapped in the terms of stational liturgy, he was even more explicitly aware of how the temporal year, and this includes the numerical "year" of the 366-poem *Canzoniere,* might be shaped by the feasts and seasons of the liturgy. Indeed, studies have shown that the central organizational datum of the collection and the foil to the poet's entire career of devotion to Laura is the Christian calendar, centered on the Good Friday commemoration of the Passion.[78] More recently, the full extent of Petrarch's use of the Lamentations text, recited during the Thursday, Friday, and Sat-

urday of Holy Week during the Matins office, has emerged in the work of
Nancy Vickers and others, including the present writer—a use that makes
clear how much Petrarch also depended on Dante's heavily liturgized poetics of mourning for Beatrice in the *Vita nuova*.[79] Thus, in a manner that
has yet to be fully assessed, the space-time of the *Canzoniere* is a paraliturgical one, in which Petrarch elaborates his own private Lauriform liturgy,
his idolatrous psalmody so discordant with that of Gherardo.

The conflict is already implicit in the infrastructure of the collection, so to speak, that is, in the working sheets of Vaticano 3196, where Petrarch characteristically dated his sessions of revision using both Arabic and
Roman numerals of the days of the month, reserving the pure classical system of Kalends, Ides, and Nones for dating the Latin letters of the well-
arranged *Familiares* and *Seniles*. Petrarch's use of this latter system has been
seen as the deliberately archaizing reimposition of classical custom. But
in fact the classical system was immediately at hand for Petrarch in the
Kalendars of missals, breviaries, and Books of Hours, where they typically
stood at or near first place. Although medieval Kalendars almost never list
the days with Arabic notation, it takes but a glance to reckon that 29 June
is the third day before the Kalends of July, which is how Petrarch signs
his letter to Pope Urban V (*Sen.* 7.1).[80] What is more, Petrarch's notations
of work done in Vat. 3196 identify the time of day or night largely in terms
identical to those for canonical hours (*mane, prima, tertia, nona, vespere, sero,
nocte*, etc.).[81] To be sure, he could hardly do otherwise in the absence of any
other complete system for dividing up the day: the point is that as Petrarch
worked on his poems about Laura he had before him as well the nomen-
clature of the canonical hours, which also entailed his habit of reciting the
Office, of recalling the stages of Christ's life as they corresponded to the
Hours, and of comparing his life with Gherardo's. With no prejudice to
the fundamental importance of Good Friday, we have seen to what extent
the daily Hours of Matins and Lauds focus Petrarchan crises of affect. The
liturgical parsing of time implicitly challenged the poet's attachment to
Laura, the *laudes* he paid to her rather than to God. These Petrarchan sen-
sitivities have manifold consequences for the *Canzoniere*.

Liturgical contexts inform what we might call cardinal points in the
collection: the opening sonnet, the canzone beginning the second part,
and the canzone "Vergine bella," naturally rich in reference to prayers to
and liturgical texts about the Virgin, and which in Valeria Bertolucci's

view rededicates the collection to her.[82] In this context, the balance of this chapter will focus on the poems in the collection that juxtapose Petrarch's erotic bondage and desire for moral freedom in terms of the rivalry between the laurel and the cross. These will include the canzone "I' vo pensando" (*Rvf* 264) and two sestine (*Rvf* 142, 214). Discussions of the four-poem sequence *Rvf* 60–63 and poem 5, the sonnet that analyzes Petrarch's utterance of Laura's name, will serve to characterize the liturgical quality of the whole collection; last of all is a short discussion of "Vergine bella" in terms of its imitation of Dante's poetic appropriation of liturgy.

The canzone opening the second part of the collection, "I' vo pensando," as Alessandro Vellutello recognized, is an anniversary poem, commemorating Good Friday, as clearly indicated by the poet's hopeful sight of the open arms of the crucified (vv. 14–15: "Quelle pietose braccia / in ch'io mi fido, veggio aperte anchora"), which encourage him to achieve a definitive conversion.[83] The image is fundamental in the poem and underpins its icastic emphasis. Petrarch returns to it in the light of his desire to embrace the truth rather than shadows (v. 72: "vorre' 'l ver abbracciar, lassando l'ombre"). The final verse, where he confesses to seeing the better course, but following the worse (v. 136: "veggio 'l meglio, et al peggior m'appiglio"), implicitly reiterates the branches of the Pythagorean lambda dividing his life from Gherardo's, and again echoes the sight of the cross, but affirms a return to the image or idol of Laura, mentioned at line 107 with a traditional vernacular pictorial metaphor for the lady's image (vv. 106–7: "et agli occhi depigne / quella che sol per farmi morir nacque"). The poem draws elaborately on Dante's text, beginning in the first stanza with the image of the crucified, echoing Manfred's hopeful use of the same image in the *Purgatorio* (3.122: "l'etterno amor ha sì gran braccia"). Note that *morir, morte* appear at lines 69 ("dopo la morte"); 89; 107 ("sol per farmi morir"); 126, ending a stanza; and 134 ("co la morte a lato"), uses that inform the poet's contemplation of imminent death (v. 89: "aver la morte inanzi gli occhi parme"). A phrase such as "son forse a l'extremo" (v. 18) suggests that it is again the *Purgatorio*, specifically the acts of repentance of Sapia (*Purg.* 13.124: "in su lo stremo") and Guinizelli (26.93: "prima ch'a lo stremo"), that have furnished Petrarch's need. The poem's emphasis on the competing images of Laura's idol and the cross is rendered by the use of *veggio* or *mirare* in four of the six stanzas, and vividly in the final verse: a frequency that recalls the importance of the sight of the "pietose braccia" on the cross, as sometimes indicated in rubrics of the Good Friday ceremony.[84] And in light of Petrarch's anxieties regarding his own death-day, *l'extremo,* the image of Christ's open arms also evokes the rituals for the reconciling of penitents, rituals that precede those for the sick and dying in thirteenth- and fourteenth-century missals and pontificals.[85] It is no exaggeration to say that the speaker here, as in the *Secretum,* imagines the scene of his own death as a spur to reform.[86] In this sense the rituals for reconciling sinners, the sick, and the dying, along with the Good Friday scenario, are sharply relevant to the poem.

Good Friday and the image of the cross leading the way to conversion is also fundamental to poem 142, hypothesized as immediately preceding 264 even as it concluded the first part of the Correggio version.[87] The sestina concludes by staging again the crisis of the temporal in the moment of choice: "ora la vita breve e 'l loco e 'l tempo / mostranmi altro sentier di gire al cielo" (vv. 34–35). The verse has been debated, with Guglielmo Gorni accepting Bernardo Daniello's sixteenth-century view that the time in question must be Good Friday; it follows that the "place" must be the space before the cross during the Good Friday unveiling of the Cross, accompanied by the singing of the *Pange lingua* Cross hymn, whose relevance to this and related poems Gorni points out. Each term descriptive of the laurel (*amor, frondi, lume, poggi, rami*) has, this critic shows, an implicit equivalent in the Crucifixion scene (the cross, Golgotha, the crown of thorns, and so on). But rather than constituting, as the critic maintains, a metamorphosis of the laurel into the cross or an ideal convergence of the two, the *tornata* in fact steps away from the Cross:

> Altr'amor, altre frondi et altro lume,
> altro salir al ciel per altri poggi
> cerco, ché n'è ben tempo, et altri rami.
> (vv. 37–39)

Describing the Cross and the offer of salvation as *altro,* as if an alien speech or *alieniloquium,* Petrarch suggests he does not yet see the Cross. It remains veiled, as if still in its shroud as presented in the Good Friday veneration ritual.[88] The poet's quotation-translation of "Nunc est tempus acceptabile," "che n'è ben tempo" (v. 39), part of the Advent as well as of the Lenten liturgies,[89] emphasizes that with respect to this sestina Christ is still to come.

The choice presented starkly in sestina 142 becomes a crisis and a petition in sestina 214, which is linked to 142 by Petrarch's scheme of coordinating the sestine across the collection so that initially distant pairings conclude with gemination (22/30, 66/80, 142/214, 237 and 239, and 332, the double sestina). In this sestina, which develops the poet's progress through the ages of man, the rhyme-words *corso* (v. 4: "fatal suo corso") and *sciolta* (vv. 18, 39: "un dì la mente sciolta"; "o l'alma sciolta") focus the conclusion of the poem on Petrarch's oft-reiterated desire to be freed of his attachment to the memory of Laura. This central theme of the collection is most dramatically manifest in the group of poems that surround the notice of Laura's death: in three canzoni and five sonnets, beginning with "I'vo pensando" (*Rvf* 264), and continuing through *Rvf* 271, a sonnet, Petrarch refers to his bondage some dozen times. My sole example here will be *Rvf* 266: "Carità di signore, amor di donna / son le catene che con molti affanni / legato son, perch'io stesso mi strinsi" (vv. 9–11).[90] These bonds are then (but in Laura's case only apparently) broken with the deaths of Laura and of Giacomo Colonna announced in *Rvf* 269 (v. 1: "Rotto è l'alta colonna, e 'l verde lauro"). The links of "I'vo pensando" and the "due cathenae" of the *Secretum* are thus much in evidence through the transition from the first to the second part of the collection.

Returning to sestina 214, which anticipates the nexus of *Rvf* 264–71 in its emphasis on the rhyme-word *sciolto* (in opposition to *nodo*, v. 20; *lacciuoi*, v. 10; *ritenuta*, v. 39), the poet's petition for release conjures the image of Christ reaching out his hand to free the speaker from attachment to his erring loves, figured as the *ombroso bosco*—akin to Dante's *selva oscura*—and to correct his fatal misstep at the *bivium* of choice (the speaker is "usato di sviarne a mezzo 'l corso," v. 15):

Ma Tu, Signor, ch'ài di pietate il pregio,
porgimi la man dextra in questo bosco:
vinca 'l Tuo sol le mie tenebre nove.

               (vv. 28–30)

Still, the last line envisions the risk of his soul remaning bound, "ritenuta al bosco" (v. 39). Implicit in Petrarch's choice of the sestina is the suitability of the form to represent bondage: not only because of the demands of the six rhyme-words, but, as David Quint argues, because of the typically six-

and seven-year intervals of bondage and liberation used in Jewish law, history, and liturgy.[91] Thus a Jew may enslave another Jew for only six years, and must free him at the onset of the seventh; thus Jacob served seven-year stints for Leah and Rachel; thus Israel was enslaved seventy years in Babylon before returning to rebuild the temple.[92] Six- and seven-year sequences of bondage and liberation are also preserved in the Catholic liturgy, which does penance on Septuagesima in anticipation of the escape from Babylon, and on Sexagesima mourns the widowhood of the Church in the absence of the spouse.[93] In the case of Catholic liturgy this is Christ, whom, we saw, is expected to come, wield his strong right arm, and free his people from servitude.

If we search Petrarch's work for the theme of bondage and desired liberation, we find texts at every stage of his career, from the metrical epistles, penitential psalms, private prayers, and *Secretum* to passages in the *Sine nomine, Familiares,* and *Seniles,* that address this issue.[94] We saw the prominence of this theme in Petrarch's letters to his brother, where the image of Christ's right arm snatching up Gherardo is especially conspicuous.[95] Petrarch repeatedly pleads for release from his moral bondage by citing Palinurus' words in the *Aeneid,* as in *Fam.* 23.12.20: "you lack no helper if not that heavenly one: He will be there and extend his right arm to you who labor, every time you call to him in that poetic vein with Christian piety: snatch me away, unconquered one, from these evils."[96] In Petrarch's use of *Aeneid* 6 we can recognize Dante's figuration, in the early cantos of the *Purgatorio,* of Palinurus in the persons of Manfred, Jacopo del Cassero, and Buonconte, a series that concludes with the allusion by Virgil to Palinurus in canto 6.[97] Yet Petrarch's instances also make it clear that he is casting his rescue in terms that allude to Christ's victory over Hell, when those who awaited in hope were freed from Limbo and borne to heaven in triumph.[98] In the liturgy this rescue was recalled, as we saw, at the time of Advent, but also during Matins and Lauds of Holy Saturday, when the harrowing of Hell is commemorated liturgically, and during Matins and Lauds of the Office of the Dead, to express the hopes of the dying of being snatched from the infernal gates.[99] Christ's victory over Hell was given narrative form in the text of the *descensus* section of the Gospel of Nicodemus (well known to Petrarch), both in the original and in versions preserved in the *Legenda aurea* and in the encyclopedia of Vincent of Beauvais.[100] For the liturgies on behalf of the dying and for the Nicodemus text as well, Psalm 23, Isaiah

9.2, and Psalm 106 represent Christ as the victorious combatant, "potens in proelio" (mighty in battle) (Ps. 23.8), who illuminates those who have long dwelt in darkness, "populus qui ambulabat in tenebris vidit lucem magnam" (The people who walked in darkness have seen a great light) (Isa. 9.1); who shatters the brazen gates, "contrivit portas aereas, et vectes ferreos confregit" (broke down the gates of bronze and snapped the bars of iron) (Ps. 106.16), and releases those in Limbo from their bonds, "et vincula eorum disrupit"; and who, extending his hand, draws Adam and the other *iusti* from the cavern of Hell.[101]

Petrarch's versions, taken together, include all principal features of this dramatic narrative. The passage from the *Secretum* is familiar; a single example from Petrarch's daily prayer will suffice: "Erue animam meam ex hoc tartaro, ubi eam vivendo sponte demersi . . . dirige gressus meos in viam pacis. . . . Ostende michi quam invictissimus sis, qui mortem vincentem omnia superasti. . . . Incute nunc vim Spiritus Sancti et dirumpantur vincula mea" (Tear out my soul from this Tartarus where, living, I have willingly immersed it . . . direct my steps in the way of peace . . . show me that you are unconquered, you who by vanquishing death vanquished all . . . send now the strength of the Holy Spirit and let my chains be broken).[102] When quoting Palinurus' plea, Petrarch, using these same three elements — the right hand, the unvanquished hero, the petition for rescue — simultaneously alludes to the liturgically informed Harrowing narrative. Indeed, Petrarch takes erudite pleasure in attaching a Christian dimension to Virgil's text when he does not actually supplement it with Psalms, as in the passage from the *Familiares* quoted above and in the *De otio.*[103] The imperatives *eripe me* (snatch me away), as well as *erue me* (tear me away), are in fact extremely common in the last weeks of Lent and Easter week, when Psalms 30.16, 70.4, 58.1, and 139.1 furnish material for antiphons, responses, tracts, and offertories beginning *eripe me* (Ps. 30.16: "de manu inimicorum mearum" [from the hands of my enemies]; 58.1: "de inimicis meis" [from my enemies]; 139.1: "ab homine malo" [from the wicked]);[104] while *erue me* is used in the Office of the Dead for the petition that Christ free the soul from the gates of Hell.[105] In addition to borrowings from the *Aeneid,* the image, so prominent in the sestina, of the right arm extended is found in the sixth reading from Job in the Office of the Dead at Matins and in the Office of the Dead at Lauds ("Me suscipit dextra" [your right hand defends me]).[106] Indeed, the reading from Job ("manum . . . porriges dexteram" [stretch out your right hand], 14.15) is closer than any other source to Petrarch's phrasing in sestina 214 (v. 29: "porgimi la man dextra"). With the Versicle "Clamantes et dicentes: venisti redemptor noster" (shouting and saying: our redeemer has come), the Office of the Dead quotes the *Descensus* narrative itself.[107] The Versicle is lifted from the narrative climax of the descent into Hell, where the ancient just welcome Christ, who draws Adam out of Limbo:

> advenisti redemptor mundi; sicut per legem et prophetas tuos predixisti, factis adimplesti. Redemisti vivos per crucem tuam et per mortem crucis ad nos descendisti, ut eriperes nos ab inferis et morte per maiestatem tuam . . . et tenens dexteram Adam ascendit ab inferis. . . . Tunc sanctus David fortiter clamavit dicens: Cantate domino canticum novum quia mirabilia fecit Dominus. Salvabit sibi dextera eius et brachium sanctum eius.

> You came, redeemer of the world, as you predicted in the law and the prophets, you fulfilled with deeds. You redeemed the living through your cross and through the death on the cross you descended to us, that you might snatch us from hell and death through your majesty . . . and holding Adam by the right hand he ascended from Hell . . . then saint David cried out loudly saying: 'sing to the Lord a new song for the Lord has accomplished marvelous things; he has won a victory with his right hand, with his holy arm'.[108]

Here, too, Dante is firmly in the background, not only in the references to the Harrowing of Hell in the *Inferno* (recalled by Virgil, as we saw, in the *possente* of *Inf.* 4.53, and reenacted in the descent of the Angel before the Gates of Dis, *Inf.* 9.64–108), but even in the imagery of Virgil's drawing the pilgrim into and through Hell by the hand, succinctly illustrated in the juxtaposition between the well-known San Marco mosaic of the *Anastasis* and the Holkam manuscript illumination of Virgil extracting the pilgrim from the *tondo* at the end of *Inferno*.[109] Dante's pilgrim, who everywhere follows in the steps of Christ, performs with his own *descensus* a narrative reenactment of the defeat of Hell, a defeat that is commemorated throughout the poem, even in the highest reaches of the *Paradiso*.[110]

As in the *Canzoniere,* in the *Triumphi* too, Petrarch refers to his attachment to the mental image of Laura as a knot, a chain, a noose, and more abstractly as servitude (*TC* 4.137: "a qual servaggio"). The speaker is haunted both by Laura's freedom from such bondage (*TC* 3.145: "preso mi trovo, et ella è sciolta") and by his own persistent failure to slip the knot (*Triumphus pudicitie* 63: "già mai mi scioglia quinci"). Only Laura's death affords the promise of freedom (*TM* 1.133–34: "il dí sesto d'aprile, / che già mi strinse, et or, lasso, mi sciolse"), but this proves an illusory release. As in other works, including the *Salmi penitenziali,* the *Triumphi* make Petrarch's bondage to love concrete by depicting it as imprisonment in a dark cage (*TC* 4.157–58: "In cosí tenebrosa e stretta gabbia / rinchiusi fummo") or jail (*TC* 4.164: "tanti spiriti e sí chiare in carcer tetro").

This imprisonment represents Love's victory over the protagonist, and over all other lovers, including the famously victorious Caesar; such continuous supersession of victors by greater powers is the pattern of the *Triumphi.* Love's dark prison is accessed through a triumphal arch (*TC* 4.140); but when Laura's chastity triumphs over Love, her victory reiterates Christ's victory over Hell and the power of darkness:

> tornava con onor da la sua guerra,
> allegra, avendo vinto il gran nemico
> che con suo' ingegni tutto il mondo atterra.
>   (*TM* 1.4–6)

Not hitherto recognized as such,[111] these verses echo Dante's language for the Satanic agents Plutus and Geryon (*Inf.* 6.115: "Pluto, *il gran nemico*"; *Inf.* 17.3: "colei che *tutto'l mondo appuzza*"; emphases mine). The allusions make Laura an imitator of the Harrowing Christ, who descends into Hell and binds Satan; in this she also imitates Beatrice, who in the *Commedia* extends Christ's saving arm by arranging the pilgrim's rescue from Hell, as recalled in the pilgrims' valediction to her near the end of the poem — a signal transformation, in the *Triumphi,* of Laura's anti-Beatrician function as Medusa in the *Canzoniere.*[112]

Another full evocation of the Harrowing pattern is found in *Seniles* 16.8, written in 1354 to Jean Birel, prior general of the Carthusian order and resident in the Grand Chartreuse, the mother house of the order, while Petrarch was residing in the Charterhouse of Garegnano near Milan.[113] The letter concludes with Petrarch's commendation of another Carthusian, his brother Gherardo, and it is thus not surprising also to find Petrarch once more expressing in the body of the letter his desire to be safely in port and freed from the bondage of sin, as he takes Jean Birel and Gherardo to be. The poet entreats the intercession of the prior in helping secure that rescue we now recognize as modeled on Christ's rescue of the just from Limbo:

> ad dominum clamans, de necessitatibus meis eripiar, & meritis tuis adiutus, Christo duce deducar in viam rectam, ac supernis civibus ascriptus, civitatem habitationis ingrediar, vel si forte primam illam tentationem ignoriantiae supergressus sum, reliquas tres evadam, quas ex ordine Psalmi textus exequitur, sedensque in tenebris et umbra mortis, vinctus in mendicitate et ferro, humiliatus in laboribus et infirmatus, iterum ad dominum clamans, ex tenebris atque ipsius umbra mortis educar, contritisque portis aereis et vectibus ferreis confractis, de via iniquitatis mea suspiciar, et de vinculis peccatorum.

> crying out to the Lord; if I were to be snatched from my straits and, aided by your merits, were to be led by Christ our Leader to the straight road, and, being enrolled among the citizens of heaven, were to approach the city of my abode, or if by chance I were to overcome that first temptation of ignorance, I would avoid the other three, which the text of the psalm lists in order. And sitting in darkness and the shadow of death, tied down in beggary and fetters, humiliated in labors and weakened, again calling to the Lord, I would be led from the darkness and shadow of death itself. And when the brazen gates have been shattered and the iron bars burst, I would be led from the path of my iniquity and from the chains of my sins.[114]

No account of liturgy in the *Canzoniere* could omit discussion of the paired sonnets 61 ("Benedetto sia 'l giorno, e 'l mese, et l'anno") and 62 ("Padre del ciel"), which vividly exemplify the conflict Petrarch experienced between praise of Laura and the recall coming from the Cross. In the case of "Padre del ciel," its close ties to the Lord's prayer, as well as to Dante's version of the *paternoster* beginning *Purgatorio* 11.1–24 ("O padre nostro, che nei cieli stai"), have been remarked; the same goes for the poem's beginning the final tercet with *Miserere,* the first word of penitential Psalm 50, also the first utterance of Dante's pilgrim in the *Inferno.* That both instances of the *Miserere* psalm are Good Friday uses emerges, moreover, from the status of Petrarch's poem as an anniversary poem (vv. 9, 14: "Or volge, Signor mio, l'undecimo anno . . . ramenta lor come oggi fusti in croce") and from the fact that the plea to Virgil of Dante's pilgrim (*Inf.* 1.63: "*miserere* di me, gridai a lui") is uttered on the Good Friday when the pilgrim begins his descent into Hell.[115] But if the liturgical framing of the sonnet derives in part from Dante, note the differences: Petrarch's petition is in the singular (vv. 5–6: "piacciati omai, col Tuo lume, ch'io torni / ad altra vita"), while Dante's, truer to the collective petition voiced in the original Lord's prayer taught to the apostles, and recited every day in the Mass and Office, retains the plural with "O padre nostro." Dante sketches a universal liturgy of all creatures in praise of God and, as often remarked, gives his prayer an unmistakable echo of the *Laudes creaturarum* of St. Francis (11.4: "Laudato sia il tuo nome e il tuo valore"), while Petrarch's poem persists in its solipsism, his discrete selfhood marked in each articulation of the sonnet (v. 4: "per *mio* mal sì adorni"; vv. 5–6: "*ch'io* torni / ad altra vita"; v. 10: "*ch'i'* fui sommesso"; v. 12: "*mio* non degno affanno"). In their respective treatments, Dante and Petrarch reflect exegesis of the *incipit* of the Psalm, where the plural is affirmed as consonant with the humility the prayer ought to manifest.[116]

The contrasting poem in praise of Laura has also been linked to a text once attributed to Dante that is a poem of malediction, not praise.[117] Petrarch's poem could rightly be seen as a refutation, not only of pseudo-Dante or Cino da Pistoia, but of what is in effect Petrarch's own malediction of the laurel at the end of the preceding *Rvf* 60: "si secchi ogni sua foglia verde" (v. 14). In so alternating curses and blessings, the poems follow precedents in the vernacular Italian tradition; commentators have not failed to note the abundance of benedictions in the Bible.[118] This is not quite enough, however. With respect to Dante, Santagata recalls Amor's invitation in the *Vita nuova* to the protagonist that he bless the day on which he was bound to Beatrice (*Vn* 24.2: "Pensa di benedire lo dì ch'io ti presi, perocche tu lo dei fare"). This allusion makes of Petrarch's poem an echo of the institution of Dante's love, and liturgy, for Beatrice. And given that *benedetto* opens each quatrain and tercet of Petrarch's sonnet, it is, as Mariann Sanders Regan suggested over thirty years ago, less to scriptural benedictions than to the formalized benedictions of the liturgy that we should look to understand how Petrarch's poem adapts sacred language.[119]

In the abundance of benediction formulas found in the liturgy, a few stand out as more likely parallels to Petrarch's use: *Benedictus dominus deus* (Blessed be the Lord) begins the Gospel canticle of Zacharias for the Office of Lauds. The lesser canticles at Lauds also feature benedictions: the canticle of the three boys (*canticum trium puerorum*), drawn from the book of Daniel, the lesser canticle during Sundays in Lent, begins: "Benedictus dominus deus patrum nostrorum" (Blessed be the Lord, the God of our fathers); its counterpart out of Lent is the canticle of Daniel, beginning "Benedicite omnia opera Domini" (Bless the Lord, all you works of the Lord); while the canticle of David, "Benedictus dominus deus Israel" (Blessed be the Lord, the God of Israel), the Lenten Monday canticle for Lauds, closely parallels the Old Testament doxology marking the Vulgate division of the psalms.[120] Although blessing and praising are in a sense metonymic of divine worship in general, that so many benediction formulas are clustered in the Office of Lauds proves significant, as we will see.[121]

These reiterated liturgical benedictions enumerate, in the case of the material derived from Daniel, the praise due to the Lord for his variegated creation. Petrarch's benedictions, on the other hand, articulate an anniversary sonnet that offers an etiology and recapitulation of the poet's amorous career, moving—according to a scheme recognized as similar to that of casting a horoscope—from the place and time of first enamorment, to the pains and sorrows of love, to voiced appeals ("chiamando il nome de mia donna"), to the written pages that earn his reputation: "Benedetto sia'l giorno . . . il primo dolce affanno . . . le voci tante . . . tutte le carte."[122] If we convert the blessings into curses, as the pseudo-Dante and the lyric tradition might suggest, the sonnet turns into an echo of Dante's *Inferno* 3.103–5, a malediction of human horoscopes for conception and birth: "bestemmiavano Dio e lor parenti, / l'umana spezie e'l loco e'l tempo e'l seme / di lor semenza e di lor nascimenti." It is by such allusive means that Petrarch prepares the contrast with the *Pater noster* imitated (but also undermined) in the following sonnet, and thus charges his sonnet of blessings with, contextually speaking, greater blasphemous potential.

But the articulatory benedictions have more to tell us. If we inspect the sonnet in the light of the Advent Tract, which consists of verses and responses, we might also espy in Petrarch's sonnet, which begins both quatrains and tercets with *Benedetto,* a trace of the transcription practices of poems in the Tuscan lyric anthologies of the late Duecento. As D'Arco Silvio Avalle points out, the Palatino and Laurenziano manuscripts include sonnets, ballate, and canzoni in which recursive elements of the ballate (*volte*) and sonnets (tercets) and the *tornate* of the canzoni are identified as Versicles (in the Palatino) or Responsories (in the Laurenziano), using the abbreviatory symbols (V for *versus, versiculus* and R for *responsorium*) traditional in liturgical manuscripts.[123] Petrarch's benediction of his sheets (*Rvf* 61, v. 12: "et benedette sian tutte le carte") may suggest that we are to think here not only of poems, but of their material support as well.[124] Thematically speaking, *Rvf* 61–62 again present us with a *tenzone* of discordant versions of psalmody such as Petrarch used to characterize his difference from Gherardo, with one Petrarchan voice speaking the penitential *Miserere* to the "Padre del ciel," while, in the previous poem, another voice refers to the scattered calls to Laura ("le voci tante ch'io / chiamando il nome de mia donna ò sparte" [vv. 9–10]) that are synonymous with the poems of the *Canzoniere* itself. This hypothesis regarding the influence of liturgical books receives indirect confirmation with the presence of the ballata that follows, "Volgendo gli occhi" (*Rvf* 63). Given its inclusion of a repeating refrain (*ripresa* or *ritornello*), the ballata, understood to be both sung and danced, is the form that most clearly mediates the extension of Responsory and Versicle abbreviations to the sonnets and canzoni of the early anthologies.[125] In fact, in light of Emilio Bigi's comparison of the peculiar arrangement of verses in the ballata to a sonnet with external quatrains and internal tercets, Petrarch seems to have given "Volgendo gli occhi" mediatory functions both formal and thematic in the arrangement of poems 61–63 in the *Canzoniere.*[126] The ballata turns the poet away once more from prayer to God and back to Laura as the source of the poet's fragile existence (vv. 5–6: "La fraile vita . . . / fu de' begli occhi vostri aperto dono"). And back to Dante as well: alluding to "novo colore / che fa di morte rimembrar la mente" (vv. 1–2), Petrarch echoes Dante's illness at the center of the *Vita nuova,* as well as, with vv. 3–4 ("benignamente / salutando, teneste in vita il core"), Beatrice's salutary effects in that same text. A phrase such as "pietà vi mosse" (v. 3) echoes Beatrice's words to Virgil in the *Inferno* (2.72: "amor mi mosse, che mi fa parlare"). In short, moments when Dante institutes his devotion to Beatrice—recall Amor's remark in the *Vita nuova,* "pensa di benedicere lo dì ch'io ti presi"—return to warrant Petrarch's reconsecration to Laura after the pious parenthesis addressing the heavenly father. Like all the anniversary poems, these sonnets confirm the institution of Petrarch's lauriform liturgy, and reflect its derivation from Dante's Beatrician ritual.

There is evidence, going beyond the year of days suggested by the 366 poems in the collection, for a quasi-liturgical model that inspires Petrarch's collection as a whole. The *Canzoniere* is nothing if not praise for Laura, and Petrarch establishes by the fifth sonnet that his poetic voice is turned, or rather attuned, to singing her praises. As part of a sequence that is markedly liturgical, the poem can be closely associated with the etiology of Petrarch's love and art that we saw in the benediction sonnet and in the reinstitution of his veneration of Laura in the ballata capping *Rvf* 60–63. Thus the third sonnet recounts the enamorment on Good Friday, and the next presents Laura's birthplace, in Dantean terms, as the equivalent of Assisi, birthplace of St. Francis (v. 12: "ed or di picciol borgo un sol n'à dato"),[127] inserting Laura, so to speak, in the Sanctoral.[128] In sonnet 5 itself, Petrarch's voice, driven by his amorous sighs, begins to utter the first syllable of "Laudando," *Lau*; the dispersed syllables of Laura's name are progressively furnished (*Lau Re Ta,* or *Laurea*); this is then repeated: "Così LAUdare et REverire insegna / la voce stessa" (vv. 9–10), with the poet's praise and reverence underlining a "liturgical" intention.[129] In the dynamics of an internal word (v. 2: "e 'l nome che nel cor mi scrisse Amore") that becomes audible (v. 3: "s'incomincia udir di fore"), we see a version of Dante's self-institutionalization as the poet of Amor in *Purgatorio* 24.42 ("a quel modo ch'ei ditta dentro, vo significando"); but we also see in the syllabification of Laura's name not only across individual verses, but in its rhythmic distribution in verses 3, 5, 7, and 9 (and possibly 14),[130] a trace of how words in liturgical manuscripts are syllabified and fitted to musical notation, and possibly of traditional mnemonics used in liturgical singing, such as the EVOVAE formula (= *sEcUlOrUm AmEn*), and even Guido d'Arezzo's didactic hymn "UT queant LAxis," where the initial syllables of the chanted text furnish the notes of the hexachord.[131]

More to the point, a reiteration of the terms for praising (*Laudando, laudare*) directs us at once to the Office of Lauds, and to the traditional account of the entire Office as the praises of God, *laus Deo,* thanks to the phrase from Psalm 118 that we recall Petrarch himself was pleased to cite ("septies in die laudem dixi tibi" [seven times a day I give you praise]). Lauds itself, we just saw, features the canticle of Zachary beginning with *Benedictus dominus deus,* and the lesser canticles at Sunday Lauds are the Canticles of the Three Boys and of Daniel, both of which begin, as we saw, with Benedictions.[132] Lauds is also the Office that daily recites that portion of the Psalter most explicitly praising God, the *Laudatio* Psalms 148–50, and it is the Office where the *Miserere,* Psalm 50, so prominent an influence in Petrarch's *Salmi,* takes pride of place. *Canzoniere* sonnet 5 also may reflect Petrarch's focus on the Matins Office that situated Petrarch's tormented meditation on Laura and his distinction from, but also attraction to, Gherardo's vocation. Matins immediately preceded and was sometimes continuous with Lauds, known as *laudes matutinas.*

It is this sense of the *Canzoniere* as the book of Laura's praises, supplanting those of God, recalled not once but many times in the collection, that requires the solemn and elaborate exorcism of "Vergine bella," by which the collection, hitherto unmistakably an *officium Laure,* bids fair to become an *officium virginis.* In that final poem, which draws heavily on Marian liturgies,[133] the name of the Virgin is invoked, rather than the name of Laura (vv. 7–8: "Invoco lei che ben sempre rispose, / chi la chiamò con fede"); the Cross, that Petrarch cannot view directly in the sestine or in *Rvf* 62, can be contemplated through the Virgin's compassion for her son (vv. 22–24: "que' belli occhi / che vider tristi la spietata stampa / ne' dolci membri del tuo caro figlio"); and the Virgin is invoked (v. 40: "Vergine santa, d'ogni gratia piena"), as a "Donna del ciel" (v. 98) who might intercede with the "Padre del ciel" whom Petrarch addresses earlier in the collection.

Petrarch's poem to the Virgin, as all readers are aware, competes with Bernard's prayer to the Virgin beginning the last canto of the *Paradiso,* using a similar incipit (cf. Dante's "Vergine madre").[134] As Gorni argues, the sheer repetition (anaphora, or *coblas capdenals*) of the initial formula of *Vergine* + modifier appears designed to displace Dante's *terza rima* with a stanzaic module for poetic prayer.[135] Given that the Virgin Mary is apostrophized twenty-one times, as many times as the years of Petrarch's bondage to the living Laura, the poem numerically and ritually displaces the years of error with a verbal act of devotion to the mother of God.[136]

But the poem takes up Dantean liturgical expressions and significations more generally as well. Petrarch's version of the angelic salutation (v. 40:

"Vergine santa, d'ogni gratia piena") resumes Dante's at *Par.* 32.95 ("cantando, *Ave, Maria, gratia plena*"); while Petrarch's verse 120 ("*miserere* d'un cor contrito humile") answers Dante's use of *Miserere* in the same canto (*Par.* 32.12, "*Miserere mei*"), thus recapping two of the liturgical phrases Dante uses most frequently in the *Commedia,* and again recalling the word Dante uses to appeal to Virgil in the first canto of the *Commedia.*

Indeed, Petrarch gives special attention to the beginning and the end of Dante's poem. His *propositio* (v. 4: "amor mi spinge a dir di te parole") echoes Beatrice's formula (*Inf.* 2.103, "Amor mi mosse, che mi fa parlare") with a formula doubly Dantean, as Gorni shows, in adopting a locution found previously in the *Vita nuova.*[137] What is often taken as Petrarch's direct subversion of Dante's lady, his reference to the Virgin as "vera Beatrice," is itself a compound of Dante's phrasing, which introduces Beatrice, in Lucia's words, as "Beatrice, lode di dio vera" (*Inf.* 2.103) and refers to Christ, in the words of the Croatian pilgrim near the end of the poem, as "Signor mio Jesu cristo, *Dio verace,* / or fu sì fatta la sembianza vostra?" (*Par.* 31.107–8). That Petrarch was attentive to this passage seems guaranteed by v. 57 of "Vergine bella": "al *vero Dio* sacrato et vivo tempio" (emphases mine).

It also treads the liturgical ground worked explicitly and elaborately by Dante, as in *Purgatorio* 6–8, where elements of the Compline Office constellate the text. Petrarch three times invokes the *Salve Regina* (vv. 22–25, "Vergine, que' belli occhi / . . . / volgi al mio dubio stato"; and compare "oculos ad nos converte" [turn then your eyes towards us], 60–62, 105), the hymn to Mary sung at Compline that Dante has his negligent princes intone in the *Purgatorio* (7.82, cf. also 6.120: "son li giusti occhi tuoi rivolti altrove?").[138] As it is with Dante's melancholy princes, the reference to Compline is consistent with the penitential theme of the whole text, as the Compline Hour corresponds to Christ's prayer in Gethsemane and his placement in the tomb.[139] Indeed, Petrarch's last line echoes the Compline Responsory ("In manus tuas commendo spiritum meum" [in your hands I commend my spirit]), also spoken by Christ on the cross, which the poet contaminates with the canticle of Simeon that is the major Canticle at Compline ("Nunc dimittis servum tuum . . . in pace" [Now let thy servant go . . . in peace]); also implicit are the several prayers for the commendation of the dead that petition the deity with *Suscipe . . .,* a close equivalent to Petrarch's "Accolga. . . ."[140]

An ideal final example of Petrarch drawing on the liturgy and Dante simultaneously is furnished by line 65, exactly halfway through the poem's regular stanzas: "et la mia tòrta   via drizzi a buon fine." Bortolo Martinelli derives the verse from Luke 1.79, "dirige pedes nostros in viam pacis" (to guide our feet into the path of peace).[141] But this text is more familiar from the liturgy, as it forms the concluding verse to the *Benedictus* or Canticle of Zachary at, again, Lauds, and is also excerpted in the Antiphon to the Canticle; a closely related phrase also characterizes the Matins Hour of the Office of the Dead.[142] But Petrarch's phraseology is also plainly evocative of Dante's: or rather, it follows Dante's vernacularization of the liturgical Latin, as in *Purg.* 10.3: "la porta / che'l mal amor de l'anime disusa / perchè fa parer dritta la via torta."[143] Petrarch in the end does not so much displace Dante, as manifest that Dante has furnished him the vernacularized liturgical language he cannot do without.

Yet for all his professed humility in "Vergine bella," Petrarch is scarcely unaware of his relative ranking as a vernacular poet, a ranking in which the prestigious Dante looms always over him. In "Vergine bella" itself, Petrarch adapts Dante's moment of self-identification at *Inferno* 23.94–95 ("I' fui nato e cresciuto / sovra'l bel fiume d'Arno, a la gran villa") to his own verse 82 ("Da poi ch'i' nacqui in su la riva d'Arno"), in this way turning the rivalry into a contestation of Dante's primacy in respect of birthplace and birthday. It thus follows that late in life Petrarch, in a pair of letters to Boccaccio, makes a bid to transform his own birthday into a red-letter day, one consciously contextualized in terms of the historical forces that determined Petrarch's status as an exile, and one that implicitly juxtaposed him to Dante's different career path and engagement with politics. Where, in the *Canzoniere,* it is the day he first saw Laura, or the time of Laura's death, that is marked with the year, the month, the day, and the hour (*Rvf* 211.12–14; 336.12–14), now it is Petrarch's own natal moment that is celebrated. Indeed, Petrarch's elucubrations on his birthday, which he speaks of as a "significant day" ("dies . . . insignis et nota") as if an important feast of the Kalendar, make it no less than the *dies natalis* of a founding saint of humanism. What *Fam.* 6.2 does for the sacred space of Rome in relation to Petrarch's projects for a hegemonic authorship, *Sen.* 8.1 consummates for Petrarch's sacralized relation to his own historical moment.

In 1366, Petrarch reached his sixty-third birthday. He wrote to Boccaccio discussing the reputation of that age, from the perspective of astrological medicine, as a dangerous climacteric. Twelve months later to the day and the hour, he wrote to Boccaccio again, congratulating himself on still being alive, and the world for the news that Pope Urban V would be returning to Rome, thanks in large measure to Petrarch's own efforts. For these reasons, these two letters to Boccaccio, *Seniles* 8.1 and 8.8, frame the eighth and central book of the *Seniles,* making Petrarch's sixty-third year, and the Petrarch-inspired return of Urban V to Rome, the fulcrum of the collection.[144] In the first letter to Boccaccio, which, logically enough, takes up the issue of the poet's mortality, Petrarch reiterates the Harrowing and Palinurus pattern with the claim that, thanks to Christ's right arm, he had been freed from Laura's influence after the Jubilee of 1350.[145] The letter also furnishes an example of Petrarch's incorporation of liturgical allusion, as he quotes, near the end of the letter, Job 14.1−2, the fifth of the familiar extracts from Job read during the Office of the Dead.

Yet, in this self-staging of Petrarch's productive longevity, the most significant adaptation of a liturgical habit of mind, and the rhetorical climax of the letter,[146] concerns 20 July 1304, Petrarch's birthdate, his advent to the world. That day was "a notable and significant day for our people," not only because of the poet's birth, at dawn, but because it coincided (to the hour, Petrarch maintains) with the defeat of the exiled White Guelphs outside the gates of Florence, an event that settled the political destiny both of Petrarch's father and, as we know, of Dante Alighieri. Although Petrarch does not elaborate, the defeat prevented Ser Petracco, and thus Petrarch himself, from resuming their roles as Florentine citizens in a collectivity whose conditions would have been starkly different from those Petrarch enjoyed as *peregrinus ubique.* Petrarch is clearly aware that the historical conditions that relegated the White Guelphs, among them Dante, to political impotence and lingering regrets, also went far to shape the individualistic and protohumanist Petrarch — after all, Urban had listened to him, while both emperors and popes had turned deaf ears to Dante. This singularity was implicit, as Petrarch sees it, in the very date of his birth, which marked a split, at the moment of origin of vernacular literature, between direct civic engagement and the pursuit of humane letters, a split embodied by the different careers of Dante and Petrarch. Petrarch's long experience adapting the spaces and times of public liturgy to his personal expression reaches fruition with the virtual proclamation, upon finishing his sixty-third year, of a singular and secular liturgy of himself.

Notes

1. The letter may refer to Petrarch's visit to Rome in 1341; for the dating, see Armando Foresti, *Aneddoti della vita di Francesco Petrarca,* 2nd ed. (Padua: Antenore, 1997), 94–97; and E. H. Wilkins, "On Petrarch's *Ep. Fam.* 6.2," in *Studies on Petrarch and Boccaccio,* ed. Aldo S. Bernardo (Padua: Antenore, 1978), 267–71; Angelo Mazzocco, "The Antiquarianism of Francesco Petrarca," *Journal of Medieval and Renaissance Studies* 7 (1977): 207, argues for an earlier date of 1337. For the γ version of the letter, see Francesco Petrarca, *Le familiari* (*Rerum familiarum libri* XXIV), ed. Vittorio Rossi (Florence: Sansoni, 1933–42, 4 vols. [vol. 4 ed. Umberto Bosco]), 2:91–94.

2. On the letter and Petrarch's periodization of the "dark ages," see Theodor Mommsen, "Petrarch's Conception of the Dark Ages," *Speculum* 17 (1942): 226–42; this view followed by Thomas H. Greene, "Petrarch and the Humanist Hermeneutic," in *Italian Literature, Roots and Branches: Essays in Honor of Thomas Goddard Bergin,* ed. Giosuè Rimanelli and Kenneth John Atchity (New Haven: Yale University Press, 1976), 201–24, and in *The Light in Troy: Imitation and Discovery in Renaissance Poetry* (New Haven: Yale University Press, 1982), 220–41; and by Philip Jack, *Antiquarianism and Myths of Antiquity: The Origins of Rome in Renaissance Thought* (Cambridge: Cambridge University Press, 2003), 35–40. More nuanced is David Galbraith, "Petrarch and the Broken City," in *Antiquity and Its Interpretation,* ed. Alina Payne, A. Kuttner, and R. Smick (Cambridge: Cambridge University Press, 2000), 17–26. The established view is critiqued in Jennifer Summit, "Topography as Historiography in Petrarch, Chaucer and the *Mirabilia* of Ancient Rome," *Journal of Medieval and Early Modern Studies* 30 (2000): 211–46, emphasizing Petrarch's placing of classical monuments within a Christian scheme of history.

3. *Le familiari,* 6.2.8–11; on Aeneas' tour of the site of Rome as a model, see Mazzocco, "Antiquarianism," 207–9; Jack, *Antiquarianism and Myths of Antiquity,* 37; Galbraith, "Petrarch and the Broken City," 20.

4. On the *possessio,* see Sergio Bertelli, *The Pope's Body,* trans. R. Burr Litchfield (University Park: Pennsylvania State University Press, 1995), 130.

5. Arsenio Frugoni, "Il giubileo di Bonifacio VIII," *Bullettino dell'Istituto storico italiano per il medio evo e Archivio muratoriano* 62 (1950): 1–121. Given the pope's absence from Rome, Petrarch was keenly interested in the Jubilee; *Epystola* II.5 helped persuade Clement VI to declare the 1350 Jubilee in 1342.

6. John Baldovin, *The Urban Character of Christian Worship* (Rome: Pontificium institutum studiorum orientalium, 1987), esp. 105–41; see 55, characterizing stational processions as "a grand, well-conceived tour of the Christian city."

7. See Summit, "Topography as Historiography," 222.

8. See Baldovin's appendix of stational lists, *Urban Character,* 285–91; also Summit, "Topography as Historiography," 222–28, on the *Mirabilia.*

9. Summit "Topography as Historiography," 219–20.

10. See Galbraith, "Petrarch and the Broken City": "the letter arose . . . from Colonna's desire to preserve a more permanent record of these discussions (18–19)." Greater account should be taken of Petrarch's playful evasiveness before Colonna's request; note esp. *Fam.* 6.2.22, "ut familiares epystolas ludens . . . scribere soleo" (as I am accustomed to writing these friendly letters almost as amusement): although Petrarch's is surely *serio ludere.* English translations of the *Familiares* are from *Rerum familiarium libri,* trans. Aldo S. Bernardo, 3 vols. (Albany: State University of New York Press, 1975; Baltimore and London: Johns Hopkins University Press, 1985).

11. For the veneration of *loca sancta,* see Summit, "Topography as Historiography," 221 and n. 34; see also Mary Carruthers, *The Craft of Thought: Meditation, Rhetoric, and the Making of Images 400–1200* (Cambridge: Cambridge University Press, 1998), 289–90 (n. 87). Jack, *Antiquarianism and Myths of Antiquity,* writes that "Petrarch envisions this tour as a metaphorical journey through time" (36). Petrarch's division of labor (*Fam.* 6.2.16: "in antiquis ego viderer expertior . . . in novis tu" [I being more expert in the ancient . . . and you in recent times]) suggests that Summit's account of the letter as a Christianization of the classical past is overstated; see Jack, *Antiquarianism and Myths of Antiquity,* 36, and Galbraith, "Petrarch and the Broken City," 18.

12. See *Fam.* 6.2.1, 5, 15. The second (5) varies the first: "Vagabamur pariter in illa urbe tam magna, que cum propter spatium vacua videatur" (We used to wander together in that great city which, though it appeared empty because of its vast size); the third (15) is "Solebamus ergo . . . sistere" (we used to . . . stop often). The pattern is noted in Galbraith, "Petrarch and the Broken City," 24 n. 27.

13. Carruthers, *Craft,* 56.

14. See Mary Carruthers, "Rhetorical *Ductus,* or, Moving through a Composition," in *Acting on the Past: Historical Performance across the Disciplines,* ed. Mark Franko and Annette Richards (Hanover, N.H.: Wesleyan University Press, published by University Press of New England, 2000), 99–117, esp. 111.

15. Galbraith, "Petrarch and the Broken City," notes Petrarch's phrase "hic elementa notis impressa," associating the traces of the city with written characters, in the parallel account of early Rome in the *Africa* (8.866) (21); see also Summit, "Topography as Historiography," 221–22 ("Petrarch's ambit among the sites of martyrdom reinscribes Rome as a network of holy places").

16. For Giovanni Colonna di Gallicano, O.P., Petrarch's fellow student of Livy and author of a *De viris illustribus* and the *Mare historiarum,* see the notes in Francesco Petrarca, *Canzoniere,* ed. Marco Santagata, 2nd ed. (Milan: Mondadori, 1997), 36 (all further references are to this edition); also Stephen L. Forte, O.P., "John Colonna O.P. Life and Writings (1298–c. 1340)," *Archivum Fratrum Praedicatorum* 20 (1950): 369–414.

17. See Albert Russell Ascoli, *Dante and the Making of a Modern Author* (Cambridge: Cambridge University Press, 2008).

18. See Dante Alighieri, *Convivio,* ed. Franca Brambilla Ageno (Florence: Le Lettere, 1995), 2:402–4. The *Seniles* are quoted from *Francisci petrarchae... opera quae extant omnia* (Basle 1554; anastatic reprint Ridgewood, N.J.: Gregg Press, 1965), 944–51, henceforth *Seniles.* For a discussion of *Convivio* 4.22.14–18, see Peter Dronke, *Dante's Second Love: The Originality and the Contents of the Convivio* (University of Exeter: The Society for Italian Studies, 1997), 60–62.

19. Petrarch's three sects are the Peripatetics, Stoics, and Academics (including Cicero); though Petrarch refers to himself as a peripatetic, his inclusion of the sects conforms to his anti-scholastic views and is possibly a shot at Dante, confessed disciple of the "maestro di color che sanno." Petrarch returned elsewhere to the active and contemplative lives in terms of the Mary and Martha episode in Scripture: see *Fam.* 3.12.8 and *De vita solitaria* 2.9 (Francesco Petrarca, *Prose,* ed. G. Martellotti et al. [Milan and Naples: Ricciardi, 1955], 504).

20. Recent views in David Hiley, *Western Plainchant: A Handbook* (Oxford: Clarendon Press, 1993), 252–63; see also O. B. Hardison, *Christian Rite and Christian Drama in the Middle Ages* (Baltimore: Johns Hopkins University Press, 1965), and Johann Drumbl, *Quem quaeritis: Teatro sacro dell'alto medievo* (Rome: Bulzoni, 1981). Karl Young, *Drama of the Medieval Church* (Oxford: Clarendon Press, 1933), 1:202–306, remains fundamental.

21. These are in part authorized, for Dante as for Petrarch, by the allegoreses in the Gregorian homilies prescribed for the liturgy; see S. J. P. Van Dijk, *Sources of the Modern Roman Liturgy* (Leiden: E. J. Brill, 1963), 2:88. Guillelmus Durandus, *Rationale divinorum officiorum,* ed. T. M. Thibodeau (Turnhout: Brepols, 1998), VI.87.5, explicitly permits inauthentic, that is, nonscriptural additions—like *Quem quaeritis* tropes—in the Matins Office.

22. See *Fam.* 6.2.1, "non etenim sectas amo, sed verum" (I do not love sects but the truth), and 6.2.2, "veramque lucem non requirerent" (do not desire the true light), and contrast these views with Dante, *Conv.* 4.22.16: "dice a ciascuna di queste sette, cioè a qualunque va cercando beatitudine nella vita attiva, che non è qui." Writing to his brother, Petrarch compared the dissonances of the philosophical schools to Gherardo's peace as a monk; see *Fam.* 10.5.6 ("totam rem tres in partes et unamquamque rursus in multas minutias secuere philosophi, unde et secte nomen creditur derivatum" [Thus, philosophers laid aside those differences that cannot be identified and divided everything into three parts; each part in turn was divided into many smaller sections, which is believed to be the derivation of the word *sect*]); also *Fam.* 17.1.36.

23. In the letter, the unusual burial sites of Trajan, Hadrian, Caesar, and Augustus are replaced by the shrines of Christian martyrs; see 6.2.11–13: "intra urbem est sepultus Traianus ... Hadriani moles ... Iulii Cesaris ossa ... sepulcrum ipsius domini [Augustus] quidam tradunt ... hic Petrus in crucem actus, hic truncatus est Paulus ... hic assatus Laurentius; hic sepultus venienti Stephano locum fecit." (There is Trajan's buried inside the city ... Hadrian's fortress ... the bones of Julius

Caesar . . . the house of Augustus, the tomb of the Emperor himself . . . here Peter was crucified; there Paul was beheaded; here Lawrence was burned, who after being buried here, was succeeded by Stephan.)

24. A few commentaries on Petrarch's debts to Dante may be noted here: Aldo S. Bernardo, "Petrarch's Attitude toward Dante," *PMLA* 70 (1955): 488–517; Marco Santagata, "Presenze di Dante 'comico' nel *Canzoniere* del Petrarca," *Giornale storico della letteratura italiana* 146 (1969): 163–211; Franco Suitner, *Petrarca e la tradizione stilnovistica* (Florence: Olschki, 1977); Michele Feo, "Petrarca, Francesco," in *Enciclopedia virgiliana* (Rome: Istituto della Enciclopedia Italiana, 1988), 4:53–78; Giuseppe Velli, "Il Dante di Francesco Petrarca," *Studi petrarcheschi* n.s. 2 (1985): 185–99; Luca Carlo Rossi, "Petrarca dantista involontario," *Studi petrarcheschi* n.s. 5 (1988): 301–16 (includes full bibliographic notes on the topic); Marco Baglio, "Presenze dantesche nel Petrarca latino," *Studi petrarcheschi* n.s. 9 (1992): 77–136; Domenico de Robertis, *Memoriale petrarchesco* (Rome: Bulzoni, 1997); Carlo Pulsoni, "Il Dante di Francesco Petrarca: Vaticano latino 3199," *Studi petrarcheschi* n.s. 10 (1993): 155–208. Santagata's annotations to Petrarca, *Canzoniere*, are indispensable.

25. E. H. Wilkins, "Petrarch's Ecclesiastical Career," in *Studies in the Life and Works of Petrarch* (Cambridge, Mass.: Medieval Academy of America, 1955), 3–32; also "Petrarch and the Cardinalate," in the same volume, 67–80. In his will (*Petrarch's Testament*, ed. Theodore E. Mommsen [Ithaca, N.Y.: Cornell University Press, 1957], 74), Petrarch acknowledged having been often absent from his duties as an archdeacon in Parma ("ubi per multos annos archidiaconus fui inutilis et semper fere absens" [where I was a useless archdeacon for many years and almost always absent]).

26. E. H. Wilkins, *Life of Petrarch* (Chicago: University of Chicago Press, 1961), 10; 130–31; 156–57; 82, respectively; see also E. H. Wilkins, *Petrarch's Eight Years in Milan* (Cambridge, Mass.: Medieval Academy of America, 1958): 17, 198–99, 139–42.

27. See Giles Constable, "Petrarch and Monasticism," in *Francesco Petrarca, Citizen of the World*, ed. Aldo S. Bernardo (Padua: Antenore; Albany: State University of New York Press, 1980), 53–99; and Jean Leclerq, "Temi monastici nell'opera di Petrarca," *Lettere italiane* 43 (1991): 42–54. Both studies emphasize the closeness of Petrarch's humanistic regimen to the religious life, based on Petrarch's discussions of *otium* and solitude in *De otio religioso* and *De vita solitaria*.

28. For Petrarch's habits in reciting the Office, associated with the poet's turn to the Fathers and the Bible, see Constable, "Petrarch and Monasticism," 85.

29. For a census, see ibid., 64 and 71, and Wilkins, *Life*, 254–56 and 264; a complete account of contacts and religious orders is in Anna Maria Voci, *Petrarca e la vita religiosa: Il mito umanista della vita eremitica* (Rome: Istituto Storico Italiano per l'Età Moderna e Contemporanea, 1983). Constable observes (86) that "Petrarch lived more like a monk than most clerics" and follows Wilkins and Cipolla in viewing Petrarch's request to Clement VI for a benefice in the gift of the Carthusians as

an indication that Petrarch once intended to establish a *"comitatus* of solitaries" (80) like the one he envisioned in *De vita solitaria* (II.14); see Wilkins, "Petrarch's Ecclesiastical Career," 14–15.

30. Petrarch's illegitimate brother Giovannino was an Olivetan monk from 1346, but has left little trace in Petrarch's writings. See Giuseppe Billanovich, "Un ignoto fratello del Petrarca," *Italia medioevale e umanistica* 25 (1982): 375–80, and M. Tagliabue, "Fra Giovannino fratello del Petrarca e monaco olivetano," *Studi petrarcheschi* n.s. 6 (1989): 225–40.

31. See poem 91 in Petrarca, *Canzoniere,* 445–46. See also *Fam.* 10.3.24.

32. See Francesco Petrarca, *Secretum: Il mio segreto,* ed. Enrico Fenzi (Milan: Mursia, 1992), 220 and 369–70 for a list of passages and bibliography (e.g., T. E. Mommsen, "Petrarch and the Story of the Choice of Hercules," in *Medieval and Renaissance Studies,* ed. Eugene F. Rice, Jr. [Ithaca, N.Y.: Cornell University Press, 1959], 156–79); Constable, "Petrarch and Monasticism," 58–59, places the *bivium* in Petrarch's life at the time of the composition of *De vita solitaria* (begun 1346) and *De otio religioso* (begun 1347), and discusses *Fam.* 4.1 as an allegory of the different choices made by Petrarch and his brother (95–99).

33. See *De vita solitaria* I.2 (Petrarca, *Prose,* 301–20). Petrarch marks several hours with liturgical elements, e.g.: Matins, referring, with "ianitorem labiorum suorum ut eggressuris inde matutinis laudibus aperiat devotus exposcit" (prays the keeper of his lips to devotedly open them to the morning lauds ready to come out), to *Labia mea Domine aperies* (Ps. 50.17, said before Vigils and every canonical hour); Terce, by referring to praise of the Trinity (probably the *Gloria patri,* or new Doxology said after each psalm); Vespers, by referring to the hymn "Lucis creator optime" (Blessed Creator of the Light) ("superni luminis poscit auxilium" [he demands the help of divine light]; see Van Dijk, *Sources,* 2:53); and Compline, with reference to the hymn "Te lucis ante terminum" (You, before the end of the day). Martellotti et al. note only the last.

34. For the norms of saying the Office, see S. J. P. Van Dijk and H. Walker, *Origins of the Modern Roman Liturgy: The Liturgy of the Papal Court and the Franciscan Order in the Thirteenth Century* (London: Darton, Longman & Todd, and Westminster, Md.: The Newman Press, 1959), 36–46.

35. Mommsen, *Petrarch's Testament,* 29; 38–39. Bought in Venice before the Jubilee of 1350, the breviary cost 100 livres and was of large format (for the codex, still extant, see Pierre de Nolhac, *Pétrarque et l'humanisme,* 2nd ed. [Paris: Champion, 1907], 1:93, and Foresti, *Aneddoti,* 255–56, with bibliography); the codex, 400 folios but incomplete (it breaks off with the Office of the Virgin), is described in Luigi Vattasso, *I codici petrarcheschi della biblioteca vaticana* (Rome: Tipografia poliglotta vaticana, 1908), 248–49; a fuller, but still incomplete, description is in Giuseppe Cozza-Luzi, *Sul codice del breviario di Francesco Petrarca acquistato da S.S. Leone XIII alla Biblioteca Vaticana* (Rome, 1893). Bocheta probably assisted Petrarch in fulfilling his duties as canon in the Padua cathedral (Mommsen, *Petrarch's Testament,* 29).

36. On the contents of liturgical books, see Andrew Hughes, *Medieval Manuscripts for Mass and Office: A Guide to Their Organization and Terminology* (Toronto: Univesity of Toronto Press, 1982), 100–244, esp. 197–202, 238–44; and Hiley, *Western Plainchant*, 291–325, esp. 320–24. Petrarch may have had a second breviary given to him by his friend Francesco Nelli, prior of the Church of the Holy Apostles in Florence; see Foresti, *Aneddoti*, 255–56, and Petrarch's letter to Nelli (*Varie*, 29). This smaller book might have been the portable type (*portos*) available at the end of the Duecento; see Van Dijk and Walker, *Origins*, 26–36.

37. Petrarch's breviary thus corresponds to the third type identified by Hughes (*Medieval Manuscripts*, 238–42), which inserts the Kalendar after the Temporal (or Office Breviary). Hughes indicates this as a type most usually of British provenance, but notes several Northern European examples and one in Italy, at the Vatican (not Petrarch's). As in the examples noted by Hughes, Petrarch's includes insertions after the various sections (the *historiae*, or Old Testament readings, after the Temporal, the Hymnal after the Psaltery, a Dedication ceremony after the Sanctoral), though Petrarch's does not coincide exactly with any of Hughes' examples. My thanks to the Biblioteca Apostolica Vaticana for their assistance in viewing this codex.

38. The psalter in Petrarch's breviary follows the common eightfold liturgical division of the psalter (see Hughes, *Medieval Manuscripts*, 225–33), with illuminated initials corresponding to Psalms 1, 26, 38, 52, 80, and 97 (68 and 109, the others in the eightfold division, are not illustrated).

39. *Fam.* 7.3.11: "surrexi demum hora solita — consuetudinem meam nosti — dumque quotidianis laudibus Deo dictis, ex more manum calamo applicuissem" [I finally got up at the regular hour (you know my custom) and after having recited my daily praises to God, I took up my pen as is my habit]; see also *Fam.* 22.10.3: "deinceps ad laudes creatoris mei media nocte consurgimus quietis tempus somnosque Illi meos fregero" (I should now rise in the middle of the night to sing the praises of my Creator, to interrupt my sleep and repose for Him); and 11: "Quos inter merito michi maximus David semper fuerit, eo formosior quo incomptior, eo doctior disertiorque quo purior. Huius ego Psalterium et vigilanti semper in manibus semperque sub oculis, et dormienti simul ac morienti sub capite situm velim." (For me the greatest in terms of merit will always be David, who is the more beautiful for his simplicity, the more learned for his purity. I desire to have his Psalter always at hand and within sight while awake, and beneath my pillow while sleeping and at the point of death.)

40. *Fam.* 10.5.28: "Ita michi placuit illud Psalmiste: 'Septies in die laudem dixi tibi' [Psalm 118.164], ut ex quo semel hunc morem sum amplexus, nulla me vel semel ab incepto occupatio diurna distraxerat, et illud eiusdem [ita mihi placuit]: 'Media nocte surgebam ad confitendum tibi'" [Ps. 118.62]. (I found so pleasing that saying of the Psalmist, "Seven times in one day I sang your praises," that once this habit was acquired, no other activity distracted me. And I have so liked that other saying by the same Psalmist, "I would rise in the midst of the night to confess to you.")

41. *Fam.* 10.3.50–53, concluding Petrarch's version of the *Improperia* or reproaches from the Cross. See Durandus, *Rationale* V.3.2: "in hac hora captus et illusus est a Iudeis" (in this hour he was seized and ridiculed by the Jews). On the liturgy at Montrieux, which Petrarch heard when visiting his brother, see *Fam.* 16.9.15 ("dum antilucanas Cristo laudes canunt" [while the monk are singing matins to Christ]), and, in a work dedicated to Gherardo, *De otio religioso,* ed. Giuseppe Rotondi (Città del Vaticano: Biblioteca apostolica vaticana, 1958), 1: "dum devotum silentium et angelicam psalmodiam stupeo" (while I wondered at your devoted silence and angelic singing) (I.i). The English translation is from Petrarch, *On Religious Leisure,* ed. and trans. Susan S. Schearer (New York: Italica Press, 2002), 4.

42. Petrarca, *Secretum,* ed. Fenzi (1992), 200–203 (III.130–32).

43. For Petrarch on the Psalms, see Francesco Petrarca, *Poesie latine,* ed. Guido Martellotti and Enrico Bianchi (Turin: Einaudi, 1976), 190–93 (*Egl.* I vv. 53–56; 72–74; 91–109). Commenting in *Fam.* 10.4.6–7 on the first Eclogue, he writes to Gherardo: "Psalterium ipsum daviticum, quod die noctuque canitis, apud Hebreos metro constant, ut non immerito neque ineleganter hunc Cristianorum poetam nuncupare ausim" (the Psalms that you sing day and night possess poetic meter in Hebrew. For this reason I dare call him both deservedly and eloquently the poet of the Christians). See also *Fam.* 10.4.17–19: "est ipse David, cui propie convenit verbum psallere propter Psalmos, suum opus; media auctem nocte propter matutinam psalmodiam, que illo presertim tempore in eclesiis vestris auditur" (It is David himself, who is worthy of the verb *sing psalms* because of the Psalms he composed. In the middle of the night, moreover, refers to psalm singing at matins, since especially at that hour they are heard in your churches); and *Fam.* 10.4.31–32; and see Petrarch, *Salmi penitenziali,* ed. Roberto Gigliucci (Naples: Salerno editrice, 1999), 7–13.

44. Cf. *Fam.* 10.3.27 "Quid cause est nisi quod contritis pari conditione laqueis, nequaquam quod sequitur pars fuit, 'adiutorium nostrum in nomine Domini'? (Ps. 123.8) cur autem hanc daviticam cantilenam tanto concentu ceptam tam dissona voce complevimus?"

45. For uses of Psalm 123.8, see Carolus Marbach, *Carmina Scripturarum* (Hildesheim: George Olms, 1963), 234, and Michel Andrieu, *Le Pontifical Romain au Moyen-Age,* vol. 3, *Le Pontifical de Guillaume Durand* (Città del Vaticano: Biblioteca apostolica vaticana, 1940), 336–38 ("De clerico faciendo" III.2).

46. See *Sen.* 10.1 (952–53) to Sagremor; to Jean Birel, *Sen.* 16.8 (1061). See the instances in *Fam.* 10.3.

47. See *Fam.* 10.3.11 ("libertati tue congaudeas et fraterne condoleas servivuti" [you are now enjoying liberty while grieving for your brother's servitude]); also 21, 26, 27, 35.

48. The point is hinted at in Bernardo, "Petrarch's Attitude," 500–506.

49. For Dante's Davidic *teodia,* see Teodolinda Barolini, *Dante's Poets: Textuality and Truth in the Comedy* (Princeton: Princeton University Press, 1984), 275–79;

cf. *Fam.* 10.4.6–7, where Petrarch speaks of the "sacrum . . . poema" of Christ's life, a reference to the psaltery (and so to the liturgy), but possibly also to the "poema sacro" of his vernacular predecessor.

50. Durandus, *Rationale* II.2.2: "Sane David, prophetarum eximius, cultum Dei volens sollempnius ampliare cantores instituit qui coram archa federis Domini musicis instrumentis et modulatis vocibus decantarent" (Well did David, best of prophets, wishing to expand the worship of God more solemnly, he instituted cantors who might sing with musical instruments before the Ark of the Covenant of the Lord); see also V.2.36, and Pope Damasus instituting "chori, in duas partes divisi, psalmos canerent alternatim" (let the choirs, divided in two parts, sing the psalms alternately).

51. "Dulcius hic quanto media sub nocte videbis / psallere pastorem!" (How sweeter you will hear a shepherd sing here at about midnight!) (*Egl.* I.55–56, in Petrarca, *Poesie latine,* 190–91); see Antonio Avena, ed., *Il bucolicum carmen e i suoi commenti inediti* (Padua: Società cooperativa tipografica, 1906), 173, cf. *Egl.* I: "et dicit psallere propter psalterium, quod fecit David, cuius psalmos in nocte debitis horis quando regulares et monaci canunt (et precipue illi monacj certose magis devote offitia eorum et misteria faciunt)."

52. In addition to Petrarca, *Salmi* (ed. Gigliucci), see also *Salmi penitenziali,* trans. Ida Garghella (Naples: Edizioni scientifiche italiane, 2002), 12, who summarizes the proposals for dating: 1342–43 (Cochin, who ties the *Salmi* to Gherardo's 1343 vocation); 1338–47 (Foresti); 1347 (Martellotti, associating them with *Bucolicum carmen* I); 1347–48 (Casali and most scholars, associating them with the *Secretum;* see below); dating also summarized in Petrarca, *Salmi* (ed. Gigliucci), 15.

53. See *Sen.* 10.1 (952–58); for the association with Gherardo, see 958. The letter to Sagremor is the fullest discussion of the *Salmi;* Petrarch claims he wrote them in a day and identifies them as rough, *rauca,* as David's verse was held to be in *Egloga* I.74 and at *Fam.* 10.4.31. See *Sen.* 10.1.53: "Psalmos septem misi quos in miseriis dudum meis ipse michi composui tam efficaciter—utinam—quam inculta . . . leges eos qualescumque sunt, idque patientius facies si hos quidem ipsos et te petisse et me, multos ante annos, luce una nec integra dictasse, memineris." (I sent the seven psalms that I long ago composed for myself in my misery. I wish they were as edifying as they are inelegant . . . You will them as they are and do so more patiently if you will remember that they are what you asked for, and that I dictated them many years ago in less than one day.) English translations from the *Seniles* are from Petrarch, *Letters of Old Age. Rerum senilium libri,* 2 vols., trans. Also S. Bernardo, Saul Levin, and Reta A. Bernardo (Baltimore and London: Johns Hopkins University Press, 1992). See also *Dispersa 73* (where the *Salmi* are alluded to as *devotiuncula*) in Francesco Petrarca, *Lettere disperse,* ed. Alessandro Pancheri (Parma: Guanda, 1994), 488.

54. See *Regula benedicti* 16 in *Benedict's Rule,* a translation and commentary by Terrence G. Kardong (Collegeville, Minn.: Liturgical Press, 1996), 191 ("qualiter

divina opera per diem agantur"): "Ut ait propheta, *septies in die laudem dixi tibi.* Qui septenarius sacratus numerus a nobis sic implebitur, si matutino, primae, tertiae, sextae, nonae, vesperae completoriique tempore nostrae servitutis officia persolvamus, quia de his diurnis horis dixit: *Septies in die laudem dixi tibi.* Nam de nocturnis vigiliis idem ipse propheta ait: *Media nocte surgebam ad confitendum tibi.* Ergo his temporibus referamus *laudes* Creatori nostro *super iudicia iustitiae suae,* id est matutinis, prima, tertia, sexta, nona, vespera, completorios, et *nocte surgamus ad confitendum ei.*" [The Prophet says: "*Seven times a day I praised you*" (Ps 118[119]:164). We will fulfill this sacred number of seven if we satisfy our obligations of service at Lauds, Prime, Terce, Sext, None, Vespers and Compline, for it was of these hours during the day that he said: "*Seven times a day have I praised you*" (Ps 118[119]:164). Concerning Vigils, the same Prophet says: "*At midnight I arose to give you praise*" (Ps 118[119]:62). Therefore, we should *praise* our Creator for his *judgements* at these times: Lauds, Prime, Terce, Sext, None, Vespers and Compline; and *let us arise at midnight to give* him *praise* (Ps 118[119]:164, 62).] English translation from *The Rule of St. Benedict,* ed. Timothy Fry, O.S.B. (Collegeville, Minn.: Liturgical Press, 1981). See also Durandus, *Rationale* V.1.2, describing the Office in general: "Verum David inquit: 'Septies in die laudem dixi tibi' et rursus: 'Media nocte surgebam ad confitendum tibi', etc."

    55. See Hughes, *Medieval Manuscripts,* 23–24. The Old Testament doxology, dividing the Book of Psalms in the Bible into eight sections, is "Benedictus Dominus" or variant.

    56. See the studies by Marino Casali, "Petrarca 'penitenziale' dai 'Salmi' alle 'Rime,'" *Lettere italiane* 20 (1968): 366–82, and "Imitazione e ispirazione nei *Salmi penitenziali* del Petrarca," *Humanitas* 13 (1958): 365–81; brief accounts in Vinicio Pacca, *Petrarca* (Bari: Laterza, 1998), 131–32, and Marco Ariani, *Petrarca* (Rome: Salerno editrice, 2000), 127–31.

    57. After *Salmi* 1.1, there are instances of *Miserere* or a closely related term at *Salmi* 1.11, 1.26; 2.19; 3.1, 3.12; 4.2, 4.20; 5.10; 6.12; and 7.22 ("Misericorditer" [mercifully]).

    58. See *Salmi* 1.27 ("eripe me de faucibus inferni" [save me from the jaws of hell]); 2.3 ("ab infernis evellere" [to lift out of hell]) and 14 ("me erueris" [you will save me]); and especially 3.7 ("eripe me servitio hostis tui" [save me from the slavery of your enemy]) and 8 ("libera me de suppliciis eternis" [free me from eternal punishment]); this last, echoing the Responsory "Libera me, domine, de morte eterna" (Free me, Lord, from eternal death) from the *Officium mortuorum* at Matins and the Requiem Mass (see Van Dijk, *Sources,* 2:193), also anchors the citations from extracts of Job used in the Nine Lessons of Matins in the Office of the Dead (see *Salmi* 3.3, "domus novissima sepulchrum" [my final house, my sepulcher] and Job 17.1, the seventh extract; also 7.16, "umbra tenuis sum, et fumus" [I am feeble shadow, and smoke] and Job 14.1–2, the fifth extract; further investigation would reveal several more, e.g., not noted by editors, Job 19.25, the eighth extract, and

Salmi 2.3 and 6.11; also *Salmi* 6.2 and Job 10.18, the ninth extract; several passages of Job used by Petrarch are closely related to the extracts, e.g., *Salmi* 5.1 and Job 7.14, and 6.10 and Job 7.5, passages which precede the first extract, 7.16; also *Salmi* 1.3 and Job 17.13, coming after 17.1–2, the seventh extract).

59. The vernacular penitential psalms once attributed to Dante are post-Petrarchan; the study by Salvatore Floro di Zenzo, *Studio critico sull'attribuzione a Dante Alighieri di un antico volgarizzamento dei Sette salmi penitenziali* (Napoli: Laurenziana, 1984), except for pp. 5–9, giving the history of the attibution, is without value. Petrarch's psalms circulated with Carthusian devotional works and with Ludolph of Saxony's *Vita Christi*; see E. Ann Matter, "Petrarch's Personal Psalms (*Psalmi penitentiales*)," in *Petrarch: A Critical Guide to the Complete Works,* ed. Victoria Kirkham and Armando Maggi (Chicago: University of Chicago Press, 2009); see also Ariani, *Petrarca,* 127.

60. Dante's instances are *Purg.* 2.46 (Ps. 113.1); 5.24 (Ps. 50.1); 19.73 (Ps. 118.25); 23.11 (Ps. 50.17); 28.80 (Ps. 91.5–6); 29.3 (Ps. 31.1); 30.83 (Ps. 30.2); 31.98 (Ps. 50.9); 33.1 (Ps. 78.1). *Purg.* 30.19, beginning "Benedictus qui venis" (Blessed is he who comes), might be taken as an instance of Ps. 117.26, but is used as an acclamation more than as a psalm.

61. Psalm 118.25, "Adhaesit pavimento anima mea" (I lie prostrate in the dust) is second; Psalm 91.5, *Delectasti,* in fourth and central position; Psalm 30.1, "In te domine speravi" (In you, Lord, I take refuge), in sixth and penultimate. The *Miserere* addressed to Virgil is of course the pilgrim's first spoken word in the *Inferno* (1.65), and the *incipit* to Psalm 50 recurs near the end of the Paradiso (*Par.* 32.12); its role is thus distributed over the whole poem. English translations of the Bible are from the *New American Bible* (New York: Catholic Book Publishing, 1992).

62. See Van Dijk, *Sources,* 2:39–40 (Octave of the Nativity, of Circumcision); 2:127 (at Vespers for the Purification of the Virgin); and 2:191 (Office of the Virgin, at all Hours). The text of the Antiphon is "O admirabile commercium: Creator generis humani, animatum corpus sumens, de Virgine nasci dignatus est; et procedens homo sine semine, largitus est nobis suam deitatem" (O wonderful exchange: the Creator of the human race, taking on himself a living body, deigned to be born of a Virgin, and coming forth a man without seed, granted us his own divinity). Vittorio Rossi (*Fam.* 13.6; Rossi edition, 2:73) points out the allusion but misconstrues it: Petrarch's point is not merely to contrast Christ with the venal pope.

63. *Fam.* 13.6.10: "erat [Cola] autem a romano rege ad romanum pontificem missus. O mirum commercium! Non audeo quod sequitur dicere, neque hoc ipsum dicere volebam, sed quod inceperam" (he had been sent by the Roman king to the Roman pontiff. What an astonoshing exchange! I dare not say what followed, nor did I wish to say this much; instead I shall continue where I left off).

64. Durandus, *Rationale* VI.26.1–4; esp. 1: "significat tempus uiduitatis Ecclesie et illius merorem propter absentiam sponsi qui peccatoribus abest per gratiam" (it signifies the time of the widowhood of the Church and her sorrow due to the

absence of her Spouse whose grace is absent from sinners); also for rogations, processions, purification; closely related to Septuagesima and the return from Babylon after seventy years.

65. For the text of *Sine nomine* 7, see Paul Piur, *Petrarcas 'Buch ohne Namen' und die papstliche Kurie: Ein Beitrag zur Geistesgeschichte der Frührenaissance* (Halle and Saale: Max Niemeyer, 1925), 192–93; for the frequency of the dialogue, see Hughes, *Medieval Manuscripts*, 53–55. For discussion of the *Sine nomine*, see Ronald L. Martinez, "Petrarch's Open Secret," in *Petrarch: A Critical Guide to the Complete Works*, ed. Victoria Kirkham and Armando Maggi (Chicago: University of Chicago Press, 2009), 291–99.

66. On Dante's use of scripture in *Purg.* 6.70–139, see M. Perugi, "Il Sordello di Dante e la tradizione mediolatina dell'invettiva," *Studi danteschi* 55 (1983): 23–135, who points out that Dante's interrogation of God relies on the rhetorically heightened figure of *licentia*; see also Velli, "Il Dante di Francesco Petrarca," and Ronald L. Martinez, "Lament and Lamentation in *Purgatorio* and the Role of Dante's Statius," *Dante Studies* 117 (1997): 46–82.

67. *Seniles* 7.1 (9–11): "o si igitur nocte hac, quae Apostolorum Petri & Pauli glorioso martyrio sacra est, & hac ipsa noctis hora, qua tibi anxius, tam fidenter nec minus reverenter haec scribo in basilica Apostolorum principis, quae peculiaris basilica tua est, divino quod nunc canitur officio, & matutinas Christi laudes interesses, quantam & quam sacram percipias voluptatem, quae suspiria, quae lachrymas dares, quam dolores, quod non longior nox esset." (Oh, if on this night, which is sacred because of the glorious martyrdom of Peter and Paul, and at this very hour that I am writing this to you so trustfully and no less respectfully in my eagerness, you were present in the basilica of the Prince of the Apostles, which is your own basilica for the divine office now being sung and the matins, what a great and holy pleasure you would experience, what sighs you would give, what tears you would shed, what regrets you would have that the night were not longer!)

68. For the liturgy of the feast, see Carolus Marbach, *Carmina Scripturarum*, 494–95; Robert Lippe, ed., *Missale romanum mediolani 1474* (London: Henry Bradshaw Society, 1899), 347; Van Dijk, *Sources*, 2:288; Durandus, *Rationale* VII.15; note especially the readings, from Acts 12.1, 7, and 11, and the pertinent Antiphons, Responsories, and Versicles ("Nunc scio vere" [Now I truly know]; "Angelus Domini" [The Angel of the Lord]; "Dixit Angelus ad Petrum" [The Angel said to Peter]; "Misit dominus angelum suum, et liberavit me de manu Herodis [The Lord has sent his Angel and freed from the hand of Herod], etc.).

69. It is also heard daily in the Canticle of Zacharias concluding the Office of Lauds (Luke 1.78–79: "In quibus visitavit nos, oriens ex alto: Illuminare his qui in tenebris et in umbra mortis sedent" [by which the daybreak from on high will visit us to shine on those who sit in darkness and death's shadow]). The text of the Antiphon "O oriens" is: "O oriens, splendor lucis aeternae, et sol justitiae, veni, et illumina sedentes in tenebris, in umbra mortis" (O rising dawn, splendor of eter-

nal light, and sun of justice, come and illumine those sitting in darkness, in the shadow of death).

70. See Durandus, *Rationale* VI.2.4 ("antiqui patres primum adventum tantum expectaverunt, secundum vero antiqui et moderni" [the ancient fathers awaited only the first coming; the second, however, both the ancient and the modern]) and VI.11.4 ("ad ostendendum desiderium antiquorum patrum, in fine Adventus cantantur septem antiphone" [to show forth the desire of the ancient fathers at the end of Advent are sung seven antiphons]). In the Nicodemus apocryphon, John the Baptist, announcing the advent of Christ to Hell, reiterates the "qui sunt in regione umbrae mortis" passage, which then recurs in varied form ("veniens sedentibus nobis in tenebris et in umbra mortis" [coming to us who are sitting in darkness and in the shadow of death]); cf. *Gesta Salvatoris* in Heerak Christian Kim, ed., *The Gospel of Nicodemus: Gesta salvatoris* (Toronto: Pontifical Institute, 1973), 37, 41.

71. Petrarca, *De otio*, 102: "Habemus quo vite cursum dirigamus, quod unum tantis illis defuit ingeniis. 'Habitantibus in regione umbre mortis lux orta est' ostensumque nobis iter in tenebris" (. . . we have the final goal, a thing which the great minds of antiquity did not have, to which we should direct the course of our life. 'The light has risen on those who live in the region of the shadow of death,' and a path has been revealed to us in the darkness). English translation in Schearer, *On Religious Leisure,* 144.

72. Indeed, the rhymes of *Inf.* 1.59–63 (*poco; loco; fioco*) are reprised at 4.68–72 (*foco; poco; loco*).

73. The whole context is Dantean in both word and number, given that Petrarch's "vinto dal sonno" (*TC* 1.11) evokes both *Inferno* 1.11 (!) "tant'era pien di sonno," and *Purg.* 9.11 (!) "vinto dal sonno."

74. Francesco Petrarca, *Trionfi, Rime estravaganti, Codice degli abbozzi,* ed. Vinicio Pacca and Laura Paolino (Milan: Mondadori, 1996), 51–52; Francesco Petrarca, *Triumphi,* ed. Marco Ariani (Milan: Mursia, 1988), 80–81 (all references to *Trionfi* are to this edition).

75. Folchetto's biography ("Folco, que' ch'a Marsilia il nome ha dato, / et a Genova tolto," *TC* 4.49–50) echoes Dante's version in *Purg.* 3.27 of the traditional epitaph locating Virgil's body ("Napoli l'ha, e da Brandisio è tolto"; not in Ariani or Pacca and Paolino).

76. See Ariani, ed., *Triumphi,* 247–48.

77. The commendation texts are in Andrieu, *Le Pontifical Romain au Moyen-Age,* vol. 2, *Le Pontifical de la Curie romaine au XIIIe siècle,* 498 ("exurgat Deus et dissipentur inimici eius et fugiant a facie eius" [let god arise and let his enemies be scattered and let them flee from his face]). *Adversarii* plausibly derives from Dante's *Purg.* 8.95, "il nostro avversaro." For the *commendatio* prayers and Beatrice's death, see Ronald L. Martinez, "The Poetics of Advent Liturgies: Dante's *Vita nuova* and *Purgatorio,*" in *Le culture di Dante: Studi in onore di Robert Hollander. Atti del quarto Seminario dantesco internazionale, University of Notre Dame [Ind.], USA,*

25–27 settembre 2003, ed. Michelangeo Picone, Theodore J. Cachey, Jr., and Margherita Mestica (Florence: Franco Cesati, 2004), 271–304.

78. *Inter alia*: Carlo Calcaterra, "La 'data fatale' nel *Canzoniere* e nei *Trionfi del Petrarca*," in *Nella selva del Petrarca* (Bologna, Capelli, 1942), 209–45; Thomas Roche, "The Calendrical Structure of Petrarch's *Canzoniere*," *Studies in Philology* 71 (1974): 152–72; Bortolo Martinelli, "*Feria sexta aprilis*: La data sacra nel *Canzoniere* del Petrarca," in *Petrarca e il Ventoso* (Bergamo: Minerva Italica, 1977), 103–48; Robert M. Durling, "Petrarch's 'Giovene donna sotto un verde lauro,'" *MLN* 86 (1971): 1–20; and *Petrarch's Lyric Poems: The "Rime sparse" and Other Lyrics*, trans. and ed. Robert M. Durling (Cambridge, Mass.: Harvard University Press, 1976), 18–26; Giovanni Biancardi, "L'ipotesi di un ordinamento calendariale del *Canzoniere* di Petrarca," *Giornale storico della letteratura italiana* 172 (1995): 1–55. See also F. J. Jones, "Arguments in Favour of a Calendrical Structure for Petrarch's *Canzoniere*," *Modern Language Review* 79 (1984): 579–88.

79. See Nancy Vickers, "Widowed Words: Dante, Petrarch, and the Metaphors of Mourning," in *Discourses of Authority in Medieval and Renaissance Literature*, ed. Kevin Brownlee and Walter Stephens (Hanover, N.H.: University Press of New England, 1989), 97–108; Rosanna Bettarini, *Lacrime e inchiostro nel Canzoniere del Petrarca* (Bologna: CLUEB, 1998), 45–60; Ronald L. Martinez, "Mourning Beatrice: The Rhetoric of Lamentation in the *Vita nuova*," *MLN* 115 (1998): 1–29, and "Mourning Laura in the *Canzoniere*: Lessons from Lamentations," *MLN* 118 (2003): 1–45.

80. On Kalendars in missals and breviaries, see John Harper, *The Forms and Orders of Western Liturgy* (Oxford: Clarendon Press, 1991), 43–56; Hughes, *Medieval Manuscripts*, 275–80; and Hiley, *Western Plainchant*, 13–17. For an example of a contemporary missal with initial Kalendar copied for an Avignon churchman Petrarch knew, see Elly Cassee, *The Missal of Cardinal Bertrand de Deux: A Study in Fourteenth-Century Bolognese Miniature Painting*, trans. Michael Hoyle (Florence: Istituto Universitario Olandese di Storia dell'Arte, 1980), 87–98. Time-consciousness in the fourteenth century was, arguably, intense because of attempts by Clement VI to correct the Julian calendar (so as to accurately fix the date of Easter); it is no accident that Durandus includes a section on *Computus* in his liturgical *summa*, the *Rationale* VIII (vol. 3, 130–75).

81. The thirty-two indications of time of composition preserved in Vatican 3196 use *matutinum* (morning), *mane* (dawn), *vesperis* (vespers), *prima et tertia* (prime and terce), *meridies et nonam* (noon and none), and *hora sexta* (sext); as well as neutral terms like *Prima face, nocte concubia, cenam, sero, prandium*. Arabic numerals predominate (e.g., "1369 iunii 21, hora 23, veneris" [June 21, 11:00 pm., Friday]), more rarely Roman numerals appear ("1351 die sabati, XXV marti, manè" [Saturday morning, March 25, 1351]; "post XXII annos. 1368 dominico, inter nonam et vesperas" [after 22 years. Sunday 1368, between none and vespers]). *Mane* or *matutinum* occurs seven times, *vesperis* nine, *prima* once, *tertia* four times, *meridies*

twice, *hora 6* once, *nona* three times, *nox* (*nocte*) three times. Data derived from *Trionfi, Rime disperse,* ed. Pacca and Paolino.

82. Valeria Bertolucci Pizzorusso, "Il canzoniere di un trovatore: Il Libro di Guiraut Riquier," *Medioevo Romanzo* 5 (1978): 254, quoted in Guglielmo Gorni, "*Petrarca Virgini*: Lettura della canzone CCCLXVI 'Vergine bella,'" *Lectura petrarce* 7 (1987): 201–18; for liturgical references see the edition by Giosuè Carducci and Severino Ferrari, *Le Rime* (Florence: Le Monnier, 1899 [rpt. 1956]), 512–21; for liturgical contexts to *Rvf* 1 and *Rvf* 366, see also Martinez, "Mourning Laura," 6–8, 32–33.

83. For the critical tradition on *Rvf* 264, see *Canzoniere,* ed. Santagata, 1043–56; a useful corrective to the attempts (by A. Foresti, H. Baron, E. H. Wilkins, Francesco Rico, K. Foster) at dating the canzone and correlating it with the *Secretum* is given by Klaus W. Hempfer, who summarizes the useful views of Bernhard Koenig; see "La canzone CCLXIV, il *Secretum* e il significato del *Canzoniere* di Petrarca," *Lectura petrarce* 14 (1994): 263–87. Whatever the dating, the verbal and thematic links of 264 with the *Secretum* and other poems such as *Rvf* 365, for example, are beyond dispute. Santagata's claim that as the twenty-first canzone the poem falls at Christmas is unpersuasive; a stronger argument can be made for marking the poem as falling on Good Friday, equally indicated by the numerological pattern.

84. Johann Drumbl, "Die Improperien in der lateinischen liturgie," *Archiv für Liturgiewissenschaft* 15 (1973): 97, cites a missal from Marseille including the rubric: "ad quam [crucem] conversi omnes, mox ut crucifixum Dominum extensis brachiis ad amplexum nos sue reconciliationis invitantem conspicimus, terre prosternimur" (to which cross all having turned, as soon as we see the crucified Lord inviting us to be reconciled with him with arms oustretched to embrace us, we stretch out on the ground).

85. See Andrieu, *Le Pontifical Romain au Moyen-Age,* vol. 2, *Le Pontifical de la Curie romaine au XIIIe siècle,* 481, "Ordo ad dandam penitentiam": "qui pro amore hominum in cruce manus expandisti." ("The order of giving penance": you who for the love of men stretched out [your] hands on the cross.)

86. Kenelm Foster gives a succinct "penitential" reading in *Petrarch, Poet and Humanist* (Edinburgh: Edinburgh University Press, 1987), 43, 56, 100; on *memento mori* in *Rvf* 264 and its correlative statement in the *Secretum,* see Fenzi ed. (1992), 70, and Hempfer, "La canzone CCLXIV," 267–73, 276–79.

87. *Canzionere,* ed. Santagata, 686–87; and Guglielmo Gorni, "La forma Correggio del *Canzoniere,*" in *Metrica e poesia* (Bologna: Il Mulino, 1993), 171–82, esp. 177–81.

88. For the veneration of the cross on Good Friday, see Durandus, *Rationale* VI.87.14–20; and Hardison, *Christian Rite,* 130–34. In *Fam.* 10.3.50–52, writing to Gherardo, Petrarch paraphrases the *Improperia,* Christ's reproaches from the Cross, part of the veneration ceremony.

89. Gorni, "La forma Correggio," 178, identifies the citation as Paul, 2 Cor. 6.2; but its uses during Lent (it furnishes the Epistle for the first Sunday in Lent) and characterizing Advent are vivid (see Durandus, *Rationale* VI.1.4; VI.32.7, 11). For Dante's use of the phrase in the context of the Advent of Emperor Henry VII, see the *incipit* to *Epistle* 5 discussed in Paola Rigo, "Tempo liturgico nell'epistola ai principi e ai popoli d'Italia," in *Memoria classica e memoria biblica in Dante* (Florence; Olschki, 1994), 33–44, esp. 40.

90. See also *Rvf* 268 (*disciolta*, v. 38; "recida il nodo," v. 65); *Rvf* 270 (*lacci*, vv. 56 and 61; *nodo*, v. 93; *sciolto*, v. 106); *Rvf* 271 (v. 1: "L'ardente nodo"; v. 6: *lacciuol*; v. 13: "rotto 'l nodo").

91. David Quint, "Schiavi del tempo: Petrarca e Ronsard," in *Il petrarchismo: Un modello di poesia per l'Europa*, ed. Loredana Chines, Floriana Calitti, and Roberto Gigliucci, 2 vols. (Rome: Bulzoni, 2006), 1:113–27.

92. See especially Deut. 15.1–3, 12–15; also Lev. 25.2–4, Deut. 5.12 (Decalogue on keeping the sabbath).

93. Durandus, *Rationale* VI.24.4 ("trademini in manu hostili, sc. Nabuchodonosor, et servietis septuaginta annis" [you handed us in the hands of the enemy we would serve for seventy years]); also VI.26.1 ("merorem propter absentiam sponsi" [sorrow because of the absence of her spouse]).

94. See Petrarca, *Secretum*, ed. Fenzi, 308; commenting on *Secretum* I (Fenzi, 128: "sed spei plenus quod Dei dextera potens promptaque sit ex tantis malis eruere" [but full of hope that the right hand of God may be prompt and powerful to deliver from so many evils]). The pattern is fully established in *Epystole* I.6, to Barbato da Sulmona (in *Poesie latine*, ed. Martellotti and Bianchi); cf. vv. 44 (gravem . . . cathenam [heavy . . . chains]); 46 (femineo . . . iugo [feminine . . . yoke]); 56 (nodus [knot]); 63 (vincla [fetters]); 109 (vincula [bonds]); 145–46 ("sic salvus ab istis / eruar" [so saved I shall be delivered by these]); 152–54 ("michi nectit Amor laqueos; spes nulla superstes, / ni Deus omnipotens tanto me turbine fessum / eripiat manibusque suis de faucibus hostis" [Love has me in its grips; no hope remains, unless almighty God with his own hands should rescue me, exhausted by so mighty a whirlwind, from the jaws of the enemy]).

95. See *Fam.* 10.3.17: "Sed te de tantis errorum tenebris eduxit repentina mutatio dextere Excelsi" (But a sudden intervention by the hand of the Almighty led you out of those serious shadows of error); other instances at 10.3.11, 23–24, and 27; also *Fam.* 10.5.23.

96. *Fam.* 23.12.20: "Non indiges adiutore nisi ethereo; Ille aderit et dextram porriget laboranti, quotiens ad eum poeticum illud cristiana pietate clamaveris : 'eripe me his, invicte, malis'" (You will need no assistance except from heaven; He will be present, extending His hand to you in your suffering as often as you direct to Him with Christian devotion those poetic words). See *Aen.* VI.365–71: "eripe me his, invicte, malis . . . da dextram misero et tecum me tolle per undas" (snatch me away, unconquered one, from these evils . . . give me your right hand, and pull me through the waters with you).

97. See Dante Alighieri, *Purgatorio,* ed. Robert M. Durling and Ronald L. Martinez (New York: Oxford, 2003), 597–600, with bibliography.

98. The Harrowing scenario is explicit, for example, in *Sine nomine* 19 (ed. Piur, *Petrarcas 'Buch ohne Namen,'* 235–38), the final letter in which Petrarch celebrates the escape of Nelli from the Inferno of Avignon: "ex inferno in se sperantes animas aducit" ([God] who guides out of the inferno the souls of them that trust in him). The English translation is from *Petrarch's Book without a Name,* trans. Norman P. Zacour (Toronto: Pontifical Institute of Mediaeval Studies, 1973), 118; see also Theodore J. Cachey, Jr., ed. and trans., *Petrarch's Guide to the Holy Land: Itinerarium ad sepulchrum domini nostri Yehsu Christi [Itinerary to the Sepulcher of Our Lord Jesus Christ]* (Notre Dame, Ind.: University of Notre Dame Press, 2002), 16.3: "dum ille mortis et inferni victor ad regna hostis spolianda descenderet" (while he descended to raid the realms of the enemy, that conqueror of death and the underworld).

99. See Holy Saturday Matins in Van Dijk, *Sources,* 2:86–88, and the Franciscan *Officium defunctorum* (Van Dijk, *Sources,* 2:192–93) for representative versions.

100. For the *Descensus* see Heerak Christian Kim, ed., *The Gospel of Nicodemus: Gesta salvatoris* (Toronto: Pontifical Institute, 1973). Much of this portion of the work was digested into Vincent of Beauvais, *Speculum Historiale* (1624; repr. Graz: Akademische Druck- und Verlagsanstalt, 1964), VII, ch. 40–63, with the *Descensus* in ch. 59–63. Chapter 53 of Iacopo da Varazze, *Legenda aurea,* ed. Giovanni Paolo Maggioni (Tavernuzze: Sismel, 1998), 1:365–69, is more condensed. Michele Feo, "Inquietudini filologiche del Petrarca: Il luogo della discesa agli inferi (Storia di una citazione)," *Italia medioevale e umanistica* 17 (1974): 115–83, does not discuss Christ's descent into Hell as an influence on Petrarch.

101. For Psalm 23, Isaiah 9.2, and Psalm 106 in the *Descensus,* see *Gesta,* in Kim, *Gospel of Nicodemus,* 41–43; for Psalm 23 and Psalm 106 in the Holy Saturday liturgy, see Van Dijk, *Sources,* 2:87, and n. 104 below. I am preparing a full discussion of this nexus of texts.

102. In *Oratio quotidiana,* in Francesco Petrarca, *Opere inedite,* ed. Attilio Hortjs (Trieste: Tipografia del Lloyd austro-ungarico, 1874), 286–87. See also *Salmi* 1.27: "et memor promissionum tuarum, eripe me de faucibus inferni" (and mindful of your promises, save me from the jaws of hell) (28 is the last verse); 3.7: "eripe me de servitio hostis tui" (free me from the slavery of your enemy); 3.8: "libera me de suppliciis eternis" (save me from eternal punishment). See also *Epyst.* I.6, 152–55 and I.14, 122–37.

103. Petrarca, *De otio,* 72: "sed in hoc, ut in reliquis omnibus mortalium bellis, sive etiam aliquanto presentius celeste auxilium sentit terrena fragilitas, itaque et in alis et in hoc maxime victoria et triumphus a deo sunt. Multa quidem, fratres, Babilonis flumina novimus magno transvadanda periculo, in quorum transitu nostri ducis dexteram poscentes cristiano ore poeticum illud exclamemus ad invictum vere, quod ad suum vere victum et profugum ille naufragus apud Virgilium exclamabat: 'Eripe me . . . quiescam.'" (but in this matter, just as in all the other wars

of mortals, if earthly frailty feels the presence of the aid of heaven somewhat more, the victory and triumph come from God in both instances, but especially in this one. Indeed, brothers, we know Babylon's many rivers which we must cross with great danger. Seeking the right hand of our Lord in crossing them, let us cry out with a Christian voice to the One Who is truly unconquered. We shall cry out as Vergil's shipwrecked who had been truly conquered and exiled: 'Rescue me . . . may I lie in a calm resting place.') See Schearer, *On Religious Leisure,* 97.

104. See Van Dijk, *Sources,* 2:80–89, passim. In the *Missale,* ed. Lippe, Psalm 139.1 furnishes the Tract on Friday and the offertory on Wednesday of Holy Week; Psalm 58.1 is the Response to the Invitatory during the week after Palm Sunday, and the Offertory on Monday of Easter week. See also *Missale,* 143, 135.

105. See Van Dijk, *Sources,* 2:192–93, *In officium mortis,* Verse and Responsory "A porta inferi erue domine" (save me from the door of hell) and "Erue domine" (Save [me] Lord).

106. See Van Dijk, *Sources,* 2:193 for the reading from Job (14.13–15) and 2:195 for the the Antiphon at Lauds, "Me suscepit dextera tua domine" (Lord, may your right hand protect me).

107. See Van Dijk, *Sources,* 2:193.

108. See *Gesta,* in Kim, *Gospel of Nicodemus,* 41.

109. The San Marco mosaic is reproduced in Charles S. Singleton, *Inferno. 2. Commentary* (Princeton: Princeton University Press, 1970), opposite p. 60; for the Holkham ms. illustration, consult: http://www.bodley.ox.ac.uk/dept/scwmss/wmss/medieval/jpegs/holkham/misc/48/500/04800431.jpg.

110. Hezekiah (*Par.* 20.49–54) and Adam (26.118–20) are examples; see Amilcare Iannucci, "Dottrina e allegoria in *Inferno* VIII, 67–IX, 105," in *Dante e le forme dell'allegoresi,* ed. M. Picone (Ravenna: Longo, 1987), 99–124, and Peter S. Hawkins, *Dante's Testaments: Essays in Scriptural Imagination* (Stanford, Calif.: Stanford University Press, 1999), 99–124.

111. It is not recognized in Claudio Giunta, "Memorie di Dante nei *Trionfi,*" *Rivista di Letteratura Italiana* 11 (1993): 411–52.

112. See *Paradiso* 31.80–81 ("soffristi per la mia salute / in inferno lasciar le tue vestige"); cf. Amilcare Iannucci, "La discesa di Beatrice agli Inferi," in *Forma ed evento nella Divina Commedia* (Rome: Bulzoni, 1984), 51–82; for Beatrice, Laura, and Medusa (*Rvf* 366, v. 111) see Kenelm Foster, "Beatrice or Medusa: The Penitential Elements in Petrarch's *Canzoniere,*" in *Italian Studies Presented to E. R. Vincent,* ed. C. P. Brand, K. Foster, and U. Limentani (Cambridge: W. Heffer & Sons, 1962), 53, and Martinelli, *Petrarca e il Ventoso,* 236–39.

113. For the date of the letter, see Foresti, *Anedotti,* 336–41; Wilkins, *Eight Years,* 139–42.

114. *Sen.* 16.8 (1061).

115. For commentary on poems 62–63, see *Canzoniere,* ed. Santagata, 316–18, where attention is also called to *Aen.* 2.143–44 and *Salmi* I.26, II.19, III.1.

116. See Durandus, *Rationale* IV.48.2: "Et per hoc quod dicit: 'Pater noster qui es in celis', dehortatur nos a duobus: videlicet a superbia, ne dicamus 'Pater mi', quasi reputantes proprium quod est commune." (And it is for this that we say: 'Our Father who art in heaven', it discourages us from two things, namely from pride lest we say 'My Father' as though we regarded God who is common to all as our private possession.)

117. See "Io maledico il dì ch'io vidi in prima / la luce de' vostri occhi traditori; e maledico; e maledico" in *Tutte le opere di Dante Alighieri*, ed. Edward Moore (Oxford: Clarendon Press, 1904), 173; the poem is now attributed to Cino da Pistoia.

118. *Canzoniere*, ed. Santagata, 312–13; cf. Boccaccio, *Filostrato* 3.83; Cecco Angolieri, poem 51, "Maladetta sie l'or e'l punt' e'l giorno" (in *Rime*, ed. Gigi Cavalli [Milan: Rizzoli, 1959], 63).

119. Mariann S. Regan, "Petrarch's Courtly and Christian Vocabularies: Language in *Canzoniere* 61–63," *Romance Notes* 15 (1974): 527–31. For liturgical maledictions common in monastic rituals (sometimes juxtaposed to benedictions) and the problematic of cursing in general, see Lester K. Little, *Benedictine Maledictions: Liturgical Cursing in Romanesque France* (Ithaca and London: Cornell University Press, 1993).

120. See Philippe Bernard, "La cantique des trois enfants (Dan. III, 52–90): Les répertoires liturgiques occidentaux dans l'antiquité tardive et le haut moyen age," *Musica e Storia* 1 (1996): 232–76; for the doxologies, see Hughes, *Medieval Manuscripts*, 23–24, 224–27. The pericope on the three boys in the furnace from Daniel 3.49–51 is part of the last of the twelve Old Testament prophecies of Christ read on Holy Saturday; as the Hymnus or *canticum trium puerorum* it is the Tract on ember Saturday in Advent and Lent after a *capitulum* from Daniel introducing it; see Van Dijk, *Sources*, 2:53; it is also a *capitulum* at Tuesday Vespers in Ordinary time, see Van Dijk, 2:57–59, 260. For the *capitulum* and tract see *Missale*, ed. Lippe, 11: "quasi ex uno ore laudabant et glorificabant et benedicebant deum in fornace dicentes" (almost as from one mouth they praised, glorified, and blessed God in the furnace saying), followed by the *canticum:* "Benedictus es domine deus patrum nostrorum" (Blessed are you Lord, God of our fathers), including eight more verses beginning with benedictions, with corresponding versicles beginning "Et laudabilis" (and praiseworthy) and "Et laudent te" (and may they praise you).

121. For formulas of praise and blessing, see Luke 24.53, the final verse of the Gospel ("et erant semper in templo, laudantes et benedicentes Deum"), and St. Francis, *Laudes creaturarum*, line 32 ("Laudate et benedicete mi' Signore"), in Nicolò Pasero, *Laudes creaturarum: Il cantico di Francesco d'Assisi* (Parma: Pratiche editrice, 1992); both scriptural and liturgical examples could be multiplied.

122. See M. Pastore Stocchi, "I sonetti III e LXI," *Lectura petrarce* 1 (1981): 1–23, esp. 10–13.

123. D'Arco Silvio Avalle, "Compendi liturgici in testi lirici profani del XIII° secolo," *Medioevo e Rinascimento* 2 (1994): 138–42; summarized in his *Concordanza*

della lingua poetica italiana delle origini (Milan and Naples: Ricciardi, 1992), clx–clxi. The *Benedicite* series is conspicious in many manuscripts with series of maiuscule *Bs* clearly emphasized, see Hughes, *Manuscripts*, 319, 331, plates 3cd and 13.

124. No trace of these designations appear in the Vaticano 3793 anthology; this might result from the reliance of the Vaticano on mercantile rather than liturgical exemplars for its concept of the book. See Justin Steinberg, "Merchant Bookkeeping and Lyric Anthologizing: Codicological Aspects of Vaticano 3793," in *Scrittura e civiltà* 24 (2000): 251–69.

125. See Avalle, *Concordanza*, clxi: "Il compendio R sembra suggerire una certa analogia . . . fra il 'responsorio' liturgico e il 'ritornello' profano (tutti e due i termini iniziano con una *r* come pure — ma si tratterà forse di puro caso — la 'ripresa', il *respos* e il *refrain* della ballata."

126. *Canzoniere*, ed. Santagata, 319–20 ("assistiamo alla ripresa, con segno invertito, della situazione del testo che precede"); cf. Emilio Bigi, "Le ballate del Petrarca," *Giornale storico della letteratura italiana* 151 (1974): 481–93.

127. Petrarch is of course evoking *Par.* 11.49–50 ("Di questa costa . . . / . . . nacque al mondo un sole").

128. Petrarca, *Canzoniere,* ed. Santagata, 25; Francis was canonized within two years of his death in 1226 and his name inserted in the Kalendar and litanies of the first Franciscan (or *Regula*) breviary by 1230; an Office for his feast was quickly arranged; see Van Dijk, *Sources,* 1:43–44. For Petrarch's attention to turmoil in the Franciscan Order, see his letter to the pope on behalf of the general of the Order (*Sen.* 11.12).

129. For bibliography on *Rvf* 5, see *Canzoniere,* ed. Santagata, 26–29, and Martinez, "Mourning Laura," 36–37.

130. For *mortal* in line 14 as part of the paragram, see Durling, *Petrarch's Lyric Poems*, 13.

131. Facsimile examples of syllabified texts may be found in Hughes, *Medieval Manuscripts*, 318–54, see esp. 336; for the mnemonics, see Hughes, *Medieval Manuscripts*, 114: for *Ut queant laxis*, see Hiley, *Western Plainchant*, 467–70. Guido's hymn is especially suggestive for Petrarch's sonnet, as its text, drawn from the feast of St. John the Baptist, concerns the act of singing itself.

132. Franciscan influence discernible in *Rvf* 4 may also be at work here, as both Psalm 148 and the *Canticum trium puerorum* were crucial influences for the vernacular canticle composed by Francis of Assisi; for a summary of the sources, see Pasero, *Laudes creaturarum*; and *Il cantico de Fratre Sole: Studio delle fonti e testo critico,* ed. Vittore Branca (Florence: Olschki, 1950).

133. Many are listed in the notes to the Carducci-Ferrari edition; see Petrarca, *Rime,* ed. Carducci and Ferrari, 512–21; see also Gorni, *"Petrarca Virgini"*; Piero Boitani, *The Tragic and the Sublime in Medieval Literature* (Cambridge: Cambridge University Press, 1989), 200–205 (on the rejection of Laura). On Dante's Beatrice compared, see Foster, "Beatrice or Medusa," 40–54.

134. Dante's *Par.* 33.1–2 and 6, "farsi sua fattura," are recalled in Petrarch's canzone, esp. vv. 1–4, 27–28, likely mediated (as Carducci-Ferrari note, *Rime,* 514) by the text of *Alma redemptoris mater* (cf. "genuisti . . . genitorem" [you gave birth to the one who made you]; also "genuisti qui te fecit" [you brought forth the one who made you] from the Mass offertory text "Beata es virgo Maria" [Blessed are you, Virgin Mary]; Van Dijk, 2:294, 297, 320). For the relation of "Vergine bella" to sestina form, see Martinez, "Mourning Laura," 32–33; see *Canzoniere,* ed. Santagata, 1402, for Bernardine inspiration, echoing the spokesman of Dante's prayer (cf. Steven Botterill, *Dante and the Mystical Tradition* [Cambridge: Cambridge University Press, 1994], 180–88). Gorni, "*Petrarca Virgini,*" points out the relation through rubricated initials both with *Par.* 33.1 and *Rvf* sonnet 1. Georg Rabuse, "Petrarcas Marienkanzone im Licht der 'Santa Orazione' Dantes," in *Petrarca 1304–1374: Beiträge zu Werk und Wirkung,* ed. Fritz Schalk (Frankfurt am Main: Klostermann, 1975), 245–54, juxtaposes "Vergine bella" 100–105 and *Par.* 33.79–85, and suggests numerological considerations (253–54).

135. Gorni, "*Petrarca virgini,*" 210.

136. *Canzoniere,* ed. Santagata, 1401–2.

137. Gorni, "*Petrarca Virgini,*" 205; note, too, that Petrarch's substitution of *spinge* for *mosse* echoes Francesca, *Inf.* 5.130: "li occhi ci sospinse."

138. Twice, too, the Marian hymn *Ave maris stella* (vv. 27, 67) and once the *Magnificat* (vv. 47–48, 52); the Vespers canticle in line 40, "vera et altissima humiltate" (true and highest humility), again echoing Dante, *Par.* 33.2, "umile e alta più che creatura."

139. Durandus, *Rationale* V.10.1: "eadem quoque hora, sanguineas guttas sudavit; et etiam in sepulcro corpus eius positum fuit."

140. See "Me suscepit dextera tua domine" (May your right hand, O Lord, defend me) from the Office of the Dead at Lauds (Van Dijk, *Sources,* 2:195), and Andrieu, *Le Pontifical Romain au Moyen-Age,* vol. 2, *Le Pontificale de la Curie romaine au XIIIe siècle,* esp. 500–503, for numerous examples of *suscipere* from the *commendatio animae.* "Vergine bella" v. 91, "e sol Morte n'aspetta," echoes Job 17.1, the seventh of the Job extracts in the *Officium mortuorum* (Van Dijk, *Sources,* II, 193).

141. Martinelli, *Petrarca e il Ventoso,* 289. Martinelli hears the same source in "Padre del ciel" (*Rvf* 62.13), *Rvf* 80.39, at the end of the *Secretum,* at the end of the letter on Mount Ventoux (*Fam.* 4.1), in Petrarch's daily prayer (*oratio quotidiana*), and in *Dispersa* 9.

142. The *Benedictus* Antiphon for the ferial Office of Lauds on Saturday, "Illuminare . . . qui sedent, ad dirigendos pedes nostros in viam pacis" (Illumine those who dwell [in darkness], and to guide our feet in the way of peace); cf. Van Dijk, *Sources,* 2:60. The Office of the Dead at Matins itself was known as *Dirige,* after the verse of Psalm 5.9 with which it begins: "dirige domine deus meus in conspectu tuo viam meam" (guide me and make straight your way before me).

143. See also *Purg.* 18.45, "se dritta o torta va, non è suo merto"; and 23.125–26: "rigirando la montagna / che drizza voi che'l mondo fece torti." See also 2.99 and 24.141 for the concept of peaceful departure.

144. 1366–67 *was* a good year for Petrarch as a writer: he completed several important works, including a version of the *Familiares,* his "image and simulacrum." *Sen.* 7.1, prompting Urban to return to Rome and 9.1, congratulating Urban on doing so, frame the two letters to Boccaccio; Petrarch is thus enshrined at the center of the *Seniles* as a world-agent who can move popes to act.

145. *Sen.* 8.1.9–15 (1554): "scit me Christus liberator meus verum loqui, qui saepe mihi cum lachrymis exoratus, flenti ac misero dextram dedit, secumque me sustulit, iuxta illud Poeticum: 'Sedibus ut saltem placidis in morte quiescam' [*Aen.* 6.731]." (Christ my Saviour knows I speak the truth, for He was won over by my tears and often gave me His right hand as I wept and groaned, and raised me according to the poet's words, 'At least in death may I rest in peaceful dwellings' [Virgil, *Aen.* 6.371].)

146. Petrarch's period is strikingly elaborate (*Sen.* 8.1.9–17): "scito enim: & sciant siqui erunt, qui tam humilem non fastidiant originem scire, me anno aetatis huius ultimae, quae ab illo qui hanc mihi spem tribuit IESU CHRISTO & initium traxit, & nomen millesimo trecentesimo quarto, die lunae vigesima Iulij illuscente, commodium aurora, in Aretina urbe, in vico qui ortus dicitur, natum esse. Quae dies, apud nostros publica, & insignis est nota, ea scilicet quae exules nostri, qui se Aretium Bononiamque contulerant, hinc illinc contractis in unum exercitibus, armati die illa, & ipsa ferme qua nascebar hora, antequam sol iugis montium erumperet, ad portas primas venerunt, siqua fors favisset, ferro exilium ulturi, isque adventus etsi inefficax fuerit, quia tam magnis motibus, & ingenti omnia terrore concusserat, nescio quidem, an adhuc est memoria hostium elapsus, sed usque ad hos proximos annos, vulgo percelebris fuit." (For let me tell you, and let others know, if there are any who do not scorn knowing about such humble origins, that I was born in the year 1304 of this last age which got its name and start from Him who provides me with this hope, Jesus Christ, on Monday, July 20, at the break of dawn, in the city of Arezzo, on what is called Garden Street. That is a red-letter day for our people, namely because our exiles, who had betaken themselves to Arezzo and Bologna, came together on that day from both place armed as a single army; and almost at the very hour when I was born, before the sun burst over the mountaintops, they came to the gates of their native city to take vengeance with the sword for their exile, if luck were with them. Although the undertaking proved fruitless, it had shaken up everything with such great tumult and immense terror that I still do not know whether to this day the enemy has forgotten it, but until these last few years it was constantly on the multitude's lips.)

Primary Works of Dante and Petrarch

Alighieri, Dante. *La Commedia secondo l'antica vulgata.* Edited by Giorgio Petrocchi. 4 vols. Milan: Mondadori, 1966–67.

———. *La Commedia secondo l'antica vulgata.* Edited by Giorgio Petrocchi. 2nd ed. 4 vols. Florence: Le Lettere, 1994.

———. *Convivio.* Edited by Franca Brambilla Ageno. 2 vols. Florence: Le Lettere, 1995.

———. *Dante Alighieri Inferno.* Translated by Robert and Jean Hollander. New York: Doubleday, 2000.

———. *Dante's Eclogues (the Poetical Correspondence between Dante and Giovanni del Virgilio).* English translation by Wilmon Brewer. Boston, Cornhill, 1927.

———. *De vulgari eloquentia.* Edited and translated by Steven Botterill. Cambridge: Cambridge University Press, 1996.

———. *De vulgari eloquentia.* In *Dante Alighieri, Opere minori.* Edited by Pier Vincenzo Mengaldo, 2:3–237. Milan and Naples: Ricciardi, 1979.

———. *The Divine Comedy.* Translated by John D. Sinclair. 3 vols. Oxford and New York: Oxford University Press, 1971.

———. *The Divine Comedy.* Translated by Charles S. Singleton. 3 vols in 6. Princeton: Princeton University Press, 1970–75.

———. *The Divine Comedy.* In *The Portable Dante.* Translated and edited with introduction and notes by Mark Musa. New York: Penguin Books, 1995.

———. *The Divine Comedy of Dante Alighieri.* 3 vols. Edited and translated by Robert M. Durling. Introduction and notes by Robert M. Durling and Ronald L. Martinez. Illustrations by Robert Turner. Oxford and New York: Oxford University Press, 1996 (vol. 1, *Inferno*), 2003 (vol. 2, *Purgatorio*), vol. 3 forthcoming.

———. *Le egloghe.* Edited and translated by Giorgio Brugnoli and Riccardo Scarcia. Milan and Naples: Ricciardi, 1980.

———. *Le egloghe.* In volume 2 of *Opere minori.* Edited by Enzo Cecchini. Milan and Naples: Ricciardi, 1979, 1989.

————. *Inferno.* Edited by Anna Maria Chiavacci Leonardi. Milan: Mondadori, 1991.

————. *Opere minori.* Edited by Enzo Cecchini. Milan and Naples: Ricciardi, 1989.

————. *Opere minori.* Edited by Cesare Vasoli and Domenico De Robertis. Milan and Naples: Ricciardi, 1988.

————. *Rime.* Edited by Gianfranco Contini. Turin: Einaudi, 1995.

————. *Tutte le opere di Dante Alighieri.* Edited by Edward Moore. Oxford: Clarendon Press, 1904.

————. *Vita Nuova.* Edited by Domenico De Robertis. In *Opere minori* I/1. Edited by Domenico De Robertis and Gianfranco Contini, 27–247. Milan and Naples: Ricciardi, 1984.

————. *Vita Nuova. Rime.* Edited by Fred Chiappelli. Milan: Mursia, 1965.

Benvenuto da Imola. *Comentum super Dantis Aldigherii Comoediam.* Edited by James Philip Lacaita. 5 vols. Florence: Barbera, 1887.

Petrarca, Francesco. *Africa.* Translated by Thomas G. Bergin and Alice S. Wilson. New Haven: Yale University Press, 1977.

————. *L'Africa.* Edited by Nicola Festa. Florence: Sansoni, 1926.

————. *L'Afrique, 1338–1374.* Edited and translated by Rebecca Lenoir. Grenoble: Éditions Jérôme Millon, 2002.

————. *Bucolicum carmen.* Translated by Thomas G. Bergin. New Haven: Yale University Press, 1974.

————. *Canzoniere.* Edited by Rosanna Bettarini. Turin: G. Einaudi, 2005.

————. *Canzoniere.* Edited by Gianfranco Contini and annotated by Daniele Ponchiroli. Turin: Einaudi, 1964, 1968.

————. *Canzoniere.* Edited by Marco Santagata. Milan: Mondadori, 1996. Rev. 2006.

————. *Canzoniere.* Edited by Marco Santagata. 2nd ed. Milan: Mondadori, 1997.

————. *The Canzoniere, or Rerum Vulgarium Fragmenta.* Translated by Mark Musa. Bloomington: Indiana University Press, 1996.

————. *De otio religioso.* Edited by Giuseppe Rotondi. Città del Vaticano: Biblioteca apostolica vaticana, 1958.

————. *De sui ipsius et multorum ignorantia; Della mia ignoranza e di quella di molti altri.* Edited by Enrico Fenzi. Milan: Mursia, 1999.

————. *Le familiari.* (*Rerum familiarium libri*). Edited by Vittorio Rossi and Umberto Bosco. 4 vols. Rome and Florence: Sansoni, 1933–42.

————. *Francisci Petrarchae operum: Tomus I–VI.* Basle, 1554. Anastatic reprint, Ridgewood, N.J.: Gregg Press, 1965.

————. *Invectives.* Edited and translated by David Marsh. I Tatti Renaissance Library. Cambridge, Mass.: Harvard University Press, 2003.

————. *Lettere Disperse.* Edited by Alessandro Pancheri. Parma: Guanda, 1994.

————. *Letters of Old Age. "Rerum Senilium Libri" I–XVIII.* Translated by Aldo S. Bernardo, Saul Levin, and Reta A. Bernardo. 2 vols. Baltimore and London: Johns Hopkins University Press, 1992.

————. *Letters on Familiar Matters. Rerum familiarum libri.* Translated by Aldo S. Bernardo. 3 vols. Albany: State University of New York Press, 1975; Baltimore and London: Johns Hopkins University Press, 1982–85.

————. *On Religious Leisure.* Edited and translated by Susan S. Schearer. New York: Italica Press, 2002.

————. *Opere inedite.* Edited by Attilio Hortjs. Trieste: Tipografia del Lloyd austro-ungarico, 1874.

————. *Opere latine di Francesco Petrarca.* Edited and translated by Antonietta Bufano. Turin: Unione tipografico-editrice torinese, 1975.

————. *Petrarch's Book without a Name.* Translated by Norman P. Zacour. Toronto: Pontifical Institute of Mediaeval Studies, 1973.

————. *Petrarch's Guide to the Holy Land: Itinerary to the Sepulcher of Our Lord Jesus Christ.* Edited and translated by Theodore J. Cachey, Jr. Notre Dame, Ind.: University of Notre Dame Press, 2002.

————. *Petrarch's Lyric Poems: The "Rime sparse" and Other Lyrics.* Translated and edited by Robert M. Durling. Cambridge, Mass.: Harvard University Press, 1976.

————. *Petrarch's Remedies for Fortune Fair and Foul.* Translated by Conrad H. Rawski. 5 vols. Bloomington and Indianapolis: Indiana University Press, 1991.

————. *Petrarch's Secretum.* Translated by William H. Draper. London, 1911.

————. *Poesie latine.* Edited by Guido Martellotti and Enrico Bianchi. Turin: Einaudi, 1976.

————. *Prose.* Edited by Guido Martellotti et al. Milan and Naples: Ricciardi, 1955.

————. *Rerum memorandarum libri.* Edited by Giuseppe Billanovich. Volume 14 in *Edizione nazionale delle opere di Francesco Petrarca.* Florence: Sansoni, 1943.

————. *Rerum vulgarium fragmenta* [*Rime sparse*]. Translated and edited by Robert L. Durling, in *Petrarch's Lyric Poems: The "Rime sparse" and Other Lyrics.* Cambridge, Mass.: Harvard University Press, 1976.

————. *Res seniles. Libri I–IV.* Edited by Silvia Rizzo with the assistance of Monica Berté. Florence: Le Lettere, 2006.

————. *Le Rime.* Edited by Giosuè Carducci and Severino Ferrari. Florence: Sansoni, 1899–1912. Rpt. 1957.

————. *Rime disperse di Francesco Petrarca o a lui attribuite.* Edited by Angelo Solerti. Florence: Sansoni, 1909. Rpt. in Florence: Le Lettere, 1997.

————. *Rime, Trionfi, e poesie latine.* Edited by Ferdinando Neri et al. Milan and Naples: Ricciardi, 1951.

————. *Salmi penitenziali.* Translated by Ida Garghella. Naples: Edizioni scientifiche italiane, 2002.

————. *Salmi penitenziali.* Edited by Roberto Gigliucci. Naples: Salerno editrice, 1999.

————. *Scritti inediti di Francesco Petrarca.* Edited by Attilio Hortis. Trieste: Tipografia del Lloyd Austro-Ungarico, 1874.

————. *The Secret.* Edited by Carol E. Quillen. Bedford Series in History and Culture. Boston: Bedord/St. Martin's, 2003.

————. *Secretum*. Introduced and edited by Davy A. Carozza and H. James Shey. New York: Peter Lang, 1989.

————. *Secretum*. Edited by Enrico Carrara. In *Prose*. Milan and Naples: Ricciardi, 1955.

————. *Secretum*. Introduced, translated, and notes by Ugo Dotti. Rome: Archivio Guido Izzi, 1993.

————. *Secretum: Il mio segreto*. Edited and translated by Enrico Fenzi. Milan: Mursia, 1992, 1999.

————. *Senile V 2*. Edited by Monica Berté. Florence: Le Lettere, 1998.

————. *Seniles*. In *Opera quae extant omnia*, 813–1070. Basle: Henrichus Petri, 1554.

————. *Le senili*. Edited and translated by Ugo Dotti. Turin: Aragno, 2004.

————. *Trionfi, Rime estravaganti, Codice degli abbozzi*. Edited by Vinicio Pacca and Laura Paolino. Milan: Mondadori, 1996.

————. *Triumphi*. Edited by Marco Ariani. Milan: Mursia, 1988.

————. *The Triumphs of Petrarch*. Translated by Ernest Hatch Wilkins. Chicago and London: University of Chicago Press, 1962.

OTHER PRIMARY AND SECONDARY SOURCES

Ahern, John. "What Did the First Copies of the *Comedy* Look Like?" In *Dante for the New Millenium*, edited by Teodolinda Barolini and H. Wayne Storey, 1–15. New York: Fordham University Press, 2003.

Alessio, Gian Carlo. "La *Comedìa* nel margine dei classici." In *Studi di filologia medievale offerti a D'Arco Silvio Avalle*, 1–25. Milan and Naples: Ricciardi, 1996.

————. "I trattati grammaticali di Giovanni del Virgilio." *Italia medioevale e umanistica* 24 (1981): 159–212.

Allegretti, Paola, and Guglielmo Gorni. "Mondo dell'oltretomba e *spelunca* in Petrarca (RVF 161–70)." In *Il Canzoniere. Lettura micro e macrotestuale*, edited by M. Picone, 383–93. Ravenna: Longo, 2006.

Allen, Judson Boyce. *The Ethical Poetic of the Later Middle Ages*. Toronto: University of Toronto Press, 1982.

Alpers, Paul J. *What Is Pastoral?* Chicago: University of Chicago Press, 1996.

Andrieu, Michel. *Le Pontifical Romain au Moyen-Age*. Vol. 2, *Le Pontifical de la Curie romaine au XIIIe siècle*. Vol. 3, *Le Pontifical de Guillaume Durand*. Città del Vaticano: Biblioteca apostolica vaticana, 1940.

Angolieri, Cecco. *Rime*. Edited by Gigi Cavalli. Milan: Rizzoli 1959.

Antonelli, Roberto. "Perché un Libro(-Canzoniere)." *Critica del testo* 6 (2003): 49–65.

Antoni, Claudio G. "Esperienze stilistiche petrose da Dante al Petrarca." *Modern Language Studies* 13 (1983): 21–33.

Aquinas, Thomas. *Summa Theologiae*. In the Blackfriars edition. 61 vols. New York: McGraw-Hill; London: Eyre and Spottiswoode, 1964–81.

———. *Summa Theologiae*. Vol. 1, *Christian Theology*. Edited by Thomas Gilby. Cambridge: Blackfriars, 1964.

Ariani, Marco. "Introduzione." In Francesco Petrarca, *Triumphi*, edited by Marco Ariani, 5–52. Milan: Mursia, 1988.

———. *Petrarca*. Rome: Salerno editrice, 1999.

Aristotle. *Aristoteles Latinus*. Edited by L. Minio-Paluello. Bruges and Paris: Desclée De Brouwer, 1953–78.

———. *Physics*. In *The Basic Works of Aristotle*. Edited by Richard McKeon. Translated by R. P. Hardie and R. K. Gaye. New York: Random House, 1941.

Ascoli, Albert Russell. "Access to Authority: Dante in the *Epistle to Cangrande*." In *Seminario Dantesco Internazionale/International Dante Seminar I*, edited by Zygmunt Barański, 309–52. Florence: Le Lettere, 1997.

———. *Dante and the Making of a Modern Author*. Cambridge: Cambridge University Press, 2008.

———. *"A Local Habitation and a Name": Essays in the Historicity and Historiography of Italian Renaissance Literature*. New York: Fordham University Press, forthcoming.

———. "Palinode and History in the Oeuvre of Dante." In *Dante Now: Current Trends in Dante Studies*, edited by Theodore J. Cachey, Jr., 155–86. Notre Dame, Ind.: University of Notre Dame Press, 1993.

———. "Petrarch's Middle Age: Memory, Imagination, History, and the 'Ascent of Mt. Ventoux.'" *Stanford Italian Review* 10 (1991): 5–43.

———. "The Unfinished Author: Dante's Rhetoric of Authority in *Convivio* and *De vulgari eloquentia*." In *The Cambridge Companion to Dante*, edited by Rachel Jacoff, 45–66. Cambridge: Cambridge University Press, 1993.

———. "The Vowels of Authority (Dante's *Convivio* IV, vi, 3–4)." In *Discourses of Authority in Medieval and Renaissance Literature*, edited by Kevin Brownlee and Walter Stephens, 23–46. Hanover, N.H.: University Press of New England, 1989.

Asor Rosa, Alberto. "Le contingenze biografiche: l'esule, l'apolide, il 'refoulé." In *Letteratura italiana V: Le Questioni*, 90–93. Turin: Einaudi, 1986.

Asperti, Stefano. "Dante, i trovatori, la poesia." In *Le culture di Dante. Studi in onore di Robert Hollander. Atti del quarto seminario dantesco internazionale, University of Notre Dame (Ind.), USA, 25–27 settembre 2003*, 67–68. Edited by M. Picone, T. Cachey, and M. Mesirca. Florence: Cesati, 2004.

Augustine, Saint. *Confessions*. Translated with an introduction by R. S. Pine-Coffin. Harmondsworth, Middlesex; New York: Penguin, 1961.

———. *Confessions*. In the Loeb Classical Library edition. Translated by William Watts. 2 vols. Cambridge, Mass.: Harvard University Press; London: Heinemann, 1976.

———. *Opere di Sant'Agostino*. Nuova Biblioteca Agostiniana. Rome: Città nuova, 1995.

————. *Soliloquies*. Translated by Gerard Watson. Warminster, England: Aris and Phillips, 1990.

Avalle, D'Arco Silvio. "Compendi liturgici in testi lirici profani del XIII° secolo." *Medioevo e Rinascimento* 2 (1994): 138–42.

————, ed. *Concordanza della lingua poetica italiana delle origini*. Milan and Naples: Ricciardi, 1992.

Avena, Antonio, ed. *Il bucolicum carmen e i suoi commenti inediti*. Padua: Società cooperativa tipografica, 1906.

Azzetta, Luca. "Le chiose alla *Commedia* di Andrea Lancia, L'*Epistola a Cangrande* e altre questioni dantesche." *L'Alighieri* 44, n.s. 21 (2003): 5–73.

Baglio, Marco. "Presenze dantesche nel Petrarca latino." *Studi petrarcheschi* n.s. 9 (1992): 77–136.

Baldovin, John. *The Urban Character of Christian Worship*. Rome: Pontificium institutum studiorum orientalium, 1987.

Balduino, Armando. "Cino da Pistoia, Boccaccio e i poeti minori del Trecento." In *Colloquio Cino da Pistoia*, 33–85. Rome: Accademia Nazionale dei Lincei, 1976.

Barański, Zygmunt G. "'Alquanto tenea della oppinione degli epicuri': The *Auctoritas* of Boccaccio's Cavalcanti (and Dante)." *Zeitschrift für Deutsche Philologie* 13 (2005): 280–325.

————. "Canto XXII." In *Lectura Dantis Turicensis. Paradiso*, edited by G. Güntert and M. Picone, 339–62. Florence: Cesati, 2002.

————. "*Chiosar con altro testo*": *Leggere Dante nel Trecento*. Fiesole: Cadmo, 2001.

————. "The Constraints of Form: Towards a Provisional Definition of Petrarch's *Triumphi*." In *Petrarch's Triumphs: Allegory and Spectacle*, edited by Konrad Eisenbichler and Amilcare A. Iannucci, 62–83. Ottawa: Dovehouse Editions, 1990.

————. "Dante Alighieri: Experimentation and (Self-) Exegesis." In *The Cambridge History of Literary Criticism*. Vol. 2, *The Middle Ages*, edited by Alastair Minnis and Ian Johnson, 561–82. Cambridge: Cambridge University Press, 2005.

————. "Dante, the Roman Comedians, and the Medieval Theory of Comedy." In *"Libri poetarum in quattuor species dividuntur": Essays on Dante and 'Genre,'* edited by Z. G. Barański, 61–99. Supplement 2, *The Italianist* 15 (1995).

————. "The *Epistle to Cangrande*." In *The Cambridge History of Literary Criticism*. Vol. 2, *The Middle Ages*, edited by Alastair Minnis and Ian Johnson, 583–89. Cambridge: Cambridge University Press, 2005.

————. "Guido Cavalcanti and His First Readers." In *Guido Cavalcanti tra i suoi lettori*, edited by M. L. Ardizzone, 149–75. Fiesole: Cadmo, 2003.

————. "'nfiata labia' and 'dolce stil novo': A Note on Dante, Ethics, and the Technical Vocabulary of Literature." In *Sotto il segno di Dante: Scritti in onore di Francesco Mazzoni*, edited by L. Coglievina and D. De Robertis, 17–35. Florence: Le Lettere, 1998.

————. "A Note on the Trecento: Boccaccio, Benvenuto, and the Dream of Dante's Pregnant Mother." In *Miscellanea di Studi Danteschi in memoria di Silvio*

Pasquazi, edited by Alfonso Paoletta et al., vol. 1, 69–82. Naples: Federico & Ardia, 1993.

———. "Notes on Dante and the Myth of Orpheus." In *Dante, mito e poesia: Atti del secondo Seminario dantesco internazionale*, Monte Verità, Ascona, 23–27 giugno 1997, edited by Michelangelo Picone and Tatiana Crivelli, 133–54. Florence: Cesati, 1999.

———. "'Per similitudine di abito scientifico': Dante, Cavalcanti, and the Sources of Medieval 'Philosophical' Poetry." In *Science and Literature in Italian Culture: From Dante to Calvino. A Festschrift for Pat Boyde*, edited by P. Antonello and S. Gilson, 14–52. Oxford: Legenda, 2004.

———. "'Piangendo e cantando' con Orfeo (e con Dante): Strutture emotive e strutture poetiche in *RFV* 281–90." In *Lectura Petrarcae Turicensis. Il Canzoniere. Lettura micro e macrotestuale*, edited by M. Picone, 617–40. Ravenna: Longo, 2007.

———. "'Prima tra cotanto senno': Dante and the Latin Comic Tradition." *Italian Studies* 26 (1991): 1–36.

———. *"Sole nuovo, luce nuova": Saggi sul rinnovamento culturale in Dante*. Turin: Scriptorium, 1996.

Barber, Joseph A. "Il sonetto CXIII e gli altri sonetti a Sennuccio." *Lectura Petrarce* 2 (1982): 21–39.

Bareiss, Karl Heinz. *Comoedia: Die Entwicklung der Komödiendiskussion von Aristoteles bis Ben Jonson*. Frankfurt and Berne: Peter Lang, 1982.

Barolini, Teodolinda. *Dante's Poets: Textuality and Truth in the Comedy*. Princeton: Princeton University Press, 1984.

———. "The Making of a Lyric Sequence: Time and Narrative in Petrarch's *Rerum vulgarium fragmenta*." *MLN* 104 (1989): 1–38. Rpt. in *Dante and the Origins of Italian Literary Culture*, 193–223. New York: Fordham University Press, 2006.

———. "The Self in the Labyrinth of Time (*Rerum vulgarium fragmenta*)." In *Petrarch: A Critical Guide to the Complete Works*, edited by Victoria Kirkham and Armando Maggi, 33–62. Chicago: University of Chicago Press, 2009.

———. *The Undivine Comedy: Detheologizing Dante*. Princeton: Princeton University Press, 1992.

Baron, Hans. *Petrarch's "Secretum": Its Making and Its Meaning*. Cambridge, Mass.: Medieval Academy of America, 1985.

Battaglia Ricci, Lucia. "Il culto per Dante, l'amicizia con Petrarca." In *Dante e Boccaccio: Lectura Dantis Scaligera 2004–2005 in memoria di Vittore Branca*, edited by E. Sandal, 21–54. Rome and Padua: Antenore, 2006.

Battisti, Carlo. "Le egloghe dantesche." *Studi danteschi* 33 (1955–56): 61–111.

Baxandall, Michael. *Giotto and the Orators: Humanist Observers of Painting in Italy and the Discovery of Pictorial Composition, 1350–1450*. Oxford: Clarendon Press, 1971.

Bellomo, Saverio. "La *Commedia* attraverso gli occhi dei primi lettori." In *Leggere Dante*, edited by L. Battaglia Ricci, 73–84. Ravenna: Longo, 2002.

———. "Introduzione." in *Dizionario dei commenti danteschi*, 1–49. Florence: Olschki, 2004.

———. "Il sorriso di Ilaro e la prima redazione in latino della *Commedia*." *Studi sul Boccaccio* 32 (2004): 201–35.

Belting, Hans. *Likeness and Presence: A History of the Image before the Era of Art*. Translated by Edmund Jephcott. Chicago: University of Chicago Press, 1994.

Beltrami, Pietro G. "Appunti su 'Razo e dreyt ay si ·m chant e ·m demori.'" *Rivista di letteratura italiana* 5 (1987): 9–39.

Benassi, Stefano. "La vertigine del sublime: Moralità della poesia e razionalità della morale in F. Petrarca." In *Petrarca e la cultura europea*, edited by L. Rotondi Secchi Tarugi, 181–201. Milan: Editrice Nuovi Orizzonti, 1997.

Benedict's Rule. A translation and commentary by Terrence G. Kardong. Collegeville, Minn.: Liturgical Press, 1996.

Benvenuto da Imola. In *"La Divina Commedia" nella figurazione artistica e nel secolare Commento*, edited by Guido Biagi. 3 vols. Turin: Unione tipografico-editrice torinese, 1924–29.

Bernard, Philippe. "La cantique des trois enfants (Dan. III, 52–90): Les répertoires liturgiques occidentaux dans l'antiquité tardive et le haut moyen age." *Musica e Storia* 1 (1996): 232–76.

Bernardo, Aldo S., ed. *Francesco Petrarca, Citizen of the World: Proceedings of the World Petrarch Congress, Washington, D.C., April 6–13, 1974*. Padua: Antenore; Albany: State University of New York Press, 1980.

———. "Petrarch, Dante and the Medieval Tradition." In *Renaissance Humanism: Foundations, Forms and Legacy*. Vol. 1, *Humanism in Italy*, edited by A. Rabil Jr., 115–37. Philadelphia: University of Pennsylvania Press, 1988.

———. *Petrarch, Scipio and the "Africa": The Birth of Humanism's Dream*. Baltimore: Johns Hopkins University Press, 1962.

———. "Petrarch's Attitude toward Dante." *PMLA* 70 (1955): 488–517.

Berté, Monica. "Introduzione." In Francesco Petrarca, *Senile V 2*, 1–69. Florence: Le Lettere, 1998.

Bertelli, Sergio. *The Pope's Body*. Translated by R. Burr Litchfield. University Park: Pennsylvania State University Press, 1995.

Bertolani, Maria Cecilia. *Il corpo glorioso: Studi sui Trionfi del Petrarca*. Rome: Carocci, 2001.

———. *Petrarca e la visione dell'eterno*. Bologna: Il Mulino, 2005.

Bertolucci, Valeria Pizzorusso. "Il canzoniere di un trovatore: Il Libro di Guiraut Riquier." *Medioevo Romanzo* 5 (1978).

Bettarini, Rosanna. "'Che debb'io far? (RVF CCLXVIII).'" *Lectura Petrarce* 7 (1987): 187–99.

———. *Lacrime e inchiostro nel Canzoniere del Petrarca*. Bologna: CLUEB, 1998.

———. "Perché 'narrando' il duol si disacerba. (Motivi esegetici dagli autografi petrarcheschi)." In *La critica del testo: Problemi di metodo ed esperienze di lavoro*, 305–20. Rome: Salerno, 1985.

Bettini, Maurizio. "Tra Plinio e sant'Agostino: Francesco Petrarca sulle arti figurative." In *Memoria dell'antico nell'arte italiana,* edited by Salvatore Settis, 1:221–67. Turin, Einaudi, 1984.

Biancardi, Giovanni. "L'ipotesi di un ordinamento calendariale del *Canzoniere* di Petrarca." *Giornale storico della letteratura italiana* 172 (1995): 1–55.

Bigi, Emilio. "Le ballate del Petrarca." *Giornale storico della letteratura italiana* 151 (1974): 481–93.

Billanovich, Giuseppe. "L'altro stil nuovo: Da Dante teologo a Petrarca filologo." *Studi petrarcheschi* n.s. 11 (1994): 1–98.

———. "Dalla *Commedia* e dall' *Amorosa Visione* ai *Trionfi.*" *Giornale storico della letteratura italiana* 123 (1945–46): 51–52.

———. "Giovanni del Virgilio, Pietro da Moglio, Francesco da Fiano." Parts 1 and 2. *Italia medioevale e umanistica,* part 1 in 6 (1963): 203–34; part 2 in 7 (1964): 279–324.

———. "Un ignoto fratello del Petrarca." *Italia medioevale e umanistica* 25 (1982): 375–80.

———. "Laura fantasma del *Canzoniere.*" *Studi petrarcheschi* n.s. 11 (1994): 149–58.

———. "La leggenda dantesca del Boccaccio." *Studi danteschi* 27 (1948): 45–104.

———. "La leggenda dantesca del Boccaccio: Dalla lettera di Ilaro al *Trattatello in laude di Dante.*" *Studi danteschi* 28 (1949): 45–144.

———. *Petrarca e il primo umanesimo.* Padua: Edizioni Antenore, 1996.

———. *Petrarca letterato. I. Lo scrittoio del Petrarca.* Rome: Edizioni di "Storia e letteratura," 1947.

———. "Pietro Piccolo da Monteforte tra il Petrarca e il Boccaccio." In *Petrarca e il primo umanesimo,* 459–524. Padua: Edizioni Antenore, 1996.

———. "I primi umanisti e le tradizioni dei classici latini." In *Petrarca e il primo umanesimo,* 117–41. Padua: Edizioni Antenore, 1996.

———. "Tra Dante e Petrarca." *Italia medioevale e umanistica* 8 (1965): 1–44.

———. "Il vecchio Dante e il giovane Petrarca." *Letture classensi* 11 (1982): 99–118.

Billanovich, Giuseppe, and F. Cáda. "Testi bucolici nella biblioteca del Boccaccio." *Italia medioevale e umanistica* 4 (1961): 201–21.

Billanovich, Giuseppe, and Claudio Scarpati. "Da Dante al Petrarca e dal Petrarca al Boccaccio." In *Il Boccaccio nelle culture e letterature nazionali,* edited by Francesco Mazzoni, 583–604. Florence: Olschki, 1978.

Billanovich, Guido. "'Veterum vestigia vatum' nei carmi dei preumanisti padovani." *Italia medioevale e umanistica* 5 (1958): 155–243.

Blanc, Pierre. "Petrarca ou la poétique de l'ego." *Revue des études italiennes* 29 (1983): 122–69.

Blumenberg, Hans. *Naufragio con spettatore: Paradigma di una metafora dell'esistenza.* Bologna: Il Mulino, 1985.

Boccaccio, Giovanni. *Amorosa Visione.* Bilingual edition. Translated by Robert Hollander, Timothy Hampton, and Margherita Frankel. Hanover, N.H., and London: University Press of New England, 1986.

———. *Carmina.* Edited by Giuseppe Velli. In *Tutte le opere,* edited by Vittore Branca, 5-i (part 1 of vol. 5). Milan: Mondadori, 1992.

———. *Il codice Chigiano L.V. 176 / autografo di Giovanni Boccaccio.* Edited by Domenico De Robertis. Rome: Archivi Edizioni; Florence: Alinari, 1974.

———. *De Montibus, Silvis, Fontibus, Lacubus, Fluminibus, Stagnis seu Paludibus et de Diversis Nominibus Maris.* Edited by Manlio Pastore Stocchi. In *Opere Omnia, Volume VII–VIII,* edited by Vittore Branca, 1815–2122. Milan: Mondadori, 1998. Pt. 2.

———. *De vita et moribus Domini Francisci Petracchi de Florentia.* Edited by Renata Fabbri. In *Tutte le opere,* edited by Vittore Branca, 1:897–911. Milan: Mondadori, 2002.

———. *Eclogues.* Edited and translated by Janet Levarie Smarr. New York: Garland, 1987.

———. *Esposizioni sopra la Comedia di Dante.* Edited by Giorgio Padoan. Milan: Mondadori, 1965.

———. *Genealogia Deorum Gentilium.* Edited by Vittorio Zaccaria. In *Opera Omnia, Volume VII–VIII,* edited by Vittore Branca, 1–1814. Milan: Mondadori, 1998. Pts. 1 and 2.

———. *The Life of Dante (Trattatello in laude di Dante).* Translated by Vincenzo Zin Bollettino. New York and London: Garland, 1990.

———. *Opere latine minori.* Edited by A. F. Massèra. Bari: Laterza, 1928.

———. *Trattatello in laude di Dante.* Edited by Pier Giorgio Ricci. In Boccaccio's *Vita di Dante.* Milan: Mondadori, 2002.

———. *Trattatello in laude di Dante.* Edited by Pier Giorgio Ricci. In *Tutte le opere,* edited by Vittore Branca, 3:423–538. Milan: Mondadori, 1974.

Boethius. *Consolation of Philosophy.* In the Loeb Classical Library edition. Edited by H. F. Stewart and E. K. Rand. Cambridge, Mass.: Harvard University Press; London: Heinemann, 1936.

Boggs, Edward L. "Cino and Petrarch." *MLN* 94 (1979): 146–52.

Boitani, Piero. *The Tragic and the Sublime in Medieval Literature.* Cambridge: Cambridge University Press, 1989.

Boli, Todd. "Boccaccio's *Trattatello in laude di Dante,* or *Dante Resartus.*" *Renaissance Quarterly* 41 (1988): 389–412.

Bologna, Corrado. "Un'ipotesi sulla ricezione del *De vulgari eloquentia*: Il codice Berlinese." In *La cultura volgare padovana nell'età di Petrarca,* edited by Furio Brugnolo and Zeno Lorenzo Verlato, 205–56. Padova: Il Poligrafo, 2006.

———. "Occhi, solo occhi (*Rvf* 70–75)." In *Lectura Petrarcae Turicensis. Il Canzoniere. Lettura micro e macrotestuale,* edited by M. Picone, 183–205. Ravenna: Longo, 2007.

———. "PetrArca petroso," *Critica del testo* 6 (2003): 367–420.

———. *Tradizione e fortuna dei classici italiani.* 2 vols. Turin: Einaudi, 1993.

Bonaventure, Saint. *De triplici via.* Vol. 8 of *Opera omnia,* 3–27. Ad Claras Acquas (Quaracchi): Collegium S. Bonaventurae, 1882–1902.

————. *Itinerarium mentis in Deum.* Vol. 5 of *Opera omnia,* 295–313. Ad Claras Acquas (Quaracchi): Collegium S. Bonaventurae, 1882–1902.

————. *The Soul's Journey into God; The Tree of Life; The Life of St. Francis.* Translated by Ewert Cousins. The Classics of Western Spirituality. New York: Paulist Press, 1978.

————. *The Triple Way, or Love Enkindled.* In *Mystical opuscula,* translated by José de Vinck. The Works of Saint Bonaventure, vol. 1, 59–94. Paterson, N.J.: St. Anthony Guild Press, 1960.

Bosco, Umberto. *Dante vicino. Contributi e letture.* Caltanissetta and Rome: Sciascia, 1966.

————. *Francesco Petrarca.* 3rd ed. rev. Bari: Laterza, 1973 [1965; 1971].

Botterill, Steven. *Dante and the Mystical Tradition.* Cambridge: Cambridge University Press, 1994.

————. "The Trecento Commentaries on Dante's *Commedia.*" In *The Cambridge History of Literary Criticism.* Vol. 2, *The Middle Ages,* edited by Alistair Minnis and Ian Johnson, 590–611. Cambridge: Cambridge University Press, 2005.

Boyde, Patrick. *Dante Philomythes and Philosopher: Man in the Cosmos.* Cambridge: Cambridge University Press, 1981.

Boyle, Marjorie O'Rourke. *Petrarch's Genius: Pentimento and Prophecy.* Berkeley: University of California Press, 1991.

Branca, Vittore. *Boccaccio: The Man and His Works,* translated by Richard Monges. New York: New York University Press, 1976.

————, ed. *Il cantico de Fratre Sole: studio delle fonti e testo critico.* Florence: Olschki, 1950.

————. *Studi in onore di Matteo Marengoni.* Florence: Vallecchi, 1957.

Brownlee, Kevin, and Walter Stephens, eds. *Discourses of Authority in Medieval and Renaissance Literature.* Hanover, N.H.: University Press of New England, 1989.

Brownlee, Kevin, et al. "Vernacular Literary Consciousness c. 1100–c. 1500: French, German and English Evidence." In *The Cambridge History of Literary Criticism.* Vol. 2, *The Middle Ages,* edited by Alistair Minnis and Ian Johnson, 422–71. Cambridge: Cambridge University Press, 2005.

Bruni, Francesco. *Boccaccio: L'invenzione della letteratura mezzana.* Bologna: Il Mulino, 1990.

Bück, August. *Der Orpheus-Mythos in der italienischen Renaissance.* Krefeld: Scherpe, 1961.

Burckhardt, Jacob. *The Civilization of the Renaissance in Italy: An Essay.* 1859. Landmarks in Art History. Oxford: Phaidon, 1981.

Burke, Peter. "Representations of the Self from Petrarch to Descartes." In *Rewriting the Self: Histories from the Renaissance to the Present,* edited by Roy Porter, 17–28. London New York: Routledge, 1997.

Cachey, Theodore J., Jr. "From Shipwreck to Port: *Rvf* 189 and the Making of the *Canzoniere.*" *MLN* 120, no. 1 (January 2005): 30–49.

————. "'Peregrinus (quasi) ubique': Petrarca e la storia del viaggio." *Intersezioni: Rivista di storia delle idee* 17 (December 1997): 369–84.

————. "Per una mappa del *Canzoniere*: *Rvf* 171–179." In *Il Canzoniere. Lettura micro e macrotestuale,* edited by M. Picone, 395–414. Ravenna: Longo, 2006.

————. *Petrarch's Guide to the Holy Land: Itinerarium ad sepulchrum domini nostri Yehsu Christi [Itinerary to the Sepulcher of Our Lord Jesus Christ].* Notre Dame, Ind.: University of Notre Dame Press, 2002.

————. "The Place of the *Itinerarium.*" In *Petrarch: A Critical Guide to the Complete Works,* edited by Victoria Kirkham and Armando Maggi. Chicago: University of Chicago Press, 2009.

Calcaterra, Carlo. "La 'data fatale' nel *Canzoniere* e nei *Trionfi* del Petrarca." In *Nella selva del Petrarca,* 209–45. Bologna: Cappelli, 1942.

————. *Nella Selva del Petrarca.* Bologna: Cappelli, 1942.

Camille, Michael. *The Gothic Idol: Ideology and Image-Making in Medieval Art.* Cambridge: Cambridge University Press, 1989.

Campana, Augusto. "Epitafi." In *Enciclopedia dantesca.* 6 vols., edited by Umberto Bosco, 2:710–13.

Capovilla, Guido. "Petrarca e l'ultima canzone di Dante." *Lectura Petrarce* 14 (1994): 289–358.

Caputo, Rino. *Cogitans fingo: Petrarca tra "Secretum" e "Canzoniere."* Rome: Bulzoni, 1987.

Carrara, Enrico. "L'epistola 'Posteritati' e la leggenda petrarchesca." In *Studi petrarcheschi ed altri scritti,* 3–76. Turin: Bottega d'Erasmo, 1959.

Carruthers, Mary. *The Book of Memory.* Cambridge: Cambridge University Press, 1990.

————. *The Craft of Thought: Meditation, Rhetoric, and the Making of Images 400–1200.* Cambridge: Cambridge University Press, 1998.

————. "Rhetorical *Ductus,* or, Moving through a Composition." In *Acting on the Past: Historical Performance across the Disciplines,* edited by Mark Franko and Annette Richards, 99–117. Hanover, N.H.: Wesleyan University Press; published by University Press of New England, 2000.

Casagrande, Carla, and Silvana Vecchio. *I peccati della lingua: Disciplina ed etica della parola nella cultura medievale.* Rome: Istituto della Enciclopedia Italiana, 1987.

Casali, Marino. "Imitazione e ispirazione nei *Salmi penitenziali* del Petrarca." *Humanitas* 13 (1958): 365–81.

————. "Petrarca 'penitenziale' dai 'Salmi' alle 'Rime.'" *Lettere italiane* 20 (1968): 366–82.

Casella, Maria Teresa. *Tra Boccaccio e Petrarca. I volgarizzamenti di Tito Livio e di Valerio Massimo.* Studi sul Petrarca 14. Padova: Antenore, 1982.

Cassee, Elly. *The Missal of Cardinal Bertrand de Deux: A Study in Fourteenth-Century Bolognese Miniature Painting.* Translated by Michael Hoyle. Florence: Istituto Universitario Olandese di Storia dell'Arte, 1980.

Cassirer, Ernst, *The Renaissance Philosophy of Man*. Chicago: University of Chicago Press, 1948.

Cavalcanti, Guido. *Rime con le Rime di Iacopo Cavalcanti*. Edited by Domenico De Robertis. Turin: Einaudi, 1986.

Cavallari, Elisabetta. *La fortuna di Dante nel Trecento*. Florence: Perrella, 1921.

Cecchini, Enzo. "Giovanni del Virgilio, Dante, Boccaccio: Appunti su un'attribuzione controversa." *Italia medioevale e umanistica* 14 (1971): 25–56.

Cecilia, Adolfo. "Eufrates." In *Enciclopedia dantesca*. 6 vols., edited by Umberto Bosco, 2:765.

———. "Tigri." In *Enciclopedia dantesca*. 6 vols., edited by Umberto Bosco, 5:604.

Ceserani, Remo. "'Petrarca': Il nome come auto-reinvenzione poetica." *Quaderni petrarcheschi* 4 (1987): 121–37.

Cestaro, Gary. *Dante and the Grammar of the Nursing Body*. Notre Dame, Ind.: University of Notre Dame Press, 2003.

———. "Giovanni del Virgilio." In *The Dante Encyclopedia*, edited by Richard Lansing, 863–64. New York: Garland, 2000.

Chenu, M. D. "Auctor, Actor, Autor." *Bulletin du Cange: Archivium Latinitas Medii Aevi* 3 (1927): 81–86.

Chevalier, Jean-Frédéric. "Introduction." In Albertino Mussato, *Écérinide; Épitres métriques sur la Poésie; Songe,* edited and translated by Jean-Frédéric Chevalier. Paris: Les Belles Lettres, 2000.

Chiarini, Eugenio. "I 'decem vascula' della prima ecloga dantesca." In *Dante e Bologna nei tempi di Dante,* edited by Facoltà di Lettere e Filosofia dell'Università di Bologna, 77–88. Bologna: Commissione dei Testi di Lingua, 1967.

Chirilli, Emilia. "Di alcuni dantismi nella poesia volgare di Francesco Petrarca." *L'Alighieri* 16 (1975): 44–74.

Cipollone, Annalisa. "'Né per nova figura il primo alloro . . .': La chiusa di *Rvf* XXIII, il Canzoniere e Dante." *Rassegna europea di letteratura italiana* 11 (1998): 29–46.

Cipriani, Giovanni. "Petrarca, Annibale e il simbolismo dell'occhio." *Quaderni petrarcheschi* 4 (1987): 167–84.

Comparetti, Domenico, *Virgilio nel Medio Evo*. 2 vols. 2nd ed., edited by Giorgio Pasquali. Florence: La Nuova Italia, 1943. First published 1872.

Constable, Giles. "Petrarch and Monasticism." In *Francesco Petrarca, Citizen of the World: Proceedings of the World Petrarch Congress, Washington, D.C., April 6–13, 1974,* edited by Aldo S. Bernardo, 53–99. Padua: Antenore; Albany: State University of New York Press, 1980.

Contini, Gianfranco. "Un'interpretazione di Dante." In *Varianti e altra linguistica,* 369–405. Turin: Einaudi, 1970.

———. "Introduzione alle *Rime* di Dante." In *Un'idea di Dante: Saggi danteschi,* 3–20. Turin: Einaudi, 1976.

———. *Letteratura italiana delle origini*. Florence: Sansoni, 1970.

————. "Petrarca e le arti figurative." In *Francesco Petrarca, Citizen of the World: Proceedings of the World Petrarch Congress, Washington, D.C., April 6–13, 1974*, edited by Aldo S. Bernardo, 115–31. Padua: Antenore; Albany: State University of New York Press, 1980.

————. *Poeti del Duecento*. Milan: Ricciardi, 1995.

————. "Postilla dantesca." In *Un'idea di Dante: Saggi danteschi*, 231–33. Turin: Einaudi, 1976.

Cooper, Helen. *Pastoral: Mediaeval into Renaissance*. Totowa, N.J.: Rowman and Littlefield, 1977.

Corti, Maria. *Principi della comunicazione letteraria*. Milan: Bompiani, 1976.

————. *Il viaggio testuale*. Turin: Einaudi, 1978.

Costa, Dennis. "Dante as Poet-Theologian." *Dante Studies* 89 (1971): 61–72.

Cozza-Luzi, Giuseppe. *Sul codice del breviario di Francesco Petrarca acquistato da S.S. Leone XIII alla Biblioteca Vaticana*. Rome, 1893.

Crespi, Achille, ed. *L'acerba*. Ascoli Piceno: G. Cesari, 1927.

Curtius, E. R. *European Literature and the Latin Middle Ages*. Translated by Willard R. Trask. Princeton: Princeton University Press, 1953. First published in German, 1948.

d'Ascoli, Cecco [Francesco Stabili]. *L'Acerba [Acerba etas]*. Edited by Marco Albertazzi. Lavis, Trento: La Finestra, 2002.

————. *L'acerba*. Edited by Achille Crespi. Ascoli Piceno: G. Cesari, 1927.

da Buti, Francesco. *Commento di Francesco da Buti sopra la Divina Comedia di Dante Alighieri*. Edited by Crescentino Giannini. 3 vols. Florence: Fratelli Nistri, 1858–62.

da Varazze, Iacopo. *Legenda aurea*. Edited by Giovanni Paolo Maggioni. 2 vols. Tavernuzze: SISMEL, 1998.

David, Michel. "Une réminiscence de Dante dans un sonnet de Pétrarque." In *Miscellanea di studi offerta Armando Balduino e Bianca Bianchi per le loro nozze*, 15–19. Padua: Seminario di Filologia moderna dell'università, 1962.

Dazzi, Manlio. *Il Mussato preumanista (1261–1329): L'ambiente e l'opera*. Vicenza: Neri Pozza, 1964.

Debenedetti, Santorre. "Per 'le disperse' di Francesco Petrarca." *Giornale storico della letteratura italiana* 56 (1910): 98–106.

de Certau, Michel. "'Mystique' au XVIIe siècle: Le problème du langage 'mystique.'" In *L'Homme devant Dieu: Mélanges offerts au Père Henri du Lubac*, 2:267–91. Paris: Aubier, 1964.

Delcorno, Carlo. "Gli scritti danteschi del Boccaccio." In *Dante e Boccaccio: Lectura Dantis Scaligera 2004–2005 in memoria di Vittore Branca*, edited by E. Sandal, 109–37. Rome and Padua: Antenore, 2006.

Del Virgilio, Giovanni. "Diaffonus." In *Atti e memorie della deputazione di storia patria per le provincie di Romagna*, edited by Enrico Carrara. Series 4, 15 (1925), 5–54.

De Nolhac, Pierre. *Pétrarque et l'humanisme.* 3 vols. 2nd ed. Paris: Champion, 1907. Rpt. 1959.

De Robertis, Domenico. *Memoriale petrarchesco.* Rome: Bulzoni, 1997.

———. "Nota al testo." In *Rime con le Rime di Iacopo Cavalcanti,* edited by Domenico De Robertis, 239–50. Turin: Einaudi, 1986.

———. "Petrarca interprete di Dante (ossia leggere Dante con Petrarca)." *Studi danteschi* 61 (1989): 307–28.

———. "Petrarca petroso." *Revue des études italiennes* 29 (1983): 13–37.

———. "A quale tradizione appartenne il manoscritto delle rime di Dante letto dal Petrarca." *Studi petrarcheschi* n.s. 2 (1985): 131–57.

Dionisotti, Carlo. "Tradizione classica e volgarizzamenti. " In *Geografia e storia della letteratura italiana,* 142–43. Turin: G. Einaudi, 1971.

di Pino, Guido. "L'antidantismo dal Trecento al Quattrocento." *Letture classensi* 5 (1976): 125–48.

Dotti, Ugo. "Miti e forme dell' 'io' nella cultura di Francesco Petrarca." *Revue des études italiennes* 29 (1983): 74–85.

———. *Petrarca e la scoperta della coscienza moderna.* Milan: Feltrinelli, 1978.

———. *Vita di Petrarca.* Bari: Laterza, 1987.

Dronke, Peter. *Dante's Second Love: The Originality and the Contents of the Convivio.* University of Exeter: The Society for Italian Studies, 1997.

Drumbl, Johann. "Die Improperien in der lateinischen liturgie." *Archiv für Liturgiewissenschaft* 15 (1973): 68–100.

———. *'Quem quaeritis': Teatro sacro dell'alto medievo.* Rome: Bulzoni, 1981.

Durandus, Guillelmus. *Rationale divinorum officiorum.* Edited by A. Davril, O.S.B., and T. M. Thibodeau, with B. G. Guyot, O.P. 3 vols. Turnhout: Brepols, 1995–2000.

Durling, Robert M. "Petrarch's 'Giovene donna sotto un verde lauro.'" *MLN* 86 (1971): 1–20.

———, and Ronald L. Martinez. *Time and the Crystal: Studies in Dante's 'Rime Petrose.'* Berkeley: University of California Press, 1990.

Eagleton, Terry. "Self-Undoing Subjects." In *Rewriting the Self: Histories from the Renaissance to the Present,* edited by Roy Porter, 262–69. New York: Routledge, 1997.

Enciclopedia dantesca. 6 vols. Edited by Umberto Bosco. Rome: Istituto dell'Enciclopedia Italiana, 1970–78.

Fanfani, Pietro, ed. *Commento della Divina Commedia d'anonimo fiorentino del secolo XIV.* 3 vols. Bologna: Gaetano Romagnoli, 1866–74.

Fenzi, Enrico. "Note petrarchesche: *RVF* 16, *Movesi il vecchierel.*" In *Saggi petrarcheschi,* 17–39. Fiesole: Cadmo, 2003.

———. *Saggi petrarcheschi.* Fiesole (Florence): Cadmo, 2003.

———. "Tra Dante e Petrarca: il fantasma di Ulisse." In *Saggi petrarcheschi,* 492–517. Fiesole: Cadmo, 2003.

Feo, Michele. "Di alcuni rusticani cestelli di pomi." *Quaderni petrarcheschi* 1 (1983):
    23–75.
———. "Inquietudini filologiche del Petrarca: Il luogo della discesa agli inferi
    (Storia di una citazione)." *Italia medioevale e umanistica* 17 (1974): 115–83.
———. "Petrarca, Francesco." In *Enciclopedia dantesca*. 6 vols., edited by Umberto
    Bosco, 4:450–58.
———. "Petrarca, Francesco." In *Enciclopedia virgiliana*. 5 vols, 4:53–78. Rome:
    Istituto della Enciclopedia Italiana, 1988.
———, ed. *Petrarca nel tempo: Tradizione lettori e immagini delle opere*. Pontedera
    (Pisa): Bandecchi & Vivaldi, 2003.
———. "Petrarca prima della laurea: Una corrispondenza poetica ritrovata." *Qua-
    derni petrarcheschi* 4 (1987): 35–50.
———. "Un Ulisse in Terrasanta." *Rivista di cultura classica e medievale* 19 (1977):
    383–88.
Fera, Vincenzo. "I sonetti CLXXXVI e CLXXXVII." *Lectura Petrarce* 7 (1987):
    219–43.
Ferguson, Wallace K. "Humanist Views of the Renaissance." *American Historical
    Review* 45 (1939): 1–28.
———. *The Renaissance in Historical Thought*. Cambridge, Mass.: Riverside Press,
    1948.
Ferroni, Giulio. "Tra Dante e Petrarca." In *Ulisse: Archeologia dell'uomo moderno*,
    edited by Piero Boitani and Richard Ambrosini, 165–85. Rome: Bulzoni, 1998.
Floro di Zenzo, Salvatore. *Studio critico sull'attribuzione a Dante Alighieri di un
    antico volgarizzamento dei Sette salmi penitenziali*. Naples: Laurenziana, 1984.
Fontana, Alessio. "La filologia romanza e il problema del rapporto Petrarca-trovatori
    (Premesse per una ripresa del problema secondo nuove prospettive)." In *Pe-
    trarca 1304–1374: Beiträge zu Werk und Wirkung*, edited by F. Schalk, 51–70.
    Frankfurt am Main: Klostermann, 1975.
Foresti, Armando. *Aneddoti della vita di Francesco Petrarca*, 2nd ed. Padua: An-
    tenore, 1997.
Forte, Stephen L., O. P. "John Colonna O.P. Life and Writings (1298–c. 1340)."
    Archivum Fratrum Praedicatorum 20 (1950): 369–414.
Foscolo, Ugo. "Parallelo fra Dante e Petrarca." In *Saggi e discorsi critici*, edited by
    C. Foligno, 279–97. Florence: Le Monnier, 1953.
Foster, Kenelm. "Beatrice or Medusa: The Penitential Elements in Petrarch's *Can-
    zoniere*." In *Italian Studies Presented to E. R. Vincent*, edited by C. P. Brand,
    K. Foster, and U. Limentanti, 41–56. Cambridge: W. Heffer & Sons, 1962.
———. *Petrarch, Poet and Humanist*. Edinburgh: Edinburgh University Press, 1987.
Frank, Istvàn. "La chanson 'Lasso me' de Pétrarque et ses prédécesseurs." *Annales
    du Midi* 66 (1954): 259–68.
Frasso, Giuseppe. "Petrarca, Andrea da Mantova e il canzoniere provenzale N."
    Italia medioevale e umanistica 17 (1974): 185–205.

Freccero, John. *Dante: The Poetics of Conversion.* Edited by Rachel Jacoff. Cambridge, Mass.: Harvard University Press, 1986.

―――. "Dante's 'Firm Foot' and the Journey without a Guide." In *Dante: The Poetics of Conversion,* 29–54. First published in *Harvard Theological Review* 52 (1959): 245–81.

―――. "Dante's Prologue Scene." In *Dante: The Poetics of Conversion,* 1–28. First published in *Dante Studies* 84 (1966): 1–25.

―――. "Dante's Ulysses: From Epic to Novel." In *Dante: The Poetics of Conversion,* 136–51. First published in *Concepts of the Hero in the Middle Ages and Renaissance,* edited by Norman Burns and Christopher Reagan, 101–19. Albany: State University of New York Press, 1975.

―――. "The Fig Tree and the Laurel: Petrarch's Poetics." *Diacritics* 5 (1975): 34–40.

Friedman, John B. *The Monstrous Races in Medieval Art and Thought.* Cambridge, Mass.: Harvard University Press, 1981.

―――. *Orpheus in the Middle Ages.* Cambridge, Mass.: Harvard University Press, 1970. Rpt. Syracuse: Syracuse University Press, 2000.

Frugoni, Arsenio. "Il giubileo di Bonifacio VIII." *Bollettino dell'Istituto storico italiano per il medio evo e Archivio muratoriano* 62 (1950): 1–121.

Fry, Timothy, O.S.B., ed. *The Rule of St. Benedict.* Collegeville, Minn.: Liturgical Press, 1981.

Fumagalli, Eduardo. "Canto XXV." In *Lectura Dantis Turicensis. Paradiso,* edited by Georges Güntert and Michelangelo Picone, 391–404. Florence: Cesati, 2002.

Galbraith, David. "Petrarch and the Broken City." In *Antiquity and Its Interpretation,* edited by Alina Payne, A. Kuttner, and R. Smick, 17–26. Cambridge: Cambridge University Press, 2000.

Galletti, Alfredo. "La ragione poetica di Albertino Mussato e i poeti teologi." In *Scritti varii di erudizione e di critica in onore di Rodolfo Renier (con xx tavole fuori testo),* 331–59. Turin: Fratelli Bocca, 1912.

Garin, Eugenio, ed. *Il pensiero pedagogico dell'umanesimo.* Florence: Giuntine, 1958.

Ghisalberti, Fausto. "Giovanni del Virgilio espositore delle *Metamorfosi.*" *Giornale dantesco* 34 (1933): 3–107.

Gillespie, Vincent. "The Study of Classical Authors from the Twelfth Century to c. 1450." In *The Cambridge History of Literary Criticism.* Vol. 2, *The Middle Ages,* edited by Alastair Minnis and Ian Johnson, 145–235. Cambridge: Cambridge University Press, 2005.

Gilson, Simon. *Dante and Renaissance Florence.* Cambridge: Cambridge University Press, 2005.

Girard, René. *Violence and the Sacred.* Translated by Patrick Gregory. Baltimore: Johns Hopkins University Press, 1977. First published in French, 1972.

Giunta, Claudio. "Memoria di Dante nei *Trionfi.*" *Rivista di letteratura italiana* 11 (1993): 411–52.

Gmelin, Hermann. "Das Prinzip der *Imitatio* in den Romanischen Literaturen." *Romanische Forschungen* 46 (1932): 83–360.

Godi, Carlo. "La 'Collatio Laureationis' del Petrarca nelle due redazioni." *Studi petrarcheschi* n.s. 5 (1988): 1–58.

Gorni, Guglielmo. "Le ballate di Dante e di Petrarca." In *Metrica e analisi letteraria.* Bologna: Il Mulino, 1993.

———. "La forma Correggio del *Canzoniere.*" In *Metrica e poesia,* 171–82. Bologna: Il Mulino, 1993.

———. "*Petrarca Virgini*: Lettura della canzone CCCLXVI 'Vergine bella.'" *Lectura petrarce* 7 (1987): 201–18.

Graevius, Johannes G. *Thesaurus antiquitatum et historiarum Italiae.* 9 vols. Leiden: 1704–23. Vol. 6, pt. 2.

Grayson, Cecil. "*Nobilior est vulgaris*: Latin and Vernacular in Dante's Thought." In *Centenary Essays on Dante, by Members of the Oxford Dante Society,* 54–76. Oxford: Clarendon, 1965.

Greenblatt, Stephen. *Renaissance Self-Fashioning from More to Shakespeare.* Chicago: University of Chicago Press, 1980.

Greene, Thomas. "The Flexibility of the Self in Renaissance Literature." In *The Disciplines of Criticism: Essays in Literary Theory, Interpretation, and History,* edited by Peter Demetz, Thomas Greene, and Lowry Nelson, Jr., 241–64. New Haven: Yale University Press, 1968.

———. *The Light in Troy: Imitation and Discovery in Renaissance Poetry.* New Haven: Yale University Press, 1982.

———. "Petrarch and the Humanist Hermeneutic." In *Italian Literature, Roots and Branches: Essays in Honor of Thomas Goddard Bergin,* edited by Giosuè Rimanelli and Kenneth John Atchity, 201–24. New Haven: Yale University Press, 1976.

———. "Petrarch *Viator*: The Displacements of Heroism." In *The Vulnerable Text: Essays on Renaissance Literature,* 18–45. New York: Columbia University Press, 1986. First published in *The Yearbook of English Studies* 12 (1981): 35–57.

Greenfield, Concetta Carestia. *Humanist and Scholastic Poetics, 1250–1500.* Lewisburg, Pa.: Bucknell University Press, 1981.

———. "The Poetics of Francis Petrarch." In *Francis Petrarch, Six Centuries Later: A Symposium,* edited by A. Scaglione, 213–22. Chapel Hill: Department of Romance Languages, University of North Carolina; Chicago: The Newberry Library, 1975.

Guidubaldi, Egidio, "Stabili, Francesco." In *Enciclopedia dantesca.* 6 vols, edited by Umberto Bosco, 3:404–5.

Hainsworth, Peter. *Petrarch the Poet: An Introduction to the "Rerum vulgarium fragmenta."* London: Routledge, 1988.

Hardison, O. B. *Christian Rite and Christian Drama in the Middle Ages.* Baltimore: Johns Hopkins University Press, 1965.

Harper, John. *The Forms and Orders of Western Liturgy.* Oxford: Clarendon Press, 1991.

Hawkins, Peter S. *Dante's Testaments: Essays in Scriptural Imagination.* Stanford, Calif.: Stanford University Press, 1999.

———. "John is with Me." In *Dante's Testaments: Essays in Scriptural Imagination,* 54–71. First published 1988.

Hempfer, Klaus W. "La canzone CCLXIV, il *Secretum* e il significato del *Canzoniere* di Petrarca," *Lectura petrarce* 14 (1994): 263–87.

Hiley, David. *Western Plainchant: A Handbook.* Oxford: Clarendon Press, 1993.

Hollander, Robert. *Allegory in Dante's "Commedia."* Princeton: Princeton University Press, 1969.

———. *Boccaccio's Dante and the Shaping Force of Satire.* Ann Arbor: University of Michigan Press, 1997.

———. "Commentary." In Dante Alighieri, *Paradiso.* Translated by Robert Hollander and Jean Hollander; introduction and commentary by Robert Hollander. New York: Doubleday, 2007.

———. "Dante *Theologus-Poeta." Dante Studies* 94 (1976): 91–136.

Hubbard, Thomas K. *The Pipes of Pan: Intertextuality and Literary Filiation in the Pastoral Tradition from Theocritus to Milton.* Ann Arbor: University of Michigan Press, 1998.

Hughes, Andrew. *Medieval Manuscripts for Mass and Office: A Guide to Their Organization and Terminology.* Toronto: University of Toronto Press, 1982.

Iannucci, Amilcare. "La discesa di Beatrice agli Inferi." In *Forma ed evento nella Divina Commedia,* 51–82.

———. "Dottrina e allegoria in *Inferno* VIII, 67–IX, 105." In *Dante e le forme dell'allegoresi,* edited by Michelangelo Picone, 99–124. Ravenna: Longo, 1987.

———. *Forma ed evento nella Divina Commedia.* Rome: Bulzoni, 1984.

———. "Petrarch's Intertextual Strategies in the *Triumphs.*" In *Petrarch's Triumphs: Allegory and Spectacle,* edited by Konrad Eisenbichler and Amilcare A. Iannucci, 3–10. Ottawa: Dovehouse Editions, 1990.

Jack, Philip. *Antiquarianism and Myths of Antiquity: The Origins of Rome in Renaissance Thought.* Cambridge: Cambridge University Press, 2003.

Jager, Eric. *The Tempter's Voice: Language and the Fall in Medieval Literature.* Ithaca, N.Y.: Cornell University Press, 1993.

Jenaro-MacLennan, Luis. "Autocomentario en Dante y comentarismo latino." *Vox Romanica* 19 (1960): 82–123.

———. "'Remissus est modus et humilis' (*Epistle to Cangrande,* par.10)." *Lettere italiane* 31 (1979): 406–18.

Jerome, Saint. *Opera Omnia Hieronymi.* In *Patrologia Cursus Completus. Series Latina,* edited by J. P. Migne. Paris: Vrin, 1844–64. Vols. 23–28.

Johannes de Virgilio Danti Alagherii [Carmen]. In Dante Alighieri, *Le Egloghe,* edited by Giorgio Brugnoli and Riccardo Scarcia, 2–27. Milan and Naples: Ricciardi, 1980.

Jones, F. J. "Arguments in Favour of a Calendrical Structure for Petrarch's *Canzoniere.*" *Modern Language Review* 79 (1984): 579–88.

Kallendorf, Craig. "From Virgil to Vida: The *Poeta Theologus* in Italian Renaissance Commentary." *Journal of the History of Ideas* 56 (1995): 41–62.

Kegel-Brinkgreve, E. *The Echoing Woods: Bucolic and Pastoral from Theocritus to Wordsworth.* Amsterdam: I. C. Gieben, 1990.

Kelly, Henry Ansgar. *Ideas and Forms of Tragedy from Aristotle to the Middle Ages.* Cambridge: Cambridge University Press, 1993.

———. *Tragedy and Comedy from Dante to Pseudo-Dante.* Berkeley: University of California Press, 1989.

Kim, Heerak Christian, ed. *The Gospel of Nicodemus: Gesta salvatoris.* Toronto: Pontifical Institute, 1973.

Kirkham, Victoria. "The Parallel Lives of Dante and Virgil." *Dante Studies* 110 (1992): 233–53.

König, Bernhard. "*Dolci rime leggiadre*: Zur Verwendung und Verwandlung stilnovistischer Elemente in Petrarcas *Canzoniere* (Am Beispiel des Sonnetts *In qual parte del ciel*)." In *Petrarca 1304–1374: Beiträge zu Werk und Wirkung,* edited by F. Schalk, 113–38. Frankfurt am Main: Klostermann, 1975.

Krautter, Konrad. *Die Renaissance der Bukolik in der lateinischen Literatur des 14. Jahrhunderts: Von Dante bis Petrarca.* Theorie und Geschichte der Literatur und der Schönen Künste, Texte und Abhandlungen 65. Munich, 1983.

Kristeller, Paul Oscar. "Un'Ars Dictaminis' di Giovanni del Virgilio." *Italia medioevale e umanistica* 4 (1961): 181–200.

Kuon, Peter. *L'aura dantesca: Metamorfosi intertestuali nei "Rerum vulgarium fragmenta" di Francesco Petrarca.* Florence: Cesati, 2004.

Ladner, Gerhart B. "*Homo Viator*: Medieval Ideas on Alienation and Order." *Speculum* 42 (1967): 233–59.

Lansing, Richard. "Dante's Intended Audience in the *Convivio.*" *Dante Studies* 110 (1992): 17–24.

Leclerq, Jean. "Temi monastici nell'opera del Petrarca." *Lettere italiane* 43 (1991): 42–54.

Lerner, Robert E. "Petrarch's Coolness toward Dante: A Conflict of 'Humanisms.'" In *Intellectuals and Writers in Fourteenth-Century Europe: The J. A. W. Bennett Memorial Lectures, Perugia, 1984,* edited by Pietro Boitani and Anna Torti, 204–25. Cambridge: D. S. Brewer; Tubingen: G. Narr, 1986.

Lippe, Robert, ed. *Missale romanum mediolani 1474.* London: Henry Bradshaw Society, 1899.

Little, Lester K. *Benedictine Maledictions: Liturgical Cursing in Romanesque France.* Ithaca, N.Y.: Cornell University Press, 1993.

Lucan. *Pharsalia.* Edited and translated by J. D. Duff. The Loeb Classical Library. Cambridge, Mass.: Harvard University Press, 1988. First published 1928.

Mann, Nicholas. "The Making of Petrarch's *Bucolicum Carmen.*" *Italia medioevale e umanistica* 20 (1977): 127–82.

Maramauro, Guglielmo. *Expositione sopra l'"Inferno" di Dante Alligieri*. Edited by Pier Giacomo Pisoni and Saverio Bellomo. Padua: Antenore, 1998.

Marbach, Carolus. *Carmina Scripturarum*. Hildesheim: George Olms, 1963.

Martellotti, Guido. "Dalla tenzone al carme bucolico. Giovanni del Virgilio, Dante, Boccaccio." In *Dante e Boccaccio e altri scrittori dall'Umanesimo al Romanticismo*, 71–89. Florence: Olschki, 1983. First published in *Italia medioevale e umanistica* 7 (1964): 325–36.

———. "Le egloghe." In *Enciclopedia dantesca*. 6 vols., edited by Umberto Bosco, 2:644–46.

———. "Giovanni del Virgilio." In *Enciclopedia dantesca*. 6 vols., edited by Umberto Bosco, 3:193–94.

———. "Mussato." In *Enciclopedia dantesca*. 6 vols., edited by Umberto Bosco, 3:1066–68.

———. "La riscoperta dello stile bucolico (da Dante al Boccaccio)." In *Dante e Boccaccio e altri scrittori dall'Umanesimo al Romanticismo*, 91–106. Florence: Olschki, 1983. First published 1966, in *Atti del Convegno di Studi 'Dante e la Cultura Veneta*, 335–46.

Martinelli, Bortolo. "Dante nei *Rerum Vulgarium Fragmenta*." *Italianistica* 10 (1981): 122–31.

———. "*Feria sexta aprilis*: La data sacra nel *Canzoniere* del Petrarca," in *Petrarca e il Ventoso*, 103–48.

———. "L'ordinamento morale del 'Canzoniere.'" In *Petrarca e il Ventoso*, 217–300.

———. *Petrarca e il Ventoso*. Bergamo: Minerva Italica, 1977.

Martinez, Ronald L. "Lament and Lamentation in *Purgatorio* and the Role of Dante's Statius." *Dante Studies* 117 (1997): 46–82.

———. "Mourning Beatrice: The Rhetoric of Lamentation in the *Vita nuova*." *MLN* 115 (1998): 1–29.

———. "Mourning Laura in the *Canzoniere*: Lessons from Lamentations." *MLN* 118 (2003): 1–45.

———. "'Nasce il Nilo': Wisdom, Justice, and Dante's Canzone 'Tre donne intorno al cor mi son.'" In *Dante Now: Current Trends in Dante Studies*, 115–53. Edited by Theodore J. Cachey, Jr. Notre Dame, Ind.: University of Notre Dame Press, 1995.

———. "Petrarch's Open Secret." In *Petrarch: A Critical Guide to the Complete Works*, edited by Victoria Kirkham and Armando Maggi, 291–99. Chicago: University of Chicago Press, 2009.

———. "The Poetics of Advent Liturgies: Dante's *Vita nova* and *Purgatorio*." In *Le culture di Dante: Studi in onore di Robert Hollander. Atti del quarto Seminario dantesco internazionale, University of Notre Dame [Ind.], USA, 25–27 settembre 2003*, 271–304. Edited by Michelangeo Picone, Theodore J. Cachey, Jr., and Margherita Mestica. Florence: Franco Cesati, 2004.

Mascetta-Caracci, Lorenzo. *Dante e il "Dedalo" petrarchesco*. Lanciano: Carabba, 1910.

Massèra, A. F. "Di tre epistole metriche boccaccesche." *Giornale dantesco* 30 (1927): 31–36.

———. "Petrarch and the Voice of Rome." Unpublished manuscript.

Matter, E. Ann. "Petrarch's Personal Psalms (*Psalmi penitentiales*)." In *Petrarch: A Critical Guide to the Complete Works*, edited by Victoria Kirkham and Armando Maggi. Chicago: University of Chicago Press, 2009.

Mazzocco, Angelo. "The Antiquarianism of Francesco Petrarca." *Journal of Medieval and Renaissance Studies* 7 (1977): 203–24.

Mazzoni, Francesco. "Giovanni Boccaccio fra Dante e Petrarca." *Atti e memorie dell'Accademia Petrarca di Lettere, Arti e Scienze di Arezzo* 42 (1976–78): 15–42.

Mazzoni, Guido. "Dante e il Polifemo Bolognese." *Archivio storico italiano* 96 (1930): 1–40. Rpt. in *Almae luces malae cruces: Studi danteschi*, 349–72. Bologna: Zanichelli, 1941.

Mazzotta, Giuseppe. "The *Canzoniere* and the Language of the Self." In *The Worlds of Petrarch*, 58–79. Durham, N.C.: Duke University Press, 1993. Earlier version appeared in *Studies in Philology* 75 (1978): 271–96.

———. *Dante, Poet of the Desert: History and Allegory in the Divine Comedy*. Princeton: Princeton University, 1979.

———. "Ethics of Self." In *The Worlds of Petrarch*, 80–101.

———. "Humanism and Monastic Spirituality." In *The Worlds of Petrarch*, 147–66. Earlier version appeared in *Stanford Literature Review* 5 (1988): 57–74.

———. "Orpheus, Rhetoric, and Music." In *The Worlds of Petrarch*, 129–46. Earlier version appeared in *Forma e parole: Studi in Memoria di Fredi Chiappelli*, edited by D. J. Dutschke et al., 137–54. Rome: Bulzoni, 1992.

———. "The *Vita nuova* and the Language of Poetry." *Rivista di studi italiani* 1 (1983): 1–16.

———. *The Worlds of Petrarch*. Durham, N.C.: Duke University Press, 1993.

McGinn, Bernard. *The Foundations of Mysticism*. Vol. 1 of *The Presence of God: A History of Western Christian Mysticism*. New York: Crossroad, 1991.

McLaughlin, Martin L. *Literary Imitation in the Italian Renaissance*. Oxford: Clarendon Press, 1995.

Mengaldo, Pier Vincenzo. *Linguistica e retorica di Dante*. Pisa: Nistri-Lischi, 1978.

Mercuri, Roberto. "Genesi della tradizione letteraria italiana in Dante, Petrarca e Boccaccio." In *Letteratura italiana. Storia e geografia. I. L'età medievale*, edited by A. Asor Rosa, 229–455. Turin: Einaudi, 1987.

Mésoniat, Claudio. *Poetica theologia: La 'Lucula Noctis' di Giovanni Dominici e le dispute letterarie tra '300 e '400*. Rome: Edizioni di Storia e Letteratura, 1984.

Minnis, Alastair J. *"Magister Amoris": The "Roman de la Rose" and Vernacular Hermeneutics*. Oxford: Oxford University Press, 2001.

———. *Medieval Theory of Authorship: Scholastic Literary Attitudes in the Later Middle Ages*. 2nd ed. Philadelphia: University of Pennsylvania Press; Aldershot: Scolar Press, 1988. 1st ed. 1984.

Minnis, Alastair, and Ian Johnson, eds. *The Cambridge History of Literary Criticism.* Vol. 2, *The Middle Ages.* Cambridge: Cambridge University Press, 2005.

Minnis, Alastair J., and A. B. Scott, with David Wallace, eds. *Medieval Literary Theory and Criticism, c. 1100–c.1375: The Commentary Tradition.* Oxford: Clarendon Press, 1988.

Moevs, Christian. *The Metaphysics of Dante's "Comedy."* New York: Oxford University Press, 2005.

Mommsen, Theodor E. *Medieval and Renaissance Studies.* Edited by Eugene F. Rice, Jr. Ithaca, N.Y.: Cornell University Press, 1959.

———. "Petrarch and the Story of the Choice of Hercules." In *Medieval and Renaissance Studies,* 156–79.

———. "Petrarch's Conception of the Dark Ages." In *Medieval and Renaissance Studies,* 106–29.

———, ed. *Petrarch's Testament.* Ithaca, N.Y.: Cornell University Press, 1957.

Monti, Carla Maria. "Per la *Senile* V 2 di Francesco Petrarca," *Studi petrarcheschi* n.s. 15 (2002): 99–128.

Morgan, Alison. *Dante and the Medieval Other World.* Cambridge: Cambridge University Press, 1990.

Munk Olsen, Birger. *I classici nel canone scolastico altomedievale.* Spoleto: Centro Italiano di Studi sull'Alto Medioevo Italiano, 1991.

Murphy, Stephen. *The Gift of Immortality: Myths of Power and Humanist Poetics.* Madison, Wisc.: Farleigh Dickinson University Press, 1997.

———. "Petrarca's *Africa* and the Poets' Dream of Glory." *Italian Quarterly* 9 (1991): 75–83.

Mussato, Albertino. *Ecérinide, Epîtres métriques sur la poésie, Songe.* Edited and translated by Jean Frédéric Chevalier. Paris: Les Belles Lettres, 2000.

Neri, Ferdinando. "Il Petrarca e le rime dantesche della pietra." *La cultura* 8 (1929): 389–404.

Noakes, Susan. *Timely Reading: Between Exegesis and Interpretation.* Ithaca, N.Y.: Cornell University Press, 1988.

Orelli, Giorgio. "Dante in Petrarca." In *Il suono dei sospiri: Sul Petrarca volgare,* 124–62. Turin: Einaudi, 1990.

Ovid. *Le metamorfosi/Publio Ovidio Nasone.* Introduced by Gianpiero Rosati. Translated by Giovanna Faranda Villa. Milan: Biblioteca Universale Rizzoli, 2001.

———. *Metamorphoses.* Translated by Mary M. Innes. London: Penguin, 1955.

Pacca, Vinicio. *Petrarca.* Bari: Laterza, 1998.

Paden, William. "Petrarch as Poet of Provence." *Annali d'Italianistica* 22 (2004): 19–44.

Padoan, Giorgio. "Il Boccaccio 'fedele' di Dante." In idem, *Il Boccaccio le muse il Parnaso e l'Arno,* 229–46. Florence: Olschki, 1978.

———. "Giovanni Boccaccio e la rinascita dello stile bucolico." In *Il Boccaccio: Le muse, il Parnaso, e l'Arno,* 151–98. Florence: Olschki, 1978.

————. "Ilaro." In *Enciclopedia dantesca*. 6 vols., edited by Umberto Bosco, 3:362–63.

————. Reviews of Aldo Rossi essays cited below. *Studi sul Boccaccio* 1 (1963): 517–40, 2 (1964): 475–507, and 5 (1968): 365–68.

————. "Tra Dante e Mussato: I. Tonalità dantesche nella *Historia Augusta* di Albertino Mussato, II. A Pisa, la cancelleria imperiale e Dante." *Quaderni veneti* 24 (1996): 27–46.

————. "Ulisse *fandi fictor* e le vie della sapienza." In idem, *Il pio Enea, l'empio Ulisse*, 170–99. Ravenna: Longo, 1977. First published 1960.

————. *L'ultima opera di Giovanni Boccaccio: Le "Esposizioni sopre il Dante."* Pubblicazioni della facoltà di lettere e filosofia, Università di Padova, 34. Padua: Cedam, 1959.

Pancheri, Alessandro. *"Col suon chioccio": Per una frottola 'dispersa' attribuibile a Francesco Petrarca.* Padua: Antenore, 1993.

Paolazzi, Carlo. "Dall'epitafio dantesco di Giovanni del Virgilio all'elogio dell' *Amorosa Visione*." In *Dante e la 'Comedia' nel Trecento*, 111–30. First in *Vestigia: Studi in Onore di Giuseppe Billanovich*. 2 vols., 2:485–502. Rome: Edizioni di Storia e Letteratura, 1984.

————. *Dante e la "Comedia" nel Trecento.* Milan: Vita e Pensiero, 1989.

————. "Petrarca, Boccaccio, e il *Trattatello in laude di Dante*." In *Dante e la 'Comedia' nel Trecento*, 131–221. First published in *Studi danteschi* 55 (1983): 165–249.

Paoletti, Lao. *Retorica e politica nel Petrarca bucolico.* Bologna: Libreria Patron, 1974.

Paolino, Laura. "'Ad acerbam rei memoriam': Le carte del lutto nel codice Vaticano Latino 3196 di Francesco Petrarca." *Rivista di letteratura italiana* 11 (1993): 73–102.

————. "Sui magdrigali di Petrarca (RVF 52, 54, 106, 121)." *Italianistica: Rivista di letteratura italiana* 30 (2001): 318–19.

Paparelli, Gioacchino. "Dante e il Trecento." In *Dante nel pensiero e nell'esegesi dei secoli XIV e XV. Atti del III Congresso Nazionale Studi Danteschi*, 31–70. Florence: Olschki, 1975.

————. "Due modi opposti di leggere Dante: Petrarca e Boccaccio." In *Giovanni Boccaccio editore e interprete di Dante*, edited by Società Dantesca Italiana, 73–90. Florence: Olschki, 1979.

Parker, Deborah. *Commentary and Ideology: Dante in the Renaissance.* Durham, N.C.: Duke University Press, 1993.

Pasero, Niccolò. *Laudes creaturarum: Il cantico di Francesco d'Assisi.* Parma: Pratiche editrice, 1992.

Pasquini, Emilio. "Dantismo petrarchesco: Ancora su *Fam.* XXI 15 e dintorni." In *Motivi e forme delle "Familiari" di Francesco Petrarca*, edited by C. Berra, 21–38. Milan: Cisalpino, 2003.

————. "Discussione della relazione di Boitani." In *Dante: Mito e poesia. Atti del secondo Seminario dantesco internazionale*, edited by Michelangelo Picone e Tatiana Crivelli, 232–33. Florence: Cesati, 1997.

Pastore Stocchi, Manlio. "Dante, Mussato, e la tragedia." In *Dante e la cultura veneta; Atti del convegno studi organizzato dalla Fondazione Cini,* edited by Vittore Branca and Giorgio Padoan, 251–62. Florence: L. S. Olschki, 1966.

———. "Petrarca e Dante." *Rivista di studi danteschi* 4 (2004): 184–204.

———. "I sonetti III e LXI." *Lectura petrarce* 1 (1981): 1–23.

Patterson, Annabel. *Pastoral and Ideology: Virgil to Valery.* Berkeley: University of California Press, 1987.

Pelosini, Raffaella. "Guido Cavalcanti nei *Rerum vulgarium fragmenta.*" *Studi petrarcheschi* n.s. 9 (1992): 9–76.

Pertile, Lino. "Dante's *Comedy* Beyond the *Stil Nuovo.*" *Lectura Dantis* 13 (1993): 47–77.

———. "Lettera aperta a Robert Hollander sui rapporti tra *Commedia* e *Convivio.*" *Electronic Bulletin of the Dante Society of America [EBDSA]* (http://www.princeton.edu/~dante/ebdsa/), October 8, 1996.

Pertusi, Agostino. *Leonzio Pilato fra Petrarca e Boccaccio: Le sue versioni omeriche negli autografi di Venezia e la cultura greca del primo Umanesimo.* Venice: Istituto per la collaborazione culturale, 1964.

Perugi, Maurizio. "Petrarca provenzale." *Quaderni petrarcheschi* 7 (1990): 109–92.

———. "A proposito di alcuni scritti recenti su Petrarca e Arnaut Daniel." *Studi medievali* ser. 3, 32 (1991): 369–84.

———. "Il Sordello di Dante e la tradizione mediolatina dell'invettiva." *Studi danteschi* 55 (1983): 23–135.

———. *Trovatori a Valchiusa. Un frammento della cultura provenzale del Petrarca.* Padua: Antenore, 1985.

Petoletti, Marco. "La fortuna di Dante fra Trecento e Quattrocento." In *La Divina Commedia di Alfonso d'Aragona re di Napoli. Commentario al codice,* edited by M. Bollati. 2 vols., 1:159–86. Modena: Panini, 2006.

Petrie, Jennifer. "Dante and Petrarch." In *Dante Comparisons,* edited by E. Haywood and B. Jones, 137–45. Dublin: Irish Academic Press, 1985.

Petrini, Mario. "Petrarca e Dante." *Critica letteraria* 23 (1995): 365–76.

Petrucci, Armando. *La scrittura di Francesco Petrarca.* Vatican City: Biblioteca Apostolica Vaticana, 1967.

———. *Writers and Readers in Medieval Italy: Studies in the History of Written Culture.* Edited and translated by Charles M. Radding. New Haven and London: Yale University Press, 1995.

Piccini, Daniele. *Un amico del Petrarca: Sennuccio del Bene e le sue rime.* Rome and Padua: Antenore, 2004.

———. "Franceschino degli Albizzi, uno e due." *Studi petrarcheschi* n.s. 15 (2002): 129–86.

Picone, Michelangelo. "Riscritture dantesche nel *Canzoniere* di Petrarca." *Rivista europea di letteratura italiana* 2 (1993): 115–25.

———. "Il sonetto CLXXXIX," *Lectura Petrarce* 9 (1989): 151–77.

————. "Il tema dell'incoronazione poetica in Dante, Petrarca e Boccaccio." *L'Alighieri* 46 (n.s. 25) (2005): 5–26.

————. "Tempo e racconto nel *Canzoniere* di Petrarca." In *Omaggio a Gianfranco Folena,* 1:581–92. Padua: Editoriale Programma, 1993.

————. "*Vita Nuova" e tradizione romanza.* Padua: Liviana, 1979.

Pierantozzi, Decio. "Il Petrarca e Guittone." *Studi petrarcheschi* 1 (1948): 145–65.

Piur, Paul. *Petrarcas 'Buch ohne Namen' und die papstliche Kurie: Ein Beitrag zur Geistesgeschichte der Frührenaissance.* Halle and Saale: Max Niemeyer, 1925.

Poggioli, Renato. *The Oaten Flute: Essays on Pastoral Poetry and the Pastoral Ideal.* Cambridge, Mass.: Harvard University Press, 1975.

Porter, Roy. "Introduction." In *Rewriting the Self: Histories from the Renaissance to the Present,* edited by Roy Porter, 1–14. New York: Routledge, 1997.

Possiedi, Paolo. "Petrarca petroso." *Forum italicum* 8 (1974): 523–45.

Pulsoni, Carlo. "Il Dante di Francesco Petrarca: Vaticano latino 3199." *Studi petrarcheschi* n.s. 10 (1992): 155–208.

————. *La tecnica compositiva nei "Rerum vulgarium fragmenta": Riuso metrico e lettura autoriale.* Rome: Bagatto, 1998.

Quaglio, Antonio Enzo, Andrea Ciotti, and Bruno Basile. "Commedia." In *Enciclopedia dantesca.* 6 vols., edited by Umberto Bosco, 2:83–86 and 99–103.

Quillen, Carol E. *Rereading the Renaissance: Petrarch, Augustine, and the Language of Humanism.* Ann Arbor: University of Michigan Press, 1998.

Quinones, Ricardo J. *The Changes of Cain: Violence and the Lost Brother in Cain and Abel Literature.* Princeton: Princeton University Press, 1991.

Quint, David. "Fear of Falling: Icarus, Phaethon, and Lucretius in *Paradise Lost.*" *Renaissance Quarterly* 57 (2004): 847–81.

————. *Origin and Originality in Renaissance Literature: Versions of the Source.* New Haven: Yale University Press, 1983.

————. "Schiavi del tempo: Petrarca e Ronsard." In *Il petrarchismo: Un modello di poesia per l'Europa,* edited by Loredana Chines, Floriana Calitti, and Roberto Gigliucci. 2 vols., 1:113–27. Rome: Bulzoni, 2006.

Rabuse, Georg. "Petrarcas Marienkanzone im Licht der 'Santa Orazione' Dantes." In *Petrarca 1304–1374: Beiträge zu Werk und Wirkung,* edited by von Fritz Schalk, 245–54. Frankfurt am Main: Klostermann, 1975.

Raffa, Guy. "Dante's Mocking Pastoral Muse." *Dante Studies* 114 (1996): 271–91.

Raimondi, Ezio. "Dante e il mondo ezzeliniano." In *Dante e la cultura veneta; atti del convegno studi organizzato dalla Fondazione Cini,* edited by Vittore Branca and Giorgio Padoan, 52–69. Florence: L. S. Olschki, 1966.

————. "Per una città nell'*Inferno* dantesco." In *Metafora e storia: Studi su Dante e Petrarca,* 39–64. Turin: Einaudi, 1970. First published in *Dante e Bologna nei tempi di Dante.* Bologna: Commissione per i testi di lingua, 1967.

————. "Petrarca lettore di Dante." In *Le metamorfosi della parola: Da Dante a Montale,* edited by J. Sisco, 173–232. Milan: Bruno Mondadori, 2004.

Regan, Mariann S. "Petrarch's Courtly and Christian Vocabularies: Language in *Canzoniere* 61–63." *Romance Notes* 15 (1974): 527–31.

Reggio, Giovanni. *Le egloghe di Dante*. Florence: Olschki, 1969.

Regn, Gerhard. "'Allegorice pro laurea corona': Dante, Petrarca und die Konstitution postmittelalterlicher Dichtungsallegorie." *Romanistisches Jahrbuch* 51 (2000): 128–52.

Reiss, Timothy J. *The Discourse of Modernism*. Ithaca, N.Y.: Cornell University Press, 1982.

———. *Mirages of the Selfe: Patterns of Personhood in Ancient and Early Modern Europe*. Stanford, Calif.: Stanford University Press, 2003.

Ricci, Pier Giorgio. "Monarchia." In *Enciclopedia dantesca*. 6 vols., edited by Umberto Bosco, 3:993–1004.

Richard of St. Victor. *Opera omnia*. Vol. 196 of *Patrologiae Cursus Completus. Series Latina*. Edited by J. P. Migne. Paris: Vrin, 1855.

———. *Richard of St. Victor: The Twelve Patriarchs, the Mystical Ark, Book Three of the Trinity*. Translated by Grover A. Zinn. The Classics of Western Spirituality. New York: Paulist Press, 1979.

Rico, Francisco. *Vida u obra de Petrarca*. Padova: Antenore, 1974.

Rigo, Paola. *Memoria classica e memoria biblica in Dante*. Florence: Olschki, 1994.

———. "Tempo liturgico nell'epistola ai principi e ai popoli d'Italia." In *Memoria classica e memoria biblica in Dante*, 33–44.

Rimanelli, Giosuè, and Kenneth John Atchity, eds. *Italian Literature, Roots and Branches: Essays in Honor of Thomas Goddard Bergin*. New Haven and London: Yale University Press, 1976.

Rizzo, Silvia. "Petrarca, il latino e il volgare." *Quaderni petrarcheschi* 7 (1990): 7–40.

Roche, Thomas. "The Calendrical Structure of Petrarch's *Canzoniere*." *Studies in Philology* 71 (1974): 152–72.

Ronconi, Giorgio. *Le origini delle dispute umanistiche sulla poesia (Mussato e Petrarca)*. Rome: Bulzoni, 1976.

Rosenmeyer, Thomas. *The Green Cabinet; Theocritus and the European Pastoral Lyric*. Berkeley: University of California Press, 1969.

Rossi, Aldo. "Il Boccaccio autore della corrispondenza Dante-Giovanni del Virgilio." *Miscellanea storica della Valdelsa* 69 (1963): 130–72.

———. "Il carme di Giovanni del Virgilio a Dante." *Studi danteschi* 40 (1963): 133–269.

———. "Dante, Boccaccio, e la laurea poetica." *Paragone* n.s. 13 (1962): 3–41.

———. "Dante nella prospettiva del Boccaccio." *Studi danteschi* 37 (1960): 63–139.

———. "Dossier di un'attribuzione. Dieci anni dopo." *Paragone* n.s. 36 (1968): 61–125.

Rossi, Luca Carlo. "Petrarca dantista involontario." *Studi petrarcheschi* n.s. 5 (1988): 301–16.

———. "Presenze di Petrarca in commenti danteschi fra Tre e Quattrocento." *Aevum* 70 (1996): 441–76.

Rossi, Vittorio. "Dante nel Trecento e nel Quattrocento." In *Scritti di critica letteraria: Saggi e discorsi su Dante*, 1:293–332. Florence: Sansoni, 1930.

———. "Sulla formazione delle raccolte epistolari petrarchesche." *Annali della Cattedra Petrarchesca* 3 (1932): 53–73.

Roush, Sherry. *Hermes' Lyre: Italian Poetic Self-Commentary from Dante to Tommaso Campanella*. Toronto: University of Toronto Press, 2002.

Sandkühler, Bruno. *Die frühen Dantekommentare und ihr Verhältnis zur mittelalterlichen Kommentartradition*. Munich: Max Hueber Verlag, 1967.

Sanson, Helena L. "*Ornamentum mulieri breviloquentia*: Donne, silenzi, parole nell'Italia del Cinquecento." *The Italianist* 23 (2003): 194–244.

Santagata, Marco. "Dante in Petrarca." *Giornale storico della letteratura italiana* 157 (1980): 445–52. Rpt. in Santagata, *Per moderne carte*, 79–91.

———. *I frammenti dell'anima: Storia e racconto nel Canzoniere di Petrarca*. Bologna: Il Mulino, 1990, 1992, 1993.

———. "Introduzione." In Petrarch, *Trionfi, Rime estravaganti, Codice degli abbozzi, edited by Vincio Pacca and Laura Paolini*, xi–lii. Milan: Mondadori, 1996.

———. "Introduzione" and notes. In Petrarca, *Canzoniere*, edited by Marco Santagata. Milan: Mondadori, 1996.

———. *Per moderne carte: La biblioteca volgare di Petrarca*. Bologna: Il Mulino, 1990.

———. "Presenze di Dante 'comico' nel *Canzoniere* del Petrarca." *Giornale storico della letteratura italiana* 146 (1969): 163–211. Rpt. in *Per moderne carte*, 25–78.

Sapegno, Natalino. "Tra Dante e il Petrarca." In *Storia letteraria del Trecento*, La letteratura italiana; Storia e testi, 169–96. Milan and Naples: Ricciardi, 1963.

Sarolli, Gian Roberto. *Prolegomena alla "Divina Commedia."* Florence: Olschki, 1971.

Sasso, Gennaro. "A proposito di *Inferno* XXVI 94–98: Variazioni biografiche per l'interpretazione." *La cultura* 40 (2002): 377–96.

Scaglione, Aldo. "Classical Heritage and Petrarchan Self-Consciousness in the Literary Emergence of the Interior 'I.'" In *Altro Polo: A Volume of Italian Studies*. Sydney: Fredrick May Foundation for Italian Studies [University of Sydney], 1984.

Schwartz, Regina. *The Curse of Cain: The Violent Legacy of Monotheism*. Chicago: University of Chicago Press, 1997.

Segre, Cesare. *Avviamento all'analisi del testo letterario*. Turin: Einaudi, 1985.

———. *Fuori del mondo*. Turin: Einaudi, 1990.

———. "Intertestuale-Interdiscorsivo: Appunti per una fenomenologia delle fonti." In *La parola ritrovata: Fonti e analisi letteraria*, edited by C. Di Girolamo and I. Paccagnella, 15–28. Palermo: Sellerio, 1982.

Serra, Renato. "Dei *Trionfi* di F. Petrarca" [1904]. Vol. 2 of *Scritti di Renato Serra*. Edited by G. De Robertis and A. Grilli. Florence: Le Monnier, 1938.

Servii Grammatici qui feruntur in Vergilii Carmina Commentarii. Edited by Georg Thilo and Hermann Hagen. 3 vols. Leipzig: B. G. Teubner, 1881–87.

Servius. *In Vergilii Bucolica et Georgica Commentarii.* Edited by Georg Thilo. Vol. 3, pt. 1 of *Servii Grammatici qui feruntur in Vergilii Carmina Commentarii.* Edited by Georg Thilo and Hermann Hagen. Leipzig: B. G. Teubner, 1887.

Simone, Franco. *La coscienza della rinascita negli umanisti francesi.* Rome: Edizioni di Storia e Letteratura, 1949.

Singleton, Charles. *Dante Studies 1: Elements of Structure.* Cambridge, Mass.: Harvard University Press, 1954.

———. *Journey to Beatrice.* Baltimore: Johns Hopkins University Press, 1977.

Smarr, Janet. "Boccaccio pastorale tra Dante e Petrarca." In *Autori e lettori di Boccaccio: Atti del Convegno Internazionale di Certaldo,* edited by Michelangelo Picone. Florence: Cesati Editore, 2002.

———. "Introduction" and "Notes." In Giovanni Boccaccio, *Eclogues.* Edited and translated eadem. New York: Garland, 1987.

Steinberg, Justin. *Accounting for Dante: Urban Readers and Writers in Late Medieval Italy.* Notre Dame, Ind.: University of Notre Dame Press, 2005.

———. "Merchant Bookkeeping and Lyric Anthologizing: Codicological Aspects of Vaticano 3793." *Scrittura e civiltà* 24 (2000): 251–69.

Stephens, Walter. *Giants in Those Days: Folklore, Ancient History, and Nationalism.* Lincoln: University of Nebraska Press, 1989.

Stillinger, Thomas Clifford. *The Song of Troilus: Lyric Authority in the Medieval Book.* Philadelphia: University of Pennsylvania Press, 1992.

Stock, Brian. "Reading, Writing, and the Self: Petrarch and His Forerunners." *New Literary History* 26, no. 4 (Fall 1995): 717–30.

Sturm-Maddox, Sara. "*Arbor vittorioso triunfale*: Allegory and Spectacle in the *Rime* and the *Trionfi.*" In *Petrarch's Triumphs: Allegory and Spectacle,* edited by Konrad Eisenbichler and Amilcare A. Iannucci, 113–34. Ottawa: Dovehouse Editions, 1990.

———. *Petrarch's Laurels.* University Park: Pennsylvania State University Press, 1992.

———. *Petrarch's Metamorphoses: Text and Subtext in the "Rime sparse."* Columbia: University of Missouri Press, 1985.

———. "Transformations of Courtly Love Poetry: *Vita Nuova* and *Canzoniere.*" In *The Expansion and Transformations of Courtly Literature,* edited by N. B. Smith and J. T. Snow, 128–40. Athens: University of Georgia Press, 1980.

Suitner, Franco. *Petrarca e la tradizione stilnovistica.* Florence: Olschki, 1977.

Summit, Jennifer. "Topography as Historiography in Petrarch, Chaucer and the *Mirabilia* of Ancient Rome." *Journal of Medieval and Early Modern Studies* 30 (2000): 211–46.

Surdich, Luigi. *Boccaccio.* Bari: Laterza, 2001.

Tagliabue, M. "Fra Giovannino fratello del Petrarca e monaco olivetano." *Studi petrarcheschi* n.s. 6 (1989): 225–40.

Tanturli, Giuliano. "Il disprezzo per Dante dal Petrarca al Bruni." *Rinascimento* (2nd ser.) 25 (1985): 199–219.

Tassoni, Alessandro, ed. *Considerazioni sopra le rime del Petrarca*. Modena, Cassiani, 1609.

Trinkaus, Charles Edward. *In Our Image and Likeness: Humanity and Divinity in Italian Humanist Thought*. 2 vols. Chicago: University of Chicago Press, 1970. Rpt. Notre Dame, Ind.: University of Notre Dame Press, 1995.

———. *The Poet as Philosopher: Petrarch and the Formation of Renaissance Consciousness*. New Haven: Yale University Press, 1979.

Tripet, Arnaud. *Pétrarque, ou la connaissance de soi*. Genève: Droz, 1967.

Trovato, Paolo. *Dante in Petrarca: Per un inventario dei dantismi nei "Rerum vulgarium fragmenta."* Florence: Olschki, 1977, 1979.

Usher, Jonathan. "Boccaccio ghirlandaio: L'incoronazione universale del *Decameron*." In *Studi sul canone letterario del Trecento: Per Michelangelo Picone*, edited by J. Bartuschat and L. Rossi, 147–60. Ravenna: Longo, 2003.

Vallone, Aldo. *Antidantismo politico nel XIV secolo. Primi contributi*. Naples: Liguori, 1974.

———. "Boccaccio lettore di Dante." In *Giovanni Boccaccio editore e interprete di Dante*, 91–117. Florence: Olschki, 1979.

———. *Storia della critica dantesca dal XIV al XX secolo*. 2nd ed. 2 vols. Milan: Vallardi, 1981.

Van Dijk, S. J. P. *Sources of the Modern Roman Liturgy*. 2 vols. Leiden: E. J. Brill, 1963.

Van Dijk, S. J. P., and H. Walker. *Origins of the Modern Roman Liturgy: The Liturgy of the Papal Court and the Franciscan Order in the Thirteenth Century*. London: Darton, Longman & Todd, and Westminster, Md.: The Newman Press, 1959.

Vasino, Augusto, Pier Vincenzo Mengaldo, and Firenzo Forti. "Bologna." In *Enciclopedia dantesca*. 6 vols., edited by Umberto Bosco, 1:660–67.

Vattasso, Luigi. *I codici petrarcheschi della biblioteca vaticana*. Roma: Tipografia poliglotta vaticana, 1908.

Vecchi, Giuseppe. "Giovanni del Virgilio e Dante: La polemica tra latino e volgare nella corrispondenza poetica." In *Dante e Bologna nei tempi di Dante*, edited by Facoltà di Lettere e Filosofia dell'Università di Bologna, 61–76. Bologna: Commissione dei Testi in Lingua, 1967.

Velli, Giuseppe. "Il Dante di Francesco Petrarca." In *Petrarca e Boccaccio* [sic]*: Tradizione memoria scrittura*, 60–73. 2nd ed. Padua: Antenore, 1995.

———. "Il Dante di Francesco Petrarca." *Studi Petrarcheschi* n.s. 2 (1985): 185–99.

———. "Il *De Vita et moribus domini Francisci Petracchi de Florentia* del Boccaccio e la biografia del Petrarca." *MLN* 102 (1987): 32–38.

———. "Petrarca, Dante, la poesia classica: *Ne la stagion che 'l ciel rapido inchina* (RVF, L) *Io son venuto al punto de la rota* (Rime, C)." *Studi petrarcheschi* n.s. 15 (2002): 81–98.

———. *Petrarca e Boccacccio [sic]: Tradizione memoria scrittura.* 2nd ed. Padua: Antenore, 1995.

———. Review of Maria Teresa Casella's *Tra Boccaccio e Petrarca, MLN* 100, no. 1 (1985): 175–77.

———. "Sul linguaggio letterario di Giovanni del Virgilio." *Italia medioevale e umanistica* 24 (1981): 137–58.

Vickers, Nancy J. "Re-membering Dante: Petrarch's 'Chiare, fresche et dolci acque.'" *MLN* 96 (1981): 1–11.

———. "Widowed Words: Dante, Petrarch, and the Metaphors of Mourning." In *Discourses of Authority in Medieval and Renaissance Literature,* edited by Kevin Brownlee and Walter Stephens, 97–108. Hanover, N.H.: University Press of New England, 1989.

Villa, Claudia. *La "Lectura Terentii."* Padua: Antenore, 1984.

Vinay, Gustavo. "Studi sul Mussato I: Il Mussato e l'estetica medievale." *Giornale storico della letteratura italiana* 126 (1949): 113–59.

Vincent of Beauvais. *Speculum Historiale,* 1624. Repr. Graz: Akademische Druck- und Verlagsanstalt, 1964.

Virgil. *The Eclogues and Georgics.* Edited by R. D. Williams. New York: St. Martin's Press, 1979.

———. *Eclogues, Georgics, Aeneid I–VI,* Edited and translated by H. R. Fairclough. In the Loeb Classical Library. London: William Heinemann, 1930.

Vlajcic, Paul. "Dante's Pastorals: The *Auctor* as Exile." Unpublished seminar paper. Newberry Library Seminar: "From *Auctor* to Author." Fall 1995.

Voci, Anna Maria. *Petrarca e la vita religiosa: Il mito umanista della vita eremitica.* Rome: Istituto Storico Italiano per l'Età Moderna e Contemporanea, 1983.

Walker, D. P. *The Ancient Theology.* Ithaca, N.Y.: Cornell University Press, 1972.

Waller, Margaret. *Petrarch's Poetics and Literary Theory.* Amherst: University of Massachusetts Press, 1980.

Warkentin, Germaine. "The Form of Dante's 'libello' and Its Challenge to Petrarch." *Quaderni d'italianistica* 2 (1981): 160–70.

Weber, Max. *The Protestant Ethic and the "Spirit" of Capitalism and Other Writings.* Edited and translated by Peter Baehr and Gordon C. Wells. 1904–5. Penguin Twentieth-Century Classics. New York: Penguin Books, 2002.

Weiss, Roberto. *The Renaissance Discovery of Classical Antiquity.* Oxford: Blackwell, 1969.

Wicksteed, Philip H., and Edmund Gardner. *Dante and Giovanni del Virgilio: Including a Critical Edition of Dante's 'Ecloghae Latinae' and of the Poetic Remains of Giovanni del Virgilio.* Westminster: Constable, 1902. Rpt. New York: Haskell House, 1970.

Wilkins, Ernest H. "Boccaccio's Early Tributes to Petrarch." *Speculum* 38 (1963): 79–87.

———. "The Coronation of Petrarch." In *Studies in the Life and Works of Petrarch,* 300–313.

————. *The "Epistolae Metricae" of Petrarch: A Manual.* Rome: Edizioni di Storia e Letteratura, 1956.

————. *Life of Petrarch.* Chicago: University of Chicago Press, 1961.

————. *The Making of the "Canzoniere" and Other Petrarchan Studies.* Rome: Edizioni di Storia e Letteratura, 1951.

————. "On Petrarch's *Ep. Fam.* 6.2." In *Studies on Petrarch and Boccaccio,* 267–71.

————. "Petrarch and the Cardinalate." In *Studies in the Life and Works of Petrarch,* 67–80.

————. "Petrarch's Ecclesiastical Career." In *Studies in the Life and Works of Petrarch,* 3–32.

————. *Petrarch's Eight Years in Milan.* Cambridge, Mass.: Medieval Academy of America, 1958.

————. *Studies in the Life and Works of Petrarch.* Cambridge, Mass.: Medieval Academy of America, 1955.

————. *Studies on Petrarch and Boccaccio.* Edited by Aldo S. Bernardo. Padua: Antenore, 1978.

Witt, Ronald. "Coluccio Salutati and the Conception of the *Poeta Theologus* in the Fourteenth Century." *Renaissance Quarterly* 30 (1977): 538–63.

————. *"In the Footsteps of the Ancients": The Origins of Humanism from Lovato to Bruni.* Leiden: Brill, 2000.

Wittgenstein, Ludwig. *Tractatus Logico-Philosophicus.* Translated by D. F. Pears and B. F. McGuinness. London: Routledge & Kegan Paul, 1961.

Wojciehowski, Dolora A. *Old Masters, New Subjects: Early Modern and Poststructuralist Theories of Will.* Stanford, Calif.: Stanford University Press, 1995.

Young, Karl. *Drama of the Medieval Church.* 2 vols. Oxford: Clarendon Press, 1933.

Zabughin, Vladimiro. *Vergilio nel Rinascimento Italiano: Da Dante a Torquato Tasso.* Vol. 1. Edited by Stefano Carrai and Alberto Cavarzere. 2 vols. Rpt. Trento: Università degli Studi di Trento, 2000. First published 1921–23.

Zaccagnini, Guido. "Il Petrarca e Cino da Pistoia." In *Convegno petrarchesco,* 1:2–21. Arezzo: Accademia Petrarca, 1936.

Zaleski, Carol. *Otherworld Journeys.* New York and Oxford: Oxford University Press, 1987.

Zanato, Tiziano. "San Francesco, Pier delle Vigne e Francesca da Rimini." *Filologia e critica* 2 (1977): 177–216.

Zimmermann, Michel, ed. *"Auctor" et "auctoritas": Invention et conformisme dans l'écriture médiévale.* Paris: École des Chartes, 2001.

CONTRIBUTORS

Albert Russell Ascoli
University of California, Berkeley

Zygmunt G. Barański
University of Cambridge, U.K.

Teodolinda Barolini
Columbia University

Theodore J. Cachey, Jr.
University of Notre Dame

Ronald L. Martinez
Brown University

Giuseppe Mazzotta
Yale University

Christian Moevs
University of Notre Dame

Justin Steinberg
University of Chicago

Sara Sturm-Maddox
University of Massachusetts, Amherst

Index of Works by Dante and Petrarch